CLASSICS IN PSYCHOLOGY

CLASSICS IN PSYCHOLOGY

GENERAL PRINCIPLES OF
HUMAN REFLEXOLOGY

By

PROFESSOR VLADIMIR
MICHAILOVITCH BECHTEREV

ARNO PRESS
A New York Times Company
New York ★ 1973

Reprint Edition 1973 by Arno Press Inc.

Reprinted from a copy in
The Princeton University Library

Classics in Psychology
ISBN for complete set: 0-405-05130-1
See last pages of this volume for titles.

Manufactured in the United States of America

Library of Congress Cataloging in Publication Data

Bekhterev, Vladimir Mikhailovich, 1857-1927.
    General principles of human reflexology.

    (Classics in psychology)
    Translation of Obshchie osnovy refleksologii
cheloveka.
    Reprint of the 1932 ed. published by International
Publishers, New York.
    "Bibliography: list of the author's scientific
works on which the present work is based": p.
    1. Psychology, Physiological. 2. Conditioned
response. 3. Reflexes. I. Title. II. Series.
[DNLM: WL106 B420 1932F]
BF186.B4413 1973   152.3'22   73-2961
ISBN 0-405-05134-4

A NOTE ABOUT THE AUTHOR

VLADIMIR MICHAILOVICH BECHTEREV (1857-1927) was, along with Pavlov, the major Russian scientist to continue Sechenov's pioneering work on the physiological foundations of the mind. Like Sechenov and Pavlov, he studied in St. Petersburg, receiving his doctorate there in 1881. Thereafter he went abroad to work with Wundt in Leipzig, with du Bois Reymond in Berlin, and with Charcot in Paris. He returned to Russia, eventually assuming chairs of mental disease in Kazan and in St. Petersburg.

Bechterev was a prolific writer. He published about 600 works in the fields of the anatomy of the nervous system, neurology, psychiatry, psychology and pedagogy. Yet his contributions are much less known than Pavlov's. The achievements of the Pavlovian school in elaborating a physiology of the cerebral cortex due to the conditioned reflex method have overshadowed Bechterev's role in the development of this procedure. Yet Pavlov acknowledged that Bechterev had described new reflexes superposed upon innate reflexes which he called associative instead of conditioned reflexes.

Among his various contributions to neurology and psychology, Bechterev was the first to elaborate conditioned motor reactions. He suggested that this method could aid in studying patients with neurological and mental diseases. He proposed the investigation of the "symbolic (verbal) movements" for the assessment of cortical centers, cortical connections, and afferent and motor pathways. Bechterev also anticipated the current Soviet interest in the orienting reflex in his study of the "concentration reflexes," a complex of muscular contractions which prepare the receptor for the best perception of a stimulus.

Bechterev sought to study the effects of physical, biological and social factors on mental functioning in a strictly objective manner by recording the external reactions—including facial expressions, gestures, and speech—and relating them to their current and prior stimuli. He took a rigorous deterministic stand—no conscious or unconscious phenomenon exists which is not manifest, sooner or later, in external behavior. Unlike the behaviorists, however, Bechterev speculated at this stage of his work about the neurological basis of mental functioning. He assumed, for example, that the obstacles encountered by the waves of ions produced by external stimulation and intensified in the brain result in a tension responsible for the "subjective tint" of the nervous current.

In 1895 Bechterev founded the first laboratory of experimental psychology in Russia. The laboratory was attached to the neuropsychiatric clinic of Kazan University. In 1904 he published an important paper, which marked the beginning of his "objective psychology." The views first expounded there were developed further in a three-volume monograph, *Objective Psychology,* published between 1907 and 1912. Finally, in 1921, Bechterev issued *Collective Reflexology* which summarized his theoretical and experimental work on group psychology. His general orientation was at first palatable to the new Soviet regime. It looked as if it met the ideological requirements for a materialistic and deterministic psychology. The Psychoneurological Institute which he helped to found, and later directed, was named the V. M. Bechterev Institute for Brain Research. In addition, a Festschrift was published in 1926 to commemorate Bechterev's forty years of teaching.

The official attitude toward reflexology has shifted markedly since Bechterev's death. In 1928 the Leningrad Society of Reflexology, Hypnosis, Neurology, and Biophysics set up a special panel to rebuild reflexology on the basis of dialectical materialism. A conference held the next year on the topic "reflexology or psychology" marked, as the title of an article suggested, the beginning of the end. Some of Bechterev's former co-workers, who later rose to leading positions in Soviet psychology, joined the critics. Included in this group was Ivanov Smolenskii who shifted to Pavlov's laboratories and developed a methodology for studying the interaction between two signal systems.

The causes of the fall of Bechterev's reflexology in Russia reside in changes in ideological positions, as well as changes in Bechterev's position. The end of the 1920's was marked by intense ideological debate and an endeavor for a more sophisticated account of the human mind than was offered by reflexology. In opposition to these trends, Bechterev, in his later years, inclined increasingly toward a mechanical reductionism. He regarded both matter and mind as derivatives of energy and this was regarded as antagonistic to the proposition that mind is a reflection of material processes. Finally, in a reversal from his earlier works, Bechterev contended that reflexology does not imply the study of the physiology of the brain. He was ready to accept any explanation of the mind, save the metaphysical. Thus he ended up at odds with the basic tenets of dialectical materialistic philosophy. Nonetheless, at the present time, Bechterev is given more credit than in previous years.

Levy Rachmani
Boston University School of Medicine

GENERAL PRINCIPLES OF HUMAN REFLEXOLOGY

VLADIMIR MICHAILOVITCH BECHTEREV
ACADEMICIAN

GENERAL PRINCIPLES OF HUMAN REFLEXOLOGY

An Introduction to the Objective Study of Personality

By

PROFESSOR VLADIMIR
MICHAILOVITCH BECHTEREV

Late President of the State Psychoneurological
Academy; Director of the State Reflexological
Institute for the Study of Brain in Leningrad

Translated by
EMMA AND WILLIAM MURPHY
From the Russian of the 4th (1928) edition

INTERNATIONAL PUBLISHERS
NEW YORK

VLADIMIR MICHAILOVITCH BECHTEREV

THE activities of Vladimir Michailovitch Bechterev, who busied himself in various branches of science and earned the title of "the hero of psychoneurology," constitute an epoch.

Bechterev was born on the 20th of January, 1857, in the Yelabuzh district in the province of Viatka. He spent his childhood in the country and attended the Viatka secondary school. At sixteen, he entered the Military Medical Academy (then called the Medico-surgical Academy), from which, at the age of twenty-one, he graduated in 1878. To prepare for his professorship, he was permitted to remain in the departmental hospital for mental and nervous diseases.

During this period, he wrote a number of prominent works on the anatomy and physiology of the brain, and on the treatment of mental and nervous diseases. In 1881, having defended his dissertation on *Results of Clinical Investigation of Body Temperature in Certain Forms of Psychic Disease*, he took the doctor's degree. In the same year, he became *privat-dozent* at the Academy, where he lectured in mental and nervous diseases. He was sent abroad to complete his scientific studies.

Bechterev worked abroad in the laboratories and hospitals of the most famous scientists of the time (Flechsig, Westphal, Du Bois Raymond, Meynert, Wundt, Charcot, and others).

While abroad on his scientific mission, Bechterev devoted himself, with especial diligence, to the conduction paths of the central nervous system, which he studied mainly under Professor Flechsig of Leipzig, studied psychology in Wundt's laboratories, and conducted clinical work in the hospitals of Charcot, Westphal, and others.

While working in hospitals and laboratories abroad, he made a number of valuable investigations in the anatomy and physiology of the nervous system, and in the treatment of nervous and mental diseases. His publications attracted the attention of the whole scientific world, and, in 1885, while still abroad, he was appointed professor at the University of Kazan in the chair of psychic diseases.

When he returned from abroad, his ardent activities continued at the University of Kazan over a period of about seven years, during which he displayed his ability for organisation and creative work. On his initiative and with his direct participation, a department for mental diseases was organised in the Kazan District Psychiatric Hospital and belonged to the University of Kazan. A hospital for nervous diseases was also organised. Simultaneously with these hospitals Bechterev founded in Kazan a psycho-physiological laboratory with histological and physiological departments, founded the Society of Neuropathologists and Psychiatrists, and a special periodical *Nevrologitchesky Vestnik* devoted to problems of neurology and psychiatry.

Bechterev's activities in Kazan are exceedingly interesting, because it was at that time that the foundations of the Bechterev school of neuropathologists and psychiatrists were laid. During this period, he devoted

5

much time to the study, at first, of the anatomy and, later, of the physiology of the brain and spinal cord, and his students, under his supervision, investigated numerous anatomical and physiological problems. The main results of these investigations constituted the foundation of Bechterev's two chief works : (a) *Conduction Paths in the Brain and Spinal Cord* and (b) *Principles of the Study of the Functions of the Nervous Centres.*

During this period, too, many papers on the treatment of mental and nervous diseases and on experimental psychology appeared.

In 1893, he was transferred to St. Petersburg to the Military Medical Academy, where he held the chair of psychic and nervous diseases and succeeded his master, I. M. Merzheyevsky.

At the Military Medical Academy, he displayed extraordinary energy and rich initiative. First of all, he organised at the hospital, which, before his time, was exclusively for mental cases, a department for nervous patients, and later, on his initiative, a separate and exceedingly well-equipped hospital for nervous diseases was built. In the latter and in the psychiatric hospital, on Bechterev's initiative, extensive laboratories were organised : anatomo-histological, pathologo-anatomical, physiological, biological, serological, and experimento-psychological. Simultaneously with these laboratories a rare and extensive special library was organised at the hospital.

At the hospital of the Academy, Bechterev's scientific activity developed from year to year, and in the hospital laboratories many doctors worked under his supervision. Some of these later occupied chairs of nervous and mental diseases at various Russian universities.

The scientific activity of the hospital for nervous and mental diseases at the Military Medical Academy reached its zenith under Bechterev's supervision. At the same time he organised " scientific sessions of the hospital doctors," founded the Russian Society for Normal and Patho-logical Psychology, and the periodical *Obozrenie psychiatrii, nevrologii i experimentalnoi psychologii.* Moreover, *Activities of the Hospital for Mental and Nervous Diseases* was published.

During the same period, he wrote a number of his more important works. Two of his chief works (already mentioned)—*Conduction Paths in the Brain and Spinal Cord* and *Principles of the Study of the Functions of the Nervous Centres*—were elaborated in detail. Besides these works, which are universally known, we must mention some other works particularly important in the development of psychoneurology, such as : (a) *Objective Psychology*, (b) *General Diagnostic of Diseases of the Nervous System*, (c) *Suggestion and its Rôle in Social Life*, (d) *The Psychic and Life*, (e) *Observations of Nervous Diseases*, and (f) *Hypnosis, Suggestion, and Psychotherapy.*

In addition to the works written by Bechterev himself, there appeared a multitude of works by his disciples—physicians of whom about a thousand worked under him during the twenty years of his supervision of the hospital of the Military Medical Academy. Forty to fifty doctors worked yearly in the hospital laboratories.

In spite of the extensive development of Bechterev's activity in the hospital of the Military Medical Academy, he was dissatisfied with work under the state restrictions there, for his extensive scientific and social plans were confined, and so in 1907 he, with his collaborators, founded the Psychoneurological Institute, the organisation of which forms one of the most brilliant achievements of his life.

According to the statutes—the approval of which Bechterev secured after a long and painful struggle—the Psychoneurological Institute was a scientific and higher educational institution. The Institute quickly gained great popularity among scientists as well as students, and the Institute Council was soon supplemented by prominent representatives of various departments of science, which were included in the curriculum. During the first ten years, about ten thousand students passed through the Institute, which attracted them by the originality of its curriculum and system of teaching, both of which satisfied the needs of the progressive youth of the time. Year by year, the Institute became a more and more powerful educational establishment with one faculty for general instruction and three special faculties : (a) a medical, (b) a pedagogical, and (c) a juridical. Bechterev took a very lively part in the work of the Institute. He succeeded in obtaining for it a large piece of land (about $36\frac{1}{2}$ acres) beyond the Nevskaya Zastava and in building there several large stone buildings, beautifully equipped and designed for the twofold task of the Institute : to impart knowledge and to investigate. In addition to the main Institute building, (a) an anti-alcohol institute, (b) a hospital for mental and nervous diseases, (c) an institute for epileptics, (d) a neuro-surgical hospital, (e) a pedological institute, and others for other purposes were built under Bechterev's supervision.

The educational, as well as the scientific, work was conducted in the various departments of the Psychoneurological Institute with extraordinary energy and enthusiasm and under Bechterev's general supervision. He continued to be president of the Institute and chairman of the council.

In 1913, he vacated the chair of mental and nervous diseases in the Military Medical Academy, ostensibly because he had worked sufficiently long, but really because of the attitude of the tsarist government, which regarded him as a " revolutionary professor," tried to oust him from pedagogical and social work, and could not forgive him for producing such expert evidence in the Beilis case as shattered the hopes of the intriguers of the Stolypin and Shtcheglovitov clique.[1]

After resigning his post at the Military Medical Academy, Bechterev devoted himself entirely to the organisation of the Psychoneurological Institute and the institutions whose activities were associated with it.

The Psychoneurological Institute, founded during the dark period of tsarism and developing on the broadest revolutionary bases, was persecuted

---

[1] Beilis, a Russian Jew, was accused of murdering a Christian child to use its blood for ritualistic purposes. Stolypin was Prime Minister. Shtcheglovitov was Minister of Justice. See *Bibliography*, no. 93.—*Translators*.

by the government. The authorities of an obsolete age regarded the Institute as a hotbed of revolution and saw in it a great and threatening danger which might undermine the foundations of the old régime.

The whole curriculum, the composition of the professorial and lecturing staff, the conditions of entrance to the Institute, which, regardless of religion and national status, admitted persons of either sex, were regarded by the government as the most undesirable and impermissible aspect of the life of the institutions for higher education, and obstacles, which only Bechterev succeeded in surmounting, were placed in the way of the Institute at every step.

The Institute, under Bechterev's supervision, endured the hard years of the imperialist war, energetically carried on its work during the civil war, and gained a secure position after the October revolution, when it was included among government institutions for higher education and obtained the same rights as these.

Simultaneous with the development of the activity of the Psychoneurological Institute, Bechterev founded a number of other institutions for the realisation of the chief aims of the Institute. The following should be mentioned here : (1) the Pathologo-reflexological Institute, the aim of which was the study of abnormal manifestations of the psychic sphere ; (2) the Pedological Institute for the study of the psychic activity of man from the day of birth to adulthood ; (3) the Children's Observation Institute, to investigate the phenomena of children's deficiencies ; (4) the Medico-educational Institute, for anti-social children ; (5) the Otophonetic Institute, to investigate disturbances in speaking and hearing in children ; (6) the Central Auxiliary School, for backward children ; (7) the Central Institute, for deaf-mutes.

Bechterev paid particular attention to the organisation of the Institute for the Study of Brain and Psychic Activity. He founded this Institute in 1918, and its chief aim was the study of the anatomy and physiology of the central nervous system, and also the study of the principles of reflexology, a new branch of science created by him. In accordance with these aims, the Institute is now called the Reflexological Institute for the Study of Brain.

In 1918, the pedagogical and juridical faculties of the Psychoneurological Institute were merged into the corresponding faculties of the University of Petrograd, and, in 1921, the medical faculty of the Institute was reorganised to form the State Institute of Medical Science (" GIMZ ") of which Bechterev, until his death, was honorary rector and a professor in the chair of psychiatry and reflexology.

After the segregation of the medical faculty, the Psychoneurological Institute, with all the other institutions connected with it, was transformed by a resolution of the State Scientific Council into the State Psychoneurological Academy, of which Bechterev was elected president.

Bechterev devoted much work to the further development of the Psychoneurological Academy. Besides the above-mentioned Institutes, other institutions were added to the Academy : (a) the laboratory for the investigation of work and a vocational consulting bureau ; (b) the clinic for the pedology and neuropathology of infants ; (c) the institute for the protection of the health of children and adolescents ; and (d) the institute for social education. Under Bechterev's guidance, the work of the Psycho-neurological Academy made vigorous progress, and had as its chief aim the objective study of human personality, with its development and manifestation in normal and pathological conditions. Bechterev was not only president of the Academy, but also director of several institutions included in the Academy. He was director of the Medico-educational Clinical Institute for nervous children. He took a very lively part in the life of each institution and interested himself in all the details of every aspect of the activity of these institutions.

Side by side with his creative organising activity, Bechterev continued till his death to labour in the wide fields of psychoneurology and published, during the whole period of his scientific activity, about six hundred works and papers : on the anatomy and physiology of the central nervous system, on the treatment of nervous and psychic diseases, on biology, psychology, philosophy, pedagogics and pedology, hypnotism, and, lastly, he devoted very much time to works on reflexology.

It is difficult to describe in detail all Bechterev's varied achievements in the many branches of science in which he worked. His investigations have procured a mass of valuable material for the treasury of scientific knowledge and brought him universal fame. Many of his writings have been translated into various languages and accepted as standard works.

Bechterev's earliest works were, as we have mentioned, chiefly devoted to the study of the conduction paths in the brain and the spinal cord and to the study of the functions of the central nervous system, so that, as a neurologist, he ranks very high.

We must enumerate some of his more important achievements in neurology : (a) investigating the structure of the cerebral hemispheres and the subcortical ganglia, he segregated the nucleus caudatus and the putamen from the globus pallidus, and came to the conclusion that the nucleus caudatus and the putamen are a cortical formation composing the internal gyrus ascending from the substantia perforata anterior to the apex of the temporal lobe ; (b) in the cortex of the cerebral hemispheres Bechterev described, in the second layer, a band of myelinated tangential fibres ; this is called " the band of Bechterev " ; (c) he succeeded in discovering the connections between the cerebral cortex and the sub-cortical ganglia (the nucleus caudatus and the putamen) ; it must be noted that before Bechterev's investigations these connections were denied by the majority of neurologists ; (d) he proved that the fibres connecting the globus pallidus with the corpus subthalamicum Luys of the opposite side enter into the structure of the commissura Meynerti ; (e) he found that in all the fundamental cortical centres (visual, auditory, tactual, etc.) there are paired distributions of efferent and afferent conductors, each centre mentioned consisting of two parts, the afferent and the efferent, these parts coinciding to some extent with each other.

In studying the grey matter and the conduction paths in the truncus cerebri, Bechterev made further important discoveries. He described, under the name of " nucleus angularis," the cellular accumulations in the medulla oblongata which lie somewhat outside the nucleus of Deiters and are the terminus of the afferent branch of the vestibular root of the auditory nerve. This nucleus has been called the " nucleus of Bechterev," and is of interest to doctors and physiologists. Besides the nucleus mentioned, Bechterev described a number of other nuclei in the pons Varolii and the medulla oblongata : such as the nucleus centralis superior, the nucleus reticularis tegmenti, the nucleus between the anterior and posterior bigemina. The latter nucleus he called the corpus parabigeminum. He also described the central tegmental bundle, the fibres of which, beginning from the subcortical ganglia (nucleus lenticularis), he traced to the inferior olives.

It must be noted that Bechterev's works touch on every part of the central nervous system, and it may be definitely stated that there is no bundle, no nucleus, in the brain or spinal cord in regard to which Bechterev has not expressed his view concerning its structure and function.

Bechterev's physiological investigations also deserve special attention. He took an extraordinary interest in the localisation of various functions in the brain and spinal cord. In this respect, his investigations of the thalamus opticus, in which he localised not only the functions of facial and other expressive movements, but also various visceral centres (vascular, perspiratory, salivary, and others) must be brought to the fore. On the basis of experimental investigations and clinical observations, Bechterev came to the conclusion that the nuclei which lie in the upper region of the truncus cerebri contain the centres regulating the act of standing in man and in animals. Bechterev studied in particular detail the localisation of centres in the cerebral cortex, and succeeded in exactly localising many cortical centres (secretion of saliva, of tears, certain motor and sensory centres, etc.). His investigations of the function of the auditory nerves, the olives, and the cerebellum must also be mentioned.

In connection with the treatment of nervous and psychic diseases, Bechterev discovered a number of new symptoms and reflexes of enormous significance in diagnosing nervous diseases, and also described several new diseases of great scientific interest. Of the reflexes he discovered and described, we must mention : (a) in the face—the orbital, chin, nose, blinking, and sound reflexes ; (b) in the extremities and trunk : the scapulo-humeral, acromial, carpo-digital, tibial, sacro-lumbar, and other reflexes, including the dorsal, which bends the sole.

In addition to reflexes, Bechterev observed many symptoms, also of considerable diagnostic value. Here belong : (a) absence of pain when the muscles of the calf are pressed, as an early symptom of tabes dorsalis ; (b) painfulness when the cheek-bone arch is rapped, in the case of diseases originating in the brain ; (c) the sensation of the presence and movement of lost or amputated extremities (pseudomelia paresthetica) ; (d) deep and superficial rappings on the skull and spinal column to discover the deep or the superficial location of a disease process ; and (e) posthemiplegial hemitonia (hemitonia postapoplectica). The " elbow phenomenon " must also be mentioned as one of the symptoms recently described by Bechterev. This phenomenon indicates the existence of latent spasmophilia in the organism.

Besides various reflexes and symptoms, Bechterev succeeded in discovering new nosological forms, which have been accepted here and abroad. To the number of such diseases described by Bechterev belong first of all : (a) the " stiffening of the backbone "—called " Bechterev's disease " ; (b) diffuse syphilitic sclerosis ; and (c) acute cerebellar ataxia, most frequently arising after alcoholism. Of the diseases of personality which have been described by Bechterev, the various phobias, which he was the first to observe, are noteworthy : fear of blushing (erythrophobia), obsessional smiling, fear of being looked at, ophidiophobia, obsessional sweating of the hands, phantasies of being hypnotically spell-bound, and others.

Bechterev was exceedingly interested in pedological problems also. In many of his scientific works he laid special emphasis on upbringing before the school age and from the very moment of birth. He busied himself with the detailed study of children and made interesting investigations in the development of language in children, attention in children, the development of children's drawings, etc. He strongly insisted on objective methods in the investigation of children and in the study of association-motor reflexes in children.

Not confining himself to his scientific writings and public speeches, Bechterev founded in 1907 a special Pedagogical Institute for the detailed, systematic, objective study of the child from the moment of birth. This institute, under Bechterev's supervision, vigorously developed its scientific investigations and, at the international exhibition in Dresden, was awarded a diploma with distinction. At the hygiene exhibition in Petrograd it was awarded a gold medal.

It is clear from this account of Bechterev's work that he brought into all the departments of psychoneurology many new and valuable discoveries accepted by the whole scientific world.

But his varied scientific activity is displayed with peculiar vividness in his creation of a new and autonomous science which he calls " reflexology." According to Bechterev's definition, reflexology is a branch of science which studies the human personality from the strictly objective bio-social standpoint. Reflexology, as Bechterev teaches, investigates all the manifestations of the " so-called psychic activity," or, in other words, " the spiritual sphere " from the objective standpoint and confines itself to the external peculiarities of the activity of man : his facial expressions, his gestures, voice, and speech, as a coherent integration of signs, in correlation with the exciting external influences—physical, biological, and, above all, social—but also with the internal, regardless of whether either of these two types of influence is referable to the present or the past. From the standpoint of reflexology, man is not only a living organism, but a " bio-social being " acting in dependence not only on the natural, but also on the social, environment. The divisions of the earlier psychology dealing with intellect, feeling, memory, will, and attention Bechterev replaces in reflexology by divisions into higher and personal reflexes, mimico-somatic reflexes, reflexes of concentration, of reproduction, etc.

He does not confine himself to the study of the individual, but utilises reflexological experiment in the study of communities, and so creates " collective reflexology."

Then, in his attempts to investigate man's life from the day of birth, Bechterev wrote a series of papers devoted to the study of the neuro-psychic life of infants, and thus laid the foundations of genetic reflexology.

Reflexology clearly illustrates Bechterev's creativeness, and is the culminating point of his scientific activity.

In tracing the development of Bechterev's scientific activity, we have seen that the first decades of his work were devoted to the study of the anatomy and physiology of the nervous system, to experimental psychology, and to the treatment of nervous and psychic diseases. On the basis of the results of his investigations in these spheres, he gradually developed the harmonious doctrine of the reflex activity of man, and, as early as 1886, remarked, in a paper devoted to the investigation of the physiology of the motor region of the cerebral cortex, that the dog's giving the paw, an act which is a motor association reflex, disappears when the motor centres of the cerebral cortex of the opposite hemisphere are destroyed. These experiments of Bechterev's show that the arcs of association-motor reflexes pass through the cerebral cortex, and not through the sub-cortical centres, as was previously supposed.

The whole of Bechterev's well-knit and harmonious doctrine of the human personality—that is, reflexology—has emanated from his preceding studies in the anatomy and physiology of the nervous system, in experimental psychology, and in the treatment of nervous and mental diseases.

Reflexology has aroused enormous interest, and, at the present time, reflexological methods are applied wherever the study of human personality is demanded : in psychiatric hospitals (pathological reflexology), in training colleges and in schools (pedagogical reflexology), and in factories and works (vocational reflexology).

Reflexology occupies an independent position as a distinct branch of science in the curriculum of institutions for higher education, and the People's Commissariat of Education[1] has established in U.S.S.R. independent chairs of reflexology in the Leningrad medical academies and faculties (" VUZ ").

[1] *Translators' note :* The so-called " Narkompros," corresponding to the Board of Education in England, but controlling the universities.

V. Bechterev's name is one of the most popular in Russia and abroad. During the last thirty to forty years, there has been no congress of psycho-neurology, pedology, or pedagogics in which Bechterev has not directed the proceedings and delivered addresses of general interest.

Not only have psychiatrists, reflexologists, and neuropathologists been in close touch with him, but also teachers, both rural and urban, have always given him a ready ear, listened to his addresses at the pedagogical congresses, and derived much of value for their pedagogical work.

Besides scientific work, Bechterev devoted much time to social activity.

Practically no students' meeting of importance was held in the Psycho-neurological Institute at which Bechterev, whom the students always received with marked enthusiasm, was not present.

For many years, the students of the State Institute of Medical Science (" GIMZ ") elected Bechterev their delegate to the Leningrad Workers' and Peasants' Soviet (" SOVDEP ").[1] It may be definitely stated that no important public event occurred in Russian life without evoking the liveliest reaction on his part.

Bechterev ardently participated in the reform of the homeless children (" besprizorniye ") and organised a number of suitable institutions. What energy he spent in the struggle against alcoholism, concerning which he published many articles ! Besides, he founded a special institute—equipped in model fashion—for the treatment of alcoholics, which cured thousands of patients, and received the highest award at the Turin exhibition of hygiene.

As Bechterev considered hypnosis particularly useful in the treatment of alcoholism, he introduced a collective method of hypnotising patients, and secured splendid results.

Bechterev was a fine fellow to work with, treated his students and collaborators with particular affection and attention, and was accorded boundless esteem and love by all who had dealings with him.

Bechterev's unlimited energy, his indefatigability (he worked not less than fifteen to sixteen hours a day), his particular interest in scientific work—hospital and laboratory—and his constant striving to link up his scientific investigations with the practical problems of life created conditions particularly favourable for work in the institutions he founded and supervised.

Bechterev's whole life was an uninterrupted service to science and mankind, and humanity, by his death, lost a great scientist and a true friend.[2]

PROFESSOR A. GERVER

[1] *Translators' note :* The legislative assembly.
[2] *Translators' note :* Bechterev died on 24th December, 1927.

TRANSLATORS' PREFACE

GENERAL Principles of Human Reflexology (Obshtchie osnovi reflexologii tcheloveka) first appeared in Russian in 1917, and reached the fourth edition in 1928, some months after the author's death, the second having appeared in 1923, and the third in 1925. The third edition was published in a German translation, under the title *Allgemeine Grundlagen der Reflexologie des Menschen* (F. Deuticke, Leipzig and Wien), in 1926. Other of Bechterev's works have appeared both in German and in French. This, we believe, is the first time that any work of his has appeared in English. The present translation has been made directly from the Russian of the fourth edition. There are no omissions. All the difficulties—and there were many—have been squarely, and, we hope, successfully, faced. Every effort has been made to render the text accurately and to eliminate various ambiguities in the original. We regret, however, that it was impossible to verify every reference.

At the outset, we wish to remove a misconception. The writer in the *Encyclopedia Britannica* (14th ed., article *Bekhterev*) refers to the present work as *General Basis of the Reflex Action of Man*. This title is entirely misleading, for here we have not merely a treatise on reflex action, but a presentation of what Bechterev claims to be a new science—reflexology—ranking among the exact sciences and consisting in the objective study of personality. Reflexology is to be regarded as a special branch of biology and as merging directly into sociology. In a word, it is the objective science of personality from the bio-social viewpoint.

This volume gives us a survey of Bechterev's life-work in the field of psychology, and, whatever the tenets of the individual reader, must be admitted to be exceedingly stimulating. The weaknesses of subjective psychology are revealed, the importance of the reflex in human development is emphasised, and an extraordinary array of facts are marshalled to hold the position. Though there is no detailed description of reflexological method, the results of the method are set down with a wealth of detail and should be ignored by no serious student of philosophy, biology, psychology, sociology, education, physiology, philology, or psychotherapy. The work should prove particularly interesting to behaviourists because of the great influence which Bechterev has exerted on behaviourism and because reflexology and behaviourism touch at many points.

Reflexology is the dominant note in Russian psychology to-day and the late Bechterev is the guiding light in humanistic science in U.S.S.R. The work he began and so ably developed is being continued by the Reflexological Institute for the Study of Brain (Leningrad), an Institute founded and supervised by Bechterev himself, and the results of the various investigations are published from time to time.

We note, in passing, that it is high time that such indefensible spellings as *Bechterew* and *Pawlow*—forms which, obviously, have been taken over from the German, a language in which they are appropriate—disappeared, in favour of *Bechterev* (or *Bekhterev*) and *Pavlov*, from the English literature of science.

We take this opportunity to record our gratitude—and, we feel sure, the gratitude of all those interested in the appearance of so significant a work—to Mrs. Ludmila Galkina, Riga, for her accuracy, speed, and unflagging energy in preparing the typescript ; to Miss Stella R. Steen, London, for her valuable and generous assistance in verifying various references ; to our Publishers (represented by Mr. H. R. Hale) for their courtesy and helpfulness, which have made our work lighter than it might otherwise have been ; and to many friends who have willingly placed their expert knowledge at our disposal.

On encountering passages of especial difficulty, we have had recourse to the German translation, mentioned above. Although we are at variance with it on certain points of detail, and have found that—wisely or unwisely —it has evaded certain knotty issues, we acknowledge considerable indebtedness to it.

The original Russian provides no index. We have remedied this rather considerable defect and append a name index and a subject index for the greater convenience of our readers.

EMMA MURPHY

WILLIAM MURPHY, B.A., etc.

RIGA, LATVIA
April, 1932

PREFACE TO THE FIRST EDITION

SINCE the appearance of my book, *Objective Psychology*, the strictly objective trend in the study of the higher activities of the human personality—activities bound up with the establishment of the relation of the person to the environment and now, in the interests of objective terminology, called correlative functions, instead of psychical or neuro-psychical—has been considerably developed.

It was found possible to discover some of the fundamental laws to which the development of processes of correlative activity conforms, and, at the same time, to throw new light on many of those phenomena which formerly seemed incapable of being fitted into the framework of strictly objective investigation.

Such is the natural course of all scientific knowledge, for each science is only gradually motivated, developed, and completed, not only in respect of content, but also of terminology.

At the present time, that branch of science, whose task is to submit to such strictly objective scientific investigation as prevails in all the other natural sciences even the finest and highest of the organism's activities, which, until recently, have fallen under the scope of subjective analysis made through direct self-observation, already finds itself in a position to use its own strictly objective terminology.

Consequently, in designating this department of science, which has originated on Russian soil, we regard it more correct to use, as more appropriate, the term " reflexology "—which we have already introduced—instead of " objective psychology."[1]

The present work is, in very compressed form, part of the theoretical course of lectures delivered during the past few years to students of the general and medical faculties of the Psychoneurological Institute, and provides a brief presentation of the general principles of human reflexology as a branch of science, the detailed elaboration of which, in special laboratories, has already afforded practical results for natural science in general and for medicine in particular.

This volume has been published in the desire to provide with a scientific, if brief, manual students, physicians, and all those striving to break the yoke of subjectivism in the scientific evaluation of those complex activities of the human organism which lead to the establishment of man's correlation with the environment.

This work is by no means exhaustive and is intended merely to introduce the reader to a scientific study which offers rich and fertile territory for further scientific exploration.

I am convinced that whoever finds this book interesting will strive to acquire practical knowledge of the methods of reflexology, and, ready

---

[1] See the German translation of *Objective Psychology*, where the term " reflexology " is used in the title of the book, while, in the French edition, the word " reflexology " occurs in the first pages of the work. I may mention here that I have used this term in a number of scientific papers.

to sacrifice some time, will be willing to join the ranks of those whose efforts have collected the material for this new branch of science.

In this respect, the present work, which contains many lacunæ in presentation, may, nevertheless, in its present form, afford such help as is necessary to the interested novice. Later, he may at any time supplement his knowledge of the subject by turning to *Objective Psychology* and the special papers devoted to the various problems of this branch of science.

PETROGRAD
   3rd July, 1917

PREFACE TO THE SECOND EDITION[1]

THE first edition of this book, published under the title *General Principles of Reflexology*, was practically sold out in the first two years, and, consequently, had already become rare last year. This shows the success achieved in Russia by the objectivo-biological study of personality.[2] Besides, in a short time, this new branch of science, which has its roots in Russian scientific thought and, in its application to man, has been developed chiefly on the basis of objective observation and laboratory experiments, especially in motor association reflexes, but also of biological data, was, as a result of the special interest taken in it by scientists and students, allowed to be taught in a number of higher medical and pedagogical schools in Leningrad, and recently, as far as I know, has begun to be taught even in one of the pedagogical institutes in Moscow and in several medical faculties in provincial towns. Moreover, after I had delivered an address, on *The Fundamental Aims of Reflexology*, to a joint meeting of the Conference on Defective Children held last year in Moscow and the Congress of Physicians for the Protection of Children and Mothers, a resolution, proposed by one of the Moscow professors, was unanimously carried : that the teaching of reflexology should be obligatory in all higher medical and pedagogical schools, including universities. Further, the medical section of the Council of Rectors in

[1] This preface has been revised by the author.

[2] The first attempts to approach the study of personality objectively were made by me as early as 1885, when I was studying traumatic psychoneuroses and hysteria (see *Proceedings of the 5th Pirogov Congress* and a number of special papers—on this and other problems of normal and abnormal personality—published in *Obozrenie Psychiatrii, Vestnik Psychologii, Vestnik Znania, Voprosi izutcheniya i vospitaniya litchnosti*, and in various foreign periodicals). In my paper, *Physiology of the Motor Sphere of the Cerebral Cortex* (*Archiv Psychiatrii*, 1886–87), I experimented, for the first time, on dogs, which had acquired association-motor reflexes by training (giving the paw, etc.), my aim being to discover the cortical localisation of these reflexes. The first paper in which I drew general conclusions regarding normal personality was published by me in *Vestnik Psychiatrii* in 1904, under the title *Objective Psychology and its Subject Matter* (translated into French in the *Revue scientifique*, 1906), and here the whole plan of the strictly objective study of personality was already outlined. In 1907, in Amsterdam, the method and principles of the objective study of personality were then divulged by me at the International Congress of Psychology, Psychiatry, and Public Care of Psychopaths. After this, my work, *Objective Psychology* (in three parts), began to appear. But, in 1912, I published in *Russky Vratch*, after a series of special papers, the paper, under the title of *The Fundamental Aims of Psychiatry as an Objective Science*, in which I arrived at general conclusions concerning the objective study of the diseased personality and I later published two further papers general in character : 1. *The Objective Investigation of the Diseased Personality as the Basis of Pathological Reflexology* in *Nautchnaya Medicina*, no. 9, 1922 ; and 2. *Diseases of Personality from the Viewpoint of Reflexology* in *Voprosi izutcheniya i vospitaniya litchnosti*, vol. 3. A brief enumeration of my investigations in the sphere of reflexology up to 1917 may be found in the article *The Objective Method in the Investigation of Neuro-psychical or Correlative Activity* in *Vestnik Znania*, 1917. It is clear that the work in the direction indicated was done in collaboration with other workers in my laboratory.

19

Moscow, 5th July, 1922, was unanimous in proposing the inclusion of re-flexology in the course of medical science at the universities. I cannot refrain from mentioning here that the reflexological section, presided over by me, of the Preliminary Conference for the Scientific Organisation of Work in Moscow, 1921, aroused special interest among the representatives of exact science—technicians and engineers. It is obvious that this science is destined to develop still further, for it is clear that man, even in the most complex manifestations of personality, is necessarily the object of natural science study, and the latter admits of only one approach—investigation by means of the objectivo-biological or reflexological method.

The study of subjective or conscious processes, which we discover in ourselves by introspection or self-observation, and with which " sub-jective " psychology, with experiments which merely aid introspection, has been occupied, can nowise be regarded as a branch of natural science, for in any science the method of investigation is primary, and the method of natural science has hitherto been strictly objective, and will remain so.

Besides, " it is not consciousness which determines existence," as the subjectivists have supposed and still suppose, but existence which deter-mines consciousness or (in reflexological terminology) human behaviour. Therefore, it may be said with certainty that the real—that is, the natural-scientific—study of human personality begins only when we introduce here a completely objective method, which gives human reflexology its motivation as the science of the objectivo-biological study of human person-ality in the social environment.

If we look into the future, we must see that " subjective " psychology will be merely a supplementary science conforming its aims to the data of the objective science of reflexology and only thus will subjective analysis (in the sense of verbal account) render services to the scientific investiga-tion of human personality. But the psychology which has hitherto developed independently has, in spite of the enormous work spent on it in the course of many centuries by a galaxy of great, and even the best, minds, really only constituted a collection of more or less interesting information, but not a science, a name which even the recently deceased psychologist and philosopher, James, denied—and with reason—to " subjective " psychology.

It must be clear to everyone that the objective study of man as an agent in his social environment, an agent establishing relations to the external world, must come first, and only in supplementary fashion may the study of the subjective aspect of man be conducted in direct correlation with objective data, and only with direct control and checking, through the objectivo-biological method, of the data thus obtained. The intro-duction of this objectivo-biological method into the study of human personality, this introduction presupposing the energic view of the mani-festations of personality, provides the motivation for the application of this method to the social life of man, as I have shown in my book, *Collective Reflexology* (Petrograd, 1922 ; publ. " Kolos ").

It is particularly significant that the introduction of the objectivo-biological method of investigation into these realms of science makes possible the discovery that the conformity of phenomena to law, a conformity prevailing in all physico-biological processes, is disclosed also in respect of human personality and society and in similar form. This thesis, which I developed in a special paper (*Universal Laws*, etc. ; see *Voprosi izutcheniya i vospitaniya litchnosti*, vols. 3 ff.), and which runs through *Collective Reflexology* and the present work, reveals the unity of all departments of science and dispenses with their division, existing to the present moment, into two main groups differing in respect of method : (1) the physico-biological group, comprising the whole of natural science with its objective method, and (2) the humanistic, comprising the sciences of man as a person and as a member of society, this group mainly employing hitherto the subjective method and being regarded by many as constituting the so-called normative sciences.

Here we are forced to the conclusion that the universal process, which consists in the continuous transformation of energy and, from the viewpoint of objective science, is an uninterrupted chain of increasingly complicated interrelations of matter, which is a latent form of the same energy, occurs according to the same fundamental principles, whether it is manifested in the movements of the heavenly bodies and in the processes occurring in them ; in the processes of inanimate or animate nature on the earth ; in particular, in the life and manifestations of the human person ; or, lastly, in human society or the so-called superorganic world in all the complexity of its external correlations.

And since this is so, the inner aspect of phenomena, too, that aspect which we discover in ourselves by introspection, cannot be an attribute peculiar to man or to those beings which resemble him—the animals. In some form, although the most rudimentary, even potential, this attribute appertains to the vegetable kingdom and to inorganic nature throughout the universe. The universe develops, changes continuously, and, at the same time, conforms to eternal, fundamental laws valid for the whole universe and each part of it, including the electron. That is the conclusion to which reflexology leads as a branch of science studying, objectively and from the objective standpoint, human personality and human society in their external manifestations ; and reflexology recognises no independent study of the subjective side of man, unless the objective data are taken into account.

V. BECHTEREV

PETROGRAD
5th March, 1923

PREFACE TO THE THIRD EDITION

ABOUT forty years have passed since, by operating on the cerebral cortex of a dog, I discovered in the sigmoid gyrus[1]—a limited area of the cerebral cortex—the precise localisation of learned movements or such association reflexes as are acquired by training, for example, giving the paw ; and more than thirty years have passed since, at the 5th Pirogov Congress in 1893 (St. Petersburg), during the discussions on traumatic neuroses and psychoses (and in a number of subsequent papers) I showed that it is necessary to introduce the strictly objective method into the diagnosis of functional disorders of the nervous system. Here I pointed out that the objective indications, reflexive in character, are of particular importance in the diagnosis of these states. Then, more than twenty years ago, in 1904, I published in *Vestnik Psychologii* the paper *Objective Psychology and its Subject Matter*,[2] in which, after a number of investigations, which led me to this method of studying man, I sketched the plan of the purely objective study of human personality.[3]

The method of dressage used in the West, for example by Goltz and Hitzig, is a method of inculcating association-motor reflexes. This method was later used in West Europe by O. Kalischer, Hachet-Souplet, and others. Concerning natural association reflexes, a number of papers, treating of their localisation in the cerebral cortex—beginning with Dr. Zhukovsky's work *O lokalizatzii dichatelnich tzentrov v mozgovoi kore (The Localisation of Respiratory Centres in the Cerebral Cortex)*—were published from my laboratory. Zhukovsky's work was published as early as 1898, twenty-seven years ago, and, in this work, he was the first to prove that the removal of the cortical respiratory centres eliminates respiratory association reflexes acquired during the animal's life (for instance, when a cat is brought near a dog's snout).

It is scarcely necessary to explain here that, at first, the study, which I began in the middle of the 'eighties, of the conduction paths in the brain and, afterwards, the elucidation, in a number of papers by me and my disciples, of the general structure of the brain, and still later, in the course of the winter 1906–7, the introduction of artificial inculcation of a motor association reflex into the method of investigating man and animals led to the foundation of human reflexology as a branch of science studying personality from the objective or, more accurately, the bio-social point of view. To think otherwise would mean to ignore the fact that reflexology is based on neurology and the direct study of man's motor reactions to internal and external stimuli, particularly those stimuli issuing from the social world. If we disregard these, the objective study of personality is unthinkable. At the present time, reflexology has reached such a point of development that it may boldly be made the basis of the study of human

---

[1] This corresponds to the præcentral gyrus in the human cerebral cortex.
[2] A translation of this paper was published in the *Revue scientifique*, 1906.
[3] See nos. 80, 81, 82, and 83 in the bibliography at the end of the present work. In these the results of pertinent investigations in my laboratory are set down.

personality, and that without our having recourse to the data of subjective psychology.

Having devoted forty years of scientific activity to the discovery and solution of the method and problems of the study of normal and abnormal human personality, having extended the same method to collective personality, and now feeling the weight of almost seventy years upon me, I can confidently hand over to my disciples and adherents the task of further elaborating this promising branch of science, which applies the bio-social method of investigation to the problems concerned with diseases of personality and to the humanistic sciences, including the important department—pedagogics. I have attempted this application (whether successfully or otherwise is not for me to decide) in other works and papers, such as *Collective Reflexology* (sep. edition), *The Objective Investigation of the Neuro-psychical Sphere in Infants* (*Vestnik Psychologii*, 1908), *Problems of the Evolution of Neuro-psychical Activity and their Application to Pedagogics* (*Vestnik Psychologii*, 1916), *The Personality of the Artist in the Light of Reflexology* (Symposium : *Arena*), and others.

It remains only to state that this, the third edition, has been revised and considerably enlarged. Chapters on genetic reflexology and creativeness have been added.

V. BECHTEREV

3rd April, 1925

CONTENTS

CONTENTS

LIST OF ILLUSTRATIONS

GENERAL PRINCIPLES
OF HUMAN REFLEXOLOGY

CHAPTER I

Anthropomorphism in scientific views of the nature of living things. The method of indirect observation of an external person ; the subjectivity of modern psychology. The use of objective data, but only for the elucidation of psychical correlations. The problem of the external ego. Different theories concerning the knowing of the external ego. Words are signs and stimuli of merely similar, and not identical, experiences in another individual. The inaccuracy of testimony. The study of subjective states may be made only on oneself.

REFLEXOLOGY, which is a new doctrine, is the science of human personality studied from the strictly objective, bio-social standpoint. It embraces a special sphere of knowledge to which human thought has not yet become accustomed, and consists in investigating, from the strictly objective standpoint, not only the more elementary, but also all the higher, functions of the human being, which in everyday language are called the manifestations of feeling, knowing, and willing, or, speaking generally, the phenomena of psychic activity—the " spiritual sphere." In this way it confines itself to the external peculiarities of the activity of man : his facial expressions, his gestures, voice, and speech as a coherent integration of signs, in correlation with the exciting external influences—physical, biological, and, above all, social—but also with the internal, regardless of whether either of these two types of influence is referable to the present or the past.

In order to assume such a strictly objective standpoint in regard to man, imagine yourself in the position of a being from a different world and of a different nature, and having come to us, say, from another planet. This being, appearing on earth and meeting man, would occupy himself with studying this living individual, who utters apparently unintelligible sounds. He would observe that man, compared to all other terrestrial beings, is endowed with a more varied and complex expression of activity, and expresses himself in movements and other reactions in two ways : some expressions are correlations, which are simpler and similar in character, with the external stimuli acting on the organism, for immediately after some given external stimulus a certain outer reaction always ensues, even in new-born infants as well as in many of the higher animals. These are phenomena which we call simple or ordinary reflexes. But in addition to these innate reflex actions, there are exhibited, on the part of man, other outward expressions, which may be found, too, in other terrestrial living beings, though in much less complex forms, and which are not so simply correlated to the external stimuli as are the ordinary reflexes, but are found correlated not so much to present stimuli as to those of the past, and sometimes even the very remote past.

So this visitor from another planet would see that man, in selecting his eatables, not only gathers berries and fruit from wild trees, but, guided by past experience, tills the soil in a certain way, grows vegetables and fruit trees, sows corn, and prepares it suitably by thrashing and grinding, and by baking from the flour bread which is eaten daily. To facilitate his work in this respect, guided again by past experience, he uses various agricultural implements which are produced in special factories, and uses the strength of horses and oxen, which he has previously domesticated for this purpose, but now breeds at home and trains in a suitable way. For the above-mentioned purpose, *i.e.* the acquiring of food and facilitating of work in other respects also, he keeps other domestic animals which he has previously tamed. He produces certain supplies which he keeps in special stores ; and, lastly, before consuming his food, he prepares many of the eatables in a special way by means of fire in specially constructed ovens, and so develops the highly complex art of cookery. For that same purpose man hunts wild animals and birds, and uses a particular kind of gun constructed on the basis of past experience, etc.

Continuing his observation of human life, this visitor from another planet would see that man, in order the better to struggle with his environment and secure food and shelter, lives in communities, and that his social life impels him, for the purpose of uniting forces, to use means of communication with others in the form of facial expressions, gestures, voice, and speech, the latter exhibiting a multitude of varieties in the form of national languages, which consist of symbolic signs or words, combined in a definite way, and composed of separate sounds. So language makes it possible for different individuals to exchange their personal experiences, and makes practicable the transmission of this experience, by means of education and culture, from one generation to the other, and thus piles up the collective experience of the ages. Lastly, language among civilised nations has a written and also a printed form, which enables man not only to preserve for posterity the experiences of previous generations, but also, by letters, and even more speedily by telegraphic communication, to exchange experiences with those who are at a great distance. Spoken language in turn may be transmitted over great distances by the telephone invented by man ; and writing and especially the printing press make it possible to spread and preserve written language in numerous transcripts for future generations, while the phonograph and gramophone invented by man communicate even spoken language to posterity.

Let us not speak of the various magnificent buildings, of technical devices for locomotion by train, steamer, motor-car, aeroplane, dirigible, etc., and of the no less amazing development of the various forms of art. But I should like to ask you now : Observing human life in all its complex expressions, would this visitor from another planet, of a different nature, ignorant of human language, turn to subjective analysis in order to study the various forms of human activity and those impulses which evoke and direct it ? Would he try to force on man the unfamiliar experiences of another planetary world, or would this being study human life and all its various manifestations from the strictly objective point of view and try to explain to himself the different correlations between man and his environment, as we study, for example, the life of microbes and lowly animals in general ? I think there can be no doubt about the answer.

It is quite obvious that a being of a higher nature can study all the various expressions of human personality only from the strictly objective standpoint, without turning to a subjective analysis of supposititious inner experiences and using for their explanation the analogy with himself, which, in the present case, is absolutely excluded.

In the same way, we, too, can and must study the various activities of man, *i.e.* his deeds, speech, facial expressions, gestures, and his so-called instinctive activities, or, rather, inherited-organic behaviour, from the strictly objective point of view, and that in the light of the external and internal stimuli, without our turning to subjective analysis and to the analogy with ourselves. In following this method, obviously we must proceed in the manner in which natural science studies an object : in its particular environment, and explicate the correlation of the actions, conduct, and all other expressions of a human individual with the external stimuli, present and past, that evoke them ; so that we may discover the laws to which these phenomena conform, and determine the correlations between man and his environment, both physical, biological, and, above all, social.

It is regrettable that human thought usually pursues a different course —the subjective direction—in all questions concerning the study of man and his higher activities, and so extends the subjective standpoint to every department of human activity. But this standpoint is absolutely untenable, since each person develops along different lines on the basis of unequal conditions of heredity, education, and life experience, for these conditions establish a number of correlations between man and his environment, especially the social, and so each person is really a separate phenomenon, completely unique and irreproducible, while the subjective view presupposes an analogy with oneself—an analogy not existing in actual fact, at least not in the highest, and consequently more valuable, expressions of a human being.

You will say that we use analogy everywhere, that in everyday life we cannot approach another man without it. All that is, perhaps, true to a certain extent, but science cannot content itself with this, because, taking the line of subjective interpretation, we inevitably commit some fallacy. It is true that, in estimating another person, we turn to subjective terminology, and constantly say that such and such a man thinks this or that, reasons in this or that manner, etc. But we must not forget that everyday language and the scientific approach to natural phenomena cannot be identical. For instance, we always say of the sun that it rises and sets, that it reaches its zenith, travels across the sky, etc., while science tells us that the sun does not move, but that the earth revolves round it.

And so, from the point of view of present-day science, there must be only one way of studying another human being expressing himself in an integration of various outward phenomena in the form of speech, facial and other expressions, activities, and conduct. This way is the method usually employed in natural science, and consists in the strictly objective study of the object, without any subjective interpretations and without introducing consciousness.

It must be noticed, however, that for this purpose it is first of all necessary to discard our usual view of the world—that view which cannot exclude the analogy with oneself and is inclined to animatism.[1]

We must emphasise that the subjective manifestations of his own personality are for man the objects of direct self-observation, and, there-fore, it is natural that man's earliest attitude to the world was anthropo-morphic in the real sense of the word. That is why, for primitive peoples, everything, beginning with the sun, is endowed with a soul; and the ancient mythology of civilised nations is full of illustrations of how man ascribes to everything that he sees around him, especially if it is capable of movement, a spirit similar to his own.

This attitude has also slipped into primitive religion, in which nature is inhabited by man-like deities possessing human feelings and passions, human reasoning-power, will, and even human form. Man himself represented the centre, as it were, or—more precisely—the alpha and omega of all animate and inanimate nature. Everything round him found in him that prototype which, simply by means of analogy with himself, with his own ego, made possible a facile solution of many world-problems which lie beyond the scope of the human mind.

That is why subjectivism is found at the root of all belief in spirits, even in the most absurd. So, if a man during an attack of insanity injures himself somehow and raves, primitive peoples explain the pheno-menon by a hostile spirit, the spirit of the devil, having entered the body of that man. The possessing spirit may also be a benevolent one, as when the " psychotic," abandoning former attitudes, preaches a better life and assumes the rôle of prophet. But that is not all. If there is question of the existence of malign and benignant spirits, obviously one has to find means to propitiate the former and to supplicate the latter. For this purpose, one may have recourse to sacrifice, absolute obedience to them, praise, flattery, glorification, etc., and, in some cases, even to threats, spell-casting, cunning, etc. All these resources of the savage result from his subjective evaluation of the external world.

According to Spencer, writing on superstitions (*Principles of Sociology*, 1898, vol. I, § 80), the root reason for the distinction between animate and

---

[1] *Translators' note :* The doctrine that part, if not all, of the inanimate kingdom, as well as all animated beings, are endowed with reason, intelligence, and volition identical with that of man. See *Folk Lore* (1900), XI, p. 171.

inanimate is the supposition that movement is identical with life. Only later is that movement which is associated with life distinguished from other movements through its spontaneity.

This hypothesis of a spirit dwelling in a body was, according to Spencer, alien to primitive man at first. In his opinion, dreams necessarily preceded the evolution of the notion of the spiritual ego; but here arises the question whether there was ever a period when man did not dream. It is my opinion that there was not, and so animatism must be contemporaneous with the very earliest periods of human life. Anyhow, Spencer does not vigorously defend his position. " In primitive thought," says Spencer, " events which are of irregular occurrence, and by this, as well as by their apparent spontaneity, suggest living agents, are ascribed to living agents deviating as little from ordinary ones as may be; and are devoid of anything like religious idea or sentiment. . . . While appearances are explained as caused by unknown living beings, we have, in the introduction here of a transfigured man, and there of a god, as instrumental, a recourse to explanations no longer of the purely natural kind."[1]

" Witnessing the temporary unconscious states of the wounded and the stunned, the savage creates, for the first time, the view that the ego, or what he later calls the spirit, is temporarily absent from the body. According to his views, when real death occurs, this ego temporarily leaves the body and roams in other worlds, just as the human spirit roams, as it were, in dreams. But the same savage assumes a reunion of the spirit with the body, and so arises the belief in a life beyond, with subsequent resurrection, a belief universally accepted. In this way, the custom of primitive peoples to leave food, clothing, and weapons in the grave of the dead is explained, for the life beyond is like real life."[2]

In the opinion of some, this also explains the custom of heaping earth copiously on the graves of the dead, so as to prevent them from coming out.

After the formulation of the idea of souls or shades of the dead, the former are soon classified into good and bad, just as we classify men in life. In the next stage of development, the idea of malignant spirits evolves, and corresponds to our contemporary notion of the devil.

Simultaneously, the idea of the participation of spirits in man's everyday life develops. Herein lies the explanation of calamities inflicted by invisible enemies, when such calamities evade obvious explanation. Savages associate even the thought of natural death with the interference of evil spirits and ascribe pathological states to the influences of such

[1] *Translators' note :* pp. 771–772, 3rd ed.; London, 1902.
[2] Examples of the last statement may be found in my paper, *The Votiaki*, published in *Vestnik Yevropi*, 1879.

Translators' note : The Votiaki, Votiaks, or Votyaks are a small tribe, Finnish in origin, living chiefly in the south-eastern part of the Viatka government, where Bechterev himself was born.

We have failed to verify the second quotation from Spencer. The earlier editions are not available to us, and the 3rd ed. is slightly abridged. See, however, *Principles of Sociology*, 3rd ed., vol. I, pp. 149, 152, 415.

spirits ; fits—epilepsy, hysteria, and other conditions—were regarded by the ancients, by many primitive peoples, and even by cultured peoples in the later periods of human history contemporaneous with the development of mysticism (*e.g.* in the Middle Ages), as a state of possession by evil spirits.

We cannot help seeing a reflection of the same mode of thinking in the fact that man, as it were involuntarily, ascribes qualities of his own ego to other living and even inanimate beings, and uses, in discriminating them, the analogy with himself. In the Persian *Avesta*, even the soil to be tilled is regarded as a person endowed with feeling and loving to be tilled. " Who gives the earth the greatest joy ? " Ahuramazda[1] answers : " He who grows most corn, herbs, and fruit trees." And again, the earth turns to man with the following words : " Man, thou who tillest me with both thy right and thy left hand, I shall always be propitious to the fields ; I shall yield all kinds of nutritive commodities—everything I can produce."

Here we may also read that demons and certain peculiar supernatural beings suffer defeat through cultivation of the corn : " When the rye is reaped the sprites utter cries ; when the rye is thrashed they turn to flee ; but when it is kneaded they perish."

In the *Kalevala*, even the road is personified and endowed with spirit, for it converses with the traveller. Here Lemminkaina, the heroine of the Finnish epic, *Kalevala*, addresses the road, which, as it were, approaches her, when she wanders in search of her son : " Road, created by God ! Hast thou not seen my son somewhere, hast thou not met my golden apple, my silver staff ? " The road, not without reason, answered her : " I have no time to care for thy son. I have many sorrows of my own, for my lot is hard, my fate is sad ; I am trodden on by dogs' feet, I am torn by ponderous wheels, I am trampled by heavy soles." That living beings of a lower order may speak human language we can see not only in children's fairy-tales, but also in the Bible (the famous biblical she-ass).[2]

We owe to the same subjectivity of primitive epochs not only a number of superstitions concerning werewolves, but also, on the one hand, an unreasonable fear of some animals, and, on the other, their worship, and even the cult of deified ancestors in the shape of various kinds of animals down to, and including, reptiles (zoolatry), and lastly the rôle of animals in ancient mythology (the eagle of Jupiter, the owl of Minerva, etc.) where they are survivals, which have become simple emblems, of some earlier cult.

On the other hand, even the Greek philosopher, Protagoras, taught that man is the measure of everything. This anthropocentric attitude has invaded science from philosophy, so that even some later writers (Haeckel,

[1] *Translators' note :* Ahurō Mazdāo (Zend) ; Auramazda or Ahuramazda (O. Persian) ; Ormuzd or Ormazd.
[2] *Translators' note :* Balaam's ass. *Numbers* xxii–xxiv.

Le Dantec, Petri, and others) attribute a psychic, consequently a conscious, not only to animals including the lowest types, but also to plants, and even to every cell (cellular consciousness) ; and extend their doctrine in this respect even to atoms (so-called atomic souls). Writers like Wundt and Espinas ascribe even complex manifestations of conscious activities such as patriotism, sense of duty, sense of property, esthetics, love, etc., to ants, bees, termites, spiders, and others. In this way even prominent scientists extend consciousness as a subjective phenomenon to the whole of animate nature, and even to the inanimate world.

The same holds good also of the infant's inner life. See how the subjectivists evolve their scientific theories of the development of the child's ego. "The child's first step in this direction is to learn to distinguish the objects of the external world as things existing independently of himself. How this step is achieved we need not stop to enquire. But we must note that all those features of the child's experience that are not thus extruded or referred to a world of external reality remain to constitute the nucleus of his idea of himself. The parts of his body, especially his limbs, play a very peculiar and important part in this process, because they are presented in consciousness sometimes as things of the outer world, as parts of the not-self, sometimes—when they are the seats of pain, discomfort, heat, or cold, or muscular sensations—as parts of the self. Thus the conception of the bodily self is in large part dependent on the development of the conception of things as persistent realities of the external world ; and the conception of those things is in turn completed by the projection into it of the idea of the self as a centre of effort, a cause of movement and of resistance to pressure." (W. McDougall : *Introduction to Social Psychology*.[1])

It is scarcely possible to doubt that here, as well as in further discussions, creative phantasy is put forward as science, because there is question of the first hours and days of the life of the infant, whose subjective world is necessarily inaccessible even to indirect self-observation. Subjective psychology and also animal psychology are full of similar fictions.

The works of such reliable investigators, as *e.g.* Romanes, are saturated with these anthropomorphic views. Here is an example of this in a work of Romanes',[2] in which we find mention of a feeling of penitence in a Spanish mule which has been punished for disobedience, and whose coronal and bells have been given to another mule ; and of a feeling of pride in the rams and bulls which wear bells and other ornaments given them as leaders of the herd.

It is true that this subjectivism is gradually being ousted from animal psychology and, from being a universal and all-embracing principle, is becoming more and more restricted, for at the present time nobody will, for example, place on an equal footing with his own ego the inner life of lower animals such as the snail or, still less, the microbe ; yet, even

---

[1] *Translators' note :* 21st ed., p. 157.
[2] *Translators' note : Animal Intelligence*, 4th ed., 1886, p. 330.

now, there is no lack of support for the establishment of an analogy between the ego and the inner life of the higher animals.[1]

It is not necessary to mention that, in the exploration of the inner world of another man, psychologists still use, as a fully admissible method, the so-called indirect method of self-observation, a method based on the analogy with oneself.

The fact is that present-day psychology, although it has become richer during recent decades through its adoption of the experimental method of investigation, still remains a thoroughly subjective science, in the sense that consciousness is regarded as the fundamental and inalienable stamp of the psychic activity not only of oneself, but also of others ; and that psychology universally uses the so-called introspective method as fundamental in the investigation of inner or psychic processes.

Even the sociologists with psychological leanings, and so great a man as Tarde (*Logique sociale* : Paris, 1904, p. 106)[2] are so infected with subjectivism that they extend the subjective method to animals. So, among other things, Tarde remarks : " Psychologists who are forced to confine themselves to the study of human psychology, and for whom it is impossible to descend to the sphere of animal psychology, or, at least, to penetrate deeply into it by the introspective method, tend to think that the idea of time, as well as of force, appears in human beings earlier than other ideas do. Does it not appear probable, on the contrary (and in the case of the lower animals even certain) that localisation in space is already quite distinct when localisation in time only just begins to be outlined,

---

[1] In this respect, passages particularly instructive and surprising of their kind are to be found, among others, in Prof. I. Sikorsky's work ; *General Psychology* (Kiev, 1901). Let us take, for example, his description of the feelings of an ox (p. 333) : " Although this quadruped may appear banal to the observer, the fact that the feeling of *awe* is found in it for the first time in the animal kingdom is not lacking in profound psychological interest. The feeling of awe in cattle may be observed in the slaughter-house. Many of the animals waiting for their turn are fully aware of the approach of their death, and, experiencing a feeling of *surprise*, caused by the unexpectedness of the event, and also a *panic fear*, do not submit to these two feelings, but rather to *compassion* for their comrades, whose flowing blood they smell. In this way the feeling of awe arises in the animals, and an ox goes to its death, not in headless terror, like other animals (pigs, sheep), but with a *noble feeling* which fills its *soul* at that moment." Other examples from the same book deserve equal attention, but it is not worth while to quote them.

Here is one more example, referring to ants. Evans (*Evolutionary Ethics*), speaking of those ants which keep slaves, which are forced to feed and to carry them, remarks that their laziness is not physical but *moral*, and results from an aristocratic contempt of work, from pleasure in being accompanied by a suite of obedient servants, and from the notion that it is incomparably more becoming and noble to travel on the backs of slaves and have food brought straight to their mouth than to move on their own legs, and themselves put the food into their own mouth. That this is really so, he continues, is apparent from the fact that, when there is question of war or plunder, these apparently helpless ants become bold and skilful soldiers.

[2] *Translators' note :* Gabriel Tarde (1843–1904). French sociologist. *Logique sociale* (1895).

and should we not recognise that they materialise the objects of their perceptions earlier than they begin to *spiritualise* them ? "

But I must say that there is not, and cannot be, any indirect self-observation, and if anything is possible in regard to an external person, it is only an *estimate* of his inner world, but this estimate, too, is based merely on analogy with oneself, and this naturally leads us into error.

It must be remarked, first of all, that the idea of the psychic is but a rather vague concept. Very often the psychic is regarded by psychologists as coterminous with consciousness, but, so far, consciousness itself has not been exactly defined, as we shall see later.

According to W. Wundt,[1] the definition of psychology as the science " of states of consciousness " is a vicious circle, for if you ask what that consciousness is, the states of which psychology studies, the answer will be—" Consciousness comprises the sum of the states of which we are conscious."

Münsterberg, who has done much in regard to the application of experiment in psychology, and who has in part created applied psychology, the so-called economic or industrial, regards psychology precisely as the science of consciousness, and, on the whole, adopts the subjective method. Thus, on page 12 of his work he says : " Practical life wants to know what feelings, what thoughts, what manifestations of will, and what emotions are to be expected under certain conditions, in what way they may be determined and regulated, and it is altogether indifferent to it whether the mechanism producing them is physiological activity of the brain cells or the process of an unconscious psychic apparatus ! "[2]

I shall not touch here on the fact that there are psychologists who widen the concept of psychical processes to embrace, in addition to conscious processes, unconscious, or, as they are sometimes styled, sub- or extro-conscious processes, for the latter, not being conscious, occur, according to the views of these psychologists, after the manner of conscious processes ; in other words, they are like extinct conscious processes (unconscious sensations, ideas, etc.).

Still, the importance of the unconscious in psychic life is, generally speaking, enormous. " The unconscious "—according to Freud[3]—" is the real psychic ; *its inner nature is just as unknown to us as the reality of the external world, and it is just as imperfectly reported to us through the data of consciousness as is the external world through the indications of our sensory organs.*"

Thus, this extension of the concept of psychical processes to include

---

[1] W. Wundt : *Einführung in die Psychologie*, 1912, p. 9.

[2] See *Psychologie und Wirtschaftsleben*, Russ. tr., Moscow, 1914, p. 11. On p. 21 of the same work, the author says : " We demand from psychology in the scientific sense that it should investigate psychic life as a content of consciousness, a content which should be split up into its elements and investigated as to its causes and effects."

[3] *Translators' note : Interpretation of Dreams*, p. 486 ; 3rd ed. ; tr. Brill.

not only conscious, but also unconscious or subconscious processes does not change the nature of the fundamental point of view ; as a result of this, present-day psychology, as I have already said, is, in the true sense of the word, a subjective science, and, therefore, sharply isolated from that province of scientific investigation which goes by the name of natural science.

Furthermore, it may be stated with conviction that, in its essence, psychic life as such does not offer any definite fulcrum for scientific analysis.

Until recently, we have adhered, in studying the psychic world, to the conventional division of the inner life into intellect, feeling, and will ; yet some condense these into two, and even one. However, Professor Petrazhitsky[1] is not satisfied with this tripartite division, but maintains that emotions or impulses which are of a bilateral, passive-active nature should rank in a separate division, while in all other psychical states we have to do with phenomena which are unilaterally active or passive in nature, such as sensations, ideas, feeling, and will, the latter to be understood as consisting of aspirations and active experiences.

Therefore he recognises the emotions as the main factors operative in adjustment to life, the other functions of the psychic playing secondary or auxiliary parts. This view is open to refutation, if we keep in mind that the division into cognition, feeling, and will is in itself of an exceedingly hypothetical character, and, besides, it is quite impossible to imagine e.g. a movement without a driving impulse ; perception and feeling without active participation of the somatic sphere (respiratory movements, the vasomotor system, etc.), or acts of volition without muscular sensations, but still the emotions may be regarded as phenomena which cannot be assigned definite places in the other spheres of psychic life known as cognition, feeling, will. And even this is disputed by some.

We must not forget that subjectivism, turning to self-knowledge, finds certain tendencies in man, and, for lack of objective analysis and, consequently, of determination of their real origin, ascribes to them a metaphysical, even transcendental, origin, as has happened in the case of Kant's categorical imperative.

As regards the method itself, some are satisfied with the subjective method and submit it to appropriate analysis, but the intuitionalists are not satisfied with it, and supplement it by the transubjective method. You will ask what is the difference between intuitionalism and subjectivism. Indeed, does not this deserve attention ? It amounts to this : the intuitionalists maintain that intuitive knowledge gives direct apprehension of the whole object, while ratiocinative analysis tackles the problem in its integral parts. Further, intuitive knowledge gives an insight into the thing itself and its real nature, and, consequently, has an absolute

---

[1] L. I. Petrazhitsky : *Teoriya prava i gosudarstva* (*The Theory of Law and of the State*), vol. I, p. 3 ; *Vvedeniye v izutcheniye prava i nravstvennosti* (*Introduction to the Study of Law and Morals*), p. 175, *et passim.*

character, while ratiocinative analysis operates through symbols, and, consequently, bears a relative character. Lastly, intuitive knowledge provides an immediate apprehension of the inexhaustible content of the object, while ratiocinative analysis is forced, in order to study an object fully, to build up an endless concatenation of concepts, but such a concatenation is impracticable. In order to illustrate both kinds of knowledge let us consider a movement of the hand. Intuitively (*i.e.* inwardly) it is regarded as a simple, unitary, and absolute phenomenon, but externally, to an observer who analyses it, it appears as a movement passing through an endless series of points. Such is the view of Bergson, the most prominent representative of intuitionalism.

The view holds undisputed sway among modern psychologists that, in investigating the behaviour of man, it is not possible to exclude the psychic altogether, because every reality and every process is first of all a psychic reality, for our knowledge of nature is secondhand, through the medium of the psychic world which the mechanists deny (Lotze).

Therefore, it is usually pointed out, as evidence of the necessity of turning to subjective analysis in the study of a human being, that our knowledge of the external world and in general our estimates of it are based on subjective process. But this ignores the fact that it only seems so, because we are forced in this case to turn to self-observation and self-analysis. But if we turn to the objective investigation of an external person and regard that individual's logical processes and his behaviour as reactions to stimuli from the external world, we shall have direct evidence that the development of these reactions is inevitable, if we take into account the individual's bio-social development under the influence of his experience, and consider his utilisation of external influences for his own preservation and for that of the community. From my point of view, logic is the result of reflexes built-in through experience. Let us say that a man swallows some fruit, say an apple, and swallows it entire. Then there is experiential evidence that the apple is edible. But this experience proves also that not only the whole apple, but also its parts, *e.g.* the peel, may be eaten together with the apple. Thus the syllogism, which is the direct result of reflexes, assumes the following form : apples are edible ; the peel—a part of the apple—is also edible. As a matter of fact, the apple is not entirely edible ; the core with the seeds, being difficult to cut, is usually discarded. This lies at the root of the analysis, and the conclusion is : apples have two parts—an edible outer part and an inedible core, etc. It is scarcely necessary to mention that the symbolism of words facilitates the conclusion chiefly in two ways : in the facilitated process of substituting certain signs for others and in their appropriate rearrangement, as in mathematical procedure.

It is important to note that logical operations may be mechanically reproduced, as has been proved by the logical machine invented by Thomson, and constructed by Chrushtchov.

If this is so, the inevitability of the subjective process in the establishing of our correlations with the environment, correlations which take the form of judgment and behaviour, is an illusion on our part. Indeed, we " comprehend " much, intuitively or instinctively, without the participation of the " conscious mind." We know of cases of perception, reasoning, and behaviour without the participation of the conscious mind, while the latter is engrossed in quite different work. Lastly, we are acquainted with phenomena of so-called unconscious creativeness, including creativeness in sleep. Many cases of such creativeness are known. Among the more recent cases may be mentioned the mathematician Poincaré's discovery of the Fuchsian functions. I myself know of a number of examples of creativeness in sleep.[1] Finally, in the subjective world of our thought-processes, we are, as you know, by no means conscious of everything, but rather only of the final result of our thinking, while the process itself by which we come to the given conclusion usually takes place to a great extent in the sphere of the unconscious or unaccountable processes.[2] And if this is so, why should we be forced to acknowledge the *a priori* inevitability of the participation of conscious processes in the establishment of our relations to the environment ?

Taking into consideration certain processes of the unconscious, *i.e.* direct knowledge in the form of intuition, and also unconscious " intuitive " creativeness, we must, on the contrary, come to the conclusion that the conscious is not at all an indispensable factor in the establishing of the appropriate correlations between the individual and the environment.

On our part, we do not think of denying " psychic " reality, but we are justified in maintaining that it is not something isolated from brain processes. We say that psychical process is inseparable from brain process, and, therefore, when studying brain processes in their higher manifestations, we study along with them the course and development of psychical processes.

Still, not every brain process is at the same time a psychical process, and, therefore, the concept of brain process is wider than that of psychical process.

Some suppose that in teleologically directed processes, such as complex activities, the result is the cause, for the goal is subjectively projected into the future, and, therefore, it is not possible to avoid subjective analysis. But we must not forget that, in some instances, the aim

---

[1] Shortly before my receiving the proofs of these lines, I. I. Lapshin, at a Conference of the Institute for the Study of Brain, mentioned more than seventy authentic cases of creativeness in sleep. I have been able to observe the same process in myself. It happened several times, when I concentrated in the evening on a subject which I had to put into poetic shape, that, in the morning, I had only to take my pen, and the words flowed, as it were, spontaneously ; I had only to polish them later. Much interesting material concerning creativeness in sleep may also be found in Grusenberg's book : *Geny i tvortchestvo* (*Genius and Creativeness*) ; Leningrad, 1924.

[2] *Translators' note : i.e.* processes of which we cannot give an account to ourselves or to others.

may be what has been previously experienced by the individual or his ancestors, as is the case, for example, in the manifestations of instinct in animals ; in other cases, the aim may be what has been reproduced on the basis of the experience of others, and, therefore, here too, the activity is directed by the reproduction of a past experience, even though it originates outside the self, and such experience is usually accompanied by a sthenic and positive mimico-somatic reaction, aiding the development of reflexes directed towards the sustaining of that same reaction. Therefore, there is no essential difference between teleological and other activities stimulated by means of the revival of similar activities which have occurred in our own past personal experience or in that of others.

Consequently, the point at issue is not concerned with consciousness, or with the idea of an aim, but with the reproduction and realisation of what, originating from past experience, stimulates sthenic or asthenic response and the appropriate mimico-somatic reaction, with aggressive or defensive reflexes. Therefore, teleological activities are proper to the simplest animals (Jennings,[1] Famintzin,[2] Metalnikov,[3] and others) and even to plants (Fr. Darwin). Lastly, man's adjustments of his outer manifestations in relation to another being, whether animal or human, do not fall under the head of psychical processes, as may be thought, but are themselves outward manifestations. This may be seen from the fact that we may merely feign to threaten somebody, and so call out a defence response on his side, or we can laugh when feeling inward sorrow, and even infect others with our laughter.

It is a well-known fact that even segments of lower animals are capable of executing exceedingly complex movements. If you dissever a ray of a starfish at its base, it continues to move to and fro, rises and falls, and if it is reversed it will right itself. Also segments of insects' bodies can perform complex defensive movements ; the segments of even one and the same insect, according to Romanes, engage in struggle with each other. Similar phenomena may be found in the vertebrates, not excluding man. Thus, a frog with its medulla oblongata transected performs complex movements with its leg in wiping a weak solution of acid off the surface of its back. If birds, *e.g.* ducks, are operated on by cutting underneath the medulla oblongata, we may, while artificially preserving their respiration, observe very complex movements of legs, wings, and rump (Tarchanoff), and, while preserving the medulla oblongata to the level of the corpora quadrigemina, it is possible for the birds even to cry. Thus the whole complex co-ordination of the various movements of vertebrates is found in the lower centres of the spinal cord. In this case the brain has only to send impulses to the lower centres in order to

---

[1] Jennings : *Behavior of the Lower Organisms ;* New York, 1915.

[2] Famintzin : *Yestestvoznaniye i psychologiya* (*Natural Science and Psychology*), St. Petersburg.

[3] Metalnikov : *K phyziologii vnutrikishetchnovo pishtchevareniya u prosteishich* (*Physiology of Intra-intestinal Digestion in Protozoa*), Petrograd, 1910.

execute certain activities. Needless to say, the function of the vegetative organs, regulated by the vegetative or sympathetic and the parasympathetic nervous system, is characterised by marked autonomy and does not require even special regulation on the part of the cerebral cortex, although an influence of the latter on the sympathetic ganglia is not excluded.

These functions, as shown by human introspection, occur without the participation of the conscious mind, or—more precisely—of the accountable activity, although in morbid states they may become conscious or accountable.[1] Here the question arises : Are those cortical impulses which shape the activity of these mechanisms necessarily accompanied by consciousness ?

It is necessary to note that modern psychology also uses the objective data of observations of the external ego, but it does so really only to approach in this way the elucidation of inner, *i.e.* subjective, experiences. In other words, it tries to discover, by means of observation of the objective manifestations, (*e.g.* expressive movements, changes in the action of the heart and in respiration, to say nothing of speech and behaviour), the correlations of these changes in the sphere of psychic activity, which is to be regarded as a series of inner processes accessible to introspection.

But we know already that even complex manifestations of our activity may occur completely automatically, without being accountable.

We know that a man in a somnambulism may perform exceedingly complex actions, and be unable to give any account of them later. He acts like an automaton. For automatic action a somnambulic state is not even necessary. It is sufficient to be distracted by something and then our activities acquire a purely automatic character.

For instance, Diderot describes such a state as follows : " He is a geometrician. Waking up in the morning and opening his eyes, he immediately returns to the solving of the problem which he has begun the previous evening. He takes his dressing-gown, dresses himself, not knowing what he is doing. He sits down at the table, takes a ruler and a pair of compasses, draws lines, writes equations, makes combinations and calculations, not knowing what he is doing. The clock strikes ; he looks at it ; then hurriedly writes a few letters which must be posted by that day's post. Having written the letters, he dresses, leaves the house, goes to dine in Rue Royale. The street is heaped with stones ; he avoids them. Suddenly he stops ; he remembers that his letters have remained unsealed and unposted on the table. He returns home, lights a candle, seals the letters, and takes them to the post office. From there he goes to Rue Royale ; enters the house where he intends to dine, and meets a circle of philosophers—his friends. They speak about freedom, and he

---

[1] In dispensing with the subjective and very vague term " consciousness," we shall use the fully objective and appropriate term " accountable activity."

Translators' note : By " accountable activity " is meant activity of which we can give an account to ourselves or others.

maintains violently that man is free. I do not interrupt his speech, but in the evening I lead him aside into a corner ; I ask him to give an account of his actions. He happens not to remember anything whatever of what he has done, and I see that he has been a pure machine passively performing various actions in accordance with the motives impelling it. He was not only not free, but did not perform a single action consciously, of his own will. He thought and felt ; but did not at all act more freely than a lifeless body or a wooden automaton which could do the same as he." (Ch. Letourneaux : *L'évolution de la morale.*)

In view of the facts mentioned, it is not without reason that the problem of the external ego so far remains a long way from solution by philosophy. There is no necessity for us to go deeply into the reasons for this, but we shall turn to the origin of modern solipsism in Russia.

This is what we read in a work by Professor A. I. Vvedensky,[1] who as early as 1892, in his article, *The Limits and Characteristics of the Animate* (*Zhurnal Ministerstva Narodnovo Prosveshtcheniya*), took up the position which he has expressed with greater fulness in more recent books : " The objective, *i.e.* the outwardly observed, indications of the possession of a mind must consist in such material phenomena in regard to which it may be unquestionably proved that they cannot originate where there is no psychic life. From these indications it will be possible to determine where it exists and where it does not. But the results of our investigations will all converge on the following conclusion : that no phenomenon objectively observed, *i.e.* no physiological phenomenon, can demonstrate the existence of a mind. Thus, psychic life exhibits no objective indications." After a number of dialectical discussions, this author says : " I am justified in boldly maintaining, without any fear of contradicting any known facts, that besides myself there is no one at all possessed of a mind in the universe." Maintaining that the existence of his own mind is an indubitable fact, this author comes to the conclusion that " where the existence of psychic life is indubitable (*i.e.* in myself) it probably flows in such a way that the concomitant bodily phenomena occur according to their own material laws, as if there were no psychic life whatever."

He regards this law as a psycho-physiological law, or the fundamental law of the absence of objective indications of psychic life. My inner experiences can, according to A. I. Vvedensky, be only objects of belief, and nothing more, for other individuals. He finds, among other things, justification for this attitude of his also in physiological investigations in regard to psychical processes in animals.

We shall not comment on the nature of the views mentioned above,[2]

[1] A. I. Vvedensky : *Psychologiya bez vsyakoi metaphysiki* (*Psychology without Metaphysics*) ; Petrograd, 1917, pp. 71 ff.

[2] A bibliography and criticism of solipsism may be found in S. O. Grusenberg's work, *A. Schopenhauer*, Petrograd, 1912, and in his *Otcherki sovremennoi russkoi philosophii* (*Outline of Modern Russian Philosophy*), Petrograd, 1910. See also my article, *What is Objective Psychology?* published in *Voprosi philosophii i psychologii.*

for A. I. Vvedensky's position is based on dialectics and speculative arguments, and these, because of the peculiar structure of the human mind, are not always reliable guides in the evaluation of truth. Let us remember the ancient sophists.

It is, for instance, clear to everybody that anyone else could deny my " psychic life " for the very same reason for which I might deny it in other people, and this clearly contradicts my inner experience, *i.e.* " the most indubitable fact " (Vvedensky's expression) which can present itself to my mind. Therefore, it is obvious that such an assertion on the part of another in regard to myself is for me an obvious absurdity ; and if this assertion is an obvious absurdity, then my assertion about others—an assertion built up by the same logical method—must be regarded as just as absurd.

One fact is indubitable : there are no suitable methods to direct us unerringly in the study of the psychic life of others. The gist of the matter is this : that the subjective may be directly known only by subjective analysis of oneself, and in no other way. If the great lights of subjective psychology are ultimately led into solipsism, it is clear what value the subjective method in general has. Still, subjectivism permeates not only subjective psychology, but also such an applied science as experimental pedagogics. To prove this let us mention the following passage from Meumann's introductory work (*Lectures in Experimental Pedagogics*).[1] " As has been shown long since by general psychology, all our observations of others consist in drawing conclusions leading to psychic experiences from the outer indications of psychic life, *i.e.* in our case—from the external indications of individuality. These external indications we regard, consequently, as symptoms of an inner life. They are either certain activities or the relations of the individual regarding which we must explain to ourselves what psychic processes and psycho-physical qualities of the individual lie at their root. But an explanation of this kind is always formulated somehow on the basis of analogy with our own inner life and its manifestations which we notice in ourselves ; and this means only that every observation (objective or external), made by us in regard to others, is founded ultimately on self-observation. (*Cp.* Bd. I ; S. 17 *u. folg.*)

From this, for the practice of observation, there results an important principle which we should never have ignored : we must, if possible, try to trace in ourselves all these individual phenomena which we find in others—trace them and attempt perhaps only to imagine an analogous development of the same qualities in ourselves. But this applies still more to experimentation, which is no more than intensive and accurate observation."

I must apologise to the reader for this long quotation, but it is pertinent to the discussion, and not to quote it fully would mean to evade an ex-

---

[1] *Vorlesungen zur Einführung in die experimentelle Pädagogik*, 2, Aufl., Bd. II, S. 36.

haustive exposition of the views of the subjectivist school. But the question is : How can we trace in ourselves the individual peculiarities of an external person, if nature has not given us these peculiarities ? Obviously, there is here a serious and radical error resulting from the subjective method of investigation.

From this it is clear that, by the use of objective data, it is not possible to have a completely accurate and quite appropriate idea of the subjective world of an external person and of an external living being in general. Of course this does not at all mean that, guided by his own experiences, man cannot reproduce the subjective world of others by means of so-called identification. That such reproduction occurs is proved by the works of the best artists of every age ; but this is the problem of artistic creativeness, consequently a creativeness that deviates from reality, and is not scientific analysis, and to be led by it would mean coming to the same logical constructions as if we judged of the real correlation of things from the creations of artists, say painters, or, for instance, accepted a theatrical representation as real life.

In fine, it must be noted that solipsism is not at all a new doctrine in philosophy. From a lecture delivered by F. I. Shtcherbatzky before the Petrograd Philosophical Society (Feb. 1916), we learn that solipsism was expounded by the ancient Hindoo philosophers, and even then gave rise to discussion, and met with severe opposition from other representatives of philosophic thought, as, for instance, Darmakirti (16th cent.).[1]

It must be noted, by the way, that for some time all the earlier theories concerning knowledge of the external ego have begun to be doubted in

[1] We give here the substance of F. I. Shtcherbatzky's lecture :

" 1. Among the works of the Buddhist idealist philosopher, Darmakirti, there is a small pamphlet devoted to the problem of the basis of our conviction that an external psychic life exists.

" 2. Its issue was evoked by the attacks of the realists, who maintained that, from the standpoint of idealism, the existence of external psychic life cannot be proved.

" 3. Therefore, the first part of the pamphlet is devoted to proving that the idealist has as much right to conclude the existence of external psychic life as has the realist ; the difference is only in this : that the realist speaks of the real manifestations of external psychic life, but the idealist only of the corresponding concepts.

" 4. Incidentally, two arguments of the realists are rejected : (a) the first concerns the doctrine that the movements and words of others must be regarded as automatic (unconscious) ; (b) the second—that in dreams it is possible to reach conclusions concerning the existence of the external psyche, because in dreams also there are images of the activities of others.

" 5. Having despatched realism, Darmakirti submits his own view, the essence of which is the recognition, firstly, of course, of one's own movements and words as real indications of psychic life, while the movements and words of others may be regarded as such only conditionally, indirectly, as a result of association because of similarity to one's own.

" 6. Then the problem : In what sense and to what degree may the conclusion founded on such similarity and concerning the existence of external psychic life be regarded as a source of certitude ? is discussed in detail."

D

psychology.[1] Thus, in the work of Lipps[2] we have a sharp criticism of the theory most in vogue : the theory of analogy.

Lipps finds the futility of this theory to consist in the fact that the physical manifestations of others are, in the majority of cases, phenomena of a different kind from our own physical manifestations. So, for instance, anger in others we observe in the form of an external visual picture, while our own anger we experience in the form of kinesthetic perceptions. Only the mirror can give us the external picture of our anger as perceived by others.

Further, assuming that the physical manifestations of others are similar to our physical manifestations, we should, even in this case, get an idea only of our own subjective state, *e.g.* anger, and not at all of that of others.

Lastly, even if we should admit the possibility of conclusions by analogy, we should be able to speak only with probability of the reason for our belief, but we should have no real proof whatever, because the argument from analogy gives us only a probable, and by no means an absolute, conclusion.

In view of the defects in the argument from analogy, Lipps has put forward a special theory : that of empathy,[3] according to which the concept of other beings as endowed with psychic life is derived from the instinct of imitation. Seeing another man yawn, I feel the desire to yawn ; seeing anger in others, I experience the tendency to similar outward manifestation. But these imitative, expressive movements are the causes of the same states in myself ; in other words, here there is question not of the reproduction of the state of another man in the form of sleepiness or anger, but of a new experience of mine.

According to the admission of Lipps himself, by the *feeling* of our own ego *into* the expressive movements of others, there results in us not the conviction of the existence of another ego, which, in his opinion, remains an inexplicable and irreducible fact of belief, but only the tendency to experience our own emotion of anger.

Needless to say, Lipps's theory, as has been justly stated by N. O. Lossky,[4] is defective in the same way as is the argument from analogy. In the perception of external yawning or external anger, we are given only the visual picture of the activity. We imitate it by means of appropriate muscular movements, which, as a result, again give kinesthetic, and not visual, experiences.

Lipps's theory is dealt with critically in M. Scheler's well-known

---

[1] See the exposition of these theories in I. I. Lapshin's pamphlet : *The Problem of the External Ego in Present-day Philosophy*, St. Petersburg, 1910.

[2] Th. Lipps : *Psychologische Untersuchungen*, Bd. I, Lief. 4, *Das Wissen vom fremden " Ich."*

[3] *Einfühlung*—feeling-into.

[4] *The Perception of the Psychic Life of Others ; Logos* (Petrograd ; Moscow, 1914).

work : *Über den Grund zur Annahme der Existenz des fremden " Ich."*[1] Thus, it has no advantages whatever over the argument from analogy.

According to Petrazhitsky,[2] the best results are achieved not by analogy, but by a combination of the methods of inner and external observation. We are firstly concerned with the establishment of a nexus between certain psychic states and certain outward manifestations. Having got this kind of general knowledge, we have the premises for deductive conclusions in concrete cases, *i.e.* conclusions not arrived at by the analogy with our own individual movements and those of others, but by subsuming the concrete movements of others under their appropriate concepts.

It must not be forgotten that, in this case also, the general concepts do not reveal individual subjective relations in the establishment of a nexus between the psychical and the external manifestations, and so we are still left in the lurch.

On the other hand, Darwin has accepted the instinctive discrimination of subjective experiences. As the expressive movements are produced in the majority of cases by means of the innate nervous mechanism, and, therefore, are produced more or less in stereotyped fashion, it is clear that, because of this, the capacity to recognise them has become instinctive.[3] On the other hand, there are theories which lead us straight into the thick of intuitionalism, to which a number of writers adhere. So, for instance, Scheler solves the problem of our knowledge of the external ego by the theory of intuitive perception. He does not make any distinction in his doctrine between that content of consciousness which represents experience, and that which is only the object of observation. Therefore, he supposes that there may be an experiencing of the " external " as if it were one's " own," and here, undoubtedly, there is a methodological error.[4]

Another kind of intuitional view is developed by N. O. Lossky, who also admits the possibility of direct perception of the external psychic life or ego.

In his opinion, it is not the visual picture, but the perception (or rather the pleasant anticipation) of the " sweet " activity of the yawn of others or the perception of the anger of others and its motor activity, which, hidden under the visual picture, impels us to the imitation of their yawn or anger. In other words, I perceive another man not simply as a combination of outward form and colour, which change their position in space, but as something vitally active, animated, and thus arises the tendency to imitate his activity and psychic life.

---

[1] See also his : *Zur Phänomenologie und Theorie der Sympathiegefühle*, Halle, 1913.
[2] *Vvedeniye v teoriyu prava (Introduction to the Theory of Law)*, St. Petersburg, pp. 30–37.   [3] C. Darwin : *The Expression of the Emotions.*
[4] See Lossky : *The Perception of the Psychic Life of Others ; Logos*, vol. I, no. 2, 1914.

Still, it is easy to understand that, in this case, too, man experiences his own activity and not that of others ; besides, here the concept of activity is replaced by that of endowment with mind, while it is clear to everybody that these concepts are not identical ; something not endowed with mind may prove to be active—such are all radioactive substances. Consequently, the theory of direct intuition also does not give us the key to knowledge of the external ego.

Intuition might be helpful as a solution of the problem only if it could be not only proved that the experience of others affects us directly (a possibility, by the way, not excluded by science), but, above all, that we reproduce it in ourselves, and reproduce it not as our activity and our experience in the perception of the activity and psychic life of another, but as his experience. Yet neither the one nor the other has been proved.

It must be noted that experiments which I have performed on animals, and later on human beings (*Problems in the Study of Personality*, 2nd vol.), prove the possibility, under certain conditions, of the direct transmission, from one man to another, of so-called latent reflexes in the form of concentration on a certain activity—a phenomenon which other writers have called telepathic transmission. From this it is clear that human and animal brains, since they are accumulators of energy, may, under certain conditions, play the rôle of transmitters and receivers, like a radio station in which Hertzian rays are used. But concerning this transmission, it is important to remember that conscious processes are not at all involved, and, consequently, there is by no means a reproduction of the latter in the form of conscious experiences, and this excludes the utilisation of telephatic phenomena as a method of scientific investigation concerning the acquisition of knowledge of the external ego.

Thus, neither the argument from analogy, nor the theory of empathy, nor the theory of intuitionalism provides us with a method of knowing the external ego, and still less of analysing it with sufficient scientific accuracy ; and the external ego itself is regarded by such representatives of philosophic thought as A. I. Vvedensky and Lipps as no more than an object of belief.

Therefore, the question is : Can a method founded on so-called indirect or direct self-observation give us a basis for a precise analysis of the psychic life of others, if the external ego itself is inaccessible to knowledge and is, in the opinion of weighty psychologists, merely an object of belief ? It is clear that the doctrine of solipsism stands in contradiction to the methods of indirect self-observation as used by its adherents and by psychologists in general.

If the external ego is only an object of belief, if I cannot prove to myself even the existence of the external ego, if I can in no way demonstrate it, how can I speak of indirect self-observation, *i.e.* the observation of what in reality cannot be proved, of whose existence I cannot be convinced, and which is only an object of belief, and, consequently, an object of possible doubt ? Let us take, as comparable, another problem : the problem of the existence of god. One may believe in god, one may reason about god, but neither, from the strictly scientific point of view, can one prove his existence nor can one be convinced of his existence for oneself. Let us assume that by turning, let us say, to the study of the prophets, to the various revelations, and to the lives of the saints, I take refuge in the method of indirect self-observation for the proof of the existence of god. This very course has been pursued by the devout, and, as is well known, has led to the anthropomorphic idea of god.

Can we derive scientific knowledge from this—can we build up a science on it ? I believe we cannot. But to continue : if it were possible to study the deity, he could be studied only through the manifestation of his power in nature, after the manner in which he is seen by primitive man, who believes in the existence of god, who is ignorant of the laws of nature, and explains *e.g.* thunder and lightning as manifestations of divine power. But cultured man does not find any miracle at all in the phenomena of nature, and studies them not from the viewpoint of manifestations of divine power, but as environmental phenomena completely conformable to law. In the same way, having no means of proving the existence of consciousness in other beings, cultured man should orient himself to the investigation of those reactions which are manifested by the organic environment, and, among others, by his fellow-men ; and the more so as these reactions of the various living beings differ ultimately from each other only in the complexity of their manifestations.

Obviously, in this rôle, *i.e.* the rôle of analysis of the external ego, indirect self-observation must be regarded from the scientific point of view as a method of little use, because, at most, we should, by using it, impose our own emotions, ideas, and experiences on the external ego, and this would lead us into serious error.

Let us take a simple visual object examined by two individuals at the same time. We might think that they would have the same visual experiences. Still it is not difficult to prove that, here too, they are far from being the same, for the one perceives colour in one way, the other in another ; the one is short-sighted, the other long-sighted ; the one looks with concentration, the other without any ; the one concentrates on one part of the object, the other on another ; the one takes interest in one thing according to his individual peculiarities, the other in another, etc.

On the whole, it must be noted that perception of the external world is not only incomplete (between the sound-vibrations, of which the highest range from 32,000 to 40,000 a second, and the heat-vibrations of several billion waves a second, there are an enormous number of rhythms which we do not perceive), but also inconstant in oneself and divergent from that of others. We shall not speak of changes in the sphere of perception under the influence of the exceedingly frequent abnormal states of the perceptive apparatus, but let us note that inaccuracies of perception depend on the very structure of our perceptive apparatus. First of all, these apparatus are adjusted each to its own special field of perception.

Therefore, they distort reception of external stimuli. A blow in the eye causes light-sensations, although the stimulus does not consist of light-waves, but is mechanical.

From the investigations of Fechner, we learn that a certain minimal strength of stimulus corresponds to a minimal strength of sensation. This threshold of sensation is not constant at different periods of life and in different circumstances, and, above all, it is not identical in different persons.

This threshold depends on outer conditions too, because the fewer the outer stimuli present, the lower it is. A weak light is readily distinguishable in darkness, whereas in a lighted hall it is imperceptible. The stars are visible at night, but the same stars are invisible in the course of the day. And if, in accordance with the Weber-Fechner law, the relation between the intensity of sensation and the intensity of the stimulus may be expressed as the relation of the logarithm to its index, it is clear to what extent our sensations are inaccurate indications of outer stimuli in general. But we know that the threshold of sensation is not identical in different persons, and, consequently, the above-mentioned relation would be proportionately unequal in different persons. Further, we know that the intensity of sensation changes very sharply according to the state of concentration, of the general mimico-somatic tone, and the greater or lesser degrees of states of consciousness, and this makes the indication still less accurate and a still less reliable standard of comparison for different individuals.

If we take into consideration the difference in concentration and in the general tone of different individuals, these factors alone are responsible for a profound difference in the sphere of sensation and perception in different persons. Again, the unequal development of the various organs of perception is known to everyone. Some have a more highly developed auditory sense (the auditory type); others a visual (the visual type); others, again, the tactual and muscular sense (the so-called muscular type); lastly, great differences are found in the receptive apparatus of smell, taste, and temperature. Therefore, our perceptions, each in its appropriate sphere, are qualitatively as well as quantitatively unequal. To realise with what sharp gradations of perception we have to do, it is sufficient to compare the attitude to music, on the one hand, of a good musician or a singer with a well-developed auditory sense, and, on the other, of a man " without an ear for music." There are, besides, types in whom not only one organ, but *e.g.* two or even three organs, of perception predominate in development. Again, the development of the motor apparatus is unequal in different individuals, and this also influences muscular perception indirectly. Setting aside the extreme importance of the muscular capacity of different individuals, the existence of two motor types, the defensive and the aggressive, has been revealed in experiments in the laboratory supervised by me. Besides, we must admit the existence of a peculiar verbal type, and as the rôle of the word as a substitute for concrete stimuli is extremely important in the development of our association-reflex activity, it is clear that this type must differ considerably from the others.

We must not forget that men grow up in different environments, and, consequently, draw unequal material from their surroundings ; and this material, in turn, is subjected to unequal elaboration because of the different conditions of upbringing and education.

And if we add to this that the innate capacity of different individuals is also unequal, we can easily understand how the inner world must differ in individual men.

In fine, we cannot have indirect self-observation, but, as we have mentioned already, only an estimate of the subjective world of another man, by our using, on the one hand, his revelations about himself and, on the other, the various other manifestations of his personality. This estimate makes possible the reproduction of the inner world of man, as an artist reproduces, for instance, a portrait of some personage whom he has not seen, but this reproduction can be only remotely similar to the reality, and not at all a copy of it, and, consequently, not identical with it.

It will be said that we have another man's speech, consisting of familiar words, as symbols to which we give a certain meaning in regard to subjective experiences. But the word as a symbol is only an indication of what is, or has been, the object of that experience. The experience itself, its character, and peculiarities depend on many pertinent conditions, such as emotions, concentration, individuality, etc. Therefore, in words as symbols we must see simply signs of the experience of another person, in its nature not identical, but only similar to analogous experiences of our own ego.

According to the well-known philologist, Potebnya, speaking does not mean the transmitting of thought from one man to another, but rather the awakening of his own thoughts in the man to whom we speak. In view of this, we must admit that what the hearer understands is only similar to what happens in the speaker.

It is clear from this that language, as a motor reaction, only sets in motion a similar thought, which develops in direct dependence on the man's personality. He who hears the speech of others thereby develops his own thought, and does not receive the external thought expressed in the words of the speaker.

According to Professor Polivanov, everything we say really requires a listener who understands the subject of discourse. If everything we wish to express were contained in the formal meanings of the words used by us, we should have to use many more words than we actually do for the expression of every separate thought. We use in speech only necessary allusions. Once these arouse in the listener the necessary thought, our goal is reached, and speaking in any other manner would be a senseless waste.

Let us take poetry—the language of images—which is much more condensed than ordinary practical language ; and yet who does not know that one or two lines of a poem arouse more thoughts than a whole treatise on the same subject ?[1]

In Potebnya's opinion, each word contains three elements : the sound, which may be divided into its parts ; the idea contained in it ; and its meaning as a symbol. The sound and the meaning remain permanently associated with the word, although, when we speak, the meaning may depend on those correlations into which the word enters with the other elements of speech, and the pronunciation depends on the dialect and accent ; but the idea, the third component of the word, is that primary inner image which has associated the given divisible sound with the given object. But this image is often lost, and, in any case, may be completely different in different individuals.

The word itself is really the embodiment of an idea and, on the other hand, the word, even every divisible sound, gives birth to an idea, but an autonomous idea, so to speak, which arises, in the head of the listener, in direct connection with the outwardly directed orientation reflex.

One and the same word in the mouth of different individuals is different, and, in turn, the meaning of it is not the same for everyone. A soldier, a scientist, an artist, a peasant, a savage, a woman, a child—all understand the same word each in his own way. Even one and the same man, in different moods and under different conditions, gives one and the same word different meanings. Then, it is clear what relativity is hidden in the words with which we express ourselves. Every word arouses in the listener an idea by no means identical, because we usually associate with every concrete word an object which has actually fallen under our experience, and every word expressing a general idea corresponds to that particular reasoning process which has happened in the individual. Further, a number of words have no strictly defined meanings, their meanings being assigned them by each person in his own way. Then there are unknown or only slightly known words, which are used in imitation of others and are given wrong or inexact meanings by each individual.

It is clear from this how little we can rely on verbal transmission, if we want thereby to study accurately the inner world of another person.

And, in reality, nobody ever studies accurately the inner life of another, but he reproduces, on the basis of the words of that other, his own inner process, and in this way deceives himself in merely apparently reproducing the experiences of the other.

The same is true of the language of expressive movements. This is why Humboldt's paradox " every understanding is a misunderstanding " has a certain meaning.

I shall even go further and maintain that it is not the idea which has associated the original word with the object, but that certain conditions

[1] See *Sbornik po teorii poetitcheskovo yazika* (*Symposium on the Theory of Poetic Language*), 1st issue ; Petrograd, 1916.

have led up to their association. The idea was my inner concomitant sign, associated with the perception of the object, and was nothing more, while the inner image was not, and could not be, the mediator.

It is obvious from all the preceding that the acquisition of knowledge of the inner experiences of another person, even if such were possible, is nothing more than a very remote approximation.

Both reasoning on the basis of analogy and empathy completely ignore the individual character of perception. And, after all, there cannot be any doubt that if one and the same object, *e.g.* a horse, is examined by a cabman, a veterinary surgeon, an amateur horse-breeder, and an artist, the inner reasoning-process of each will be by no means identical. Accordingly, the further development of the inner process in the form of secondary associations will vary considerably. It will be objected that this variation is taken into account in the verbal transmission, but here, too, we must not forget that not only words, but also the facial expressions, the gestures, the actions, and the conduct must be considered part and parcel of the manifestations of human personality. And, finally, even if we should utilise all of these in aiming at knowledge of the inner world of another, we should not succeed, for a man may be attentive or distracted, tell untruths intentionally or unintentionally, control his gestures and facial expressions, and avoid betraying his intentions.

In general, it may be said that although the visible identity of the outward manifestations of two individuals may make us suspect the possibility of similar inner experiences, they are not similar, even if the condition of similar reasons for these outward manifestations is present. The point is this : if equal external stimuli produce, at the outset, sensations which, though not identical, are at least similar in character, the further development of the inner experiences, which depends on individual set, already exhibits more or less considerable variations.

Let us assume that we see two laughing faces looking at one and the same event. Can you be convinced that in both cases you have the same inner experiences ? Of course not, for one thinks one aspect funny in the given event, and the other another. It is clear that the difference is conditioned by the individual set to one and the same outer influence, and this set is not identical in different persons.

Let us take another example. A man laughs and infects another with his laughter. Thus, both laugh ; but it is obvious that again their inner experiences are not identical. It is clear that, if the different individual sets to the outward stimulus, when there are identical outward reactions, lead to different inner experiences, the more does a different external cause with identical outward reactions condition a difference in inner experience.

It is obvious that we are concerned here not with indirect observation, but with a judgment concerning the subjective world of another person, and, moreover, a judgment which is far from being precise.

Some of those infected by subjectivism overvalue the importance of the subjective method in another direction. So Woltmann, in his work, *Die Darwinsche Theorie und der Sozialismus* (p. 8, Düsseldorf, 1899), says that " in his personal concerns, man has created, as it were, a mirror, in which, by means of analogy, he observes and comes to know the external world. Man had first to become conscious of his own development, and only then could he recognise evolution as a scientific principle necessary for the explanation of the universe. Before the investigation of the creative force of the struggle for existence in the animal and vegetable kingdoms, this struggle had been already recognised in the world of man," etc.

I must, however, decisively contradict this statement. The progress of thought met the greatest obstacles precisely when man made his own mirror his starting-point. The abandonment of the Ptolemaic system, according to which the earth, on which man lives, is the centre of the movement of all the celestial bodies, the rejection of the absolutely free will of man, the discarding of the idea of a deity externally similar to man, and the abandonment of subjective factors as important have been considerably delayed in the history of mankind, just because man looked, and still looks, into his own mirror, projects his own ego on to the external world, and thus retards the progress of human thought.

Lastly, it may be thought that the narration of subjective experiences guarantees the accuracy of the reproduction of one's own inner world. But, as we have already said, a word is only a symbol, a sign, and, therefore, here too, we are far from the truth. This refers in still greater measure to those cases in which the narration does not occur immediately after the experiencing of the external event, but only after some time has elapsed, for the narration is then inevitably incomplete in its transmission of subjective experiences, is distorted, and is supplemented by products of the imagination, as has been proved in a number of experiments carried out in our laboratory.

The experiments of Binet, the later investigations of Stern, and, especially, the experiments of Claparède on adults, the object of which was to discovery the rôle of testimony, are particularly instructive in this respect.

They disclose the striking unreliability of testimony and its being supplemented by products of the imagination, while, in certain cases, false testimony is rather the rule than the exception.[1]

A. F. Koni, an undeniable authority on judicial cases, expresses himself very emphatically on this subject. " Testimony," says A. F. Koni,[2] " even given under conditions calculated to ensure its reliability, is often unreliable. The most conscientious testimony, given with the genuine desire to tell the whole truth, and nothing but the truth, is based on an

---

[1] For details of these experiments see V. Bechterev : *Objective Psychology*, 3rd part.

[2] A. F. Koni : *Psychopathy and Testimony* in *Noviye ideyi v philosophii*, no. 9, p. 67, St. Petersburg, 1913.

effort of memory, which reproduces that to which the witness has paid attention at the moment. But attention is a very imperfect aid to perception ; and memory, in the course of time, distorts the images impressed by attention, and sometimes allows them to fade out completely. Attention is not paid to everything that the witness ought to remember later, and that to which incomplete and insufficient attention has been paid is, for the most part, feebly conserved by memory. This fading of memory gives rise to an unconscious filling-in of the gaps which have been formed, and, gradually, invention and self-deception furtively enter into the transmission of what has been seen and heard. Thus, there is, in nearly all testimony, a kind of ulcer, which gradually poisons the whole organism of testimony, not only against the will, but also without the knowledge, of the witness himself."

As I am at present making collective experiments on the verbal reproduction of pictures shown to subjects, I have been able to see for myself frequently how the subjects themselves, whenever they are given the opportunity to compare their reproductions with the original picture, are surprised at the distortions which they allow to creep into the immediate reproduction of what they have just seen.

Let us take an historical example : Thousands of persons were present at the famous cavalry charge in the Battle of Sedan ; still, because of the most contradictory testimony of eye-witnesses, it is impossible to discover who led this attack. The English general, Wolseley, in his new work, shows that, up to the present, the most erroneous ideas exist concerning the main facts of the Battle of Waterloo, notwithstanding that these facts have been witnessed by hundreds (Le Bon : *Psychologie des foules*, p. 183).[1]

G. Le Bon even asks himself in this connection : " Can we know, concerning any battle, how it fared in reality ? I doubt it strongly. We know who the victors and the vanquished are, and our knowledge probably does not go further than that." This is a confession of the unreliability of subjective testimony concerning events. On the other hand, objective data may be reliable, and are not merely limited to a statement of who the victors and the vanquished were, but disclose how many were lost by being taken prisoners, by being wounded or killed on both sides ; how many guns and how much ammunition were captured by the victors ; how and whither the vanquished withdrew, etc. In a word, the objective data, derived from various calculations, will give a full and objective account of the battle, such as can never be given by the subjective testimony of eye-witnesses.

It is clear that, on the basis of narration alone, we shall miss the truth ; and, in general, we cannot be even more or less accurate in regard to the investigation of the subjective experiences of another man, if the narration is not accurately recorded in writing immediately after the external event,

[1] *Translators' note :* Translated into English as : *The Crowd : A Study of the Popular Mind.*

and, in addition, with full attention on the part of the narrator to his inner experiences.

Moll is right when, in discussing the *libido sexualis* (p. 125), he says : " We cannot help noticing that self-observation often leads to self-deception, because we can have self-observation only of what we are conscious. But it does not follow that, when we are conscious of certain sensory impressions, these latter are true from the objective standpoint."

As a result of all this, it is necessary to bear in mind that the self-observation of an external person, as it takes its value from the angle of vision of that other, is, in reality, not self-observation, even indirect, but is actually an interpretation of the self-observation of the other, a self-observation made under certain conditions. Nevertheless, the analogy with oneself is applied everywhere to external human beings, regardless of the fact that, in this case, it is not permissible to consider indirect self-observation a scientific method.

We shall be still farther from the truth when we aim, by such a method, at the investigation of the subjective experiences of children, psychopaths, and such speechless beings as animals and infants. Here the beloved analogy with oneself will help us still less, for the inner world of these beings is, in its development and manifestations, too remote from our inner ego.

But subjectivism knows no limits and gladly indulges in flights of phantasy. As is well known, even the doctrine of inter-subjective spiritual continuity, which may be studied by means of a special science—intermental psychology (*psychologie intermentale*)—has been evolved. The most prominent exponents of this doctrine are Foulié and Boodin. In regard to this, P. Sorokin (*Sistema sotziologii—System of Sociology* : vol. i ; p. 245) says, not without reason : " One may invent various words. But it is necessary that these words should mean something. To change the phrases of Duprat, the methods of Foulié, Boodin, and others may be described thus : first endow the whole of interstellar space with spirit, or ascribe consciousness to it, replace the simple atom by the spiritual and conscious monad, replace all the elements of the inorganic world by consciousness, then ' form ' them according to the recipe of ' psychisation,' give every ' psychisised ' element in the world a tendency to collective life, to association ; add to this higher ruling centres of consciousness as monarchs, etc., and, in this manner, you will get, simply and easily, not only inter-subjective soul and collective consciousness, but also anything you like : god, the devil, cosmic spirit, logos, consciousness ; in fact, anything you wish, ' reason,' ' universal consciousness,' ' the atomic soul,' and hosts of other ' impersonal personalities,' ' wooden iron,' ' black whiteness,' and other logically incongruous, empirically absurd notions. These will have about as much value as ' wooden iron.' The sphere of telepathy, theosophy, and mysticism, but not the region of science, is the right place for such methods."

But the matter does not end here. We come across flights of phantasy

just as daring in connection with the problem of the extent of consciousness in nature.

Thus, Haeckel, Le Dantec, Petri, de La Grasserie, and others regard
the psychic, and, consequently, consciousness, as resident in every cell
and even in every molecule and atom (cellular consciousness, cellular
souls, atomic souls). Haeckel and de La Grasserie, in speaking of
the psyche of molecules and atoms, have created the " psychology
of minerals." A number of others, *e.g.* Bergson and James, speak of
" cosmic consciousness " ; and, consequently, a " cosmic psychology "
could also be evolved, as Bergson does, in effect, in his philosophy.

Let us quote a passage from the work of Dr. R. M. Beck, the author of
the book, *Cosmic Consciousness* (p. 25) : " Certain individuals of some
advanced species, in the course of the slow development of life on our
planet, become conscious beings one fine day for the first time, *i.e.* they
realise that a world exists—something subsisting outside themselves.
Even a cursory glance at this transition from the unconscious to the
conscious state may produce in us the impression of a phenomenon as
magnificent, wonderful, and divine, as the transition from the inorganic
world to the organic."

The same remarks apply to the higher form of consciousness known
to subjective psychology as self-consciousness. " Here," says the same
writer, " we again encounter another gap similar to the earlier ones, a gorge,
rather an apparent abyss, yawning between simple consciousness and
self-consciousness—a deep gulf or ravine, on the one side of which roam
the animals, on the other dwell men." " In the so-called *alalus homo*,
the fundamental human quality, self-consciousness, and its twin, language,
have developed from the highest form of simple consciousness."

But can the subjectivist psychologist or philosopher confine himself
to this in his quasi-scientific faddishness ? He extends the flight of his
phantasy still further, and speaks of a " comsic consciousness " as developing and as already reached by at least some men. This new step is not
a simple extension of our self-consciousness, but something as different
from it as self-consciousness differs from simple consciousness, or as the
latter differs from the capacity for life apart from consciousness, or, lastly,
as consciousness differs from the world of inorganic matter and force—
the world which has preceded it and from which it has originated.

It is clear that the question of " cosmic consciousness " borders on
that creative imagination which characterises the so-called inspiration
of the poets, which represents a special enhancement of their association-
reflex activity[1] with a simultaneous heightening of the so-called mimico-
somatic tone or the so-called emotional sphere.

All this leads us to the establishment of the principle that the study of
subjective states may be prosecuted really only on oneself, and that the
experience should be recorded in writing immediately after the external

[1] *Translators' note :* What Bechterev calls " association reflex " corresponds
to what Pavlov and the behaviourists call " conditioned reflex."

event. Data derived in this way may be supplemented only by data derived from the narration of the subjective states experienced by others ; but in the latter case, it is necessary to deduct, on the one hand, such inaccuracies of a general character as are contained in every narration of another person, and, on the other, the special inaccuracies accruing from the personal evaluation of the other ego. Therefore, narration is untrustworthy unless checked by objective data.

CHAPTER II

THE inadequacy of the subjective method may be disclosed not only concerning the impossibility of a more or less accurate elucidation of the inner experiences of an external person, but also concerning such fundamental questions as the freedom of the will and as the ontogenetic and the phylogenetic development of consciousness.

Subjectivism has always led, and still leads, mankind in all spheres of science to the standpoint with which science continuously struggles. Let us take primitive cosmology, in which it was thought that the whole world revolved round the observer, to whom his accidental position served as the starting-point of the evaluation of the movement of the heavenly bodies. How much trouble and how many victims were necessary to expel from science this erroneous view, which originated in primitive subjectivism, and was later supported by the Christian religion ! Let us remember the death at the stake of Giordano Bruno, who extended the doctrine of Copernicus to the universe in general. The same is true of the unfortunate problem of the absolute freedom of the will, a doctrine which has led mankind into serious errors concerning the eradication of evil and criminality. In fact, it is well known that human consciousness does not reconcile itself to the idea of the limitation of the will. Subjectively, it seems to man that he is quite free in his actions and conduct. From this has originated the doctrine of the absolutely free will, according to which the will of man determines itself, and, at the same time, is the cause of changes in the external world, although it is not itself determined by anything whatever in the external world. As is well known, this doctrine, which has sprung chiefly from the jungles of subjective views in psychology, has been upheld until recently by prominent jurists and accepted by them as the foundation of the severest juridical oppressions. Meanwhile, we know, from the time of Quetelet, that the activities of man are in direct dependence on certain external conditions, and that national calamity is reflected in the number of crimes and even in the number of slips in the addresses of letters.[1]

[1] One example, among others, of the conformity of the activity of a human being to certain laws may also be seen in the fact that, as statistics prove, in France, of 1000 sentenced by the correction police, nearly 45 cases appeal yearly, while protests on the part of the public prosecutor continuously decrease. We must note here the determination, arising from certain conditions of temperament, which gives boldness and confidence in the success of the petition, the making of which has to be seriously considered, for failure may result in something worse for the petitioner. For details see my work : *The Objective Method Applied to the*

There is, as is well known, an endless quarrel in subjective psychology between two camps—the determinists and the indeterminists—in regard to the freedom of the will.　The former maintain that the character of our actions is determined by the motives, and if the motives and their greater or lesser strength are known, it is possible to predict, with certain accuracy, the line of a man's behaviour.　The indeterminists contradict this view, and hold that neither past nor present psychic states predetermine the line of behaviour, for one and the same psychic state may cause one set of results to-day, and another to-morrow.　O. Christiansen (*The Philosophy of Art* : Fedotov's edition, p. 17)[1] has the following pertinent to this problem : " The individual has no independent subsistence : he is woven into the system of the universal life."　And a little earlier (p. 16) : " The individual, like every other scrap of reality, is the point of intersection of various processes : the phenomena originating in the individual are examined from the standpoint of causality ; so then the individual is neither the beginning nor the end, but only a junction.　The question of the causes of everything he experiences, everything that is happening in him, arises, and these must be looked for beyond the individual."　" In everything that happens in himself, the individual participates only as far as any machine ; what is happening in every machine is produced partly by environmental influences, partly by the peculiarities of the machine itself.　The individual in this sense is not something fundamental or self-contained, but a point of intersection of mechanical processes, only a very complicated psychical mechanism.　Everything he is, and everything he experiences, is ultimately conditioned by his environment and his past, and, in turn, influences the environment and the future."

In another place (p. 17), the same author says : man " cannot maintain of himself that he is the *fons et origo* in respect of causality ; try to think over seriously the proposition that a new series of processes could arise without any cause in the individual, and you will abandon it with terror ; and if causeless phenomena should arise in the individual, confidence in oneself and in others would disappear ; it would be replaced by the terror of events, the mere possibility of which outstrips the wildest monstrosities of insanity.　And the more free will in this sense man possessed, the more reason he would have to fear the future, for he does not know beforehand what inner processes might begin to dominate him.　The greatest absurdities would be possible."

This point of view is decisive in the dispute between determinists and indeterminists in favour of the former, for it states that human activities are governed by causality, and although man is regarded as the inde-

Study of Crime : Sbornik, posv. pamyati D. Drilya (Symposium Dedicated to the Memory of D. Dril) ; St. Petersburg, 1912.
　Translators' note : The figures given in the footnote do not agree with those in chap. XXIII.
　[1] *Translators' note : Philosophie der Kunst*, Hanau, 1909.

pendent source of phenomena in his creativeness and actions, he is by no means their causal and original source.

But here comes the intuitionalist and transubjectivist, Bergson, who maintains that both camps talk nonsense, for " neither the one nor the other touch upon the problem of the freedom of the will." " All the difficulty arises from the fact that both parties picture the deliberation under the form of an oscillation in space, when it really consists in a dynamic progress, in which the self and its motives are, like real living beings, in a consistent state of becoming." If there is question of a progression, any fluctuation, in the sense of a return to the old, cannot occur, for the self does not remain unchanged, but, on the contrary, continuously changes. And that is why the determinist is wrong, for the progression of psychic life is not subject to the pressure of the strongest motive ; but the indeterminist is also wrong, for in a progression there is no freedom in the sense of a limitless possibility of choice. Still Bergson establishes freedom of action from his own point of view : " We are free," he says, " when our acts spring from our whole personality, when they express it, when they have that indefinable resemblance to it which one sometimes finds between the artist and his work."[1] On the other hand, the same author does not admit the possibility of the prediction of personal behaviour, for predictions are based on causation, and, according to Bergson's words, the psychic life is not subject to causation.

It is not necessary to say that Bergson has not made the question any clearer, for to maintain that in the progression of man's experience there is no freedom, but that in the actions of his complete personality he is free, means that Bergson merely gives us a vague solution or really none at all.

We have already mentioned that accurate objective data testify that the actions and conduct of man are subject to general external laws, and, for instance, the number of criminal actions in the form of thefts varies from year to year in direct proportion to the prices of such essential food-products as rye.

A table (on page 66) comparing the prices of rye and the number of thefts in Prussia may serve as an example. It shows, for each year, a complete parallelism between an increase in the price of rye and in the number of thefts committed.

In my work, *The Objective Method Applied to the Psychological Study of Crime* (Symposium Dedicated to the Memory of D. A. Dril, St. Petersburg, 1912), I have shown the complete dependence of the development of criminal actions on the totality of factors influencing the person at the moment of the crime, as well as those which have influenced him earlier, even from birth, and, lastly, those which, in their influence on the ancestors, have determined the conditions of the conception and the pre-natal life of that person. A man who has fallen into criminality is, to some extent, the

[1] Bergson : *Time and Free Will* : (*Essai sur les données immédiates de la conscience*), 1889, pp. 183 and 172. Tr. Pogson, London, 1912. (*Translators.*)

E

victim of economico-social conditions and, in particular, of alcoholism, pauperism, loneliness, and isolation from his home and coterie ; not rarely is he the victim of acute intoxication, of temptation, of an environment conducive to crime, of interference with established personal relations, of bad example, of unfavourable heredity influencing the formation of his personality, the victim of insufficient education, of mental debility, and, lastly, of various diseases which weaken man physically and morally, to say nothing of psychic illness.

Year.	Price of rye in marks per 50 kilograms.	Number of thefts per 10,000 inhabitants.
1854	10·40	33·4
1855	10·64	35·5
1856	11·45	38·6
1857	6·87	24·6
1858	6·38	21·2
1859	6·79	21·8
1860	7·65	22·3
1861	7·71	22·9
1862	7·97	23·1
1863	6·78	20·5
1864	5·69	20·0
1865	6·24	22·5
1866	7·30	23·0
1867	9·84	26·5
1868	9·87	29·2
1869	8·08	21·3
1870	7·78	21·2
1871	8·50	23·6
1872	8·40	22·2

As for the crime itself, which also must be studied exclusively from its objective, *i.e.* external, side, for it is a complex action which develops under certain conditions and in direct dependence on a number of previous factors which have influenced the neuro-psychical sphere of the person in question, it proves to be predestined and inevitable under the given conditions, which complete a cycle of previous influences of a general, and also a particular or individual, character.

Its prevention is, of course, not impossible, but is already beyond the power of the person who commits the crime, and depends on a change in the external conditions which lead to the commission of the crime. It would be sufficient to change any one of the external influences and introduce a new and favourable factor, and the crime would not be committed ; but as the change does not occur, the crime happens in a predestined and inevitable manner, just as every external phenomenon is produced by a definite series of antecedent conditions.

Therefore, in order to explain a crime, it is necessary to study, quite objectively, all the external conditions under which it has happened, as well as the personality of him who has committed the crime, and, at the same time, his whole past history. After such an investigation, the crime will be intelligible and clear to us, as is every human action performed, under the given external conditions, as an inevitable act resulting from a number of external influences both of most recent and more distant dates.

Thus, the objective method, in its application to every single crime, aims at revealing, in their totality and sequence, the whole chain of past and recent influences which lead up to the development of the crime, and so at making the given crime perfectly clear from the objective point of view, and without any reference to the subjective experiences which have been, and still are, usually emphasised by criminologists. Those facts must be kept in mind also in regard to suicide. In my work on the causes of suicide, I have written the following : " Suicide is scarcely ever the result of a single cause, but, in the vast majority of cases, of a con-catenation of causes, which are operative at different times and among which it is difficult to determine the decisive factor."

Finally, there is no doubt that, in such cases, each factor has played some part in leading up to the suicide, which, as I have said before, is the predestined and inevitable result of all the previous unfavourable condi-tions, and is committed only under the influence of the last motive, as a slight push easily topples over an undermined stone.[1]

Is it necessary to mention how many victims and what streams of blood our self-deception concerning the absolute freedom of the will has cost humanity ? It is just this which has darkened the pages of history with the disgraceful Inquisition and the countless terrible tortures, the descrip-tion of which makes the blood run cold in our veins.

We shall see, however, that self-deception concerning the absolute freedom of the will is not unparalleled in the subjective sphere. We may point out another example—alcoholism, to which mankind has sacrificed countless victims. As is well known, man, under the influence of alcohol, feels more fit for work, both physically and mentally, but, on the con-trary, strictly objective experiments (the investigations of Kraepelin and his school) show that, in actual fact, his capacity is diminished. In reality, it comes to this : it is not that his capacity for work is heightened, but that his higher controls or inhibitions are removed, and their removal leads to the emergence of association reflexes completely uncontrolled and unregulated. In this way, those tendencies and actions, which could formerly be controlled from motives, say, social in character, are now deprived of these controlling forces and emerge entirely unchecked. According to the words of V. Danilevsky, " the intellect, backed by edu-cation and culture, should hint to man how many illusions and deceptions are included in the ' usefulness ' of alcohol, e.g. in that feeling of strength,

[1] See V. Bechterev : O pritchinach samoubistv i o vozmozhnoi borbe s nimi (The Causes of Suicide, and the Possibility of Preventing it), sep. ed., 1912, pp. 19–20.

freshness, and enthusiasm, which is so easily evoked by it, and so decep-
tively lures man into all kinds of heroisms, inordinate undertakings,
excessive struggle and work. In reality, all this proves to be merely a
trick of the feelings and imagination, and equivalent to such forgetfulness
of the unhappiness and bitterness of life as is sought for in wine and
found there. Our sensory organs, our perceptions of reality are blunted
by alcohol, and so we imagine that the world has become better and life
easier. The same self-deception again ! When the poisonous vapours
pass, the man will be still weaker and reality still harsher."

On the other hand, we are subject at every step to physiological illusions, inevitable notwithstanding the fact that we know that the reality
does not correspond to the illusion. On the basis of strictly objective
measurement, we convince ourselves of the equal length of two lines ;
and, still, it is sufficient to draw from both sides, at the ends of one line,
two auxiliary lines at an angle of 45 degrees—these auxiliary lines being
turned inwards, *i.e.* towards the middle from the end—and two similar
auxiliaries on the other line, but outwards, from each end, and the
former line seems shorter, the latter longer (the Müller–Lyer illusion).[1]
The subjective factor which leads us to this self-deception cannot be
corrected by any means.

This is a new example of how subjective evidence does not correspond
to reality. Such illusions are inevitable, even when their origin, discovered by objective investigation, is known.

Thus we definitely know that some illusions stand in close relation to
life experience. Man, being social, develops his reflexes in his contact
with his fellow-man and in their continual interaction with the environmental stimuli. On this basis, those reflexes which are in general more
adapted are retained. The greater part of what is unadapted is discarded
by means of natural selection, but some of the unadapted orientation
reflexes are retained, as not having been very injurious to the individual
and as making possible an appropriate correction by means of other
receptive apparatus. Thus, reflexology explains the origin of the majority
of the so-called physiological illusions. Let us take, for example, Aris-
totle's illusion of the double sensation produced by a little ball placed
between two crossed fingers. It shows us that subjective judgment is in
direct dependence on experience and practice, which, when we take hold
of some object, bring certain receptive surfaces into juxtaposition with
others. In this way, the singleness of the stimulus is determined, but

[1] *Translators' note :*

sometimes represented thus :

two skin surfaces, which are not juxtaposed in our experience, duplicate the object even when the stimulus is single. Our knowledge of these facts does not enable us to escape the illusion.

It is clear from the above to what extent we may rely on subjective evidence in other cases too.

So, at present, few can be found to defend not only the doctrine of the absolute freedom of the will, to belief in which we are led by our inner consciousness, but also the reality of self-control in general.

As we know, the definition of the consciousness of processes has itself not been sufficiently elucidated, for some understand by it those higher processes of the so-called psychic activity which transcend what is included in the sphere of instinct ; others do not deny some consciousness to the instincts ; others again include under conscious processes everything that is accompanied by subjective mainfestations. The latter are, from our point of view, more justified than the former, for if we do not refer to consciousness the most primitive processes in the form of feeling and sensation, and, in general, everything that refers to the so-called inner experiences, we are in danger of losing every means of determining logically which processes to call conscious and which not.

Even the wider definition of psychical activity is open to objection. So, for some, the psychic is equivalent to the conscious ; for others it is coterminous not only with conscious, but also with nervous and even vital, processes ; and some, as we have mentioned already, extend it even to inorganic processes.

How can so much vagueness in such fundamental concepts of subjective psychology be explained ? The reason is to be found precisely in the use of the method of self-observation where it should not be used, *i.e.* outside the self, for, here, in this method of so-called indirect self-observation, everything is untrustworthy and, therefore, vague.

Needless to say, all sorts of unfounded hypotheses have been constructed around the origin of the psychic, and there are writers who think it demonstrated that the physico-chemical processes are the direct source of the psychic. (Prof. Yushtchenko : *Soul and Matter : Priroda*, 1914.) There are also writers who advance an " oxygen " theory of the origin of consciousness. Others, again, regard it as equally certain that the psychic can on no account be referred to material processes.

Consciousness itself cannot be appropriately defined by the school of subjectivist psychologists.

Placing ourselves on the evolutionary plane, we must maintain, as has been already mentioned in one of my works (*Consciousness and its Limitations :* Speech delivered at the *Actus* of Kazan University, 1885),[1] that by consciousness is to be understood everything subjective that man discovers in himself. This definition is wider ; and, at the same time, it satisfies the evolutionary process, for we can construct complex forms of consciousness from the very simplest, *e.g.* the elementary feelings, which,

---

[1] Published in *Actus of the University of Kazan*, 1885.

as we may suppose, lie at the root of the more complex forms of consciousness, and which must be in general the earliest form of consciousness.
Besides, we can also assume that the subjective (or psychism) is inseparably
associated with life, in as far as the latter manifests itself in irritability.[1]
If it is possible for us, by relying on experiments on human beings, to
say for certain that association-reflex activity is accompanied by subjective phenomena, there is no reason why the subjective aspect in regard
to the association reflexes of other and lower animals should be denied.
Meanwhile, experiments on animals standing on the border-line of life
show that in them, too, association reflexes may be inculcated. This has
been proved in Dr. Israelson's experiments, carried out in my laboratory,
by the artificial inculcation of the association-motor reflex in infusoria,
and by Metalnikov's investigations on the feeding of infusoria with
suitable and unsuitable foods (see below). We may assume that a living
unicellular organism, characterised by irritability, must also manifest a
subjective aspect, although in a completely elementary and impersonal
form.

From the point of view indicated, we can understand, on the one hand,
the gradual development of complex forms of consciousness through
differentiation of the various forms of the feeling and perception of the
movements themselves as responsive reactions, and, on the other, their
interrelations. If we admit that the irritability of tissue in general is
associated with subjective process, it naturally follows that the nerve
process of the higher animals also may be associated with subjective
process. In this case, we regard the subjective as the direct result of
energy manifesting itself in the complex albumen formations, for otherwise it is by no means possible to exclude consciousness from processes
of the material order. In this respect, Huxley is right in saying that that
arrangement, which, by means of stimulating the nerve tissue, results in
something as wonderful as the state of consciousness, is just as inexplicable
as the appearance of the sprites, when Aladdin rubbed his lamp. Therefore, we shall say simply that the energy which manifests itself in complex
formations containing phosphoric albumen is accompanied, in addition to
its physical aspect, by general subjective states, which, when we observe
them in ourselves in a developed form, we define as our consciousness.

Otherwise the concept of consciousness resists definition. This definition does not detract, to any extent, from the mechanistic view of conscious processes as brain processes. Experiments have been made which
elucidate the mechanism of defensive movements : cries evoked by
severe irritation of the skin. Thus Amsler (*Arch, f. exper. Path. u.
Pharmakol.* Bd. 90 ; H. 5–6 ; 1921) has made the following experiments :
the animals are given an appropriate dose of morphium, which, by
depressing the receptive cortical centres, stops the cries and other defensive movements accompanying severe cutaneous (painful) irritations. But

[1] For details see my work : *The Psychic and Life* ; St. Petersburg ; Pub. K
Ricker.

if these animals get an injection of chloral hydrate, which paralyses the depressing activity exercised by the cerebral cortex on the appropriate centres, but without counteracting the effect of the morphium, the animals begin to cry during the chloral narcosis. It is obvious that the above-mentioned defensive movements are executed, in the form of reflexes of a lower order, by the subcortical ganglia, but are they accompanied by consciousness or not ? Can that be discovered, and is it of any special importance whatever in the given case ? I suppose not. We have already mentioned that the definition of psychology as a science of states of consciousness is, according to the words of Wundt, a vicious circle, for if we ask what consciousness is, the states of which psychology studies, the answer will be : "Consciousness comprises the sum of the states of which we are conscious" (W. Wundt : *Einführung in die Psychologie*). Similarly, Höffding, speaking of consciousness and its elements, says : "Their description or definition is impossible" (*Grundriss der Psychologie*, S. 56). Haeckel speaks of consciousness thus : "Consciousness does not admit of definition. To explain any phenomenon, we must describe it in terms of some other phenomenon. But there is nothing in the world similar to consciousness, therefore we can define it only in terms of itself, and this is like trying to lift oneself by one's own belt. Consciousness is the greatest mystery which confronts us."

Consciousness is indefinable and scarcely admits of description, says Natorp (*Einleitung in die Psychologie*, 1888, S. 12). According to Rickert, the definition of the psychic presents great difficulties, as is well known. (*Psycho-physical Causality and Psycho-physical Parallelism*, in *Noviye ideyi v philosophii*, No. 8, p. 3.)

A vicious circle in the definition of consciousness is to be found also in other writers, who aim at a more limited definition of the concept of consciousness, or we come across the contention that consciousness is either indefinable or difficult to define.

It is not less difficult to define consciousness in the activities of other beings. It is quite clear, therefore, that the subjective method cannot solve the problem of the stage of the animal world at which consciousness originates. If we use the hackneyed method of analogy, admit the existence of consciousness in the higher animals, and descend the ladder of the animal world, we shall, in the end, arrive at a stage where we shall have to doubt the existence of consciousness. Would everyone who admits the existence of consciousness in the higher animals allow its existence, say, in a cuttle-fish ; and if someone posits its existence in these animals, would he acknowledge its existence in insects ? Daring writers would find no food for thought here. So, for instance, Sighele (*La foule criminelle* : Paris, 1901), speaking of the manifestations of moods in insects says : "A wasp, for instance, buzzes in a particularly expressive way, and this state corresponds in it to a state of anger and alarm ; other wasps hear this sound and envisage it, but they cannot do so without greater or lesser excitation of the nerve fibres which usually produce it."

I let the reader judge whether all this is scientific. But if anyone admits consciousness in insects, he should be asked whether he admits it also, e.g., in snails, the amorous intimacies of which Mantegazza has described so graphically, and then let us ask whether, and in what form, he admits consciousness in microbes, including cocci or bacilli, and also in plants.

Neither can the analysis of particular activities in the animal world give us a criterion of consciousness. We know of countless examples of protective colouring in insects, fish, reptiles, birds, and higher animals. It is difficult to speak of consciousness in the case of mimicry, at least when the animal changes its apparel at a certain season. But the chameleon changes its colour in accordance with the environmental conditions. On the other hand, the female crane, which completely changes its outward appearance during the egg-laying season, deserves our attention. How does it change it? The bird covers its back and wings with a layer of mud, which, when dried, gives the bird a reddish colour corresponding to the surroundings and thus protects it from enemies. Is that consciousness or the opposite?

Some tend to the former opinion. But why? If this is a manifestation of " instinct," do we not know from our own experience that instinct does not require conscious thinking for its manifestation? This question remains unanswered in spite of the greatest efforts of our reason to solve it. But the important point is: that neither a positive nor a negative answer to this question would help us in the elucidation of the activity itself.

Some birds imitate the cries of animals and thus frighten away their enemies, and the important point is that they imitate the cry of an animal which is stronger in comparison with the beast of prey, the enemy of these birds. Thus the chalcophans of North America, when they see a hawk, imitate the cries of animals or other birds and so deceive their enemies. The question is: Do they do so consciously or unconsciously? Who can decide it? And is the answer to this question necessary when we aim at the development of that knowledge which elucidates the correlations of certain animals with the environment? And such an elucidation alone may serve as the aim of knowledge. Whether we say that this act is conscious or unconscious, there is no change in our objective knowledge, but only the satisfaction of our completely aimless curiosity, and nothing more.

In general, who of the subjectivists can indicate that plane in the animal world where consciousness first arises, and how and why it arises?

" On the side of (its) philosophy," writes Romanes,[1] " no one can have. a deeper respect for the problem of self-consciousness than I have ; (for) no one can be more profoundly convinced than I am that the problem on this side does not admit of solution. . . . I am as far as anyone can be from throwing light upon the intrinsic nature of that the probable genesis of which I am endeavouring to trace."

[1] Romanes : Mental Evolution in Man, pp. 194–195, 1888.

Huxley says : " I really know nothing whatever, and never hope to know anything of, the steps by which the passage from molecular movement to states of consciousness is effected."[1]

Thus we encounter one of those world-riddles which Du Bois Raymond, in his famous speech, designated by the words : " *Ignoramus et ignorabimus.*"

Here is what Du Bois Raymond says concerning this : " At a stage unknown to us in the development of life on the earth, there emerges something new, something previously unheard of and—like the nature of substance and movement—incomprehensible. This incomprehensibility is ' consciousness.' An abyss already opens with the first awakening of pleasure or displeasure felt by the simplest being on earth, with the first perception of quality, and the world becomes doubly incomprehensible."

It must be noted, however, that, as the method of analogy does not guarantee the possibility of a correct delimitation of consciousness of activity in other beings, writers use other and indirect criterions for this purpose.

The development of the central nervous system is recognised in biology as such a criterion of consciousness.[2] Here the conclusion is accepted that where there is a developed nervous system, there is also consciousness, and where there is no nervous system, there cannot be consciousness either. Thus consciousness is admitted only in the higher animals and man ; and, on the other hand, consciousness is excluded in the lower nerveless animals and in plants.

But if we take into consideration that we can convince ourselves, by self-observation, of the existence of unconscious complex activities in man, and learn by observation the strikingly varied activities of protozoa, the conditional character of this criterion is more than obvious.

The same conditional character is to be found in the criterion which relies, for consciousness of activities, on the presence of the grey cortical matter, which is present in man and the higher animals and is absent in invertebrates.

Other indications of consciousness are derived from the data of ontogeny. The processes of consciousness exhibit a capacity for evolution or consecutive development, while unconscious or instinctive processes are complete at birth, and do not evolve, it is said ; but if they do change, then the change is as sudden as change of scene on the stage. Thus, a child learns to understand a language strange to it, to speak, behave, live, etc., while a chicken, straight from the egg, already understands the language of the hen, and all its behaviour is, as it were, predictable. The same is true of the behaviour of the bee and the canary, whether they are isolated from birth or have grown up in the society of others. Thus, it would seem that it is not imperative for them to learn.

It is necessary, however, to keep in mind that there is no absolute

---

[1] *Contemporary Review,* 1871, Nov. ; Essay : *Mr. Darwin's Critics.*
[2] See V. Vagner : *Biopsychology* (Russian), vol. I.

consistency of reaction even in the instincts. If, for instance, a starfish is turned on its back, it tends to turn over, but this turning over does not always happen in the same manner (Preyer). It is further known that European bees transported to Australia, where there is eternal summer, do not provide stores of honey in their hives for posterity, as they do in Europe. Consequently, in this case, the instinct of the European bees is destroyed in its very essence through change of climate.

Dunant Hennop describes the following case. A canary has laid an egg on the ground. After that, the male canary brings grass, moss, wadding, wool, hair, and other material, pushes it all under the egg, and so makes something like a nest.

I doubt whether it is necessary to cite other examples of this kind.

But even assuming the above-mentioned hypothesis to be irrefutable, we shall come to the conclusion that, although such a criterion makes it possible to distinguish " instinctive " from " volitional " actions, it does not definitely answer the question of their consciousness or unconsciousness, for we know from our own experience, on the one hand, that instincts are not absolutely unconscious, and, on the other, that activities which seem volitional may prove to be unconscious.

Further, it has been pointed out that the difference between instincts and rational actions is the stereotyped nature and the impersonality of the former, and a certain individuality in the others. Besides, the latter are educable, while the former are not. But in regard to these definitions the same objections hold as in regard to the previous.

One can, for instance, often observe that bitches, in the beginning of the period of heat, if they remain unsatisfied, jump on dogs, and perform those sexual movements characteristic of the male. Cows, at the same period, when in a herd, jump on other cows.

According to V. Vagner : " One should understand by conscious activity only such acts of animals possessing a nervous system as evidence the capacity to utilise the results of their personal experience, and so control their actions."[1] Here, personal experience, as we see, is identified with consciousness. But are actions based on personal experience always conscious ? Thus, all piano-playing is a result of personal experience, but is it conscious in all cases and in each detail ? Who will maintain that it is ?

It is obvious from what has been said above that the view of subjective psychology does not harmonise with the law of evolution, if it cannot tell at what level of development in the animal kingdom the phenomenon called consciousness begins. And if it maintains that consciousness is proper to every living cell and every living being, down to, and including, plants, what reason is there to deny that the inorganic world possesses some degree of consciousness ?

But in this case we overstep the limits of plausibility in our conclusions.

In other words, if we construct a scientific system based on conscious-

---

[1] V. Vagner : *Biopsychology* (Russian), p. 94.

ness as the foundation, we meet at some point in the evolution of the world a completely new phenomenon, to which there is nothing similar in the phenomena that have preceded it in the evolutionary sequence, or we must posit a ubiquitous consciousness in the world, and even go as far as to admit a " cosmic " consciousness.

The correct attitude towards this question must take cognisance of the fact that the capacity for the reproduction of past experience should not be the criterion of consciousness, for it frequently happens, as we are well aware, that events consciously experienced by us cannot be reproduced. That is because certain conditions may arise which inhibit the states experienced, and the removal of the inhibitions, which is essential for reproduction, demands, in turn, certain conditions which may not be present at the moment. On the other hand, if we agree to understand by consciousness the first manifestation of subjectivity, we must admit, as a result of experiments in association reflexes, that the latter, as everyone can convince himself by experiment on himself, are accompanied by the subjective process of the expectation of stimulation by an electric current, although there may be no such stimulation, after the association reflex has been already established, and sometimes, too, there may be even self-deception in the form of a sensation of a stimulation by a current, when in reality there is none.

In this way, the assumption that a cerebral cortical process is simultaneously a subjective process is proved.

If, thus, the association reflex is simultaneously a cerebral and a subjective process, it is clear that we have reason to assume the subjective wherever the inculcation of an association reflex is possible.

Later, we shall see that, on the border-line of the animal world, *i.e.* in protozoa, the origin and development of association reflexes may be proved and, along with this, the development of the subjective process.

In considering subjective processes abstractly, psychology is deprived of every means of deciding when consciousness first arose. Therefore, it is natural that subjective psychology cannot solve such problems as those of the first awakening or the *primum cognitum* of conscious activity. Thus, for instance, subjectivists cannot, so far, give a final answer to the question in what consciousness primarily consists : whether in differentiation, as some think (Spencer, Bain, Schneider, and others), or in the apprehension of similarity, as others think. This problem cannot be solved by subjective psychology, because the object of investigation evades observation. In the mind of the adult, as we know from the data of self-observation, both processes nearly always go more or less hand-in-hand, but what happens on the first appearance of consciousness at the infantile stage is not known, and there are, in the realm of subjective psychology alone, no data which give hope of its solution.

The subjectivists experience many difficulties also in the elucidation of the question whether animals can reason, and when judgment first evolves in the child.

Further, let us ask ourselves how is the mentality of past ages, of primitive man, studied ? Are we right in turning to our personal inner experience as the index of the subjective world of prehistoric man ? Is the objective material alone insufficient for us to judge of the mental development of primitive man ? " The flints and arrowheads, the celts and the hammers of early man," says H. Drummond, " are petrified mind."[1] The question is : Would it be at all scientific, if, directed by the analogy with ourselves, as the subjectivist psychologists so willingly are, we were to reconstruct, on the basis of these remnants, the inner experiences of primitive man ?

The subjectivist is also helpless in regard to the elucidation of the question of the origin of consciousness in man's individual life. From self-analysis we know that fragments of memories are preserved in us from the age of two to three. But the question arises whether that means that an infant up to the age of two or three is completely devoid of consciousness in his activity, and if he is not completely devoid of consciousness, I ask you : When do conscious processes originate in the head of an infant, and when does his subjective life begin ?

Needless to say, these questions remain unanswered and the subjective method is just as helpless in their elucidation as in the question of the origin of consciousness on the phylogenetic plane of the animal world ; and, consequently, the problem of the evolution of consciousness in man remains unsolved.

Attempts to establish the correlations of the individual psychic or conscious processes with the material processes will remain fruitless, if we insist on the necessity of studying all our higher processes from the inner aspect only.

Further, we must not leave out of consideration that the application of the subjective method to others demands two conditions from them : frankness and truthfulness, which are by no means found in all ; and, in some cases, there may be not only a pathological tendency to lying or to the aggravation of one's condition, as may particularly often be observed in children and hysterics, but also interestedness, for various reasons, in being untruthful, as happens, e.g., in a juridical medical investigation. In these cases subjective investigation usually proves helpless in discovering the truth, and sometimes only a trick proves useful. The application of objective methods of investigation is the decisive factor.[2]

In this case, the reflexological method, worked out in our laboratory, of investigating simulation deserves special attention. Let us assume that we have a case of feigned deafness. For its detection an association sound-reflex must be inculcated under ordinary conditions, and it is desirable

---

[1] *The Ascent of Man*, p. 187.

[2] V. Bechterev : *The Application of Association-Motor Reflexes in the Treatment of Nervous and Psychic Diseases ; Obozrenie Psychatrii*, no. 8, 1910 ; and *The Application of the Method of Association-Motor Reflexes in the Investigation of Simulation ; Russky Vratch*, no. 14, 1912.

to arrange the experiments so that the sound of an electric bell begins a little before the discharge of an electric current into the sole of the foot or the fingers of the hand, this discharge stimulating the reflex of withdrawing the hand or the foot.

On the establishment of the association reflex, the sudden withdrawal of the extremity will occur when the bell begins to ring, although the electrical stimulus is completely absent, while in the case of the really deaf the sound will establish no association reflex whatever. The experiment also succeeds when the stimuli are simultaneous and not only single, but are those of light and sound. In this case, on the establishment of the association reflex, the light-stimulus is suddenly eliminated, and then the simulator exhibits an association reflex to the sound stimulus only ; but a deaf person would not exhibit any reflex in these circumstances. Reflexological investigations, carried out in an analogous way, make it possible to detect when blindness, paralysis of cutaneous or muscular perceptivity, and motor paralysis are feigned.

Partial deafness, partial blindness, anesthesia, and hypesthesia may be detected in just the same way, but the association stimuli selected must be of such a degree of intensity, as, according to the words of the subjects themselves, is not perceived. In a similar manner the aggravation and decrease of the pathological symptoms in question and also of hyperesthesia may be investigated.

We must not overlook also the deceptive character of subjective evidence as an illusion of a special kind. Let us take the case of fatigue. Can the subjectively unpleasant feeling of fatigue be an index of real fatigue ? Of course not. We know very well that people do not notice fatigue, and, as a result, often ruin their health and even their life, and, on the other hand, others complain of considerable fatigue after the slightest effort, obviously because the feeling of fatigue seems to be somehow accentuated. Imagine what would happen if the problem of fatigue were solved by science on the basis of subjective evidence. It is obvious that here, too, the strictly objective method alone can lead us along the right path.

Another example has been already advanced : under the influence of wine, man subjectively feels a flood of energy, while in reality his productivity is decreased, and that not only quantitatively, but also qualitatively.

Professor W. McDougall[1] is partly right when he says : " Psychologists must cease to be content with the sterile and narrow conception of their science as the science of consciousness, and must boldly assert its claim to be the positive science of the mind in all its aspects and modes of functioning, or, as I would prefer to say, the positive science of conduct or behaviour. Psychology must not regard the introspective description of the stream of consciousness as its whole task, but only as a preliminary part of its work. Such introspective description, such ' pure psychology,' can never constitute a science, or at least can never rise to the level of an

[1] *Introduction to Social Psychology*, 21st ed., p .13.

explanatory science ; and it can never in itself be of any great value to the social sciences."

The above definition, contained in the beginning of this extract, has been expressed by the same author in his work *Primer of Physiological Psychology*, 1905, consequently after the publication of my paper, *Objective Psychology and its Subject Matter*.[1]

It is regrettable that McDougall, immediately after this definition, ceases to be an objectivist, for he speaks of the study of consciousness as introductory to the fundamental task of psychology, and later mentions the existence of " innate tendencies to thought and action that constitute the native basis of the mind," and then, abandoning the objective standpoint in science, speaks of science, of human spirit, of psychic qualities, of consciousness and other subjective processes.

Here is what we read in the same author : " The basis required by all of them " (the social sciences) " is a comparative and physiological psychology relying largely on objective methods, the observation of the behaviour of men and of animals of all varieties under all possible conditions of health and disease. It must take the largest possible view of its scope and functions, and must be an evolutionary natural history of mind. Above all it must aim at providing a full and accurate account of those most fundamental elements of our constitution, the innate tendencies to thought and action that constitute the native basis of the mind. . . . A second very important advance of psychology towards usefulness is due to the increasing recognition of the extent to which the adult human mind is the product of the moulding influence exerted by the social environment, and of the fact that the strictly individual human mind, with which alone the older introspective and descriptive psychology concerned itself, is an abstraction merely and has no real existence."[2]

We cannot help noting the fact that man, in his subjective evidence, does not realise that he acts under the influence of some mood ; he does not see that, at another time and in another mood, he would not have said or done what he has. Subjective evidence leads him into deception, and he supposes that he defines, quite exactly, his relation to the fact and event, however strange his actions may appear to an external observer. There is a peculiar self-deception, such as is completely excluded in an objective evaluation of a person and his actions. It is at least quite clear to an external observer how a man reacts in one case or the other, although he does not notice it himself, as, for instance, when he is in a state of elation or depression, these being reflected in his facial expressions, gestures, intonation of voice, etc.

And there is another sphere where subjective analysis proves quite helpless : the formation of concepts. " Although everybody knows," says Dr. Beck (*l.c.* : pp. 32–33), " that at the present moment we possess notions which we had not a few days before, the wisest of us is probably not able to say, on the basis of personal experience, from what process

---

[1] See *Vestnik Psychologii*, 1904.   [2] *l.c.*, pp. 13, 14.

precisely these new concepts have originated, whence and how they arise. But although we cannot apprehend this by means of direct observation either of our own mind or the mind of others, there is, nevertheless, a method of tracing this latent process, namely, language." This is an admission which proves the superiority of the investigation of the objective manifestations of association-reflex activity over subjective self-observation or self-analysis in such an important sphere as that of the formation of concepts.

In general, it must be regarded as a great mistake to maintain that the study of consciousness is the fundamental task of psychology. Thus psychology will not advance far in knowledge of the psychic world, which consists not only of consciousness, but also of the unconscious, and here we must admit that the unconscious are more important quantitatively than are the conscious processes.

In this respect, it is useful to quote the words of Freud[1] : Consciousness " is only a remote psychic product of the unconscious process. . . . The unconscious is the larger circle which includes within itself the smaller circle of the conscious ; everything conscious has its preliminary step in the unconscious . . . *the unconscious is the real psychic ; its inner nature is just as unknown to us as the reality of the external world, and it is just as imperfectly reported to us through the data of consciousness as is the external world through the indications of our sensory organs.*"

Freud has indicated, among other things, the method of revealing the unconscious by means of so-called " psycho-analysis," based on intensive concentration on certain psychic phenomena ; but an extensive and crushing criticism of this method, a criticism into which it is not possible to enter here, shows how faulty this subjective method is. In particular, a certain " pan-sexualism," artificially discovered, by the method of psycho-analysis, as the origin of the common neuroses, has now, as is well known, been partly replaced by the doctrine of the conflict of the individual with the social environment (Adler).

The view, once commonly accepted, as held, for example, by Herzen and others, that conscious processes differ from unconscious by dynamic peculiarities, *i.e.* the degree of intensity of the process itself, is also open to objection.

According to Freud, the rôle of consciousness consists in the perception of qualities, *i.e.* affectivity in the form of pleasure or pain. Bleuler,[2] however, holds a different opinion similar to that which I advanced long before him in my paper, *Personal and General Consciousness (Vestnik Psychologii)*, and later in a series of other papers, and also in *Suggestion and its Rôle in Social Life.*[3]

---

[1] *Translators' note :* Freud : *Traumdeutung :* Brill's translation : *The Interpretation of Dreams*, 1927, pp. 485–486.

[2] Bleuler : *Journ. f. Psych. u. Neur.*, Hf. 1.

[3] There is a translation of it in German and French. The French enlarged edition is the later.

According to Bleuler, those processes are conscious which are associated with our ego, *i.e.* those contents which, at a given moment, form our personality.

On the other hand, " if an unconscious complex absorbs an ever-increasing number of elements from our ordinary ego, at the same time not associating with it as a whole, it ultimately becomes a second personality."

Be that as it may, do we submit everything to self-observation when we explicate our psychic activity by means of introspection ? Ultimately, that of which we are conscious is often a product of preceding unconscious activity. On the other hand, along with conscious processes, there constantly go on in us also unconscious processes, of the existence of which we have only indirect information.

The problems of so-called second consciousness or sub-consciousness have only recently become subjects of scientific investigation, chiefly from the period of the study of hypnosis. Now we know that second consciousness manifests itself generally throughout everyday life, too. Thus, A. Moll mentions Barkworthy, who added up long columns of figures while he engaged in animated conversation, which he did not interrupt for a single minute.

F. Myers sometimes forgot, while lecturing, that he was delivering a lecture, and imagined that he was chatting to acquaintances in the lecture hall. But after a minute, he realised that he was standing at the desk and delivering the lecture quite coherently (Beck, *l.c. :* p. 254). Such cases, according to my observations, are not rare. It is well known, too, that a musician plays at his best when he does not concentrate on the piece, but renders it unaccountably.

It will be said that all this lies beyond the pale of objective study. By no means. There is, indeed, little room for subjective psychology here, for how can one speak of self-analysis, when there is question of another consciousness which does not submit to self-analysis, and which is lost to memory ? There remains only the statement of the fact ; further, the analysis itself cannot proceed, if it does not utilise, to a certain extent, the artificial method of psycho-analysis. Reflexology, however, in this case, analyses all the external manifestations of the individual, including complex actions, and uses the narration only to explicate which actions are accountable, and which not, and examines the narration itself from the viewpoint of objective analysis.

Further, many other problems of a more particular, yet far-reaching, character cannot be solved, only because subjective analysis is taken as the criterion. Take, for instance, the above-mentioned question : Have animals the power of reasoning ? For some, the answer is in the affirmative on the ground of the data, for it has been proved that animals can count, but others will not even hear of this. Further : Try to answer the question : Are the processes which relate to the so-called instinctive manifestations quite unconscious ? Lastly, the question : What phenomena, accompanying affects, are to be regarded as primary—the material, the somatic, or the psychic ? also remains unanswered.

Thus, the subjective method is helpless in regard to the study of psychic activity, even at any given moment, and requires to be supplemented by objective observation. That is why we contend that an external human being should be studied first of all from the strictly objective standpoint, *i.e.* in his outer manifestations, and thus, in reality, is determined the precise value of the individual in his environment. Yet, the strictly objective method does not force us to turn to the elucidation of subjective experiences, but has in view merely the study of the outer manifestations of human activity, defining its dependence on certain external causes, present as well as past, and on certain inherited characteristics.

It may be said for certain that in order to have a sufficiently complete knowledge of a human individual we must least of all be guided by the individual's narrations about himself, but we must know his personality, firstly from his actions and conduct, from the form and content of his speech, from his facial expressions, his gestures, and, in general, from his relations to his environment and from his behaviour, for, ultimately, personality represents the whole individual complex of higher, *i.e.* association, reflexes, including also those of their peculiarities which are to a certain extent the reflection of inherited conditions, such as innate dispositions, temperament, the motor tempo in general, the individual type (auditory, visual, motor, etc.), the so-called instinctive or inherited-organic manifestations, greater or lesser talent, etc.

It is obvious from the above that personality is thus a result of racial and individual or acquired experience in the social environment ; in other words, is a bio-social entity.

Therefore, it is clear that the new science, which we call reflexology, has for its aim the study of personality by means of objective observation and experiment, and the registration of all its external manifestations and their external causes, present or past, which arise from the social environment and even from the framework of inherited character. In other words, the aim of reflexology is the strictly objective study, in their entirety, of the correlations of the human being with the environment through the mediation of man's facial expressions, his gestures, the content and form of his speech, his behaviour, and, in general, everything by which he manifests himself in the environment.[1]

---

[1] Because of its absolute objectivity, I prefer the term " reflexology " to the terms " psycho-reflexology " and " objective psychology " which I formerly used. The term " objective psychology " is also inconvenient, because it gives ground for confusing reflexology with the method of a school of psychologists who call themselves objectivists only for the reason that, in occupying themselves with the study of consciousness, they use objective methods, but in reality do not cease to be subjectivists, while for reflexology the focus of study is the external manifestations of personality and the explication of those external and internal causes, past and present, which condition them in their particular social environment.

Some writers have taken as indicating consciousness or intellect those cases in which activities are teleological or pursuing a definite aim ; but, doubtlessly, there are conscious activities which do not pursue a definite aim ; and, on the other hand, there are purely automatic activities of which man can give no account, and which, nevertheless, are teleological in character.

So this index, too, does not give us any ground, on the basis of external manifestations, for regarding certain activities as conscious or unconscious.

According to Petrazhitsky, more precise results are secured, not by the method of analogy, but by a combined method of inner and external observation. In such cases, a nexus between certain inner and external manifestations in certain individuals would be first established. Having accumulated such data, " we have the premises for deductive conclusions in concrete cases," consequently not by analogy, but " by subsuming the concrete movements of others under their appropriate general notions." [*Introduction to the Theory of Law* (Russian), St. Petersburg, p. 35.]

However, it is easy to disclose the weak points of this method, too. First of all, there is question of a previous study, which is not always possible and practicable. In any case, it is absolutely out of the question on first meeting with a strange man. Secondly, is it really so simple, and is it at all possible, to study the nexus between certain inner or psychic experiences and external manifestations ? For inner experiences may be known only by external manifestations ; consequently, in reality, we shall here, too, study the correlation of only the external manifestations with external stimuli, and not at all with the inner or psychic phenomena, which will, anyhow, remain unknown in their full extent.

By the way, the intuitionalist theory of investigation of another mind (Scheler, Ellwood, Bergson, Lossky, and others) was advanced, in the first place, by Darwin. According to him, as the expressive movements must become instinctive, it is *a priori* probable, to a certain extent, that the capacity for recognising them has become instinctive. But here there is question of such expressive movements as the expressions (facial, etc.) of anger, sorrow, etc., but not of the symbolic forms, the most important in the world of man, of expression in the form of speech. Nevertheless, only our own anger and our own sorrow, and not those of others, are accessible to us.

Finally, if we do not know the psychical experiences of others, but are conscious only of our own, which we put into the heads of others, and if, in the degree of emotion and in the character of the associations, our psychical experiences, as belonging to us as peculiar individuals, cannot be identified with the experiences of some other individual, it is obvious that we understand each other each in his own way, exchanging signs and constructing, according to these signs, our own conscious experiences, which doubtlessly diverge more or less in degree, as well as in character, from the conscious experiences of others. After all of this, can the subjective method satisfy scientific precision? The answer is, undoubtedly, in the negative.

Everything we have said leads us to the conclusion that objective science not only can, but also should, be built up exclusively on the objective method and without any help from the subjective method.

The question is : Shall we exclude the latter altogether from the realm of science? Not at all, but it finds its place only in conjunction with the data of the objective method and under its control, a subject to which I devote the last few pages of my book. In any case, the use of self-observation is possible only on oneself and only at the moment of the experiencing of the event, or just after it.

Referring to the applicability of the method of self-observation only to the self, I admit that it can be applied not only by myself, but also by others, but each one of those who use this method is an independent observer of his own experiences, and must himself immediately write down the results of his observations, or dictate them to another who records them. These results I can later compare one with the other, so as to note their individual peculiarities, or explicate the most significant points, all of which process will be my own judgment, but not indirect self-observation as the subjectivist psychologists contend.

Let us suppose that several subjects are shown an impressive picture, e.g. the picture of John the Terrible's murder of his son. They are required to describe in writing both the picture itself and their inner experiences. Their notes will give me purely objective material, which will be expressed in the more or less accurate description of the picture, in the pointing out of certain characteristics in that description, in the character of the description itself, etc. These same descriptions may also serve me to estimate the subjective states of the subject while looking at the picture, and I can also compare the data of their respective inner experiences evoked by seeing the given picture. But, in the last two cases, I shall have judgments, as I have mentioned already, which have for their special aim to investigate the inner or psychical experiences of the subjects, but for objective knowledge, the strictly objective evaluation of the material which I derive from the notes of those who have looked at the picture is sufficient for me ; and my objective material will not gain anything if I add to it the subjective evaluation of the same material in the sense of a judgment concerning the subjective experiences of the subjects, but, rather, it will lose to a greater or lesser degree.

We must not forget that the application of the objective method must be appropriate to that material with which the science has to deal. Thus, if a physicist applies a physical criterion to living individuals, and investigates them as physical bodies, he will doubtlessly fall into error, even though he fascinate an entire galaxy of pure physiologists. In this case, we must keep in view the incorrect application of the method, and that is all ; the resulting error does not force on us a condemnation of the method itself. That is why I cannot agree with V. Vagner, who condemns the method itself, instead of the mode of its application. Criticising the physiologist Professor I. Pavlov, who attacks animal psychology, he says : " The reactions of the nervous system, although it is completely homogeneous in its morphological structure, may, as a result of a number of inner and external causes, be different in one and the same organism. It follows from this that, by studying the reaction mechanisms of the nervous system of a given organism, we do not learn what is necessary for the delimitation and explication of its psychology. That is one point. Secondly, we know that the nervous system is a mechanism by means of which work of the most varied kind can be performed. As a loom, set in motion by a definite mechanism and fed with one and the same material, can manufacture various fabrics according to the hands which manipulate it, so also the mechanism of the nervous system, which is constructed in given organisms according to one pattern and receives the same kind of stimuli, can elaborate reactions different in character and content."[1]

All this is doubtlessly true theoretically, but it ignores the fact that a method has been discovered by which we learn why exactly, in a given animal, one and the same stimulus now calls out one, and now another, reaction. V. Vagner is right in one point : that, by the objective study of the activities of the higher centres, we cannot yet solve the problems of biology. But if the objective method is applied not in the study of the activities of the nervous system only, and not in the study of the innervation of the salivary gland only, but directly in the study of all the reactions which we observe in animals, then the matter will appear in a different light, and the above-mentioned views will be shed as unseasonable.

In the same way, when a physiologist tries to solve the complicated problems of sociology on the basis of experiments on the salivary gland, as attempted by Dr. Zeliony, he quite naturally meets with sharp opposition from the American sociologist, Ellwood (*The American Journal of Sociology*, t. XXII).[2] According to the latter, the method of physiologists " will answer very well for the behaviour of a rat or for the interaction of a colony of rats. It conceivably even would be adequate to describe the social life of a human group which lived half a million years ago . . . in a *perceptual* world. Civilised man, however, lives in an *ideational* world. For him the world of real objects is largely replaced by a world of ideas, standards, values. These ideas, standards, values have gradually developed and accumulated during the whole of human history. . . . Human history thus presents itself as a growing tradition or ' social mind,' which cannot be understood apart from its content. . . . Human culture is essentially a psychic matter, and culture has made the human societies we know."

[1] V. Vagner : *Physiology and Psychology in the Solution of Psychological Problems* in *Noviye ideyi v biologii*, St. Petersburg, no. 6, p. 6. See also his : *Animal Psychology before the Tribunal of Physiology* in *Vestnik Psychologii*, 1911, pts. 3–5 and *Biopsychology*, vol. I.

[2] *Translators' note :* pp. 302–303.

Further, the objective method is regarded as insufficient by Ellwood, also because, according to him, it is impossible to establish a strict correspondence between the psychic and our external manifestations. He contends that, because of " the organising activity of the mind, knowledge, beliefs, and standards " may have been " completely transformed so that they issue in new behaviour complexes. . . . This is not to deny that a purely physiological statement of human behaviour is possible, but to substitute in our description of social processes the hypothetical activities of the cells of the central nervous system, which have not yet been observed and of which we know little, for ways of thinking and feeling which are well understood and which are *ex hypothesi* the exact correlatives of these physiological processes, is sheer pedantry ! " On the other hand, " we know the opinions and beliefs of others as clearly and as accurately as we know many physical objects." Such is the substance of Ellwood's objections to the objective method.

Here, again, we see merely a condemnation of the pretensions of the physiologists to solve the complicated problems of the sociology of modern cultured man by means of the " salivary " method alone, which is, according to this writer, valid only for the study of the " behaviour of rats," or a man-animal who is only a little higher than a rat ; but, for all that, we can on no account agree with Ellwood's view that sociology is the science of man living in a world of ideas, and that the history of mankind is the history of a " social mind " which cannot be understood apart from its ideal contents, and that human culture bears an essentially psychic character. In all of this, we see that spiritualistic dogmatism which, to the present day, has retarded the development of all the so-called humanistic sciences, including sociology, instead of directing them along the path of science. The kernel of the problem lies, of course, not in the different character of the view of these two writers, and not in psycho-physical parallelism, which, although accepted as fact, has, by the way, not been demonstrated at all,[1] and, lastly, not in replacing the description of social phenomena by the hypothetical activity of cells, but in the evaluation of sociological facts as the objective reactions of communities or as forms of interaction between classes and individuals, as agents who have individual past experience and, besides, have certain potentialities, and are born under given conditions. There is, and there should be, no room here for subjectivism and its ideas, for an idea is symbolically expressed by a word or some other sign, and the corresponding ideas will appear, on analysis, dissimilar in every social individual, because of his different individual experience. To speak of the knowledge, opinions, and forms of belief of others does not, however, mean paying tribute to subjectivism, which begins from the moment we mention " the organising activity of the mind " or " the social mind," for then everyone is free to put his own ideal content into the corresponding signs, and so to complicate facts quite unnecessarily. At the same time, the

[1] See V. Bechterev : *General Principles of Reflexology*, St. Petersburg, 1918

elucidation of reactions and also of the mutual relations between human beings will be fully possible, if, besides the external character of the reactions, on the basis of which relations between individuals are established, their individual past experience is taken into account. It is just this experience which is usually not taken into account, and, as a result, some writers, although they approach the problems objectively, still cannot master the complex social phenomena, while others do not regard it at all possible finally to abandon the subjective method.

The same must be said concerning the study of diseased personality. The subjectivist psychologist can by no means dispense with the subjective method, for he imagines that it is not possible to proceed without it in the study of the diseases of personality, and so he falls into gross errors in not objectively evaluating the words and actions of the diseased subject, and in applying to them no other than his own subjective norm, for the subjective experience of the diseased is not directly accessible to him. (See V. Bechterev : *Diseases of Personality ; Problems in the Study and Education of Personality*, 2nd vol.)

What has just been said refers to those descriptions, which the diseased themselves leave on record, of pathological states. From such records, the objective material, which alone has scientific value, should be extracted, but the subjective aspect, which is hidden beneath the spoken or written signs, is of interest rather to the literary artist or the poet than to the scientist, who must submit to analysis not only the speech, which consists of words as signs or symbols, of the diseased, but also their other reactions expressed in their expressive movements, in their behaviour, and inherited-organic reflexes. Therefore, leave it to the painters, the writers, and the poets to study and reproduce the soul of others, with its experiences and emotions, but leave to science occupation with the higher reflexes and all sorts of other reactions in correlation with the external influences, present as well as past, of the environment. With the subjective or inner reactions science must occupy itself only in their correlation with the external reflexes, and, then, only to that extent to which they may be directly observed by self-analysis.

In fine, I must state that the difference between subjective psychology and the objective study of personality lies in the fundamental opposition of the views of the nature of the phenomena studied. Thus, subjective psychology regards language as an instrument for the expression of thought, action as an expression of will, expressive movements as a manifestation of feeling and emotion, conditioned by vasomotor changes (according to the James–Lange theory), while reflexology regards language, actions, expressive movements, cardio-vascular and respiratory phenomena as reflexes developed, on the basis of ordinary reflexes, by up-bringing and experience, and as subject, dependent on certain conditions, to processes of inhibition, release, differentiation, generalisation, etc. Of course, analogous phenomena in animals, phenomena which establish the relations of a living being to its environment and may be called in their totality the correlative activity of the organism, should be studied in the same way.

Needless to say, the subjectivists are not very satisfied with this aim of objective investigation, for the scope of subjective psychology has recently been extended, as we have seen, not only to include the external personality, but almost the whole animal world, or at least an extensive part of it, and also the whole world of the child, including the age of infancy, and, lastly, the world of the psychopath.

Nevertheless, truth must be based on accurate facts, and must be attained by strictly objective methods as exact as possible, but not on analogies and assumptions ; therefore, subjectivism must abandon the field in favour of the objective study of a subject.

Can there be a complete and real science which does not make prediction possible ? Try to drag prediction out of the data of pure self-observation. Try to show that a man guided by indirect self-observation may determine, with appropriate accuracy, the actions of another man. I fancy that, in this way, there can never be accurate prediction, for circumstances may prove stronger than any intentions. It is true that subjective psychology has itself already recognised the insufficiency of the subjective method unaided, and has recourse to objective methods of investigation, but, as we know, only to supplement self-observation and to utilise them for the elucidation of the subjective experiences of another individual. This widens the psychological perspective, but in no case does it secure for subjective psychology that completeness of knowledge which may be attained by the science of the correlative activity of man, the science called reflexology.

Do not forget that reflexology, generally speaking, does not exclude any hypothesis of consciousness and of the psychic.[1] If one is pleased to regard consciousness as simply a function of the brain, reflexology may take it as a conclusion deduced from certain scientific data, but even other hypotheses of consciousness, of course excluding the metaphysical, are not in opposition to reflexology. I have developed above the energic point of view, which I defend, of nervous processes in the light of the ion theory, and this seems to me to be the nearest to the truth. But this is really the realm of physiology. Reflexology does not study directly the functions of the brain ; it rather investigates the association-reflex activity of man, independently of the understanding of it, and of whether this association-reflex activity has some particular basis in the brain as an apparatus which establishes the relation of the individual to an external person.

[1] In the second edition, as a result of such inattention as may occur in any work, the words " of the soul " were used instead of " of the psychic." This must be noted here, for some subjectivist psychologists, for instance, Basov (and, I regret to say, Kornilov also) have made appropriate use of the slip, and imagined that, by utilising isolated passages from a work saturated with mechanistic views, they could minimise the importance of reflexology in the study of human personality and so enhance their own position. Futile defence !

Besides, the naturalist psychologists have already clearly recognised the inadequacy of such a subjective psychology as is still taught in the lecture hall. " Psychology," says Forel, " cannot be content with the study, by means of introspection only, of the phenomena of our higher consciousness, for then psychology would be impossible. Each individual should have only the psychology of his own subjectivism, according to the principle of the old spiritualist scholastics, and should doubt the existence of an external world and of his fellow-men." " Finally, such a subjective psychology, regarded independently of our activity, in the world in which we live, is something incomprehensible, full of contradictions, and, above all, obviously opposed to the law of conservation of energy. From these fairly simple considerations, it also follows that a psychology which ignores brain activity is an absurdity." (Prof. A. Forel : *Der Hypnotismus*, Russ. tr., p. 8, Petrograd.) And yet this same writer actually contents himself with the so-called physiological psychology, which co-ordinates that very subjective or introspective psychology, which he rejects so resolutely, with brain-activities, and such a procedure is, in reality, nothing but an absurdity also.

Everything we have already stated renders it possible for us to include in the circle of the biological sciences, which are concerned only with the purely objective method, the study of the organism's highest activities, which establish its relations to the environment, or that activity which we have above styled correlative.[1]

An investigation of correlative activity is possible without an appeal to consciousness, because all, even the most complex, conscious activities may occur, as shown by subjective analysis, without consciousness, or, at least, outside the field of personal consciousness, and, in consequence, we cannot give an account in our subjective world of the course of these complex activities. However we explain this fact, it testifies that the process remains intrinsically the same, whether or not it is reflected by any phenomena in the subjective world.

Besides, we must bear in mind that subjective processes have not in reality the same completeness as objective. If we take a man suffering from an affection of the spinal cord, we shall see that, although a prick in the foot will cause a reflexive withdrawal of the limb, the prick will not be felt. So the passage of the nerve impulses, along the afferent nerves, the cells of the spinal cord, and the efferent nerves, is not accompanied by consciousness. There is consciousness when the impulses reach the highest brain centres or the centres of the cerebral cortex. Thus, by investigating consciousness, we can judge only of the central part of the process, but by studying the process as a reflex, we get an idea of the whole process from beginning to end.

---

[1] In the following treatment, we shall everywhere use, in the interests of objectivity, the terms " correlative activity " and " correlative processes," and understand by them the sum of the reflexes of an individual in response to external stimuli.

Justification for the study of the external manifestations of correlative activity in conjunction with their external causes, past and present, and also the organic conditions, is to be found in the fact that, according to modern views, there is no psychic and no conscious or subjective phenomenon which is not accompanied by a nervous current passing through the neurons and their axons or through the fibres of the brain, while there are neural processes which are not accompanied by the phenomena of consciousness. And this naturally leads to the conclusion that the observations of the external manifestations of personality, in the form of behaviour and movements in general, including facial expressions, and gesticulations, as well as verbal, vascular, and secretory reflexes in connection with certain external conditions, present or past, will give us a more complete and accurate picture of the whole personality than will the elucidation, by the introspective method, of the subjective experiences of the given personality.

It may be said, however, that there are subjective experiences which remain, as it were, latent inner experiences, which man does not reveal to his fellow-man, but it is quite clear, naturally, that these latent subjective experiences, which are unexpressed thoughts, are inaccessible to indirect self-observation also From the objective standpoint, they should be regarded as processes of inhibition or temporary blocking of correlative activity, which manifest themselves, as is well known, in weak external effects (so-called inner speech, controlled expressive movements, slight respiratory changes, vasomotor reactions, galvanic current in the skin, etc.). To see that this is so, it is sufficient to remember that, when a man thinks with concentration, he necessarily whispers. Some cannot concentrate at all without pronouncing words, but when a man is excited, when the association reflexes in general are released from inhibition, he cannot help expressing his thoughts audibly. On the other hand, a man reading with strained concentration whispers, and even speaks aloud, what he reads. Thus it is quite clear that we are concerned, in the one case, with the overt association reflex in the form of speaking or reading, and, in the other, with the inhibited association reflex in the form of thinking to oneself or reading to oneself.[1]

---

[1] It has been often shown that concentration of thought in a definite direction or " wishing " is accompanied by certain bodily movements, and, even recently, Pfungst has shown, in a number of laboratory experiments, that such movements must have been executed by those present at the reception of answers from (the horse) " clever Hans " in von Osten's experiments. Whether or not the explanation of von Osten's experiments is correct—that the horse observed such movements—is a different question, but these movements are always produced. Besides, all our data show that the movements in this case are, in character, nothing other than the minimal manifestation of those actions which should correspond to the given thought or wish. For instance, invite a subject to take note of one card of many placed in a row, and ask him to concentrate intensively on it. Offer to indicate the card in question. Take the subject's hand, which should be relaxed ; pass it quickly along the cards, and you will immediately notice a resistance on his part when his hand reaches the given card. This will make it possible for you to

But if this is so, it is obvious that thought and subjective experiences in general must be understood as inhibited reflexes, which, sooner or later, having freed themselves from inhibition, will enter the objective world either in the form of narration or in the form of actions or other reactions. Thus, in the course of time, the completeness desired in the objective study of personality will be secured.

Adopting the attitude indicated, we must first of all discard the view that correlative activity is an activity *sui generis*, and having nothing in common with the environment, that it is, to speak in philosophic language, a manifestation of " mind." On the contrary, all scientific data indicate that correlative activity is ultimately a result of that manifestation of energy which we know, in its simplest form, as the irritability of protoplasm, but, in its more complex manifestations, as the so-called nervous current derived from it and accompanied by the negative oscillation of the electric current in the nervous and central organs.[1]

guess the particular card, but this also proves that the concentration of thought on the given card produces a straining of the muscles of the hand, when it delays over the card in question, as if to indicate its position. Thus we have in this, as well as in analogous cases, really inhibited motor acts or inhibited mimico-somatic manifestations, or, which is the same thing, inhibited reflexes. The latter, among others, may be revealed also by special objective methods, under which fall the scales of A. Mosso, the skin current of Tarchanoff (the so-called psycho-galvanic reaction of Binswanger, Veraguth, and others).

Translators' note : O. Pfungst : Clever Hans, pp. 1–29. *Animal Intelligence.*

[1] See V. Bechterev : *The Psychic and Life*, St. Petersburg, 1904. In this book there is a bibliography of the question discussed. (The French and German editions of the book are much fuller than the Russian.) See also bibliography in Dr. Trivus's *Dissertation* (my laboratory), St. Petersburg, 1900 ; also Dr. Kaufman : *Dissertation* (my laboratory), St. Petersburg.

CHAPTER III

The problem of the relation of the " spiritual " world to the physical. The doctrine of psycho-physical parallelism. The hypothesis of interactionism. The notion of the unity of the material and the " spiritual " world.

AS is well known, philosophy has hitherto paid much attention to the problem of the relation of the " spiritual " world to the physical, and many writers still make vain endeavours to solve the problem of the relation of the so-called mental processes to the bodily processes and *vice versa*. In this respect, two main trends are observable—the dualistic and the monistic. The first posits the existence in the world of two substances different in kind—matter and mind—while the second is the standpoint which unifies the physical and the spiritual or psychic world.

But the clear-cut distinction drawn between these two " entities " is a product of the mental culture of later times. In Greek, as we know, the same term stands for both " mind " and " word."

Recall : " In the beginning was the word, and the word was with God, and the word was God." According to the ideas of the ancient Greeks the soul was looked upon as rarefied and higher substance, like vapour. Only later the concept of ideas was formulated, and thus subjectivism in philosophy and psychology was given a stable basis.

Before Plato, a gross materialism, which derived the idea of human personality from unverified experience and drew its data from the external world, prevailed in philosophy. Thus, six centuries before the Christian era, Greek philosophy, represented by Thales, regarded water as the principle of the universe, but later, in the doctrine of Anaximenes, air was regarded as the principle. According to the notions of that time, everything originated in air, and also everything on earth changed into air. By inhaling air, man was supposed to draw in a part of the universe, and this gave him life and energy.

From the time of Plato and the later philosophers, who first formulated the concept of human personality as a spirit, men have made various and strenuous attempts to solve the problem of the interrelation of the material and the spiritual world and to adopt one or other standpoint in problems concerned with the understanding of the universe. Ultimately, we get, on the one hand, gnosiological idealism, and, on the other, critical realism. The former maintains that, in the first place, consciousness exists, and that consciousness alone may be regarded as indubitable in the world, while the whole environment is represented to us in the form of ideas, and we do not know, and cannot recognise, anything except ideas. Realism, on the contrary, maintains that an external world exists as the cause of our ideas of it, and some regard the external world as being such as it is represented to our mind (so-called naïve realism), but others hold that the world is reflected in us not in the form in which it exists in reality ; that the colours of nature do not exist objectively in the form of colours, and that there are really no sounds in nature, but, in both cases, there are only forms of movement of the material particles, in one case of ether, in the other, of air.

The dualistic attitude towards the world was developed by Descartes in particular, who held that there is a sharp distinction between the material and the psychic, and that these two have nothing in common.

The nature of our soul, according to Descartes, is quite independent of our body, and, therefore, it cannot die with the body. Descartes, as we know, held that the soul, by which he understood thinking principle, exists prior to the body. But in view of his doctrine that only man can think, he denied the existence of a soul in animals, which he regarded as machines.

According to Descartes, matter is extended, occupies a certain position in space, and is measurable, but lacks the power to think, while thought is an attribute of mind, but mind is not extended, and does not admit of measurement, *i.e.* it is non-spatial. Mind is, thus, not material, not corporeal, not sensible. In other words, the psychic is the " spiritual," *i.e.* something that is not perceptible to objective observation.

It is clear that this doctrine has its source in the notion of " bodiless spirit," and in those religious doctrines which personify, in spiritual form, a being of a higher order. In fine, we are here standing on the threshold of occultism, and exact science, in spite of the other merits of Descartes, has nothing to do with his doctrine.

Because of the establishment of the above-mentioned distinction between the material and the mental, a true interrelation is in reality impossible, but, since everyday observation teaches the contrary, the adherents of this doctrine were forced to take final refuge in the thought that this interrelation is a kind of miracle, an interference on the part of a supernatural will, an interference on the part of God. As such a miracle would be necessary every second, for our wishes associated with the execution of actions are incessantly operative, Leibnitz, so as to abolish a great miracle in the logical structure, advanced the doctrine of pre-established harmony, according to which, in the nature of the human organism, a definite harmony between mind and body is established once and for all. As a result of this harmony, the body always executes what the mind wills, and the mind always knows the state of the body.

Needless to say, both doctrines—that of Descartes and that of Leibnitz —have now an historic importance, but their influence is still noticeable everywhere, and even the familiar hypothesis of psycho-physical parallelism may be regarded as, to a certain extent, a reflection of the views of these two philosophers.

Psycho-physical parallelism must be regarded as one of the most widely accepted doctrines at the present time. This doctrine, in substance, is that both the mental and the physical represent two sets of phenomena running parallel, although both are different in nature. Fechner is considered the father of this doctrine. According to him, the material and

the spiritual are really one process. The parallelism of both sets of phenomena is illustrated, by the exponents of this doctrine, by similes which
really do not illustrate anything, as, for example, when they say that a
number of bowls put into each other will, if looked at from the outside,
appear convex, but from the inside, concave. Another simile consists in
the comparison to the inner and the outer side of a clock. Needless to
say, no matter how clever these similes may be, they cannot bring us
nearer to an understanding of the intimate connection of what is various
in its manifestations, and, therefore, this hypothesis is regarded by many
as simply a working hypothesis and nothing more.

Some, championing the doctrine of psycho-physical parallelism, maintain a causal dependence between mental and material processes. So
some, for instance, Büchner and Haeckel, regard the material process
as fundamental and make the mental dependent on it. (According to
Haeckel, thought is a result of the movement of material particles.[1])
Others give preference to the psychical process, make it fundamental,
and regard the material process as dependent on it.[2] Arising from this
difference in views, there is the attempt to solve the contradiction unilaterally—either materialistically or spiritualistically.

It is not necessary to dwell here on either of these doctrines, for they
have both really become obsolete, and if they now find their exponents,
they have no fewer antagonists.

A. Kronfeld, criticising Freud's doctrine, says : " From the standpoint
of epistemological criticism, we must admit the intrinsic impossibility
of a physical explanation of separate psychic phenomena, and abandon,
as a psycho-physical dogma, the doctrine of inhibition." But, at the
same time, a new objection arises which has been neatly formulated by
Münsterberg : " Does the problem of a connection between brain and
consciousness disappear because of this ? Does the very raising of the
question cease to be justified, because we know that it is meaningless from
the metaphysical standpoint ? "

Up to quite recent times, fruitless attempts to explain consciousness,
i.e. to direct it away from the material world, have been made. The
hypothesis of oxygen as the source of consciousness has been recently

---

[1] " The theory of atoms endowed with souls—an ancient idea, which has
found expression 2000 years ago in Empedocles' doctrine concerning the hate and
love of elements—may be regarded as, in some sense, an essential component of
this type of monism. Our contemporary physicists and chemists in general have
accepted the atomistic hypothesis, first proposed by Democritus, and, regarding
every body as a combination and aggregate of atoms, ascribe all changes to the
transposition of such separate particles. All these changes in the organic as well
as in the inorganic world seem to us really intelligible only if we see in the atoms
not little masses of dead matter, but *living* elementary particles, endowed with the
power of attraction and repulsion." (Haeckel : *Vorträge uber Naturwissenschaft
und Philosophie. Der Monismus ;* S. 14 ; Bonn, 1898.)

[2] According to Fichte, for instance, " Consciousness is the only proved real
principle of the prime force which is operative in everything."

advocated ; but there is nothing more obvious than that these attempts do not advance the problem a single step.[1]

Lastly, some place both processes in functional interdependence. Mathematics defines functional dependence as the interrelation of two given quantities. If we say that the area of a circle is $A = \pi r^2$, this means that, between A and r, there is a certain interrelation, which makes it easy to determine A, if we know r, and, on the other hand, given A, to determine r. Yet, it is not difficult to understand that, although between the objective or material process in the brain centres and the subjective phenomena a certain interrelation, conformable to law, may exist, it is, so far, impossible to say in what way we can determine the objective process from the subjective data, and *vice versa*.

It deserves attention that the Ionians in ancient Greece accepted animatism. Later, Spinoza preached the idea of oneness or, more correctly, the unity of the material and spiritual worlds. Maintaining the impossibility of comparing one with the other, and the difference in the laws by which they are governed (one is endowed with the attribute of thinking, the other, of extension), Spinoza posits the existence of a close connection between them, as both orders of phenomena are manifestations of one substance. The latter is nothing else than the unitary, universal entity, the absolute, god ; everything that is in the universe is only a manifestation of this unitary, universal entity.

Thus, both the material and the spiritual are only separate aspects of the one higher substance, and where the material is, there also is the spiritual. From this it is clear why Spinoza is considered the founder of the pantheistic attitude towards the universe, an attitude which is widespread even now.

The famous philosopher, Spencer, has developed a view similar to Spinoza's. He also regards the material and the spiritual as manifestations of an absolute unknown power, which he identifies with God. He, however, does not ascribe to the latter the attribute of personality, for the concept of personality is a human one ; but the deity embraces something higher—super-humanity.

We shall not enter into a detailed examination of these partly obsolete

---

[1] I. A. Sacharov (Honorary Member of the Caucasian Medical Society), in his work, *Tchto takoye soznaniye ?* (*What is Consciousness ?* Tiflis, 1917), develops in detail this " oxygen " hypothesis for the explanation of psychic phenomena. This author has formulated his views in the following way : " Oxygen is the source of psychic life. It organises a central complex which receives the stimulations issuing from the external world, and, by welding them, changes them into sensations. It also gives these sensations a feeling tone, and arranges, in accordance with its various relations to the reducing substances of the cerebral cortex, the whole scale of sensations, beginning with the pleasant and unpleasant, and ending with feelings of pleasure, pain, desire, etc. It also produces the movements which arise with these feelings." Needless to say, this attempt at the mechanisation of consciousness does not advance us a single step either, apart from the generally accepted view that, without oxygen, there is no consciousness as there is no life whatever.

doctrines. We shall, however, note that the hypothesis of parallelism meets with opposition on the ground of the incommensurateness of the intensity of subjective processes and of the accompanying external movements.

Thus, the more a man concentrates on something, the more intense become his inner experiences, while his external movements are the more inhibited, and, on the contrary, speed in the performance of an action leads to automatism or unconscious execution. But even if this argument should appear unconvincing, the hypothesis of parallelism is open to yet another objection.

The most recent investigations maintain the existence of a splitting of consciousness itself, for writers distinguish between the so-called " higher " and the " lower " consciousness, and these are by no means co-ordinated. In a nutshell, the lower consciousness is not subject to the higher consciousness, which does not know " what interests and occupies the former at a given moment." (Pierre Janet : *Automatisme psychologique.*) The problem is how to harmonise the hypothesis of parallelism with these two forms of consciousness. We shall not touch on other objections to the hypothesis of parallelism.[1]

On the other hand, the hypothesis of interactionism meets with obstacles because of its admission of interaction between the phenomena of the physical and those of the psychic or spiritual order.

As a matter of fact, from the standpoint of subjective psychology, the problem of the transformation of ideas into movement or action remains insoluble. " In reality, an idea," says Ribot,[2] " cannot produce movement : so complete and wonderful a change of function would be something miraculous. It is not the state of consciousness itself, but the corresponding physiological state which is transformed into movement. I repeat that the correlation does not take place between a psychic state and movement, but only between two physiological states not different in kind, between two groups of nervous elements—the sensory and the motor. If we continue to regard consciousness as the cause, everything remains vague ; but if we regard consciousness as a simple concomitant of a certain neural process, which alone has real importance, everything becomes clear and the artificial difficulties vanish."

To illustrate this problem by an example, let us take violet rays, which, as is well known, act chemically on the retina. The question is whether their activity is associated with the colour-sensation, as a conscious act, or with the amplitude of their vibrations and with their wave-length I feel sure that the answer will favour the view that the active principle in this case is really not the sensation as such, but a special kind of radiant energy. In general, what interaction can there be between spirit and

---

[1] Those who desire a fuller treatment of the criticism of this doctrine we refer to Stumpf's paper : *Leib und Seele*—speech at the opening of the International Conference of Psychology in Munich, 4th August, 1896.

[2] Ribot · *De la volonté*, 1883.

matter ? How can one reality pass into another which is quite incommensurable, and *vice versa*? But even allowing this, although it is logically inconceivable, we must further allow that between two incommensurable realities, an interrelation, fully determined and conformable to law, is established by a miracle. On the same grounds, it is impossible to produce logical arguments in favour of Spinoza's theory also, which, by the establishment of a correlation of both with one absolute or god, merely conceals the interrelations between the two orders of phenomena. That is why we cannot rest content with any of those theories mentioned above.

Recently, some writers, dissatisfied with the doctrine of psychophysical parallelism and the hypothesis of interactionism, have begun to speak of psycho-physical causality. To the ranks of these belong Rickert and, partly, Stumpf. But the concept of causality in itself cannot satisfy natural science, for a cause presupposes a force which we should have to subsume under the notion of the psychic ; and then we should encounter the inapplicability to animate organisms, in so far as their psychic activity is concerned, of the law of conservation of energy, a law which is general for the universe.

CHAPTER IV

Energy as the basis of active processes in general, and of correlative processes in particular. The psychic processes of the higher animals are brain processes. The organs
of the ganglial and particularly of the central nervous system of higher organisms
are a kind of accumulators of energy.

IN spite of Descartes' view, science has demonstrated that the so-called
thought-processes are accompanied by objective manifestations.
In concentration, thought is reflected in facial expressions, in the
vocal cords, in the increased flow of blood to the brain and to the head in
general, in the more profuse excretion of phosphates, in respiratory and
cardiac changes, etc.

In Lehmann's famous work,[1] we may find detailed, though by no means
complete, references to these.

Now, apparently, it must be admitted that there is no thought-process
which is, as it were, incorporeal, *i.e.* lacking in external physical expression.

Recently, Ponzo (*Arch. ital. de Biologie*, t. LXIV, Nov. 1916) has
proved by experiments, in which respiration was recorded, that reading
aloud and reading to oneself manifest themselves in the same form of
respiratory movements. In the reading of a foreign language, the respiratory changes are still more marked, and the less familiar the language, the
more marked they are.

Investigations carried out in my laboratory do not leave any doubt
that even the mere listening to music is reflected in appropriate changes
in respiratory movements.

Here it is necessary to keep in mind that scientific data have firmly
established the view that so-called psychical processes occur only in the
brain, and occur in time, just as do all physical processes.

The physiology and the anatomy of the brain, in following this direction,
have already established an unconditional connection between the psychic
processes and certain physico-chemical processes occurring in the brain ;
as a result of this, increased psychic activity is accompanied, on the one
hand, by increased disintegration of phosphoric substances excreted by the
kidneys, and, on the other, by concomitant changes in the cells of
the cerebral cortex (so-called chromatolysis), by electrical phenomena in the
cortex, by increase in the temperature of the cerebral cortex, by its acid
reaction, etc.

Nevertheless, Haeckel's view, for instance, with its materialistic roots
in the atomic theory, cannot explain psychical phenomena, for the psychic
cannot be deduced from atoms. But, more recently, with the development
of the doctrine of energy, it has become possible to regard psychical
processes, too, as a manifestation of energy, while some writers, such as
Lasswitz, Grot, Krainsky, and others, hold the existence of a special
psychic energy. We, personally, consider it more correct to speak of
neuro-psychical energy,[2] which determines not only the movement of

---

[1] A. Lehmann : *Die körperlichen Äusserungen psychischer Zustände*, German tr.,
Leipzig, 1899.

[2] V. Bechterev : *Psyche und Leben,* Wiesbaden. *L'activité psychique et la vie*, Paris.

the nervous current, but also the manifestation of the specifically psychical processes in the brain, is the creative molecular energy of the lower animals, and is characterised by the contractility of protoplasm.

According to the latest view, the material universe is built up of positive and negative electrons, and the latter revolve in the atoms round a positive nucleus in orbits like a planetary system.[1] The latest investigations in this direction by Bohr, Rutherford, and Rozhdestvensky have deepened still further our knowledge of the structure of the atom. Thus, all the earlier philosophical views built on the basis of the antithesis of energy to matter fall to the ground. Matter, as studied by physics and chemistry, proves to be merely a fiction, as it were, for, instead of atoms, they discover energy, and, at that, energy of enormous power, and incapable of being harnessed because of the relatively low power of resistance of the best insulators.

But if matter is a fiction, and only energy is real, there is no ground for the contraposition of the psychic to the material and *vice versa*, and we have to ask ourselves : Is it not possible to reduce psychic activity, too, to physical energy ?

First of all, we must maintain that all psychical processes are brain processes, at the basis of which lies the movement of the nervous current. But the nervous current is, in reality, energy ; and we have every reason to speak of the transformation of those energies, which are known to us and which are acting on the outer and inner surfaces of the body, into a nervous current, and of the transformation of the latter into the molecular activity of the muscles, which, in turn, is transformed into mechanical work.

Everything that is referred to the subjective or psychical process obviously represents the result of a higher tension of the same energy, or of its capacity to manifest itself under appropriate conditions.

This higher tension of energy occurs usually in the case when the process, reaching the higher brain centres, is inhibited.

In any case, reflexology draws its general premises from the final generalisations of the natural sciences.

In the understanding of the universe, we must begin with what is given to us in experience in general, and the essence of this experience is that every phenomenon and every thing are the products of previous phenomena.

Our subjective world, like all our brain-processes, is a result of influences coming from outside. Therefore, we cannot assume the standpoint of gnosiological materialism. In this way, also, the external world —of course, not that which we perceive and imagine, but that which exists in reality—is subject to the law of causality or, more accurately, to the law of relations. And when we prosecute our analysis to the end, we must acknowledge one fundamental and first principle of all being, and this we call energy. In the concept of energy we have the idea of various

[1] A. Righi : *The Modern Theory of Physical Phenomena*, 1907.

manifestations of movement under the form of great masses, which are the heavenly bodies ; and under the form of smaller masses, sometimes larger, as, for instance, individuals constructed of cells, or smaller, as, for instance, molecules, atoms, and electrons ; but electrons apparently do not represent the ultimate division of substance. To the basis of this movement, a basis which must be common to all the phenomena of nature, including ourselves as a part of the universe, we give the name of universal energy.

Energy as such is often defined by physics, according to external manifestations, as the capacity for work ; and in this definition, of course, there is nothing material, but also nothing explanatory.

We shall content ourselves with defining energy as movement, and shall not enter into a further analysis. We shall only remark that " the thing-in-itself," or that noumenal which is unknown to us, lies beyond the confines of perception, is regarded as metaphysical, and is merely potential energy, and thereby we exhaust the concept of " the thing-in-itself," about which so many pages have been written in various philosopical works.

We may thus speak of energy as a movement which permeates the universe, and is exhibited under one peculiar form in living nature.

The forms of energy assumed by physics are various, but among them must be reckoned also the molecular energy of the complex and exceedingly mobile colloidal structures of living matter. The nervous current and the so-called neuro-psychical or, objectively speaking, brain processes are also products of this molecular energy.

When we see an object of a certain size and colour, this means that light-rays of a definite frequency act on our eyes ; when our body is touched by a hot or a cold object, when there is mechanical stimulation of the surface of the skin, or when sound-waves in the air reach the organ of Corti, etc., this means that the external energies, acting on the ends of our sensory organs, are transformed into molecular energy, which, in the form of a nervous current, passes along the centripetal conductors to the brain, this nervous current being itself a special kind of energy. This energy, on reaching, as a result of increased resistance to its movement, a certain tension in the centres, is accompanied by subjective manifestations, yet does not cease to be a nervous current, but later, returning by way of the centrifugal fibres in the form of a nervous current to the periphery, to muscles, and to glands, the same energy is transformed into the molecular energy of the muscles, on the one hand, and that of the glands, on the other.

Regarded from this point of view, molecular energy lies at the root of that irritability which characterises such an unstable composition as living cellular protoplasm. This irritability of protoplasm finds in the higher organisms further and intenser expression in the form of the various response reactions to external stimuli.

There is the protoplasm of a unicellular being. A stimulus is applied as a result of which we get the effect of contraction. If the stimulus is repeated at short intervals, the effect is, in the course of time, gradually weakened as a result of exhaustion, but may be exhibited again after some rest. The same is true of organisms of a higher order. What is the underlying principle ? The stimulus sets off the discharge of stored energy accumulated during the time when the protoplasm has been resting. When the recuperation is not sufficient, and there are repeated and frequent stimulations, there is a gradual and more or less complete exhaustion of the stored energy. But as a result of nourishment, the supply is replenished, and, besides, external stimulations also are a source of replenishment, if they do not lead to the discharge of stored energy.

As all of this is applicable to the activity of the nerve tissue, we have reason to assume that completely analogous phenomena must occur in our retina, in the organ of Corti, in the neural apparatus of the surface of the skin, in the bipolar cells of the Schneider membrane, in the papillæ of the tongue, etc., and equally in the appropriate central localities which are connected with the periphery by a chain of afferent conductors and send out centrifugal conductors, while the whole process occurs not in one element, but consecutively in the whole chain of neurons linked to each other.[1]

These processes of life, or, more accurately, life reactions, are maintained by a definite organisation, which causes a constant metabolism based on the redintegration of energy dissipated by previous disintegration. This self-regulation, which ultimately means a constant transformation of energy in the organism, is accomplished, on the one hand, by the taking of food from the environment, which, in its ultimate constitution, is merely a chemical product containing the stored radiant energy of the sun, and, on the other hand, by the impact of external energies on the receptive organs, as transformers of external energy—this impact leading to the disintegration and subsequent redintegration of organic substance, and all of this activity leading to the development of the nervous current. But as the redintegrative processes, as a result of nourishment with appropriate periods of rest, mostly prevail over the disintegrative, energy is finally stored in the organism in general, i.e. in its cellular protoplasm, and, in particular and especially, in the organs of the ganglial and central nervous system, which are, along with the muscles, more powerful accumulators of energy than are any other tissue elements of the higher organisms.

To make all this clearer, we shall state that, if we relate the stimuli impinging on the surface of the body to the subjective phenomena which we observe in ourselves, we shall find, first of all, that the sensation is proportional to the logarithm of the stimulus. This is known as the Weber–Fechner law. Although it cannot sustain searching criticism in all its

---

[1] The author is " accountable " to himself for the fact that all neurologists do not acknowledge the neuron theory, but suppose that the neuro-fibrillæ of one cell merge into the others. In the brain of higher animals, however, neurons are facts hitherto not disproved, even by the latest investigations.

details, this law gives us general indications that, with an increase in the intensity of the stimulus, the intensity of the sensation increases, though in lesser proportion, that is, while the intensity of the stimulus increases in geometrical progression, the intensity of the sensation increases in arithmetical progression. This means that the inertness of living matter manifests itself relatively to increase in the intensity of the stimulus, and, consequently, the difference between the figures of the geometrical and the arithmetical progression represents the expenditure of energy on resistance. The intensity of the sensation is conditioned by the extent of the resistance offered to the activity of the stimuli in the neural apparatus, and, as a result, there is a slight decrease of resistance when the same process is renewed in the future. In this decrease of resistance and the preparation of the way for future stimuli of the same kind, in this development of " molecular set," is to be found the basis not only of that activity by which we reproduce the past, but also of the mechanisation of the nervous process.[1]

It is clear from this that not only the external manifestations of association-reflex activity, but also its subjective manifestations, are a

[1] Therefore, we cannot agree with Krainsky's so-called energic theory of memory (Dusha i energiya : Soul and Energy, Vilna, 1911, p. 31). According to him, part of the energy of the external stimulus, which, according to the Weber–Fechner law, exceeds the intensity of the sensation, in other words is unproductively expended in the overcoming of resistances in the cellular protoplasm, like friction in mechanical apparatus, must correspond to the process of memory. This " surplus energy of the external stimulus at the moment of its activity is not relived," according to this writer, " subjectively in the form of sensation, but is laid aside in a potential state, obviously in the form of chemical energy of dynamic combinations, which are preserved in the accumulators of the psychic centres ; the accumulators periodically discharge, and then the potential energy of memory is again transformed into psychic energy which possesses a subjective form, and a series of memories develop in our psyche. The store of the potential energy of memory is a definite given quantity, and is expended together with the discharging of the accumulator. Ridding itself of some images, the memory accumulator is continuously charged with the energy of new impressions ; and, thus, a mobile equilibrium constant in time is established."

In advancing his theory, Krainsky naturally meets with what he calls that absurd notion that " the oftener and longer we reproduce a given image in our memory, the sooner we forget it, for the potential energy which is at its basis is spent." But he evades this difficulty by allowing " a certain power of containing to the organ of memory," on the one hand, and " a capacity to rid itself automatically of the surplus of impressions stored in it," on the other. This automatic discharging of accumulators he finds in " the magic world of imagination, which, in the shape of phantasy and dreams, bedecks our soul," and consists in transformed memories. And the " discharged psychic energy is again transformed into other forms of energy." (l.c., p. 12.) Such is Krainsky's somewhat fantastic explanation of memory.

We shall not enter into a criticism of this hypothesis, the artificiality of which is more than obvious. But however that may be, we stand for the energic viewpoint in the explanation of subjective processes, which, from our viewpoint, are a result of a special tension of energy caused by its inhibition or temporary blocking in the central organs of the nervous system, for it has been shown by experiments that the more an association reflex is inhibited, the more intense is the subjective state accompanying it.

product of the same energy, which conforms, like all other forms of energy, to the law of conservation of energy first advanced by Mayer and Helmholtz.

We do not stand for the theory of interactionism, according to which the physical nervous process becomes subjective or psychic, and then, at one point, this same psychic process is again, as a whole, replaced by the physical nervous process. We say that there is one process from beginning to end, the neuro-psychical, but when resistances in the peripheral apparatus are insignificant, this process does not manifest itself in subjective form, while, in the central sphere, on account of great resistances to the movement of the current, this same process is " neuro-psychical," with an obvious subjective colouring, which, on the return journey of the current-wave and its passage along the motor and secretory conductors, is again reduced to a nervous process merely. The essence of the problem, therefore, lies not in interactionism, but in the theory of complete and incomplete manifestations of one and the same neuro-psychical process, which depend on the greater or lesser resistance of the particular tissue along which it flows.

Thus, reflexology, adopting the energic viewpoint, investigates association-reflex activity as a consecutive superstructure of inherited and acquired reflexes, which become more and more complex and varied. The subjective manifestations which we discover in ourselves are thus regarded as a result of the same energy as are the external manifestations ; but between both manifestations there is a direct relationship, and for this reason we may say that the less the resistance to the external mani-festation of energy, the less the expression of the subjective phenomena, and *vice versa*. This provides us with an explanation of the fact why not all neural processes are accompanied by subjective phenomena. It is obvious that, if the processes of ionisation, which occur in the appropriate neural environment, because of the resistances encountered in it reach a certain tension, and so condition the appearance of subjective phenomena, the same may, in other conditions, go unobserved even in the same neural environment on the establishment of pathways, when the so-called mechanisation of the neuro-psychical processes has occurred, and when we have practically only physical processes without concomitant psychical phenomena.

Another argument for the energic theory is to be found in the fact, proved by Féré, that every kind of sensation, whether or not it reaches consciousness, is accompanied by an increase in the dynamic equivalent, in other words, is recorded on the dynamometer as an increase in muscular strength.[1]

It is clear from this that the subjective act of sensation is not always only a " mental given quantity " in our nervous system, because, behind it, energy is invariably concealed in the form of a nervous current, which,

[1] Cited from Dr. L. N. Voitolovsky in *Jubilee Symposium in Honour of I. A. Sikorsky : Yubileiny sbornik I. A. Sikorskovo*, p. 348.

reaching the periphery through the centrifugal communications, expresses itself in an increase of muscular activity.

It is also obvious from the aforementioned that every organism, since it is an agent, because of the stored energy which it has acquired, to a certain extent even from its ancestors, but chiefly by accumulating it in the course of life by the process of nourishment and of the transformation of external energies influencing it, reacts in some way or other to all those external influences which are adequate to evoke discharge of this energy in the form of certain reflexes. So all aggressive reflexes, under the influence of external stimuli of medium intensity, which maintain a strict metabolism in the appropriate organs, are accompanied by a sthenic inner reaction, which, in turn, leads to the renewal and maintenance of aggressive reflexes, until a sufficient degree of stimulus-fatigue occurs, and leads to a general asthenic reaction.

It is clear that our central organs are accumulators of energy, every one of which possesses at least a pair of conductors. One of the latter, being afferent, connects them with the receptive organs and the centripetal tissues ; the other, being efferent, leads from these central organs in the form of centrifugal tissues. The impact of the external stimulus is accompanied by a process of ionisation in the receptive apparatus, and this process, by stimulating the centripetal conductors and disturbing the equilibrium of the potentials in two neurons which are in contact, acts in a stimulating manner on the nucleus of the nearest neuron, and so develops in it the same process of ionisation. Thus the process is carried to muscles, which, because of the discharge of energy, undergo contraction. When the store in the accumulator is growing less, it is replenished chiefly through nutrition and gaseous metabolism by means of the blood carried to the brain, but it is in part maintained by influences from other surfaces of the body. In this consists the theory of discharges already described by me in 1896 in connection with the neuron theory.[1]

The subjective phenomena which we discover in ourselves by self-analysis, or what are called our experiences, are, as we have mentioned above, a result of the energy which lies at the root of the association-reflex (neuro-psychical) functions of the organism as its productive vital processes. Therefore, there is no reason to regard subjective processes as superfluous or subsidiary phenomena in nature (epiphenomena), for we know that everything superfluous becomes atrophied and obliterated, while our own experience tells us that the subjective phenomena reach their highest development in the more complex processes of correlative activity.

This forces us to admit that the subjective and the objective in correlative activity are phenomena closely associated in one process, which is, in reality, the manifestation of a given form of energy. It is clear that, in the investigation of the association-reflex activity of an external

[1] See, for instance, Zimmel : *The Concept and Tragedy of Culture ; Logos,* 1912–13.

individual—an activity revealing from the outside the full extent of his energy—conformity to law in the development and manifestations of this activity can, and should be, investigated by the method of objective analysis.

In the physical world, we have not only the quantitative, measured more or less by the speed of the vibrations of molecules, atoms, and electrons, but also the form and quality of the vibration, which vary in different cases.

In the psychic, we have again a series of quantitative changes in the sense of varying intensity, and so we have the form of the psychic, but it is the form which, in this case, conditions the quality of the subjective elements.

Therefore, I do not see any incompatibility which, as it were, forces us to assume two closed and interlocked circles of phenomena, one physical and the other psychical, between which, according to the general admission, psycho-physical parallelism, or the still more marvellous interactionism, operates miraculously.

As we have already stated, we regard the physical and the psychical as a unitary phenomenon in one process of nervous current, as energy passing through the higher ranges of the nervous system. From experience, we know that this phenomenon as such can reveal itself in man in its complete form—with the participation of the psychic ingredient—only by means of active concentration, which is usually closely associated with the stimuli which issue from the somatic sphere. If we call one reflex conscious, and others subconscious or unconscious, this does not mean that the latter are not accompanied by the element of the psychic, or by consciousness, during their activity, but only that they are not reproduced as are other activities, and, consequently, are not " accountable." To the category of the accountable belong all reflexes which occur when active concentration participates.

When we speak of association-reflex activity as based on the manifestation of energy, it must be borne in mind that we imply not only a difference in terminology in respect of previous views, but also a difference in the very nature of the problem. Even now, we run across serious scientific papers in which there is mention of an " essentially pure spirit," or of the pure " bodiless " psyche and of its contraposition to the body.[1]

Let us take, for example, an extract from the work of P. Sorokin,[2] commended by the late Professor M. M. Kovalevsky : " The nature of social manifestation is dual : the purely subjective self-existence of spirit and the objectified existence of the same spirit, yet not ' bodiless,' but incarnate in some ' substantial ' and ' perceptible ' form. In the first case, it can live according to its own laws ; in the second it ceases to be ' free,' and

---

[1] See for instance, Zimmel : *The Concept and Tragedy of Culture ; Logos*, 1912–13.

[2] P. Sorokin : *Crime and Punishment : Prestupleniye i kara*, St. Petersburg, p. 333.

becomes bound by the ' heavy ' and ' inflexible ' laws of the objective world, which sometimes radically change its own laws."

This extract renders comment superfluous.

As an example of the abuse of subjectivism in scientific spheres, where it should not enter at all, let us take the case of an investigator, who, in dealing with the bio-chemistry of psychopathological conditions, maintains that " the higher living organisms are so constituted that everything favourable to the current and to the redintegration of energy, if it does not threaten the stability of the store of energy, is accompanied by a positive or pleasant feeling. Every phenomenon not complying with these conditions is accompanied by a negative or unpleasant feeling. According to fundamental biological laws, the positive and negative feelings serve as a means of self-preservation,"[1] etc.

Another investigator, and one of the most authoritative, holds that " thought exists for the prediction of phenomena." Applying Darwin's evolutionary doctrine, he states that " thoughts, just like individuals, strive for self-preservation, and those which are best adjusted to the given conditions are victorious."[2]

According to A. Comte, the human mind in its development inevitably passes through three phases : the theological, the metaphysical, and the positive. This law, obviously, is demonstrated also by the study of human personality itself, for, at the beginning, the so-called psychic activity of man, his soul, was regarded as a divine gift, and the human soul was accorded a supernatural origin, as something entering the body from outside at birth and leaving the body at death. After this theological period, we have the metaphysical philosophy of the spirit, and contemporary psychology with its metaphysical concepts of will, attention, faculties, etc. ; lastly, the reflexological method of investigation of the phenomena of conscious activity as a manifestation of energy—the method adhered to in this work ; and allow me to regard it as the positive method in the true sense of the word.

Thus, in the consecutive phases of the investigation of human personality, the law of dialectical development is illustrated, for the metaphysical method of studying personality is the antithesis of the theological attitude ; empirical psychology, of the metaphysical method ; and, lastly, the reflexological method, in turn, is the antithesis of empirical psychology, and, eventually, having created the science of human personality, will give us the final synthesis through the objective method.

---

[1] A. I. Yushtchenko : *Soul and Matter ; Priroda*, p. 356, 1914.
[2] *Priroda*, 1914, p. 356.

CHAPTER V

The reproductive activity of living protoplasm. Pathways in the nervous system.
The dependence of reproductive activity on inner conditions. The reflex as the
creative factor in individuality. Every activity of the organism is a resultant of
two factors : the specific environmental stimulus, and the inner conditions. The
significance of reflexes in individual evolution.

SOME writers, who, like Sergi, have employed the subjective method,
have already been forced to admit that " psychic activity is activity
of a general type, and all other organic activity without exception is
of the same type. He who is more or less familiar with activity of such a
kind knows that all organic tissue reacts to stimulation ; stimulated by
some external agent, it acts according to the nature of the energy
of the stimulus." (Sergi ; *ap.* S. Sighele : *I delitti della folla*, p. 46,
Torino, 1902.)

That is why the elucidation of the fundamental qualities of correlative
activity must be sought in the nature of living matter.

A living being of the simplest form (for instance, the rhizopodal
astrorhiza, which may attain a size of 1 cm.) feels viscid to the touch,
is ductile, and has no constant shape. In these qualities it resembles
sponges. According to the investigations of Schultz, artificial elongation of the plasma divides the astrorhiza into fibrils surrounded by
remnants of plasma. The locomotion of such beings occurs by means of
elongation of the adhesive pseudopodia, which perform circular, groping
movements, and are then drawn in, but not in the form of a contraction,
for the movement of the component parts of the pseudopodia occurs just
as if each part were a complete amœba. The emergence of the pseudopodia
is caused by tumescence, which, being a form of expansion, leads to the
formation of fibrils, which are a result of the differentiation of living
matter.

The catching of food and its digestion is continued even by the pseudopodia apart from their nucleus, and they can live several days.

Acids and alkalis promote tumescence by making the plasma more
plastic. In an acidless environment no tumescence takes place, and movement is absent. (T. Schultz : *Minutes of the Society of Investigators of
Nature*, Kharkov Univ. ; No. 3, sep. ed.)

It is clear from this that, even in the early stages of life-development,
we encounter a change in size of living matter in the form of tumescence
and absence of tumescence or contraction. This change, conditioned by
external influences, is a kind of aggressive and defensive reflex.

A peculiarity of this colloidal substance, which we call living protoplasm,
is that it tends to reproduce later and in similar form, when there is fresh,
even though slight, external stimulation, the changes which occur in it
under the influence of external conditions. In other words, a change,
which has once occurred as a result of an external influence, so weakens the
power of resistance to the renewal of a similar change that such a change is
repeated as a result of a slight external cause capable of dislodging the
protoplasmic molecules in a certain measure.

Obviously, because of external influences, a molecular change in the substance takes place, and this leads, to a certain extent, to the clearing and beating of a track for the reflex. We know that the nerve cells are accumulators, while the nervous current passing through them leaves a trace behind it, in the sense of a lessened resistance to the renewal of the same process. Thus, under the influence of reflexes, which establish minute structural changes in the living substance of the cellular elements, paths of least resistance or beaten tracks are constituted in this substance. It is clear from this that the reflex itself is a creative factor in individuality. In other words, past experience leaves its vestige ; it inevitably facilitates the future reaction, by changing the form of the irritable protoplasmic matter and producing the conditions for facilitated reaction. This is doubtlessly an asset to the individual in question.

An insufficiency of activity and absence of reflexes lead, in turn, not only to the obliteration of the beaten tracks and their conforming to the general structure of the substance, but also to the inner inhibition of reflexes.

To supplement what has been said, we shall remark that inorganic matter also reacts to an external impact, but this reaction is purely mechanical, and does not essentially influence the composition of the substance and its subsequent reaction, but if it does so in a certain case, then it does so only after numerous and more considerable external influences, which fundamentally change the very structure of the substance, while a living being changes, on each occasion and in accordance with the external influences, not only its form, but also the structure of its substance by means of change in metabolism of the part stimulated.[1]

One cannot help seeing, in all that has been said above, a certain distinction between living and dead matter, for even if the latter permits of the reproduction of a reaction which it has once experienced as a result of an external impact, the degree of reaction stands in a definite, constant relationship to the intensity of the external influence. Thus the compression of a ball by external pressure applied to it can be reproduced, to the same degree, only by pressure of the same intensity, while protoplasmic contraction, which has once occurred under an external influence, or a reflex produced by a given intensity of the external stimulus, will occur later as a result of a less considerable stimulus, a phenomenon which we cannot observe in the inorganic world. It is clear from this that reproduction is not exact repetition.

However, we may find an analogy with this in the action of light-energy on living matter. There are substances which absorb light and have the capacity of emitting rays when these substances have been

---

[1] It is scarcely necessary to add that everything in the universe is relative, and, therefore, this distinction is not, generally speaking, absolute. For instance, steel will change on being heated, although this substance consists of dead matter. But, here, the activity of the temperature is so drastic that, under its influence, the very nature of the substance changes.

previously exposed to the influence of light. This may be proved by the following simple method. Let us take an engraving which hangs on the wall, and expose it to the influence of direct sun-rays. Then, after placing it on a sensitised photographic plate, let us leave it in the dark. After twenty-four hours, we get, in the form of dark shadows, a reproduction of the white parts of the engraving. Probably the sunlight has produced, in those parts of the engraving exposed to the light, a more or less durable vibration of particles, and so gives them, as it were, an invisible phosphorescence which has an influence on photographic plates. But this is, indeed, a conservation of the traces of a definite stimulus, such as we meet, to a much greater extent, in the organic world, but in its highest degree in the nerve cell. The latter must, at the same time, be regarded as the most perfect accumulator which we know in the organic world.

But if the central organs of the nervous system with their cells are accumulators of energy, it becomes intelligible how organisms are capable of realising independent movement, or, which amounts to the same, of translating their potential energy into kinetic or manifest work in the external world.

There are, as we know, in inorganic nature, the radioactive qualities of matter, but there we must emphasise that there is a slow and independent disintegration of substance, consequently a process of decay, which, to a certain extent, characterises all bodies in nature, but living bodies, by a redintegration which maintains their life, counteract this disintegrative process. This is the second fundamental quality of living beings which distinguishes them from the category of dead matter.

On these two peculiarities rests the living organism's reproductive activity, which is realised in external reactions.[1] Independently of what has been said, we cannot help mentioning the important fact that the reproductive activity we have discussed is subject not only to external, but also to internal, influences, the latter being dependent on nutritional and metabolic conditions, and being capable of inhibiting and activating it. In this is included what are sometimes called the inner powers of the organism, and what produce such manifestations on its part as are dependent, not on external, but precisely on internal, conditions.

These facts may be proved even in the lowest animals. Let us take the protozoa, which have no nervous system. The investigations of Famintzin and the American biologist, Jennings, lead to the conclusion

[1] In speaking of the difference between living and dead matter, we do not wish thereby to imply that there are no gradual transitions. On the contrary, we have at the present time an array of facts which force us to the conclusion that living matter is ultimately only a further complication of dead matter. I shall merely mention the works of Di Brazza and P. Pirenne (*Revue scientifique*, 1904), Prof. R. Dubois (*Soc. de biologie*, t. LVI), Butler-Burke (*Nature*, 1905), and others. Much material, founded too on pertinent laboratory investigations, may be found in the work of one of my former pupils, Dr. M. Kukuk of Leningrad, under the title : *L'univers être vivant—La solution des problèmes de la matière et de la vie à l'aide de la biologie universelle*. Genève, 1911.

that the behaviour of unicellular organisms, which have no nervous system, does not really differ in any way from the behaviour of the higher animals, for they react to external stimuli in the same way as do all other animals. It is clear from this that the various responsive reactions may occur without the participation of special sensory organs and in the absence of a nervous system. According to Jennings, some parts of the body of unicellular animals are more sensitive than others, and, thus, may be compared to the sensory organs of the higher animals ; the reactions and reflexes of unicellular animals may vary with variation in the impinging stimuli.[1]

A simple amœba is attracted, like worms and insects, by weak stimuli and repelled by stronger. In unicellular animals, just as in the higher animals, reactions may vary while the stimulus remains constant ; in other words, the organism may react to a stimulus, first in one way, and later quite differently, in spite of the fact that the stimulus remains the same. And these variations in reaction are not explained by fatigue, but depend on the inner state of the organism. All this shows that between the behaviour of protozoa and other cellular animals there is no essential difference.[2]

Loeb, in his work, *Comparative Physiology of the Brain and Comparative Psychology*, arrives at analogous views. This writer comes to the conclusion that the nervous system has no specific qualities which we cannot discover in protoplasmic structure. It has been demonstrated that the qualities of the nervous system are the qualities of protoplasm. Therefore, we observe also in unicellular organisms devoid of a nervous system those fundamental vital manifestations which are usually regarded as characteristic of the nervous system. Lastly, the physiology, too, of the higher organisms shows that in these also many functions prove possible without the participation of a nervous system.

It is clear from this that the nervous system is an apparatus which merely perfects the whole system, exhibited by the protoplasmic structure itself, of the organism's correlations with the environment, and, at the same time, makes possible, in complex organisms, the manifestation of the co-ordinated reaction of various parts of the body to external stimuli.

Further, the interesting experiments made in America by L. Day and M. Bentley[3] deserve attention. These placed a paramecium in a closed capillary tube, the diameter of which was such that the infusorium could not easily turn round. Swimming forward in its usual manner, the infusorium backed on reaching the end of the tube, and trying to take another angle—right or left—and encountering an obstacle, repeated the same movement. These movements were repeated 30–50 times before

---

[1, 2] *Translators' note :* The Russian is so free that we have reported Jennings indirectly. See the latter's *Behavior of the Lower Organisms*, p. 262 ; Columbia University Press, 1906.

[3] *Translators' note :* See Wheeler : *The Science of Psychology*, pp. 120–121 ; Jarrolds, 1931 ; and also *Journal of Animal Behaviour*, 1911, vol. I, pp. 67–73.

the infusorium backed[1] in the opposite direction. When it reached the other end, it made not 50, but only about 15, vain attempts. The next time there were still fewer attempts, and lastly the infusorium, as it were, learned to reverse more quickly.

The experimenters concluded that the reactions of the infusorium are exceedingly modifiable, and that it uses previous experience in its manifestations.

Jennings[2] comes to the same conclusions when he says that the same organism reacts to one and the same stimulus in a very different manner, and that, if we take into consideration that in all these cases the external conditions remain the same, the modification of the reactions must be the consequence of some changes in the organism itself.

Metalnikov, in collaboration with L. Galadzhiev, has shown that, in regard to the reflex of swallowing food and to the passage of the food through the oral tube and the digestive vacuole, which then opens and circulates in the protoplasm of the slipper animalcule (paramecium caudatum), the modifiability and variety of reactions which depend on individual peculiarities are marvellous. This modifiability, as has been shown, depends on the nature of the food given to the infusorium or on the quality of the stimulus.

So, for instance, when infusoria are fed with easily digested food (bacterial emulsion, yolk of hen's eggs), 15–20 vacuoles are formed in the course of 30 minutes, and these vacuoles remain 2–5 hours and longer circulating in the body ; but when the infusorium is given indigestible products (emulsion of carmine, Indian ink, carbon), the vacuoles are formed in smaller number and circulate not 2–5 hours, but only 20–50 minutes.

Change in the external conditions of the environment (chemical composition) is reflected in a marked manner in all the manifestations of the nutritional functions of infusoria. But there is another reason which influences the modification of reactions or reflexes. It has been found that infusoria gradually swallow less of the indigestible food (carmine emulsion), and finally cease to swallow it at all. They are driven, as it were, to make efforts, by means of their cilia, to repel the carmine, so that no particle of it enters their mouth, while they readily ingest Indian ink. Thus the infusoria have learned the trick of distinguishing carmine from Indian ink and other substances.

It is obvious that the physiological condition of the infusoria has undergone a change in the given case, and, therefore, their reaction also has changed, and this modified reaction is directed against harmful conditions.

Thus, previous experience has not passed without leaving its trace, but has created conditions for a purposeful direction of reactions towards the advantage of the organism.

Not less instructive in this respect are Jennings's remarks, which

[1] *Translators' note :* By reversing its cilia.   [2] *l.c.*

Metalnikov mentions in a paper of his.[1] According to the words of the
latter : " the modifiability of reactions, of course, often depends on
external factors,—but I shall discuss this later ; what interests us here is
the fact that the reaction of an organism to every definite external stimulus
depends on the organism's inner physiological state.

The physiological state may change under the influence of various
factors, first of all under the influence of metabolism in the organism.
Well-fed hydras, sea-anemones, or infusoria differ in a marked manner
from those which are hungry. While the well-fed animals usually react
negatively, the hungry react positively.

In proof of this statement it is possible to quote numberless examples."

Not less instructive in regard to the influence of modifications of the
physiological conditions of infusoria on external reactions is the following
observation, which we set down here in Metalnikov's words : " When a
large, attached infusorium (stentor roeselii) is stimulated by a jet of water
directed on its front part, there is always a definite reaction. The infusorium, wishing to get rid of the unpleasant stimulation, turns to different
sides. If this does not help, if the stimulus continues to operate, the
infusorium contracts its body and hides in a small, slimy tube, which it
usually builds from its mucous excretions. After some moments, it
emerges from its house. If the stimulus is continued, it hides again, but
if it is repeated many times, the infusorium finally emerges from its house,
abandons it, and swims to another place, where it begins to build a new
house."

Here we have one and the same infusorium, the same external conditions, and the same stimulus. The reactions on the part of the infusorium vary markedly. This variation in the reactions may be explained
only by variations in the inner physiological condition of the infusorium
itself. The infusorium which turns its body to different sides is not the
same after these turnings. The infusorium which contracted and hid in
its tube is not the same ; therefore, its further manifestations are
different.

Finally, on the basis of all these data, we cannot help coming to the
conclusion that every activity of the organism is a resultant of two
factors : the specific stimulus issuing from the environment, and the
inner conditions, which represent the sum of the given individual's
qualities, consisting in turn both of qualities which are inherited and such
as have been acquired through life experience.

Metalnikov advances a mathematical formula for individuality. He
writes : " If we denote by the letter ' N ' all the inherited qualities which
the organism gets from its ancestors, every individual may be expressed
in the following formula : $N \times a, b, c, d, e, f, g, h, i \ldots$ in which the
small letters represent all the manifestations of the organism, whatever
they may be ; and so, in accordance with the growth, development, and,

[1] Metalnikov : *The Reflex as a Creative Act—Russkaya Misl*, November,
1916, p. 98 ff.

in general, the life of the organism, the number of these letters will go on increasing."

Further, Metalnikov, generalising about the modifiability and the uniqueness of the reactions of an organism, not only of the lower but also the higher animals, comes to the conclusion that a reflex, and, in general, every reaction, produces something new, and, since it changes, according to Lamarck's doctrine, the structure of the tissues and the forms of the organs, is a creative act, for it creates individuality and peculiarity of the constitution. Finally, according to Lamarck, the form is, as it were, the expression of functions, for the form changes with change of functions. Metalnikov refers here to the works of Brank, who has observed individual features in the seminal glands of individual men, to the investigations of Nemilov, who has noticed individual features in the milk glands of cows, and to B. I. Slovtzov, who has pointed out the individual peculiarities of metabolism in different individuals.

It is not necessary to demonstrate that Metalnikov's ideas are quite correct in regard to the modifiability and the uniqueness of the organism's reactions. It is clear that the organism's wealth, which has been amassed in such a way and is called individual experience, is that factor in individual evolution which characterises all organisms from the lowest to the highest ; at the same time, we must not leave out of account that the law of modifiability is a general law for the universe, where everything changes and evolves. Further, Metalnikov, together with Lamarck, brings forward individual variations to support the theory of the evolution of species and recognises the importance of individual experience in the origin of those slight individual changes and variations of which Darwin has spoken. But here it is necessary to set certain limits.

We suppose that if the conditions of individual life lead to such modifications as extend to that same organisation which serves for the production of offspring, there is not only no reason to deny its importance in the evolution of species, but it is necessary to regard this fact, which I have discussed at length in my paper, *Bio-chemical Systems and their Rôle in the Development of Organisms*,[1] as one of the most important in evolutionary process. But to probe deeper into this problem would not be wise.

We shall not here touch on those cutting remarks, which Professor Timiryazev has made in the periodical *Lyetopis*, concerning Metalnikov's paper, which has appeared on this subject in the *News of the Academy of Science*.[2] But we, personally, maintain that individual experience, in so far as it influences the organisation and chemical composition of the reproductive (sex) secretions of every individual, is a factor of peculiar significance in evolution ; but, apart from this, acquired peculiarities do not die on the death of the organism, and if they are not so deep as to be transmitted to posterity through biological heredity, they are handed down

[1] V. Bechterev : *Russky Vratch*, no. 7, 1913.
[2] *Izvestia Akademii Naük.*

through imitation and adoption from generation to generation, as a result of the social life of organisms playing a rôle in social selection.[1]

If we take into account, on the one hand, that irritability and, consequently, the reflex are the fundamental quality of every living being— for the cell, which constitutes the tissue of complex organisms, reacts to external stimuli in a manner which can, and must, be understood as reflex —and, on the other hand, that metabolism is impossible without cellular reaction or cellular reflex, which are synonymous, for which reason the cellular reflexes lie at the root of the so-called trophic phenomena, we shall naturally conclude that on the reflex itself are based the organism's creative powers, which lead to its growth and the development of its organs, and play such an important rôle in the law of individual evolution.

Special and considerable importance in respect of the growth and development of the organism is to be attached to the endocrine organs in the form of glands—the thyroid, the parathyroids, the thymus, the pituitary, the sex glands, the adrenals, and others. As is well known, they secrete a special product in the form of a chemical substance which enters the blood and acts, through the latter, on other organs, including the other endocrine organs, and so excite or depress the cellular elements of the latter. As a result of these conditions, a certain equilibrium between the organs of inner secretion is established on the basis of their interrelations which are conditioned by the inner chemo-reflexes. Thus, the gist of the matter is that, as a result of the chemo-reflexes, development or retardation of various departments or systems of the organism is attained.[2]

At the present time, we know that the formation and development of the skeleton is dependent on the secretion, first, of the thymus gland, later, of the thyroid, sex, and pituitary glands, while the secretions of the thyroid and adrenal glands are necessary for the development of the brain. The sex organs develop chiefly under the influence of the thymus and thyroid glands, and perhaps the pituitary (hypophysis). The pineal (epiphysis), on the contrary, retards their development. The sex glands (according to Steinach—the interstitial puberal glands contained in them) and the *corpora lutea* produce the secondary sex indications and even sexual characterological peculiarities. We know, on the other hand, that every movement is based on the contractility—a primitive reflex-action —of the cellular elements.

Every movement of a lower living being is ultimately the effect of that protoplasmic contractility which characterises every reaction of cellular elements, not excluding the secretory cells. Even the treatment of abnormal processes is based on the excitation of appropriate reflexes ; in some cases, by the introduction of suitable substances into the organism, the

[1] V. Bechterev : *Social Selection and its Biological Significance* (*Vestnik Znania* and *Nord and Süd*, 1912) ; also the same author's *The Significance of Hormonism and Social Selection in the Evolution of Organisms* (*Priroda*, Nov., 1916).
[2] Further details may be found in my work : *Diseases of Personality*, etc. ; *Problems in the Study and Education of Personality*, 3rd vol., 1922.

H

reflexes which evoke the organism's plastic processes are aroused ; others stimulate its metabolism ; others again strengthen the defence reflex (immunisation). In other cases, when a substance, either alien in nature to the organism, or in doses unacceptable to it, is introduced into the organism, the latter mobilises all its defensive reflexes, and, in certain cases, produces antibodies, so as to liberate itself as speedily as possible from the noxious agent. Thus, the introduction of alcohol increases the oxidising process, by which the alcohol is subjected to quick combustion, and causes extension of the peripheral vessels, through which it is excreted by the skin, the lungs, etc. Strychnine produces muscular tension, causing cramps, while this muscular activity, in turn, causes increased disintegration of muscular tissue, forms lactic acid, which depresses the nervous system and lowers the contractile activity, as a consequence of the absorption of water by the muscle colloids. Cordials cause diuresis, etc.

Here we find operative the same defensive reflexes as we observe also in the case of unfavourable natural influences : high external temperature —extension of peripheral vessels ; the action of cold—constriction of the peripheral vessels ; the activity of light—favourable sun-burn, etc.

On these defensive reflexes are based so-called auto-serotherapy and auto-hemotherapy, because serum or defibrinated blood, taken from a diseased individual and containing pathogenic products, leads, when injected subcutaneously into the same individual, to the production by the organism of antibodies useful to him in his struggle against the fundamental disease process within him.

In general, there are, in the organism, exceedingly complex relations which re-establish impaired equilibrium, and this equilibrium is established only by reflexes, among which must be included the various chemical reactions occurring in our body. The point of special interest here is the scheme of the parallelo-intersectional influence of the endocrine glands (Dr. Belov : *Problems of the Study and Education of Personality*, 4th vol., 1921), which, from the reflexological standpoint, must be understood thus : heightened chemism of the endocretory organ A, arouses, by its secretion, a chemo-reflex in the organ B, but the product of this reflex acts inhibitorily on the chemo-reflex of the organ A. On the consequent weakening of the chemo-reflex of the organ A, the inadequacy of the secretion inhibits the chemo-reflex of the organ B, but the inadequacy of the secretion of B inhibits the chemo-reflex of A. In this way, the necessary equilibrium of the impaired processes of the organism is restored as a result of the complex-reflexive interrelations of the endocrine organs. Such are the relations between the pituitary and the thyroid gland, between the pituitary and the seminal glands, or the ovaries, between the ovaries and the mammary glands, between the ovaries and the *corpora lutea*, between the seminal glands and the prostate gland, etc. In the work just mentioned, Dr. Belov refers to my investigations carried out in the years 1914 and 1916—investigations which, by approaching the problem from a different angle, made it possible for me to formulate even then

" the analogical thesis " indicating the parallelo-intersectional course of the conjunctive and disjunctive processes.

It is clear, from everything said above, that the capacity to accumulate changes occurring under the influence of stimulations which facilitate the future influence of similar stimulations is the fundamental or primal manifestation of the activity of every cell.

Nerve cells, as we have said, are, to a greater extent than other cells, accumulators of energy, which they acquire both by the afflux of nutritive material and by the impact of external energies on the sensory organs, especially under conditions of the inhibition of nervous excitation in the centres. Moreover, they are characterised by special molecular motility, as a result of which every stimulation so changes their molecular condition that a stimulus similar to one which has previously occurred arouses the reflex with particular facility.

So it appears that even the neuron connections in the central organs adjust themselves appropriately, as a result of which, after frequent repetitions, beaten tracks are established as paths of least resistance, which can, to a certain extent, be hereditarily transmitted in the form of certain dispositions or tendencies.

CHAPTER VI

The fundamental activities of all living beings are reflexes of aggression or defence.
Examples of the activity of the cell and of the activity of lower and higher animals.
The concentration reflex. Imitation and symbolism as reflexes. The irritability
of plants as a manifestation of the same reflexes of aggression and defence.

THE fundamental activities of all living beings are acts of aggression
and defence ; in other words, they are aggressive and defensive
reflexes, which are to be found not only in the lower animals, but
even in plants which are tied by nature to a definite spot and get food
from the environment.[1]

In general, the concept of reflex has been recently regarded from two
points of view : On the one hand, we have begun to understand by reflex
not only such mechanical acts as writing, reading, etc., but also tropisms
in the vegetable world, as, for instance, the turning of a plant and its
blossoms to the sun, etc., and the responses of bacteria to increased
stimulation. On the other hand, reflexology regards all the organism's
more complex correlations with its environment as higher reflexes, which
we call " association " reflexes. In reflexology, we go further than biology,
and reduce to reflexes, on the one hand, such phenomena as morphogenesis and propagation, and, on the other, the social interrelations between
human beings.

In the animal kingdom, even the simple cell exhibits an aggressive, as
well as a defensive, reflex, for every cell contracts under the activity of
unfavourable external conditions, and expands again under favourable
nutritional conditions. All of this applies not only to the cell body, but
also to the protoplasmic projections or dendrites of the neuron, for these
projections shorten in the first case, and become elongated in the second.

It is obvious that the contraction of the cell and its projections is an
act of self-defence or protection, because by this very activity the cellular
surface is decreased, and so, simultaneously, becomes, on the one hand,
more dense and less permeable, and, on the other, is withdrawn to a
certain extent from the unfavourable stimulus, while, in the case of cellular
expansion, we have the activity of aggression and absorption, for the
absorptive surface of the cell and its projections becomes, under favourable
conditions, more extensive and permeable, approaches the favourable
stimulus to some extent, and finally absorbs it.[2]

Similar phenomena may be observed also in the simplest animals. Even
in higher animals, for instance, the hedgehog, the armadillo, and others,
the contraction of the body into a ball is a mode of self-defence.

The contractions of the pigmented cutaneous coat, which lead to a
change, protective in character, in the colour of the skin, as we observe in

[1] As is well known, plants are capable of the activity of sucking in, sometimes even of seizing (for instance, the well-known fly-trap, fish-catching sea-
weeds, and the like) and of acts of defence in the form of drooping, shedding
leaves in autumn, so-called gall-nuts, etc.

[2] An excellent example of acts of aggression and absorption is found in the
phagocytosis of the white blood-corpuscles.

some animals, for instance, in reptiles (especially chameleons), amphibians (the green-frog), fish, and molluscs of the cuttle-fish family, also develop as a result of a certain activity which is doubtlessly useful to the animal, and has, therefore, been transmitted through heredity.

Besides, the shrinkings of the lower animals and the formation of a dense surface, as a result of the contraction of the body, have led in the majority of animals to the development of a more or less dense external envelope, which in some of them attains the hardness of a horny coat of mail. But apart from this, many animals use either holes artificially made or natural holes in the ground or in trees, and there the dense external environment which covers them serves them as a defence.

Lastly, consecutive contractions of the muscular tissues in animals capable of locomotion lead, as a mode of defence and self-defence, to the activity of withdrawal from noxious influences and of flight from enemies. For this self-defence by flight in the face of danger, there have been evolved various organs—pseudopodia, cilia, flagella, shells which close, but in the higher animals, beginning with insects : wings and legs ; in vertebrates : limbs ; in primates, and especially in man : feet. In man, and to an extent in the apes, hands are important weapons of active defence in the repulsion of enemies.

Along with defence reflexes, there develop everywhere in the animal kingdom reflexes of aggression or attack and of seizing, the former of which often serve simultaneously for active defence, although the fundamental aim of the reflex of attack is both the finding and seizing of food as a stimulus, and the satisfaction of other demands.

It is scarcely necessary to say that aggression and defence, inasmuch as they are fundamental functions of the organism, must represent the earliest reflexes in animal phylogenesis, and, consequently, as we have seen, we find these reflexes in the simplest unicellular organisms, beginning from the amœba, and even in plants. Besides, the organs of movement serve simultaneously for both functions on the most divergent planes of the development of animal life. Thus, the octopus both catches its prey and propels itself by means of its arms. In the crustaceans, the same organs serve for locomotion along the ground, for swimming, and for catching prey. In insects, the jaws have evolved from organs of locomotion, and their legs also serve for seizing food and for defence by repulsion and locomotion, as in many vertebrates. Similarly, the hands of primates serve simultaneously for seizing food, for the satisfaction of other demands, and for defence.

The so-called nematocysts[1] of some cœlenterata, for instance, the medusæ, hydras, sea-anemones, and also of coral polyps, and others, serve equally for defence and aggression. Even the ejection of sepia by the cuttle-fish serves simultaneously both for defence and aggression.

In many animals, organs used in feeding, for instance, jaws, which in arthropoda are transformed legs, serve for defence and aggression.

[1] *Translators' note :* Tentacular and stinging organs of hydrozoa.

But there are also more specialised organs of defence and aggression, such as the chelæ of the cray-fish, the sting of bees (ovipositor), the poisonous sting of the scorpion, the stinking fluid of the skunk, the horns of some mammals, and even the horny bristles (as in the porcupine and the hedgehog) which, by the way, serve rather for defence than aggression.

Even prostration, which results from suppression of all the organic functions when an animal is faced by danger, is an act of passive defence in some animals (so-called playing 'possum) including insects. Shamming real death, they thus frequently escape real danger.

It is necessary to keep in mind here that acts of aggression and of defence do not operate suddenly, and, besides, it is not always advantageous to the animal to have recourse to defence or aggression, but it is necessary for it to be in readiness for some time, to be alert, and this leads to a temporary check of the act of defence or aggression. This preparation for aggression or defence, a preparation often associated with lying in ambush for enemies, is originally a special concentration reflex found extensively throughout the animal kingdom. It is essentially based on the inhibition of all motor activity, but not of the muscles which serve the organ stimulated by the given stimulus, and in which, therefore, the greatest muscular tension is manifested. Here, obviously, the important point is the excitation of one of the centres, for instance the visual or auditory, and the inhibition of all the other centres, in accordance with the general law of the functional correlations in the brain centres, the law according to which the stimulation of one centre is accompanied by suppression of the others.

But, in the act of increased concentration, we have also the character of that physiological process which Professor Uchtomsky has recently styled the dominant, and which I have as early as 1911 explained in the same manner.[1] According to this, in concentration, not only is the excitation of one centre accompanied by inhibition of the others, but this particular centre is also stimulated by all incidental stimuli, yet they do not, as usual, arouse local reflexes. An example of the physiological dominant may be seen in spring in the embrace reflex of frogs during copulation, in the act of defæcation, in the interrupted activity of swallowing, etc. The point to be emphasised here, just as in heightened attention, is not only excitation of one centre and simultaneous inhibition of the other centres, but, doubtlessly, also, increased activity of the particular centre as a result of incidental stimulations.

It is self-evident that acts of concentration acquire great significance in association-reflex activity; consequently, inadequate concentration is characterised by inadequate orientation and adjustment.[2]

---

[1] See V. Bechterev : *Vestnik Psychologii*, 1911 : *Objective Psychology*, ed. 1917.

[2] By the way, acts of concentration (attention) form a basis of K. Kornilov's work on the subdivision of the motor reactions of man into seven fundamental types, which he calls the reaction scale. Under these types of reaction he places also the various work activities which form the work process scale. The facts,

In connection with the act of concentration, the reflex of alertness develops, in which the appropriate muscular apparatus is mobilised in the form of its preparation for aggression or defence. At the Congress of Psychoneurology in Petersburg, January 1924 (see *Minutes of the Congress* and *New Scientific Achievements in the Sphere of the Reflexology and the Physiology of the Nervous System*), a special paper, published in a symposium of reflexology, was devoted by me, in collaboration with Dr. Shumkov, to the detailed investigation of the character of this reflex so important from the biological and social points of view.

Lastly, the social character of animal life leads to the development of imitation reflexes, as well as of reflexes of expressive movements and of symbolism, as signs which, on the one hand, express the inner state of the organism, and, on the other, serve to denote external objects and their correlations.

In the animal world, various kinds of movements serve this purpose : the antennæ of ants, various forms of facial expression, expressive movements in general, gestures, and even light and colour phenomena (the glow-worm's lamp, the reddening or the becoming blue of bare parts of the body in some animals) and, lastly, sounds produced by different organs, and, in particular, by the throat and mouth.

The highest development of the latter kind of reflexes is human speech, which, based at first on simple vocal reflexes and echoisms, has developed gradually into the complex form of speech signs by means of differentiation and selective generalisation.[1]

In conclusion, let us remark that, on the ground of reflex activity, plants must be classified with animals, and this is comprehensible, for " the kingdom of living beings forms one harmonious, coherent whole, which in its primitive stages can only artificially be divided into animals and plants " (Strasburger). But also, on the highest planes of both kingdoms, we find processes which are, in many respects, identical in character, especially when there is question of such fundamental vital functions as feeding, metabolism, respiration. As regards special reflex activity, that irritability, which in the vegetable kingdom represents acts of defence or aggression, seizing or attracting, is also a long-established fact, known already from the time of Haberlandt's[2] and Pfeffer's experiments.

communicated by this writer and founded on his investigations in regard to the types mentioned, as well as in regard to attitude and persistence during work, are of some interest, but I am sorry to say that the author has not abandoned the subjective point of view in treating the subject. (See : *Voprosi Truda—Problems of Work*, no. 1, 1921.)

[1] See V. Bechterev : *Vestnik Psychologii*, 1910. Also his : *Objective Psychology*, 3rd part ; and *The Evolution of Neuro-psychical Activity* (*Russky Vratch*), nos. 14, 15, 1913.

[2] *Translators' note* : *Die Lichtsinnesorgane der Laubblätter*, Leipzig, 1905. *Physiologische Pflanzenanatomie* (Leipzig, 1909).

Cinematographic representation of the movements of plants produces, as is well known, the impression of quick animal movements. According to the words of Pfeffer,[1] we should see, if our eye were constructed like a microscope, that growing stems and roots execute groping movements, and, in any case, we should discover prompt reactions as results of stimulation.

It may be thought that there is a difference between the contraction of muscles in the movements of animals and growth which depends on the swelling, grouping, and differentiation of cells and is the essence of morphogenesis. But the movements of animals, too, do not always depend on the contraction of muscles, for instance, in the case of the rising and descending movements of ciliophora, the gliding movements of gregarines,[2] etc.

Some even draw parallels between actions and morphogenesis. " Morphogenesis occurs in different ways : by growth, differentiation, extrusion, the wandering of cells, destruction, etc. All these ways, however, have something in common, and this common factor is the essence of the process, and manifests itself in the fact that a process, directed along any one of these ways, becomes operative under the influence of a definite stimulus, and leads to a definite result, creates something definite, aims at it in spite of interference, *i.e.* is a teleological process."[3]

There are carnivorous plants which, in their functioning, very much resemble carnivorous animals. Such is the sundew (drosera rotundifolia), which has a leaf with tentacles which secrete a viscid fluid from their glands. The point of interest here is the seizing reactions, which are quite analogous to those we have in the animal kingdom, but only considerably slower, since the transmission of the stimulation from one protoplast to the other occurs by means of cytoplasmic projections. The leaves of the sundew, being supplied with pin-shaped tentacle-glands of different lengths, secrete a transparent, viscid fluid, which plays the rôle of digestive juice. Tiny insects alight on the drops of this fluid, stick to them, and are finally drowned in them, for this viscid fluid closes up their tracheæ. At the same time as the insect alights on a drop of the sundew's secretion on the leaf, slow but systematic movements, which radiate to different sides from one protoplast to the second, to the third, etc., begin on the surface of the leaf. It is interesting to note that various mechanical stimulations by grains of sand, little lumps of earth, rain-drops, and non-nitrogenous substances sprayed in solution, etc., produce no result. But it is sufficient that the leaf be touched by nitrogenous substances, especially a piece of meat or albumen or a midge, for the tentacles of the leaf to

---

[1] Pfeffer : *Die Reizbarkeit der Pflanze : Verhandlungen der Gesellschaft Deutscher Naturforscher und Ärzte*, 1873.

[2] *Translators' note :* The movements of gregarines have been ascribed by Crawley to a succession of contractions of the myocyte layer. See : *Encyc. Brit.*, 13th ed., vol. XII, 557 d.

[3] T. Schultz : *The Organism as Creativeness. (Organism kak Tvortchestvo)* Kharkov, 1915.

begin movement in the course of about ten minutes, and the pin-shaped ends of the tentacles to bend towards the surface of the leaf, and after ten more minutes the more distant tentacles to begin to be inflected in the same way, till after about two to three hours all the tentacles have bent over their prey. Then occurs the secretion of a fluid which reminds us of gastric juice. The digestion of such food, so unusual for plants, requires a few days, and after three days the tentacles unbend and again glitter with their transparent drops, which in the sun resemble dew and attract new victims.

Further, Bose's[1] experiments have shown that all plants are characterised by irritability, as are animal organisms. It is not necessary to describe here his exceedingly interesting experimental investigations based on accurate recording by means of a special interrupter contact devised by himself. But we shall point out that Bose's experiments have proved that all plants and every plant organ manifest irritability to some extent and respond to the stimulus issuing from a definite electrical discharge.

The familiar sensitive plant (mimosa pudica) can, as experiment shows, exhibit greater irritability than does man. If stimuli are applied without giving the plant rest, it shows all the signs of fatigue. On less sensitive specimens, one can find, when the plant is fatigued, that physiological phenomenon known as " ladder reaction." The sensitivity of plants stands in direct dependence on light. If we take the plant to a dark room, its sensitivity is lost in the course of an hour. The same depression occurs during rain, and is explained by the absorption of water. Various gases act in a depressing or exciting manner. Thus, carbonic acid has a depressing, but nitrogen a stimulating, influence. Alcohol vapours cause first stimulation, then depression ; ether, and especially chloroform, cause depression. An analogous condition results from carbonic disulphide, ammonia, and sulphuretted hydrogen. Nitroxide and sulphurous gas act fatally like poison. A high temperature of 60° C. causes death to the plant after a spasmodic contraction.

Bose's experiments have also shown that the stimulation, being accompanied by peculiar polar phenomena (stimulation on the shutting of the cathode and the opening of the anode), spreads, with a definite speed, along the petiole of the plant. The various physiological agents influence this transmissibility in an inhibiting or activating manner. Thus, decrease in temperature first weakens, and then paralyses, the transmissibility, tetanising electric shocks re-establish transmissibility, but the local application of poison (e.g. potassium cyanide) destroys it again.

Lastly, in some plants, for instance in the so-called telegraph plant, there are phenomena of independent rhythmical pulsation like that of the heart. In this plant (desmodium gyrans) we can trace the inhibitory

[1] Bose : *Researches on the Irritability of Plants*, London, 1913. See also *Vestnik Znania*, June, 1915.

influence of ligature, cold, alcohol, weak carbonic acid, ether vapour and carbonic disulphide. Sulphate of copper and especially potassium cyanide promptly and completely destroy the plant's irritability. On the contrary, warmth and fresh air have a stimulating and reviving influence.

Everything said above shows that, in the vegetable kingdom, we encounter phenomena essentially the same as in the animal world, for life on both planes is subject to the same laws.

It is obvious from this that we have a right to say that the reactions of the simplest living being and even of the plant, as well as the most complex activities of man, have, if regarded strictly objectively, a common origin and are of an essentially identical biological nature common to all living organisms.

It must be clear from the foregoing that every reflex is closely associated with morphogenesis. We see the clearest examples of this in the amœbæ which form pseudopodia under the influence of external stimuli. Another no less clear example is the imitative colouring (mimicry), fairly general throughout nature, of the animal envelope. From this it is obvious that the reflex secures morphogenesis.

According to Spencer, all development is an accumulating of substance with corresponding loss of movement, and every disintegration, on the contrary, is associated with loss of substance and increase of movement. But we cannot help taking into account that, in general, movement lies at the root of normal metabolism, and only excessive movement leads to exhaustion or to a more or less sustained loss of substance and to the atrophy of the organ operative, while moderate movement is associated with the development of the organ. From this the dependence of morphogenesis on the reflex is obvious.

Generally speaking, morphogenesis and the reflex go hand-in-hand, frequently conditioned by one and the same cause which has an organic basis. Such are, for instance, the secondary sex characteristics and sex reflexes, which are a result of the function of the sex glands.

Morphogenesis, like all other reflexes, may be, in some cases, a result of external stimuli; in others, a result of inner stimuli. As an example of the significance of external stimuli we may take the reaction of living matter to colours. Thus, if we place the sensitive plant in glass cases of various colours, it will be seen that the petioles of the leaves will droop and the leaves fade in the violet and the blue, but in a lesser degree in the green cases, while in the yellow, the orange and the red cases, the petioles become erect, and the leaves recuperate, but remain half-shut.

Further, the works of a number of authors illustrate the unequal influence of various kinds of coloured light on growth, blossoming, fruit-formation, and on the development and colouring of the blossoms and fruit. Flammarion's experiments on the sensitive plant are particularly interesting : " In a blue hot-house the plants did not develop at all in the course of three months, but were torpid, as it were ; in a white hot-house they attained a size of 100 mm. ; in a green one up to 152 mm. ; in a red, up to 423 mm." Only in the red did they blossom and show extraordinary sensitivity, while in the blue the mimosæ were completely insensitive. Analogous phenomena have been observed in other plants also. Rays of different colour influence unequally the form, the colouring of the leaves and blossoms, and even their size. The influence of temperature is also not without significance in this respect. The influence of various kinds of coloured light on the development of animals is also well known and a number of scientific investigations have been made in this sphere.

It is not difficult to reveal colour reactions also in protozoa, not excluding bacilli and other microbes. Volvox globator, which is a colony of polyps inside and on the surface of the water-filled, spheroid membranous wall, also exhibits an exceedingly marked colour reaction. According to Ehrenberg, it is sufficient to lower a blue or a red object into the water and an excitement begins, which is similar to the movement of a herd or of a flock of birds or a crowd of people ; the polyps are attracted by the coloured object and begin to swim towards it.

We have also P. Beer's experiments on small crustaceous daphnia. When the rays of the spectrum are directed on them through a crevice in a dark vessel, they gather on the spectrum, and, moreover, gather in the largest numbers on the area from the orange to the green bands, in somewhat fewer numbers on the red band, still fewer on the blue, and in very few on the violet. In a word, a peculiar living scale was formed in the colour spectrum. It proved also, under the influence of separate coloured rays, that these crustaceans were attracted most of all by yellow and red rays, and less by other coloured rays. The daphnia are quite indifferent to dark violet and dark red rays.

Let us pass on to the consideration of that morphogenesis which is associated with inner stimuli. The homology of organ-structure, for instance, the development of the organs of plants according to the type of the leaf, the structure of vertebræ, of teeth, etc.—all of these point to definite internal conditions which manifest a certain creative activity, while external influences play a subsidiary rôle here. But, in general, in regard to morphogenesis, both functional adjustments (Roux) and, consequently, the functional activity associated with them, assume great importance. There is reason to think that some structures, such as the distribution of bony substance, of connective-tissue fibres, of blood vessels, etc., are explained by the fact that cells functioning more intensively get greater nourishment, while cells which have little or no part in the given process perish.

On the other hand, the activity of the endocrine glands, which plays such an important part in the morphogenesis of tissue, must also, as we have said before, be reduced to reflex phenomena, for every gland is chemically stimulated by the hormone of other glands, and reacts to it by increased or decreased secretion ; in other words, by excitation or depression of the chemo-reflex peculiar to it.[1]

Further, fertilisation processes must also be subsumed under the formula of reflex, the spiral movement of the tail of spermatozoa being ultimately merely a form of reflex, as a result of which the meeting of the spermatozoon with the ovum is realised, and is followed by the morpho-genetic process which develops on the basis of the welding of the two elements.

[1] See V. Bechterev : *Diseases of Personality from the Viewpoint of Reflexology ; Problems in the Study and Education of Personality*, 2nd vol., 1920.

CHAPTER VII

The dependence of the external reactions of the organism on conditions of past experience. The fallacy of regarding animal organisms as inert bodies. The phenomena of taxes and tropisms. Criticism of the theory of taxes and tropisms.

LET us note that reflexes of aggression and defence may be traced to the most fundamental biological processes which occur in the organism, where we meet with the absorption and assimilation of certain substances—these activities are reflexes of an aggressive character —and the refusal and ejection of certain other substances—these are defence reflexes. Moreover, everything that promotes the life-activity of the cell is imbibed or absorbed, and, on the contrary, everything that acts unfavourably in regard to the cell is rejected and sets in motion the contractile processes of the cells. Thus, here, the contractility of protoplasm and decrease of surface is a defence reflex of the cell against the intrusion into it of harmful products. But the organism has also elaborated inner chemical processes, which take the form of reflexes aggressive and defensive in character. The former are represented by the formation of activators, the latter by the formation of antibodies. As soon as an albuminous body foreign to it is introduced into the organism, the appropriate organs immediately develop an appropriate antagonist or antibody as a defence of the organism against the harmful influences of such intrusion. The whole doctrine of hormones, the Wasserman and Abderhalden reactions, and many other bio-chemical processes are based on the defence reflexes of the organism, for they are just as much reflexive processes in our sense as are the expansion of the vessels and the arrival of white blood-corpuscles at the wounded area, as well as the struggle of the phagocytes with foreign products which disturb the integrity of the organism's activities and the harmony established with the processes of its life-activity.[1]

[1] The doctrine of heredity or genetics reveals the conditions of the organic reproduction of forms of temperament and definite tendencies. The general similarity of offspring to their parents is, as is well known, based on the fact that the former originate from the material prepared by the parental organisms—by the female in the form of egg cells, and by the male in the form of seminal cells. Thus, in a fertilised egg there are already contained in a potential state those qualities which pertain to the parental organisms. Not associating them with any parts of the cells, Johannsen called these germs of future qualities " genes," as hereditary units. But there are reasons for regarding the chromosomes (i.e. that substance of the cellular nucleus of the female and male organisms which greedily absorbs colour) as the carriers of hereditary qualities. The number of chromosomes is different in different animals. In man, every cell contains twenty-four chromosomes ; in fertilisation, two nuclei, one of the female egg cell, the other of the male seminal cell, are welded. But before fertilisation, the reproductive cell loses half of the chromosomes through reductive division, and only such a cell, with half the number of chromosomes, can be fertilised. The chromosomes, being qualitatively unequal, are apparently the chief carriers of hereditary qualities, although there are facts which lead us to think that other parts of the cell also are not indifferent in this respect. In the cell itself, chromatin (Lundegard's carotin) is the sum of the genes or the " hereditary matter," but in the protoplasm the " plastosomes " or chondriosomes must be regarded as hereditary matter. (See Meves : *Eine Plastosomentheorie der Vererbung*, 1918.)

Let us further remark that the reproductive capacity which we discover in the world of living nature, and which is based on the release of previous reflexes from inhibition, conditions the dependence of the external manifestations of the organism at every given moment on past influences which have issued from the external world, all of which creates in living organisms the conditions of past individual experience.

Without past experience, there is no reflexological scheme, for inner compulsion, just as external, can be overcome by that inhibitory force which is inculcated by past experience. Thus, whether I may be threatened with punishment for theft or may be driven by hunger to the criminal act, I, who am guided by habits formed in me by education, may still refrain from the crime.

In the same way, no matter how much I may be incited to some action or other by encouragement, I, who am guided by past experience, refuse to be lured. In this case, we are concerned with an inner inhibitory force, which has arisen as a result of past experience. Apart from the influence of past experience, it is quite impossible to understand the actions of man, and also of other beings.

That is why one cannot agree to the full extent with such a purely mechanistic view as has been recently advanced concerning the lower animals and regards organisms as some kind of inert bodies exclusively dependent on external influences.

As is well known, de Réaumur, Lubbock, Forel, and other naturalists, experimenting on lower animals, have used in their investigations a method based on some simple irritation. They have carried out their investigations almost exclusively on insects. In their experiments, they hid some fruit under leaves, and when they saw that the insect found it, they concluded the existence of a perceptive apparatus. If the insect, after an operation, did not find the hidden fruit, they concluded that the animal had used the removed organ in finding it. They carried out similar experiments on butterflies—by hiding the females which have a specific odour, and, after having performed an appropriate operation for the removal of the olfactory organ, by making the males search for the females. For instance, Frisch[1] studied the orientation of bees by the fragrance of flowers. In places frequented by bees, he placed little boxes with apertures or doors. Some of the boxes were empty, others filled with sweet acacia-flavoured syrup. He proved that the bees frequented only the boxes scented with acacia.

In order to show that the bees associated the given odour with food, i.e. that they had acquired an association reflex in regard to a definite smell in the acquisition of food, the investigator changed the positions of the boxes, leaving them empty, but one of them, also empty, was scented with acacia. The result was that the acacia-scented box was visited by seventy-one bees, but the other three unscented ones only by three bees. When boxes with attar of roses and essential lavender oil were then placed

[1] *Translators' note :* Prof. K. von Frisch.

beside the box scented with acacia, it happened that, also in this case, the acacia box was visited by 133 bees, and no bee visited the other boxes. But Frisch succeeded later in similarly training the bees to rose and lavender oil, and even to lysol.

The same investigator proved that the bees distinguish colours. After the bees had been trained to fly to the smell of acacia into a violet-coloured box, he replaced it by two boxes—a yellow acacia-scented one, and a violet one without any fragrance. It was found that the bees made from afar for the violet box, but, when they approached it, some of them turned to the scented yellow box. The experimenter was justified in coming to the conclusion that bees at a distance are guided in their choice by colour, and, when near, by smell, the olfactory stimulations being more differentiated in them than are colour stimulations.

Thus the objectivo-biological method unquestionably gives much to the study of the correlative activity of the lower animals. But some writers, especially Loeb and Bohn, have gone further, making use of an analogous method.

It is well known that unicellular organisms react in a completely identical manner to very different external influences. Thus, chemical agents, light and mechanical stimuli, often produce the same effect. But, on the other hand, various unicellular organisms react unequally to external influences. The reader may find examples of this in Vagner's book : *Comparative Psychology*, v. i, pp. 190 ff. (*Sravnitelnaya psychologiya*).

By the way, the movements produced in unicellular organisms by the influence of light are called phototaxis by Strasburger, and he distinguishes positive and negative phototaxis according to the direction of the movement to the light or away from it.

Needless to say, the intensity of light is not without significance in regard to the movement, because light of one intensity produces positive phototaxis, and light of another, negative phototaxis.

But not only light produces taxic movements in unicellular organisms. Favourable temperature, for instance, attracts them ; unfavourable repels them. This is the so-called thermotaxis, also positive and negative.

Further, we know of phenomena of chemotaxis or of the attraction and the repulsion of unicellular organisms by chemical substances, *e.g.* infusoria are attracted by oxygen and repelled by a solution of common salt.

Further, for the same reasons, we must recognise galvanotaxis, which again is positive (attraction to the cathode) and negative (attraction to the anode). It is possible to distinguish, further, other kinds of taxes, such as geotaxis (attraction along the line of gravitation to the ground), etc.

Apart from taxic, there are also tropistic movements, which are observed particularly in plants and do not lead to a change of place, but express themselves in change of position and in direction of growth. These tropisms, in turn, are positive and negative and, according to the external influences, may be called photo-, helio-, or geotropisms, etc.

It must be stated, by the way, that not all writers distinguish between both kinds of movement, for some call both kinds of movement tropisms, others taxes.

According to Verworn, all these movements, which are completely automatic (unconscious), are conditioned by the influence of physico-chemical irritations, because, for instance, substances with which the organisms have never formerly entered into correlation sometimes prove to be chemo-tropistic. In general, tropisms are explained by one-sided or partial irritation of the protoplasm, this irritation producing a reaction of a certain kind, *i.e.* contraction or expansion of the body of unicellular organisms. Loeb[1] also holds the same view of the movements of pro-tozoa, *i.e.* that they are quite automatic, but he extends this view to the whole animal kingdom, including also the higher animals.

J. Loeb isolated the animal to be studied and tried on it the effects of various physical agents, especially light-stimuli, in regard to its movement. Here the animal was actually regarded as a physical body and the effect as a result of physico-chemical agents. It is this effect which Loeb sub-sumes under the concept of tropism.

According to J. Loeb,[2] animals (such as moths) with a quick forward movement, under the influence of heliotropism, enter the flame before the heat of the fire has time to inhibit their movement. Animals with a slow forward movement and on which the increasing heat can act while they are approaching the flame, but before they enter it, when, as a result of their positive heliotropism, they are close to the flame, have their forward movement inhibited by the high temperature, withdraw from the flame, and again orient themselves, etc.

Loeb comes finally to the conclusion that the life not only of lower animals, but also of vertebrates, is regulated by attraction and repulsion caused by temperature, light, and electricity, without any correlations with the inner conditions of the organism.

Taking his stand on the thesis that the irritability of protoplasm is an indisputable law of all living matter, and that this same irritability is exhibited in multicellular organisms also, Loeb comes to the conclusion that the activities of the latter must be also reduced to taxes and tropisms. The presence of a nervous system in animals does not change the nature of the phenomena. Thus, the phenomena of heliotropism in animals possessing nerves and in those devoid of them are produced by the same causes as they are in plants which have no nerves, *i.e.* by the form of the body and the irritability of cellular protoplasm.

In any case, tropistic phenomena do not depend on special qualities of the nervous system, as some suppose, when, for instance, they explain by instinct or reflex the attraction of moths to the light. Moreover, keeping in view that the activity of the nervous system may be reduced to the irritability of living matter in general, this investigator supposes that

---

[1] Loeb : *Comparative Physiology of the Brain and Comparative Psychology.*
[2] Loeb : *l.c.*

this one attribute is really sufficient to explain the behaviour of the higher animals.

According to Loeb, the reason for animal movement, such as reproduction, defence, and the seeking for nourishment, consists merely in orientation in regard to the " lines of force." The animal is subjected to the influence of various forces and its posture is determined by equilibration of these. For instance, a definite position of the animal must be explained by the identical morphological and chemical structure of the symmetrical points of its surface. Thus, according to Loeb, the directing influence which sets the animals in motion depends on physico-chemical agents which act on them as inert, though irritable, bodies.

In other words, the responses of animals in this case are completely explained by external influences. Finally, Loeb regards heliotropism, chemotropism, geotropism, and others[1] as the most important forms of tropism.

Jennings, dissatisfied with Loeb's tropisms, supplements the doctrine by the trial and error method. In other words, according to him, the organisms are not simply subjected to attraction and repulsion, but, by the help of trial and error, find the right way.

The view of Loeb, who does not accept Jennings's amendment in regard to trial and error, has served as the foundation for its further development in biology, but has its adversaries also. According to the words of V. Vagner, " one of the representatives of this trend in science describes the phenomena of galvanotaxis in frogs and fish ; another describes the phenomena of phototaxis in birds ; another offers quinine to crayfish, experiments on actinia with sulphuric acid, on worms with salt and sugar, etc., and then calls every taxis or tropism by a new or the old name, and prefixes positive or negative signs." (*l.c.*, pp. 198–199.)

The former craze for anthropomorphism in animal psychology has thus been replaced by a crude physico-chemical trend, in which animals have been denied even the so-called instincts, which have been replaced by the concept of tropisms well known in the vegetable kingdom.

But the nature of tropisms itself has not yet been investigated even in regard to plants. Is it only a matter of simple physico-chemical relations in the plant, or may we here speak of an active, *i.e.* reflexive, process ? Let us take as an example the light which makes the stem bend towards the sun. This phenomenon is, from the point of view of tropism, usually understood as a phenomenon of decreased capacity for stretching or an increased contraction on one side (Loeb).

But is this very capacity of cells to stretch or contract the result of a greater or lesser drying-up process or of an active contraction of the protoplasm under the influence of an external agent ? This is the essence of the problem.

---

[1] Loeb has more fully expressed his conclusions concerning tropisms in his address to the Sixth International Congress of Psychologists in Geneva. Of this we shall speak later, when we discuss the law of gravitation.

I

Analogous phenomena may be observed, as is well known, in the stem of the polyp eudendrium. Here, too, we may speak of growth or of orientation produced by cellular contraction, consequently of physiological phenomena, by which similar phenomena may be explained in other cases also.

Needless to say, the theory of tropisms encounters a number of weighty objections in other respects also, and its weakness becomes the more obvious, the higher we rise on the ladder of the animal world, where we can see, in almost every movement of the animal, not a direct response to external stimuli, but a response based on past inherited or individual experience.

Metalnikov's investigations, which we have already mentioned, leave no doubt about the fact that even the simplest animals are guided by past experience in their relations to the external world.

Notwithstanding this, investigations in different directions in regard to the theory of tropisms are now being made. It is sufficient here to point to the work of Bohn on photo- and chemotropism in cœlentera, although the same investigator has discovered in actinia memory phenomena which indicate the rôle of past individual experience concerning ebb-tides ; to the investigations of J. Bell on crayfish, of A. Mayer and Caroline Soules on the caterpillar of Danais plexippus, of Loew on insects which frequent the blossoms of one and the same plant (oligotropism), and those which frequent the blossoms of many plants (polytropism), and to the investigations of Rádl and many others.

Hachet-Souplet, however, doubts the very facts which lie at the root of the doctrine of tropisms, explains them differently, and gives them a different meaning. It is, in general, necessary to keep in mind that, in addition to the cellular changes which lie at the root of metabolism, reflex activity, which is closely associated with the latter and is to be understood in a wide sense of the word, is a characteristic of the organism.

Tropism is based on the assumption that there is a quantitative correlation between the external stimulus and the reaction.

But it is not possible to admit the existence of only such a correlation in the more complex manifestations of the animal organism, for here we encounter the reproductivo-association activity, as well as a number of influences which depress or excite, and, at the same time, revive past inhibited reflexes, and, on account of this, the external effect of influences on the animal organism is a result of the sum of all these factors.

It is obvious that the doctrine of tropisms, regardless of the existence of inherited and individual experience in the animal kingdom, stands in contradiction to the law of evolution, for it completely subjects living beings to external influences, and this excludes the process of development which depends on the organism's previous life conditions. A criticism of tropisms and taxes, which produce, in one case, attraction, in another, repulsion, may be found in the work of Hachet-Souplet, as well as in

V. Vagner,[1] and in other authors.[2] Without going into the details of this criticism we shall say that, according to Hachet-Souplet, an animal governed by tropisms would inevitably perish, for their influences cannot harmonise with the demands of life. Life would not be properly secure, and, consequently, could not exist under tropisms.

In general, although we must admit that both the activity and the development of organisms are subject to the external forces of nature, still we must not forget the circumstance that the external forces of nature are transformed by the organism at its surfaces, not excluding the alimentary canal, into internal forces, and thus there is created in the organism an enormous store of energy, through which living beings can transform the inorganic environment. With the acceptance of the theory of tropisms, one should not, in our opinion, at the same time leave out of account that the animal, drawing its energy from the external world through its food and through the external influences impinging on the receptive organs, utilises it for the purpose of its existence. We must not forget either that Jennings's experiments (see above) force us to admit that, while tropisms exist, the habitual modes of reaction to a certain stimulus are acquired by means of so-called trial and error, i.e. past experience. This is also supported by Yerkes's[3] observations, who, making frogs and crayfish crawl from one point to another according to certain indications, has noticed that at first they took circuitous routes, but later followed a shorter path.

But, in addition to the abovesaid, we cannot help taking into account also other peculiarities in the relations of living beings to the environment. It is easy to see that all bodies in existence must be divided into two different orders, the movements of the one being in exclusive dependence on external influences, and, consequently, in complete dependence on certain incidental external conditions. These are the inanimate or inorganic bodies. In the movements of the other—organised—bodies, we encounter such a kind of reaction to external influences as is eloquent to a relation to the environment, but a relation peculiar to, and characteristic of, a living being, the essence of this relation consisting in aggression, defence, concentration, and, in certain cases, imitation and symbolism. Thus there is question of an active relation of these organised bodies to the environment in respect of the store of energy contained in them, and although this relation is doubtlessly directed by external influences, its reactions are by no means completely proportional in their intensity and direction to these external influences. On the contrary, organised bodies are also directed, in this relation to the surrounding influences and forces, by the results of experience based on previous influences. It is precisely

---

[1] V. Vagner : *Comparative Psychology* (*Sravnitelnaya Psychologiya*), v. I, p. 200 ff.

[2] See, for instance, W. Buddenbrock : *Berliner Klinische Wochenschrift*, p. 923, 1921.

[3] R. Yerkes : *Biol. Bull. ;* Woods, Hall ; Mass., vol. III.

this teleological-active relation to the environment which lies at the root of the behaviour of living organisms, while tropisms, too, are utilised by them in accordance with their needs determined by past experience.

The behaviour of man as a living being, behaviour correlated to the past and present influences of the environment, reaches those more complex forms which, by common agreement, are called conduct, and which are characterised by a number of interconnected activities directed by a clearly defined aim, *i.e.* a stimulus which has occurred earlier in the experience of the given person, or of other persons, or which is an inevitable conclusion from previous experience as its direct consequence.[1]

From this we must conclude that behaviour in general and the conduct of higher beings in particular presuppose such a mechanism as, in contradistinction to the bodies of inanimate nature, has at its disposal, in addition to the activity of tropisms, a store of energy which it acquires partly from the environment itself and partly through heredity, for a new-born being is already capable of manifesting elementary forms of behaviour.

Professor McDougall[2] characterises it thus from the external point of view :

" 1. A creature must not merely move in a certain direction, like an inert mass impelled by external force ; in its movements there is implied an end that subserves the life of the individual or of the species, for its movements do not cease when it meets with external obstacles ; such obstacles rather provoke still more forcible striving.

2. The striving, however, is not persistent in a given direction ; though the striving persists when obstacles are encountered, the kind and direction of movement are varied so long as the obstacle is not overcome. Thus behaviour is a trial towards an end with, if necessary, variation of the means employed for its attainment.

3. In behaviour the whole organism is involved, or, I would say, the organism as a whole, for ultimately behaviour is not merely a partial reaction, in the form of a simple reflex movement, which is of an almost

---

[1] Man, being social, develops his reflexes in the society of man and in their continuous interaction with the stimuli issuing from the environment. On this basis, those reflexes which are, in general, more adapted are retained. The greater part of what is unadapted is discarded by means of natural selection, but some of the unadapted orientation reflexes are retained, as not having been injurious to the individual, and as making possible an appropriate correction by means of other receptive apparatus. Thus, reflexology explains the origin of the majority, if not all, of the so-called physiological illusions.

[2] *Translators' note :* Bechterev here uses the Russian translation (Moscow, 1916) of Prof. W. McDougall's *Introduction to Social Psychology.* Our translation is a faithful rendering of the Russian, and is made, as far as possible, in the words of the original English text. While the Russian translation, as quoted by Bechterev, is in substance identical with the original, yet the two texts do not altogether tally, and, that he may not be led into any misinterpretation of McDougall's ideas, the reader is referred to the *Introduction to Social Psychology*, 21st ed., enlarged, pp. 304–305 (Methuen).

mechanical character ; rather, in every case of behaviour, the energy of the whole organism is concentrated on a definite end : all its parts and organs are subordinated to and co-ordinated with the organs primarily involved in the activity.

4. Although, on the recurrence of behaviour, the creature behaves again in a similar manner, yet the activity is not repeated in just the same fashion as on the previous occasion (as is the case with mechanical processes) ; there is as a rule some evidence of increased efficiency of action, of better adaptation in respect of the gaining of the end—the process of gaining the end is shortened."

Having cited this analysis of behaviour—an analysis obscured by McDougall's subsequent subjectivist remarks—I should like to indicate that behaviour is a result, on the one hand, of inner, i.e. organic, phenomena and, on the other, of external influences, and is directed in both cases towards the maintenance of the general well-being of the organism.

The objective study of human behaviour and also of human language, facial expressions, and gestures under various conditions comprises the fundamental subject-matter of reflexology.

The individual experience of everyone indicates that behaviour is usually accompanied by peculiar inner phenomena or phenomena psychic in character, which are called conscious experiences, and which usually, to some extent or other, accompany behaviour.

This makes it intelligible why we involuntarily associate the behaviour of other human beings with a so-called soul, for we allow in them inner experiences similar or analogous to those which we experience in ourselves, but the study of the behaviour of others in no case compels us to turn to their inner or psychic experiences, which may not exist ; otherwise, we should not only lose objectivity in observation, but should also be guided by phenomena the character of which we know only from our own subjective experience, and, even then, by no means in all cases, and this inevitably leads us into error.

Besides, the relations between human individuals do not at all correspond to inner or psychic experiences, but to their speech, facial expression, gestures, and conduct, i.e. the external manifestations of personality.

Correlative activity, as experience shows, already manifests itself in the vegetable kingdom in the development, growth, and direction of roots in accordance with the character of the soil, its dampness, etc. ; in the opening and closing of the blossoms—at sunrise and sunset respectively ; in the stretching and bending of the plant towards the light, or the so-called tropisms ; in the drooping of the leaves of some plants when you strike their stem, and sometimes even when the leaves are mechanically irritated ; in the shedding of leaves as winter approaches ; etc. But the fixation of plants to a definite place, as a result of the nutritional conditions under which the plant derives its nutritive material from the soil, is responsible for the low grade of development of correlative activity, realisable to its proper extent for the different species of the vegetable kingdom only under appropriate conditions of climate and locality, and this explains the geographical distribution of the various species of plants.

The conditions of animal life, which have made locomotion necessary chiefly for the satisfaction of the nutritional function, have for that very reason produced a greater development of correlative activity in animals. But here, too, this development, because of the different conditions of climate, environment, and nutrition to which the various species of the animal kingdom are subjected, is by no means uniform. Thus, animals living in the ground, for instance, worms, since they possess an organism appropriate to their environment, cannot possibly develop their correlative activity to the proper extent, for this environment is devoid of light-stimuli, conducts sound badly, and, at the same time, renders impossible the development and differentiation of specialised organs of locomotion, *i.e.* of limbs such as other animals have. It is obvious that, on the one hand, the primitiveness of the structure of worms and, on the other, the limited character of the development of their correlative activity are a result of unfavourable environmental conditions.

In this way also is explained the atrophy of some organs, for instance, eyes, in animals forced to spend the greater part of their life underground. On the other hand, animals which have evolved from worms and are vermiform in the embryonic stage of their existence evince, as insects, which in their full development pass into an overground, airy, or aqueous environment, a considerably more developed correlative activity, as well as a more perfect structure in comparison with worms.

The aqueous environment has a great advantage over the subterranean, and, therefore, the representatives of the aqueous kingdom, such as fish, and fish-like animals, should, and in fact do, exhibit a more highly developed correlative activity as well as a more perfect structure. However, this environment, too, since it is a bad conductor of mechanical irritation, considerably absorbs light rays, and hinders the diffusion of olfactory stimuli, must be still regarded as but little favourable to the development of correlative activity—the more so because the environmental conditions limit the differentiation of limbs to oar-shaped and rudder-like forms, by no means perfect as limbs. Therefore, the very important rôle of the active tactual sense of other animals has not been able to reach a high degree of development in fish, and their visual sense can establish correlations only with objects not very distant from them.

Amphibia have no great advantage over fish, for, as has been already mentioned, water, because of its poor conduction of mechanical irritation, its strong absorption of light, its resistance to the diffusion of olfactory stimuli, is, in general, an environment but little favourable to the development of correlative activity, while the locomotion of amphibia on land is, in general, exceedingly imperfect and limited, for differentiation fails to secure appropriate adjustment of the organs of locomotion, as well as other organs, to both environments.

Reptiles have all the advantages of a land over a water environment, but the absence of special organs of locomotion, realised, in this instance, by movements of the body, demands such an expenditure of energy on locomotion, catching prey, and avoiding danger, that their correlative activity is retarded in its development by rather unfavourable conditions. But from the time when the reptile developed legs and stood up on these legs, it acquired by this very means—facilitated capacity for locomotion on land—an advantage in regard to the development of its correlative activity, and simultaneously created the conditions for a more varied correlation of its organism with the world around it.

On the other hand, an air environment has every advantage over a subterranean because of the relatively fast locomotion, and, therefore, insects, evolved from these same worms, reach a high grade of development in their correlative activity, although, it seems, they must overcome greater, and, certainly, more varied, obstacles for the securing of their existence. Compared with those animals previously mentioned, birds, also, because of their locomotion in air, have every advantage in respect of the development of correlative activity. But this environment affords no specially favourable conditions for the development of correlative activity, chiefly because a number of correlations with external conditions, met with on the surface of the earth, do not exist for the inhabitants of the air, and, besides, their expenditure of energy on locomotion in the air must be enormous.

It is clear from this why quadrupeds, which live their life overground on land, must have a great advantage in regard to the development of correlative activity over feathered creatures, notwithstanding the fact that the differentiation of limbs (wings and legs) is more perfect in birds than in quadrupeds. And, indeed, animals living their life on land enjoy the most favourable conditions for the development of their correlative activity both because of the more varied external influence of the environment, as well as of the comparatively smaller expenditure of energy on locomotion.

It is clear that there is greater variety among quadrupeds in the development of their correlative activity, and that this is in direct dependence on the conditions of their habitats, on the greater or lesser richness of the latter in nutritive products, on the mildness or severity of the climate, on their living together with other living beings, and on many other conditions.

Correlative activity has been brought considerably nearer to perfection, from the time when, under the stress of life's demands and the differentiation caused by them, the organs of locomotion, without abandoning their original function, have assumed other functions, such as grasping and defence. Therefore, the apes, for instance, exhibit a more highly developed correlative activity than do other quadrupeds.

Even the differentiation arising from the special life conditions of such a peculiar prehensile organ as the elephant's trunk gives this animal a peculiar advantage in regard to the development of correlative activity.

But it is indisputable that, since the time when land quadrupeds evolved into bipeds and simultaneously set free a pair of upper limbs for grasping and defence functions, these limbs began to differentiate, concomitantly with their varied use, into the form of a human hand, and thus, notwithstanding certain limitations of the speed of locomotion on two legs, made possible the better utilisation, for their needs, of the various conditions of the environment ; and all of this has necessarily influenced the greater development of correlative, and particularly association-reflex, activity.

In addition, the gradual development of the upper limbs into the human hand has led to the extensive use of suitable objects as implements (sticks, sharp flints, etc.), then to the appropriate elaboration and perfecting of these implements, later to the development of craftsmanship and the facilitation of the procuring of food and to its appropriate preparation (chopping, etc.), and to inventions of various kinds (*e.g.* producing fire, etc.). All of this has considerably widened the circle of interrelations between the organism and the environment and, thus, inevitably led to an extraordinary development of correlative activity in the world of man.

Further, the development of the human hand has led to considerable extension of expressive movements, as a result of the development of gesticulation, and this, in turn, has considerably helped both communication between individuals and interchange of individual experience.

Simultaneously, the so-called social environment, or the environment of the interaction of individuals, which may be reasonably called the superorganic world, acquires great significance in respect of the development of association-reflex activity. It is true that this environment is not something new in this case, for it exists in the form of temporary approaches to each other among the lower organisms, but the important point is that, because °f the temporary character of the approaches, these organisms have not had sufficient means and implements for the appropriate utilisation of this environment.

But, wherever this environment has been utilised to a greater extent, the development of correlative activity has reached a considerable stage of development. As examples of this we may cite, on the one hand, termites and our ants and bees among insects ; and, on the other, beavers, monkeys, and others among vertebrates.

Further, along with the development of the hand as a convenient instrument of intercommunication and with the appropriate preparation of food by means of the same hand (preliminary chopping, cooking by fire, etc.), the whole oral cavity, in respect of its bony substance, including the teeth, and of its soft structures, especially the tongue, underwent appropriate changes, so that it became possible to supplement the language of facial expression and gestures by vocal communication, which gradually developed into verbal language in the form of human speech with all its nuances of intonation and striking differentiation of composite sounds—up to, and including, the production of complex sounds.

There is no necessity to indicate here what advantage man has derived from vocal language which has developed *pari passu* with facial expressions and gestures and at first merely supplemented the languages of gesticulation and facial expression, and later, as a result of its peculiar development, acquired its supreme significance as a means of communication among different individuals.

In any case, along with the development of oral language, after which followed the development of picture-writing and written language, man could, to a greater extent than any other being on earth, organise and utilise the social environment, which consists of individuals similar to himself, and this, consequently and inevitably, led to a peculiar development of the association-reflex activity of man, a development beyond the reach of other animal species and leading man to those pinnacles of human culture manifested in the form of technical, esthetic, and social creativeness.

It is clear from the above that the development of correlative and, in particular, association-reflex activity stands in direct relation to certain environmental conditions ; and, in dependence on the change in means of utilising the environment—a change arising from certain conditions—the association-reflex activity progresses or regresses : whenever wider possibilities of utilising the environment open up to a living being, the association-reflex activity receives an impetus to further development and, as a result of these conditions, reaches its climax in man.

CHAPTER VIII

The necessity of studying the activity of all living beings in its objective manifestations in connection with past experience and conditions of heredity. The inadequacy, for objective study, of the definition of reflex as propounded by subjective psychology. The division of reflexes into innate and inherited or ordinary, on the one hand ; and, on the other, acquired or associated. The difference between them.

ULTIMATELY, in consideration of the fact that all living beings are subject to the same laws, we insist that it is necessary to study this activity first of all from the purely external side—in its objective manifestations, and then not merely in dependence on current external influences, however the activity of these influences may be explained, but also in dependence on the results of past influences both on the organism itself—influences leading to the creation of past individual experience in the form of acquired reflexes—and on its ancestors—influences manifested in the particular constitution of the individual, his temperament, the degree of general and special endowments, and inherited reflex movements in the form of a large number of ordinary and instinctive reflexes of varied complexity.

We must keep in mind, therefore, that subjective psychology regards reflexes as unconscious processes, but this definition, on account of its subjective character, can have significance only for a man who is subjected to test, and even then only to a very limited extent. But, in the case of animals, it cannot, because of its subjectivity, be regarded as adequate, for there are, in the case of animals, no objective data to help us to determine whether given movements are conscious or unconscious. Independently of this, biology began to take the term " reflex " in a wider sense, as comprising various kinds of reactions of the organism. Thus it is regarded by Driesch, Jennings, and others. Therefore, we may speak of reflexes even in protozoa (Metalnikov), in microbes in general, and even in plants. It must be noted, however, that some propose the term antikinesis for the reactions which occur with the participation of a differentiated nervous system, but for those reactions occurring in the absence of a nervous system the name antimia has been suggested (Beer, Bethe, Uexküll). To this, however, it has been justly objected that the concepts reflex and reaction are physiological concepts and, therefore, should be based on physiological, and not on anatomical, data. Besides, we cannot maintain that because hitherto no nervous system has been discovered in an organism, it may not, in view of the constant progress of science, be discovered to-morrow.

On the other hand, the same investigators propose to call reflexes only those reactions which are recurrent in the same form, but all reactions which change in dependence on previous influences it has been suggested to call antiklises.

But this definition, too, does not sustain severe criticism, as has been shown by Ziegler, for all reflexes can really be subsumed under the abovementioned concept, because all of them may, to some extent or other, be subject to change resulting from previous conditions.

As a matter of fact, it is not possible to discover, from the objective standpoint, an essential difference between the manifestation of responsive movements in nerveless animals and those in animals supplied with nerves. It is true that the former movements are more simple and stereotyped ; the latter, complex and varied. The former are pre-established and conditioned by certain external stimulations ; the latter seem to be less conditioned by external influences. But experiment shows that, if all previous influences are investigated, we encounter, in those latter movements, a strict conditioning by the results of past individual and inherited experience. Thus, it would be difficult to indicate an essential difference in this respect also.

Although the more complex and apparently independent movements are more easily inhibited by external stimuli, this does not constitute a a radical distinction from ordinary reflexes. Besides, as we shall see later, they are ultimately reproductions of simple reflexes only under other conditions, as a result of the association of a primary stimulus with a secondary one. For this reason also, complex motor acts may be called reflexes. However, these reflexes are acquired, and not innate or inherited. In this lies their peculiarity and their distinction from ordinary reflexes. This I have pointed out already in my first contributions to reflexology.[1] Ziegler, Metalnikov, and others also work on this basis when they classify animal reactions as inherited and those acquired by individual experience.

Before proceeding to explicate the problem further, I should like once more, dwelling on certain details, to clarify the distinction between ordinary reflexes and other higher reactions.

As we have already seen, all the external manifestations of the correlative activity of individuals may be regarded as reflexes, either (a) inherited or (b) complex-organic, or (c) those acquired in the course of life as a result of individual experience and exercise. Inherited reflexes, being an acquisition of the species, reveal themselves in a perfected form either at birth, or after a certain time, and without previous individual experience. These reflexes we divide into two main groups : exogenous and endogenous. To the former belong those reflex reactions which arise under external influences. Here belong a number of ligament, skin, bone, muscle, and other reflexes, more or less perfect at birth or appearing some time after birth, but always independently, without any special life experience. Here, too, belong some reflexes of the sensory organs, for instance, the pupil reflex.

However, we must keep in mind that some cutaneous reflexes, and also the blinking reflex, seemingly do not belong to the order of inherited, but of acquired, reflexes. We shall return to this later.

Reflexes which arise under the influence of internal or organic causes,

[1] V. Bechterev : *Objective Psychology and its Subject-matter*—in *Vestnik Psychologii*, 1904. Also the same author's *Objective Psychology*, 1907, and other works.

and which are, therefore, called organic reflexes, belong to the category of innate or inherited reflexes endogenous in character.

These organic reflexes which have a specific *modus operandi* are usually called instincts in scientific literature.[1] However, the term " instinct " must be excluded because of its vagueness and subjectivity. All organic reflexes presuppose an innate or inherited biological need manifested in the form of a tendency, which subserves the existence of the individual and, consequently, the existence of the species. Such are the organic reflexes in the form of the need for food and self-preservation in general, for warmth, light, oxygen, movement, and, when the organism is tired, for rest ; and, lastly, urges sexual in character, which ensure the life of posterity.

In connection with the organic reflex of nutrition, a responsive reaction, which may be called the parent reflex, is developed on the part of the parents, and especially of the mother giving suck. This reflex is really acquired, but it has a partly organic basis in the mother's nursing the child at her own breast, and in the procuring by the parents of other forms of nutrition for the child, and, in general, the care exercised by the parents for his welfare. Thus, here we have really to do with a reflex partly organic, partly acquired.

Another organic and, at the same time, acquired reflex results from the child's need for companionship, because of his helplessness and the insecurity of his existence when he is deprived of the society of others, and, above all, of the mother. These reflexes, which, on the one hand, develop under conditions of family life, and which, on the other, are sustained by the conditions of adult social life, may be called, the first, the family or family-social reflex, and the second, the social reflex.[2]

It is necessary to keep in mind that inherited or acquired organic reflexes have organic impulses at their basis only, but are realised partly on the basis of personal experience also. Thus, the organic reflex of nutrition would not appear if new-born infants were not offered the mother's breast, for this creates for them conditions under which they acquire personal experience in this respect. We must keep this in mind in regard to the sex reflex also and those reflexes which secure the utilisation of air, light, warmth, rest, etc.

Now we must note that both the exogenous and the endogenous reflexes are the source of the higher, or association, reflexes, because the stimuli which accompany the primary reflexogenous stimuli acquire the qualities of the latter. Thus, under the influence of a burn or prick, an association

---

[1] In the first edition of this book we called them inherited-organic reflexes, but they may be more simply called organic reflexes.

[2] Besides the above reflexes which arise in a natural way, man acquires, in the course of his life, because of the habitual introduction of certain narcotics into his organism, artificial organic reflexes or habitual organic reflexes in the form of the smoking of tobacco, the drinking of wine, etc. Also many other habits, because of numerous repetitions, are special acquired organic reflexes, the action of which is accompanied, to a certain extent, by biological satisfaction.

reflex, defensive in character and based on a simple defence reflex, is produced for the first time at the sight of any hot object or pricking instrument ; on the other hand, when the infant reflexively squeezes some object with its hand, a higher or association-grasping reflex develops and belongs to the class of reflexes aggressive in character.

In precisely the same way, higher or association reflexes originate on the basis of organic innate or organic acquired reflexes. Thus, on the basis of the simple organic reflex of sucking there gradually develops a visual association-sucking reflex, so that the nipple of the breast need not be put into the infant's mouth, but he himself, under the influence of visual impulses, seizes the nipple or some similar object, for instance, the finger, etc., with his lips. Later, with the development and increased variety of nutritional conditions, a complex of association reflexes aggressive in character develops, and these are associated with nutrition, the acquisition of nutritive products and of other objects. In a similar way, a complex of association or higher reflexes is developed on the basis of organic reflexes in the form of the need for warmth, light, and fresh air, and they lead to the appropriate acquisition by the individual of warmth, light, and fresh air. Since, in this acquisition, the presence of monetary signs is, among others, an anterior and concomitant stimulus, these signs, in turn, become stimuli which lead to the excitation of appropriate aggressive reflexes associative in character, reflexes which lead to the acquisition of money.

Professor I. P. Pavlov, in his paper, *The Aim Reflex* (*Vestnik Yevropi*, April, 1916), maintains that teleological activity, as a whole, is a special primary, inherited reflex, which must be included, under the term " aim reflex," in the other instincts or reflexes recognised by biology. The nature of this reflex consists, according to him, in the tendency to the possession of some stimulating object, for here we have a " mysterious, primary, irresistible tendency—an instinct or reflex." What proofs have we of this ? The author sees a proof in the frequent occurrence of disparity between the importance of the aim and the efforts made to achieve it. Example : The collecting mania, observable not only in man, but also in animals, is that mysterious force which makes the miser tremble at the sight of a heap of money.

Genetically, this " aim reflex " is expressed in the child in the form of a tendency to grasp and put into his mouth everything that his eye sees. Collecting, as an " aim reflex," corresponds to the digestion reflex—the desire to eat. Like an eater, who is satisfied when sated and then loses his appetite, so in the collector the " aim reflex " temporarily abates when the object is secured, but only to reawaken later, just as the eater's appetite returns in due course. We shall not discuss the author's other views.

It is scarcely possible to admit that the " aim reflex " in the collector temporarily abates in a manner similar to the eating reflex. In my opinion, the former reflex is still more inflamed and enlivened by the acquisition of objects, but however that may be, according to Pavlov, the " aim reflex," which develops under the influence of an external object, for instance in the form of collecting, may arise, subside, and again revive, like other organic reflexes. Now the question is : Do the reduction of the most complex biological act to such a simple scheme and the supporting of this position by expatiating on why exactly we, Russians, have, under the influence of centuries of slavery, lost our volitional busyness, while the Anglo-Saxons, in contrast, have for a long period freely developed their " aim reflex "—do these afford a solution of the problem in the sense of explaining the given biological phenomenon ? It is scarcely necessary to point out that very little is gained in this way and that the adversaries of the objective method in its application to the investigation of human personality are given a weapon. All who wish to learn more about how psychologists evaluate the " aim reflex " we refer to the critical article on it by V. Kravkov in *Psychologitcheskoye Obozrenie*, part I, p. 153 ; Moscow, 1917.

According to our data, along with the simple reflex phenomena, including the more elementary muscle reflexes (the so-called ideo-muscular excitability in the form of contraction of the muscle bundles and of general muscular contraction), and also various inner reflexes of a simple type down to, and including, cellular reflexes and chemical reactions or chemo-reflexes, a number of more complex reflex phenomena must also be classed as innate or ordinary reflexes. The complexity of these reflexes in animals demands special attention. Thus, for instance, a chick which has just come out of the egg can stand, walk, and even peck, imitating its mother. If its leg is seized, it pulls it out of the hand ; it swallows food which is put into its mouth. According to my observations, a lamb just born (one to two hours old), stands on its legs, fearlessly approaches man, runs, gambols, bleats, and responds by bleating to the bleating of its mother. Now and then it makes quick (wagging) movements with its tail. It is guided in its movements by visual, auditory, cutaneous, and muscular irritations. It pulls away its leg when grasped by the hand. When its body is scratched, it tries to prolong and intensify the scratching by inhibiting its other movements and pressing the body against the hand. When a sudden movement is made with the hand towards its muzzle, it jerks back. When the hands are clapped in its vicinity, it starts and jerks back! It pulls back its ear when seized, and begins to suck and lick, if the fingers are put into its mouth. When it is separated from the mother for some time and then given back to her, and she does not recognise it at once, it remains apart from her for some time.

My observations of new-born kids, calves, and sucking-pigs are in general accord with the above-mentioned data. For instance, it was discovered that a goat had littered two kids. Although the latter could not have been more than a few hours old, they could run astonishingly well, and orient themselves in their movements, although they sometimes fell when turning clumsily. In spite of threatening movements, no blinking reaction was evoked, the ears stood upright and moved freely. They reacted to scratching by turning their head. On the following day, both kids ran playfully around each other, licked each other's muzzle, and sometimes knocked their foreheads together in a butting manner. They reacted to loud sounds by retreating, crouching, and setting their ears back. They retreated when their muzzle was touched. The surprisingly quick development of association reflexes in these animals deserves attention. Here is an example :

A kid was born on the 6th of March, 1921. Investigation showed that the ears drooped. The eyes did not blink when threatened or when objects approached them. They closed when mechanically irritated ; the tail wagged quickly when the animal ate ; the kid sucked milk from a rag immersed in milk ; when the cheeks and head were irritated, it nuzzled ; it could move its ears when mechanically stimulated ; it walked ; and it bleated when hungry.

The next day, the kid had learned to drink alone, began to run after the girl who fed it, and even gambolled ; when hungry, it ran to the milk when it heard the sound of the plate ; it jerked back its head when a rag was waved at it or when it was mechanically irritated. The ears were already raised. On the third day, it began to jump out of the box in which its bed was, scratched its cheek with its foot, ran after the farmer's wife, jumped, asked for food by bleating, caught and ate cockroaches from the kitchen oven. It was quite indifferent to its mother. Now it showed a blinking reaction when the hand approached its eyes.

Thus, it is clear that the above-mentioned mammals immediately after birth display a number of complex innate orientation, defensive, aggressive, imitative, mimico-somatic, and vocal movements, executed under the guidance of sensory organs, and they quickly learn a number of movements which are association reflexes.

New-born puppies and kittens, which are born blind, crawl about, and are guided in their movements by cutaneous and muscular stimuli, and immediately suck the mother and execute pressing movements with their paws on her mammæ. However, they have no native inclination for food of a particular kind and begin to feed on milk only from the moment when their muzzle comes into contact with the mother's teats.

The above-mentioned data, set down in the briefest form, show that animals, in comparison with infants, are born more perfect as reflexive beings. But there are differences among animals, too, and the higher the type of the animal, the less in general is it born fit for life. In this respect, the comparative study of the greater or lesser perfection of various reflexes from birth and also their successive development in different animals and in man afford many instructive data, useful for generalisations which make possible the foundation of a specially important comparative method in genetic reflexology.

As regards the organic reflexes or the so-called instincts, everything necessary has been said above and it is not necessary to offer fresh explanations now. It is sufficient to say that there is question here of a chain reflex which originates, in the first place, under the influence of organic stimuli of an inherited character and requisitions the results of past individual experience.

In the case of acquired reflexes, there is question of the manifestation of an association or, to be more exact, reproductivo-association activity, which is characterised by the revival, under appropriate conditions, of traces of former reactions—traces which have been established in previous experience. These reactions lay down beaten tracks, which link up the area of excitation by the secondary stimulus with the area of the primary reflexogenous stimulus. One of several proofs of this may be seen in the shortening of the time-interval in the pronunciation of familiar and unfamiliar words, as has been proved by experiments made in my laboratory. (Prof. Astvatzaturov : *Dissertation*. St. Petersburg.)[1]

The association reflex is usually a reproduction of either the whole or a certain part of an ordinary reflex, but a reproduction under conditions given in previous experience and based on the associative activity of the brain.

By the way, for the establishment of an association reflex, it is not necessary to link up the primary reflexogenous stimulus with an indifferent one, for the former may be replaced by such an indifferent stimulus as itself, because of previous experience, arouses an association reflex. In this case we have to do with an association reflex of the second order, and so, in the same way, we may have an association reflex of a still higher order.

Let us note here that some (*e.g.* Dr. Lenz) call "super-reflexes" those association reflexes which develop on another association reflex, and these "super-reflexes" may be of the second, third, and lastly, the $n + 1$ order. But it is not proved that these "super-reflexes" are distinguished by any peculiar qualities from association reflexes of the first order ; and, in everyday life, it is not possible to discover under which category a particular reflex falls. Therefore, we do not adopt this division of association reflexes into primary association reflexes and "super-reflexes" ; from our point of view, it has no practical significance. We regard all association reflexes as reflexes of a higher order in comparison with ordinary or inherited reflexes and we have described them as such in various parts of the present work. Besides, a verbal stimulus, in its character of command or prohibition, plays the rôle of a primary reflexogenous stimulus. Under the conditions of social life, this stimulus acquires the greater force, the more the power of one man over another is displayed.

The external distinction of association reflexes from ordinary is this : that, in the latter, the reaction always occurs on definite excitation and

---

[1] In as far as it conditions the transmission by heredity of dispositions to more prompt acquisition of ancestrally acquired reflexes, the development of beaten tracks under the influence of long exercise may be reflected in posterity. There are superabundant proofs of this in the animal world.

according to a definite, strikingly sterotyped pattern, and *ad libitum* when the stimulus is repeated ; while, in the former, the reaction evoked by the stimulus depends on previous individual experience, and, because of the development of inner inhibitions, is weakened and disappears on frequent repetition, but in other cases is revived under stimulating influences. Moreover, the reaction depends to a large extent on external conditions, which have sometimes an inhibiting and sometimes an activating influence.

Up to the present, the opinion holds in scientific literature that complex personal reactions (the volitional, in the terminology of subjective psychology), which only gradually become automatic by becoming simple reflexes, are primary. Ribot also holds this view. We read in his work : " It is obvious that, from the viewpoint of development, all reactions were first volitional. They became organic-racial only because of countless repetitions in the sphere of individual and racial life." (*De la volonté*, Russ. trans., p. 27.) This is obviously one of those errors into which science has fallen as a result of the subjective method of investigation. It is necessary to keep in mind that even personal reactions are association reflexes which always originate on the basis of ordinary reflexes by means of the association of a primary stimulus with secondary or by-stimuli. On the other hand, there is no case on record in which the complex personal has changed into an ordinary reflex.

On the contrary, we know that, on the very lowest levels of ontogenesis, simple reflexes, but not association or personal, are the first to appear. Also in the phylogentic order of living nature, we find, in the first instance, reactions in the form of ordinary reflexes, on the basis of which association reflexes develop later. There are no cases to the contrary. Thus, reflexology excludes the above-mentioned opinion as in opposition to the law of evolution.

Besides, we must bear in mind the correlation between ordinary and association reflexes in regard to the influence of concentration, for experience shows that ordinary spinal—for instance, ligamental—reflexes are strengthened when concentration is distracted. A clear proof of this is Jendrassik's well-known method of producing weakened knee reflexes. Also experiments on association reflexes testify that the distraction of concentration by incidental stimulation usually releases from inhibition an association reflex already inculcated.

It is true that cutaneo-tactual reflexes (*Strichreflexe*) are intensified under concentration on them and weakened when concentration is distracted. But we shall see, in another context, that many such reflexes may be regarded to a certain extent as association reflexes which have developed in the course of life and occur with the participation of the brain cortex.

Let us note here also that simple association, reasoning, volitional process, and attention, as the subjectivists understand them, may be subsumed under the scheme of association reflex with its stimulation and inhibition. We shall speak of this later. By an association reflex in

K

general is to be understood every acquired reaction regardless of what inner processes take place during its occurrence.

Let us enter into detailed investigation of the innate reflex.

There was a time when problems of the first magnitude were approached without an adequate empirical basis and when scientists requisitioned speculations the plausibility of which, in their eyes, depended not so much directly on their objective significance as on the extent to which they supported preconceived notions.

Such is, for instance, Descartes' doctrine that animals do not possess such qualities of psychic activity as man does, for they are devoid of a human " soul," and, in consequence, all their activities are merely reflexes, and, of course, innate reflexes, because at that time there was no mention of any acquired reflexes such as we call association reflexes. Thus, from Descartes' standpoint, all external animal manifestations, even the most complex, were regarded as simple, *i.e.* innate and inherited reflexes.

But science has long ago discarded Descartes' view, and with the establishment of the law of evolution, it has become obvious that there is no radical difference between the higher activities of animals and of man. Having stated this fact, we encounter a question not less important : Which of the manifestations we include in the correlative activity of man must be referred to innate or inherited phenomena and which to phenomena acquired in the form of association reflexes in the course of life ? This is a radical problem. Here, too, extreme exaggerations have not been wanting and one of several of these is Lombroso's doctrine of the " born " criminal.

Gradually, however, science has abandoned such extravagances in this direction as have led to the exaggeration of the rôle of hereditary transmission in regard to human actions and, nowadays, most authorities regard human criminality as a phenomenon socio-economic in character.[1] A number of congresses devoted to problems of criminality have elucidated this aspect of the problem in the way just mentioned.

It is quite obvious that such problems as what man and the animals inherit from their ancestors and what they acquire in the course of life cannot be solved by speculations which have nothing in common with exact science.

When conducting an objective investigation of human activity, it is essential to distinguish between those manifestations of the human organism which are referable to inherited phenomena, those which are referable to complex-organic and mimico-somatic reflexes, and those which are a result of individual experience and are referable to association reflexes acquired in the course of life.

It is not necessary to dilate on the point that all cellular reactions, including the reactions of the white corpuscles and the movements of

[1] See V. Bechterev : *The Objectivo-psychological Method in its Application to the Study of Criminality—Sbornik, posv. pamyati D. A. Drilya (Symposium Dedicated to the Memory of D. A. Dril)*, and published separately, 1912.

spermatozoa, must be referred to an order of reflexes which are native characteristics of the cell.

All tissue reflexes are innate reflexes, as are also reflexes of the visceral organs, and also the glandular chemo-reflexes produced by internal stimuli vested in the life conditions of the organism itself.[1]

But the same kind of reflexes, when produced by external stimuli which originally did not arouse these reflexes, are association. For example : the secreting of gastric juice produced by ingested food is an innate reflex, but the secreting of gastric juice at the sight of a piece of meat is an association reflex.

The exact elucidation of the problem : What precisely in the sphere of so-called external reflexes must be referred to the one order of phenomena and what to the other ?—demands careful treatment, the more so because, since the time of Ch. Darwin, the problem of the significance of heredity in biology has come to the fore and although Darwin himself admitted the hereditary transmission of acquired characteristics, his adherents, with Weismann at their head, deny any such transmission, as everyone knows.

Besides, the problem of mimico-somatic manifestations deserves attention. From the viewpoint stated above, it may be seen that all mimico-somatic movements are innate. But data advanced by me in my work on expressive movements force the conclusion that, in addition to reflexive expressive movements, many such movements are association reflexes and thus are acquired by learning, and are not innate. For instance, laughter produced by tickling is a simple reflex, but in all other cases laughter is an association-reflex movement. The same is true of weeping and a number of other movements.[2] In particular, what Professor I. Pavlov (*loc. cit.*, pp. 303 ff.) regards as an innate slavery reflex in the dog (see below) is an expressive movement, which is, as must be supposed, the reproduction of behaviour acquired through experience, and is observed in dog fights ; the position of the defeated dog, with his belly turned upwards, is reproduced also when there is no real fight, but, in the latter case, the guilty dog assumes the vanquished posture as an association reflex.

A number of appropriate experiments have been performed on animals and have led to the conclusion that only those characteristics or peculiarities which depend on external influences affecting the sex-cells are hereditarily transmitted. All other acquired characteristics which depend on influences not affecting the sex-cells are not hereditarily transmitted (Weismann's theory). As an example of characteristics acquired through the influencing of the sex-cells, we may take the nutritional change resulting from the animal's moving into a new district or from changed life conditions. Resulting changes in the functions of the endocrine

[1] V. Bechterev : *Diseases of Personality ; Problems of the Study and Education of Personality*, 3rd vol.

[2] V. Bechterev : *The Biological Foundations of Expressive Movements* in *Vestnik Znania*, 1910, and published separately. St. Petersburg.

glands lead to change in the sex-cells. Another example : intense external influences which cause a considerable mimico-somatic reflex influencing the function of the endocrine glands and, consequently, also the function of the sex-glands and their secretion. We shall not cite other examples, but there are many.

There are also experimental investigations in regard to association or conditioned reflexes. (See Dr. Tzitovitch's *Dissertation*, St. Petersburg.) These investigations were carried out on dogs to elucidate the problem to what extent association reflexes are transmitted to posterity. The results, however, did not lead to an absolutely positive solution of this problem and the matter requires further elaboration. On the basis of Dr. Studentzov's investigations on mice, I can conclude, being guided by personal information from the investigator himself, that when association reflexes are fixed, there are transmitted to posterity, as was to be expected, not the acquired reflexes themselves, but a disposition to their more prompt formation under appropriate stimuli.

In regard to man, the elucidation of this question is complicated by the impossibility of performing experiments similar to those mentioned above on animals. Still, here too, science utilises facts derived from experiments made under certain circumstances. Thus, the problem of what belongs to the sphere of inherited phenomena and what to the sphere of acquired phenomena in the act of vision has, as we know, been elucidated by investigations on persons blind from birth and on whom operations have been performed. Here it has been shown that the distinguishing of visual objects is impossible without the appropriate practice necessary for the establishment of individual experience.

What belongs to the phenomena of higher brain activities acquired with participation of the auditory organ has been elucidated by special investigations and the education of those congenitally deaf, those who have become deaf-mutes, and also those who are blind-deaf-mutes. To what extent speech depends on individual experience is shown by the fact that, when an infant of one nationality is placed in a family of another nationality, he acquires, as his own, the language of the latter, but retains nothing of the speech of his parents and of that accent which characterises those who learn a strange language at a later age.

That man learns not only to speak, but also to walk and to manifest certain other activities, not by heredity, but by education is shown by the well-known case of Gasper Hans,[1] who, from his early childhood to the age of fourteen, was isolated from human society.

We also know that a child of some savage tribe, when it is placed in its infancy with a civilised family, acquires by education everything that is given to him by the new family, and does not betray the least sign of savagery. On the other hand, history shows that a slave's child, when educated in a family of free citizens, becomes just as freedom-

---

[1] *Translators' note :* The German translation, made from the 3rd ed., gives " Kaspar Hauser," for whom see *Encyc. Brit.*, 13th ed.

loving as his fellow-citizens and does not betray any signs of inherited slavery.

All these facts are universally known to an extent which would make it unnecessary to mention them here, if this problem had not been recently touched upon by the authoritative physiologist, Professor I. Pavlov (*Russky Vratch*, 1918), who, disregarding the long and instructive history of this important problem, solves it negatively. Professor Pavlov founds his conclusion exclusively on his observations of one lively dog, with abundant and spontaneous salivary secretion, and maintains of a similar dog that its peculiarties have not been duly accorded their proper scientific evaluation.

On the basis of the above-mentioned data, *i.e.* the observation of a dog, which secreted saliva spontaneously and which could not possibly inhibit the reflex, Pavlov posits a special " innate freedom reflex " and also gives the criterion of the innate reflex as one which is incapable of being extinguished or inhibited irrespective of any kind of other conditions. Needless to say, association or conditioned reflexes are usually easily inhibited, in contradistinction to the innate, which, if they are inhibited, are inhibited only with much greater difficulty. But it has been already proved on man, by the application of our method of investigation of the association-motor reflex, that also association, *i.e.* indubitably acquired reflexes, are characterised in some exceptional cases, to the extent to which they depend on the constitution, by amazing persistence, and cannot be inhibited even by the usual methods in the course of a considerable time. This fact has been demonstrated by Dr. Platonov's investigations (*Dissertation*) and by Dr. Vasilyeva's investigations in the laboratory supervised by me, and the latter has even made it the subject of a special paper.

It is clear from this that it is not possible to solve the problem of the innate character of a reflex merely on the basis of the inability of the usual methods to inhibit it, but it is necessary to turn in this case to an examination of the problem of its origin, for, only when we state the fact that the given reaction has originated independently of the animal's life conditions and of the external activities which have influenced it, have we the right to regard it as an innate reflex. Such are, in man, all complex-organic reflexes, the ligamental reflexes, many cutaneous reflexes produced by pricking and stroking stimuli, the so-called mechanical excitability of the muscles, the pupil and cornea reflexes, the reflexes of the visceral organs, tissue reflexes, etc.

When we read Professor I. Pavlov's paper, it is not difficult to see that the data which he cites in favour of the existence of an innate " freedom reflex " and a " slavery reflex " in dogs are absolutely inadequate ; we have still less reasons for extending these conclusions to man, who, according to Pavlov's statement, also possesses an innate " freedom reflex."

The opposite reflex—the " slavery " or " submission reflex," which is expressed in the dog by a cringing posture and by turning on its back, and

to which the kneeling posture in man is analogous—is, according to
I. Pavlov, an innate action both in the dog and in man. But also in this
case no appropriate evidence has been cited in regard to man. There is
only mention of the case of Kuprin's story of the student who became
implicated with the secret service (*ochranka*), who was the son of a parasitic
woman, and finally committed suicide.

Here the betrayal of his friends to the *ochranka* is, as it were, an expression of the innate slavery reflex inherited from the mother. Thus,
according to Professor I. Pavlov's doctrine, not only the dog, but also
man, is born with " freedom reflexes " and " slavery reflexes," and it is
possible to counteract these innate reflexes later by education.

It is unnecessary to criticise this view and we have dilated on it only
because of the authoritativeness of its exponent as a physiologist, and
because of the significance which he attaches to his discovery in the
sphere of social relations, as is obvious not only from the above-mentioned
statement about the unfortunate student supposed to have inherited the
" slavery reflex " from his mother, but also from the generalisation with
which the paper concludes.[1]

It is, however, indubitable that, apart from all cellular and tissue reflexes,
reflexes of the internal organs, and ordinary external reflexes, including
vocal reflexes, man at birth derives from his ancestors a general constitution, reflexive expressive movements, complex-organic reflexes (instincts),
special qualities or dispositions, a certain anthropological type (auditory,
visual, etc.), and greater or lesser giftedness.

As regards dispositions, we know that, from ancient times, the so-called
temperaments were distinguished into sanguine, choleric, melancholic,
and phlegmatic, and these were characterised according to subjective
indications.[2]

From the objective standpoint, the doctrine of temperaments has little
significance in that form in which it is usually propounded, but we must
not forget that, generally speaking, men enter life with dissimilar innate
constitutions.

Judging by external manifestations, we may so far distinguish the following human types : the quick, the slow, the aggressive (with aggressive
reflexes prevailing), the defensive (with defensive reflexes prevailing), the
alert (with alertness reflexes prevailing). Apart from these, we may distinguish special types : the auditory, the visual, the tactual-motor, to
say nothing of such subdivisions as, for instance, the sexual type.

In conclusion, let us mention that K. Kornilov (see *Doctrine of Human
Reactions—Utchenie o reaktziyach tcheloveka*, and his paper in *Voprosi
Truda—Problems of Work*, nos. 1 and 2, 1921) distinguishes seven funda-

---

[1] Let us note that, under the title of the paper, the exact date of the delivery
of the address to the Biological Society is given as November 1916, but it was not
delivered then because of the illness of a collaborator.

[2] K. Sotonin's book, *Temperamenti*, has been recently published (Kazan,
1921). This is based exclusively on the subjective attitude to the subject.

mental types of human reactions and calls them the scale of reactions. Corresponding to these, seven types of work-processes are assumed, as we have already mentioned. Two fundamental forms of reaction are characterised by the speed and the intensity of their occurrence, and by the form of the movement of the organ. These are the well-known sensory and motor reactions conditioned by difference in the direction of concentration. The work of the miner and the agricultural labourer comes under this type (our muscular type). The activities of a lathe-worker or watchmaker, a book-binder, a compositor, etc. (our sensory type) correspond to the sensory reaction. According to his opinion, we may distinguish, as special types, on the one hand, the sensory-passive type, which exhibits slow and weak reactions, and the sensory-active type, which exhibits slow and strong reactions (our slow type), and, on the other hand, the muscular-passive type, which exhibits quick and weak reactions, and the muscular-active type which exhibits quick and strong reactions (our quick type). In the same way, also all those engaged in work of any kind may be grouped by means of a chronoscope and a specially constructed dynamoscope, both of which make it possible to measure the expended energy in milligram-millimetres.

Kornilov has also investigated the capacity to pass from one type of reaction into the other. It has been discovered that the ease with which the slow type pass over to quickened reactions is proportional to the difficulty with which the fast type pass over to slow. Thus, the slow (sensory) attitude is the less stable and, on the contrary, the quickened (muscular), the more stable.

As regards its dynamic side, the passive attitude is the least stable and those characterised by it comparatively easily change from a weak reaction to an active one. On the contrary, the active attitude is more stable and the transition from it to the passive mode of reaction presents greater difficulties.

Kornilov remarks, as a result of his investigations, that the transition from mental work to physical is easier than the reverse process.

The special interest of these investigations cannot be denied, but it is regrettable that they are not devoid of subjective colouring (sensory, sensory-passive, and sensory-active types). It would be of the highest importance to know to what extent these types may be regarded as associated with innate conditions, for instance with the so-called constitution, or whether they are acquired under the influence of the development of a certain facility by exercise. In any case, there is foundation for the supposition that innate dispositions are not without some significance here.

CHAPTER IX

Natural association reflexes with the external characteristics of ordinary reflexes. Inhibitory conditions in the development of reflexes. Every area in the cortex is an area of association reflexes. Orientation, defence, and aggression reflexes.

EXPERIENCE shows, however, that a distinction between both kinds of reflexes cannot be drawn so sharply as might at first have appeared possible. There is a group of reflexes usually regarded as innate, which exhibit the characteristic peculiarities of association reflexes. Let as take the defensive reflex of the eye. Everybody knows that, if a threatening gesture of the hand is made before the eyes of another man or if we obtrude some object close to his eyes, the man blinks. But this reflex quickly weakens on repeated stimulation and in the end disappears completely, but it reappears after a time. In this respect the defence reflex of the eye has all the peculiarities of those reflexes which we call association reflexes, and which, being inculcated by exercise, are gradually inhibited, and disappear on frequent repetition, but then revive in time—a phenomenon which we do not observe in simple reflexes, as, for instance, the patellar, the ligamental, and other reflexes.

Guided by what has been said, we have every reason to regard the defence reflex of the eye as an association reflex, but one which has been inculcated under natural conditions, in other words, a natural association reflex. The fact that this reflex cannot be observed in new-born infants is a confirmation of this.

There is reason to suppose also that some tactual reflexes, which are regarded as ordinary reflexes, must be regarded as natural association reflexes, which develop in dependence on certain anatomo-physiological conditions. Such are, for instance, some cutaneous reflexes. These reflexes, too, are distinguished by the peculiarity that, on repetition, they are often inhibited to some extent and sometimes even disappear completely, but revive after some time.

A proof of the statement that these are natural association reflexes may be seen in the fact that these reflexes manifest themselves only when aroused by stimuli issuing from other individuals. Such reflexes as the defence eye reflex, the tickling reflex, and some cutaneous reflexes cease completely, when the same stimuli issue from the subject's own hand. It is clear that they are associated with the action of an external person and have been inculcated in the course of life as defence reflexes against external stimulation.

It is well known that cutaneous defence reflexes are evoked on definite somatic zones which we call reflexogenetic. This may be explained by appropriate anatomo-physiological conditions. But when the irritability is heightened, the reflexogenetic zones usually become much more extensive suddenly and, as a consequence, defence reflexes may be produced in zones which usually do not serve as localities where cutaneous reflexes may develop.

On the other hand, external cutaneous stimuli produce in infants a multitude of reflexes which are gradually weakened and, in the end, become confined to certain zones.

It is obvious that, as we grow up, inhibitory conditions begin to prevail gradually and, as a consequence, many reflexes are suppressed.

It may be thought that aggression reflexes, which are so highly developed in infancy, are, in the course of time, suppressed still more than are the defence. But while aggression reflexes are usually inhibited in adults, they are easily released from inhibition under appropriate conditions of brain activity, and especially on the direction of concentration to the zone stimulated.

Thus, for instance, the movement of the eyes in the direction of food remains inhibited until active concentration is directed on the need for food.

Lastly, the defence or protective and aggressive association reflexes, which develop on a certain receptive surface, are established in a natural way in life experience.

Let us take the organ of vision. The process of seeing is conditioned by the light-stimulus falling on the different parts of the retina and also on the *fovea centralis* ; and thus, causing a light-effect of varied intensity, the light-stimulation serves as the source of a reflex which, under the influence, from one side or the other, of a moderate light-stimulus acting favourably on the retina, results in an appropriate turning of the eyes, so as to place the more sensitive *fovea* opposite the light. This reflex of turning the eyes is, as observation shows, present in man from the day of birth, but in the form of a slow, intermittent movement of the eyes to the source of light.

As regards the appropriate establishment of accommodation, it cannot be perfect in an infant from the very first. But gradually, on the movement of the eyes for the purpose of accommodation, a reflex is established in the form of a definite contraction of the accommodative muscle in regard to the spatial situation of the object focused. It is this process which is manifested when the orientation visual reflex in the form of seeing is being realised.

The auditory, olfactory, gustatory, tactual, static, and other orientation reflexes are established after the manner of visual orientation reflexes.

Let us explain here that orientation association reflexes are those as a result of which any local stimulation is associated either with a certain form and measure of movement or with the mobilisation of the receptive organ and its vascular and secretory effects, this association serving the more favourable utilisation of the stimulation by leading to the focusing of the receptive organ on the object.

If the stimulus, because of its intensity and other peculiarities, should act harmfully on the organ itself, defence or protective reflexes are developed.

Thus we understand by defence reflexes such reflexes as manifest themselves in the appropriate organs and are established by life experience for the purpose of the defence of the receptive organ from harmful influences. Such are, for instance, the shutting of the eyes in strong light, blinking on the approach of a hand to the eyes, the jerking back of the hand when pricked, etc.[1]

As regards the aggression reflexes, first of all the orientation reflexes must be classed among them, next reflexes of attack, seizing, approach to the source of stimulation, etc. They develop under the influence of stimuli which act favourably on the receptive organ and, in general, on the whole organism.

Simple association reflexes are those in which the reflex is produced directly after the stimulation without any other complicating processes. For example : the threat of a prick—scream. Those reflexes, in which there is a series or complex of various reflexes associated with certain conditions of past experience, are more complex. The inhibition of reflexes must also be regarded, in the majority of cases, as an association reflex. Thus it seems that a stimulus should evoke an appropriate effect, but past experience has associated this stimulus with an inhibitory reaction, and therefore the effect is not produced, just as past experience may associate this stimulus with a defensive movement and we get defence instead of aggression. For instance, a dog reacts by barking to its reflection in the mirror, but a more experienced dog does not do so ; a child stretches

---

[1] Sleep, which is characterised by general inhibition in the form of the temporary loss of a number of reflexes of the higher order, must be also regarded as a kind of defence or protective reflex inhibitory in character—a reflex which has been biologically evolved for the purpose of protecting the brain from further poisoning by the products of metabolism, and which may be evoked, as an association reflex, under conditions of fatigue (for instance, the falling asleep at a certain hour, etc.). By the way, this view agrees with the views of Claparède on this subject. But it must be kept in mind that there is a complex mechanism which lies at the basis of sleep. Doubtlessly, a rôle is also played by the bio-chemical processes which lead to the production of hypnotoxin (Legendre and Piéron) inhibiting the activity of the cortex in the frontal regions of the brain, and so causing corresponding changes in the cellular elements. The theory of the separation of the cellular projections of the cortex as a cause of sleep (Duval's famous histological theory) has been exploded by Stefanovskaya, although V. M. Narbut's investigations in my laboratory are rather in favour of the contraction of the cellular projections during sleep. Besides, it is necessary to take into account that sleep is associated not with functional change in the cortex alone, but also with functional change in the diencephalon, as has been already pointed out by Mauthner (Trömner—the so-called sleep-centre) and has been confirmed by cases of so-called sleepy sickness (encephalitis lethargica). See in regard to this Fr. Luckasch's paper in the *Zeitschrift fur d. ges. Neurologie*, Bd. 39, H. 1–21. In general, the nature of sleep has not yet been finally discovered. Thus E. Küppers (*Zeitschrift f. d. ges. Neurologie & Psychiatrie*, Bd. LXXV, Hft. 1–2), adopting the bio-chemical theory which posits the development of toxic deposits as a result of fatigue, has recently maintained that the latter act stimulatingly on the nerve fibres of the vegetative nervous system (*binnenvegetative Nervenfasern*) which end in the brain in the central grey matter, and that, as a result, the vegetative system is separated from the central system and that inner parasympathetic system which serves the large visceral organs.

out his hand to his reflection in the mirror, but an adult, as he is guided by past experience, inhibits this reaction ; a child stretches towards the fire and may be burned, but an adult duly withdraws his hand from the flame.

We know further that the association reflexes in the motor system of certain organs have as stimuli not only those which issue from the receptive surface of that same organ, but also those from other receptive surfaces which are connected with the former as a result of the associative connections of the brain cortex. Such are, for example, the turning of the eyes in a certain direction at a sound coming from a certain point in space, listening towards the spot where we have seen some living thing moving, smelling to a bottle at sight of the label which denotes that it has contained, or still contains, eau-de-Cologne.

It is obvious that we are here concerned with the co-ordination of the association-reflex activity of the cortical areas—an activity which establishes an interrelation between the acquired reflexes of a different kind, whether they are aggression or defence reflexes. We know of a similar co-ordination in regard to complex-organic reflexes transmitted by heredity.

It is a biological fact that certain insects prepare food useless to themselves, but necessary for their pupal posterity which they will never see, as they themselves have not seen their parents.

Thus, for example, the sphex, by stinging a beetle, paralyses it, drags it to its larva, and places it so that the perforated point of its body is close to the larva's mouth. In this way, the sphex makes it possible for the larva to suck the juices out of the beetle. Here we are obviously concerned with the insect's reproduction of its own experience on the larval stage of its development and with the transference of this experience on to its larva. The reproduction of the manner in which the larva feeds is realised in the adult stage of the insect in accordance with such conditions of feeding as have been previously experienced, and, as a result of this reproduction, posterity is supplied with food. Such is my explanation of this instinctive reflex. It is impossible to explain the fact otherwise.

We know, further, that young bees, having freed themselves from the cocoon, are already capable of gathering honey and building cells. They require no education. There is question here not only of inborn tendencies to work, of attraction by certain fragrances of flowers, an attraction arising from the reproduction of larval life conditions, but also of the imitation of adult bees.

A fly, having grown from a larva placed in putrid meat, itself during the egg-laying period looks for rotten meat in which, guided by smell, it deposits its eggs. This sense of smell, however, may be deceived and, as a result, the fly has been often known to lay its eggs on the fœnopodium fœtidum, a plant which smells like putrid meat.

Also a hen, at the egg-laying period, reproduces the period of brooding, which, during her development, she has experienced from her mother and she obeys an organic impulse which ties her down to her eggs for a long period. Here, too, instinct, guided by past experience and cutaneous stimulations, may be deceived, if other eggs, or even smooth round stones, are substituted for hens' eggs.

I repeat that, in these and similar cases, under appropriate organic conditions associated with a certain condition of the organism and under external influences of an appropriate kind, there is reproduction of an experience from the larval period or an initial period of development.

In other cases, there may be even the reproduction of ancestral experience.

We know that a migratory bird, which has never flown and has grown up in a cage, begins to be very restless and flutters in its cage at the migration period, and that a salmon, which should go to spawn at a certain time, jumps out of the tank. Observations of the reaction, which our domestic animals experience in regard to wild animals which they have never seen before, afford convincing examples of how the reproduction of ancestral experience by posterity occurs in the animal kingdom. We know what restlessness horses show at the sight of a chained bear. Birds, when they see a hawk for the first time in their life, show still greater distress. Here is a characteristic story illustrating this : " A young turkey, which I brought home when it was still chirping in its intact shell, was picking food from my hand on the tenth morning of its life, when suddenly a young vulture shut up in a cage uttered a shrill cry : ' ship, ship, ship ! ' The poor turkey shot like an arrow to the other end of the room and remained there without uttering a sound and motionless with fear, until the vulture cried again ; then it jumped through the open door to the very end of the corridor, where, bunched and trembling, it huddled itself into a corner. It heard the same alarming cries several times in the course of the day and each time exhibited the same fear."[1] There is no necessity to cite analogous examples, of which there are a countless number.

These facts are explained by the persistent transmission, through numbers of generations, of the appropriate reactions which are stamped in the nerve centres of the ancestors by their experience, and take the form of a particular tendency or predisposition to similar reactions under appropriate conditions, just as man inherits certain tendencies.

Everything said above shows that we have in correlative activity a certain natural analysis characterised by a selective principle in reactions to the external world. Even in the vegetable kingdom we come across the simplest analysis with the character of selection, for the insectivorous plant, dionæa, gives preference to certain of the bodies coming into contact with it. The amœba's feeding on organic particles is also selective. No subjectivist will dare to maintain unflinchingly that this is conscious selection. In any case, this is a reaction of just the same character as that which we observe on higher planes of the animal kingdom.

By what is selection conditioned in general and on the very lowest

[1] Ch. Letourneaux : *L'évolution de la morale ;* Russian trans., p. 4 ;   St. Petersburg.

biological plane in particular ? Obviously by the preference of that stimulus which is most favourable to the given life conditions and, consequently, this stimulus is capable of producing an appropriate aggressive reaction, while stimuli unfavourable to the life conditions produce a defensive reaction, but stimuli indifferent in this respect produce none.

Thus we have, as one of the fundamental manifestations of a living being, the capacity to react unequally to different external influences, some of which may produce a favourable effect on the organism, others an unfavourable. At the same time, both favourable and unfavourable stimuli, though different in nature, are linked together by their capacity to produce the same reaction when they act on the organism, but this is synthesis.

When an object is explored by touch, we have both selection and co-ordination or synthesis of muscular contraction in accordance with the form of the given object and the resistance created by this object. But this is a primary orientation, cutaneo-muscular association reflex based on experience. The same is observed in seeing, hearing, etc. We know, further, that the muscles adjust the intensity of the contraction to the intensity of the resistance and analyse it, as it were. This adjustment is also conditioned by appropriate selection and, on the other hand, every weight acts on the muscles, as on any elastic body, by stretching them and at the same time exciting their contractility. But here, too, we are concerned with the co-ordination of muscular contraction with the weight of the object.

It is clear from what has been said that all motor reflexes, in respect of the conditions of their stimulation, may be divided into visual, auditory, olfactory, gustatory, tactual, muscular, and somatic association-motor reflexes.

The last-mentioned complex of reflexes, being genetically the oldest, arises under the influence of inner somatic influences usually leading to organic needs. This complex represents the fundamental group to which all other groups of reflexes are subsidiary, and this because organic needs mobilise, when necessary, all other reflexes for the achievement of that biological satisfaction which secures the defence of the organism against destruction. Thus, under the guidance of active concentration, the complex of somatically conditioned reflexes, which consists of a series of active movements aggressive or defensive in character, directs the latter towards certain objects in the external world and simultaneously requisitions a series of reflexes evoked through other perceptive organs—those of vision, hearing, touch, etc. Moreover, as a result of the participation of active concentration, not only the somatic association-motor reflexes, but also other reflexes which form a nexus with them may be reproduced, through the same active concentration, together with a group of somatically conditioned association-motor reflexes, a group which may be always revived independently under the influence of inner causes. Besides, man can, at any moment, give an appropriate account of all such reflexes as a result of their established connection with the somatic sphere and he does so through speech or symbolic reflexes, but he cannot do so in the case of a number of other reflexes which have not formed a nexus with the somatically conditioned association-motor reflexes.

It is clear from what has been said that correlative activity, executed with the participation of the cerebral cortex, is a complex co-ordination of more or less differentiated association-motor, -vascular, and -secretory reflexes, the forms and laws of the manifestation of which, co-existent with a certain inherited constitution of the organism, constitute the subject-matter of the science which I call reflexology.

CHAPTER X

Complex-organic or instinctive reflexes. Their difference from other association reflexes. Examples and discussion. The origin of organic reflexes.

A S we have seen, there are, in the animal kingdom, complex reflexes which bear indubitable characteristics of the nature of innate or inherited reflexes, for their general direction does not depend on individual experience; but, on the other hand, the external manifestations of these reflexes usually bear, in certain aspects, the characteristics of acquired association reflexes. We shall call these reflexes, usually termed instinctive, complex-organic reflexes.

Although animal psychologists maintain that instincts are executed by some special mechanism which differs from the reflexive mechanism, there is no reason to distinguish this mechanism from the mechanism of reflex movements; yet it must be kept in mind that the source of these reflexes is not external, but internal. And as instincts may be inhibited by inner conditions, it happens that, under the same external conditions, they may manifest themselves in one case and be absent in another. This is not possible in the case of simple reflexes. Thus, the instinct of nutrition manifests itself when the blood becomes impoverished, and is absent on satiation; the sex instinct is evoked under the influence of the elaboration and accumulation of sex products, and is weakened or ceases to be evoked after coitus, etc. It is clear that there is question of the changing composition of the blood and that this acts directly on the centres by automatically exciting them, as has been proved by experiment (for instance, according to Steinach's experiments, the injection of an extract from the mid-brain of the male green-frog stimulates the embrace reflex). Professor Vasilyev[1] agrees with me in regarding simple reflexes and automatism as insufficient for the initial realisation of instinctive acts. He distinguishes a chain of reflex acts: for instance, under the influence of the stimulating activity of increasing improverishment of the blood, the animal abandons its state of rest and manifests the aggressive food reflex in the form of searching movements of the lips. When the lips are stimulated by the nipple, the act of sucking ensues and is accompanied by a new stimulus—milk, which leads to the reflex of feeding. Lastly, the imbibed food products annul the impoverishment of the blood, and the animal returns to its starting-point.

In my opinion, we have here a manifestation of the general biological law of interaction between stimuli and organism. One stimulus— improverished blood—leads to the aggressive act of sucking for the purpose of the utilisation of the source of food, and this utilisation inhibits the act of sucking according to the degree of satiation.

There is reason to believe that, although the basis of these reflexes lies in the inherited organic nature of the living being, their realisation, in many cases and especially on the higher levels of the animal world,

[1] Address at a Session of the Conference for the Study of Brain, in 1923, Leningrad.

occurs to a certain extent under the guidance of past individual experience. Thus, what is known by the name of instinct and is inherited reflexes develops in dependence on organic conditions and is, as it were, in its nature, the middle link between ordinary reflexes and association reflexes in the true sense of the word.

The fact that, contrary to the opinion of some writers, the so-called instincts are not something completely unchangeable in their manifestations is explained by the participation of individual experience in the execution of instinctive activities. As a matter of fact, examples of the variability of instincts may be cited. Thus, according to Evans, many birds have, within living memory, made great progress in the art of building and have invented new and improved methods of nest-building. Such progress is specially noticeable in Californian swallows from the time of the settling of emigrants in that country. In all cases, the younger generation utilised the knowledge acquired by the elders, and so improvement in building methods has become an inherited accomplishment of the species. For instance, in places where they were specially subject to attacks from quarrelsome sparrows, they began to close the aperture in front of the nest, but, instead, made an entrance at the back, near the wall. In some cases, this purely protective and defensive change in the structure of the nest was adopted by all swallows in the district after its utility had been tested in the case of one nest. In a similar way, the oriole, finding that the branch from which its nest hung was too weak to hold the weight of all the young ones, fastened it, as Dr. Abst assures us, to the upper branch by means of a structure of loops and twigs. The Baltimore oriole adapts the material and the structure of its nest to the demands of the climate. In southern states, it selects the site of its nest on the northern side of the tree, and builds it of the very flimsy Spanish moss and without a lining, so that the air can circulate freely. More to the north, it selects sunny spots and uses soft material for lining. The same bird now uses cotton and woollen fabric, instead of vegetable material, for its nest (Evans : *Evolutionary Ethics*).

In the majority of cases, these organic reflexes differ from ordinary reflexes by their complexity also, as they are expressed in a certain peculiar character of the animal's behaviour, a character conditioned by its organic nature, while ordinary reflexes, including physiological automatism, have the character of a simple activity (jerking back of the foot, respiratory movements, the secretory activities of glands, etc.).

As regards association reflexes, their complexity may be very different, beginning from the simple reproduction of an ordinary reflex, consequently of some simple activity, and ending with complex activities, which consist of a series of separate reflexes connected by conditions of the achievement of a definite aim.

If we compare complex-organic or instinctive reflexes, in the form of definite behaviour transmitted by heredity, with association reflexes in the form of complex activities, *i.e.* also behaviour, but behaviour which is being adjusted to the most varying external conditions, we may still discover no inconsiderable difference between them.

When there is question of complex-organic or instinctive activities, the aim is reached as a result of organic conditions hereditarily transmitted, and this aim is accomplished chiefly through the mediation of an inherited mechanism, but partly, at least in the higher animals and in man, also by means of movements acquired by life experience, and guided by an organic impulse hereditarily transmitted. In complex activities, however, the aim appears as a result of past individual experience or is derived from the experience of others and, as a result of experience, it may be achieved, in dependence on circumstances, by various methods.

This is why stereotypy and hard-and-fast sequence are so striking in instinct, while in complex movements, in the form of association reflexes, only a general guidance by a definite aim derived from past individual experience is to be detected, but the achievement of the aim is ever changing in dependence on external conditions and under the guidance of past experience.

An example of complex-organic reflexes, which are very extensively found throughout the animal world, is the squirrel which has been taken out of its nest, separated from its parents, brought up in a room, and, towards the end of the summer, begins to hide nuts under the carpet somewhere in the corner. As another example we may take migratory birds. Some of these migrate singly, as we know. Submitting merely to a natural tendency, they start southwards at a certain time of the year and without any guidance as to the direction, while, at another time, they go northwards.

Take bees or bumble-bees, which cannot distinguish objects at a distance of a few feet, as has been proved by special experiments ; confine them in a box and carry them a long distance from the nest, for instance several miles ; dye their wings a special colour, so as to distinguish them, and then let them out of the box, and after a short time you will find them in their nest again. Analogous experiments with pigeons give the same result.

In all these cases animal behaviour cannot be explained by means of ordinary reflexes, for these are elementary activities realised in a too stereotyped and stencilled manner, as is not the case here. Neither are they association reflexes, for the fundamental tendency is not the result of life (individual) experience. However, it may be definitely maintained that impulses leading inevitably to a definite aim (the squirrel's tendency to store nuts for the winter, the searching for warmth by migratory birds in autumn, the finding of the old place of abode by means of circular flights, etc.) are hereditarily transmitted, but the realisation of the inherited impulse occurs to some extent by means of actions derived from individual experience (the squirrel's using the carpet instead of dry leaves, the young birds' imitation of the old during migration, etc.).

As regards man, we encounter in his life three main organic reflexes—

L

self-preservation, nutrition, and propagation. And again we may say with full certainty that the basis of these instincts is the organic conditions hereditarily transmitted (biological dissatisfaction and the tendency to procure food when one is hungry, the lack of outlet for sex products, and the tendency to secure outlet through the mediation of the opposite sex, etc.), and that the reflex is realised by movements and actions which are partly inherited in the form of mechanism and partly derived from individual experience.

We shall not discuss here the family-social " instinct," for we have said everything necessary about it in another place.[1] We shall only remark that, in the form of the family instinct, it is inculcated and developed with the mother's milk, as it were, for the mother is the first companion of every new-born child ; later, this instinct develops and is perfected by the unintermittent influence of the social environment.

We shall not touch here on the question of the origin of organic reflexes. Their origin, like that of all reflexes, may be explained by natural selection, which fixes in the offspring variations which arise somehow or other and bear the character of adaptive reactions. In this sense, they are essentially a result of racial experience extending over generations. The latest data of biology prove a striking tendency to the development of reflexes in the offspring of parents who have acquired the same reflexes through experience. Not entering into the details of this subject which have been discussed by me elsewhere,[2] we shall only note that the ambling to which the Arabs train their horses is, in some cases, as maintained by experts in this sphere, very easily acquired by the offspring. The training of some Bologna dogs to fetch and carry is so easy that they appear to learn it effortlessly from their earliest days. The pointing of spaniels and setters is sometimes acquired without special training. Tendencies proper to their kind are manifested in other dogs, as for instance sheep-dogs, watch-dogs, and divers. We have elsewhere mentioned experiments on mice. These facts give the clue to the explanation of the origin of instincts, which are chain reflexes. The fundamental impulse for these reflexes always comes, as we know, from organic stimulations (lack of food, warmth, etc.), and is, therefore, a stimulus hereditarily transmitted which brings certain centres into operation. These centres mobilise the muscular apparatus so as to remove conditions unfavourable to the organism (defensive or aggressive movements adapted to the purpose mentioned). All of this belongs to the category of pure reflex. But as such a reflex manifests itself in certain, though changing, life conditions, association reflexes supplement this organic reflex, and these association reflexes are repeated with certain frequency and so create hereditarily transmitted

---

[1] V. Bechterev : *Objective Psychology*, 3rd part.
[2] See V. Bechterev : *The Psychic and Life*, St. Petersburg. A bibliography of this subject is given in Dr. Tzitovitch's *Dissertation*. See also my work, *Zoo-reflexology as a Scientific Doctrine*, etc. ; in *Problems of the Study and Education of Personality*, 2nd vol. and 4–5, St. Petersburg.

tendencies to execute the act in a certain direction. In this sense, we must consider the extension of the theory of heredity, which transmits to posterity not only innate qualities, but also fixes frequently repeated individual experience in the form of a tendency or predisposition. There can be no doubt that in man, too, we have the hereditary transmission not only of constitution, but also of greater or lesser giftedness and talents, and even of certain tendencies, in accordance with the laws of Mendelism. If this hereditary transmission does not manifest itself so simply in man as in the animal world, this is explained merely by the considerably greater individual differences between men. The following fact may, perhaps, serve as an example of the transmission of a disposition in man to the retention in the offspring of reflexes acquired by the parent : on the Polynesian Islands, the consumption of human flesh is, according to the accounts of travellers, strictly prohibited to women ; as a result of this, the latter, in contrast to men, always react to it with organic disgust. Moreover, for a few days they avoid those men who have taken part in orgies where human flesh has been consumed. Similar examples are encountered even in the life of cultured peoples.

CHAPTER XI

General plan of the structure of the nervous system and the area of the development of ordinary, association, and complex-organic reflexes in the nervous system.

LET us now turn to the problem of the area of development of reflexse in general. But first let us say a few words concerning the structure and functions of the nervous system.

We may divide the whole nervous system into the vegetative, the para-vegetative, and the animal. The first, in the form of a tissue system represented by intratextural cells and ganglia, serves the nutrition and the functions of the tissues, by supplying with fibres the blood-vessels, the tissue itself, and the glands. The animal nervous system has for its main function to serve the peripheral receptive, as well as the external motor, organs, the locomotion of the body, and the utilisation of the bodily organs as instruments (movement of the foot, the hand, etc.). The visceral or paravegetative system,[1] which serves the visceral organs of the body, such as the respiratory organs, the esophagus, the stomach, the intestinal canal, the bladder, the uro-genetial organs, etc., must be regarded as a special branch of the animal system. Thus, instead of the sympathetic, parasympathetic, and central nervous systems, formerly so-called, we shall distinguish the fundamental tissue nervous system, which serves the organic interstitial spaces ; the visceral nervous system, which serves the inner surfaces or cavities of the body ; and the animal nervous system which serves the external surfaces of the body. The first nervous system is the oldest phylogenetically and may be discovered even in some infusoria ; the second nervous system presupposes the development of permanent inner cavities intended for the organism's vegetative functions and is more recent phylogenetically ; and, lastly, the animal nervous system, which begins its development with the appearance of permanent organs of movement in the form of instruments, and with which the visceral nervous system enters into close correlation, must be regarded as still more recent phylogenetically.

The vegetative nervous system has the peripheral cells and ganglia as its chief centres and, therefore, manifests its activity in the form of reflexes, even when the tissues are completely severed (for example, ideo-muscular excitability, some reflexes which are manifested during the severing of organs from the body, contractions of isolated parts of the body, etc.).

In order to establish connections with the other divisions of the nervous system, the vegetative system has its own centres in the cerebro-spinal axis, and these centres are placed in the closest proximity to the cerebro-spinal canal and take the form of the so-called central grey matter, beginning from the central *substantia gelatinosa* in the spinal cord and extending upwards through the grey matter of the base of the fourth ventricle and of the aqueduct of Sylvius up to, and including, the grey central matter of the third ventricle. Along the whole of this route are situated secondary

[1] Küppers : *Zeitschr. f. d. ges. Neurologie u. Psychiatrie*, Bd. 75, Berlin, 1922.

vegetative centres, which are connected with peripheral tissue ganglia serving the tissue functions and are, at the same time, mediators in the transmission, by means of reflexes, of stimulations, developing in the tissues, to the peripheral tissue cells and ganglia.[1]

The visceral nervous system has special centres in the form of special peripheral ganglia, which are inlaid in the walls of the inner cavities or near them and which condition, in the innervated organs, vitally necessary co-ordinated reflexive movements. These movements occur with the participation of centres in the cerebro-spinal axis, centres which are isolated parts of the central grey matter ; such are the nuclei *n. vagi* in the medulla oblongata, the nuclei *n. phrenici, n. splanchnici*, of the cervical *sympathicus* (the centre of Budge in the area of the lateral horn, at the level of the first thoracic pair) ; *n. erigentis* in the spinal cord. These centres are in direct correlation with the animal system, but are subject to the latter only in proportion to the influence of external stimuli on the visceral organs, stimuli received by special receptive organs.

Lastly, the animal nervous system, in turn, consists of two systems—(1) the lower or fundamental, which is derived, in the form of special ganglia, from the same central matter of the cerebro-spinal axis and secures the lower co-ordinated reflexes for the external receptive organs ; and (2) the higher system which is represented by the hemispheres of the cerebrum and cerebellum. To the former system belong the ventral horns of the spinal cord, the nuclei of the medulla oblongata and of those parts of the brain which lie higher, the cerebellum, the mesencephalon or corp. quadrigeminum ; and the diencephalon or thalamus opticus. To the second or higher system belong the cortex of the cerebrum with the

---

[1] It has been proved, in accordance with my theory (see *The Study of the Nervous Centres*, 3rd vol.), by the latest investigations by one of my pupils (A. G. Molotkov), that the trophic function of tissues is conditioned by a reflex transmitted along the centripetal paths and through the centres of the spinal cord to the periphery, by means of the nearest nerve supplying the same area. As a result of this, old ulcerous processes, which do not heal for a long time and which are a result of traumatic affection of some nerve, heal quickly (in the course of a few days or two to three weeks) after the severing of the centripetal conductor and its subsequent suture above the affected nerve area ; also other chronic ulcerous processes, not excluding osteomyelitis, heal quickly through the same operation carried out on the upper regions of the centripetal conductor or on the dorsal radices which correspond to this conductor. Even processes of new formation accompanied by processes of decomposition, as, for instance, cancer, are known to be healed by the same operation. Thus it is clear that trophic processes in the external coats and in tissues connective in type are subject to reflexive influence with participation of the centres of the spinal cord. The remarkable fact here is that, in the case of bilateral ulcerous processes in tissues, the severing of the nerve on one side is sufficient for the healing process to appear on both sides. If we take into consideration that the nutrition of muscles is known to depend on nervous impulses transmitted through the spinal cord, but through the mediation of its ventral radices, it is clear that the formation of tissues in higher animals stands in direct dependence on reflexes, but reflexes of the lower order, or simple reflexes, in other words, inherited or racial reflexes.

corpus striatum (the so-called neo-striatum, with its two members—*n. caudatus* and *putamen*). The centres of the first, *i.e.* the lower, division of the animal system are phylogenetically the older. These are the only centres of the animal system in amphioxus lanceolatus. The higher centres—the brain cortex with the corpus striatum (neo-striatum)—develop later.

In view of the fact that the animal nervous system effects various and complex co-ordinated reflexes, including the complex activities of man, we are concerned here with a number of co-ordinated centres, of which the highest in function are the cortical areas. The middle centres are those of the mesencephalon and the diencephalon, together with the cerebellum which develops in supplementary fashion as the organ of equilibratory co-ordination. The lowest centres are those of the ventral horns of the spinal cord and the nuclei of the medulla oblongata.

The higher areas of the animal nervous system are, in turn, co-ordinated with the cortex and nuclei of the cerebellum, which serve the function of animal locomotion (statics and dynamics), and with other ganglia, the cortex of the cerebrum, in association with lower centres, establishing a correlation of the organism with the environment on the basis of individual experience and, consequently, executing all more or less complex acquired association reflexes.

As a result of this, all functions, which are innervated by the vegetative or tissue nervous system and also by the visceral and the fundamental or lower animal systems, and which are somehow concerned in the execution of acquired association reflexes, stand in a certain co-ordination with the cortex of the cerebrum—the fundamental area of the development of association reflexes ; for the rest, the above-mentioned areas of the nervous system are independent nervous apparatus, the dependence of which on the cortex of the cerebrum is less, according as the functions which they perform participate to a lesser extent in the realisation of acquired association reflexes.

It has been mentioned already that association-motor and other reflexes in man and in higher animals are, as experiments show, reflexes which occur with the participation of the cerebral cortex. At least, the contrary has not been proved in the case of higher animals. (We do not refer here to the lower.) It is true that other reflexes also, which we are accustomed to regard as ordinary, develop in the cortex. Such are the nail and the hair reflex in dogs, blinking (under threat), and some local cutaneous reflexes. But as we have already mentioned, there is reason to suppose that these are natural association reflexes, which develop at an early age simultaneously with life experience and arise under the influence of appropriate exercise.

Thus, the sympathetic ganglia are the area of development of the primary vegetative reflexes. The spinal cord and the subcortical ganglia must be regarded as the area of development of ordinary-simple, and ordinary-complex reflexes, but the cerebral cortex is the surface which serves as the area of development of association-motor reflexes. This, however, does not at all exclude the participation of the subcortical regions of the brain in the development of association reflexes, as is obvious without further explanation.

It must be noted that, in regard to the orientation association reflexes in man, which are evoked by complex external stimuli, it may be regarded as established that they begin to develop from the very day of birth in many animals, and that, in the infant, too, they may be posited from the first few days after birth, and, on the basis of a number of pathological data, it has been proved that visual impulses are transmitted to the sub-cortical regions through the mediation of the occipital lobes of the cerebral cortex. Auditory stimuli are also transmitted to the sub-cortical regions through the mediation of the temporal lobes of the cerebral cortex, and chiefly through the mediation of the gyrus of Heschl, and of a part of the superior temporal gyrus. Analogous data apparently are to be found in regard to other kinds of stimuli. Thus, cutaneous and muscular stimuli produce reflexes through the mediation of the postcentral and præcentral gyri. The same is true also of the olfactory cortex in the *lob. olfactorius*, and *g. uncinatus*, and of the taste cortex in the region of the upper coat (operculum).[1]

These data determine the afferent aspect of a number of association reflexes, which, in accordance with the character of the stimulus, is localised in the occipital, temporal, and central lobes ; in the upper coat ; and in the olfactory areas of the cerebral cortex.

In the same areas of the cortex there is also the efferent aspect, by means of which the appropriate orientation reflex, under the influence of visual, auditory, tactual-muscular, gustatory, and olfactory stimuli, is realised. There is a mutual functional connection between the areas of the cortex ordained for the realisation of orientation association reflexes, as has been proved by clinical observations. A particularly close connection exists between visual and tactual orientation reflexes. Thus, Goldstein thoroughly investigated a man suffering from psychic blindness and the complete loss of visual imagery.[2] (*Zeitschr. f. d. ges. Neur. u. Psych.*, 1918.[3]) The essence of Goldstein's conclusion is : (1) In those whose

---

[1] The localisation of the taste centre in the region of operculum was first established by me in 1900 ; now it has been authoritatively confirmed, as may be seen from the following words of K. Goldstein : " The taste centre was formerly localised almost universally near the olfactory centre, and this is certainly not correct. The recent investigations of my Boernstein Institute leave no doubt that the localisation of the taste centre in the operculum, as Bechterev had already assumed in 1900, is perfectly justified. The proximity of the taste area in the lower region of the postcentral gyrus, the masseter centres in the corresponding area of the præcentral gyrus, and the gyrus of Heschl may here lead to a characteristic triad of indications, as the centre of operation is fairly small."

[2] In order to render the text accurately, we preserve the author's subjective terminology.

[3] *Translators' note :* The German translation has : *Zeitschr. f. Psychol. u. Physiol. d. Sinnesorg.*, Bd. 83, 1920.

vision is normal, the complete loss of visual images removes the capacity for spatial localisation of objects, and this holds good for all the activities of the spatial sense and for the capacity to distinguish two points, as well as the form and extent of areas touched. (2) The complete loss of visual images destroys the perception of separate limbs and the perception of passive movements, notwithstanding the retention of sensations of active movement. (3) The loss of visual images destroys the capacity to execute deliberate movements without looking at the moving limbs. (4) Sensations experienced through the skin are not qualitatively different and, in general, afford no local indications. (5) The normal person localises visual images by means of kinesthetic processes associated with them, processes which, though they do not reach consciousness, yet are necessary, in as far as they represent local indications. (6) The impairment of spatial sensation of the skin, in spite of the integrity of the sensory apparatus, an impairment arising from the loss of visual images, must be regarded as transcortical impairment of sensibility. (7) In spite of the integrity of the sensory apparatus, there was, in the given case, a certain lowering of sensibility for touch or pressure, and this lowering gave the impression of a peculiar sensory impairment. However, this destruction of the spatial sensation of the skin does not occur when the subject makes movements having reference to the place touched. As soon as these movements are executed (the so-called *Tastzuckungen*—spasmodic groping movements), the feeling of place, spatial feeling, capacity to determine the direction of movements, etc., remain intact and, at the same time, the patient can determine the size and form of objects put into his hand.

Thus, Goldstein recognises a special form of tactual paralysis conditioned by the loss of visual images. It is worth noting that, in everyday life, too, the determination of the extent of objects is expressed in tactual forms, for instance, a finger's thickness, a finger long, etc. A close connection between visual and auditory orientation areas, on the one hand, and tactual-muscular areas, on the other, is proved also by the establishment of visual-motor and auditory-motor association reflexes. So, as early as 1886, I showed that the localisation of the efferent path of those reflexes must be assumed in the sigmoid gyrus in animals, which corresponds to the central gyrus and the posterior area of the superior frontal gyrus in man. A dog, which has been trained to give the paw either when we say " Give the paw ! " or when we stretch out our hand, permanently loses the power to execute this movement, which is a typical association-motor reflex, when his sigmoid gyrus has been removed. I have proved this.[1]

Dr. Protopopov, who has more recently experimented in my laboratory on artificially inculcated association-motor reflexes defensive in character (jerking back of the paw at the sound of an electric bell, which has been previously accompanied by electrical stimulation of the animal's paw),

---

[1] V. Bechterev : *The Physiology of the Motor Area of the Cerebral Cortex.* *Arch. psychiatrii*, 1886–1887.

has also proved that this reflex is irrevocably lost after the destruction of the sigmoid gyrus. (See his *Dissertation*.) As regards association reflexes manifested in the area of the vegetative functions, there can be no doubt that their afferent areas, at least when the stimulations are complex, are the same visual, auditory, and other cortical areas, but the rôle of efferent areas for these reflexes can be taken over by the cortical areas (discovered in our laboratory—myself and N. Mislavsky, Dr. Spirtov, Prof. Gerver, Prof. Nikitin, and others) of salivary secretion (gyrus compositus anterior and the supra-Sylvian area, but partly also a considerable part of the parietal gyri), of gastric juice secretion (behind and outwards from the *g. sigmoideus*), and of lactic secretion (near the facialis area in sheep) ; but apparently extensive compensation on the part of the subcortical areas is possible here, because, for example, a speedy re-establishment of the association reflex ensued after the removal of the above-mentioned cortical salivary and gastric-juice-secretory areas (Dr. Spirtov, Dr. Gre-ker).[1] Thus, it may be explained why the investigation of secretory association reflexes, which was made not earlier than one or two weeks after an operation for the extensive removal of the frontal part of the cortex of dogs, has again afforded a positive result in regard to the association-reflex secretion (Dr. Tichomirov). Another explanation, to the effect that the efferent aspect of the reflex is partly executed through the cerebral cortex, and partly by means of the subcortical formations of the optic thalamus and the striated system, is, of course, admissible.[2]

However this may be, the cerebral cortex is the territory on which the experience of the whole of life is stamped and through which the analysis of external stimuli occurs, and through which, at the same time, the co-ordination or synthesis of the various association reflexes realised in the life environment is established. It is clear from this that man's individual features also, in as far as they are a result of education and of the influence of the environment, and are expressed in his speech, in his expressive movements, actions, and conduct, are represented mainly in the cerebral cortex. In contradistinction, on the various areas of the cerebro-spinal axis and the peripheral ganglia devolve those manifestations of the activity of the nervous system which are a result of racial experience transmitted, from generation to generation, as inherited or innate reflexes in which, in turn, certain individual constitutional peculiarities are expressed.

The question now is : Where is the localisation of the complex-organic or so-called instinctive reflexes ? If inherited reflexes are executed, as we have said, by the spinal cord and the subcortical ganglia, and association reflexes with the participation of the cerebral cortex and probably

---

[1] Relatively speedy compensation has been observed in dogs in regard to the functions of movement also, which is usually re-established in the course of a short time after the removal of the sigmoid gyrus.

[2] From my point of view, the direct transmission of the stimulation, on conditioned secretion of saliva and secretion of juice, from the occipital areas of the hemisphere directly to the medulla oblongata and evading the subcortical ganglia, a view regarded as tenable by the school of I. P. Pavlov, is not very probable.

also the cerebral ganglia, the question arises : Which part precisely of the nervous system executes the complex-organic reflexes or their complexes in higher animals and in man ? If, in discussing the so-called instincts, we speak of an impulse which arises in organic fashion, we can scarcely doubt that this impulse arises chiefly, if not exclusively, from the organism in general, *i.e.* from its tissues or organs which are concerned in the given complex of reflexes. Thus, in the complex of reflexes connected with nutrition in the higher animals, the impulse emanates from the body tissues in general, including the stomach and intestinal canal, which, as a result of the composition of the impoverished blood, are deprived of the necessary nutritive material ; and in the complex of reflexes connected with propagation, it emanates from the sex organs which secrete the appropriate hormones, etc. From the two examples mentioned, it may be seen that the same must be held true of other organic reflexes also.

It is clear that, under certain conditions, and sometimes at a certain period of development (the period of sexual maturity), and at a certain season, there issue from tissues and organs impulses which, by evoking local stimulations, transmitted with the participation of the vegetative system to the cerebral centres, exert definite influences here. But as these influences, at least in the higher animals, lead to the realisation of appropriate association reflexes, which, as we have seen, are produced with the participation of the cortex in the higher animals, we must admit that the execution of so-called instinctive movements in the higher animals and in man, in as far as they are a result of individual experience, also occur with the participation of the cortex, but the invincibility of " instinctive " action is rooted in the conditions of the life activity of certain inner organs and tissues, which are innervated by the vegetative system and serve as primary sources of impulses transmitted to the brain. Another source of impulses which lead to the realisation of complex-organic reflexes is the secretion of hormones into the blood by the organs of inner secretion, these hormones exerting an influence on the brain.

Thus, complex-organic reflexes, not only because of their nature, but also of their mechanism, must be distinguished both from ordinary reflexes and acquired association reflexes, for these complex-organic, in contradistinction to ordinary, reflexes are complex acts executed in the higher animals with the participation of the subcortical ganglia, and partly of the cerebral cortex, but in contradistinction to acquired association reflexes, they have, as their fundamental impulse, stimulations which, emanating from the inner organs and tissues and being associated with their life activity, are transmitted to the cerebral cortex partly through the mediation of the vegetative nervous system, and, to a certain extent, directly through the blood flowing to the brain.

CHAPTER XII

Aims of reflexology. Objective observation and experiment.

AFTER all that has been said, it is obvious that that science which I have duly called reflexology consists in the study of the organism's correlative activity in the wide sense of the word, and by correlative activity we mean all the organism's inherited and individually acquired reactions, beginning from innate and complex-organic reflexes up to, and including, the most complex acquired reflexes, which in man go by the name of actions and conduct and comprise his characteristic behaviour.

Comparative reflexology embraces the correlative functions of all living beings, but in what follows we are interested mainly in problems of human reflexology, and chiefly in those of the higher manifestations of man's correlative activity characterised by association reflexes.

As we know, every external influence acting on the organism is capable of producing, in addition to physico-chemical reactions, local reflexes in the form of simple or ordinary reflexes. Moreover, external influences produce general reactions of an inherited character, in other words, racial reactions in the form of urges or the so-called instincts, or, synonymously, complex-organic reflexes, but they also produce acquired or association reflexes based on past experience. The aim of reflexology as a scientific study is the explication and investigation of response reactions in general, and, in particular, of association reflexes, the study of which must be made in relation to current, past, and, also, hereditary influences.

It must be noted that ordinary reflexes in the animal world, not excluding man, have been comparatively well investigated, and continue to be studied, and, therefore, we shall not dilate on this subject.[1] Recently, as we have seen, acquired reactions, too, in the animal world have been submitted to objective investigation in various directions. But, as we have already said, the centre of interest in the following exposition is human reflexology, which has as its aim to study not only man's constitutional conditions, but also his external reactions of an inherited, complex-organic, and also acquired character—reactions which develop under the influence of external or internal stimuli either present or past. In this direction reflexology may achieve its aim in the following ways :

1. By the objective, bio-social study of all the external manifestations of a human being, and by the noting of their correlations with the external and internal influences, present and past, and also by the study of the consecutive development of the correlative, and particularly the association-reflex, activity from the day of birth.

2. By the experimental and observational investigation of the conformity to law of the development of association-reflex activity under various conditions.

[1] A description of the most important reflexes of this kind in man may be found in my book : *General Diagnostic of the Nervous System*, Part I, pub. Ricker, St. Petersburg.

3. By the study of that mechanism through the mediation of which is established the correlation of certain association and other reflexes with the external and internal stimuli, present and past ; this study is prosecuted by experiments in which areas of the brain of the animal are destroyed and by the observation of pathological conditions in men.

4. By the study of the ontogenesis and the phylogenesis of the correlative, and particularly the association-reflex, activity in relation to the purely genetic development of the cerebral hemispheres.

5. By the study of the correlation of the objective processes of the association-reflex activity with man's verbal account of the experiences connected with them.

The first aim is difficult to achieve in the case of an adult. Anyhow, it may be achieved only by means of a detailed and elaborate scheme in which all possible external reactions are set down under the categories of their external manifestations (speech, actions, facial expressions, gestures, organic or instinctive manifestations) and in which are, at the same time, set down the external stimuli which have produced them. Besides, there is required a careful collection and objective analysis of material concerning the human individual in the past and the present. This aim is much more easily achieved in the case of new-born infants, if trouble is taken to record, in strictly objective fashion and according to a definite scheme, all the infant's external manifestations in relation to the past and present influences, external and internal, acting on him.[1]

The second aim naturally follows from the analysis of the material mentioned, but it is also achieved by present-day laboratory methods of artificially inculcating association reflexes, methods through which both the development of these reflexes, as well as certain alien influences acting on them, may be studied in strictly objective fashion. Nevertheless, observation of the behaviour of man and animals under various conditions also provides much pertinent material.

The third aim is achieved mainly by experimentally investigating association reflexes in animals when various areas of the nervous system have been destroyed, and in man in cases of affection of the brain and of the nervous system in general.[2]

The fourth aim is concerned with genetic and comparative reflexology.

The fifth aim is achieved through comparison of the objective investigation of external reaction with the verbal account of the unexpressed or latent reflexes which are studied chiefly on oneself.

[1] See V. Bechterev : *The Development of Neuro-psychic Activity in the Course of the First Half Year of the Child's Life—Vestnik Psychologii*, 1912. Also his *Early Stages of the Evolution of Children's Drawings—Vestnik Psychologii*, 1910. Also his *Objective Investigation of the Neuro-psychical Sphere in Infants—Vestnik Psychologii*, 1909. Also his : *The First Six Months of the Child's Development—Vestnik Psychologii ;* and *Symposium on the Reflexology and the Physiology of the Nervous System*, ed. V. Bechterev, 1924.

[2] V. Bechterev : *The Application of Association-motor Reflexes as the Objective Method of Investigation in the Treatment of Nervous and Psychic Diseases—Obozrenie Psychiatrii*, 1910.

Let us note in conclusion that man is an agent whose mechanism is set in motion by external and internal stimuli, for he is a product both of the past life of his ancestors (racial experience) and of his own past individual experience. In accordance with this, and in dependence on it, he develops reactions to certain external and internal influences, and these reactions take the form of various—sometimes complex, sometimes more simple— concatenated reflexes produced by external, as well as internal, stimuli not only present, but also past. Thus, for reflexology, man is not distinguishable into subject and object, but is a unitary being, both object and subject at once, in the form of an agent, whose external aspect alone is accessible to scientific investigation by an external observer. This external aspect is comprised of the totality of the various reflexes, and primarily appertains to objective study, while the subjective aspect does not appertain to direct observation, and, consequently, cannot be studied directly ; but what we can study is the objectively given verbal account of the inner or latent reflexes, an account which has to be taken into consideration, but must be invariably checked and tested against objective data.[1]

---

[1] During the reading of the proofs of this work, I became acquainted with Calkins's paper (*Psych. Rev.*, 28 ; 1921). She finds three trends in behaviourist psychology in America. None of these is completely co-extensive with reflexology, which I began to elaborate (beginning from the middle of the 'eighties) before the development of behaviourist psychology, and which must, therefore, take an independent place in scientific thought.

CHAPTER XIII

The nervous current as a qualified kind of protoplasmic irritability. The source of the energy which lies at the basis of the nervous current. Receptive organs as transformers of external energies. The hypothesis of discharges in the transmission process.

AS we have reason to suppose that the existence of all living beings depends on the irritability which characterises their protoplasm, an irritability which is an energic manifestation at the basis of which processes of ionisation lie, we must keep in mind that the nervous current which develops in the nervous system of the higher animals and man is only a derived phenomenon which is a qualified kind of irritability of the cellular protoplasm.

But if the nervous current is a qualified kind of irritability of cellular protoplasm, the question necessarily arises : What is the source of that energy which is manifested in the form of nervous current as a special kind of cellular irritability ?

It is obvious that the primary source of this energy lies outside the organism, and is to be found in food and those stimuli which exert their influence on the organism through its internal surfaces, the cutaneous and mucous coats, the movement of the limbs and the whole body in space (muscular stimuli, the semicircular canals) and through special receptive organs (eye, ear, nose, mouth).

As regards the nutritional source of energy, there is no necessity for us to dilate on that. It is sufficient to say that the investigations of Rubner and W. Atwater, by their calculation of the calories contained in food and of the expenditure of heat, a topic to which we shall refer later, have proved the applicability of the law of conservation of energy to the living organism. On the other hand, Berger (*Zeitschr. f. Psychol.*, 82, 1919) has calculated that in mental work 1196 metre-kilograms[1] are converted in one hour into "psychic," or—synonymously—cerebral, energy. Therefore we have here only to touch briefly on the problem of the organism's derivation of energy through its receptive organs.

As early as 1896,[2] I advanced the hypothesis that our receptive organs are merely transformers of external energies, so that these energies produce the nervous current when they impinge on the receptive organs. The nervous current must be regarded as a manifestation of one kind of the universal energy.

At that time, the transformer hypothesis advanced by me was only a theory which explained the origin of one of the sources of nervous energy. It was already known then that the severing of the dorsal radices produces a weakening of the tonus of the muscles as a result of the stoppage of impulses transmitted to the muscles through the mediation of the ventral radices and the motor nerves, and that the severing of the latter also

---

[1] *Translators' note :* One metre-kilogram represents the energy required to raise 1 kilogram or 2·2046 lbs. to a height of 1 metre.

[2] See *Obozrenie Psychiatrii*, 1896, and *Neur. Centralbl.* of the same year.

weakens the tonus of the muscles, as one may prove by a muscle artificially stretched by means of a special weight. As we know, the tonus of the muscles becomes weaker also in locomotor ataxia (tabes dorsalis), which is accompanied by degeneration of the dorsal radices, and also in pathological conditions accompanied by degeneration of the cells of the ventral horns to which are transmitted all impulses, both from the periphery of the cutaneous surface through the dorsal radices and from the cerebral areas which lie higher, along the efferent conductors. Since that time, new facts have been discovered which confirm the above-mentioned theory. Thus, Ewald has proved that when the semicircular canals of the ear have been severed, muscular atonia is observed. So this organ produces a constant tonic muscular tension. The same is known to be true of the cerebellum.

The question now is : What is the source of the tonic impulses which flow unintermittently to the brain from the semicircular canals ? Can there be any doubt that this source implies, in turn, a constant influx of energy through the sound waves which continuously invade the ear, and through the constant percussions which the pressure of the endolymph in the vestibule and in the semicircular canals of the labyrinth undergoes as a result of these sound waves and of the constantly changing positions of the head. The influence of the aural labyrinth on the muscles of the body has, as we know, been proved by a number of experimental and clinical data concerned with affections of the labyrinth, and also by observations of the deaf and dumb, who, when revolved, do not exhibit the objective phenomena of dizziness, such as head movements in the opposite direction and the characteristic eye movements.[1]

It is clear that the cutaneous coats, the muscles, the tendons, and the ear, with their nervous apparatus, and also the cerebellum are reflexive-tonic organs of muscular activity.

Can there be any doubt that the organ of vision also and, to a certain extent, the organs of smell and taste must be regarded as organs reflexive-tonic in regard to our muscles ?

In the case of the organ of vision, this may be proved in the following way : if one of a dog's cerebellar peduncles is severed, he begins, as is well known, to make vigorous, violent movements around the long axis of his body. But if the animal is blinded, his revolving movement either ceases completely or is at least appreciably weakened, as I have proved in my experiments. Besides, the influence of vision on the muscular tonus may be particularly well seen in the so-called symptom of Romberg. When a patient, who, as a result of that illness called locomotor ataxia (tabes dorsalis), has lost cutaneous and muscular sensitivity in his legs, can still stand with relative surety when he fixes his eyes on something in front of him, he immediately begins to sway from one side to the other as soon as he shuts his eyes, and this results from the weakening of the

[1] *Translators' note :* Periodic movements of the eyes to right and left—*nystag-mus* movements, as they are called.

tonus of the muscles and the loss of a certain orientation in their tension the source of which is vision.

There is no doubt that also the muscles which move the eye receive their tonus to a considerable extent from the retina. If you take a man suffering from atrophy of the retina, you can see for yourself that he is, to a certain extent, devoid of the power of effecting such vigorous side-movements of the eye as can one endowed with vision.

Besides, it is necessary to keep in view that the life processes which occur in the tissues, the phenomena of endosmosis and exosmosis, the blood pressure, and also the friction produced by the movement of the lymph and the blood in the vessels, excite the activity of the vegetative nervous apparatus, and transmit, along the centripetal conductors, the nervous current and, consequently, the energy to the central organs, which, in turn, transmit impulses to the centrifugal conductors of the external and internal organs—the motor, vascular, and glandular organs.

Lastly, pathology tells us that the severing of the peripheral nerves leads to consequent degeneration of the nerve fibres and the muscles, and this can be explained only by the stoppage of impulses which sustain the function and nutrition both of the nerve fibres and the muscles, and, consequently, by the cutting off of that energy which is expressed in these impulses. It is well known that a rupture of the central conductors leads to their secondary degeneration, which is explained in precisely the same way.

In some cases, it is now possible for us to determine even the equivalence of external energy to nervous energy, if the lowest threshold of stimulation is taken as indicating the norm of nervous energy, as may be seen in the case of audition. Having taken into account the definite correlation, discovered by experiments carried out in my laboratory, of the lowest thresholds of stimulation which set up an association reflex, with the lowest threshold of sensation, it is possible to determine what degree of expenditure of external energy is necessary to produce an association reflex. This can be discovered also in regard to cutaneous and other qualified external stimulations. Thus, we know that when energy of $1/1,000$ erg is expended, we still hear a fairly loud sound ; even when $1/10,000$ erg of energy is expended, we hear a sound distinctly, and an erg corresponds approximately to the energy expended in lifting 1 milligram to a height of 1 cm., i.e. the very smallest weight capable of being weighed by the most sensitive scales (more precisely $= \frac{1}{681}$ gr.).

Furthermore, the equivalence of the increase of the expended external energy in relation to the increase of the nervous energy is determined by the Weber–Fechner law, according to which the external energy expended must increase in definite geometrical progression whenever the intensity of the sensation increases by a scarcely perceptible unit, i.e. increases in arithmetical progression, as, probably, the energy of the nervous current also increases.

The above-mentioned hypothesis, together with my scheme of the cerebral structure as consisting of various pairs of afferent and efferent conductors,[1] and my hypothesis of the transmission of the nervous current from one neuron to the other as a result of discharges produced by difference in tension of energy in two adjacent and connected neurons,[2] explain to us the uninterrupted movement of the nervous current from the receptive organs to the appropriate afferent area in the cerebral cortex (visual, auditory, olfactory, gustatory, muscular, tactual-muscular, etc.). Thence the nervous current is transmitted, through the association cells, partly to the nearest cells with an efferent conductor, partly to cells of other areas of the cerebral cortex, hence it is transmitted to efferent conductors leading towards the periphery again, if, of course, the current is not temporarily impeded by some inhibitory conditions, external or internal in character, in cells which lie on its route.[3]

In the above-mentioned course of the nervous process one cannot fail to see the scheme of a reflex with its centripetal, central, and centrifugal conduction, and all association-reflex processes may thus be regarded as reflexes of a higher order, and based on reproduction and association.[4]

At the present time, it is possible to determine not only the velocity of the nervous current which travels along the central and peripheral conductors—this velocity being approximately 28–30, and, at the maximum, 60 metres, a second—but also the rhythmical frequency of waves in the nervous current.

Thus, it has been calculated that normal muscle-waves, which are basic in our movements and are produced by rhythmical nervous current, occur

[1] See V. Bechterev: *Conduction Paths in the Spinal Cord and the Brain*, St. Petersburg, 1906, 2nd part, p. 311. *Scheme of the Functions of the Cerebral Cortex*—Address to the Scientific Conference of the Institute for the Study of Brain, 1921.

[2] V. Bechterev: *Obozrenie Psychiatrii*, 1896. *The Psychic and Life*, St. Petersburg, 1896. *L'activité psychique et la vie*, Paris. *Psyche und Leben*, Wiesbaden.

[3] The investigations of Ramon y Cajal, Bethe, and others have shown that, in the centripetal conductors themselves, contrary, *i.e.* centrifugal, fibres exist, which, in my opinion, serve to dilate the vessels in the receptive organs, as do similar fibres in the dorsal radices.

[4] The conception of " psychic " processes as reflexes has been duly advanced by Spencer, and introduced into physiology by Prof. Setchenov (*Reflexi golovnovo mozga—Reflexes of the Brain.*—St. Petersburg, 1866). It is a pity that both Setchenov and Spencer assumed the subjective standpoint when they treated of problems of psychic activity. Nevertheless, Setchenov's acknowledgement of cerebral reflexes at the back of " psychic " processes is his indubitable merit. " The whole endless variety of the external manifestations of brain activity," says Setchenov, " may be finally reduced to one phenomenon—muscular movement. Whether a child laughs at the sight of a toy, whether Garibaldi smiles when he is exiled for excessive love of his country, whether a girl trembles at the first thought of love, whether Newton creates universal laws and writes them down on paper—everywhere muscular movement is the ultimate fact " (*l.c.*, p. 9). It must be noted, however, that, in addition to external muscular movement, cardio-vascular effect and effect on the part of the internal organs—an effect caused by the contraction of the smooth musculature—and certain secretory effects may also be the ultimate result of association reflexes, as has been shown by observation and experiment.

M

with a frequency of 120 to the second.[1] If we do not normally notice these muscular pulsations, it is because of simultaneous inhibitory influences on the part of the nerve centres. But when these inhibitory influences are removed, as may be observed, for instance, in some illnesses accompanied with fever, or in a nervous condition, we know that a nervous trembling appears in which every nervous impulse is distinguishable, and in so-called organic trembling the muscular wave is occasionally interrupted for some time, with convulsive contractions as a result.

As regards the character of the nervous wave, which, generally speaking, occurs with considerably greater frequency, as telephonic phenomena prove, there is reason to believe that, at least for the centripetal conductors, it is not the same. This results from the different conditions of peripheral stimulation of the wave itself in the receptive organs which vary considerably in their structure.[2]

Let us now turn to the investigation of the nature of nervous conduction.

The study of nervous process has developed slowly and gradually. The earliest views in this sphere were that there are mechanical processes in the form of a wave travelling along the nerve. From the time of Galvani's and Volta's investigations, the nerve was regarded as the same as any other electrical conductor. However, the slowness in the movement of the nervous current, as proved by Helmholtz, necessitated the abandonment of such a simple explanation of the nervous process.

We owe to Du Bois Raymond our knowledge of the fact that the excitation of the nerve is associated with negative electric vibration and the phenomena of catelectrotonus and anelectrotonus. From that time, the nervous process has begun to be regarded by some scientists as a physical, by others, as a chemical, process. But certain data force us to accept the physico-chemical nature of the conduction.[3]

On the basis of the analysis of all the data, I have, in my work, *Technique and Life*, already come to the conclusion that the nervous current is a physico-chemical process in the sense that in the cells it is predominantly chemical, but in the nerve, as a conductor, physical, while in both cases it is accompanied by the development of a negative electric vibration of the current or by that of action-current. Besides, it has been proved in my laboratory that local excitation of the cortex, under the influence of specific stimulation of the receptive organs, is characterised by the development of action-current in the cortex. (Dr. Larionov in *Nevrologitchesky Vestnik ;* Dr. Trivus, *Dissertation*, St. Petersburg.)

[1] E. Boss and W. Trendelenburg : *Zeitschr. f. Biol.*, Bd. 74, H. 1–2, 1921. An approximately equal number of vibrations was ascribed by Garten and Dittler to the " will " rhythm (" Willensrhythmus "), which is, however, distinguished by an irregularity which depends on the irregularity of impulses issuing from the central cortical areas.

[2] V. Bechterev : *Principles of the Study of the Nervous Centres*, 1 vol.—*Die Functionen der Nervencentra*, Jena, H. 1.

[3] See V. Bechterev : *The Psychic and Life*, St. Petersburg.—*Psyche und Leben*, Wiesbaden.—*L'activité psychique et la vie*, Paris.

The essence of the process is now reduced to its electro-chemical nature, for the explication of which the doctrine of osmosis, semi-permeable walls, and colloids has been recently introduced.

The famous chemist, Ostwald, has already pointed out the rôle of semi-permeable walls in the process of nervous excitation. But an important addition to the theory of the nervous process has been made by his disciple, Nernst, after whom the works of Loeb, and, in Russia, of Vvedensky, Tchagovetz, Verigo, Kaufman, Lazarev, and Vasilyev followed, not to mention other works of secondary importance.

At the present time, we may hold that the nervous process is the movement of a constant current. This was developed by Nernst in connection with the nature of semi-permeable walls. The development of the current depends on the process of ionisation which takes place in the nerve. In view of the fact that the cathode produces a nervous current, it is maintained that the concentration of the cations in the form of Na is accompanied by excitation, and, on the contrary, that the concentration of anions produces depression. This theory has given us the explanation of the inefficacy of currents of high tension and greater frequency for nervous excitation. Loeb then assumed that not only the ions Na, but also other ions, produce excitation through concentration, and that the relation between the concentration of univalent and bivalent ions is of paramount importance. Finally, transposition of, and change in, concentration condition excitation.

The academician Lazarev, accepting the theses of Nernst and Loeb, and taking his stand on his own experiments, has found that excitation occurs in dependence on change in the relation of the ions. As cations are not equally mobile, for univalent move more quickly in comparison with bivalent, so the former are predominant in the cathode, and, as a result, their relation is changed.

Dr. Vasilyev,[1] a collaborator at the Institute for the Study of Brain, however, finds that the arguments of the academician Lazarev cannot stand severe criticism in all details. It is indubitable, however, that Nernst and Loeb have afforded the correct bases of the theory of the excitation which travels along the nerve. In any case, there can no longer be any doubt that, under the influence of appropriate external stimuli— light on the eye, sound on the ear, etc.—the basis of a nervous process is an electric current produced by ionisation of the disintegrating matter contained in the peripheral receptive apparatus.

The transmission from the centripetal to the centrifugal conductors occurs as a result of periodic chemical reactions which are—according to Lazarev—midway between radio-active and photo-chemical processes, and every periodic process produces an electric current which has been discovered in the appropriate areas of the cortex, for instance in the auditory when a sound acts on the organ of Corti, in the visual when

[1] See his Address at the Conference of the Institute for the Study of Brain, 1922.

light acts on the retina, etc.[1] This current, apparently, may also extend outside the brain and the cranium.

Further data regarding the nature of the nervous current may be gathered from a later work of the academician Lazarev.[2] According to him, the excitation consists in the incessant disintegration of nervous matter into ions, and the current can be detected also outside the coats of the head, and this paves the way for the explanation of the influence of thought across space, an influence which I have subjected to laboratory experiments on animals and partly on men.[3]

The phenomena of excitation and inhibition are now being explained from the physico-chemical aspect also. Nerve tissue is a complex aggregate of albuminous particles saturated with salt solutions. It must be taken into account that salts, acids, and alkalis, as well as albuminous substances, disintegrate into cations and anions. The salts of Na and K (the first group of metals) excite the nerve conductors, while the salts of Ca and Mg act in a depressing manner (the second group of metals) ; therefore, when different ions, *i.e.* chemical groups differently charged, which result from the disintegration of albumen, salts, acids, and alkalis, act simultaneously, the effect of the activity will depend not only on the character of the ions, but also on the numerical correlation of some ions which act antagonistically and in unequal degree. It has also been proved that the speed of transposition of different ions is unequal. Thus the salts of Na and K travel more quickly to the cathode when the nerve is electrified than do the salts of Ca and Mg. Therefore, the excitation of the nerve at the cathode is at first more marked than later when the salts of Ca and Mg have accumulated. It is clear from this that the functional process in the sense of excitation or depression is, in every time-unit, directly dependent on the qualitative and quantitative correlations of the influent ions, and so also excitation and depression are active processes,[4] dependent on the disintegration of the tissue elements and conditioned by the varying correlation of ions different in quality. But if excitation and depression are active processes distinguished only by their physico-chemical character, inhibition also, as well as excitation, may arise as an association reflex. In other words, we shall have an associative inhibitory force, which develops like an associative excitation in its association with some reflexogenous

[1] Not only the current itself, but also its vibrations, have been discovered in investigations carried out in my laboratory by Dr. Trivus and Dr. Larionov.

[2] Academician Lazarev : *Visshaya nervnaya deyatelnost v svete sovremennoi naüki.* (*The Higher Nervous Activity in the Light of Present-day Science*), Moscow, 1921. *Fiziko-chimitcheskiye osnovi visshei nervnoi deyatelnosti* (*The Physio-chemical Foundations of the Higher Nervous Activity*), Moscow, 1922.

[3] See V. Bechterev : *Problems of the Study and Education of Personality*, 2nd vol., 1921.

[4] In N. Vvedensky's opinion, inhibition in the form of parabiosis is really over-excitation, but it is possible to grant that there is another form of inhibition, as a state contrary to excitation, *i.e.* excitation decreased to the minimum, a form which would correspond to what we call " fatigue." Fatigue is really a reflex of inner inhibition in the form of a defence reaction against the danger of toxicosis.

stimulus. To distinguish them from association-motor reflexes, we shall call reflexes of this kind association-inhibitory reflexes, which, under life conditions, correspond to the negativistic attitude towards certain objects, or to abstention from certain actions on the existence of a definite stimulus.

It must be borne in mind here that nerve cells contain complex chemical substances which carry an enormous quantity of potential energy bound up in chemical form. These stores of energy are expended in the disintegration of these complex substances. Oxygen, which is supplied by the blood and has strong chemical affinity, oxidises the products to be disintegrated, and releases energy which passes over into the mechanical activity of the muscles and the activity of the glands both external and internal. At the present time, we may assume that the main source of stored energy in the cells is the tigroid, or, in other words, the chromatin substance, or Nissl's granules, which disintegrate when the nerve centres are exhausted and redintegrate when they have rested, but to this we shall refer elsewhere.

Recently, Dr. Kronthal[1] regards the nerve cell as an element formed from two parts—neuro-fibrils, and white blood-corpuscles—of which the first part is the fundamental conductive part of the nervous system in general. The cell itself he deprives of its meaning as an organism, and regards its body merely as an insulator for the intersecting conductors— the neuro-fibrils. My embryological investigations, made before Kronthal's (Address to the Scientific Meetings of the Hospital for Psychic and Nervous Diseases in 1896; paper in the *Neur. Cent.*, p. 1130, 1896), are in agreement with the view which maintains the origin of the nerve cell from fibrils and germ cells, or preformed white blood-corpuscles. However, the body of the cell is not, as Kronthal assumes, merely an insulator for the conduction of the intersecting neuro-fibrils. Without doubt, it actively participates in the functions of the nerve tissue, for the summation of the nervous excitation which travels through the nerve cell is an indubitable fact, and not less certain are the phenomena of fatigue in the wave of excitation travelling through the cell, while the nerve itself is (1) incapable of summation of the excitation, and is (2) untiring, or practically untiring. In my laboratory, experiments were made in which the so-called motor areas of the cerebral cortex of a dog were stimulated over a long period after the severing of the spinal cord behind the cervical swelling. The results were cramps of the front limbs and the muscles of the neck, cramps manifested by means of the cells of the ventral horns of the cervical swelling, while the hind extremities remained quiet. On dissection of the animal when it had been killed, and on examining bits of the spinal cord from the cervical swelling and from the lumbar swelling, a marked difference in the cells of the one and of the other was observed; the cells of the cervical swelling were, as a result of prolonged activity, in a state of marked chromatolysis with disintegration of Nissl's granules and

[1] *Neur. Centr.*, no. 10, 1919. *Originelle Mitteilungen.*

with other phenomena, while there was nothing similar in the lumbar swelling. The relations between these two swellings must be the exact opposite when the hind limbs of the animal operated on in the manner described are stimulated for a long time, the stimulation producing in them incessant reflex movements and leaving the front limbs quiet at the same time. It is clear that the tigroid substance of the cell, a substance consisting of Nissl's granules, is subjected to disintegration or expenditure in dependence on the activity of the cell, and this forces us to recognise, on the one hand, the activity of the nerve cell in the process of nervous excitation, and, on the other hand, the rôle of Nissl's granules as the containers of those products necessary for the activity of the cell.

CHAPTER XIV

The subsumption of psychic processes under the scheme of reflexes. The centres of the cerebral cortex as the areas of association reflexes. Their afferent and efferent aspects. Orientation, aggression, and defence reflexes : visual, auditory, olfactory, gustatory, muscular, tactual, static, etc.

THE functions of the higher nervous system were first reduced by the physiological school of I. P. Pavlov to analytic activity in regard to external stimulations, and to an integrating activity which establishes the connection of the organism with the resolved or analysed stimuli of the external world. " The activity of the higher areas of the central nervous system establishes more detailed and more refined correlations of the animal organism with the environment ; in other words, a more perfect equilibration of the system of those substances and forces which constitute the animal organism with the substance and forces of the surrounding world."[1]

But as early as 1909, I pointed out the law of the differentiation of association reflexes in general, while many of them were still regarded as " specific " by several physiologists.[2] Nevertheless, I consider inadequate the definition which regards the cortical areas as playing the rôle of analysers. The higher functions of the nervous system do not consist in analysis or differentiation and in integrating activity alone, the more so as analysis appertains, to a certain extent, to the lower organs of the nervous system also.

There can be no doubt that the analysis of external stimulations begins even in the peripheral areas of the nervous system, and in the subcortical ganglia. The organ of Corti, the retina, the Schneider membrane, the papillæ, and the cutaneous nervous apparatus are themselves analysers of external stimulations, since the establishment (secured by racial experience) of the integrating functions (in the form of innate or inherited reflexes) of the lower centres of the nervous system produces reactions when the external stimulations have already been resolved by analysis. Thus, a decapitated frog adjusts its reflex movements to the spot stimulated on the cutaneous surface, and reacts in unequal degree according to the character of the external stimulations.

The higher, *i.e.* the cortical, areas of the nervous system are thus only an apparatus more perfect in this respect and reacting with a more refined analysis and a more mobile character.

But I see a no less, if not more, important characteristic of the activity of the higher centres in that process which I call selective or associative generalisation. The latter is reducible to synthesis or union of different external stimulations in the sense of a single reaction to two or more different stimuli, and thus establishes the relation of proximity and

[1] Professor I. Pavlov : *The True Physiology of the Brain—Priroda*, January, 1917.
[2] See V. Bechterev : *The Significance of the Motor Sphere—Russky Vratch*, 1909.

succession among the external stimulations. In a word, not only analysis, but also synthesis, is an inalienable attribute of the higher functions of the nervous system.

If two different stimuli are presented, and a definite responsive reaction to one of them is already present so that this stimulus is reflexogenous, the same reaction will be established in time to the other accompanying non-reflexogenous stimuli, whether one, two, or more, and this is obviously synthesis. This synthesis is particularly important, because it makes possible the adjustment to future stimuli which stand in a relation of proximity to each other.

The integrating and the disintegrating rôles of the higher centres are of equal importance, for if, in the one case, the responsive reaction to a given external stimulus is important, in the other case, not only the temporary retardation or inhibition of the external reaction to the given stimulus, which formerly evoked an appropriate reaction, but also the more or less complete disappearance of the given reaction, is of no less importance.

Thus, differentiation or analysis, on the one hand, and selective generalisation or synthesis, on the other, and, before these, excitation and inhibition in connection with the integration and temporary disintegration, or even complete disruption, of earlier associations—these are the fundamental functions of the cortical areas of the brain.

Thus, the analytico-synthetic activity of the cortical areas bears the stamp of those temporary adjustments to the environment which develop in accordance with temporal variation in the needs of, and things advantageous to, the given individual who has grown up in certain conditions and, consequently, bears the stamp of those adjustments which have, in each individual, peculiar traits having a certain relationship to inherited tendencies also.

On the other hand, in the process of excitation of association-motor reflexes, we constantly encounter the fact that, in the period of the initial development of the reflex, the excitation invariably spreads over the whole cortical area of the receptive organ stimulated, and only on repetition of the reflex is it more and more confined to the area nearest the influence of stimulation.[1] This confining process invariably occurs in the cerebral cortex when a motor or some other association reflex is being inculcated, and it is accompanied by the inhibition of other parts of the cortex, while the inhibition of an association reflex is again accompanied by the diffusion of the excitation over the cortical area.

It is necessary to keep in mind that, indeed, there is none of the higher brain processes which may not be subsumed, from the external viewpoint, under the scheme of reflex. This scheme makes it possible to embrace all processes of association-reflex activity, because nervous

[1] See the Dissertations, from my laboratory, of Dr. Protopopov, Dr. Shevalev, Dr. Israelson, and others.

processes which, as a result of certain stimulations, have begun at the periphery are, after appropriate differentiation, establishment of connections, and generalisation, ultimately discharged at the periphery again in muscular movement, cardio-vascular effect, or secretion.

If a man, while occupied in writing, is asked about some acquaintance, he writes that other man's name although it stands in no relation to what he is writing. Here it is perfectly clear that the slip of the pen is a reflex arising under the influence of the sound-stimulation which is received by the ear and on which the writer concentrates for a moment. The same is true of slips of the tongue when the speaker inserts into the text of his speech a completely irrelevant word only because it happens to be in the field of his concentration at the moment of utterance. In both cases, there is question of a reflex associative in character, for, in language both oral and written, some of the words are doubtlessly connected with the act of concentration, but others are developed through an habitual association of one word with the other. This has been confirmed by experiments in my laboratory.[1]

Even such general states as hypnosis, which is produced by suggestion, and also suggestion itself must be subsumed under the same scheme of association reflexes.[2]

As regards sleep, there is no doubt that it cannot be reduced to auto-suggestion, as some hypnologists would have it. Still, such causes as monotonous, frequently repeated stimuli, even the habit of going to sleep at a certain time, and concentration on the imminence of sleep are sure to be not without significance in the induction of sleep, which is, as we know, a biologically developed defence reflex against the accumulating products of fatigue (hypnotoxins), which depress the active part of the personality localised in the frontal lobes. Thus, in regard to the process of falling asleep, the development of processes of inhibition, on the one hand, resulting from constant stimulation of one and the same centre by a monotonous stimulus, a stimulation which leads to consequent general inhibition of other cortical centres, exerts an indisputable influence ; and, on the other hand, the influence of association reflexes, which have been established through exercise and have originated as a result of life conditions, is not without significance.

We must remember that, from birth, there goes on an accumulating of inculcated association reflexes in the most diverse directions ; and a number of reflexes of this kind, by becoming associated with certain inner states, are produced by the latter, and, on the other hand, certain external influences, by becoming associated with certain inner states, serve to stimulate the latter.

Verbal and written signs, which play the rôle of symbols, are of paramount importance among association reflexes.

[1] See V. Bechterev : *The Causes of Slips of the Tongue—Golos i retch*, nc. 9, 1919, St. Petersburg ; *Objective Psychology*, 3rd pt., St. Petersburg.
[2] See W. Bechtereff : *La suggestion et son rôle dans la vie sociale*, Paris.

As a matter of fact, every word, being a sign, is, in accordance with the association-reflex scheme, associated as a secondary stimulus either with an external or internal stimulus, or with some state, posture, or movement of the individual in question, and consequently plays the rôle of an external stimulus, and becomes a substitute, according to the association established, for an external influence or a certain inner state.

So the word assumes the capacity of an agent, as does every secondary stimulus which originates from the inculcation of an association reflex. Both the immaturity of personality in children and the repression of personality in pathological states—for instance, in hysteria and alcoholism—and also artificially produced states such as hypnosis, which is a peculiar biological state resembling sleep,[1] considerably enhance the influence of words as stimuli, and thus is explained the phenomenon of heightened suggestibility in these cases. From this viewpoint, both pathological states concerned with repression of personality and the hypnotic state are of special interest for reflexology, particularly as they make possible the deeper exploration of the mechanism of association-reflex activity.

Besides, what is usually called a need must be subsumed under the scheme of association reflexes, for a need is a striving towards a certain end, which, as a stimulus, when it was attained in the past, was accompanied by a general sthenic reaction. Therefore, a need may be regarded as an habitual reproduction of a stimulus definitely associated with that same sthenic reaction. It is self-evident that a need is an association reflex reproduced, on the appropriate occasion, as a result of exercise and habit.

The initial stage of the process known in subjective psychology as perception and arising under external influence is effected in the form of a pure reflex and not otherwise. The influence of external stimuli on the organs of vision, hearing, smell, taste, and touch forces us to see, hear, smell, taste, and touch ; and all movements which are inseparably connected with these acts are merely association reflexes which may be called orientation association reflexes. It is obvious that these reflexes are based on the reproduction of those associations which have been established from the first days of the child's life, when light, sound, olfactory, gustatory stimulations, and mechanical influences were acting on him, and, consequently, the cortical centres which execute these reflexes must be regarded as areas of association reflexes.

I have elsewhere developed in detail this view of the function of the cerebral cortex.[2] I shall remark here that the formerly accepted division of the cerebral cortex into a number of sensory and motor centres, and

---

[1] See V. Bechterev : *Hypnosis, Suggestion, and Psychotherapy—Vestnik Znania*, and sep. ed., St. Petersburg.

[2] See V. Bechterev : *Principles of the Functional Activity of the Cerebral Cortex* in *Russky Vratch*, no. 33, 1913.

associative or psychic centres, must now give place to another view, according to which there are neither sensory, nor motor, nor specifically " psychic " centres, but only cortical areas of certain association reflexes, for instance, visual-motor in the occipital lobe, auditory-motor in the temporal lobe, cutaneous-motor in the central and adjacent frontal gyri, gustatory-motor in the lower area of the central gyri, olfactory-motor in the olfactory bulb and the gyrus uncinatus, the posterior statico-motor in the temporal, and partly in the occipital, lobe ; the anterior statico-motor in the frontal areas ; and the organic-motor in the frontal regions of the hemispheres and in the fronto-central areas. Not only are association-motor reflexes executed with the participation of the cortex, but so are also partly vasomotor and secretory association reflexes. In particular, the extensive associative area of the central and the adjacent post-frontal gyri, an area which we call the coat-muscular-motor area, stand in relation to the establishment, by means of association reflexes, of certain correlations between external influences received by means of special nerve apparatus of the external coats, on the one hand, and, on the other, muscular influences and the activity of the inner organs, as, for instance, the respiratory organs, the cardio-vascular system, the spleen, the digestive tract, the uro-genital system, the endocrine and the exocrine glands, etc.

Each of the above-mentioned regions contains afferent parts which receive the centripetal conductors ; and efferent parts which send out centrifugal conductors. The former are not excitable by electric current, and their destruction leads to the loss of external influence through the appropriate receptive organ, while the latter, being excitable by current, thus produce vascular effects or secretion in the appropriate organs, and their destruction means the destruction of the effect of the external influence, in the sense that it eliminates local orientation reflexes, without at the same time eliminating the more general and distant reflexes, which condition, for instance, locomotion under the guidance of the receptive organ (so-called psychic blindness and psychic deafness). The same is true of the visual-motor, auditory-motor, and coat-muscular-motor associative areas, and also, apparently, of the other associative areas.[1]

As regards the " associative " or essentially " psychic " centres which some authors assume, I have reason to believe, on the basis of my investigations, that the so-called posterior associative centre of P. Flechsig, which stands in correlation with the visual-motor and the auditory-motor area, executes partly a vasomotor, and partly a secretory, function, for instance, the saliva and gastric juice secretory function ; and so the

---

[1] See V. Bechterev : *La localisation des psychoreflexes dans l'écorce cérébrale ; Scientia*, vol. XX, Dec. 1916. Also his Address to the Conference of the Institute for the Study of Brain, 1921. Also his *Vom Bogen der Associationsreflexe im Zentralnervensystem*, etc. ; *Zeitschr. f. d. ges. Neur. u. Psych.*, Bd. LXXXVIII, H. 1–3.

efferent functions of the above-mentioned associative areas are supplemented. But the anterior associative centre of P. Flechsig, which receives the fibres of the anterior cerebellar peduncle and the fibres of the anterior nucleus of the thalamus opticus, and contains the statico-motor area and the area controlling the movement of the eyes and head, serves for the execution of active concentration, as well as for the direction of motor reflexes in connection with stimulations coming from the somatic sphere.

It is well known that subjective psychology bases the process of reproduction on the so-called associations or connections—more or less close—of one idea with another. However, experiments made in the laboratory on the development of artificial association reflexes have suggested a new viewpoint, according to which we are concerned here either with the release from inhibition of association reflexes, which have temporarily become obliterated in regard to certain external stimuli, or with the process of concentration, which, as a dominant inhibiting the other cortical areas, attracts to itself the excitations which are revived on the basis of the connection previously established. In this case, there is question of that physiological process in which the more excited area simultaneously possesses a greater attraction for the nerve energy, while it inhibits the other areas.

Thus, according to what we know from the data of reflexology, the point in reproduction is not, indeed, association, but release from inhibition or the draining of the excitement from the other cortical areas to the area most excited. There is expenditure of energy in the excited area, and, consequently, there occurs a disturbance of the potential, as it were, between the neighbouring unexcited or but slightly excited areas and the more excited areas, and the excitations flow to the latter from areas functionally connected with them.

Let us assume that a man has heard the word " mustard." As this word is manifested in the form of a certain excitation in the receptive auditory area, which is situated in the speech centre of the superior temporal gyrus of the left hemisphere, a nerve current from the gustatory and visual areas of the brain immediately travels to it, and, by increasing the excitation of the first area, translates it into appropriate action through the efferent, or Broca's motor-speech, area which is connected with it and is situated in the posterior part of the inferior frontal gyrus of the same hemisphere.

Every fresh excitation, as a result of the path of least resistance which has been formed, travels along the path which has previously been traversed.

In fine, let us remark that the most complex processes of correlative activity in the form of association reflexes are realised with the participation of the cerebral cortex, where the subjective side of the whole process mainly develops. Less complex processes of this activity in the form of simple reflexes are executed through the vegetative and the central sub-cortical nervous system with its peripheral afferent and its efferent conduction, with or without the participation of the cortex, but, in organisms of a lower order, the more simple correlative activity is executed with the participation of the vegetative nervous system alone, or even of protoplasm alone, as a result of its irritability.

CHAPTER XV

Reflexology rests on the law of evolution. It deduces the whole of correlative activity from experience. Space, time, number, the establishment of relationship, interaction, and causal correlation as results of experience. Directive symbols.

COMPARATIVE and genetic reflexology, inasmuch as they have for their aim the tracing of the development and manifestation of correlative activity from the amœba to man, and from the germ to adult existence, rest on the principle of evolution, which is general for everything living and dead.[1]

In particular, human reflexology forces us to look upon man as a being whose actions are subject to external laws to the same extent as a manifestation of an agent which disposes of a store of borrowed energy constantly being replenished from the outside. In this case, having recourse to " free will " would mean admitting that in some cases there may be interference on the part of some supernatural power.

But we know that natural science does not admit anything miraculous or supernatural, and, therefore, also in the sphere of correlative activity, which is reduced to movement, activity, cardio-vascular changes, and glandular secretion, there cannot, and must not, be any special mysterious power.

On the contrary, reflexology is a science which deduces the whole of correlative activity from experience.

The concepts of space, time, number, states of relationship, interaction, and dependent or so-called causal correlations are not regarded by reflexology as data given from above, or as transcendental, or ready-made by nature, but it deduces them from the collectively generalised experience of human personality on the establishment of its relation to the surrounding world.

The first measurements of space arose through the application of parts of the body as measures of surrounding objects : ell (elbow), foot, pace, span (the space from the tip of the thumb to the tip of the little finger when the fingers are extended—nine inches), fathom (the arms extended). It is clear that all these measures have been established through experience, but their further sub-divisions and elaborations into larger measures have been attained through multiplication and perfection of the same experience which has been the basis of spatial relations in general. Besides, our eye is accommodated through experience to the determination of spatial relations, and the precision of spatial determinations by means of the eye may be investigated by reflexological methods through differentiation of the smallest spatial differences. As regards the capacity of our

---

[1] This principle, in its application to living nature, assumes that all new forms arise on the basis of previous ones, which becomes vestigial because they have no justification in changed conditions. New organs originate as they are useful to the individual, and are retained only as long as they are useful to him. The moment their utility disappears, they gradually atrophy, but they do not cease to exist until their existence in the atrophied state brings more harm than good to the organism.

cutaneous transformer to determine spatial relations, works have been written on this topic by Dr. Shevalev (*Dissertation*, St. Petersburg), and Dr. Israelson (*Dissertation*, St. Petersburg), and from these works it follows that the regions of the so-called nervous areas or neurozones, and later the regions of Weber's circles, serve the primary determination of spatial relations by the cutaneous surface.

Just in the same way, the determination of time in regard to the alternation of seasons, of day and night, in regard to the sequence of rhythmic movements, to a period of time corresponding to a distance travelled, etc., is a result of experience. Life experience, which makes it possible also to mark smaller intervals of time on the basis of respiratory movements and heart-beats, and, among cultured humanity, on the basis of the movement of the hands of the clock, accommodates our cerebral apparatus to the measurement of time, and to such an extent that we can distinguish with fairly great precision the time intervals occurring in everyday life,[1] but this precision varies in accordance with many external and internal conditions. Counting is first learned on the fingers of the hands. Beginning from these primitive reckonings, all the more complex forms of calculation have arisen through experience and its direct results.

Further, the establishment of relationship and interaction has been deduced from experience of a lever of the first order.[2]

Dependence or causality or, more precisely, dependent correlations are established as a result of movements performed and of consequences thus produced in the organism itself, as well as outside it, for instance, the action of the hands, of hammer and anvil, the action of a lever, etc.

Further still, the reproduction of external experience is facilitated by symbolic, and particularly linguistic, signs, which, by denoting the various parts and qualities of external objects, and also by being combined in a particular way, make it possible to formulate general and abstract definitions, which are thus a result of external experience. In precisely the same way, primitive counting on the fingers is replaced by numbers, and numbers, as signs or symbols, facilitate combination and analysis in endless variations, and this has ultimately led to the development of present-day mathematics.

The mechanism of calculation is thus based originally on the quantitative correlation of objects, and then on the correlation of numbers as signs. It is a striking fact that there may be extraordinary calculators who are not capable of creative work in mathematics. In 1887, during a demonstration at the Paris Academy of Science, an uneducated Italian shepherd boy of ten did not take more than half a minute to extract the cube root of 3,796,416 ($=156$). Another example is the blind Fleury. He lived from the age of ten in an asylum for the blind, where he was taught Braille,

---

[1] Prof. V. Tchizh's investigations show that during sleep the hour fixed for awakening is fairly accurately determined.

[2] *Translators' note :* That is, with the fulcrum between the weight and the power—a two-armed lever.

some mathematics, and geography. As a result of extraordinary irascibility arising from degeneration and of other pathological phenomena, he was then put into a psychiatric clinic. At that time he calculated with extraordinary skill. In one minute and fifteen seconds he calculated how many seconds there are in 39 years, 3 months, and 12 hours, and did not forget to take the leap years into account. He had no idea of raising a number to a power, but when it was explained to him what the square of a number meant, he immediately calculated the squares of three- and four-digit numbers. After the explanation of the concept of square root, he faultlessly extracted, without instruction in the classical method, the square roots of four-digit numbers and gave the remainder.[1]

Placing side by side the extraction of roots as calculated by him and by another famous calculator, Inaudi, as given by Claparède, we get the following :

				Fleury.	*Inaudi.*
$\sqrt{625}$	$= 25$			instantaneously	1·49 seconds
$\sqrt{837}$	$= 28$, remainder 53			1·5 seconds	2·56 ,,
$\sqrt{640}$	$= 25$	,,	15	1·0 second	1·68 ,,
$\sqrt{4,920}$	$= 70$	,,	20	2·0 seconds	3·00 ,,
$\sqrt[3]{728}$	$= 8$	,,	216	3·0 ,,	
$\sqrt[3]{5,564}$	$= 17$	,,	651	20·0 ,,	

I have had the opportunity of meeting the calculator Diamandi, who was endowed with a similar extraordinary capacity for extracting roots, raising numbers to a power, and calculating on a big scale. He possessed, too, the striking ability to reproduce long series of figures. After reading and repeating once to himself five rows of five-digit numbers, he could repeat them by heart not only seriatim from beginning to end, but also backwards, and every row separately horizontally and vertically, and could reproduce all the figures along the diagonals.

Another calculator whom I have observed was a youth of about twenty, who exhibited signs of degeneration and delinquency, and was consequently lodged for a long time in a psychiatric institution. When he was demonstrated like Diamandi by Professor Merzheyevsky, he amazed everyone by immediately telling the number of seconds in any given number of days, months, and years, immediately multiplied five- and six-digit numbers, and extracted the square and cube roots of very large numbers. All these striking mathematical capacities were, as I have said, united in him with defective moral development. It is not less striking that, under the influence of moderate quantities of alcohol, he made the calculations with still greater speed than usual. Similar capacities for calculating were possessed by the equally famous calculator, Arago, who, by the way, immediately gave the total of five rows of five-digit numbers written on a blackboard.

[1] Desruelles : *Un calculateur prodige, aveugle-né. L'encephale*, p. 518, 1912.

Notwithstanding their striking capacities for calculating, these and similar calculators, although they mastered the mechanism of calculation, have given nothing to mathematics, while Poincaré, the renowned creator in the sphere of mathematical science, used to say of himself that he could not add without making mistakes.

However this may be, all correlative activity is a result of experience —whether this experience is an acquisition of the individual or of many generations of a species. And if Locke in his time has maintained that there is nothing in consciousness which is not also in sensation, we shall say that there is nothing in correlative activity which is not in personal experience, in the experience of others, or in the experience of the ancestors.

Thought itself is, in reality, nothing but a sub-vocal reflex or a reflex unexpressed in words. We shall refer to this later, but if it is so, then the more complex processes of reasoning must also be understood, from the viewpoint of reflexology, as a series of association reflexes impeded in their efferent aspect, that is, as latent association reflexes. It is clear from this that reflexology does not exclude complex processes of reasoning from its province, but regards them not as products of purely psychical activity, but as complexes of symbolic, motor, and other externally unexpressed reflexes which arise on the basis of past experience, and later are verbally expressible.

Even in custom, religion, belief, and art, we find reflected the leading complexes of symbolic reflexes, which, as a result of their associations with motor reflexes, determine the definite character of man's behaviour. But the origin of complexes of this kind is found in past experience, which makes it possible to reject what is harmful and retain what is useful, to turn towards what arouses a positive reaction, and to turn away from what arouses a negative general or local reaction, to be attracted by what is good for all, i.e. the general good, and shrink from what is bad for all, i.e. the common evil. It is precisely experience which establishes correlations between the given behaviour and its results, and, consequently, between behaviour which produces useful results for the individual as well as for others, or only for the individual, and the other type of behaviour which generally produces harmful results in some respect or other. In accordance with education and life experience, results useful for others are accompanied in some by a positive mimico-somatic reaction, and this guides their activities towards the common good, which sometimes does not at all correspond to the needs of the particular organism. Besides, the future behaviour of man is predetermined to a considerable extent by complexes of reflexes which have become fixed. This behaviour reflexology understands as the establishment of a definite complex of association reflexes, an establishment which is based on experience and must be accompanied by consequences which are, in some respect or other, the best.

It is clear from the above that ethical problems also can, and must, be examined from the standpoint of reflexology, but this is not the place to

N

go into details concerning this. It is sufficient to remark that, in the aforesaid, the directive significance of symbolic complexes religious, social, moral, political, and national in character is determined. Even the worship of a deity, as an assumed origin of origins, is ultimately of empiric source, if we keep in mind the fetishism and totemism of savages, and it must be understood as a result of collective experience in the establishment of correlations, vague to man, between certain phenomena. The worship of a deity in the individual's life is most frequently a result of education and imitation.

The objective of activity, *i.e.* the end which is established through experience and in accordance with which the personal association-motor reflexes are directed, originates in precisely the same manner as do the directive complexes of symbols. There is no goal whatever which ultimately is not a result of the past experience either of the individual himself or of somebody else, and, consequently, an experience derived by imitation, an experience which makes it possible to establish a definite mode of action, which leads, as the same kind of experience shows, to a definite result, *i.e.* to the given end.

In accordance with the aforesaid, we are compelled to accept Marx's principle of the direct correlation between the economic basis and the development of society. We know that all the so-called superstructures of social life : law, science, morals, religion, and even art are also now subsumed under this formula. There cannot be the least doubt that the economic situation is reflected in all these superstructures, nor can it be doubted that the majority of these superstructures, such as law and science, directly flow from the economic situation. Still, art, for instance, contains so many specific elements independent of the economic situation that it cannot be entirely, and without special constraint, traced back to this basis.

There are, in social conditions, other factors also which are not less powerful than the economic basis, and which must be taken into account in addition to the economic situation, as, for instance, the correlation of the sexes. In this factor, too, as well as in the economic situation, one of the main sources of the development of art must be sought.

CHAPTER XVI

The special experimental method of reflexology. Its historical development. Experiments on trained animals (dressage). Experiments in which cortical centres are destroyed and the natural association reflexes consequently eliminated. Artificial motor, secretory, and vasomotor association reflexes.

THE establishment of reflexology as a special department of science is justified not by its new subject-matter alone. It is generally agreed to regard as a special science any study which has not only a special subject-matter, but also a special method of investigation.

If we take the special subject-matter of reflexological investigation as having been unfolded in the previous chapters, it is essential at the very outset to examine whether a special method of investigation appertains to reflexology. In this respect, it is necessary to keep in mind that reflexology as a scientific doctrine began to collect its first material by means of a special experimental method. The necessity to take refuge in the strictly objective method of investigation in the so-called traumatic neuroses served as a special incentive.[1]

Then in 1886–1887, when experimenting on the motor area of the cerebral cortex,[2] I used dogs in some of which were inculcated by training, *i.e.* in an artificial way, movements in the form of giving the front paw when demanded by the master, in others, dancing movements on the hind paws when some inducement was offered (sugar, etc.). At that time, the opinion prevailed that learned movements are localised in the subcortical ganglia which are known as the striped body (corp. striatum). However, on the basis of my experiments, I proved that these artificial association reflexes are localised in the so-called motor or coat-muscular-motor area of the cerebral cortex, for, with the destruction of the latter, these reflexes permanently disappeared.

Subsequently, other writers also began to use trained animals in their experiments directed towards the investigation of the localisation of acquired reflexes in the cerebral cortex, and also for other purposes (Franz, Kalischer, Hachet-Souplet, and, in Russia, Afanasyev, and others).

Then a series of investigations (in my laboratory) made by me and also by my collaborators were devoted to the investigation of the rôle of the cerebral cortex in regard to the activity of the inner or vegetative organs, such as respiration, heart-beat, movements of the spleen, bladder, bowels, secretion of saliva, gastric juice, bile, tears, excretion from the kidneys and through perspiration.[3]

Further, the disappearance of natural association reflexes in the organs

---

[1] See V. Bechterev : *Proceedings of the 5th Pirogov Congress,* 1885–86. See the Debate on the Lecture on Traumatic Neuroses and Psychoses.

[2] See V. Bechterev : *The Physiology of the Motor Area of the Cerebral Cortex*—*Archiv. Psychiatrii,* 1886–87.

[3] See Bibliography in my *Principles of the Study of the Nervous Centres,* vol. VI. *Die Functionen der Nervencentra,* Hft. 3, Jena. Preliminary hints concerning the influence of the cerebral cortex on some of the vegetative functions had been already made by Bochefontaine.

indicated, as a result of the destruction of certain areas of the cerebral cortex, was described, beginning from 1898, in a series of dissertations and other works from my laboratory. Thus, in experiments on dogs, it became evident that the respiratory changes, which they develop on the approach of a cat, disappeared after the removal of the cortical respiratory centres, the electrical stimulation of which was accompanied before the removal by marked respiratory changes (Professor M. N. Zhukovsky). In all other respects, respiration remained unchanged. Then it was shown by special experiments in my laboratory that the lactic secretion of sheep through a tubule inserted in the dug—a secretion observed on the cry or sight of a lamb—stopped after the removal of a certain cortical centre (near the facialis) the stimulation of which formerly produced lactic secretion in the same sheep. (Professor M. P. Nikitin.)

Similar phenomena were discovered through experiments in my laboratory also in regard to other association reflexes such as sex reflexes, in the form of cessation of libido in a male dog (Professor L. M. Pussep), gastric juice secretion reflexes (Professor A. V. Gerver), and others which disappeared during the period immediately after the removal of certain areas of the cerebral cortex, while the animals retained the same functions in the form of ordinary reflexes.[1] Finally, my experiments have shown me that local (orientation) reflexes also are lost when the appropriate areas of the cortex are removed ; for instance, movement of the ear disappeared when the cortex of the gyrus angularis was removed, etc.[2] The same is true also of the pupil expansion in the case of sudden associative stimulations. This reflex disappeared when the cortical area expanding the pupil was removed in a dog.

It is clear that natural association reflexes occur with the participation of the cortex, and that their localisation is discoverable by the method of ablation. Thus the foundation was laid for the experimental investigation of natural association reflexes, an investigation which promises results of significance in the direction mentioned.

On the other hand, in the physiological laboratory of Professor I. Pavlov, a series of investigations were made on the conditions of the salivary secretion association reflex (" conditioned reflex "—according to the terminology of Pavlov's laboratory) which appears when the animal is shown nutritional products, and which has been already known since the end of the eighteenth century (Siebold). As early as 1833, Mitscherlich (*Poggendorffs Annalen*) made interesting investigations in regard to this reflex on a man suffering from fistula. In 1904–1905, Dr. Boldriev, in the physiological laboratory of the Military Medical Academy, succeeded in securing the artificial inculcation of the salivary secretion association or

[1] The contradictory results secured by Professor Gerver and Dr. Tichomirov and also Dr. Spirtov concerning the salivary secretion reflex on removal of the cortex are best explained on the ground that the subcortical ganglia speedily compensate for the function of the cortical area which has been removed.

[2] See V. Bechterev : *Nevr. Vestn.*, vol. XV, no. 1, 1908.

conditioned reflex, and a communication concerning this appeared a year later in the Papers of the Society of Russian Physicians. Numerous investigations, which afforded a number of important scientific data, were then made on this reflex in the same laboratory (and partly in ours and in others).

Being dissatisfied with this method, especially because of its inapplicability to man, I made a communication, in the spring of 1907, to the Society of Physicians of the Hospital of Nervous Diseases, and proved, on the basis of experiments made by me in collaboration with Dr. Spirtov, the

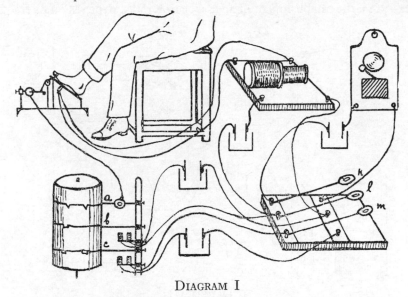

DIAGRAM I

Scheme of the arrangement of experiments in the inculcation of an association-motor reflex with electro-cutaneous stimulation of the sole of a man's foot.

possibility of producing an artificial association-motor reflex in the respiration of a dog. (See *Minutes* of these Meetings.)

A little later, the same reflex was produced in my laboratory on a man also (Dr. Anfimov), and then an artificial association-motor reflex was produced in my laboratory by the electrical stimulation of a dog's paw (Dr. V. P. Protopopov), and this experiment essentially improved the methodology of investigation of association-motor reflexes in dogs. After this, the artificial inculcation of an association-motor reflex from the sole, and later from the fingers, of a man (see diagrams I and II) was secured in my laboratory (Dr. Molotkov, *Dissertation*, St. Petersburg), according to a method suggested by me.

From this time, progress in the elaboration of this subject began to be swift as a result of the establishment of a new method, and gradually it became possible, in my laboratory, to produce in man an artificial association-motor reflex to a sound—an association-motor reflex in the form of the reflex which is obtained by knocking with a little hammer on the patellar ligament (Dr. Shevalev), and another reflex to a sound—a reflex after electric stimulation of the palm or the finger-tips (Bechterev and Shtchelovanov). In the following period, it became possible in our investigations to inculcate an association-motor reflex to any stimulus by other means also, for instance a verbal reflex or a reflex in the form of a certain movement, for instance a movement of the humerus. In this case, too, the establishment of an association reflex depends on its frequent

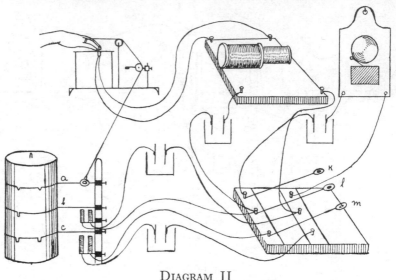

DIAGRAM II

Scheme of the arrangement of experiments in the inculcation of an association-motor reflex with electro-cutaneous stimulation of the fingers of a man's hand.

repetition simultaneous with some stimulus, for instance, a sound. Such reflexes were investigated in my laboratory by myself, Fedorin, Dobrotvorsky, Kunyaev, Protopopov, Dernova, and Shnirman, and then, on my suggestion, a method of investigation of the artificial cardio-vascular association reflex in man, by the plethysmograph,[1] and the differentiation of this reflex were successfully realised in my laboratory (Dr. Tchaly).[2]

[1] *Translators' note :* See Wheeler : *The Science of Psychology*, p. 230, Jarrolds, 1931.

[2] Dr. Tchaly lectured on the cardio-vascular association reflex and its differentiation to the neuro-psychiatric section of the Psychoneurological Institute at the beginning of 1914. These experiments have shown that cardio-vascular association reflexes also are subject to the law of differentation, just as association-motor reflexes are. (See below, on the law of differentiation.) The paper by Prof. Tzitovitch on the same subject appeared much later (*Physiologitchesky Vestnik*, 1918).

A very valuable asset in the investigation of association-motor reflexes is that it is possible, simply and conveniently, to register the reflexes on a recording drum, thanks to the mechanical transmission of the movement of the limb, to the air-water transmission (through a manometer) of respiratory excursions, and to the recording, by electric signs, of the funda-mental (electro-cutaneous) and the associative (sound, light, touch, etc.) stimuli, as is represented by the above diagrams (Diagrams I and II). The object of investigation—whether man or animal—is, for the purpose of precision in investigation, placed in a separate room in my laboratory, and only the organ to be investigated (hand or foot) may remain under the observer's control through a special window through which also the

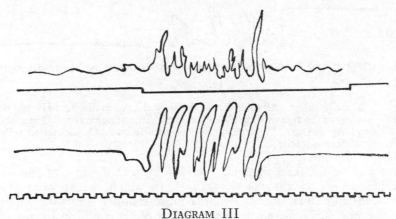

DIAGRAM III

Association reflex inculcated in a dog. The highest curved line denotes the record of respiration ; the second line along its depression denotes the sounding of a note of 564 vibrations on an Appun apparatus ; the third line shows the movement of the right paw ; the fourth repre-sents the time.

electrodes to the recording apparatus are drawn. All stimuli are applied to the subject by an electric switch which supplies current from the accumu-lators, and lies on a table which is outside the room, just as is the kymo-graph, which can even be taken into another room so as to avoid noise. Thus, the experiments concerned with the application to the subject of certain stimuli by means of a special electric switch can be performed in completely noiseless surroundings. Papers written by collaborators in my laboratory provide examples of records (see Diagrams III–VIII) of reflexes to show with what care the experiment is performed in regard to the reflexes obtained.

On the basis of the study of the totality of artificially and naturally inculcated association reflexes—motor and others—as well as on the basis of the objectivo-biological investigation of an individual human being in general and his constitution in particular, human reflexology really began to be built up as a science. It is regrettable that the method of secretory or saliva-secretory association reflexes, in the form in which it has been elaborated hitherto on dogs, is not applicable to man, because it demands an operation. The observation of the swallowing of secreted saliva in man, as has been made on children by Professor Krasnogorsky, may not be regarded

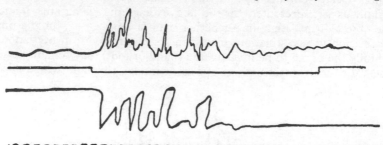

DIAGRAM IV

The same dog. All lines denote the same data as in diagram III, but the note is one of 632 vibrations on the same Appun apparatus. Thus both diagrams III and IV demonstrate an undifferentiated association reflex for different pitches.

as a sufficiently exact method. Besides, even in the case of animals, the technique of experiments on animals, in which the saliva is made to flow, through operation, along an artificial channel, limits the application of this method to mammals of a certain size. It is subject for regret, too, that this method is not applicable to particularly valuable or expensive animals, and also to all the smaller and lower animals.

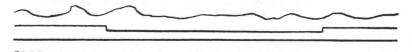

DIAGRAM V

The same dog. All lines denote the same data as in diagram III, but the previous note of 564 vibrations is produced on a 'cello; it may be seen that the dog makes no movement with the right paw, and his breathing is clearly impeded. Here there is already a differentiation in regard to the different timbre.

Besides, the necessary application of an acid solution as a stimulus in this method may affect the mucous membrane of the animal's mouth, because of the possibility of the development of stomatitis which prevents further investigations for a long time. To avoid this it is necessary to establish a certain shorter or longer interval between the applications of the stimuli (about one quarter of an hour) to the animals experimented on. The very procedure of opening the mouth by force, and even the bruising of the animal's lips if it resists (see Dr. Burmakin's *Dissertation* from the laboratory of I. Pavlov at the Military Medical Academy), in order to apply the acid stimulus to the animal, must be regarded as a condition

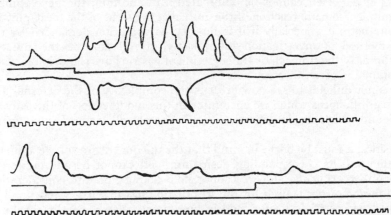

DIAGRAMS VI AND VII

Further experiment with the same dog. All lines denote the same data as in diagram III, but in the record of diagram VI, a fundamental note of 574 vibrations was sounded, and produced an association-motor reflex of the animal's right paw and of its breathing, while in the record of diagram VII, a note of 498 vibrations was sounded, and it is clear from this that a differentiation occurred not only in regard to the timbre of the instrument, as in the previous experiment, but also to a different note.

which sullies the purity of the experiment—the more so because the animal grows exceedingly restless during this procedure. The other kind of stimulation of the animal's oral cavity through its licking up pulverised

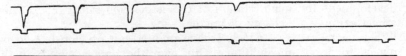

DIAGRAM VIII

The upper line represents the association-motor reflex of a human foot, a reflex inculcated to two simultaneous stimulations—light and sound. The second line represents the application of the light-stimulus, the third, of the sound, and the fourth, of the electrical. It is clear from the diagram that both factors of the composite stimulus produce an association reflex which, gradually, but not in the same period of time, disappears if not sustained by the fundamental electrical stimulus.

meat offered to it—a method later introduced—is associated with the opening of the jaws by the animal itself, its protruding its tongue, movement of its head, and, what is still more important, with olfactory stimulations. The consequent swallowing of the pulverised meat is here inevitable, just as the animal's licking its snout after the swallowing of the powder, the movement of the animal's head, and the visual stimulation from the meat-powder itself cannot be eliminated ; in addition, the development of a mimico-somatic reaction of the animal at the sight of the meat-powder is quite natural, especially if it is hungry—a condition demanded by the very method of investigation—and, lastly, stimulation of the mucous membrane of the stomach by the secretion of gastric juice is inevitable when the animal is given meat-powder.

It is not difficult to see how great is the complexity of the external and internal influences which we encounter in this modification of the salivary reflex and which are, in general, difficult to make allowance for in experiments.

Besides, it must be borne in mind that the unequal degree of the animal's satiation and its corresponding desire for food cannot be an indifferent factor in experiments, and we cannot help taking this into consideration when meat-powder is used for the stimulation of the salivary reflex. The unequal degree of desire for food in an animal must, generally speaking, vary very considerably in accordance with a multitude of conditions often untraceable, and this very fact inevitably influences the results of experiments employing the saliva method of investigation. All this must be borne in mind when conclusions are drawn from the comparison of results obtained from different experiments.

In regard to all of this, it must be remembered that, for accuracy in the investigation of the saliva association reflex, it is necessary to take into account various conditions which influence the manifestation of the saliva reflex produced by stimulation of the oral cavity, because, as we know, this reflex, on the basis of which the association reflex must be inculcated, varies widely, not only in regard to the quantity, but also the quality, of the secretion, and this circumstance necessarily influences also the development and manifestation of the association-saliva reflex which sometimes assumes a " chaotic character."

All these facts, many of which I have pointed out previously,[1] do not permit us to apply unconditionally to man the data secured by this method.

Again, we must note the circumstance that secretion is a function which is outside the active influence of the individual investigated, and therefore, in general, cannot serve for the thoroughgoing investigation of correlative human activity—an investigation which also embraces the inner (volitional —according to subjective terminology) stimulation of the excitation or inhibition of association reflexes. Nevertheless, we must not forget that the investigation of secretory, as well as cardio-vascular, reflexes has special significance in mimico-somatic states.

The saliva reflexes of dogs have also provided material for numerous investigations which have made possible the detailed study not only of the

[1] V. Bechterev : *The Significance of the Motor Sphere—Russky Vratch*, 1909, nos. 33, 35, and 36

various conditions of inhibition and its release, but also other peculiarities in the manifestations of the correlative activity of dogs.

Luckily, in all animals, and especially in man, who particularly interests us in regard to the study of correlative activity, the secretory activities play a much smaller part than do motor activities, and, as a result of this, and for other reasons also (the absence of an operation, the possibility of exact recording, the possibility of frequent repetition of the stimuli—after 10–20 seconds—and the absence of any complications as a result of frequent stimulation in experiment) we give unconditional preference, in view of the above-mentioned defects of the saliva method, to the method of investigation of association-motor reflexes of the extremities and of respiration—a method developed in my laboratory.

This method, which is equally applicable to animals and to man, and consists in the electrical stimulation of the front paw of the animal, and in man, of the palm or fingers of the hand, or the ball of the foot, with simultaneous visual, auditory, cutaneo-muscular, and other stimulations, has, as far as I know, not met with any opposition in scientific literature from the time of its publication.

There are only some brief remarks made by Dr. Eliason, who, having met with opposition because of his application of the saliva method in his experiments, has remarked in his address to the Oto-laryngological Society that the general conditions of the organism are more or less intensely reflected in respiration, which is studied through the method of the motor association-reflex, and that the sphere of consciousness (?) is reflected in movement in general.

The first remark is perfectly justified, because such phenomena as respiration and blood pressure, and also the secretory processes, including saliva secretion, necessarily reflect the general conditions of the organism. But from the records of respiration by my pneumograph (a tubular belt filled with water or a flat rubber balloon) it is not difficult to see what the condition of respiration is at a given moment, and it is understood that changes in respiration are recorded relatively to the general respiratory wave, which is more or less constant throughout a certain period of time.

The investigation of respiratory association reflexes and of association-motor reflexes of the extremities is particularly valuable for us, because we are enabled to trace in the record of respiration the slightest deviations indicating whether the external stimuli are reflected in it in an activating or a depressing manner, and this is, in some cases, an irreplaceable convenience.

Thus, it has been proved for the first time, by records of respiration, that, in the period of development of a differentiated association reflex, that stimulus which was previously presented simultaneously with the electrical, produces an association-motor reflex in the dog's paw, while all other stimuli, without producing a reflex in the paw, have an effect on respiration in the form of a clearly expressed depression. (Diagram V.)

Curves which convince in this respect may be seen also in Professor V. P. Protopopov's *Dissertation* which has issued from my laboratory. Facts of a similar kind can scarcely be represented in a clearer manner than in the respiratory function. Besides, it is a factor of great value that the respiratory curve is a nicer and, therefore, more demonstrative reaction than other motor reactions. But in order to remove or isolate the influence of general conditions on the motor functions under investigation, we use, simultaneously with the investigation of respiration, a record of movements of the extremities, and it is clear that, whenever necessary, in some experiments both the change in respiration and the movement of the extremity can be recorded simultaneously ; in other experiments we may rest content either with the record of the movement of the extremity merely or the record of the change in respiration merely.

It is scarcely necessary to mention that, in regard to the association-reflex movement of the extremity in the conditions prevailing in the arrangement of our experiments, there is not, and there cannot be, any objection in respect of the influence of the general conditions of the organism. It remains for us to examine the influence of " consciousness," *i.e.* (as far as we can gather) the influence of the knowledge both of the aim of the experiments and of the expected result, which may be changed, because of that knowledge, by the personal interference of the individual experimented on.

It is scarcely necessary to remark that this question does not arise in regard to animals, and is significant only in regard to man.

But by special experiments performed in our laboratory, it has been proved that a firmly inculcated association-motor reflex cannot be suppressed by personal efforts, and, consequently, its investigation is applicable, as I have frequently pointed out, to the detection of simulated blindness, deafness, anesthesia, and paralysis.[1] Only a reflex as yet not fixed can be subject to any extent to inner inhibition by personal efforts.

Another question arises : Is it possible to produce, by personal efforts, an imitation reflex through a " volitional " movement of the foot or hand ?

This question, too, has been listed for solution in my laboratory, and there are data which lead us to suppose that the times at which a true

[1] The method of detection of simulated deafness by association reflexes, a method developed in my laboratory, was published by me as early as 1912 (see no. 67 in the appended bibliography) and, on being demonstrated at the Dresden Physiological Exhibition, was there awarded first prize. Later investigations in the same direction and by the same method, investigations by Dr. Arendarenko : *The Conditioned Motor Reflex to Sound Stimuli in the Detection of Simulated Deafness* in *Vestnik ushnich, gorlovich i nosovich boleznei*, 1913, and by N. Paütov : *Conditioned Reflexes in the Detection of Simulated Deafness* in *Naütchnaya Medicina*, no. 11, 1923. In the latter work, the writer, in his bibliography, does not even mention my paper, notwithstanding the fact that both the application of the method itself and the results of the work are essentially a repetition of the results of my work.

association reflex and an imitation reflex are manifested give a clue by which to distinguish the one from the other.

As a result of my experiments, I am convinced of the influence of suggestion on the development and manifestation of the association reflex.[1] But this fact, although interesting in itself, does not detract from the automatic character of the reflex. It must be noted, however, that the above-mentioned question is significant only when those to be experimented on have been initiated into the character and aims of the investigation; but under the conditions observed in experimentation in my laboratory, this does not happen. Such investigations are made, should the necessity arise, in such a way that the person experimented on, usually a stranger to the laboratory, is not at all initiated into the method of the experiments, or their aim, or the course of the investigation itself.

As regards the reflexology of man, it has developed gradually like other sciences. As early as 1893–1894, at the 5th Pirogov Congress in St. Petersburg, during the discussion of the question of the medico-legal significance of traumatic psychoneurosis—characterised almost exclusively by subjective symptoms at that time—I proposed that a strictly objective investigation of these abnormal states was necessary, and also pointed out a number of objective indications which a more thorough investigation reveals in these patients. (See *Proceedings of the 5th Pirogov Congress*, 1896.) In 1896, in the *Obozrenie Psychiatrii*, I proposed to regard the external receptive organs as transformers of external energies (p. 89), and put forward the theory of discharges for the transmission of energy from one neuron to the other (p. 23), and so established the energic viewpoint of the functions of the brain and its " psychic " activities. After the study of the objective manifestations of hypnosis (*Nevrologitchesky Vestnik*, 1893 ; *Obozrenie Psychiatrii*, 1902, pp. 12 and 96) and of various manifestations of common neuroses and psychoses, such as the traumatic psychoneurosis and others (*Nevrologitchesky Vestnik*, 1895 ; *Neur. Centr.*, 1895 ; *Obozrenie Psychiatrii*, 1889 ; *Neur. Centr.*, 1900 ; *Obozrenie Psychiatrii*, 1901, p. 19, and others), I published a general outline under the title of *Objective Psychology and its Subject-matter*, in *Vestnik Psychologii*, 1904 (translated into French in the *Revue scientifique*, 1906). In 1907, an experimental method of investigation of association-motor reflexes was developed in my laboratory, first on animals and then also on men. After that, the application of the strictly objective method in general, and, in particular, of the experimental method of association-motor reflexes, to the investigation of the neuro-psychical sphere in general, was systematically elaborated. (See my papers : *The Methods of Objective Investigation of the Neuro-psychical Sphere*—Address to the Scientific Meetings of the Hospital, 1907, 24th May ; *Objective Investigation of Neuro-psychical Activity*—Speech delivered at the International Congress of Psychiatry and Experimental Psychology in Amsterdam, 1907 ; *Proceedings* of this

[1] See my address in the *Minutes of the Scientific Conference of the Institute for the Study of Brain*, 1921.

Congress and *Obozrenie Psychiatrii*, 1907 ; *The Reproductive and Associative Activity of the Nervous System,—Obozrenie Psychiatrii*, 1908 ; *Early Stages in the Evolution of Children's Drawings*—Communications to the Russian Society of Normal and Pathological Psychology in 1908, published in *Vestnik Psychologii*, 1910, and separate edition ; *The Objective Investigation of the Neuro-psychical Sphere in Infants*—Address to the Committee of the Pedological Institute in April 1908, published in *Vestnik Psychologii*, 1909 ; *The Aim and Method of Objective Psychology*—Speech on the Anniversary of the Opening of the Hospital for Nervous and Psychic Diseases, November, 1908—*Novoye Slovo*, 1909, February ; *What is Objective Psychology ?—Voprosi philosophii i psychologii*, 1909 ; *The Significance of the Investigation of the Motor Sphere for the Objective Study of the Neuro-psychical Sphere in Man—Russky Vratch*, Nos. 33, 35, 36, 1909 ; *The Individual Development of the Neuro-psychical Sphere from the Standpoint of the Data of Objective Psychology*, 1910 ; *The Fundamental Manifestations of the Neuro-psychical Activity in their Objective Study—Russky Vratch*, 1911 ; *The Evolution of the Neuro-psychical Sphere—Russky Vratch*, 1913. A list of other works is appended at the end of the present work. In 1906 began the printing, and in 1907 appeared the first part, of *Objective Psychology :* the second part appeared a little later.)

It must be noted that, in the course of some years, beginning from the foundation of the Courses of the Psychoneurological Institute (1908), I delivered a series of lectures there on reflexology. Later, I delivered a similar course of lectures at the State Institute of Medical Sciences, in the Petersburg Medical Institute, and in the Pedological Courses of the Psychoneurological Academy. These Courses later developed into the Psychologo-Reflexological Faculty of the Institute of Pedology and Defectology.

I shall also mention that, after my address on the fundamental aims of reflexology (in Moscow) to the General Congress for the Protection of Children's Health and to the Conference on Defective Children, both congresses unanimously passed a resolution that the delivery of a course of reflexology in all medical and pedagogical institutions was necessary. Also, the latest Congress of Psychoneurology, which met at Leningrad in January, 1924, passed the following resolution : " It is necessary to introduce into S.S.S.R. instruction in the science of the behaviour of animals and man studied from the objective standpoint, and the fundamental content of this science must be the investigation of those internal (biological, physico-chemical) and external (physical and social) factors which determine the development of the human being and his behaviour." The Congress also emphasised in another resolution the importance of genetic reflexology in the study of the child.

All this shows what a secure conquest the new department of science, which I call reflexology, has made here in S.S.S.R.

It must be remembered that, after us, the Americans also have followed the line of objective study of human behaviour. Especially illuminating in this respect are the works of Weiss, Russell, Watson, and many others in the *Psychological Review*, and the monographs by Meyer, Bernard, Mod, Benthli, Kenagy, and others on so-called behaviourism.[1] There are also works by Dutch scientists referring to a later period.

[1] *Translators' note :* The original has these names, printed in Latin type, in the form in which they are here reproduced.

CHAPTER XVII

The significance of the method of training (dressage) in the investigation of correlative activity. The investigation of animal behaviour in artificially created surroundings. The aim reflex.

THE method of training, which, as has been already mentioned, we used for the first time for the cerebro-cortical localisation of learned movements, which are a kind of motor association reflexes, is recently acquiring new significance.

The following extract from Mendus, the author of the work *Du dressage à l'éducation* (p. 23, Paris, 1910), shows that this method is a kind of artificial inculcation of association reflexes.

" The method remains the same whether there is question of teaching a bear to dance, of making a parrot draw a little cart or throw somersaults on the table, of teaching an elephant to blow a trumpet, to act the waiter, or to walk on wooden bottles, etc. It is necessary to connect in the animal's mind the idea of the given movement with a given stimulus, which, during the repetitions of the exercise, must remain unchanged all the time, whatever its nature may be (a gesture of the trainer, the tone of his voice, a melody, a tit-bit received, etc.), and it is only necessary that the connection between the stimulus and the idea of the movement should be sufficiently strong for the stimulus inevitably to produce the appropriate reaction."

The development of obedience is achieved through education thus. In the case of a conflict between the teacher and the pupil, *i.e.* the animal, it is necessary that the former should prove the victor at all costs. If the trainer " succumbs even once to the resistance of the horse, it will never properly submit to training."

This is confirmed by V. L. Durov, from conversations with whom I have been convinced that the so-called " breaking of the will " of an animal can be achieved only if the trainer, in no circumstances, allows the animal to evade anything that appertains to its training.

It must be kept in mind that by training it is possible to direct the animal along the path of its natural bent, or to inhibit the manifestation of certain tendencies, but we cannot expect new tendencies to arise as a result of its training. Trainers can correct defects, but training is powerless to create in animals special endowments which have not been bestowed on them by nature. The special significance of the method of training consists in the unfolding of the individual peculiarities of certain species of animals and also in their association-reflex development.

The defects of this method are that the training itself, because of its exacting character, depends partly on skill, and also that this method does not lend itself to being precisely recorded ; lastly, that it is applicable to animals, but, for perfectly obvious reasons, comparatively little to man. However, within certain limits, it may be applied to man also : for instance, the training of sportsmen and the like conforms to precisely the same principles as does the training of animals, and education itself is, to a considerable extent, reducible to the acquisition of habits and to training, identical with the training of animals.

Comparatively recently, Hachet-Souplet[1] in France made extensive investigations in which he applied this method.

In his investigations on animals, he partly used our method also, and that with complete success.

However that may be, the method of training is not devoid of valuable scientific significance, and, as we know, noteworthy facts have been revealed by means of this method.

Hachet-Souplet has extensively used the method of training in his study of the development of the so-called instincts.

By training in this context is to be understood the art of teaching animals to obey words, signs, or other stimuli which had previously no influence whatever on them. Synonymously, there is question of learned movements produced on a definite signal. This teaching of animals is achieved either by their attraction to a definite object by means of some allurement, or by incitation to the performance of the act by means of a whip or some other intense (for instance, electric) stimulus. We may distinguish between training in the true sense of the word, when the effects produced are habit phenomena, and other procedures, in which, although they are related to habits, man participates only in the general preparation of the experiment and without using the method of real training. Thus, for instance, a crab goes towards the light of a candle through a small aperture, and so gradually acquires the habit of passing through it more and more quickly.

Really these methods are not training in the true sense of the word, for the light-stimulus acts directly on the crab, and this stimulus is not replaced by any other signals in the experiment.

Here there is question of the establishment of an association without obedience to a human signal and, consequently, this does not appertain to training in the true sense of the word. Similar examples may be found in self-education.

A pigeon, for instance, flying round a horse's head, at first frightened the horse by the whirring of its wings and thus made him spill grain from his nose-bag. Led by this casual experience, it repeated the trick several times and for the same purpose.

We shall also cite the famous example of the pike in Moebius's experiment. This pike, having been isolated from fish by a glass, bumped its snout against the glass every time it wanted to seize a fish. At length, it broke its habit of rushing at the fish and, afterwards, when the glass was removed and the pike remained in one aquarium with the other fish, it did not touch them.

In the first example, that of the pigeon, there was question of an independently inculcated action; in the second example, of an inculcated inhibition of an action. Returning to our terminology, we say that, in the

[1] Hachet-Souplet : *La genèse des instincts*, Paris.

o

first case, a natural association reflex was formed ; in the second case, a natural association reflex was inhibited as a result of an artificially created condition.

According to Hachet-Souplet, elementary training consists in a stimulus producing an effective dynamogenous excitation, associated, by the mechanism of " recurrence," with the idea, which in turn becomes dynamogenous.

The same phenomena occur in the natural life-conditions of animals. As the trainer regulates the order of the stimuli according to the task, and is guided by a certain plan, so also the external world regulates the order of stimuli which are presented to animals in freedom.

Needless to say, the method we are examining has enormous significance for the reflexology of animals, in the sense of studying those phenomena which the same author (Hachet-Souplet), for some reason or other, and without sufficient ground, refers to the category of " instinct." He uses the term " instinct " or " instinctive action " not in our sense, but in the sense—general in animal psychology—of the contraposition of these actions to those which are known to belong to the category of the so-called " rational." Consequently, his concept of " instinct " is widened to such an extent as to include all association reflexes, with the exception of personal reflexes.

Hachet-Souplet's method of investigation is, in principle, quite analogous to our method. " Let us assume "—says he—" that the animal has been taught by training to perform a reaction after affective stimulation. If we want to discover whether it is susceptible to auditory, olfactory, visual, and other stimuli, we must several times produce, by means of the given affective stimuli, affective states accompanied by a definite motor reaction. When, at a given moment, affective stimuli, which on their initial application produced no reaction, at last begin to produce it without the excitation of the affective stimulus, it will be proved that a nexus has been formed between the motor impulse, on the one hand, and, on the other hand, the sensation produced by that stimulus the effect of which we wish to discover. If, on the contrary, the subject remains inert under these conditions, the absence of the appropriate sensations is proved."

It is clear that we have here, in subjective terminology, a description of the foundations of the same method as we have used in our earlier investigations.

The same author employs, in the training of animals, as we have already mentioned, not only allurements, but also electric discharges as a means of producing a suppressing effect in regard to certain " instinctive " actions.

" Having determined the sensory capacity (*faculté sensorielle*), the experimenter, in order to determine its intensity, has only to repeat the same experiments and decrease the intensity of the stimulus in each test. The minimal intensity of stimulation necessary for a noticeable reaction denotes the lowest threshold of sensation."

It must be noted that the preface to Hachet-Souplet's book is dated January, 1911 ; consequently, the work was published many years after our works on objective psychology. And in it there is also mention of our method of producing association-motor reflexes. It is obvious, therefore, that Hachet-Souplet's method is in this respect a borrowing from the work of the Russian school.

It is evident that, as regards its content, Hachet-Souplet's method deserves no reproach from our side.

I regret to say that Hachet-Souplet assumes the subjective standpoint in general, as may be seen from the passages quoted. On p. 112, he writes thus :

" Having such a constitution, man can never regard anything in the subjective sphere as simpler than sensation." " When attempts are made to explain it objectively, they are nothing more than dreams."

Then the same author speaks of " affective sensations " or " feelings " and of " feeling ideas " and, of course, extends these phenomena to animals. In another passage, he says : " We think that Loeb is wrong when he writes that one advances a useless hypothesis when, in respect of the lower animals, one assumes sensation as a necessary mediating link between external excitation and the effect. The lower animals surely experience pain and pleasure."

Further in his work Hachet-Souplet speaks, at every step, of the consciousness and intelligence of animals.

Even in the experimental section, the same author does not proceed without subjectivism. These " subjective " explanations naturally lead him into error. So, touching on the problem of associations, he speaks, for instance, of the method of investigation through training with the participation of self-observation. Besides, in regard to the law of association, he thinks, being guided by self-observation, that reproduction in man always occurs in the same succession as do the stimuli. In higher and intellectually developed animals, for instance in apes, he assumes that the same is probably true, but, in the vast majority of animals, he assumes that associations occur in a succession which is the reverse of the order of events.

Needless to say, this is one of those errors which cannot be avoided by the " subjectivist " psychologists, who arbitrarily furnish the animal kingdom with experiences derived from their own psychic world.

" Let us assume," says the same author, " that an animal is being trained to approach on hearing the words : ' Come here ! ' At first it is indifferent, and does not manifest any reaction. But then it is offered pleasant food as an allurement which makes the animal come, and this is a natural reaction. Later, the allurement may be removed, and the words ' Come here ! ' which preceded the allurement, call out, in turn, the same reaction." He calls this the " law of recurrence," which, in its objective nature, was studied long before him in my laboratory, and which I call the " law of signals."

To speak of a contrast between man and the lower animals is impermissible, because, when the experiments are identically arranged, we get the same phenomena in man.

Thereby, we do not wish to depreciate the generally very valuable methodological hints of the same author in the sphere of the manifestation of those animal reflexes which he calls "instinctive."

Still, the subjective trend of his work isolates him from a number of other writers who adhere to the strictly objective method in the study of animal behaviour.[1]

In America, the objective study of animal psychology has recently taken hold, and almost every large university has founded a chair of animal behaviour. Even a number of text-books on this subject have been published—Holmes, Jennings, Washburn, Watson, and others ; and, in addition, special periodicals are issued such as *The Journal of Animal Behaviour*.

The general character of the investigations is based on the behaviour of an animal trying to reach some allurement in the form of food, while the animal's efforts meet with some obstacle placed in its way. The overcoming of these difficulties, in terms of the time necessary for reaching the food and of the number of deviations made by the animal in reaching the goal, serves as the measure of the animal's mental capacity.

One kind of apparatus used in such investigations is the maze. This is a box divided into corridors and blind alleys, and in the middle is a food box, from which the animal, let into the labyrinth, gets food. In this labyrinth, the animal learns, after a more or less long series of trials, to find its food quickly and without error.

What organs serve, in this case, as guides in finding the food may be determined either by an operation for the removal of certain organs or by the introduction of certain external stimuli. Watson, for instance, has proved in this way that rats, when finding their food in the labyrinth, use kinesthetic stimuli chiefly, but partly touch ; while blind rats, and those devoid of smell, generally reach the goal as quickly as do normal rats.

However, vision also is not indifferent here. This has been proved by the work of Stelly Vincent, who, in her maze experiments, painted the walls and floors of the corridors of the labyrinth in different colours ; for instance, the right way was painted a brilliant white, and the blind alleys black. It happened that in such a labyrinth the rats found their food more quickly than in an ordinary one. So if, for instance, in learning in an ordinary labyrinth, the rats, to reach their goal, require 1,804 seconds in the first experiment and make 149 errors, in a painted box the rats

---

[1] Investigations of lower animals have, for a long time, been made from the strictly objective standpoint, as we have already mentioned. We in S.S.S.R. have also made beautiful investigations on insects, from this standpoint. I shall indicate, as an example, the valuable works of Professor V. Vagner, not to mention many others.

reach the same goal in 1,342 seconds and with 5–7 errors. Besides, the number of errors decreases more rapidly in subsequent trials.

However, visual guidance had no special influence on the end-results, for at the end of the learning period the rats followed the correct route without mistakes in the same time-interval. The experimenter concludes from this that vision helps only during the period of learning, but the automatism which results is directed, at the end of the learning period, by kinesthetic impulses mainly. Smell and, later, touch, as shown by analogous experiments, play a similar auxiliary rôle.

Experiments made on crabs by Schwarz and Saphir have shown that maze experiments are successful in the case of invertebrates also, although A. Bethe is sceptical about their capacity to learn. Other apparatus were used in experiments to investigate the organs of perception, for instance, by Jensen and Hunter in their investigation of hearing in dogs and rats. Both investigators have come to the conclusion that dogs and rats do not distinguish pure tones ; and Hunter's experiments have led to the conclusion that rats are guided by noises and soon learn to localise them. However, experiments on dogs, in regard to sounds, contradict Dr. Zeliony's experiments in Leningrad, and Dr. V. P. Protopopov's experiments in my laboratory. These used more accurate methods, and, therefore, the former experiments must be subjected to appropriate test.

Experiments in the distinguishing of colour by animals are also interesting. Such are obviously among the most difficult experiments of this kind.

Formerly there was no doubt about the animals' capacity to distinguish colours. On this fact the theories of protective colouring or mimicry and of sexual selection were built. Also the symbiosis of insects with flowers was based on the supposition of the insects' capacity to distinguish bright colours. But Jesse began to prove experimentally that invertebrates do not distinguish colours at all. However, Frisch has decidedly opposed Jesse's views and come to the conclusion that bees, for instance, distinguish colours excellently. In Professor I. Pavlov's laboratory, his disciple, Professor Orbeli, maintained, as a result of experiments on the saliva reflex, that the dog does not react differently to different colours (see his *Dissertation*, St. Petersburg), while, in my laboratory, Dr. Valker has shown, by means of the association-motor method, that dogs react differently to different colours (Address to the Scientific Meetings of the Hospital for Psychic and Nervous Diseases, St. Petersburg). Other investigators, also, have, in this case, secured results which do not agree with Professor Orbeli's.

Not long ago, in America, Yerkes painstakingly investigated, by means of a special apparatus he constructed, the capacity of wild pigeons to distinguish colours. After many experiments, this investigator came to the conclusion that pigeons decidedly choose red out of two colours—red and green. However, he does not solve the problem whether their choice depends on difference in the intensity of the colours.

The investigations of Lashley, Watson's disciple, who worked on Bantam chickens, may serve as a supplement to Yerkes's experiments. It was discovered first of all that the chickens were from the very beginning positively phototropic.

This investigator first inculcated an association reflex to the intensity of light, and then he went on to the investigation of the influence of chromatic stimuli. Ultimately, he came to the conclusion that hens distinguish 4–6 different colours, for instance, green, red, reddish-orange, and yellow. Parrots, also, distinguish the fundamental colours (N. N. Ladigina-Kots). De Vosse and Rosa Hanson, who experimented on cats, came to the conclusion that they are incapable of distinguishing colours. The cats were at large, and the stimuli consisted not of spectrum light, but of pieces of coloured paper with which the opening of the box was covered. Ultimately, the investigators came to the conclusion that cats react to the intensity of light, but not to colours.[1]

Further, R. Yerkes's investigations by the method of natural selection deserve attention. This method consists in the following : the animal experimented on must learn to select one of a number of mechanisms, and the correct choice gives him some satisfaction, for instance food. Immediately after the selection, the number and position of the mechanisms to be selected is changed. Experiments were made on birds and on mammals including anthropoid apes. According to the opinion of the investigator, this method makes possible the comparative evaluation of the mental development of animals. But from my point of view, the method itself does not give much certainty.

We must also call attention to the investigations concerning the imitative capacity of animals—investigations first made, with negative results, by Professor Thorndike and later, with positive results, on cats by Dr. Barry in R. Yerkes's laboratory ; Kinnaman's experiments on apes, and N. N. Kots's on chimpanzees—also with positive results.[2] We shall not enter into the details of these and many later investigations which have their objective trend in their favour. I shall only remark that, recently, the literature on the objective study of animal behaviour has grown considerably and in America an approach is being made to the study of human behaviour, a study which has first been set on a scientific basis on Russian soil in my laboratories at the Military Medical Academy and at the Psychoneurological Institute.

In all the above-mentioned experiments on animals, the investigators used allurements in the form of food, which the animals had to get.

[1] Is this peculiarity connected, perhaps, with the fact that the cat's eye is adapted for vision not only in the day time, but also at night, when colours in general are merged ? However that may be, Dr. Studentzov's investigations, made in my laboratory by the method of training, have shown that even such larval vertebrates as caudata distinguish both sounds and fundamental colours.

[2] My paper on the imitative speech of parrots refers to the investigation of the imitative capacity of the lower animals—birds. *Voprosi izutcheniya i vospitaniya litchnosti*, 4–5, 1922.

Thus, in these investigations on animals, there was question of an " aim " reflex. In the case of the adult, in whom higher interests are prevalent, the above-mentioned arrangement of experiments is, for quite comprehensible reasons, impossible, but in infants and children the food allurement may be utilised as the primary stimulus in experiments. Besides, the maze may be used for experiments in the form of children's games. But in the case of an adult, the aim may be created either by offering him some prize or by previous agreement with the experimenter. Thus, he can, under these conditions, perform some task, for instance select some objects from a number, make calculations, solve jig-saw puzzles and other problems, form sentences from words, exhibit creative activity in a certain task, etc. Moreover, a pictorial representation on paper of the maze, as modified by Dr. Ivanov-Smolensky, who worked in my laboratory, may serve, as experience shows, as a method of experimenting on human beings, especially in childhood. The task, the solution of which is required, consists in finding the shortest way, avoiding blind alleys, from the periphery to the centre of the maze. In experiments of this kind the time necessary for the performance of the task must be noted, and also the quality of the performance, expressed in the number of errors, must be taken into account.

We must mention that the maze method can be considerably improved. For this purpose I have proposed to construct a sectional maze in which the food is visible to the animal through wire-netting or glass. The investigation begins with a fewer number of obstacles and, when these are overcome, the number is increased. The obstacles are marked with numbers. The number of the obstacles surmounted determines the degree of the animal's resourcefulness. In this manner, I could investigate the resourcefulness of hens at different ages.

Needless to say, " aim " actions are more complex than other association reflexes, for in them we see a co-ordinated connection of a number of association reflexes or a complex of the latter, directed towards the achievement of a certain end as a stimulus. But in this case, we find greater dependence on individual—positive or negative—attitude on the part of the subject to the performance of the experiment and this must be taken into account by the experimenter—the more so as man cannot be put into the position of an animal forced by hunger to strive towards the attainment of food.[1]

A similar attitude may be found especially in cases where the subject is interested in preventing the attainment of correct results. That is why the experiment, in such cases, must be invariably supplemented by appropriate observation of the subject, and this observation must, of course, be just as strictly objective as the experiment itself.

Besides, the irreproachableness of the method of investigation by the

---

[1] And again, in experiments on animals, we must take into account the circumstance that the investigation must be made under conditions of moderate hunger for it would obviously give different results if made on sated animals.

association-reflex method is evident from the fact that, as soon as we began the investigation, it was revealed, during the inculcation of association reflexes, that the central excitation produced by the stimulation very quickly extends to all stimulations of the given organ and to all degrees of intensity of those stimulations. After this, the subsequent differentiation of these reflexes begins in the sense that they are produced by only one stimulus with which the primary stimulus, in the form of an electrical current, has been associated. Thus, the theory of the specificness of conditioned stimuli was excluded, a theory which at that time was supported by those who used the saliva method in Professor I. Pavlov's laboratory. The same process of initial eccentric extension or generalisation of the excitation and its subsequent differentiation holds good also of the responsive reaction. This can easily be shown in experiments on dogs. In experiments in which an association reflex in respiration was recorded, it was not difficult to show that the initial, eccentrically extended process of excitation is replaced by a process of inhibition, which spreads concentrically ; and thus, precisely, the process of differentiation is effected.

Further, it was discovered in our laboratory that if we have a composite stimulus, for instance, light and sound, to which a reflex is inculcated, the latter may be produced also by the individual components of the composite stimulus, although in weaker and unequal degree (Professor Platonov).

The same has been recently discovered in our laboratory also in regard to the individual colours which constitute a composite colour stimulus. This process is analysis. However, it has been shown by Professor Platonov's investigations that the composite stimulus can be differentiated from its components, so that the association reflex is obtained only by the activity of the composite colour stimulus, but not by its individual constituent parts. This process we call synthesis or generalisation. Besides, an association reflex to two or more different stimuli, for instance tones of different pitch, can be inculcated by the usual method, while the reflex will not appear to other tones. This phenomenon we call selective generalisation.

Lastly, our attention is drawn to the interesting fact that if a dog is prevented from realising an association reflex in that extremity in which it has been inculcated, it is replaced by a reflex in the extremity on the other side.

These are the main characteristics discovered even in the first experiments in the inculcation of association-motor reflexes in dogs and in man. All the other points will be discussed later. The great individual differences, which appear in different persons, in the speed of the appearance and in the durability of association reflexes also deserve attention. Here one may meet with types characterised by great sluggishness in regard to association reflexes and others characterised by the speed of the appearance and by the special durability of association reflexes.

CHAPTER XVIII

The relation of reflexology to experimental psychology. The experimental method usually employed in the exploration of the higher manifestations of correlative activity.

AN important problem presents itself for immediate solution : the relation of human reflexology to contemporaneous experimental psychology. More accurately expressed, the problem is : whether the data arrived at by the experimento-psychological method have special significance for reflexology ; and if so, what is this significance.

Here we must first of all note that by experimental psychology we are to understand that sphere of subjectivo-psychological knowledge which has been secured by means of experiment, for experimental psychology has no other aims than the investigation of subjective (inner) experiences. Like observational psychology, it really studies the same processes of perception, ideas, memory, attention, association ; volitional process, etc., but utilises experimental conditions in their study. Experiment supplements and refines observation and, anyhow, observation is merely experiment under natural conditions, and, therefore, experimental psychology, while remaining an essentially subjective science, supplements observational subjective psychology with which mankind has been long acquainted, and which, because of the experimental method which it has adopted, has, for some time, been receiving more steady support for its tenets.

In other words, contemporary experimental psychology and subjective observational psychology, as sciences prosecuting the same end—the study of man's inner world, one, by observation, *i.e.* natural experiment, the other by experiment, *i.e.* artificial experiment—form between them that scientific doctrine which we call " subjective " psychology, but we must keep in mind that its fundamental aim is the study of subjective processes or processes of consciousness, a study which relies chiefly on the introspective method.

Therefore, it is natural that the conclusions of contemporary experimental psychology, in as far as they refer to the study of processes of consciousness, cannot have direct significance for our doctrine, which has as its fundamental aim the study of the objective manifestations of correlative, and, in particular, association-reflex, activity, as an integration of higher reflexes, and these conclusions may be used only when checked against the objective data of reflexology.

But the material acquired in the experimento-psychological investigations may be of some value to reflexology, if the results of the experiments are examined quite independently of subjective processes or processes of consciousness and only from the strictly objective viewpoint, just as they are given in the experimental conditions.

Let us take the well-known correction method which consists in the crossing out of certain letters of the text—a method which was first introduced by Binet, and which is so much used in experimental psychology for the study of processes of attention. Needless to say, the results obtained by this method do not depend on attention alone and, besides, may occur almost automatically, and, therefore, the method does not give quite irreproachable results in regard to attention. But for reflexology, this method, improved in my laboratory by Dr. Ilyin,[1] Dr. Anfimov, and others, determines the capacity to choose or, rather, to designate certain objects, and, in as far as we shall evaluate, as a method applied in work, the results obtained by this method from the viewpoint of choosing, we shall get quite objective data which characterise the given person.

Let us take another example. Mental arithmetic, consisting in addition and subtraction, is a method much used in the investigation of complex processes of mental capacity for work. If, however, we shall not evaluate, from the point of view of conscious processes, the results obtained by this method, especially as there is question not only of so-called reflection, but also of memory, associations, and other subjective processes here,

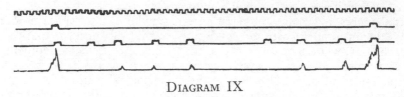

DIAGRAM IX

The upper line—time indication ; the second line from top—electrical stimulus on the ball of the foot ; the third line from top—indication of sound-stimulus ; the fourth line—reaction of the sole of the foot. Experiment on man : demonstrates the phenomena of inner inhibition, and also of release of inhibition on increase of the interval between the stimuli. The diagram should be looked at from right to left.

but shall study them from the strictly objective viewpoint, understanding them as a synthesis of complex symbolic reflexes in the form of mathematical calculation, which is work, the results of such an investigation may be utilised by reflexology also. In other words, reflexology may utilise the same method simply as the making of a calculation, and we shall remain on the strictly objective plane, and limit ourselves to the results of the given calculation in the case of a given problem, and under given conditions. We cannot doubt that the result will be different on the repetition of the same calculation under different conditions of experiment and, consequently, the objective result of the calculation will stand in a certain correlation with certain inner and external conditions. It is clear that the result will be different in accordance with the individual and other conditions.

The same must be true of the so-called simple reaction and of all other methods of experimental psychology including the most complex processes. The results obtained by these methods on other human beings must be

[1] See A. V. Ilyin : *Dissertation*, 1901, St. Petersburg.

investigated, for our purpose, first of all without reference to processes of consciousness, but as an expression of a certain series of association reflexes which manifest a certain activity, and only in this case will they prove to be quite suitable for utilisation by reflexology.

Thus, if reflexology, in the investigation of an external person, does not

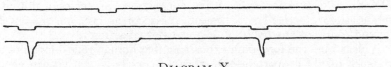

DIAGRAM X

The upper line—indication of a cutaneo-tactual stimulus applied to a spot not usually stimulated ; the second line—indication of the same kind of stimulation in the usual spot, where the reflex was inculcated ; the third line—the reaction of the sole of the foot. The experiment demonstrates the topographical differentiation of a cutaneo-tactual stimulation in an association reflex in man.

introduce into the sphere of its study such subjective states as feeling, sensation, idea, perception, and even such semi-metaphysical notions as attention, memory, imagination, will, etc., it regards as extremely valuable the experimental method introduced into modern psychology, but uses it on external persons not for the exploration of certain subjective

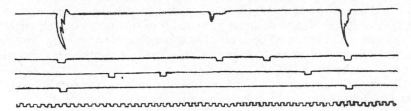

DIAGRAM XI

The upper line—the reaction of the sole ; the second line from top— the sound-stimulus ; the third line—the light-stimulus ; the fourth line —the primary electrical stimulus ; the fifth line—indication of time. The experiment, with the application of a double stimulus—sound and light—shows greater reactivity to sound than to light.

states as such, but for the study of the external manifestations of association-reflex activity, as complex higher reflexes.

Therefore, in the utilisation of the methods of experimental psychology for the purpose of the objective study of the association-reflex activity of an external person, no reflections whatever concerning consciousness, feeling, sensations, ideas, will, attention, etc., are permissible, for the result of the investigations must be interpreted in this case from the viewpoint of the objective data which surround the investigation.

But we must not forget that, in this case also, the material obtained by the experimento-psychological method, which had as its fundamental aim the revelation of the inner or subjective side of personality, does not solve those fundamental problems in which reflexology, which studies man in his activity and work, is particularly interested. For instance, it elucidates neither the formative processes of new connections, processes of inhibition, differentiation, selective generalisation, replacement, etc., nor the development and course of any habitual or non-habitual activity, etc.

It is clear from the foregoing exposition that human reflexology not only has a special subject-matter—the study of correlative activity in general, and, in particular, of the association-reflex activity of man from the objectivo-biological side—but that it also uses special and peculiar objective methods of experimental investigation, methods which have already made possible the attainment of various generalisations in this new sphere of knowledge, and all of this taken together gives reflexology a sufficient justification for existence as an independent department of science in the circle of the other sciences.

It is exceedingly important that reflexology, as distinguished from subjective psychology, really directs the investigation of an external person towards the unfolding of his external manifestations, and not towards the explication of the inner processes of consciousness which occupy contemporary psychology. From the standpoint of reflexology, subjective investigation is permissible only on oneself and as providing data in the form of a verbal account, supplementary to the objective investigation ; and for full and accurate knowledge of the individual, the results of the verbal account must be invariably subordinated to the data provided by the objective method and, at the same time, must be appropriately checked against the latter.

Clearly, the investigation may be made under certain conditions, for instance inhibiting or stimulating, and this will influence the results obtained.

As, from the viewpoint of reflexology, a person is an agent who has developed under bio-social conditions, it is natural that the reflexological investigation of a person must consist above all in the recording of his activity or work, but for the evaluation of activity the comparative method must be utilised. It is obvious from this that it is not sufficient to limit oneself to the positing of a certain phenomenon as characteristic for the person or of the so-called capacity, as psychologists usually or frequently do, but it is necessary to lead objective study in the direction of the investigation of different forms of activity in which personality is somehow expressed.

CHAPTER XIX

The objective observation of behaviour and, in general, of all the correlative processes of a human being. The significance of the recording of these manifestations in the child. The results of investigations made in this respect.

THE material of reflexology does not consist of experimental data alone. Strictly objective observation may not be excluded from its sphere.

If we assume a strictly objective standpoint in regard to a human being, we may say, with certainty, that all his external manifestations may be subsumed under the scheme of the development of association reflexes, as dominants, and must be regarded as such.

The explication of the correlation between the external manifestations of a person with the external influences, current and past, and also with inner stimulations is arrived at by means of careful and strictly objective observation of all the actions, conduct, speech, and other manifestations of that person. Not those data derived from subjective analysis, but the results of the objective observation of all the external manifestations of personality should really lie at the root of the characterising of a human being. In simpler language, the truest characterisation of a man should be his actions, conduct, relation to the environment, speech, gestures, facial expressions, and inherited-organic manifestations in correlation with some present or past external conditions and in connection with inherited peculiarities.

Not only the detailed and careful observation of all the objective data regarding the human being in his correlation with all the internal and external, current as well as past, causes which have led to his external manifestations, but also the exploration of the whole past of the given individual, *i.e.* of the conditions of his life and education, and also the conditions of heredity, do not leave any doubt that a person is a bio-social being, whose biological nature, transmitted by heredity from the ancestors, contains the degree of potentiality of development ; inherited tendencies, innate gifts ; the constitution which, together with the development, determines the temperament ; the anthropological or racial type in the sense of the prevailing development of certain receptive organs (hearing, vision, active touch, etc.). Everything else appertains to the external influences both physico-cosmical and social, and especially the latter. The material for the characterisation of a person should be gathered in the light of what has just been said. The possession of such material makes it possible to foresee with certainty how a certain man will act in certain circumstances.

It is true that such an investigation, although possible, is, in the majority of cases, rendered difficult by the fact that it is not easy to have sufficiently complete and exact knowledge of a given individual's past, and that all the motives of actions in adults are, in individual cases, difficult to discover, but still this investigation is possible. The conditions are specially favourable for this purpose when we observe a developing personality, especially in the period of infancy, and, consequently, beginning from 1908, I devoted to this subject a series of papers, published in *Vestnik Psychologii*. If, as we have already said, all the infant's external manifestations, even the slightest, are, in their different circumstances, recorded in writing from the day of birth, and if, at the same time, note is made of all the external motives, current and past, of his reactions, irrespective of whether they are natural or artificially created, it is possible to secure a sufficiently complete inventory in both cases and then to state that his actions are conditioned both by external influences and those influences which have acted on him in the past, but some peculiarities of the external reactions must be ascribed to heredity.

Immediately after birth, the new-born infant exhibits reflexes of two kinds : on the one hand, local reflexes ; and on the other, general reactions, which are most intense of all to unfavourable stimuli, such as a damp and cold bed, hunger, etc. To these the child reacts by crying, by various movements of the hands, legs, trunk, and head, by grimaces, etc. This restlessness, which takes the form of a number of random movements defensive and mimico-somatic in character, is inhibited under favourable general influences, for instance warmth and after feeding, and is replaced by complete quiet of the body, the smoothing of all the wrinkles of the face, and by sleep.

In the course of time, the same phenomena are produced not only by peripheral stimuli, but also by other external influences. For instance, the child much later performs the same series of movements, and cries when the mother withdraws from him and, on the other hand, is pacified immediately when he sees in front of him his mother, who is feeding him at her breast. This is already the beginning of the development of association reflexes.

In the same way, we can trace how in the child all association reflexes, of whatever kind, first develop on the basis of ordinary, *i.e.* innate, reflexes, how they gradually differentiate, manifesting themselves only in response to a definite kind of stimulus from among that class of external influences which at first produced them. Besides, it is not difficult to trace how they are subjected to synthesis or selective generalisation, when one and the same association reflex is the reaction to a number of various stimuli, which stand in certain correlation with the personality of the child.

For the sake of completeness, I shall quote here a résumé of my earliest observations concerning the development of the association-reflex activity in the course of the first half-year of the child's life.[1]

" The association reflexes develop in the child really through the reproduction of ordinary reflexes produced by certain sensory stimuli which initially do not call out the ordinary reflex, but which, as a result of frequent concurrence, have become associated with the primary stimuli (which call out the ordinary reflexes). Observation shows that reflexes

---

[1] V. Bechterev : *Vestnik Psychologii*, 1912.

which appear under the influence of internal stimuli are the first to be reproduced (sucking, crying, smiling, etc.).

The reproduction of association reflexes may be temporarily inhibited under the influence of various external and internal stimuli, but reappears in full force.

After the association reflexes have originated, their differentiation sets in and the reflex is reproduced in response to a component part of the stimulus, precisely as it was formerly reproduced in response to the whole stimulus.

Simultaneously, the differentiated association reflexes by way of new combinations are reproduced in response to various external stimuli which bear a certain relation to the fundamental stimulus which calls out an ordinary reflex, and this may be called selective generalisation.

At the same time, the differentiation of the responsive (efferent) aspect of the reflex occurs and, instead of general movements, a more and more localised motor effect gradually appears, an effect adjusted to the particular stimulus ; in other words, in response to a given stimulus, the reproduction of the appropriate part, instead of the whole reflex, occurs. Simultaneously greater co-ordination of separate movements is achieved, a co-ordination which has at its root the selective combination of separate muscular contractions.

Let us also note that the conditions of inner inhibition make possible, in the course of time, the reproduction of association reflexes precisely when it is appropriate to the organism's needs, which are the chief guides of the organism's reactions and thus, later, the predominance of the so-called personal reflexes develops."

From these observations of human personality in the infantile period of man's existence, it is already not difficult to draw the conclusion that the gradual development of correlative activity, through increasing enrichment of the personality by association reflexes, is entirely conformable to law. Further observations in this respect will be published by me later. Now I shall merely note that the infant is, in general, an exceedingly favourable object not only for observation, but also for experiments, " natural " in character, in association-motor reflexes, as, by the way, has been proved by investigations made according to a method (suggested by me) of natural experiment in which the child reacts to colours. These investigations have been made in the Pedological Institute which was founded by me and Zimin, and is now the Pedological Department of the Institute for the Study of Brain.[1]

Let me quote here also a short résumé of later observations concerning

---

[1] V. N. Brazhas : *Exp. psych. issledovaniya tzvetov. vpetchatleny u detey* (*Exp. Psych. Investigations of Colour Impressions in Children*).—*Minutes of the All-Russian Congress of Experimental Pedagogics*, St. Petersburg, 1911. Other earlier investigations, objective in character, have been made on children in the same Institute by me (*Vestnik Psychologii*, 1909, 1910) and by Dr. K. P. Lifshitz (see *Minutes of the Scientific Meetings of the Hospital for Psychic Diseases*, 1910).

the development of the child, observations described in a common address by me and N. Shtchelovanov (*K obosnovaniyu Genetitcheskoi Reflexologii—Principles of Genetic Reflexology*) at the Plenary Session of the General Congress of Psychoneurology in Leningrad, 3rd January, 1924 :

After a preliminary reflexological study of the infant, a study made first by V. Bechterev in a number of papers dating from 1908 (*Vestnik Psychologii*), a special Department of Reflexology was organised in 1922 in the Leningrad Pedological Institute ; and there, under the supervision of V. Bechterev and of the departmental superintendent, N. Shtchelovanov, systematic work is being carried out by a number of collaborators (Dr. M. Denisov, N. Figurin, Dr. A. Lukin, and others) employing the method of uninterrupted systematic observation and the recording of the child's every reaction produced under the influence of external and internal stimuli, those collaborators also applying reflexological experiment and other methods. As a result of this work, there is an enormous amount of factual material in the form of diaries and records of experiments on several infants in the first half-year of life who were kept in the Department. The present address is a result of the elaboration of part of these factual data.

Needless to say, psychology has no genetic method, because it is impossible to study empirically the infant's sphere of consciousness, and thus psychology is deprived of the most important method of the natural sciences.

At the present time, the general reflexology of adults has been considerably elaborated as a result of numerous experimental investigations made in V. Bechterev's laboratories, where, for the first time, dating from 1907, a special reflexological experiment was applied to man, an experiment which makes possible the formation of new functional connections in the central nervous system and the discovery of the fundamental conformity to law of the development of higher reactions or association reflexes in man. On the basis of these investigations, V. Bechterev has published papers in which he cites pertinent methodological, general-biological, and empirical data concerning the reflexology of man.

But the cerebral mechanism of the adult is exceedingly complex. Its functioning is conditioned not only by external and inner (chiefly chemical) stimuli direct in their influence, but also by the individual's whole past experience, as a result of which complex functional connections in the nervous system have been formed. Therefore, it is exceedingly difficult, even on the application of reflexological experiment, not only to investigate thoroughly all the complex functional interrelations in the nervous system —interrelations which determine the reactions and, in general, the whole behaviour of an adult—but also to fix the general principles and the individual peculiarities of the functioning of the nervous system.

In view of this, the genetic method acquires specially important significance for reflexology. The object of the genetic method—the child—is born the least perfect, in his development, of the new-born offspring of all living beings. His nervous system, especially in its higher ranges, is, at the moment of birth, both morphologically and functionally undeveloped in considerable measure, and its development, like that of the whole human organism, is gradual throughout the course of a comparatively long time. This great simplicity, which distinguishes a child from an adult, and makes impossible the explanation of its reactions on the basis of analogy with the experiences of an adult, is exceedingly valuable in objective investigation. The carefully organised study of the development of the child's reactions from the moment of birth, a study prosecuted in the environs of a special institution—The Pedological Institute—where everything is adapted to the end of working through appropriate method, and, secondly, the investigation of the histogenesis of the nervous system—an investigation which is being made at the Institute for the Study of Brain and runs parallel to the investigation of the development of complex reactions—make possible an avenue to the explication of the most important problems of development. The determination of the gradual change of the reactions towards complexity, differentiation, increase in variety and compass, establishment of complex interactions among reactions, gradual change in the general character of reacting and in the fundamental functional states, such as sleep and wakefulness, makes possible the elucidation of the significance not only of the external stimuli which can be directly observed—stimuli which evoke reaction—but also the inner conditions of the formation and activity of these reactions. Physiologo-neurological analysis discovers the fundamental principles of the development of the nervous system in its physiological aspect, and determines the interdependence between its functioning and the ontogenetic development of cerebral connections.

In as far as the development of personality is a result of native qualities, on the one hand, and the interaction of the personality with the physical and, especially, the social environment, on the other hand, the genetic method discovers what, in the development of personality, is referable to biological, and what to physico-social, factors, i.e. what reactions or separate elements of complex reactions with their physiologo-neurological basis are heredito-organically predetermined reactions, and what are formed as a result of personal experience, and also on the basis of what hereditarily conditioned reactions of simple reflexes, in what order, at what time, and under what conditions the higher reactions or complexes of association reflexes develop.

In the empirical part of the address, we were able to characterise the content and the development of the fundamental types of reactions in the course of the first five months of a child's life, and to state the most important principles governing their development. Special significance must be attached to the gradual development in the central nervous system of processes of a dominant character, or—more briefly—dominants.

The principle of the dominant has been recently advanced by Professor Uchtomsky as one of the general and most important principles relative to

P

the activity of the nervous centres, and he has backed it by data derived from experimental investigations on warm-blooded and cold-blooded animals. But relative to association-reflex activity, it was discussed by V. Bechterev as early as 1911 in his *Objective Psychology*, in the chapter on concentration. The essence of this principle is that the centre of excitation, irrespective of the area of the central nervous system in which the excitation arises, determines the paths of discharge of the nervous excitation. This centre, as it were, attracts their excitation from other nerve centres, and this produces inhibition in some, and heightening of excitability in other, areas of the nervous system.

In the analysis of factual data relative to the development of the child's reaction, the most important problems arise from the investigation of the increasing complexity of the interaction among reactions. In the elaboration of the materials of the Pedological Institute, a special type of reactions was segregated. To this type belong the infant's nutritional reactions from the very beginning; then with gradual development, reactions which, in the form of visual concentration, arise to stimuli impinging on eye and ear, and which, according to their physiological characteristics, must be regarded as functionally predominant. These functionally predominant reactions were segregated as a special type, not only because of their physiological peculiarities, but also because they have a specially important significance in the genesis of all complex reactions. The principle of the dominant in the activity of the nerve centres, a principle so wonderfully backed by experiments on animals, completely explains the physiologo-neurological basis of these functionally-predominant reactions, and it may be stated that the dominant processes in his nervous system, which exist from the first in a new-born infant, and also the new dominants which develop gradually, are the fundamental factors in the development of the complex reactions which arise later and, in general, in the functional perfecting of the infant's nervous system.

A new-born child has only one quite clearly expressed dominant, which arises during sucking or, in general, during the activity of positive nutritional reactions, among which we must include, in addition to sucking, the primary orientation nutritional reactions. The latter reactions are expressed in the turning of the head to one side, with the mouth open or " groping," as it were. Sucking and " groping " arise under the influence both of external stimuli (during the first days, touching the lips and, simultaneously, the tip of the tongue produces sucking; touching the corners of the mouth or the cheek near the lips produces " groping ") and also of inner stimuli, for in a hungry child not only a general reaction arises, usually in the form of movement and shouting, but also specific nutritional reactions : sucking and groping. When these reactions occur in the absence of an external stimulus, they obviously afford evidence that hunger (" hungry blood ") acts as a chemical stimulus, firstly, on the whole nervous system and so calls out a general reaction and, secondly, predominantly or selectively on the nutritional centres, and, consequently, specific nutritional reactions arise apart from any external influence. Selective influence on the nutritional centres occurs also in satiation during which positive nutritional reflexes often do not arise, even under the influence of the usual or external stimuli, which in this case produce a defence reaction in the form of pressing the lips together. During the occurrence of nutritional reactions, all general reactions, which had hitherto existed as movements and shouting, are retarded or inhibited, and it may be also often observed that sucking which is weakening or ceasing is again renewed, and even strengthened, under the influence of external stimuli, for instance, cutaneous (slapping), and this affords evidence of extensive functional connections and of the dominant process in the nervous system. Thus, the positive nutritional reactions in a new-born child are physiologically very strong and complete, and this is fully in accordance with their biological significance for the child. Another dominant more weakly expressed arises in a new-born infant during quick change of posture (for instance, the change from the horizontal to the vertical position) and under the influence of this, the infant, who is crying and moving, becomes temporarily calm and motionless. In the given case, the dominant process in the nervous system arises from the influence on the semicircular canals, since various muscle-joint stimuli, operative in all kinds of passive movements, do not produce inhibition of movement and shouting.

All the other various reactions of a new-born babe have a different character ; they differ from the dominant reactions mentioned in that, on their occurrence, they do not inhibit other reactions and bear, as it were, a local character. To these belong those reflexes which arise under the influence of external stimuli acting on the various receptive surfaces : cutaneous, mucous, ligamental, optic, aural, etc. It is expedient to divide these reflexes into two groups : (a) simple specific and (b) complex specific reflexes. Complex specific reflexes, which occur in response to an influence on the eye (light) and on the ear (sound) and take the form of turning the eyes and head to the impinging stimulus, and of movement of the eyes and head after a luminous object moving before the eyes, are, in a new-born infant, completely identical with simple reflexes in that, during their occurrence, they do not exert any appreciable influence in the form of inhibition of other reactions present ; in other words, they bear a local character. Complex specific reflexes differ from simple not only in their greater complexity, but chiefly in the fact that, while simple reflexes (cutaneous, ligamental, etc.) suffer comparatively little change in their further development, complex reflexes change in the direction of the establishment of their interaction with other reactions, when (under the influence of stimulations of eye and ear) extensive dominant processes are present in the nervous system. The dominants are expressed in the form of positive functioning of the organ stimulated, while there is simultaneous general inhibition of all other reactions (concentration). This condition appears for the first time between the ages of fourteen days and two months. Beside the reflexes mentioned, there arise in the new-born child general or complex non-specific reactions in the form of general movements—often accompanied by shouting—under the influence of external as well as inner stimuli (hunger ; and among external influences, chiefly temperature affecting a considerable part of the cutaneous surface, as happens in changing the napkins). The causes of such general reactions are to be found in the peculiarities of functioning of the central nervous system, which is inclined to irradiation of excitation.

Side by side with the development of the infant, a gradual change and improvement in the reactions takes place. We shall cite some facts important for the characterisation of development. Here belongs first of all the gradual change of the reactions of eye and ear, and these are expressed in the following way : in a new-born infant these reactions, as has been already mentioned, are local complex specific reflexes, but, beginning from the third week, the first association reflex is established as a response to the usual feeding posture, when the infant makes groping movements of the lips before he is drawn to the breast ; and, beginning from the second to the third month, perfectly defined visual and auditory dominants, in the form of concentration, are exhibited.

The general conclusions from the empirical part of the address are as follows :

(1) A new-born infant exhibits, in addition to innate simple and complex specific reflexes and general non-specific reactions, innate reactions of a dominant type—the nutritional dominant and the posture dominant.

(2) The first important stage in the child's development consists in the origin of dominants from other receptive surfaces, and of these the most important are the visual and the auditory dominants.

(3) For the development and further perfecting of the dominants, their exercise under the influence of external stimuli is important.

(4) The dominants of the organs of vision and audition develop on the basis of the gradually developing functional complexity of the originally local reflexes, which are already being produced in the new-born infant from the same receptive surfaces, and which then, as a result of the maturing of complex nervous mechanisms, both the cortical and the sub-cortical regions of the nervous system participating, enter into complex interactions with the other reactions.

(5) Dominant correlations in the functioning of the complex nervous mechanisms are the fundamental conditions of the formation of differentiated motor reactions which are formed on the basis of the primarily existing general motor reactions and simple reflexes, and also through the further formation of new functional connections, and this leads to the establishment of higher reactions of the type of association reflexes.

(6) The time and the order of the formation of those association reflexes which are genetically the earliest correspond to the time and the order of the formation of dominants. The establishment of new functional

connections, *i.e.* the formation of association reflexes, is possible only on the presence of appropriate dominant processes general in character (on concentration), which occur not only in the cortex, but also with the participation of the lower parts of the nervous system, and, as a result of this, the mechanism of association reflexes is not limited to cortical processes. Therefore, the subcortical regions also, as well as other parts of the organism innervated by them, for instance the vascular system and the glands, have an influence on the formation of association reflexes and their activity. We have to admit also the possibility of the formation of new connections either in the subcortical regions or with their direct participation, as, for instance, in the case of the establishment of the nutritional reaction, which occurs in the feeding posture as early as in the course of the first month.

Let us further note that the genetic method propounds as one of the most important problems the problem of the development of wakefulness as such a general functional state as is the fundamental premiss of all higher reflexes. Since the state of sleep or, rather, the absence of wakefulness is the initial state of a new-born infant, so, in genetic investigation, it is possible both to trace the quantitative increase of wakefulness as well as the deepening of the sleep, and also to elucidate the external and internal conditions of its origin and development. It is clear from this that the problem of sleep also can be ultimately solved only in conjunction with the explication of the nature of wakefulness, because sleep ensues when the conditions necessary for wakefulness are removed.

The further development of the child takes the direction of the successive acquisition of new association reflexes, together with the establishment of appropriate dominants, and this is essentially facilitated by the development of speech. Counting, *i.e.* the denoting of numbers of objects by certain words, develops, however, much later than the simple denoting of objects by words, for here there is question of the numeral relations of the objects themselves. Houzeau says in this context : " At first, the child distinguishes only a single object from a multitude. At eighteen months, he distinguishes one, two, or several objects. At the age of three, or a little earlier, he distinguishes one, two, and four ; and only later does he begin to count correctly in order : one, two, three, four. At this point he remains very long. That is why the Brahmins teach the pupils of the first class to count only to four, and postpone counting up to twenty to the second class. It has been observed in regard to European children of average capacity that they count to ten not earlier than at the age of six, and to 100 not earlier than the age of ten. Of course, the child at this age can repeat the numbers which we have taught him, but knowledge of numbers, *i.e.* capacity to determine the numbers of objects, does not consist in this." (Quoted from Ribot : *L'évolution des idées générales*, Paris, 1897, p. 43.) B. Pérez also agrees in general with Houzeau's opinion.

Pérez observed a child of $2\frac{1}{2}$, who could count to 19, but had no idea of the meaning of 3 days, and had to have it explained to him that it does not mean to-morrow, but to-morrow and another to-morrow. Binet's experiments are significant in regard to the development of counting in children. The results of these experiments have been reduced by Ribot to the following (*l.c.* p. 44) : " A four-year-old girl, who could neither read nor count, learned the names of several numbers, and these she applied without a mistake to one, two, and three objects ; when the number was higher, she named the higher numbers at random and, for instance, counted four objects as six and twelve indiscriminately. If two groups, one of 14 and another of 18 counters, of the same size are spread unheaped on the table, she quickly recognises the more numerous group. Then, both groups are changed by increasing the number of counters by one on the right and then by one on the left, so that the proportion of 14 to 18 remains. In six experiments, the answer was always correct. If the proportion is 17 to 18, there are eight correct answers, and one wrong one. But if the counters in question are not equal in diameter, everything is changed. The green counters have one diameter, and the white another. On one side there are 18 green counters, and on the other 14 white. The child constantly makes mistakes and thinks the latter group more numerous ; the number can even be decreased from 14 to 10, and she still does not change her opinion. Only when 9 remained does the group of 18 green counters seem more numerous to her." It is obvious that the child judges not by number, but by extension, and this agrees with Binet's other experiments with lines, the differences between which are generally well determined by children.

Preyer's observation must be understood in the same way, when he says of one of his children that " it was impossible to take away one of ten ninepins without his noticing it ; and at the age of 18 months, he knew perfectly well whether all his ten animals were present or whether one was missing." Preyer's son, a child of 17 months, who could not speak, reached for a toy which had been placed in a cupboard too high for him to reach, but having looked around, he pushed a little suitcase to the cupboard, climbed on the case, and captured the toy. Ultimately, we are concerned here precisely with an association reflex based on the need to get the given object and on the satisfaction of this need by a certain device. Let us also note that, from the time that the child begins to react to social stimuli and thus begins to be a social being, he co-ordinates his activities more and more with the social environment, and subjects himself to the activity of social, and later socio-economic, factors as stimuli which inculcate complex reflexes expressed in his behaviour. These factors acquire exclusive significance for the developing individual, especially from the time when he frees himself from the guardianship of the parents and begins to follow the path of independence.

CHAPTER XX

The development of natural association reflexes in adults. Examples of natural association reflexes produced from the cutaneous surface, from the motor and static organs, the organs of vision, hearing, smell, and taste.

IN precisely the same way, man, as a result of continuous life experience, has inculcated in him, in the course of his later life and without any active intervention on his own part, a number of association reflexes which hitherto could not have been properly evaluated because of insufficient knowledge of their development. In this respect, the appropriate elucidation of these phenomena is not devoid of significance for us.

A typical phenomenon belonging here is the experiment in touching, without the participation of vision, objects placed in a closed box. Let us assume that among the objects placed in the box there are also living beings, such as a crawfish. When the latter quite suddenly manifests its presence, even by a simple movement, everyone knows how the hand is immediately and suddenly withdrawn from the box, because the possibility of being pinched by the creature's claws, although such a pinch is quite innocuous, is associated with the crawfish.

A peculiar phenomenon also belonging here consists in the fact that if a pedestrian quite unexpectedly touches even some insignificant obstacle with his head, that is sufficient to call out a reflex in the form of ducking the head and the whole body.

In a third case, it is sufficient for someone to touch another man's belly unexpectedly, and the man touched immediately and suddenly springs back with his whole body.

Further, if a man, while going on his way, suddenly and slightly touches some obstacle with the point of his foot, he immediately jerks forward to keep his body on his feet.

In all these cases, the disproportion between the effect and the external stimulus is striking, for a mere touch is sufficient for the motor reflex to grow into a complete and complex defensive movement.

The above-mentioned defence movements, which arise on certain cutaneo-muscular stimulations, may not be regarded as simple reflexes, for they can in no case be evoked when the subject is prepared for them. Consequently, these reflexes are usually inhibited ; and only when the external stimuli act unexpectedly, when the subject is not prepared for them, or concentration is distracted, are they evoked under the appropriate conditions.

We observe here, just as in other association reflexes, a peculiarity consisting in the fact that, on repetition, they are inhibited even when concentration is distracted. This relatively facile capacity for inhibition obviously indicates that these are association reflexes in their nature.

Apparently, the development of the latter must be understood thus : in the course of life, under the influence of appropriate mechanical stimuli, association reflexes have arisen—reflexes which, defensive in character, arise when a foreign object even ever so slightly touches the body, this touch giving, as it were, the signal for a possibly more considerable impact. In other words, we are concerned here with cutaneo-muscular association reflexes defensive in character.

Let us take an example from another sphere. A man who is accustomed to sit on chairs of a certain height will inevitably fall if, without being prepared, he tries to sit on a very low chair.

Everyone knows the result of the wicked practical joke which consists in removing the chair, when the person who has risen from it intends to resume his seat.

The case of a sudden false step is a no less striking example : when a man, with his concentration distracted, while he is walking on a smooth surface, steps into a hole.

Lastly, we know that a man, who, without effort, has overcome some obstacle many times, makes an exaggerated effort when the obstacle is suddenly removed.

In all these cases, there is question of a certain cutaneo-muscular association reflex, which is adjusted in its intensity to the conditions usual in man's life, or of that phenomenon which may be called the fixing of a reflex. A sudden change in these conditions leads to the continuation of the usual realisation of the reflex, without adjustment to the changed conditions, and, as a result of this, the above-mentioned consequences occur.

Here we are obviously concerned with the same fact as is observed in the laboratory investigation of personal association reflexes, by a method developed in my laboratory.[1] When the personal association reflex has been set in a certain direction, this personal reflex is, for some time, manifested in its former direction and at its former time-intervals, when the conditions are suddenly changed.

This is why, if we arrange with the subject of experiment that he should press a rubber ball with his finger at every beat of a quickly ticking metronome, he invariably presses superfluously when the metronome is suddenly stopped. The number of such surplus pressures stands, as experiment shows, in a certain correlation with the number and frequency of the beats of the metronome to which the subject presses the rubber ball with his finger.

But in addition to cutaneous and muscular association reflexes, there are in man's life a multitude of other fixed association reflexes—visual, auditory, etc.

We know that, if some obstacle suddenly appears before the eyes, a jerking back of the head and body ensues immediately. On the other hand, the sudden approach of a hand or some foreign body to the eyes leads to the shutting of the eyes and the jerking back of the head. We

---

[1] See V. Bechterev : *The Reproductive and Associative Reaction in Movements—Obozrenie Psychiatrii*, 1898. See also the investigations made by Dobrotvorskaya in my laboratory : *Vestnik Psychologii*, 1910.

know that when an eatable is shown, abundant secretion of saliva and also of gastric juice appears, as experiments on those who have been operated on convince us.

It is not difficult to imagine that a man will begin to flee at the sight of a snake moving towards him, even if it is not poisonous. Many animals, for instance nervous horses, cannot help shying at the sight of a mere piece of paper. In precisely the same way, a man recoils from the muzzle of a gun or revolver pointed at him, even if the weapon is not loaded. Every man, on seeing a handkerchief or some other object falling from another man's hand, immediately jerks forward to pick it up, even when this is not necessary. When a companion, or a man who happens to be walking beside one, falls for some reason or other, a hand is inevitably stretched out to support him.

We know further that the mere sight of a vomit causes nausea.

Many fixed association reflexes of the auditory organ may also be pointed out. A hunter seizes his gun and makes ready to shoot when he hears a mere rustle in the bushes. Everyone immediately begins to flee on hearing the roaring of a wild beast in the wood. One involuntarily starts back on hearing a shot. When the sound of a familiar voice becomes audible, one immediately turns in its direction. At the sound of a familiar song, one, without being aware of it, begins to hum it. At the sounds of a march, one involuntarily adjusts one's steps to the time of the march. The sounds of dance music incite one to dance.

The olfactory organ plays a lesser rôle in man's life than do the other organs, but it is indubitable that in this case also numerous examples of similar association reflexes may be cited. So, at the mere smell of a savoury dish, the eyes turn in its direction and saliva begins to be secreted ; a disgusting smell often causes nausea, etc.

Lastly, in connection with stimulation of the gustatory organ, association reflexes may also be discovered. So it is sufficient to put a pacifier into the new-born infant's mouth, and, immediately, not only the reflex act of sucking, but also the act of swallowing, is produced.

All the above-mentioned phenomena would be rather incomprehensible without the experimental study of association reflexes, and, on the contrary, from the standpoint of these experiments, they receive a quite natural explanation.

It is especially important to note here that the social milieu, as a result of the conditions of social life, is, in its various forms, the chief stimulus which inculcates in the individual a countless number of reflexes which are being stratified on the innate or inherited reflexes, and, consequently, an adult personality is, in the true sense of the word, a bio-social being.

CHAPTER XXI

Imitation, facial expressions, concentration, speech, gestures, and personal movements as association reflexes. The active and the passive aspect of personality.

IT must be kept in view that also the more complex manifestations of correlative activity can, and must, be understood and explained from the viewpoint of the same theory of association reflexes.

Let us take the process of imitation—a process based on the fact that the visual impression of a certain posture and movement produces in another the same posture and movement in the form of an association reflex, and that the hearing of a song excites in another the singing of the same song in the form of an association reflex. The mere sight of yawning is well known to infect others, because the visual impression excites, by association, the appropriate muscular contractions which lead to a yawn, which, as a result of organic character, is in a state of readiness for realisa-- tion. Imitation, which is the simplest association reflex, has at its root past experience in the social milieu. Let us assume that we beat time with our feet at the sight of one dancing. But we, in our experience, have frequently, during our own movements, performed the same movements under our visual control; and, consequently, an association reflex to visual rhythmical stimuli, in the form of movement of our own feet simultaneously with the accompanying kinesthetic stimulations and the movements themselves, has been already inculcated and fixed. This is sufficient for the sight of the rhythmical movement of feet like our own in the dancing of an external person to excite in us the accompanying kinesthetic stimulations, which produce the beating of the appropriate time with our feet. The same happens in other cases of imitation. Self-imitation passes over into imitation.

Various kinds of imitation, on which education is based to a considerable extent, are well known to be extensive throughout the animal kingdom also. According to Hachet-Souplet, so-called " rational " imitation is not excluded in the higher animals, but, in the majority of cases, there is question of " instinctive " or, more precisely, reflexive imitation, for the existence of an " instinct " of imitation has not been proved. Imitation among individuals of the same species does not differ essentially from associations by similarity. An individual, situated beside another of the same species, has a tendency to act like his neighbour. For example, a peacock, on whose leg a ribbon had been tied several times, pulled off the ribbon tied round the leg of its fellows, as if it were tied to its own leg. Pigeons placed without food in a cage and separated by a grating from another cage of pigeons began to peck the floor when the other pigeons in the neighbouring cage ate grains.

The inanity of such imitation is still more obvious in the fact that when strange bees enter a bee-hive and begin to devour the larvae, the workers of this colony discontinue their duty of driving out the intruders, and themselves begin to devour the larvae which they have fed. (Büchner, Siebold, and Künckel.)

In birds, the acquisition of habits occurs not through training or special lessons taught to the younger ones by the old, but, to a considerable extent, through mere imitation on the part of the fledglings, which see the actions and the mode of living of older birds. How imitation in birds is developed may be seen from the following : Magde d'Aubusson has published a military pilot's observations of the flight of birds. It was seen that, for instance wild duck, which fly in a chain, exhibit striking co-ordination of movements. The least deviation of the foremost bird to one side or the other leads to the same movements in the other birds. The duck were flying at a speed of 110 kilometres an hour at a height of 105 metres.

Dogs which have been brought up with cats acquire certain feline peculiarities, for instance the washing of the face (Romanes).

Hachet-Souplet cites numerous examples of imitation in trained animals.

The fact that higher animals, for instance apes, imitate less than other and lower animals is explained by Watson as due to the interference of inhibiting impulses produced by the greater development of the association-reflex activity of higher animals.

I must state here that imitation is one of the most extensively studied phenomena in living nature and is encountered everywhere in the animal kingdom, beginning from the lowest organisms and ending with man. For instance, the imitation of adults by children is universally known. We know of equally striking facts of imitation also in adult idiots. But we find imitation, too, in the daily life of normal people. There is no necessity to dilate here on this phenomenon, which the French sociologist, Tarde, has regarded as the foundation of social life in general. It is sufficient to say that imitation is one of the fundamental manifestations of correlative activity and that this manifestation is, from my viewpoint, a result of social life, which it pervades. Although imitation is a reproduction of the actions, words, gestures, facial expressions, and other external manifestations of one or of many men by other persons, one or several, it must be borne in mind that imitation, in many cases, cannot be " blind," without any correctives on the part of the individual, who, through imitation, notes certain phenomena which are new to him. These correctives are conditioned by what constitutes the experience of the person, and everything that is not opposed to this experience may be readily acquired through imitation, while everything opposed to the results of past individual experience, which has left its traces on the personality, or on what the subjectivists call " mind," encounters opposition, on the part of the person, in regard to imitative reproduction ; and even if it should be taken over and assimilated by him, then this happens only with appropriate correctives, which are results of partial inhibition and of the process of substitution.

Under life conditions, two cases may arise : (1) when the inhibition is complete and ousts imitation, the reproduction of the model being quite excluded, since it excites a negative reaction of protest and evokes the reflex of rejection ; and (2) when the inhibition of imitation is not complete and, consequently, the acceptance and assimilation of an external influence is modified by correction provided by the experience of the person.

It is clear from this that the weaker the experience of the person, the stronger the imitation. Animals in general, the lower they are in the development of correlative activity, the more imitative they are. It is also intelligible why children imitate one another to a greater extent than adults do and, on the other hand, why young nations imitate older nations to a greater extent than the older do the young.

The question arises : What really lies at the root of the development of imitation ? Why does one animal, living in community with another, begin to imitate it ? It must be noted that imitation lies in the nature of the orientation reflex, in as far as this reflex reproduces the form and peculiarities of the object towards which it is directed. Thus, on hearing a rhythm, we split it up in an appropriate manner and, consequently, imitate it. In the tactual reflex, we follow the contour of the object with the finger, and, consequently, in the tracing of its form, there is again question of imitation, as we imitate in seeing, when we explore with our eyes the various outlines of the object, and when the object moves, our look, as well as our head, reproduces its movement. Thus, imitation is, as it were, a further development of the orientation reflex. On the other hand, we are concerned here with the fact that movement and activities in general are a normal condition of existence for every organism, and, therefore, they are accompanied by a general sthenic reaction, at least up to the moment when indications of fatigue begin to appear. Those movements which arise through reproduction, which participates both in self-imitation—numerous repetitions of the same movement—and in the imitation of others, are facilitated and, as a result, their execution is accompanied by a still greater sthenic reaction, and the latter, as we know, always sustains the movements and activities which arouse it.

If we grant that imitation in itself, as a reproduced movement, is accompanied by a general sthenic reaction, then it becomes comprehensible to us why imitation is often manifested simply for the sake of imitation : why a man laughs unnecessarily when another laughs, why a man yawns on seeing another yawn, etc.

We must remember that imitation is obviously a characteristic of the whole animal kingdom, beginning from the lowest animals. Here belongs the so-called mimicry of the lower animals when they imitate the environmental conditions.

Imitation is well developed in insects, birds, and mammals. In the higher animals, it is manifested not in the colouring of the cutaneous surface, but in the manifestations of voice, in expressive movements, and in actions, and many examples may be cited of imitation which is not useful, but is imitation merely for the sake of imitation. So, for instance, the thrush can imitate the crowing of a cock so perfectly as to deceive even hens. Naturally, imitation plays an enormous rôle also in the development and formation of the so-called " instincts." Details of this may be found in Romanes (*Animal Intelligence*).

We encounter imitation for the sake of imitation in savage peoples also, and in some cases, because of special conditions, it reaches an abnormal degree (" emeryatcheniye ") as has been observed, for instance, in the peoples of the north of S.S.S.R., in Siberia, and North America.

In view of the comparatively complete study already made of the phenomena of imitation in the animal kingdom, we do not think it necessary to dilate on this subject.

The question arises, however : What sustains the development of imitation in the biological scale of animal life ? First of all, it is necessary to bear in mind that imitation, as a reflex, is a result of selection, for, in many cases, imitation of the environment or of the leader of the herd means safety from enemies or escape from attack. On the other hand, the various favourable influences, by which nature affects the living being, naturally serve as stimuli to his reproducing the same phenomenon. This may be one of the causes of mimicry, irrespective of conditions of natural selection. Imitation also serves as a basis of social life, which is a necessary life condition for all living beings, for without imitation there could be no expressive movements, no language, no co-ordinated activities, no fixed categories. It is natural that the social life conditions are stimuli to the imitation reflex. Thus, some prey secured by collective efforts excites, in a more or less equal degree, all the members of the group, all of which perform more or less similar gestures and expressive movements. Fatigue resulting from joint expeditions and from collective work led to the development of drowsiness in all the members of the group, and this they expressed by yawning. This, in turn, makes comprehensible why the yawn of one person infects another and why, in other cases, the smile on one face infects others. The collective work itself demands harmonious, often even identical, movements, and this is the beginning of imitation. Generally speaking, correlation among people, as among individual animals, occurs on the basis of external manifestations, and not of inner experiences, as the subjectivist psychologists assume, and imitation is the first step in the establishment of such correlation.

Expressive movements also must be regarded as association reflexes. We must note that many external influences arouse in us a general reaction in the form of a general mimico-somatic reflex. Originally, this reflex appears on the satisfaction of the organism's daily needs : when the hungry individual becomes satiated, when the thirsty gets sufficient drink, when one tired of continuous and long walking rests at last, when the victim of intense sufferings gets relief from them, a general mimico-somatic reaction, which corresponds to organic satisfaction, invariably ensues in the form of an association reflex. This mimico-somatic reaction consists in the heightening of heart activity, in appropriate changes in respiration, and in the arterial afflux of blood to the cutaneous coatings of the face and to the brain. This afflux is seen in the flushing of the face, increased moistening of the eyes, which, consequently, shine, the smoothing out of the facial wrinkles as a result of the enhancement of muscular energy, and in the stretching of the corners of the mouth, which thus manifests a smile. This mimico-somatic reaction also consists in the general enhancement of muscular tension, this enhancement leading to increased straightening of the body and thus creating a corresponding dignified air. In addition, the more thorough irrigation of the brain enlivens all the correlative processes, particularly the processes of reproduction ; and this leads to increased vivacity in the sphere of speech, facial expressions, gestures, and movements in general, also to enlivened metabolism and the enhancement of the neuro-muscular activity, and this is expressed by a relatively greater capacity for work.

This general mimico-somatic reaction, which corresponds to the reaction connected with the process of the satisfaction of biological needs, lasts for a shorter or longer time before it passes over into the usual state of rest. This state, which accompanies those subjective phenomena which take the form of good mood, may be called the positive mimico-somatic tonus.

This positive mimico-somatic tonus is accompanied, as we have already seen, by the arterial afflux of blood to the brain ; consequently, the latter receives more oxygen and nutritive material (albumen, carbohydrates, phosphorus, salts, lime, etc.), is more thoroughly irrigated, and duly gets rid of its metabolic products. The heart-beat and the respiration are also changed in a corresponding manner. Primarily, as a simple reflex, this state arises, as we have said, on the necessary nutritive material being supplied, and during physical well-being in general ; secondarily, as an association reflex, it arises on our learning of some improvement in our social position, in our material circumstances, etc.

That mimico-somatic reaction which is the opposite to this state, a reaction characterised by phenomena of an opposite nature on the part of cardio-vascular, secretory, and muscular activity, of metabolism, processes of correlative activity, facial expressions, movements, and of the general posture of the body must be called the negative mimico-somatic tonus. There is reason to believe that the negative or depressed mimico-somatic tonus is accompanied by a constriction of the cerebral arteries with the result that the brain receives less oxygen and nutritive material, is less thoroughly irrigated, and is, consequently, poisoned by its own products, and so the nerve centres are weakened in their activity and the heart-beat and respiration are disturbed. This leads to complaints of tightness in the chest and of physical and mental weakness.

Primarily, as a simple reflex, this state, conditioned by acute anæmia of the brain, may be a result of hunger and also of the efflux of blood from the brain because of copious bleeding, of certain forms of poisoning, or of certain diseases. Secondarily, as an association reflex, we observe it when we learn that we have suffered a heavy loss.

In a special paper, I dilated on this subject and proved that all expressive movements, not conditioned by immediate stimuli, are merely association reflexes. Let us take weeping. As a simple reflex, it is evoked by a sharp, pricking stimulus. But the reproduction of weeping when we receive very depressing news is an association reflex. Laughter on our being tickled is a simple reflex, while the reproduction of laughter caused by some external stimulus is an association reflex. The same is true of all other mimico-somatic movements.[1]

The dog bites the stick which has beaten it, the angry child beats the object against which he has accidentally knocked himself. The savage acts in the same manner, and even the educated man scolds an object which has hurt him. All these are examples of the development of the mimico-somatic association reflex, which, obviously, is not always pertinent to the occasion.

Only the theory of association reflexes can give an explanation of these phenomena. Dr. Schneerson,[2] working in my laboratory, has proved that a mimico-indifferent[3] stimulus, associated with a stimulus mimico-somatic in character, itself assumes a mimico-somatic character. Such mimico-somatic reflexes, like all other association reflexes, are subject to conditions of inhibition and its release. This fact has a bearing on my papers concerning the reflexology of the psychoneuroses as abnormally increased mimico-somatic association reflexes.[4]

Besides, all mimico-somatic states may be distinguished according to their intensity in the sense of excitation or enhancement and inhibition or depression. All the data which we have, bearing on the mimico-somatic excitation or enhancement of the general mimico-somatic tonus, are reducible, on the one hand, to the novelty of the influences which evoke a reaction of a general character favourable to the organism ; in other cases, the excitation is manifested during the solving of a knotty problem beyond one's powers, the solution being demanded by the given circumstances. Dr. Parfenov discovered this reaction during a change in the ticking of the metronome from a frequency of 100 beats—a frequency associated with a reflex—to a frequency of 104 beats, a frequency not easily distinguishable from the former, and not previously associated with this reflex. The same has been observed in analogous experimental conditions, in which a circle was replaced by an ellipse closely similar to it. The inhibition and lowering of the general mimico-somatic tonus is conditioned by sudden and intense stimuli to which the individual has no time to adjust himself, and also by stimuli destructive in character.

[1] For details, see V. Bechterev : *The Biological Development of Expressive Movements from the Standpoint of Objective Psychology—Vestnik Znania*, 1910, Sep. ed., St. Petersburg, 1910. *Objective Psychology*, 3rd pt., 1913.

[2] Schneerson : *The Emotional Association Reflex—Vestnik Psychologii*, 1917.

[3] *Translators' note :* That is, a stimulus which does not call out expressive movements.

[4] See also Kempf's paper, *Journ. of Abnormal Psychology*, vol. XVII, no. 1 ; April, May, 1917.

Translators' note : See also Kempf : *Psychopathology*, St. Louis : Mosby, 1920.

It is necessary to note that the primary mimico-somatic reflex, as well as the mimico-somatic association reflex, is accompanied, in some cases, by excitation of the vegetative or sympathetic nervous system, or sympathicotony ; in other cases, on the contrary, by excitation of the visceral or parasympathetic nervous system. It is obvious that, in this connection, the harmony of the endocrine glands also is more or less abruptly disturbed, and this has been proved by experiments. We have said already that, in my laboratory, an experiment was made in which a cat was caused to approach a dog. As a result, the dog's respiration immediately showed an exceedingly violent reaction, which completely disappeared on removal of the cortical centres. In Cannon's[1] laboratory, an experiment of a similar kind was made, but for the purpose of determining the amount of adrenalin in the blood. In this experiment, the approach of a dog to a kitten's nose led to a marked increase of adrenalin in the blood.

Thus, in some mimico-somatic reflexes depressive in character, we find, as a result of the heightening of the sympathicotonus, a marked adrenalin increase, which leads to asthenia with constriction of the peripheral vessels and weakening of heart activity ; in other cases : in mimico-somatic reflexes sexual in character, we shall find increased secretion of sex hormones—a secretion leading to a sthenic state—expansion of the vascular walls, and increase in heart activity. In mimico-somatic reflexes aggressive in character, we shall find still other modes of behaviour on the part of hormone secretion and of the cardio-vascular system.

I must say here that, up to the present time, there has been offered no satisfactory explanation of the biological development of mimico-somatic movements. The principle of utility advanced by Darwin has received the greatest measure of recognition in this respect. However, I must say that, if this principle were to explain everything, it should be general and not particular—applicable only to one series of cases—for how can a useless characteristic be retained along with a useful one ? Still, Darwin himself regards the principle of utility as explanatory only of some mimico-association reflexes and by no means of all.

From my point of view, the utility of mimico-somatic reflexes does not at all consist in, for instance, causing fright (according to Darwin) as in the case of the standing on end of the hairs on the neck and body, but consists in the fact that some expressive movements were originally indispensable, in general, to the individual for the purpose of aggression and defence, preparation for aggression or defence, acceptance or refusal of food, approach for sexual intercourse, certain forms of activity, and rest, but are now reproduced, on appropriate occasions, as association reflexes, and are simultaneously signs of these states, signs which serve as a primitive language among individuals.

Gestures and ejaculations supplement man's facial expressions and are

---

[1] *Translators' note :* The original has *Keunan ;* the German translation *Kennan,* but the reference seems to be to Cannon, W. B. (*Bodily Changes in Pain, Hunger, Fear, and Rage,* New York, 1922).

an expressive language which probably satisfied primitive man during many thousands of years, before articulated speech arose and developed from the language of ejaculations and echoisms.

Two other principles of Darwin's, the principle of antithesis and of direct nervous influence, do not sustain searching criticism and, in general, do not find adherents. Therefore, it is unnecessary to dilate on them here.

It is obvious that, for the origin of expressive movements, we must assume such a principle as would not only explain the utility of expressive movements, but would give an appropriate explanation of their origin and of their development into complex forms.

The principle of the reproduction of certain ordinary reflexes in the form of association reflexes affords an explanation of the origin of all mimico-somatic movements.

When the reproduction refers to movements of aggression, defence, and concentration, they could not help being useful, from the very nature of things; otherwise, aggression, defence, and concentration would not sustain life.

But other mimico-somatic movements reproduce movements which obviously were never useful, for instance, wringing the hands, beating the breast, tearing the hair. They would even be harmful if they were fully realised, for they reproduce movements of aggression against oneself. This clearly is an argument against Darwin's theory and for our explanation.

Tears are a result of an afflux to the lachrymal sacs and this afflux is produced by strong physical stimulations. Nowadays, this is an association reflex which reproduces the same secretory phenomenon, but under external influences indicating the possibility of some privation. A sigh is a reproduction of the reflex act of sobbing. The standing of the hairs on end in fright is a reproduction, at the moment of danger, of the defensive movements of the cutaneous appendages. Laughter is the reproduction of a mimico-somatic defence reaction with spasmodic contraction of the expiratory muscles, and has for its purpose the defence of the body against cutaneous stimuli to which one is unaccustomed, and which, consequently, have not led to appropriate adjustment.

Thus, we regard as the only true explanation of the origin of mimico-association reflexes that derived from the principle of the reproduction of ordinary reflexes as fixed association reflexes.

According to this principle, movements realised in different states of the organism's life activity are later reproduced, according to the law of association reflexes, as signs of the same states, and thus subserve communication between different individuals not only of the same species, but also of different species.

In view of the fact that mimico-somatic reflexes are manifested in the most marked manner in the cardio-vascular and respiratory spheres, they can be experimentally investigated by records of these movements, as has

Q

been done in the laboratory supervised by me. In experiments in respiration, I have proved that the association reflex in respiration is very easily produced by sharp sound-stimuli simultaneous with stimulation of the cutaneous surface by an electric current. When we have many times synchronised both stimuli, we get a respiratory association reflex which, as experiments show, not only arises more quickly, but is more durable than the defence reflex of a dog's paw or of a man's hand. Dr. Sreznevsky has experimented in my laboratory, with a plethysmograph, on the cardio-vascular system. By means of intense sound-stimuli, he produced changes in the cardio-vascular system, changes with the character of association reflexes.[1] On the other hand, Dr. Tchaly used, for the same purpose, an electric current and associated its influence on the cardio-vascular system with an indifferent stimulus, and so obtained in a human being a vascular association reflex which, after many repetitions, could be differentiated just like any other association reflex. Finally, Dr. Schneerson, working in my laboratory, approached the investigation of this problem from another side. He found that, in some particularly impressionable people, the usual method of calling out an association reflex is accompanied by a mimico-somatic state, which is reproduced also to the associated indifferent stimulus. (See *Vestnik Psychologii*.)

Various gestures are also association reflexes, which are reproductions of movements which man uses in the appropriate circumstances, and are symbolic reactions of a certain kind.

These symbols, known as gestures, are imitative, descriptive, indicatory, aggressive, defensive, and other movements.

In reality, they are reproductions of corresponding reflexes in complete or incomplete form, *i.e.* movements which serve as expressions of a certain attitude on the part of man to some object or phenomenon. Thus, we perform a beckoning movement with the hand and so reproduce the movement which draws the object towards us ; in another case, we perform a repelling movement with the hands, as if pushing something away from ourselves ; we bend the head forward to indicate acquiescence, and this is a reproduction of the movement of the head in bowing a salute and in taking food ; on the contrary, we move the head from side to side, and so reproduce the movement of refusing food ; we make a threatening movement with the index finger, and thus reproduce the movement of a blow, while the finger plays the rôle of stick ; in another case, we perform an indicatory movement with the finger, and thereby reproduce the movement of poking at an object ; in anger, we clench our fists and throw up our hands ; in complete despair, the fists are directed towards our own breast and thus reproduce blows of the fists on the one responsible for the misfortune, in the given case—ourselves, etc.

In my paper, *The Biological Development of Expressive Movements* (*Vestnik Znania*, 1910), I have cited an enormous number of examples

[1] See Sreznevsky : *Ispug* (*Fright*), etc., Dissertation : St. Petersburg.

which are convincing in this respect. An analogous explanation must be adopted also in other cases. I shall add to all these examples only the three following which have not been cited in the paper mentioned. We know that, in every hopeless situation, men shrug their shoulders. This strange phenomenon has baffled Darwin in his time. But from the viewpoint of association reflexes, this movement is a gesture which reproduces the jerking back of the arms when there is question of a phenomenon dangerous to some extent, one which we cannot master, and with which we are powerless to struggle. When we hear some terrible news, we clutch our head, and this is a reproduction of the defensive movement of the hands in protecting the head. Lastly, when men are in a difficult position, they perform a peculiar movement in the form of scratching the back of their head. This movement is based on the fact that, in every difficult situation suddenly arising, contraction of the cutaneous vessels and tension of the *erectores pilorum* take place ; this tension, being accompanied by the standing on end of the hair, produces a peculiar irritation in the hairy part of the head. The movement of scratching is, in such a case, a defence association reflex, which removes this irritation by causing extension of the vessels of the cutaneous coats of the head. Consequently, in every difficult situation, when a solution of the difficulty does not present itself immediately, the scratching of the back of the head is reproduced, as a fixed mimico-somatic reflex.

Let us also remark that, precisely because they are a result of the reproduction of certain motor reflexes, expressive movements teem with symbolism. Thus, for instance, slavish submission assumes the form of what happens in real slavery. We know, for instance, of cringing movements in the ceremonies with which their subjects approach the petty African kings (Spencer). " A sign of humility in ancient Peru was to have the hands bound and a rope round the neck."[1]

---

[1] Spencer : *Principles of Sociology*, vol. II, p. 126.
" In Dahomey, when approaching royalty, they either crawl like snakes or shuffle forward on their knees." (Spencer : *Principles of Sociology*, vol. II, p. 117.) Also in the Bible (3rd Book of Kings xx, 32) there is mention of winding ropes round the head when going to the King of Israel.

> " and all his powers do yield,
> And humbly thus, with halters on their necks,
> Expect your highness' doom, of life, or death."
> (Shakespeare : *Henry VI*, pt. II, IV, 9.)

In our language, the same symbolism remains in the words : " your most obedient servant," " Merciful Sir," etc. Darwin says : " I have noticed that persons in describing a horrid sight often shut their eyes momentarily and firmly, or shake their heads as if not to see or to drive away something disagreeable " (*Expression of the Emotions*, p. 32). Humility is expressed by bowing and kneeling down ; prostration signifies submissiveness or a submissive petition ; crossing oneself denotes the fixation on the body of the cross as a means of defence against the spirit of evil, the cross having received this significance in the Christian religion.

Translators' note : " Merciful Sir " or " Gracious Sir " was the usual mode of address in formal commercial letters, petitions, etc., in Russia.

This is a reproduction of how the prisoners were brought from the battlefield in ancient times.

So-called concentration, which plays such an important rôle in the various correlative processes, similarly arises as an association reflex, which appears in infancy and is based on organic impulses. Let us take visual concentration. Every one knows that we can walk along the street without being arrested by a multitude of incidental impressions. But when we meet acquaintances, our concentration is immediately directed on them and this is a reproduction of the reflexive concentration experienced during our first meeting with them. In another case, among the multitude of sounds which we hear at an opera we are attending for the first time, a familiar melody is distinguished, and our hearing immediately concentrates on it. In life, concentration is aroused by many other influences also, but in the form of an association reflex.

The process of concentration must be understood as a dominant, *i.e.* as a process of concentrated excitation of one nerve centre and of one muscular apparatus with simultaneous inhibition of the others; collateral stimuli, such as do not suppress the dominant, promote mobilisation of the muscular apparatus.

It must be remembered that various forms of external influence stimulate the act of concentration, which consists in appropriate excitation of the receptive organ and in the inhibition of other centres, as occurs in the case of a real dominant. In life conditions, we may speak of visual, auditory, tactual, olfactory, gustatory, and other forms of concentration. Visual and auditory concentration acquire peculiarly important significance in life, while other forms play a subsidiary rôle, and are, to a greater or lesser extent, associated with visual concentration, which, as a result of the connections established, participates in auditory, tactual, olfactory, and other influences.

It is clear that reflexes evoked with participation of the act of concentration, as a result of the connection established, may be released from inhibition or reproduced by means of concentration, which is originally associated with all those influences which satisfy the organism's biological needs; and, therefore, with the development of the latter, the act of concentration is aroused and is directed towards those influences which formerly satisfied these needs.

Thus, a person, thanks to his accumulated store of past experience and of directed concentration, gathers from the environment only whatever can somehow stand in correlation with the data of past experience, whether the new influences are in accord with them or even otherwise. And it is perfectly obvious that one and the same environment will have an unequal influence on the person according to the general state of the person concerned, and even to what the person is occupied with at the given moment, *i.e.* what complex of influences from past experience is being revived at the given moment, in accordance with certain external or inner stimuli.

From this it follows that a person may be regarded as comprising such an integration of complexes of higher reflexes as promotes, by means of concentration, the segregation, as it were, of external influences, and does so in accordance with the stimulated complexes of past influences—complexes which are a result of experience previously accumulated. Here, naturally, the question arises : What happens to those external influences which, for some reasons or other, do not enter into correlation with complexes of reproduced past influences associated with concentration ? Do they pass without leaving a trace on the person, or have they some influence on him ? As, in the cases cited, the influences mentioned remain outside the pale of concentration, these, although they call out the usual reflexes, cannot be reproduced by active concentration and, consequently, are unaccountable.

Concentration may be external or internal. By external concentration we understand that concentration which is a dominant of receptive organs stimulated by external objects, as stimuli leading to the mobilisation of the muscular apparatus of these organs. By internal concentration must be understood a similar act of concentration on reproducible, but unexpressed or inhibited, speech and other reflexes.

Keeping in mind that various forms of external influence stimulate the act of concentration by appropriate mobilisation and adjustment of the receptive organ to external stimuli, we may speak, as we have already mentioned, of visual, auditory, tactual, olfactory, gustatory, and other forms of concentration. Therefore, internal concentration also may be divided into corresponding categories, and each of them is accompanied by a scarcely appreciable mobilisation of the muscles of the appropriate receptive organ.

As daily biological needs lie at the root of all other needs which develop later in connection with the biological, the act of concentration, as well as the reflexes associated with it, are, as it were, at man's permanent disposal. By means of language, man can give himself and others an appropriate account of all such reflexes, as well as of the influences which have produced them, while other influences and reflexes not associated with the act of concentration are not at the disposal of the person himself, and, consequently, cannot be reproduced and are verbally unaccountable. Thus, we have two orders of influences and also of reflexes produced by them. Those which one is capable of reproducing at any moment and of which one is able to give a verbal account may be called accountable. Those which one cannot reproduce and of which one can give no account may be called unaccountable.

And, indeed, in some cases, a man can give no account of his behaviour, at least not immediately, and this serves as an indication that his behaviour was conditioned by influences which did not arouse active concentration, and which, therefore, like his behaviour, are unaccountable to the individual himself.

However, concentration is still the chief guide in personal behaviour in the waking state, and so past personal experience is utilised to subserve the acquisition of new life experiences, while in states of incomplete sleep, in states of deep hypnosis, and in some pathological conditions (somnambulism, epileptic automatism, hysterical somnambulism, mediumistic trance, etc,) the habitual, *i.e.* firmly fixed, association reflexes often, without arousing concentration, acquire predominant significance and guide personal behaviour to a certain extent. It must be noted here that, in these states, the accumulated experience, in connection with the biological and other needs of the person, does not lose its influence on behaviour; on the other hand, in the normal waking state also, personal behaviour is guided not by the influences of past experience alone— influences which form complexes of reflexes associated not only with biological needs, but partly also with other needs which sustain the habitual reflexes.

The data given above may be tested by experiment on hypnotised persons, and here our attention is drawn to the fact that a man under hypnosis, a state characterised by inhibition of the active manifestations of personality, can avail of all his past experience and loses nothing of it, while, on awaking, he cannot give an account of his state during the hypnosis. In hypnosis, the individual's passivity is striking, notwithstanding his orientation in regard to external stimuli, and he submits, without the least resistance, to all the hypnotist's commands, for, in deep hypnosis, one word from the hypnotist can produce appropriate actions, imaginary impressions, distortion of external influences, and even reincarnation of the personality, etc. Thus, here there is question of more or less complete inhibition of the active side of personality, for there remains a personality which cannot manifest an active relation to the environment, notwithstanding the fact that past experience is not lost. Moreover, external influences, in the form of suggestions made by the hypnotist, may, as a result of the rapport which the very act of hypnotising establishes between the subject and the hypnotist, influence even the subsequent waking state of the person concerned, for, after the passing of the hypnosis, there may remain unconquerable tendencies or imaginary stimulations, the origin of which remains unknown to the person when awake. In general, the person in the waking state cannot give any account of his passive hypnotic state. But, on being induced again into the passive hypnotic state by the same means, he becomes capable of reproducing everything that happened in the previous hypnotic state and of giving an appropriate account of it.

In the examples cited, there is artificial inhibition of the active state by the inducing of an hypnotic state, either through suggestion or certain physical methods. But there are some who can fall into such a state by the reproduction of suggestion or by auto-suggestion. Here we have the phenomena of auto-hypnotism and mediumism, which have not yet been sufficiently investigated by science.

On the other hand, the person may be absorbed by certain external influences or by reproductive activity on which the entire concentration is directed. This will be a state of distraction of concentration with suppression of the other sides of the active state, and here automatism in actions produced by incidental stimuli becomes possible. Here belongs the well-known automatic writing of hysterics. If such a state is evoked by conditions which produce an intense mimico-somatic reaction, it is called ecstasy, such as is easily observed, for instance, in those who are deeply religious and whose concentration is directed on prayer or an object of adoration. If concentration, as a dominant, is based on a functional interrelation of different centres of the cerebral cortex, and, consequently, the excitation of some centres leads to the inhibition of others and *vice versa*, we must not overlook the correlation of the centres on the basis of the co-ordination which exists between the cortical and subcortical centres, and also between the frontal cortical areas and those lying farther back. The subordination of the subcortical centres to the cortical has been revealed by observations which show that cortical excitation, in the form, *e.g.*, of active muscular tension, reinforces the reflexes of the lower extremities (Jendrassik's method), and thus causes release of the function of the spinal centres from the influence of the motor centres of the cortex. The same reinforcement of reflexes occurs also in pathological cases of dissociation of the centres of the spinal cord from those of the brain. On the other hand, the suppression of the frontal areas in hypnosis is accompanied by the development of greater functional activity of the cortical areas lying farther back and is characterised by the appearance of hallucinations during suggestion.

As regards speech, we have to do here with a real symbolic reflex, the reflexive nature of which is revealed by the fact that a man must not be asked a question when he is swallowing food, for his food may at once go down the wrong passage, because of his insuperable tendency to answer immediately.

Speech itself consists of verbal symbols associated with a certain object, action, or state ; and, consequently, we are concerned here with a real association reflex, which is acquired by children chiefly by imitating the sounds made by their parents, but partly by the formation of association reflexes from ordinary vocal reflexes (*och ! ach ! nu !* etc.).

By the way, so-called slips of the tongue and of the pen are explained by concentration on a certain reproduction of words, this reproduction being consequently translated into action, *i.e.* into pronouncing or writing. For instance, the sentence : " Professor V. associates hysterical swellings with auto-intoxication resulting from disturbance in the function of the glands of inner *contusion* "—(he means *secretion*)—" a disturbance produced by air contusions," was written because the word " contusion " occurred subsequently in the sentence, and, at the moment of writing the word, concentration was directed to it.

In other cases, slips of the pen are a consequence of compensation or substitution, *i.e.* through inhibition of one word and its replacement by another as more closely associated with the previous. In the same way, in general, slips of the tongue occur.[1]

In my earlier works, I discussed in detail the phylogenetic development of speech, and proved that primitive speech-sounds were originally simple reflexes, which were later manifested as association reflexes in the form of ejaculations ; but, in time, in the course of further evolution, these reflexes, through differentiation and associative generalisation, changed into those complex movements which we call articulate speech.[2] It is obvious that echoism also plays a particularly important rôle in the phylogenetic development of speech.

This theory of the origin of language shows how speech arose step by step from simple reflexes. According to this theory, the sound of swallowing gave rise to the root " gar," and so we have the word " garknut " (to shriek). The sound of water when swallowed gave rise to the root of the word " glotat " (to swallow), where, by the way, there may also be echoism, as in the words " grom " (thunder), " chrip " (rattles in the throat). In other cases, words are developed from simple sounds produced as reflexes, for instance, from the sound " brrr," we get " brezgat " (to nauseate), " bryuzzhat " (to grumble), " brikat " (to lash out or to kick). In the same way from the word, " nu " (now then !), we get " nukat " (to urge a horse on ; to repeat " now then ! " frequently), " ponukat " (to egg on), " nu-te " (come now !) ; from the sound " uch," we get " uchat " (to jolt or to whoop), etc. Finally, some roots have arisen as further developments of defensive vocal reflexes, such as " fu," " frr," from which have developed " fuknut " (to say " pshaw ! "), " firkat " (to snort, burst into laughter), and as " ach," from which we get " achnut " (to express surprise ; to groan and moan).

We must keep in mind that there are gaps in the dictionaries of savage tribes, and these gaps are explained by the fact that in actual speech the missing words are supplied by signs or gestures, and, besides, many words are rather simple signs than words. On the other hand, as I have seen from observation, a child, before the development of speech, expresses, by means of bodily movements, facial expressions, and intonation of voice, all his requirements in such a fashion that every mother or nurse understands his language as clearly as if he spoke. In the speech of the adult also, gesture and intonation, which are, as it were, survivals of primitive language, play a considerable part, and we have recourse to gestures usually in cases when we wish to supplement our description of an object by the plastic method of graphic representation, and we turn to intonation when we wish to express our own attitude towards the object.

A proof of the fact that echoistic language is the primitive language may be found in children's speech, which usually begins with echoism : such

[1] V. Bechterev : *Golos i retch*, no. 2, 1913. Also the same author's *Objective Psychology*, 3rd pt.

[2] V. Bechterev : *Objective Psychology*, 3rd pt.

words as " mew " for cat, " tick-tack " for clock are formed by the child himself and, together with gestures, serve him at an early age as a simple kind of speech.

Children in general name many things echoistically, for example, "cock-a-doodle-do " for cock, " ding-ding " for a little bell, " boom-boom " for a big bell, " moo " for a cow, etc.

Echoistic forms are retained, as we know, also in language already developed. The Egyptians call the ass " eo," the Chinese call the cat " mau," the Persians call the nightingale " bulbul," the Australians call the fly " bumbero," the Greeks call the flute " umole," the Yagasaks call a little bell " qualyal," in Sanskrit a drum is called " dundu," etc.

It is obvious from the aforesaid that speech reflexes, being names of objects, of phenomena, or of correlations between them and certain sound-signs, comply with the requirements of economy, for, otherwise, the reproduction of the forms and correlations of objects would require considerable expenditure of time.[1]

Speech intonation—which, in turn, consists of stresses on certain words of the spoken text, of raising and lowering the voice, of separating and lengthening syllables, of quickening and slowing down the speech tempo, of pauses—harmonises to a certain extent with gestures and facial expressions, and partly replaces them, since it is, as it were, vocal gesticulation. The development of the intonation of the voice is indubitably correlated with the development of gestures and facial expressions and may be also subsumed under the scheme of association reflexes, but it is unnecessary to dilate on this subject.

As echoistic signs have served as the basis of language, so signs which imitate visual impressions lie at the root of writing. Writing has actually originated from signs similar to the corresponding objects, for primitive painting consisted in the graphic representation of animals, objects, and actions. Events which people regarded as necessary to preserve for posterity were, at first, crudely represented graphically, as we find in the chronicles of the North American Indians. According as the records of events became more extensive, the drawings began to be contracted and generalised, and more and more lost their resemblance to the objects and actions, until, at last, because of the need to express proper nouns, some of the latter began to be expressed phonetically, and so arose signs for sounds.[2] Writing has thus developed from pictographic representations.

Hieroglyphic writing also, which has many signs similar in form to the

[1] The above-said does not exhaust what is really necessary to be said here concerning the development of language, but further information may be drawn from philological works. Very much of interest in this respect may be found in the recent investigations of the Academician N. Marr in the Japhetic languages—*Yaphetitchesky Kavkaz i trety etnitchesky element v sozidanii sredizemnomorskoi kulturi* (*The Japhetic Caucasus and the Third Ethnical Element in the Creation of Mediterranean Culture*), Petrograd, 1920.

[2] Spencer : *Principles of Sociology*, vol. II. See also Denzel : *Die Anfänge der Schrift*, 1912, pp. 1–9.

objects depicted, confirms this. Even now we use graphic representations in mathematics—triangles, squares, etc.

Finally, let us note that words, in as far as they are symbolic and substitutional reflexes, correspond, in some cases, to aggressive actions, and here belong exclamations such as : " Forwards ! " " it must be," " it is necessary," etc. To defensive actions correspond : " Stop ! " and " back ! " ; to reflexes of alertness corresponds the exclamation : " Careful ! " As in actions we have often a chain of reflexes or a chain reflex, so also, in words, we have chain reflexes in the form of deliberation.

Lastly, it is necessary to say something here about personal movements and so-called actions and conduct as intricate complexes of these reflexes.

Personal movements are at first difficult to regard as association reflexes, for they are most frequently produced by inner incitations. But we must keep in mind the twofold nature of our correlative activity, in which some reflexes arise on the basis of external influences, while others are produced by internal organic stimulations.

We have seen above that the so-called " instincts " arise as a result of certain organic stimulations and become operative by means of a mechanism hereditarily transmitted. But apart from this, internal stimuli contitute a directive principle also for other external movements co-ordinated with certain biological needs, the satisfaction of which is accompanied by a general sthenic reaction.[1]

On the other hand, in complex personal reflexes, we are really concerned with the co-ordination of several association reflexes. Let us take some kind of simple work, say, chopping wood. It is a co-ordination of muscular contraction of the arms with the act of visual concentration which is a particular association reflex, as is the muscular contraction of the arms, but both reflexes are here closely co-ordinated with each other (see Diagram XIX). To what extent work, like every activity, is a durable co-ordination of two reflexes—acting and seeing—is seen in paralysis of the external rectus, a condition resulting in deviation of the stroke, and, consequently, in such cases, the smith strikes his own hand with the hammer.

If a man suffers from hemianopsia, he cannot bisect a straight line, but always deviates to the side in which the field of vision is retained.

Some suppose that the group of those complex movements, which subjective psychology calls rational or teleological, cannot be subsumed under the category of association reflexes, because they presuppose an aim which may be foreseen, but, in reality, the aim is always given in the person's past experience or in that of others, or is deduced from it by a logical process or a certain connection of association reflexes—a connection established by experience—and the aim is in this case a stimulus.

Here it is necessary to keep in view that every repetition of acts accompanied by a general sthenic reaction, when the repetition has grown

[1] Concerning sthenic reactions, see my *Objective Psychology*, 2nd and 3rd pts.

habitual, becomes a need characterised by reproduction of the same sthenic reaction whenever an appropriate stimulus is presented, and the sthenic reaction is, as we know, always associated with aggression reflexes.

Naturally, the satisfaction of a need is secured by the reproduction, under certain external influences in direct correlation with the given need, of previously established association reflexes.

It is clear from the above-said that the group of movements which we call personal movements, and which, in their complex forms, constitute so-called actions and conduct, may, and must, be understood as association reflexes, which stand in a certain connection with the demands of the environment and the needs of the organism, not only those needs which have been transmitted by heredity, but also those fixed by education ; however, these reflexes have not that imperative significance which appertains to all instinctive or complex-organic movements, which are more closely connected with certain physiological states.

Thus, if we take into account that those association reflexes, which we may call reflexes personal in character, develop in connection with certain needs of the individual, we shall have concluded our brief survey of the chief forms of association reflexes manifested in the higher animals and in man.

Generally speaking, the usual exciters or stimuli of actions in life are external compulsion or the stimulating of a need. The need which results from inherited organic impulses in some cases, and from formed habits in others, is also really a form of stimulation or compulsion, but an internal compulsion, while the external compulsion is a stimulus which issues from external conditions, whether this compulsion be the inevitability of a given way of escape from the existing circumstances, or whether its source be an external living force—based on the power to punish—in the form of the demands of society, for instance laws and the executive or of the demands of a stronger man with whom the fate of the given individual is somehow interlocked, such as the demands of parents from children, employer from employee, etc.

Thus not only the need, which is a result of organic impulses or of a formed habit, but also every external compulsion, is an associative stimulus. Originally, this stimulus arises on the basis of bodily influences or their symbols. So, the force of circumstances has arisen from inevitable extinction accompanied by the development of the physical processes of disintegration. Compulsion issuing from a living force has arisen from physical measures punitive in character.

In this way, the whole of man's activity is, from the objective standpoint, reduced to the influence of an internal or external compulsion as a stimulus, or internal and external stimulation, leading to the development of a more or less complex reflex expressed in a certain action, and this reflex itself is a result of past experience and exercise, both of which may lie at the basis of the inner impulse or inhibitory force. In addition, we must keep in mind the existence of incidental stimuli, some of which may stimulate a complex reflex in the form of an action, while others may impede or inhibit it.

All favourable conditions and encouraging measures, such as reward, praise, etc., must be included among external stimuli, exciting in character. But there may be also internal incidental stimuli, exciting in character, which are a result of the innate peculiarities and the acquired proclivities of a person and his character, for instance persistence, enhancement of energy, the desire to assert and distinguish oneself, etc. Both classes of stimuli quicken and intensify the effect, *i.e.* the complex reflex or action, and make possible the overcoming of all kinds of difficulties.

As regards incidental inhibitory stimuli, they may take (*a*) the form of external inhibitory forces, to which belong : unfavourable conditions, and compulsion, which acts in a direction contrary to the individual's own needs, etc. ; and (*b*) the form of internal inhibitory forces, for instance innate sluggishness in reaction or acquired internal inhibitory conditions, general temporary depression, negativism, etc. These inhibitory forces may be so strong as to exclude completely possibility of action and manifestation of reactions.

Applying this scheme to human activity, we shall see that it embraces all actions personal in character and all speech reactions, reactions of concentration, all mimico-somatic manifestations, and all inherited-organic reactions, often called instinctive.

It has been already mentioned that association reflexes enter into co-ordination with each other and form a number of complexes in dependence on those needs and correlations which develop as a result of individual experience. In this respect, it is first of all necessary to distinguish two chief complexes of reflexes : those individual and those social in character, each of which may be further subdivided. Thus, complexes individual in character are constituted of complexes associated with the need for food, with marital needs, self-preservative or egoistic needs, needs for narcotics, etc. On the other hand, complexes social in character may be formed under the influence of the family, of comradeship, the social environment or milieu, nationality, humanity in general.

It must, however, be kept in view that, if the individual and social experiences create a number of association-reflex complexes, which, in their integration, form a complete personality, the framework, on which the structure of personality is built, is provided by the individual's nature acquired by heredity. Here belongs a degree of natural giftedness, the individual type (auditory, visual, motor, etc.), and the general constitution, which depends on conditions of metabolism and of inner secretion, and all of this produces not only a greater or lesser development of the higher processes of correlative activity and individual tendencies, but also the so-called temperament, the tempo of movement, etc.

If the biological framework of correlative activity in the form of innate reflexes, inherited-organic reflexes (instincts), and many mimico-somatic reflexes, is a direct inheritance of racial cosmo-social experience or phylo-genesis, everything superimposed on it in the form of association-reflex activity is a result of individual or personal experience developed in fellow-ship with others of the same species, and consisting both in continuous adjustment to the environment and in the utilisation, for one's own organisation, of the means which nature provides.

In order fully to elucidate the subject, it is also necessary to investigate here the creative activities of the human individual, as they are looked at from the reflexological standpoint.

CHAPTER XXII

CREATIVENESS as an activity is essentially the creation or production of something new. There is no creativeness at all unless something new is derived from something given. But the new in creativeness is only a purposeful change of some previously existing combination of stimuli or relations between them. The breaking up of a complex object, as a stimulus, into its components is creativeness through analysis. Selective generalisation or the purposeful building up of a whole from its separate elements is also creativeness, but through synthesis. The purposeful combination of new movements (for instance, dancing) is also creativeness. The representation on canvas of some typical face or the representation of a typical scene is creativeness synthetic in character. A new combination of sounds in the form of a melody is musical creativeness synthetic in character.

Mathematical analysis and the combination of numerical data in a new form are also creativeness.

The creation of a new poem, a new publication, is also creativeness, just as is the performance of every new complex action. As thought and, in general, all psychic processes are regarded by reflexology as reflexes not efferently manifested, the expression of a new thought is also creativeness, verbal in character. Lastly, every physical work which results in something new, if only it has not become stereotyped, also necessarily implies creativeness.

Creativeness understood in this manner is a complex act aggressive in character, and, like every search after truth, often demands great expenditure of work and time. Reflexology regards this act as a complex chain of association or higher reflexes, directed towards the achievement of something new in the given sphere, either through analysis (differentiation of stimuli) or synthesis (selective generalisation), and exciting the enhancement of energy under the favourable influence, in the mimico-somatic sphere, of the act itself and of the results achieved. Thus, creativeness is a series of reflexes linked together for the achievement of a certain aim, and the aim, in turn, is always given either in the individual's own analogous past experience or in the experience of others. Here, too, the question arises : What stimulus is the source of these reflexes ?

The opinion prevails among the physiologists of the Leningrad school that the exploration reflex is innate, but I do not hold this opinion, for neither the new-born infant nor the new-born puppy manifests a single explorative activity, but only a number of reflex movements adapted to seizing and evoked by internal or external stimuli, and neither the infant nor the puppy manifests attempts at exploration, even for the purpose of finding the necessary food.

Only contact with a mother's breast or with a nipple will first evoke the act of sucking in the infant. This is perfectly obvious, and it may be proved by the direct observation of infants[1] that the discovery of the source of food occurs through an association reflex, and not through an innate act which makes the discovery. Only gradually do reflexes, which are subject to differentiation (analysis) and selective generalisation (synthesis), as they develop and increase in complexity, lead to the rise of visual and auditory concentration, which affords the new-born infant the possibility of active analysis and synthesis of external stimulations or the resolution and combination of his own movements, and, consequently also, new external forms of both. It is with this act of concentration that creativeness is essentially associated, for, as a result of concentration, all material, which lends itself to the investigation of the given object and is reproduced from past experience, is drawn to the centre excited in the given case. In the contraposition and selection of this material consists that association-reflex activity which is often described in everyday language as " the throes of creativeness," and which, for it is closely connected with the process of active inhibition and excitation, is accompanied by a corresponding disturbance of the mimico-somatic tonus.

But every new product obtained through one's own activity, like every success, evokes a sthenic or enlivening reaction in the form of a general reflex, which is mimico-somatic in character, and is manifested by an enhancement of energy, and all this creates, on repetition, the habit of creative activity, draws the individual into it, and creates, for whoever devotes himself to it, a certain set towards creativeness, a set characterised by a special appetite for creative activity.

There is reason to believe that the above-mentioned mimico-somatic reflex is accompanied, through the mediation of the vegetative nervous system, by an inner secretion which is favourable to the activity of the brain, enters the general blood stream, and causes an afflux of arterial blood to the cerebral hemispheres.

It may be admitted hypothetically that we are concerned here chiefly with excessive production of secretion of the sex and adrenal glands.

However that may be, as a result of the above-mentioned mechanism, favourable endocretory conditions, which promote striving towards this activity, develop, in connection with creative activity, in persons who work in a certain sphere and have more or less talent, without which real creativeness is out of the question.

But, in my opinion, the direct stimulus of creativeness is always a problem or aim, which, as the fundamental stimulus, may arise as a result of a perfectly definite conclusion drawn from an investigation, as happens in the systematic study of various objects. The problem, in such a case, is a working hypothesis, which is later tested by synthesis and analysis. In another case, a man suddenly, as a result of association activity, gets an

[1] See V. Bechterev and Shtchelovanov : *Principles of Genetic Reflexology :* Address to the Congress of Pedology, Experimental Pedagogics, and Psychoneurology. Leningrad, 1924.

idea, *i.e.* an externally unexpressed reflex, and this idea is made the starting-point of a problem.

In both cases, consequently, the first incentive to creative activity is a problem arising, in the one case, as a direct conclusion from existing facts, in the other, as a result of association activity called out by an incidental stimulus. In such cases, the subjectivists are fond of speaking of a sudden illumination, after which follows an exaltation, *i.e.* an appropriate enhancement of energy, a topic to which we have already referred.

But illumination is merely a thought which arises through association activity, *i.e.* through a number of reflexes which are externally unexpressed and often even unaccountable—a thought which in itself is a hitherto unexpressed reflex, and often precedes the attainment of the final goal of the investigation. Exaltation is merely the development of cerebral activity in the form of hitherto unexpressed association reflexes, a development associated with the above-mentioned enhancement of energy.

However that may be, in both cases, the problem is the stimulus ; and the responsive reaction to it or a series of response reflexes are the activity which leads to creative achievements.

What is the mechanism of the action of the problem-stimulus ? Like every powerful stimulus, it first of all stimulates concentration on the problem—stimulates, as it were, the directing of the working mechanism to the given problem. This directing is a kind of dominant in mental activity, *i.e.* such a process of excitation as attracts to it, as to a centre, excitations from other parts of the brain, gathers to itself by reproduction the whole store of past experience, and, at the same time, inhibits all other inadequate excitations.[1] Besides, the very presentation of the problem evokes a positive, mimico-somatic reaction, as a result of the possible consequences (indicated by past experience) to be derived from a correct solution of the problem—a reaction which leads to enhancement of energy and, consequently, to increased activity. The material gathered because of the presentation of the problem is then subjected to analytic sifting of the relevant from the irrelevant ; and, after this, the relevant material is submitted to further analysis and subsequent synthesis, and, as a result of both, a new product is created. It is of no importance whether this is a new conclusion, or a new combination, or a hitherto unachieved resolution of some complex whole into its component parts. That is the usual way of scientific creativeness.

In artistic creativeness also, a problem is first of all set, and it is indifferent whether it is a product of accountable or unaccountable activity, unaccountable activity being often called intuitive. The problem again plays the rôle of the direct stimulus to creative activity, and the answer

[1] The physiological definition of a dominant may be found in the works of Uchtomsky and other representatives of the school of N. E. Vvedensky (see the communication of Professor Uchtomsky to the Congress of Psychoneurology, January, 1924), but I have independently approximated to his conclusions in my *Objective Psychology*, 1907–12.

to this problem, in this form of creativeness, may be more unaccountable or intuitive than accountable. In this case, the response takes the form of pictures which transform the environment in an appropriate way, and are reproduced by the painter's brush as colour combinations on canvas, or by the sculptor as figures moulded in clay, or by the composer as rhythmically combined sounds drawn from a musical instrument, or by the dancer as symbolic bodily movements of a certain tempo, intensity, and force, or, lastly, by the architect as rhythmical or symbolic forms in architecture.

Since creativeness, as a complex act, demands for its realisation not only native giftedness, but also considerable exercise by way of training and preparatory mental work, exercise which creates a certain skill in work, it is natural that, even in geniuses, the initial creative activity is, to a certain extent, imitative. As an example of this we may take Peter the Great, who partly imitated foreign countries in building up his state ; Pushkin and Lermontov, who began by imitating Byron. Only gradually does the experienced creator-thinker, creator-technician (inventor) or creator-artist approach originality in creation, and create not only something new, but also original, *i.e.* unique.

It must be borne in mind here that, in the foregoing, creativeness has been examined only in its biological aspect ; but all creativeness is an act intended for the social environment, and the chief impulses to creativeness, apart from all inherited, *i.e.* biological, aptitudes, are derived from the physico-cosmical and social environment of the creator in science, the creator in technique, or the creator in art. That is why the activity of creators in science and technique takes its direction from contemporary conditions, as well as from those of education and environment, these conditions having directed association-reflex activity into one, rather than another, direction. Every artist is also the child of his own time, and reflects, through the glass of his social environment, the climate around him ; simultaneously, he reflects the social conditions in which he lives, and which determine the predominant character and the direction of his creativeness. In this sense, creativeness is as much a product of biological, inherited qualities of cerebral activity or of giftedness, as of physico-cosmical influences (climate and natural environment), and, especially, the influences of the social environment. In particular, the general set to creativeness is not only an ego-centric reflex (self-satisfaction accruing from success achieved), but is predominantly a social reflex, which incites the individual to creative activity, so as to promote his social standing and society in general.[1]

It is clear from the foregoing that two kind of creativeness must be distinguished.

1. The unaccountable or intuitive—sudden illumination. An idea is glimpsed, the problem is presented for elaboration, and is then gradually solved. This initially unaccountable creativeness subsequently becomes accountable.

[1] V. Bechterev : *Collective Reflexology,* 1921.

R

2. The systematic, when a problem is presented as a working hypothesis, *i.e.* as a possible conclusion whether from a truth received or facts obtained.

In both cases, the problem plays the rôle of stimulus, but in the former case, the incentive is a by-product, arising, as it were, spontaneously out of the work in the form of association activity, while, in the second case, it is presented as a result of concentration on a work developing according to plan and assuming the form of analysis or synthesis, and is an hypothesis in so far as it is a possible conclusion from the given data.

Thus, to sum up : the problem plays the rôle of stimulus ; creativeness is the responsive reaction to it ; and the product of creativeness is a result of the final solution of this reaction, which is an integration of reflexes.

How does the stimulus operate ? It excites the concentration reflex, which, in turn, produces a mimico-somatic reflex which is favourable to the activity, and secures enhancement of energy through vasomotor activity and the secreting of endocrine hormones, which excite cerebral activity. Concentration, as a dominant in the cerebral activity, and being accompanied by the mimico-somatic reflex, on the one hand attracts co-excitations from all other cerebral regions, and collects round itself, by the reproduction of past experience, all the stored material which stands in relationship to the stimulus, *i.e.* to the problem, and, on the other hand, inhibits all irrelevant processes of cerebral activity. The problem itself becomes, for some period of time, the object of concentration—the dominant, and the material reproduced is subjected to appropriate sifting, analysis, and subsequent synthesis on the basis of relevant experience previously obtained.

As has been mentioned above, some degree of giftedness, with appropriate training and environment, both of which create skill in the work, are necessary for all creativeness. Training develops the bent towards the display of natural gifts, and, consequently, a well-nigh insuperable tendency or urge to creative activity ultimately arises. The direct determinant of its goals is the environment consisting in the natural surroundings, the material culture, and the social circumstances, particularly the latter. The social environment gives its direction to the individual's creative activity also.

This is, in a nutshell, the general scheme of creative activity from the standpoint of reflexology.

Thus, if the framework of correlative activity, both in the form of innate reflexes (instincts) and of many mimico-somatic reflexes, is a direct inheritance of racial cosmo-social experience or phylogenesis, all super-structures in the form of association-reflex activity are a result of individual or personal experience, which is elaborated in the society of others of the same species and in continuous adaptation to the environment, as well as in the perpetual utilisation, in the interests of the individual's organism, of the means which nature provides.

CHAPTER XXIII

The scheme of association reflexes embraces all correlative processes from the lowest to the highest. Where responsive reactions are absent for a prolonged time, as in personal movements, we are concerned with processes of inhibition. The conformity to law both of all the external manifestations of a person and also of all historical events.

IT is clear from the above-said that the concept of correlative activity embraces all reflexes from the very simplest to the most complex, the complex being placed in a scheme of reflexes of a higher order which, in the higher animals and in man, are based on the associative activity of the nervous system.

As we know, reflexes may arise as a result of stimulations from the surface of the retina, from the organ of Corti, from the Schneider membrane, from the mucous membrane of the tongue and soft palate, from the cutaneo-muscular surface, from the semicircular canals of the labyrinth, and from the inner surfaces of the body. But wherever these stimulations arise, they can, on the one hand, produce—by means of the shorter transmission of impulses through the sympathetic ganglia, the spinal cord, and the cerebral ganglia—the ordinary organic or vegetative, vascular, secretory, and motor reflexes, and, on the other hand, by reaching the appropriate centres of the cerebral cortex and being then transmitted through associative connections to motor and other centrifugal conductors, they produce certain response reactions more complex in character—the so-called higher or association reflexes in the motor, vascular, or secretory sphere.

Everything said above will become perfectly comprehensible to us if we adhere strictly to the fundamental principle that, without a nervous current, there is not, and cannot be, any association-reflex process in the higher animals and as the nervous current, which is excited from the periphery by external stimulation, wherever the latter arises, is ultimately discharged to the periphery again, it is quite natural that the scheme of association reflexes or reflexes of a higher order, *i.e.* reflexes which, in comparison with ordinary reflexes, have a longer arc, because of the participation of the cortical centres and of the associative connections between them, is applicable to all manifestations of association-reflex activities in the higher animals and in man.

It is true, we encounter here phenomena characterised by the fact that the final outcome, by means of a responsive reaction, is often separated in time from the initial external stimulus by a longer or shorter interval. It is universally known that a man, who, under the influence of an external stimulus, has taken a definite decision, sometimes carries it out a considerable time after the presentation of the stimulus, for instance after days, weeks, or even years. In this manner, these responsive reactions seem to contradict the scheme of association reflexes, but, in reality, these facts are explained from the viewpoint of inhibitory conditions, to which we shall refer later. It is necessary to keep in mind that, in addition to external stimuli, which produce association reflexes, internal stimuli, determined by the composition of the blood and by hormone secretions, which influence the general state of nervous activity in respect of its excitation or depression, have a special influence on the character of a person's external manifestations, his actions, and conduct. We must not forget here that the composition of the blood may be accompanied by specific reactions also ; for instance, impoverished blood at first evokes in infants groping movements of the mouth, and later a general reaction in the form of shouting ; but in adults it evokes processes of concentration and actions directed towards the obtainment of food, while the secretions of the sex glands produce an afflux of blood to the sex organs, and cause subsequent erection, etc. But hormonism as such depends not only on direct stimuli of an external or internal order, but also on higher or association reflexes, especially reflexes, mimico-somatic in character, which excite or depress the activity of the endocrine glands, and which also directly influence the cardio-vascular system and respiration, and this, in turn, acts, in a stimulating or a depressing manner, on the activities of the nervous system. All of this taken together, and not merely external stimuli as such, finally determines a person's behaviour. Incontrovertible statistics prove that all these phenomena are, like all other phenomena of association-reflex activity, conformable to law.

As we have stated already, from the time of Quetelet,[1] it has been recognised that human actions, even as subtile as slips of the pen in addressing letters, are conformable to law in respect of their dependence on various external conditions. Since that time, it has been accepted as a fact, proved by irrefutable statistical data from all civilised countries, that increase in various types of criminality, of suicide, and even in the number of births is dependent on social conditions.

It follows from this that the human activities and conduct of the herd are externally determinable, if all the previous and present determinants of its behaviour are taken into account. However, it may be thought that there is question here of predisposing socio-economic factors, which determine only the general statistics of criminality or other social phenomena without reference to the units included in these statistics. In a word, it may be thought that, in the herd, certain general conditions cannot remain without influence on the increase of crimes, suicides, and births, but that all this does not exclude the free self-determination of the individuals in their actions and conduct. I have dealt in detail with this problem in a special paper previously referred to.[2]

" Why exactly a given individual becomes a criminal is determined—I maintain—by the totality of the conditions which surround him and have surrounded him from the moment of birth, and determine the more or less favourable conditions of his conception and gestation. In the analysis of a crime, it is not difficult to be convinced that, in addition to the general

---

[1] *Translators' note :* 1796–1874.

[2] V. Bechterev : *The Objectivo-psychological Method in its Application to the Study of Crime ; Symposium Dedicated to the Memory of D. A. Dril ;* St. Petersburg, and published separately.

socio-economic factors, there are particular factors which really decide the given individual to the commission of the crime. Let us assume that socio-economic causes have shaken the man out of his usual rut and deprived him of his usual earnings. Having looked for work for a long time, and having exhausted all his resources, this man is forced to search for work in another district ; here, then, a new factor is introduced— separation from his circle, from acquaintances who could sustain him by advice, and, in an extreme case, help him with money also. Further failure to find employment next robs him of the means of living his life in surroundings which satisfy the minimal requirements of a human being. Pauperism inevitably ensues as a consequence of the above-mentioned conditions. But this pauperism is still borne with for some time, until the individual falls morally under stress of the surrounding conditions, until he becomes the victim of alcohol, until temptation, in the form of the possibility of easy gain, overcomes him, or, lastly, until the more weighty motive of the extreme need, in the form of gnawing hunger, arises.

Ultimately, crime is the fated outcome of the influence of a number of general predisposing and directly-acting or proximate factors. That is why not only the influence of the proximate external factors on the individual, in any given case, but also his character, in which are reflected his whole past life and the conditions of his development in the sense of the influence of heredity, can in no case be ignored, no matter what figures socio-economic statistics advance in favour of various general influences in the development of criminality among the population."[1]

But whatever is applicable to so-called criminal acts or—in objective terminology—such anti-social activities as are provided for in legal codes, is applicable also to all other human activities, only with this difference : that, usually, external influences less imperative in character are required for the latter than for the former.

Tarde (*Les lois de l'imitation*, p. 223, Paris, 1895) draws our attention to the fact that, in the course of half a century, those sentenced by the correction police appeal in nearly 40 cases out of 100,[2] while the public prosecutor, in the same period of time, appeals in a constantly decreasing progression. The latter fact is explained, according to Tarde, as the result of professional imitativeness, but the question is how to explain the former fact. The following is the only suitable explanation : as hope of success and fear of failure are equal in this case, the chief impulse which decides the course taken is boldness, which is an expression of the native temperament of those sentenced, and the result is that the same number of the sentenced appeal.

It may seem that an action which I perform, for instance the stretching or lifting of my hand, is not conditioned by anything except myself ; consequently it is externally indeterminable ; still, the fact that this

[1] V. Bechterev : *l.c.*, pp. 36–37.
[2] *Translators' note :* These figures do not agree with those given in the footnote in Chap. II.

movement has a certain goal, for instance to show my capacity for self-determination in the execution of the movement, points to the fact that this movement is conditioned by a certain stimulus, created by the individual's past experience and taking the form of a need to show independence of movement. Thus, these actions also must be regarded as externally determinable.

However this may be, we must admit that all an individual's activities are, without exception, externally determinable, the conditions producing them being not only current external influences, but also all influences which have acted on him in the past, and, equally, those hereditary influences which have conditioned his innate peculiarities through influencing the circumstances of conception and gestation.

The viewpoint outlined above inevitably leads us to conclude strict causation in all the activities of a human being, as well as in all historical events.

This conclusion of reflexology in regard to each individual person is fully in accordance with the view which recognises the conformity to law of the activities of a human herd both in the present and in the past.

We must admit that not only the number of births, suicides, crimes, and indifferent, and seemingly capricious, activities, such as slips of the pen in addressing letters, are subject to certain laws, but also that certain politico-economic, geographic, and other conditions determine both the peculiar form of government and the customs of nations. On the other hand, the historical sciences also tend, at the present time, to discover the conformity to law of the various historical phenomena. Relevant to this, L. Tolstoy, in his famous work, *War and Peace* (p. 272), has brilliantly formulated the law of historical determinism in the following words : " To regard human freedom as a force capable of influencing historical events, *i.e.* as non-conformable to law, is the same, in the sphere of history, as the according of freedom of movement to the heavenly bodies in astronomy.

" To do so would destroy the possibility of the existence of laws, *i.e.* knowledge of any kind. If only one body moves freely, there is an end to the laws of Kepler and Newton, and we can form no conception of the movements of the heavenly bodies. If man is free in a single action, there is no historical law or any conception of historical events."[1]

---

[1] It is regrettable that the moralist, L. Tolstoy, later changed the views he advanced in *War and Peace*, but he changed them through sophistries quite unsuited to his artistic nature. Here are his words as recorded on the phonograph : " It is said that man is not free, because everything he does has a cause preceding it in time. But man always acts only in the present, and the present transcends time, for it is only the point of contact of the past and the future, and, therefore, at any moment in the present, man is free." Is this not sophistry in which the present is regarded not as a direct consequence of the past, but is, as it were, isolated from the concept of time by means of a special designation, " the point of contact " of the past and the future ? And only such a perfectly artificial

Needless to say, as a result of scientific investigations in the sphere of history, these theses have been more firmly and deeply based. We must particularly keep in mind here so-called historical materialism, which is a strictly objective science.

isolation of the concept of present time permits him to speak, for some reason or other, of the freedom of man's activities in the present, while, in this case, there can be question only of lack of proof that human actions are not free. Needless to say, from the logical point of view also, this reasoning cannot sustain any criticism whatever.

CHAPTER XXIV

Processes of inner and external inhibition. Discussion and examples.

WE have already in the previous chapter mentioned processes of inhibition. Generally speaking, processes of impediment or inhibition have been known for a long time in physiology. We know of the inhibitory influence of the nervus vagus on the heart-beat, the inhibitory centres of Setchenov in the thalamus opticus, the inhibitory influence of the brain on the spinal cord, the inhibitory influence of the frontal lobes in respect of the other regions of the hemispheres, etc. But, on the other hand, there are a number of physiological phenomena from which it is obvious that the stimulation of one and the same region of the brain, for instance its cortex, produces excitation of certain muscles and inhibition of the activity of others—their antagonists ; or the excitation of certain centres leads to the inhibition of the activities of other centres. If, in some cases, there is question of special conditions of adaptation in the nervous system, in other cases we have phenomena of a different kind, since it is clear that we are concerned not with such centres as would be specially predetermined for the inhibition of certain functions, and so would be special inhibitory centres, for such do not really exist, but with the correlation of the exciting and inhibitory influences of any given area, as well as with the appropriate relation of the central and other areas of the nervous system to certain influences. Often inhibition occurs, as it were, of itself, as a result of work ; for instance, we throw aside some work that has become boring, abandon the reading of an uninteresting book, etc. In other cases, we bring into action the antagonist muscles, so as not to permit a certain movement. Thus we inhibit yawning, laughter, etc.

Lastly, distraction of concentration plays an important part in the suppression of certain processes of association-reflex activity, for concentration, as a dominant process exciting the given centre, is accompanied by inhibition of all other centres.

We may observe the same phenomenon when association reflexes are inculcated under different conditions. Every differentiated association reflex is accompanied by the inhibition of such reflexes as are evoked by other stimuli. On the other hand, every association reflex, on frequent repetition, is subjected to inner inhibition ; consequently, not being sustained by association with the primary stimulus, it gradually weakens in intensity on each repetition.

It is in this gradual weakening of the motor reaction to external stimuli that the inner inhibition of association reflexes is manifested, and this inhibition occurs when the inner resistance in the nerve tissue does not counterbalance the force of the external influence.

As is well known, inhibition is a physiological process proper to all reflexes. This process, however, must be distinguished from exhaustion and fatigue resulting from auto-intoxication. Processes of inhibition are characterised by the fact that, if the source of this state of depression of function is weakened, the latter is enhanced. (N. E. Vvedensky.) But if, in the given case, depression of the function is followed by its excitation, we are right in regarding such a depression as an inhibition. Lastly, if some centres are depressed, but others interconnected with them are in a state of excitation, we are right, in this case, too, in regarding the depression of the function as inhibition. Parabiosis, discovered by N. E. Vvedensky, as a state of hyperexcitation, is a special form of inhibition. Any reflex can be inhibited under the influence of an external stimulus, and, consequently, it will not be externally expressed until the inhibitory condition is removed, and, so, conditions for the release of inhibition of the reflex will ensue, as a result of the removal of depressing or inhibitory conditions.

But in ordinary reflexes and under the usual conditions of their production, inhibition of their manifestation usually occurs for some time as a result of strong or weak, but uniform and sustained, external stimuli ; and only in rare cases do phenomena of inhibition as a result of internal causes ensue, while in association reflexes, inhibition from external, as well as internal, causes occurs in a considerably more marked degree and with much greater ease.

To illustrate this, let us take the patellar reflex, as an example of ordinary reflexes. It is not difficult to prove that, under the usual conditions, it can be produced *ad libitum* without being inhibited. Only when a state of exhaustion of the nervous system has set in as a result of special conditions does the repeated production of the patellar reflex lead to its inhibition, which disappears after an interval.

On the other hand, particularly strong peripheral or central stimuli can temporarily inhibit the patellar reflex, but on the removal of these stimuli, the reflex immediately reasserts itself and can be again produced incessantly *ad libitum*.[1]

However, the same cannot be said of association reflexes. These are easily inhibited even under usual conditions, and also for a long time. Let us take the blinking reflex in response to a feint with the hand. In this association reflex, as in all similar reflexes, the reproductivo-associative activity of the nerve centres plays a part, for the ordinary blinking reflex is produced by mechanical stimulation of the conjunctiva and the cornea, but when there is a feint, the reflex occurs because of the association of the visual stimulus of the hand approaching the eye with previous mechanical stimulation of the latter under the same conditions.

We find that such a reflex is easily weakened by frequent stimulations, and, at last, temporarily disappears. To revive it, it is necessary to produce fresh mechanical stimulation of the eye in the same way, and then the reflex in response to a feint reappears.

Another example : Let us assume that an animal, for instance a dog, has got a cut of a whip. He naturally turns to flee ; afterwards he will run on a mere flourish of the whip. But assume that you overdo the flourishing of the whip ; the animal grows accustomed to it, and no longer runs away.

[1] For bibliography of this question see my work : *Diagnostic of Nervous Diseases*, 2nd ed., St. Petersburg.

However, a fresh cut on the dog's body will revive the reflex of defensive flight when he sees the raised whip.

It is clear that, in the world of man also, examples of the action of the same principle are not difficult to find. Let us assume that a man has lost a dear friend. At first, every external influence which reminds him of his loss produces an intense reaction, which vents itself in tears, but as time goes on, the same stimulus produces a weaker and weaker reaction, until, at last after a longer time, the man assumes a tranquil attitude towards such external stimuli.

The loss of what we have learned, as we always observe under certain conditions, is also a phenomenon of inhibition. Inhibition by no means always occurs from the outside. It may be internal also. Both external and internal inhibition lead to indecision and inactivity. In this case, there is sometimes question of what are known as " inner contradictions." Such are cases of clash of belief with scientific knowledge, a clash causing internal conflict, etc.

Here also belong those cases of a man struggling between two contrary tendencies, for instance between amusement and passion for science, etc. ; lastly, those cases when a tendency encounters some obstacle which makes its satisfaction impossible or when there are facts to show that its satisfaction will not bring good results.

In general, wherever there is a clash of two mutually exclusive factors, processes of inhibition or of suppression of reaction become operative.

If, in the laboratory, we have artificially inculcated an association reflex, through a method elaborated by us, by electrically stimulating the skin of the sole or of the fingers and associating this stimulus with one of light or sound (see Diagram I), we shall notice, in either case, that, on repetition of the artificially inculcated reflex at certain time intervals, it becomes weaker and weaker, its period of abeyance is gradually increased, and, finally, the reflex is completely blocked or inhibited.

If there are no external incidental influences, this disappearance of the reflex occurs quite regularly, and, on each repetition, the reflex is more and more weakened up to the point of complete inhibition (Diagram VIII).

It is clear that association reflexes have a tendency to grow weaker on repetition under the influence of internal causes, in other words, under the influence of inner inhibitory conditions, but they are also easily revived under certain conditions, one of which is the fresh association of the stimulus to which the association reflex has been inculcated with the primary reflexogenous stimulus, which produces an ordinary reflex. Moreover, a number of other conditions, as for instance temporary rest from stimulation, and also the influence of other incidental stimuli, may cause release of the inhibition of association reflexes, but we shall refer to this later.

Nevertheless, inhibition does not exclude minimal reflexive effects. In other words, an association reflex is usually inhibited only to a degree of minimal manifestation, which is either not observable at all or observable only with difficulty. Thus, for instance silent reading and other motor-association reflexes, which are inhibited in their external expression, are accompanied by weak movements, in the first case, of the speech apparatus, in the second, of the remainder of the motor sphere. The same occurs in regard to other functions, for instance, vascular and secretory activity, when there is question of association reflexes in these spheres.[1]

Thus it is clear that the existence of a minimal motor effect, which, under conditions of complete manifestation of the association reflex should be expressed in a more marked manner, signifies inhibition of the association reflex.

In view of the aforesaid, what we subsume under the concept of "desire" and is usually accompanied by minimal motor effects must, from the viewpoint of reflexology, be regarded as an inhibited association-motor reflex. It is well known that intense desire is always accompanied by weak motor impulses, which, however, are easily detected by good "thought readers" and can also be well recorded on an apparatus. It is clear from this that such processes as, for instance, activities produced by inner inhibitory effort—activities always accompanied by certain motor impulses—are merely inhibited association reflexes.

In this respect, so-called internal speech also, which is characterised by minimal motor effects in the speech apparatus, by weakly expressed gesticulation, and facial expressions, must be regarded as an inhibited symbolic association reflex.[2]

Obviously, all the so-called psychic processes also, since they are accompanied by weak vasomotor and secretory effects, which can be detected by special apparatus, are inhibited or latent association reflexes. In all the cases mentioned, the association processes receive a complete verbal or other external expression on removal of the inhibitory force, and they are cast in the mould of more explicit association reflexes.

Thus, inner processes in general are merely association reflexes of a verbal, motor, or other character, which have been inhibited in their external manifestation. This thesis obviously contradicts the views of those who are accustomed to think that thought is a purely internal phenomenon, and merely finds expression in words, while reflexology is based on the energic doctrine according to which the subjective is inseparable from the objective, and thought is an energic process which, in the one case, is transformed into muscular activity, in the other, into the molecular activity of the centres.

In general, it is necessary to recognise that inhibition of an association

[1] If silent reading may be regarded with perfect justification as a speech association reflex inhibited in its motor part, then, with equal justification, thoughts, since they are accompanied by scarcely perceptible movements of the tongue, the vocal cords, and sometimes also the lips, must be regarded as inhibited association-speech reflexes. We shall dilate on this elsewhere.

[2] V. Bechterev : *The Biological Development of Speech—Vestnik Psychologii.* See also *Objective Psychology,* 3rd pt.

reflex usually reduces the reflex to the minimum and by no means results in its final disappearance. Consequently, the inhibited reflex is always and under appropriate conditions ready, as it were, to be released from inhibition, the release being equivalent in this case to enhancement of a reflex which has been reduced to the minimum.

Needless to say, examples of the inhibition and release of association or higher reflexes may be found everywhere, including personal movements. Let us say that you intend to take something from the next room, but on the way you become distracted. That is sufficient to inhibit the associativo-reproductive activity, and, consequently, you lose the aim of looking for the object you want. But then it is sufficient to come back to the room you have left, and immediately the reproductivo-associative activity in regard to the given object is revived, and the reflex is again released from inhibition. We find interesting examples of inhibition in cutaneous reflexes, which develop easily on stimulation of certain spots of the cutaneous surface by some external agency, while the same stimulation issuing from one's own hand does not produce the same effect. Consequently, when we associate with a stroking or pricking cutaneous stimulus another simultaneous cutaneo-muscular stimulus arising from the active movement of the hand, these reflexes which, as we have proved elsewhere, are really association reflexes, are inhibited.

Further, it often happens that a man temporarily forgets a familiar word, that is, there is temporary inhibition of a learned speech-reflex. This usually happens under conditions which distract his attention. But then he runs across objects or words closely associated with the object the reproduction of the name of which is temporarily inhibited ; then the speech reflex, in the form of the word which has been temporarily inhibited, is immediately revived, and the word is uttered.

Thus, in speech reflexes also, inhibition and revival or release from inhibition occur in a manner analogous to that of all other cases.

It is obvious that there are also other conditions which lead to the inhibition and revival of association reflexes. For instance, the appearance of a new incidental stimulus is sufficient to produce inhibition of an association reflex, and after inhibition has taken place, the presentation, after some time, of the earlier stimulus revives the association reflex, which seemed to have disappeared. In any case, it is necessary to accept as a fundamental thesis that higher reflexes, which we call association reflexes, differ from ordinary reflexes by a special facility for inhibition, from which, however, these reflexes are released under certain conditions, and this makes the association reflex apparatus especially mobile, as a result of the continuous alternation of inhibitory and stimulating influences.

CHAPTER XXV

CASES of inhibition in the animal kingdom must be regarded as universal, and, therefore, deserve our special attention.

Even the very lowest unicellular beings (Vampyrella and Arcella) exhibit inhibitions and contractions, as Engelmann has shown, and regulate these movements so as to avoid conditions harmful to them ; even the mobile cells of an organism exhibit inhibitory phenomena.

In just the same manner, there is an element not only of revival, but also of inhibition in all the movements of animals and of man. If the speech apparatus were not regulated by inhibitions, we should talk incessantly, as may be observed in persons in a state of excitement. In children, movements are less inhibited, but as the children develop, their movements are gradually inhibited more and more.

In general, the greater the fatigue, the weaker the inhibition, and, consequently, a stimulus, which at first impeded the manifestation of a reflex, may later, in a state of fatigue, strengthen it. Instructive examples of such phenomena are to be found in infants, for fatigued children become exceedingly irritable before sleep and begin to cry on the least provocation. This results from the tendency, manifested here, of local processes to irradiate.

Concentration, as we have seen, is accompanied by inhibitory activities also, the latter being phenomena of the dominant.

In the logical flow of speech reflexes also, we must recognise, in addition to the excitation of speech reflexes, the existence of inhibitory conditions, which regulate the course of these reflexes in accordance with a definite plan.

At the same time, we have all the data which favour the statement that inhibition is an active process, and not simply the cessation of movement or of some other reaction. This is easily shown in the case of such functions as manifest themselves in rhythmic movements, such as respiration, heart-beat, the movements of the internal organs, etc.

Rhythm itself is the expression of oscillation between exciting and inhibitory processes. Indeed, every reflex, as we have seen above, is based on the consecutive development of processes of inhibition and excitation, which are not equally balanced in the various stages of the process, for, in the latent period, processes of inhibition prevail ; next, processes of excitation are strengthened, and, after this, processes of inhibition again prevail.

It is obvious that the movement of the nervous current, too, consists in alternation of waves of excitation and inhibition, but these waves are so slight that they are not externally manifested, and only in some cases, for instance increased nervousness or fever, do they become more intense and are expressed in muscular trembling.

As we have already said, we must distinguish between internal and external inhibition. The former is manifested on the repetition of the stimuli, and also on the operation of general causes which interfere with the course of association-reflex activity (for instance, sleep, influence of narcotics, etc.). External inhibition of association-reflex activity is conditioned by the influence of an external stimulus.

We have seen above that inhibition of a reflex does not at all mean its complete disappearance, as may be proved by the fact that the inhibited reflex is often manifested in minimal reflex movements, and, on the other hand, revives in the course of time. But a certain interval of time must be allowed for the revival.

For instance, if an association reflex is inhibited as a result of repeated stimulations, it is sufficient to renew the stimulation after a twice longer interval and the same association reflex is revived ; as a result of renewed stimulation, it will disappear again, but when the interval between the stimulations is again doubled, it will reappear, etc.

Apart from conditions of inner inhibition, various external influences also may, as we have said, lead to inhibition of an association reflex. It is sufficient to apply, at the period of the complete differentiation of an association reflex, a new external stimulus, and the reflex inculcated is immediately inhibited for some time (Diagrams V and VII), after which it may be revived.

This experimental fact accords with everyday observation. For instance, when someone is reciting poems learned by heart or is saying a prayer, it is sufficient to apply some irrelevant stimulus of a kind to distract him from the theme and, immediately, he has difficulty in continuing the recital. But some time elapses, and the words learned by heart are again reproduced with the same ease as before.

Everything said above shows that in inhibition there is a state in which an association reflex exhibits a readiness to be manifested again at any moment.

Consequently, we may formulate the thesis that every association reflex inhibited under certain conditions can be released from inhibition, when the appropriate influences are present.

This release from inhibition may, as we have seen, be a result of inner conditions which promote increase of excitability, and consist, for instance, in recuperation from previous fatigue, or, under the influence of certain internal conditions, lead to increase of nervous excitability, and, lastly, it may be a result of mimico-somatic states accompanied by enhancement of the general tonus.

Every one knows that a fatigued man cannot perform learned movements, cannot reproduce what is easily reproduced after rest or, generally, during a period of liveliness, for instance after fortification by food or, lastly, in a state of heightened general tonus.

Observation and experiment show that external stimuli also often promote release of inhibition. We all know that sometimes, in spite of all our efforts, we cannot reproduce a familiar word, but it is sufficient for the individual to be distracted by something, and reproduction of the word temporarily lost ensues.

Every association reflex, once it has developed, does not disappear without leaving a trace, but, as a result of leaving its trace in the nerve centres, it reveals a tendency to reproduce a similar reflex under the influence of the same or a similar external impact, or of one somehow associated, even if weaker compared with the first, and, in cases of frequent repetition, even in accordance with the tempo to which it was evoked.

When an ordinary reflex, for instance the patellar reflex, is frequently produced when the eyes are shut, one can observe that it is sometimes called out at the correct moment and independently, as it were, before the ligament has been tapped.

This may be explained only by the assumption that, in the production of the patellar reflex, the centripetal impulses from the tap on the ligament reach the appropriate centres in the cerebral cortex, and remain as a trace, which, being revived after a definite time interval, is transmitted from the afferent areas to the efferent, and so serves as the source of reproduction of the same reflex. Such a reflex independently reproduced, without the participation of any external stimulus, may be called a reproductive reflex, although, in reality, this reflex is the same association reflex, but produced through release of inhibition. In this case, the muscular stimulation, which is a result of the reflex, is closely associated with muscular contraction, which occurs after definite time intervals, and, consequently, the reproduction of this stimulation at the appropriate moment serves as a source of the production of the reflex.

We can show, in another manner also, that every reflex leaves, in the centres, a trace which may be revived. It is sufficient if we repeat a movement many times after we have arranged to cease from the movement at a certain signal, for instance a sound. As shown by experiments performed in my laboratory, this cessation cannot be procured immediately when the movements follow each other quickly, but one, two, or several superfluous movements, according to the rapidity of their succession, will be performed after the signal. This case, too, may be explained by the trace which has been left in the centres by the movements performed, and which may be revived under appropriate conditions.

Let us further assume that an association reflex is inculcated according to the method in vogue with us. If we stimulate this reflex without sustaining it appropriately by means of the primary stimulus, it will, as we know, gradually disappear. However, it does not disappear without a trace. It is sufficient to allow the working centres to recuperate, for instance by omitting the stimulus at the end of one time interval, and the reflex will reappear, as we know. It is obvious that the apparently extinct reflex remains as a trace in the centres, and this trace, under appropriate conditions, can be revived, and leads to the renewal of the reflex.

All processes of release from inhibition are based on the retention—in the centres—of the traces of reflexes. As a matter of fact, we know that a reflex once inculcated may be inhibited under the influence of an external stimulus, and thus temporarily ceases to be manifested, but even weak stimulation by the original stimulus is sufficient for its reappearance.

It is obvious that this fact also may be explained on the assumption that the inhibited reflex has left a trace apt to revive.

Let us take another case. Ten very simple pictures, for instance, figures of animals, are passed in succession before the eyes of an observer. As shown by investigations in my laboratory, the observer can reproduce only about half the names of the animals he has seen in these pictures. The next time, we submit a number of pictures half of which are new, the other half consisting of those whose names were not reproduced when the pictures were previously submitted to the observer. This experiment shows that the names of those pictures submitted in the first experiment, but not then reproduced, are reproduced in considerably greater number compared with the names of the new pictures. Thus, here the result of the experiment cannot be explained otherwise than by the assumption of a trace left in the centres by every reflex.

Reproduction, since it is a process of release from inhibition, may be external or internal. By external reproduction we understand that which realises external movements previously performed. By internal reproduction we understand that which is externally unexpressed and is manifested by external movements scarcely perceptible to the eye (internal speech, etc.), but which, at the same time, is accompanied, as verbal account shows, by appropriate internal or psychic phenomena (such as a new idea, etc.).[1] Thus, there is question here of release from inhibition of a past reflex which has not been externally expressed.

All habitual movements, the adjustment of movements to certain resistance, and the inertia of movements in general are based on the principle of the reproduction of a reflex which has once occurred, and, consequently, no movement can be instantaneously suppressed.[2] Besides, some characteristic slips of the tongue, slips with which every speaker is familiar and which have their origin in the reproduction of an irrelevant word, must also be explained by the leaving of a trace and by the reproduction of a past reflex. Convincing facts in this respect are provided by the experimental investigations which were carried out in my laboratory and which I have already mentioned above.[3]

[1] Let us note that internal reproduction is manifested in the same manner as external, and that internal reproduction can be suppressed by other internal reproductions, just as if we were concerned with external reflexes.

[2] Investigations in this respect are described in my work : *The Reproductive and Associative Activity of the Nerve Centres—Obozrenie Psychiatrii*, 1908 ; and in Dr. Dobrotvorskaya's paper—*Vestnik Psychologii*, 1910, vol. VI, pt. V.

[3] V. Bechterev : *Objective Psychology*, 3rd pt. See also V. Bechterev : *Golos i retch*, no. 9, 1912.

Here also belongs the inculcation of habits in animals, habits useful not to themselves, but to their master—man, and the propensities to certain activities in this case are even transmitted by heredity. Here belong the pointing of sporting-dogs, the watching of the flock by sheep-dogs, etc.

Examples from the life of tamed animals which have become wild again, as happens, for instance, in the case of elephants which regain freedom by escape, show how great is the tendency to exhibit association reflexes acquired through training. According to Franklin, it often happened that an Indian boldly approached a wild elephant and ordered him to take him up on his neck. Hearing the man's order, the animal immediately recognised the authority of his former master. Another fact is still more striking. One of the elephants in London began to show signs of paroxysmal fury. It was decided to shoot him. It was noticed during the execution, when shots were already being fired, that the animal still obeyed the keeper's voice.

Let us note here also that reproduction is obviously based on the fact that every excitation of one area, an excitation which arises as a result of stimulation from the periphery, creates, through the overcoming of resistance to the transmission in the given area, a condition as a result of which a new excitation moves with relative ease along the same path, and so dynamic connections are created. This resembles the process of dominants, a process in which the irrelevant stimulations come to the assistance of the excited centre, and increase its excitation still more.

By the same process we must also explain the well-known self-imitation which takes the form of perseveration, and the so-called " circular reaction " which is particularly often observed in children.

On the other hand, so-called active reproduction, *i.e.* reproduction conditioned by inner efforts associated with an established need, presupposes a process of concentration, which is really a cerebral process in the form of a dominant.

Lastly, the association reflex produced in the usual way is also conditioned by the fact that the excitation-trace, which remains after the primary stimulation and is a centre of attraction, draws to itself the nervous current arising from the secondary external stimulation.

The reproduction of reflexes by means of secondary external stimulations, which are associated with the primary stimulation, proves that the primary stimulation, just like all other stimulations, produces in the cortex a dynamic change, which serves as the point to which the nervous current is attracted from the areas of the reflex which has already occurred.

In general, we must not conceive of the trace as an anatomical imprint resembling, let us say, a typographical cliché, as I have already mentioned many times in my papers, but we must understand it in the sense that every nervous excitation, on reaching the cortical centres, overcomes a certain resistance in them and, after the cessation of the reflex, results in a trace, in the form of a path of least resistance. Consequently, every new nerve wave, after reaching the appropriate nerve centre, concentrates around

S

itself the nervous energy which streams to it along the paths of least resistance, and so, under different external conditions, reproduces the previous reflex.

We observe the same process in laboratory experiments in association reflexes. An inhibited reflex is, during the period of its inculcation, usually released from inhibition through the influence of any sufficiently strong external stimulus, which attracts concentration to itself. Thus we are concerned here with stimulative influences.

We encounter the stimulation of reflexes at every step. Let us assume that a man has discovered a fact new to him. This makes it possible for him to make a supposition. All other facts confirmatory of this supposition strengthen it, give it greater significance and force, and also all data which lend colour to this supposition revive it and strengthen it more and more, and, consequently, it becomes a securely founded conclusion.

Every discovery, every new undertaking, arises in precisely this way : some external influence produces a number of reflexes which are revived and supplemented under the influence of other stimulations standing in associative connection with them, etc., until the integration of reflexes attains its requisite fulness. Even every backing from another man encourages the carrying out of a decision formed, and, consequently, the subsequent reaction is fuller and intenser. Any fact harmonising with the decision always strengthens and confirms it. Thus, in the case of gross overestimation of one's own personality, an overestimation based on self-analysis, any superflous praise is sufficient to lend this self-assessment still greater confirmation and to develop it further. In some cases, unlimited self-deception results on this basis.[1]

It must not be forgotten that processes of inhibition and of release from inhibition depend on the state of the nervous apparatus, fatigue of which is accompanied by inhibition ; recuperation, on the contrary, by revival or release from inhibition. On this precisely is based the fact that frequent repetitions of an association reflex at certain time intervals lead to its temporary inhibition.[2]

[1] The conditions stimulating association-reflex activity have been, in many respects, insufficiently investigated. The fact has recently been discovered in my laboratory that stimulation of mental activity, in the form of calculation, has occurred under the influence of preceding sound-stimuli produced by the metronome vibrating 100 times a second.

[2] Fatigue, as we know, has been explained by the humoral-toxicological theory. But this theory does not embrace all the facts concerning fatigue, for, in some cases, fatigue cannot be explained either by the direct influence of the toxic products of disintegration on the organ operative, or by these products making their way by means of the blood to the organ operative. From Dr. V. I. Kabanevitch's work at the Institute for the Study of Brain supervised by me, it follows that fatigue under natural conditions is a function of the association-reflex activity—a reflex of inner inhibition. According to its inner physiological mechanism, it is produced by ionic processes which lie at the root of nervous excitation. The character and degree of fatigue in the individual organs at any given moment depend on the qualitative and quantitative concentration of ion groups both stimulative and

On the other hand, the state of general excitation, irrespective of what has produced it (for instance, favourable lighting, sound-stimulations, etc.), promotes release from inhibition, and, on the contrary, the state of general depression leads to the inhibition of association reflexes.

Moreover, processes of inhibition and of release from inhibition depend on conditions of stimulation. For instance, if we too often associate the primary, *i.e.* reflexogenous, stimulus with the secondary stimulus, the association reflex cannot be inculcated. On the contrary, when the interval between the stimulation is greater, the association reflex is easily inculcated. Investigations made in our laboratory (Dr. Schwarzman) show that there is a certain limit to the time interval between a new stimulus and a previous reflexogenous stimulus and, within this limit, the association reflex is not produced, but beyond this limit the reflexogenous stimulus, if associated with an indifferent stimulus, leads to the development of an association reflex.

It is clear that the problem is thus reduced to a certain effect of the primary stimulus, an effect accompanied by inhibition lasting for a certain time. The latest experiments in our laboratory have shown that the activity of inhibition is subject to considerable individual oscillation.

Further, phenomena of inhibition and of release from inhibition depend on the temporal relation of the secondary to the primary stimulus.

Thus, if the secondary stimulus precedes the primary reflexogenous stimulus by some seconds and is, as it were, a signal, it easily produces an association reflex after numerous associative repetitions. However, later investigations made in my laboratory (Dr. Shirman) have shown that secondary stimuli presented a few seconds after the reflexogenous stimulus can, with equal facility, produce an association reflex after repeated associations with the reflexogenous stimulus. But when the stimulus to be associated is far removed in time from the primary stimulus, an association reflex cannot be produced.

It must be kept in view that new stimuli introduced as inhibitory forces to supplement those to be associated are necessarily not uniform in their operation, this lack of uniformity depending on whether they precede in time the stimulus to be associated, or closely coincide with it in time, or follow it, but this problem has not yet been sufficiently investigated.

Next arises the question of the significance of the strength of the newly introduced stimulus and of its correlation with the stimulus to be associated.

As regards the strength of the newly introduced stimulus, it obviously does not remain without influence on inhibition, for every inordinately strong, as it were, stunning, stimulus usually (if the individual oscillations, always possible, are not taken into account) inhibits a reflex, while weaker

inhibitory. Fatigue is really a defence reaction from the threatening danger of toxicosis as a result of waste products, but toxicosis, of course, is not thereby excluded. However, these two processes are irreducible one to the other. (For details see *Vestnik psychophysiologii, reflexologii i gigieni truda*, Symposium, no. 1.)

stimuli have no such absolute inhibitory influence, although they may appropriately be made an inhibiting force.

Obviously, a strong stimulus, in the case of overstimulation, produces a contrary effect in the form of inhibition instead of excitation. This reaction is characteristic for states of overstimulation, states reducible to fatigue of the cerebral apparatus.

If we turn to the energic viewpoint, all the various forms of inhibition are ultimately reducible to expenditure of energy in the overcoming of inner resistances in the case of inhibition or to transmission of energy to other centres and conductors, and, consequently, the energy manifested in one direction is accompanied by its diminution and inadequacy in another.

The delayed production of association reflexes, as is sometimes encountered, stands in connection with processes of inhibition. Although there are some relevant laboratory data afforded by our experiments both on animals and human beings, they are inadequate to provide a secure basis for conclusions and, therefore, we shall not touch on them here.

CHAPTER XXVI

IT is necessary to dilate here on the problem of the varied character of association reflexes. These have as their prime source not only the external surface of the body with its receptive organs which arc really transformed epithelial coatings, but also the internal surfaces of the body which also are covered by epithelial or endothelial layers, provided, just as are the external coatings of the body, with receptive nervous apparatus.

The latter watch, as it were, over the correct functioning of the internal organs—the heart, the lungs, the stomach, the intestines, and other vegetative apparatus. Any functional change in these organs is immediately reflected in peculiar stimulation of the receptive nervous apparatus with which they are inlaid. This stimulation, being transmitted through the sympathic ganglia, results in regulation of these changes, and being also transmitted to the higher centres, subserves the development of internal or organic reflexes, but the integration of these reflexes in association with external stimuli determines the organism's so-called organic needs.

It is obvious that association reflexes, which develop on the basis of simple reflexes, may be of different kinds : some are external association reflexes, of which we have already spoken ; others may be internal association reflexes, to which belong association reflexes which develop on the basis of internal stimulations and are spent in the internal organs. Gastric secretions, associated, in the case of hunger, with the appearance of external stimuli in the form of nutritional products, may serve as an example.

In this case, we may speak of externo-internal association reflexes, by which must be understood association reflexes evoked by external stimuli, but manifested in the internal organs. Here belong, for instance, not only the above-mentioned gastric juice secretions stimulated by the sight of food or by sounds associated with its preparation, but also a considerable number of mimico-somatic reflexes.

Lastly, it is necessary to keep in mind also those association reflexes which, though produced by the internal organs, are expressed in external manifestations, for instance in certain activities. Here belong not only the complex-organic or instinctive activities, for instance, eating, sexual activities, etc., which arise from inner impulses, but partly also activities personal in character and associated with acquired, habitual needs.

The development of association reflexes of this kind occurs in the same manner as that of external association reflexes, which are caused by stimulations of the external receptive organs. Let us take, for example, the alimentary canal, the function of which consists in the receiving and mincing of the nutritive material, in the mechanical and chemica elaboration of the nutritive pulp, in the assimilation of its products, and the excretion of the unelaborated parts as offal.

From the first moments of infantile existence, stimulation arises as a result of impoverishment of the blood in respect of products necessary for the nutrition of the organism, and this leads to general excitation of the organism, which begins to announce its needs. But this stimulation produces merely waking up from sleep, shouting, vague restlessness, movements of the infant's lips, and of its head from one side to the other. But now the lips touch the mother's breast and the mouth is moistened by her milk. The nipple, seized by the lips, immediately arouses the innate reflex of sucking, and the nutritional need, which was marked by general excitation, is soon satisfied, and this results in tranquillity and sleep, that is, in phenomena of general inhibition. Henceforward, an association reflex begins to be established between impoverishment of the blood in respect of albumen and other products, stimulation in the region of the stomach ("gnawing in the stomach") as a result of hunger, the smell and sight of the breast as the source of milk which satisfies the nutritional need, and also the sight of the mother herself. Consequently, the infant very soon, on the first appearance of internal stimulation in the form of hunger, begins to make groping movements with its lips, and being drawn to the breast, finds the nipple by smell and sight, and seizing it with its lips, begins the process of sucking. Later, the infant, when shouting with hunger, becomes calm when it is placed in the feeding posture and, still later, when it sees its mother approaching.

Thus, the "instinct" of nutrition, the fundamental process in every living being, is promoted by personal experience, based on association reflexes which develop in connection with it.[1]

In the course of time, individual experience makes possible the creation, on the basis of internal stimulations, of further association reflexes in the form of activities personal in character, which form the fundamental complex of association reflexes in every individual human being—a complex which, as a result of its relation to internal stimulations, comes to play the leading rôle in man's life.[2]

In a perfectly analogous manner, the manifestations of sexual urge arise in due time. This urge is based on the development of the hormones of the sex glands. These hormones produce tension in the sex organs, this tension resulting from afflux of blood to them, and leading to the search for a sex object. Success in the attainment of this object is achieved through the individual's experience in the social environment, which, on all sides, indicates the opposite sex as the object of future mating.[3]

[1] See V. Bechterev : *General Scheme of the Functioning of the Cerebral Cortex from the Viewpoint of Reflexology*—Address to the Scientific Conference of the Institute for the Study of Brain, 1921.

[2] See V. Bechterev : *Objective Psychology*, 3rd pt.

[3] V. Bechterev : *Sexual Perversions and Inversions ; Problems of the Study and Education of Personality*, vols. iv and v.

CHAPTER XXVII

The conformity to law of correlative activity in the artificial inculcation of association reflexes. Association reflexes develop on the basis of ordinary reflexes through their reproduction under conditions whose connection has been previously established in the experiment by means of an association formed with the primary, reflexogenous stimulus. All manifestations of association-reflex activity have ordinary reflexes as their prototypes. The interrelation of excitation and inhibition. Concentration as a dominant. Complexes of association reflexes.

IT must be remembered that any science may be regarded as a science only if it renders possible the prediction of phenomena as inevitable consequences of certain correlations revealed by experiment and observation. In this respect, reflexology has a special advantage over psychology, which, if we exclude the Weber-Fechner psycho-physical law, by which we can predict the intensity of subjective phenomena in their dependence on the intensity of the stimulation, posits, as conformable to law, practically no other correlation between subjective phenomena, while the objective study of correlative activity reveals, in the most varied directions, the strictest conformity of phenomena to law.

The conformity of correlative activity to law may be studied most simply of all in the artificial inculcation of association reflexes.

We shall now pass on to the exposition of conformity to law, a conformity revealed by strictly objective method in the artificial inculcation of association reflexes.

One of the fundamental facts on which we must dilate is that every association reflex develops on the basis of an ordinary reflex, by the reproduction of the latter under influences whose connection has been previously established in the experiment through their associations with the primary, reflexogenous stimulus.

In this fact, *viz.* that the ordinary reflex which has previously occurred is reproduced under the influence of a different external stimulus, which is, as it were, an alien impact, the basic, developmental process of association reflexes is expressed. The essence of this process consists in the fact that, if a stimulus, incapable of evoking a reflex, approximately coincides in time with a primary stimulus, that is, one which produces an ordinary reflex, the reflex is, after some repetitions, produced not only by its proper stimulus, but also by the collateral external stimulus associated with it, a stimulus previously indifferent. Thus, we can reproduce all motor and secretory reflexes, and, as shown by investigations in my laboratory (Dr. Tchaly), cardio-vascular reflexes also. It is easy to see that there is question of the formation of previously non-existent connections in the central nervous system, and this formation results from co-excitation of two topographically different nerve centres and conductors. Thus, both centres of excitation become concatenated with the inter-central cortical link ; and, along the resulting chain, the path of the movement of the nervous current in the direction of the reflexogenous centre is henceforth established.

As we have already said, the child becomes calm as soon as its lips touch the mother's breast, and it begins to suck, but, later, it is quietened by the mere approach of the mother. In all other cases also, association reflexes are based on the reproduction of ordinary reflexes, under conditions determined by the association-reflex activity of the centres. Such are, ultimately, speech, expressive movements, and all movements which we call personal.

We have mentioned that speech arises from primitive sound-reflexes, such as : " och," " ach," " uch," " oi," " ai," " hmm " (humph !), " nu," " uvi " (alas !), etc., and from reflexive echoisms, but both kinds of sound are originally simple sound-reflexes, which occur in certain normal states and under certain external influences. The reproduction of these reflexes under certain conditions forms primitive, symbolic speech, which consists of association sound-reflexes which take the form of ejaculations, and of echoistic designations. From both of these, articulate human speech has developed through various kinds of sound-complications, doublings, affixes, suffixes, etc.

The same holds good in other cases too. Let us assume, for instance, that a nervous man has once been frightened by a dog which has attacked him. He then experienced a mimico-somatic reaction accompanied by severe palpitation and so the mere barking of a dog is sufficient to produce attacks of palpitation. In another case, a man has experienced sickness because of having taken putrid, stinking meat into his mouth. Henceforth, the mere sight of meat is sufficient to produce the phenomena of sickness. Needless to say, we could cite similar examples *ad libitum*.

It must also be kept in view that, in addition to special influence arising through the mediation of the appropriate receptive organ, external stimulation usually, or at least often, produces a general influence exciting or depressing the activity of the circulation of the blood in the tissues, respiration, and the action of the heart, in other words, by acting favourably or unfavourably on the nutrition not only of the local, *i.e.* the stimulated, organ, but also of the whole organism. The character of the influence in this case depends primarily on the intensity and quality of the external stimulus and secondarily on the condition of the individual himself. Influences which promote nutrition and metabolism are favourable ; those which impede them are unfavourable. These influences are relative, for, in some cases, an influence which is usually favourable may prove to be unfavourable when acting on a tired organism, and *vice versa*. It is clear from this that the influence of one and the same stimulus on nutrition and metabolism may be unequal at different times, and is determined by the general state of the organism and of the receptive organ at the given moment.

But we already know from other data that everything acting favourably on the organism evokes a reflex aggressive in character, while everything acting unfavourably produces a reflex defensive in character ; but whatever does not excite a general reaction of some kind does not in itself excite a reflex in the form of an activity. It can produce such a reaction, but only

indirectly in association with another stimulus, which exerts a favourable
or unfavourable influence on the organism ; consequently, in the form
of a so-called association reflex.

During the repeated influence of every stimulus, the general reaction
which it evokes is gradually blunted as a result of inhibition ; consequently, the reflex is gradually weakened and at last disappears, but only
temporarily.   In the course of time the reflex is revived.

Another process conformable to law, a process discovered in the investigation of higher reflexes, is the interrelation of the phenomena of excitation and inhibition.   We have already, in detail, discussed the phenomena
of inhibition.   Here we shall deal precisely with the interrelation of both
processes, an interrelation characterised by the fact that every time a
centre is in a state of excitation and the system of conductors which serve
it are operative, other centres not functionally connected with the first
are depressed or inhibited to a greater or lesser degree.   This fact has
been proved by a number of physiological investigations to be described
later and is easily revealed by an appropriate experiment on man, for
every human activity in one direction is accompanied by its weakening
or depression in another.   Moreover, when the excitation of one of the
centres reaches its climax, as in a dominant, not only are all other centres
inhibited, but also incidental stimuli do not produce local reflexes ; they
rather stimulate the excited centre still more : in other words, enhance
its excitation.   This principle, which I have already formulated in my
Objective Psychology, 1907–1912, and the physiological basis of which I
have there explained, has recently received the name of dominant (Professor Uchtomsky).   The process which we call concentration, and which
is so important in the sphere of the functioning of the higher centres, is
really only a typical dominant, for here we have excitation of the concentration centre and inhibition of all other forms of movement, and simultaneously, any irrelevant stimulation, which does not completely suppress
concentration, not only does not destroy the latter, but, on the contrary,
strengthens it still more.   Observations of infants, as we have already said
in the appropriate context, do not leave any doubt about the fact that the
sucking reflex in infants is a real dominant, for, during the act of sucking,
all other movements are inhibited, but irrelevant stimulations still further
intensify the act of sucking.

In precisely the same manner, sexual intercourse, from the age of
puberty onwards, affords all the indications of a real sex dominant.   We
have seen elsewhere that the excitation of any centre, under the influence
of an external stimulus, may be a dominant.   But, in this case, appropriate
adjustment of the central nervous system occurs.   In cases when concentration on an external stimulus is impossible, for instance, because of the
suddenness of the stimulus, a marked effect occurs in the mimico-somatic
sphere, an effect characterised by shock or so-called fright.

All stimuli with a favourable general reaction, when they are repeatedly
renewed at certain time intervals, lead to the establishment of a habit in

respect of these stimuli, and evoke an organic need for them, a need characterised by an appropriate set to the stimulus to be presented at a certain time. This set is similar to that observed in experiments on movements personal in character.[1] Lack of habitual stimulation in this case leads to a contrary effect, *i.e.* to the development of an asthenic reaction. We see examples of this in the action of all narcotics : tobacco, alcohol, morphium, etc.

Every new stimulation, if it does not act exclusively in an inhibitory manner on the organism, either because of specific influence, or of extra-ordinary intensity, usually produces a general sthenic reaction. There-fore, all new and moderate stimuli usually evoke aggressive reflexes sustaining the development of a general sthenic reaction.

In general, every stimulus which presents an element of novelty attracts concentration to itself, and concentration, since it produces some kind of general reaction, is associated with excitation of appropriate motor im-pulses in the direction of the object of concentration. If this excitation is not inhibited by some conditions, it is expressed, in one case, by aggressive, in another, by defensive, reflexes.

Let us turn now to mimico-somatic reflexes. We have already stated that mimico-somatic association reflexes are simply reproductions, under certain conditions, of ordinary reflexes.[2]

Apart from facial expressions, gesticulatory expressive movements, which are merely the language of gestures and bodily movements, in the form of so-called pantomimic movements, play an enormous rôle in life.

These gestures, as we have already said, are ultimately a number of descriptive, imitative, and, sometimes, indicatory and groping bodily movements, and are reproductions of personal movements which are manifested in certain cases, and which are now only signs or symbols of a similar attitude of the individual to new external influences.

We know that an indicatory gesture is a reproduction of an indicatory movement of the hand ; beckoning movements of the hands are reproduc-tions of those movements by which we draw an object towards ourselves ; threatening movements are reproductions of movements of aggression ; rejecting movements are reproductions of movements of defence, etc.

Obviously, these are the movements which we use in appropriate cases, but these movements, or their more characteristic parts, are here repro-duced under different conditions and as symbols which denote the par-ticular individual's attitude to external influences.

A rich development in imitative and descriptive gesticulation may be observed in the social intercourse of primitives, in the gestures of children

[1] See V. Bechterev : *The Reproductive and Associative Activity of the Cerebral Cortex—Obozrenie Psychiatrii,* 1910. N. I. Dobrotvorskaya : *Vestnik Psychologii,* 1910, vol. VI, pt. V.

[2] V. Bechterev : *Biological Development of Expressive Movements—Vestnik Znania,* nos. 1–4, 1910, and published separately. Also the same author's : *Objective Psychology,* 3rd pt.—*Objective Psychologie oder Reflexologie,* Leipzig und Berlin, 1913.

who cannot speak, in the language of deaf-mutes, and, lastly, in everyday life, when we describe movements, sounds, and peculiarly shaped objects. Doubtlessly, here too, we are concerned with the reproduction of personal movements.

Further, we know that concentration, which results from the maturation of intracortical connections, develops in infancy as a reflex which ensures better utilisation of the action of the external stimulus on the organs of sight, hearing, taste, smell, and of the external coatings. In the course of time, the reproduction of this reflex, under the influence of internal causes, conditions so-called active concentration on certain objects and the latter is merely an association reflex, which develops chiefly in connection with the personal needs of the organism.

The reflex of active visual concentration, a reflex developed in infancy, consists in directing the gaze to that stimulus which exerts a favourable general influence on the organism. Such stimuli are all nutritive objects and objects which create conditions of well-being in the organism in general, and, so, evoke reflexes aggressive in character. But influences of a contrary character also, such as excite a defence reflex, produce active visual concentration, which is thus closely associated with all external stimuli within the field of vision, and capable of producing reflexes aggressive or defensive in character.

However, there may be not only one reflexogenous stimulus present, but several may present themselves simultaneously and, therefore, active concentration primarily accompanies that external stimulus, which, at the given moment, is strongest or most active as a result of past experience, but other influences remain outside the pale of active concentration.

As external stimuli, which produce visual concentration, may be concomitant with auditory, olfactory, and tactual stimuli, active visual concentration is naturally produced by stimuli of sound, smell, touch, etc., so that each of these stimuli separately can produce visual concentration, just as can stimulation of the visual apparatus itself. Moreover, even previous orientation reflexes, when they are released from inhibition or revived, simultaneously revive the act of visual concentration which has accompanied them ; the same is true of all other kinds of concentration— auditory, tactual, etc.

It is not difficult to prove that various personal movements also are basically reproductions of ordinary reflexes. A child stretches for the candle and, burning his finger, quickly withdraws his hand. But when his hand happens to approach the flame the next time, he duly withdraws it and so exhibits an association reflex personal in character.

Let us assume that a nipple is put into a hungry child's mouth. He will execute various movements with his hands and finally grasp the nipple. On another occasion, when he sees the same nipple, he stretches out his hands for it and so reproduces, in the form of an association reflex, the original reflexive movement.

As regards complex actions and conduct, these really consist of a number of separate personal movements and, therefore, they too are basically reproductions of a consecution of ordinary reflexes.

There is question here of a complex of concatenated reflexes associated, in a certain sequence, for the attainment of a certain aim, which is a stimulus given in the individual's past experience or is reproduced as a result of the past experience of others and is, at the given moment, a dominant stimulus.

The above-mentioned experiments on animals, which obtain food by overcoming artificially created obstacles in the maze, may serve as examples of such a complex of association reflexes, *i.e.* reflexes which are, in reality, reproductions of several ordinary reflexes. Needless to say, in human actions also, we encounter complexes of purposeful personal reflexes which develop in the same manner as in animals in general.

We shall not multiply examples, but what has been said above is sufficient to convince that association or higher reflexes are basically reproductions of ordinary reflexes.

This fact, as we have seen, may be traced in the development of the child also, for this development consists precisely in the consecutive formation and complication of association reflexes on the basis of ordinary or innate reflexes, which are proper, as we know, to the very lowest organisms. Since, as is well known, the embryo passes through the various developmental stages which we find in the ascending phylogenetic scale of the animal world, the child later, from the day of his birth, begins to construct his personality through the stratification of association reflexes on the basis of ordinary reflexes.

We must remember that, from the time that the association-reflex activity has developed to such an extent that it has begun to dominate the adjustment of the so-called " bodily " nature, the clever, through the operation of natural selection, begin to be preferred to the stronger, for highly developed association-reflex activity makes possible the introduction of new devices in the struggle for existence and, gradually, the evolution of association-reflex activity begins in man to prevail over the evolution of his organic nature.

Thus, we are forced to recognise that all the higher manifestations of association-reflex activity have as their prototypes ordinary reflexes, which are transmitted from generation to generation by heredity and are reproduced as a result of the reproductivo-associative activity of the higher centres. Consequently, the general character of the manifestations of association-reflex activity assumes essentially the same forms as do ordinary reflexes, and as the latter bear the character of preparation, aggression, defence, and reflexive imitation, the higher reflexes also are ultimately reducible, in their external manifestations, to preparation or alertness, aggression, defence, and association-reflexive imitation, as well as to symbolism, which develops in connection with this imitation. However, they respond to stimuli not according to a previously established pattern, but are adjusted to conditions of stimulation which, in life, are various and often change. Yet, their more complex forms, that is, personal reflexes, are adapted to the prosecution of a certain aim, which is sometimes labile, and sometimes even evades prosecution. This aim is a stimulus producing a dominant process.

It is clear from this that there is, in complex association reflexes, not only a quantitative, but also a qualitative, aspect, and that the latter characterises all the activities of living beings as much as it does the inner world of man. Here we are really concerned with a transition from quantity to quality.

Let us further remark that man, not only as a living being, but also in his social or collective life, is not exempt from subjection to universal laws, for the development of the universe proceeds in the same fashion both in the sphere of inorganic nature, in the world of living beings, and in the social conditions of life. But, as unequal conditions prevail in the inorganic, the organic, and the super-organic or social environment, the development of these general laws in their particular environment manifests peculiarities and exhibits specific correlations and a peculiar conformability to law. Example : The law of inertia, which is manifested everywhere throughout inorganic nature, is represented in organic nature by the biological law of the inheritance of characteristics ; in the life of the individual, it is represented by set or by habitual movements ; and in the social world, by the inheritance of survivals from the past (customs, etc.), by so-called routine, etc.

The objective study of human personality, as we have already said, gives its position to this science among the exact sciences and, consequently, reflexology must be regarded as a special department of biology and as merging directly into sociology. And if this is so, it is obvious that all the fundamental physico-biological laws may be applied to the sphere of correlative activity.

I have shown, in a special paper, that the fundamental laws are the same both for the inorganic, the organic, and the super-organic or social world[1] ; consequently, the development and the manifestations of personality also must be subject to the same general laws to the operation of which the universe conforms. And it cannot be otherwise, if we take into consideration that the universe is really one, complete, living organism, and that we are all infinitesimal and mobile cells in it. The study of personality, in connection with the various manifestations of the one universal process, gives its position, in the best manner possible, to the science of human personality within the general circle of the sciences which investigate the nature of the universe.

Keeping in mind that the concept of substance is now reduced to latent

[1] For details in regard to the manifestations of these laws in the super-organic world, see V. Bechterev : *Fundamental Laws of the Universe in Connection with the Investigation of the Social World from the Point of View of Reflexology—Voprosi izutcheniya i vospitaniya litchnosti*, vols. II, III, and ff., 1921. Also the same author's *Collective Reflexology*, Petrograd, 1921.

energy, and that what we call correlative activity is, like life itself, merely manifestations of energy, for at the basis of both lie processes of ionisation, it is perfectly comprehensible that the general or fundamental laws of the universal process must be manifested in a way more or less identical in nature in all three worlds—the inorganic, the organic, and the super-organic—for the universal process is everywhere ultimately reducible to various manifestations of energy.

Such a view of the world, a view which dispenses with futile meta-physics, ensures for reflexology its significance as a biologo-social branch of science, and this we cannot say of subjective psychology with its method of self-observation and so-called indirect self-observation. In view of this, we shall engage in a brief and orderly investigation of the application of universal laws to the development and manifestations of personality. It is self-evident that this does not exclude other and particular laws manifested especially in correlative activity, laws which have been discovered in sociology and in the various branches of natural science, and which are really developments of the same universal laws which we shall call *principles* in the subsequent discussion.

Even the inorganic environment, in its various forms—solid, fluid, and gaseous bodies—provides conditions for the manifestation of particular laws issuing from the general law, as, for instance, Mariotte's law,[1] which is applicable to the conditions of the inorganic environment, and inapplicable to other conditions. The same is true also of such particular conformity to law as is manifested in the organic and super-organic environments.

[1] *Translators' note :* Boyle's law : the volume of a gas varies inversely as the pressure.

CHAPTER XXVIII

The principle of conservation of energy.

MANY attempts have hitherto been made to harmonise the principle of conservation of energy, as demonstrated in the physical sciences, with so-called psychic activity. But, from the very nature of the case, all such attempts have been unsuccessful, for the fundamental view of the psychic as something different from the physical, and as running parallel to physical phenomena, or as interacting with them, has not afforded suitable ground for the application of this principle to the sphere of neuro-psychical energy.[1] The pertinent theories may be divided into three chief groups. One group completely excludes the applicability of the law of conservation of energy to animate objects ; another, while admitting the existence of special " psychic " or " spiritual " energy, regards the significance of the principle of conservation of energy as summary for physical and " psychic " energies, and not for physical energies only ; and, lastly, the third admits the law of conservation of energy only in respect of the organism's physical energy.

There is no necessity for us to enter into a discussion of all those works which are characterised by speculation rather than by facts. Those who wish to make closer acquaintance with these problems may turn to works dealing with the given subject. Of these, the following may be indicated : Schwarz : *Über das Verhältnis von Leib und Seele* (*Monatshefte der Comenius–Gesellschaft*, Bd. VI, 1897) ; L. Busse : *Geist und Korper, Seele und Leib*, Leipzig, 1903 ; Elsberg : *Leib und Seele*, Leipzig, 1906 ; A. Klein : *Die modernen Theorien über das allgemeine Verhältnis von Leib und Seele*, Breslau, 1906 ; Erich Becher : *The Law of Conservation of Energy and the Hypothesis of Interaction between Soul and Body* (*Noviye idei v philosophii*, No. 8, St. Petersburg, 1913) ; Heymans : *Über die Anwendbarkeit des Energiebegriffs in der Psychologie*, Leipzig, A. Barth, 1921, IV ; and others.

We shall conduct the investigation of this problem quite independently of the above-mentioned speculations and views, and shall first of all dilate on those facts which leave no doubt about the applicability of the law of conservation of energy to the exchange of the energies derived by the organism from the environment and expended by the organism.

The organism receives its chief supply of energy from the food which is introduced, in the form of albumen, fats, carbohydrates, etc., into the stomach and from the oxygen of the air inhaled by the lungs ; it also acquires energy, in the form of warmth, by the conduction of heat and also in the form of mechanical and radiant energy, which is absorbed by special organs : the skin, the ear, the eye, the nose, the tongue, etc. Energy is expended in the form of loss of heat, in the form of offal and excretions, which contain chemical energy, and in the form of the mechanical energy

---

[1] Lehmann's view of a special energy, the expression of which is both cerebral and psychic activity, is equally fruitless.

of bodily movements. In some animals, we may also speak of expenditure of electrical energy (in man, this is practically negligible) and light-energy. The balance between the energy absorbed and expended has provided food for investigation for physiologists, hygienists, and bio-chemists, among whom we shall name Pettenkofer, Paskutin, Rubner, and Atwater, not to mention many others. But Rubner[1] and Atwater[2] have made particularly valuable investigations in this respect and these we shall now discuss in their broad outlines.

The investigations were made by a calorimeter, in which the animal does not absorb radiant energy ; all the heat which it expends remains in the calorimeter, including the heat resulting from transformation of the animal's movements. As the animal remains almost immobile in the calorimeter, almost the only source of energy at the animal's disposal is those chemical processes which occur in the organism, but the energy expended is heat. Consequently, the problem was reduced to the investigation of the correlation between energy absorbed and expended in the forms mentioned above.

For this purpose, Rubner, in his experiments to determine the heat expended by an animal during digestion, placed in the calorimeter an animal which had been fed with a particular kind of food. The energy expended during oxidation of the food is determined by the difference between the heat resulting from combustion of excretions, urine, and offal and that resulting from combustion of the food. The experiment, which lasted 14 days, showed that 96 per cent of the energy was eliminated in the form of heat in the calorimeter.

Arranged in this way, the experiment was not exact, because the process of disintegration in the organism is reducible not alone to the quantity of food taken and, therefore, the animal's weight should have been taken into account. Also, because of faulty choice of food, great differences arose between the quantity of food ingested and the quantity of substances disintegrated.

Thus, a more accurate method consists in determining, from the products of metabolism, from excretions, and air exhaled, the quantity of substances digested. Having taken into account the composition of the food and the quantity of nitrogen and carbon eliminated, it is possible to determine, as has been already shown by the investigations of Voit and Pettenkofer, the quantity of protein, fat, and carbohydrates disintegrated, and the products of exhalation can be accurately determined by means of Renoir-Rens and Pettenkofer respirators. It is also possible to determine the heat of combustion of the organic material of the nutritive products, and of the products of excretion. Rubner adopted this method in his experiments.

In these experiments, the heat given off by the animal was determined

[1] M. Rubner : *Die Quellen der thierischen Wärme—Zeitschr. f. Biologie*, 12 (30), 1894.
[2] See F. Friedländer und Asher : *Ergebnisse der Physiologie*, 1904.

by means of a special respiration calorimeter ; the products of metabolism were collected, and the quantity of carbonic acid and water excreted was determined by control experiments. Thus, it was possible to determine accurately which substances were really metabolised in the animal's body. The food given was suitably warmed. Moreover, the influence of the difference in the temperature of the food was experimentally investigated and an appropriate interval was allowed to elapse before the calorimetrical determinations were begun. Thus, the influence of the temperature of the food was counteracted. The influence of differences in the animal's temperature at the beginning and the end of the experiments was counteracted by the protraction of the experiment over a whole day.

In a word, all the biological factors in the experiments such as : disintegration of the substances, the production of heat, and the evaporation of water, were taken into account, and all the values of the process of the "disintegration of substances" were determined.[1]

The table obtained from experiments on dogs is as follows :

Food.	Number of days.	Total of heat calculated.	Total of heat directly determined.	Difference %	Average difference %
Hunger . .	5	1,296.3	1,305.2	+6.69	−1.42
	2	1,091.2	1,056.6	−3.15	
Fats . .	5	1,510.1	1,495.3	−0.97	−0.97
Meat and fats .	8	2,492.4	2,488.2	−0.17	−0.42
	12	3,985.4	3,958.4	−0.88	
Meat . .	6	2,249.8	2,276.9	+1.20	+0.43
	7	4,780.8	4,769.3	−0.24	

The average of all the experiments for 15 days gave the quantity of heat obtained by the calorimetric method as only 0.47 per cent less than the quantity obtained by the calculation of the heats of combustion of the disintegrated and the nutritive materials.

If we take into account the relative insignificance of the differences, which do not exceed the margin of probable error, we cannot help agreeing with Rubner that the fund of energy introduced as food into the organism "is externally expended by the same organism in quantities accurately measured—in this household there is neither abundance nor deficiency."

The third series of experiments are, as it were, control experiments and their purpose is to prove that, if the law of conservation of energy is applicable to the animal organism also, oxidation of nutritive materials

[1] Rubner : *Die Quellen der thierischen Wärme—Zeitschr. f. Biologie,* 12 (30), 1894.

T

can be carried on in it for the investigation and determination, by the calorimetric method, of the heats of combustion of these materials, for it is clear that, if the oxidation of the same materials will occur, on the one hand, inside the body, on the other, outside the body, and the heats obtained from both are equal, we shall have a new proof of the applicability of the law of conservation of energy to the animal body. The results of such experiments are in full accord with what has been previously known from physical measurements, an accord " rarely attained by analysis of biological processes." Thus has been provided " a proof of the passage of energy, in unchanged quantity, through the animal's body " and so the law of conservation of energy, which has been duly discovered by Mayer and Helmholtz, has doubtlessly been further developed and supplemented.

Rubner's experiments have been later confirmed by Laulanie,[1] who also made his investigations on animals.

If the equivalence between the chemical energy introduced into the animal's body and the vital energy expended by the animals is thus proved, it is, of course, to be expected that man also must give the same results. Nevertheless, it is essential that this law should be confirmed in the case of man in particular ; and this task has been performed, in the course of twelve years of untiring work under complicated technical conditions, by W. O. Atwater[2] in collaboration with many scientists, of whom we shall mention E. B. Rosa and F. G. Benedict. Besides, these were not control experiments, but a development of the problem which Rubner had set himself. The previous experiments by Rubner and Laulanie were performed on small animals and in comparatively small numbers ; the time for each experiment was short, the analyses of the food, drink, and excretions were not sufficiently thorough, and in none of these experiments was external muscular work performed. It is especially important that, for the sake of completeness in these experiments, external muscular work should be taken into account also. In these experiments, there were compared : " (1) the quantity of potential energy in substances really oxidised in the body with (2) the quantity of the kinetic energy expended by the body either only in the form of heat, in those experiments in which muscular work was not performed, or in the form of heat plus external muscular work, the latter also measured and calculated in the form of heat, in those experiments in which work was performed."

In experiments of the first kind, i.e. without muscular work, the calculations were made in the same way as in Rubner's experiments. But in experiments in which work was performed, the quantity of energy expended on external muscular work was added to the heat eliminated by the body, so as to calculate the total of energy expended. Thirty-two experiments were made altogether in the course of 107 days.

If we consider the mean of all these experiments, of which 32 were made

[1] *Arch. d. Physiol.*, 1898.
[2] A description may be found in F. Friedländer and Asher : *Ergebnisse der Physiologie*, 1904, 1, pp. 497–622.

in 107 days with ordinary food, the daily income amounts to 3748 calories and the daily expenditure to 3745 calories ; consequently, the difference does not exceed 0·1 per cent of the whole.

In experiments without work and with special diet, the average daily expenditure exceeded the income by 15 calories, while in experiments with work, expenditure exceeded income by 17 calories.

In general, as a result of considering 45 experiments made during 143 days, a difference of 55 calories was obtained in a total of 500,000, which makes 1 : 10,000. In the later experiments, which were more accurate, the difference decreased to 1 : 20,000. Of course, such differences do not exceed the margin of probable technical error and do not affect the general conclusion that the totals secured in such experiments tally.

Thus, these experiments demonstrate the applicability to man of the law of conservation of energy.

It must be noted that those writers, who regard the " soul " as a peculiar entity and psychic activity as a peculiar force, maintain that proof of the applicability of the law of conservation of energy to animal organisms is not valid for such of the life-activity of a living being as has, as it were, a peculiar source. Therefore, it has been found necessary to adjust, somehow, to the new facts the two hypotheses which prevail in regard to psychic activity and which we have already mentioned—the hypothesis of parallelism and the hypothesis of interactionism. We shall not enter on a long discussion here, or refer to those views which still exclude the principle of conservation of energy in regard to man with his neuro-psychical activity. These discussions may be found, together with some bibliographical sources, in, for instance, Erich Becher's paper.[1] In his résumé, he remarks that, if we accept the principle of conservation of energy as proved for " animate " objects, the hypothesis of interactionism may accord with this principle in different ways. If we recognise the principle of conservation of energy throughout the whole sphere of physical processes, we arrive, according to him, at the hypothesis of dualism of causes and of effects. Of all forms of the hypothesis of interactionism, this form is closest to the theory of parallelism, but does not pass into it. It is, however, not free from defect ; it is, he maintains, forced to have recourse to an auxiliary assumption, which remains to be proved, and which the theory of parallelism does not require. The boldest hypothesis of interactionism must have recourse to this auxiliary hypothesis. If, according to Becher, the " soul " could change physical systems even by leaps and bounds with interruptions, it should be forced to choose those comparatively rare forms of influence in which the quantity of physical energy remains intact. On the whole, the principle of conservation of energy, according to this writer, supports the theory of parallelism.[2]

[1] Erich Becher : *The Law of Conservation of Energy and the Hypothesis of Interaction between Soul and Body—Noviye idei v philosophii*, St. Petersburg, no. 8, 1913.
[2] A. Klein : *Die modernen Theorien v. d. allgem. Verhältnis von Leib und Seele*, Breslau, 1906.

A. Klein acknowledges that "the advantages of parallelism lie in the empirical aspect of the problem" and maintains that parallelism, "without straining, fits in with the law of conservation of energy," while the "hypothesis of interactionism" does not so easily accord with the principle of conservation of energy as does "parallelism." But parallelism is a reflection of dualism, with which the conception of the universe as unitary does not accord.

The reflexological point of view, which does not recognise two distinct energies, psychical and nervous, but only one neuro-psychical energy, becomes involved in no contradictions by accepting the principle of conservation of energy. It is obvious that this principle, as proved for physical processes, does not exclude somatic cerebral processes, which occur through metabolism of the blood and the lymph in the cerebral cellular elements, with their granules, which store energy, just like the muscular and other cellular elements of the body. But in addition to protoplasmic granules, the nervous cellular elements contain a conductive or fibrous part, which, as has been proved in regard to peripheral nerves (and between these and the central conductors there is no intrinsic difference), is indefatigable[1] and, consequently, may be compared to a physical conductor, such as a telegraph wire, with only this difference : that nervous conduction is not always uninterrupted, but, on the contrary, in the cerebral areas of the higher animals and of man, is interrupted at the synapses and connected by conditions resembling those of contact. But I have duly advanced a theory of transmission of excitation, in the form of discharges of energy, along the chain of neurons. This theory satisfactorily solves the problem of the movement of the nervous current.

If we now assume an unstable state of all the active elements of the body, including the substance of the nervous and glandular cells and of the muscular fibres, we find, during the production of a reflex, external energy (light, sound, mechanical, and other[2]) which is changed in the receptive transformers into nervous current or neuro-psychical energy transmitted by discharges from one neuron to the next ; and, ultimately, if it is not inhibited by other influences, it reaches the muscular or glandular tissue, and here produces, in one case, kinetic, in another, chemical energy at the expense of potential energy.

The acceptance of the principle of conservation of energy demands, in the particular instance of cerebral activity, the assumption that external energies, while acting on the receptive organs as transformers, result in an equivalent amount of nervous current or neuro-psychical energy, which,

[1] The indefatigableness of the nerve conductor has been proved by N. E. Vvedensky's investigation (*Tormozheniye, vozbuzhdeniye, narkoz.—Inhibition, Excitation, Narcosis*), St. Petersburg. Such opposition as exists concerning this subject in physiological literature (Herzen and others) is not sufficient to shake the main points of Professor N. E. Vvedensky's conclusions.

[2] V. Bechterev : *Obozrenie Psychiatrii*, and *Neur. Centr.*, 1896. See also my work : *The Psychic and Life*, St. Petersburg.—*Psyche and Leben*, Wiesbaden.— *L'activité psychique et la vie*, Paris.

when inhibitory influences are absent in the muscles, undergoes a further transformation into an equivalent amount of kinetic energy. It is obvious that the assumption of this principle is not only fully licit, but also inevitable, and it is just as inevitable to acknowledge the applicability of the principle of conservation of energy in the transmission of electric energy over a wire as it is to recognise the same principle in the transmission of nervous excitation arising from electrical stimulation of the neuro-muscular preparation of a frog.

Keeping in view the ion theory of nervous conduction, we may regard the development of kinetic energy from stored energy in the muscle or gland as a result of a discharge, as it were, which is produced simultaneously with the afflux of nervous current to the muscle or gland.

It is clear from this that the application of the principle of conservation of energy to the activity of the nervous system does not, from the reflexo-logical viewpoint, conflict with any facts, but, on the contrary, it quite accords with scientific data.

Let us develop our views more fully in this respect.

We have already stated that our receptive organs are merely transformers of external energies, and translate the latter into nervous current : (1) light energy—influence of light rays on the retina ; (2) sound energy—influence of sounds on the organ of Corti ; (3) mechanical energy—influence (a) of mechanical impacts on the cutaneous surface ; (b) of transposition and straining of parts of the body on the muscular tissue, the ligaments, and the joints ; (c) of the percussions of the endolymph, in change of bodily posture, on the semicircular canals ; (d) of mechanical influences on the cutaneo-muscular equilibratory apparatus ; (4) heat energy—influence of heat on the cutaneous and mucous surfaces ; and (5) chemical energy—influence of volatile substances on the Schneider membrane and of solutions on the papillae of the tongue and on the soft palate. Thus, the nervous current which lies at the basis of correlative activity may be regarded as a special kind of energy, which, as a result of difference in potentials, is transmitted from one neuron to the other, and is manifested externally as a negative electric oscillation or action-current. As has been already mentioned, it has been found by investigations in my laboratory that this is also manifested in the appropriate centres of the cerebral cortex, when the peripheral receptive organs are specifically stimulated.

Now, as we know, there are data which permit us to reduce the development of nervous current to the process of ionisation and this makes it possible for us to probe more deeply into the nature of the nervous current.

On the other hand, those nervous apparatus which, in the muscles, consist in nerve endings and, in the glands, in the peripheral endings of the efferent nerve fibres are mediators through which the nervous current produces discharges of energy at the expense of the supplies in the muscles and glands.

Thus occurs a cycle of energy, various forms of which, by influencing the periphery of the body, are transformed by the receptive organs into nervous current and, after passing through a number of centres, are again transmitted to the periphery along the efferent fibres, and evoke in the muscles and glands discharges of the energy which appertains to them.

We know from physiology, however, that the nervous centres summate the stimulation arising from external influences and this leads to the conclusion that the central areas store energy, and are thus real accumulators of energy.

But energy is stored in the central organs not exclusively under the influences of external stimuli. Internal stimulations, issuing from the bodily organs, play a no less significant rôle in this respect, for every heartbeat, every respiratory movement, all kinds of stimulations issuing from the region of the gastro-intestinal tract and depending on the passage of food through it, stimulations of the vascular walls under the influence of the blood current, and also the phenomena of osmosis and endosmosis, and other processes in the organism give rise to the nervous current, which, along the sympathic conductors, reaches the ganglia and higher centres and, accumulating there, is partly transmitted again, in the form of discharges, along the centrifugal conductors, to the periphery.

Besides, as we know, a specially important source of energy in the organism is food, which is solar energy stored by plants. Nutritive substances, after appropriate mechanical and chemical elaboration in the gastro-intestinal tract, enter the blood and then permeate, through the interstitial spaces, to the bodies of the nerve cells. As a result of this, the nerve cells accumulate an enormous quantity of energy chiefly at the expense of the nutritive material, and this energy is then expended in the form of intellectual or physical work, but it is transformed into external work[1] in such a way that the store of nervous energy spent is gradually replenished chiefly at the expense of the elaborated nutritive material flowing with the blood to the brain.

Assuming that there are no subjective or conscious processes without cerebral processes, consequently without nervous current, which comes to the same, we must admit that all correlative activity occurs at the expense of transformation of energy, the various forms of which are changed into nervous current by the peripheral receptive transformers. After this, the current, travelling along the efferent conductors, is again transformed into mechanical and chemical energy, and a certain store of unexpended energy is always retained in the nerve centres.

Now we even know that the main storehouse of the accumulated energy in the nerve centres is the granular part of the cellular protoplasm or the

---

[1] It must not be left out of account that mental work, as well as concentration, consists of a number of excitations and inhibitions, both of which occur in the cerebral centres, and, therefore, it is quite natural that mental work should exhaust the energy of the cerebral cells more quickly than does physical work, in which the performance of the work, as well as the comparatively simple activity of the nerve centres, is realised mainly through muscular tension.

so-called Nissl's granules, in other words, chromatin or tigroid. Indeed, a number of observations leave no doubt that, in the exhaustion of the nerve cell, as we have seen, phenomena of chromatolysis ensue, *i.e.* disintegration of Nissl's granules. But this chromatolysis of the cells disappears after appropriate rest, for they are replaced by the normal structure of the nerve cells with Nissl's granules complete, and this as a result of the subsequent rehabilitation, at the expense of the composition of the blood flowing to the brain, of the nutrition of the nerve cells heretofore exhausted.

It is perfectly obvious that every living cell in the organism, as a result of its being supplied by the blood with nutritive material, is an accumulator of energy, and there is no doubt that the nervous system, on account of its functions as the organ of correlative activity and its being furnished with receptive apparatus, plays the primary rôle in this respect and may be regarded as an accumulator of specifically nervous energy.

We have seen above that, between the work performed by man and the quantity of calories consumed in food, there is complete correspondence, for a man who does not work, or who does easy work, needs a daily consumption of not more than 2400–2900 kilo-calories, while an organism which performs hard work requires 5000–6000 kilo-calories. But we must not forget that the successfulness of work is always increased under favourable external influences on the receptive organs, for instance music in a major key, good lighting, etc., and this must depend on the stimulating influence of the external energies on the centres. The energy of the latter is then transmitted to the periphery ; and, on the one hand, directly excites the muscles and glands, and, on the other, influences both by changes in the cardio-vascular system. It has been calculated that the human organism may produce 21 per cent efficient work, an efficiency greater in proportion than that of an ordinary steam-engine, which is 13 per cent to 15 per cent efficient.[1] Moreover, 21 per cent of efficiency is not the maximum which a human being can develop ; healthy people, under favourable conditions, can develop as much as 36 per cent. All of this depends on the organism's native constitution, and also on various external influences, for there are certain indications of the dependence of productivity in work on the general condition of the organism at any given moment, as well as on the appropriate external conditions.[2]

Everything said above shows that the general principle of conservation of energy is fully applicable to human correlative activity, not only in regard to caloric metabolism arising from the ingestion of digestible food, but also in regard to the energy which is received by the brain and the nervous ganglia in general through the receptive organs and considerably enhances caloric metabolism. Obviously, we are concerned here with

[1] By the way, Diesel engines give a considerably higher percentage of efficiency.
[2] Omare : *Le moteur humain*, Paris. V. Bechterev : *The Rational Utilisation of Human Energy during Work*—Address to the Preliminary Conference for the Scientific Organisation of Work, January 1921 ; *Voprosi izutcheniya truda.* (Problems of the Study of Work), Petrograd, 1922.

problems of the transformation of external energies into cerebral, and *vice versa*. It is true that these problems are still waiting for investigators who will express these forms of transformation in exact, quantitative units.[1]

[1] The law of conservation of energy, in its application to association-reflex activity, inevitably advances the problem of the correlation of the latter with the activity on our planet of the main source of energy—the sun, and this not only in the sense of a cycle of energy, through its being stored in the vegetable world, and through its further transformation as a result of the ingestion of food, but also through the direct influence of solar activity on the earth. (See Sviatsky's and Tchizhevsky's papers on the influence of sun-spots on human life.)

CHAPTER XXIX

The principle of the proportional correlation of the speed of movement with the moving force. The principle of similarity.

THE well-known principle in mechanics—that every increase in speed of movement is caused by a force proportional to it and in the same direction as it—is limited when applied to the organic world, for here there is question of closed systems. Nevertheless, it is applicable within certain limits to correlative activity also.

Let us take the development of association reflexes. Let us assume that in laboratory experiments a secondary stimulus operates along with the primary reflexogenous stimulus. This is a condition necessary for the accompanying secondary stimulus to become adequate through a fixing of its connection with the primary stimulus, and this fixing process we are justified in regarding as a growth of the moving force of the primary stimulus. It transpires that the more associations we form with both stimuli, other conditions being equal, the sooner a reflex is evoked which overcomes the inertia of the nervous centres. If we continue the experiment under strictly determined conditions, which exclude any unnecessary inhibition, we see that the fixation of the association reflex is in direct dependence on the number of associations formed, and the fixation of a reflex is bound up with the overcoming of resistance. In this case, this is equivalent to acceleration. In both cases, the influence of the secondary stimulus as a force is equal, in respect of direction, to the reflexogenous process as movement, and produces its proportional acceleration in the sense of fixation of the association reflex.

In everyday life conditions also, we know that the oftener a secondary stimulus is associated with a primary, the more strongly the former stimulus operates, and, other conditions being equal, the more it acts in an exciting manner on the appropriate function, by overcoming all obstacles to its manifestation.

There are examples on all sides. Every prize, as an external stimulus in the execution of some work, is an auxiliary stimulus, *i.e.* a stimulus which acts in the direction of the stimulus as a moving force which conditions the work. It is obvious that the acceleration of work in this case, other conditions being equal, will be proportional to the intensity of this moving force, of course within the limits determined by the structure of the organs operative.

We shall cite another example in illustration. Let us assume that some work, necessary in itself and, consequently, having its primary reflexogenous stimulus, is being done, for instance cleaning a room, the stimulus being the need for cleanliness, this work will be performed the more quickly, the oftener some secondary stimulus is associated with it (praise, monetary reward, etc.). It is perfectly clear that the character of the secondary stimulus has its own special sigificance here and has a certain influence on the work to be done, but this belongs to another order of phenomena.

Along with the above-mentioned principle, it is necessary to take into consideration the principle of similarity, a principle known in mechanics and according to which equal causes, acting under equal conditions, lead to similar phenomena. In accordance with this principle, biology explains, for instance, the origin of an eye similar in structure both in molluscs and in vertebrates, the similarity of the organs of fishes and fish-like mammals, etc. In the sphere of association-reflex activity, we have simultaneous discoveries by different scientists in two different places and these discoveries are a result of the same scientific material being at their disposal and of equal social conditions ; the similarity in the conclusions arrived at by various investigators in the same sphere very often affords ground for suspicion of plagiarism. We know that even among the peoples of two continents, the Old and the New World, between which there was no intercommunication, similar religious rites and a striking similarity in certain myths were disclosed on the discovery of America.

Even the customs of certain peoples sometimes seem to be derived one from the other, notwithstanding that, as we have mentioned, there could not have been any intercommunication, throughout the period of human existence, between the peoples of both continents.

The latest—the neo-positive—school of sociologists (De Roberti and others) maintain that the so-called general categories, for instance time, space, etc., owe their origin to collective experience. However, we must not forget that, if human beings did not possess more or less similar organs and if their development did not move through similar stages, there could have been no similar results accruing from the experience of separate individuals and, consequently, collective experience also could not have found appropriate footing.

If we turn to the sphere of experiment, we once more discover that, if we establish the same experimental conditions in regard to some activity, we shall obtain approximately uniform results.

This same law of similarity explains why the development of correlative activity, under similar external conditions and similar innate dispositions (for instance, in twins), takes more or less the same form, and, on the contrary, why, when there are deviations in the developmental conditions of this activity, corresponding deviations or anomalies are revealed in the development.

Besides, the principle of similarity makes it possible to check scientific results obtained by the same methods when the same objective conditions are present, as may be done, for instance, in mathematics and in all the exact sciences and, consequently, the development of science is, to a considerable degree, due to this principle.

It is clear from this that the reproduction of some work and, consequently, imitative activity also are based on the principle of similarity, which, therefore, acquires enormous significance in the social life of peoples.

CHAPTER XXX

THE principle of continuous change in inanimate nature is as follows : nothing in the world is constant : everything moves, flows, changes.

" Is there anything common to all the events, in all the processes, which occur in the universe ? " Professor Auerbach asks. " This common factor is *change*, and the objects which change are exceedingly various : place changes in space ; the speed and direction of movement ; form ; colour ; the cells and organs of living beings—all change ; through change, movement is transformed into heat, electricity into light, life and death alternate unintermittently. And all these changes occur without oscillation in the quantity of matter and energy : the principle of conservation remains intact."[1]

We observe the same in processes of correlative activity.

No sufficiently strong external stimulus goes without exerting an influence on the mechanism of correlative activity. This mechanism reacts with an appropriate reflex, but this reflex changes the state of the organs which participate in its execution and, at the same time, changes, in some degree, the very mechanism of correlative activity, and this change, in turn, changes the form of the reaction to the same stimulus in the future, for the modified mechanism cannot manifest the same reaction previously evoked by the given stimulus.

We have dilated above on this subject and shown that every reflex effects something new and is really a creative act, and this is in accordance with Lamarck's doctrine, that the form of the organs is the expression of their functions.

The same is certainly true also in regard to the nervous system in general and to its central organs in particular. These undergo change in the sense of the formation of new connections and the fixation of connections, or in the sense of the beating of tracks on the occurrence of each and every reflex and even on the influence of every stimulation, although, as a result of inhibition, this stimulation does not lead to the development of a reflex.

We must admit that every organic reaction in the form of an acquired or association reflex is something irreproducible, for if a given reaction changes the executive mechanism in some degree, every new reaction will be different, although the difference may consist merely in the speed with which it is manifested, and we know, from experience, that, as a result of exercise, the speed of every reaction is changed in the sense that it is accelerated.

---

[1] Professor Auerbach : *Tzaritza mira i eyo ten (The Queen of the Universe and Her Shadow)*, Leningrad, 1919. Matter, however, as we know, changes into energy and, therefore, one may truly speak of absence of oscillation in the quantity of energy only.

It is clear from this that the human individual also is nothing constant, but changes on every new influence, on every manifestation, on every new reflex, for if this reflex is a reproduction of a former reflex, the individual is enriched by the facility he has acquired, irrespective of the fact that this reflex is not quite identical with its predecessor.

But if the reflex, because of combinative activity, is new in character, the individual is enriched also in regard to the quality of external manifestation. Thus, in both cases, the correlative activity, which lies at the basis of the development of the person, changes and, as the manifestation of reflexes is unintermittent, it is obvious that the person himself is being unintermittently changed and, indeed, at every moment, the person changes as a result of the realisation of reflexes.

It is clear from this that a person, since he is original as a result of hereditary conditions and the peculiarities of his social education, is, at any given moment, something changing and irreproducible, and each moment invests him with something he has not previously experienced and which, therefore, is creative of habit.

.   .   .   .

Along with the principle of change, we must keep in view also the principle of evolution, which consists in the production of new forms.

As we know, the metaphysical materialism of former times maintained that the world consists of a countless number of atoms, which are the chemical elements. According to Ludwig Büchner's view, an atom of carbon always remains an atom of carbon and was such from the very beginning; an atom of hydrogen was, is, and will be always the same as we know it to be. But who will maintain this at the present time ? Do we not now know that the atom is a complex body consisting of electrons revolving in orbits round a nucleus (proton), and that atoms are divisible, and that all electrons are qualitatively alike.

The apparent difference in the qualities of visible bodies has begun to disappear, especially since hydrogen and oxygen have been changed, by freezing, into solid bodies and since liquid air has been obtained.

Man naturally began to enquire : What will become of the " eternal " qualities of various substances if the temperature should be reduced to absolute zero ? And will matter not lose its fundamental quality of impenetrability, on the final analysis of matter, and will it not be identified with physical energy as such ?

On the other hand, the axiom that all the various forms of energy are transformations of the same energy which manifests itself in unequal manner in different physical conditions has been long established.

The atoms themselves are regarded as centres of potential energy in the form of electrons revolving in orbits.

Crookes' hypothesis posits the existence of a hypothetical protyle from which he deduced all the atoms successively, and the chemical elements are merely aggregates of atoms held together under the influence of positive and negative forces. According to Crookes, the development of the universe may be represented in the form of a spiral situated in the great ocean of protyle ; and, according to the measure of its gyrations around an invisible axis, the chemical elements successively originate, these elements deriving from the environment the materials of which the visible universe is built. This hypothesis is now of merely historical significance, but it has affected the later development of science.

There is no necessity to cite other and later hypotheses and we shall not further discuss what form the principle of evolution now assumes in regard to inorganic nature. It is sufficient to say that here, just as in the organic and the super-organic, the universality of the principle of evolution is incontrovertible and it remains for us only to discover to what extent this principle is manifested in processes of correlative activity.

Therefore, we shall touch here neither on the form in which this principle, already accepted by Lamarck in respect of the development of organic forms, and definitely established, with modifications, by Darwin and Spencer, was advanced by these two founders of this principle nor on the manner in which this principle was later supplemented and modified by de Vries, who propounded the so-called principle of mutations or sudden leaps.

Our business is merely to elucidate how the principle of evolution is manifested in regard to correlative, and particularly association-reflex, activity.

If the study of the person is approached through the subjective method and processes of consciousness are investigated, as is done by every psychologist, the principle of evolution becomes inapplicable. As we have seen, it is not possible adquately to solve, by the empiric method, the problem when and how conscious activity first arose, for there are here no direct methods to enable us to decide unerringly when a process is conscious and when unconscious.

But if we approach the problem from the strictly objective viewpoint, we shall observe how locomotion by means of pseudopodia develops from the simple irritability of plants and from the contractility of protoplasm in protozoa, and how, in the later developmental stages, the movements of organs—movements which are fundamental manifestations of correlative activity—grow more and more complex *pari passu* with the development of the various organs of locomotion ; and how association reflexes develop from simple reflex actions.

This development of association reflexes under natural conditions is clear also from the investigations of Jennings, Metalnikov, and others on protozoa, and the artificial association reflex in infusoria has been already observed by Dr. Israelson in my laboratory.

In addition to the development of various forms of movement, we may observe, in animal phylogenesis, not only how the appropriate mimico-somatic tonus, as well as the corresponding mimico-somatic movements in the form of reflexes, develop from simple reflex phenomena, which characterise the well-being or otherwise of the organism, its satisfaction or dissatisfaction with the nutritive material, but also how various acts of defence, aggression, orientation, concentration, and imitation have served as the foundation of the development of expressive bodily movements in the form of gestures.[1] Likewise, it becomes possible to investigate, with equal accuracy, the serial development, in different species of animals, of sound signals for communication with each other and later to investigate the further development of vocal signs in the form of human talking.

In this case, as we have already seen, we can quite definitely trace how original language, in the form of ejaculations and simple roots which denoted some object or action, gradually developed, on the one hand, from discrete and purely reflexive sounds, and, on the other, from echoisms ; how real language gradually developed from these ejaculations and roots by means of affixes, doublings, combinations, inflections, etc. ; how this language grew gradually differentiated and complicated through selective generalisation ; how the language of one people became different from the language of another as a result of the peculiar conditions of the social environment and the equally peculiar life conditions ; how, by the mixing of the original simple languages, new languages originated, etc.

In a word, it is possible to trace all the stages in the evolution of language, this most important instrument of the social life of man, just as we can also trace the gradual development of the various forms of human activity in general, including artistic creativeness. There is justification for maintaining that this development occurs in accordance with the dialectical method, but it is not necessary to dilate on this topic.

Let us note that the theory of discontinuity is applicable to the development of association-reflex activity. So, for instance, differentiation does not always occur gradually. Often, on the contrary, as shown by experiments in our laboratory, the undifferentiated reflex, when left unexercised for a period, differentiates spontaneously in the course of time and without any exercise (so-called latent differentiation—see below).[2]

If we take the ontogenetic development of animals and man, it is again possible to trace, by attentive observation, how, on the basis of simple reflexes in the infant, as well as in any new-born animal, association reflexes develop ; how concentration, which is a real dominant, develops ; how association reflexes differentiate, and are combined with other reflexes ; how they thus become more and more intricate, by becoming complexes of reflexes, conduct, and action, as we have already said.

In precisely the same way, we may observe in the child the development of mimico-somatic movements, of speech, of drawing,[3] and of artistic creativeness in general, etc.

[1] See V. Bechterev : *Expressive Movements and their Biological Significance, Vestnik Znania*, 1916.

[2] Polonsky, one of the investigators at the Institute for the Study of Brain, also develops the theory of discontinuity.

[3] See V. Bechterev : *Early Stages in the Evolution of Children's Drawings*.

Thus, in regard to drawing, I have, on the basis of my personal investigations,[1] come to the conclusion that, at the beginning, the child draws lines and next scribbles. Here we find the beginning of symbolic drawing, for the child associates a certain object with certain scribblings. Gradually, the first drawing of the child originates from these scribblings, and most frequently in the form of an irregular ring with one or two additional lines. This drawing may, at first, denote a man, a berry, an animal, or any kind of object. Next follows the gradual differentiation of separate representations of various objects from one generic drawing, and, consequently, the graphic representation of objects develops gradually, a representation in which, by the way, many details, not corresponding to reality and determined by the child and his life conditions, appear over a long period. Combinatory drawing develops later. Still later, the esthetic element develops in the child's drawing. Perspective drawing is one of the latest achievements and perspective is to be found only in parts of the drawing. Moreover, proportion between the parts of the drawing is, comparatively, a very late achievement. Needless to say, in independent drawing, children reflect parts of their daily environment.

We must keep in mind that the development of the person generally occurs by no means uniformly, but in sudden leaps at certain periods, for instance at the periods of 6-7 years and 12-14 years there is delay followed by accelerated development.

Thus, also in the ontogenetic development of the human person, it is fully possible to trace the serial development of the various manifestations of correlative activity and the formation of some forms from others, as we find in regard to all the other manifestations of nature.[2]

It is obvious from the above-said that the principle of evolution is completely and unconditionally applicable to the manifestations of correlative activity, and in particular of association-reflex activity, and is thus a universal principle valid not only for all the phenomena of organic life, including correlative activity, but also for all the phenomena of the inorganic and super-organic worlds.

[1] V. Bechterev : *Early Stages in the Evolution of Children's Drawings*, pp. 49–50 *Vestnik psychologii, kriminalnoi antropologii i pedologii*, 1901, and sep. ed.
[2] For details of this see my paper : *The Evolution of Neuro-psychical Activity—Russky Vratch*, 1912.

CHAPTER XXXI

The principle of interaction. Discussion and examples.

THE principle of interaction is a general principle manifested in the inorganic, the organic, and the super-organic world. In the inorganic world, we find interaction of bodies, and interaction between one kind of energy and another. Interaction in the animal and vegetable kingdoms is universally known and does not call for illustration. Interaction between human individuals is also universally known. Life itself is nothing but a constant interaction, on the one hand, of external energies influencing the organism and, on the other, of the energy developed by the organism at the expense of its stores obtained from the nutritive material and from the unexpended brain energy previously transformed by the receptive organs.

Passing on to correlative activity, we must keep in mind that here there is question of interaction between the person—as an integration of racial and social experience—and influences issuing from the environment. In the social environment also, interaction between individuals and social groups grows more and more complicated side by side with the differentiation of social classes, of forms of work, of trade, and industry. But also between the separate manifestations of a human person there is constant and uninterrupted interaction, for, side by side with the differentiation of association reflexes, the development of interaction proceeds and becomes more and more complicated.

In respect of association-reflex activity, we must keep in view interaction between accountable and unaccountable manifestations of personality; between processes occurring in sleep or hypnosis and manifestations of personality in the state of wakefulness ; between complexes of reflexes in general ; and even between certain separate reflexes constituting the same complex ; and, lastly, between inhibition of reflexes and their release. Let us take as an example the integration of reflexes defending the oral cavity from the intrusion of a foreign body. First, the lips are pressed together, but, when their resistance proves insufficient, they are opened and the teeth are pressed together ; when this also proves insufficient, the jaws are parted, but the tongue is firmly pressed against the palate, etc. If we encounter aggression, the initial defence consists in a repelling movement of the hands, but if this does not help, the repelling movement of the hands ceases, and we turn to flee. It is obvious from this that, in the chain of previously formed defence reflexes, the excitation of one centre is replaced by its inhibition at the moment when another centre is brought into action.

By strictly objective experiment in laboratory investigations, the complete conformity to law of interaction between excitation and inhibition in the activity of the cerebral cortex, as an apparatus of correlation, was discovered ; and it was proved that the excitation of the given cortical area, an excitation produced by external influence during the period of the inculcation of an association reflex, at first diffuses from the given area of excitation over the whole cortical area capable of being stimulated by influences of the same kind or by those similar to that stimulus to which the association reflex is being inculcated, for instance, sound, light, colour, or touch, etc. But, after this initial diffusion of the excitation, a contrary wave of inhibition necessarily follows and this wave, beginning from the more distant parts of the scale of related stimulations, gradually reaches its nearer parts. In other experiments in our laboratory, it was proved (Dr. Protopopov) that the general qualities of a given order of stimulations (for instance, in sounds, the timbre) are inhibited earlier than are the more particular qualities of the same stimulations (for instance, in sounds, the pitch and intensity). On the other hand, external inhibition, in turn, diffuses in the form of a wave over the whole scale of related stimulations, and, beginning from the nearest, diffuses to the more distant. Afterwards a wave of excitation follows, and is characterised by release of inhibition, travelling from the more distant to the nearer parts of the scale.

Even in the association reflex, just as in the ordinary reflex, we encounter, as I have observed in my investigations, interaction between exciting and inhibiting forces, and here we have, in the latent period, the prevalence of inhibitory processes, but, from the beginning of the manifestation of the reflex, exciting processes begin to prevail and this prevalence first reaches a certain limit, is then weakened, and the prevalence of inhibitory processes ensues.

In the inculcation of an association reflex, we attract, as it were, the nervous energy to that part of the reflexogenous apparatus to be stimulated and, as a result, the inertia of the nervous conductors is overcome, this inertia representing the inhibitory conditions; then excitation begins under the influence of the afflux of energy, but, with the increase of the latter, inhibitory conditions develop in the form of products which obstruct the excited centre. These inhibitory conditions at last overcome the excitation, and the reflex disappears, but, after recuperation, which removes the inhibitory conditions produced by the obstruction of the path, a new stimulation may again turn the scale in favour of the exciting forces and, after this, inhibitory conditions gradually preponderate. Then a new stimulus, similar to the previous, proves insufficient appropriately to evoke the exciting forces. So it is necessary again to effect a breach in the obstructed path through supporting the association reflex by an electric stimulus simultaneous with that stimulus to which the association reflex is being inculcated.

Thus, in the development of the association reflex, we have a process of interaction between exciting and inhibitory conditions, and the reflex is a result of the prevalence of certain conditions over others. Interaction between processes of excitation and inhibition has been proved by a series of physiological investigations (Sherrington and others) and may be easily demonstrated by suitable experiments on man, for every human activity in one direction is accompanied by its relaxation in another. Moreover,

U

when the excitation of one of the centres reaches its highest point, not only are all the other centres inhibited, but also collateral stimulations still further stimulate the given centre and do not produce local reflexes—in other words, they increase its excitation.[1] This process, which we call concentration and which is so important in the sphere of the functioning of higher reflexes, is really nothing but a typical dominant, for here we have excitation of one centre, while all other forms of movement are inhibited and, at the same time, any collateral stimulus not only does not suppress and remove concentration, but, on the contrary, reinforces it.

In conditions of interaction between excitation and inhibition, we encounter the general principle which is manifested in all association reflexes without exception, and which leads to the greater or lesser development of aggressive or defensive reflexes in a certain direction—conditioned by external stimulations—together with the simultaneous inhibition, to some extent, of muscular contractions in other directions. As external stimulations excite association reflexes, first of all in the appropriate receptive organs, it is obvious that, in dependence on the character of the external stimulus, orientation muscular contractions may be manifested predominantly or exclusively in the appropriate receptive organ, and may be raised in it to the highest tension, while the muscular tension in all other parts of the body is relaxed or suppressed, and *vice versa*.

In fine, the principle of interaction may be expressed thus : the more limited the muscular apparatus brought into action, the more energy it can develop under tension, and the more work it can do compared with the case when a more extensive muscular apparatus is contracted. Every muscular tension in one of the apparatus is accompanied by a process of inhibition in other muscular groups and this tension is obviously secured at the expense of the recuperation of other muscular groups, the principle of economy thus operating.

Under these conditions, those peculiarities, which, in the activity of the nervous system, are associated with the phenomena of dominants, are expressed. Further, the manifestation of the principle of interaction in regard to muscular contractions depends, in considerable measure, on exercise and habit in respect of certain movements. We know that some movements promote one another, while others are mutually inhibitory, and this fact depends mainly on the conditions of the activity of these muscles throughout the course of life. To these movements which promote one another belongs, for instance, the contraction of muscles working together ; while to the mutually inhibitory movements belongs, for instance, the movement of one hand in a perpendicular direction to the chest and the movement of the other in a horizontal direction to the chest. As we know, the attempt to perform these movements simultaneously and without special practice proves quite unsuccessful. In regard

[1] See V. Bechterev : *Vestnik psychologii*, 1911, and *Objective Psychology*, 3rd part, 1912.

to the problem of the influence of some movements on others, special investigations were made, at my suggestion, in my laboratory by Dr. Solovtzova and, later, Professor Osipov. These investigations afford pertinent details.[1]

I shall merely note here that the process of concentration based on the principle of interaction can be manifested not only in regard to external objects, but also in regard to unexpressed reflexes, which are revived by means of reproduction, and which we call processes of thought. Such concentration, which may be called internal concentration and is manifested by the usual external indications of the mobilisation of the muscles of the appropriate receptive organ, obeys the same principle of interaction and of the dominant, as a result of which all other motor acts are inhibited.

Let us, however, enter into further details regarding experimental data pertinent to the problem of interaction between association reflexes.

First of all, because of the frequency with which, in everyday life, we use two extremities, one on either side of the body, let us turn to the problem of interaction between association reflexes simultaneously inculcated in opposite sides of the organism.

In experiments on association-motor reflexes, this interaction may be studied under such conditions as secure the inculcation of association-motor reflexes, in each extremity separately, to two different stimuli, for instance, sound and touch, or light and sound. As a result, one extremity, for instance the right, during the inculcation of an association-motor reflex, will manifest the reflex to one stimulus, and the left to another.

Such experiments have been made in my laboratory on dogs (Dr. Afanasyev) and on men (Dr. Zhmichov). In the former experiments, one of the stimuli was an electric bell, to the sound of which a reflex in the dog's front right extremity was established, while the other stimulus was a prick, to stimulation by which, in the form of pricking the left side, an association-motor reflex in the front left extremity was inculcated. At first, in the experiment, the inculcation of the sound-association-motor reflex in the front right extremity was secured and, then, in the usual way, the inculcation—by means of a prick—of an association-motor reflex in the front left extremity. Then it was seen that, from the time the reflex was obtained isolated and always appeared in the appropriate extremity on the application of the particular stimulus, alternation in the application of these stimuli did not, at first, produce a fully isolated association reflex, since, for instance, to stimulation by the ringing of the bell, not only the reflex in the front right extremity was obtained, but sometimes it was preceded by an association-motor reflex in the front left extremity.

Further, when one stimulus, for instance, the sound-stimulus, was supported by simultaneous stimulation by a faradic current, especially when the intensity of the latter was considerable, and the second stimulus was unsupported by the current, the influence of the second stimulus

[1] The results of these investigations are given in my *Objective Psychology*, St. Petersburg.

usually produced an association-motor reflex not in the extremity corresponding to the reflex, but in that previously stimulated by being supported by the current. It is clear that the latter stimulus has an influence on the realisation of the association-motor reflex in its extremity, even when the stimulus, which, as a result of previous inculcation, usually produced an association reflex, is applied to the other extremity.

Moreover, the following circumstance was discovered during the experiments : if an association-motor reflex to the ringing of a bell is evoked several times in succession in the front right extremity, a sudden change from one stimulus to the other—for instance, from the ringing to the prick, which should produce a reflex in the front left extremity—results in the association-motor reflex being at first obtained as before in the right extremity. Thus, the influence of previous excitations of the association reflex is displayed in the sense of a tendency to manifest the reflex in the same extremity.

It is clear that, in both cases, the responsive centre of the association-motor reflex is raised to a state of dominant excitation and this determines the realisation of the reflex through that centre precisely, and not through another, even if the stimulus operative at the moment should have been previously associated with another responsive centre. This is merely the consequence of dominant excitation.

Thus, the responsive reaction is conditioned not only by previously established association of a certain stimulus with the given reaction, but also by the state of greater or lesser excitation of the responsive centre, an excitation which, after previous stimulation, leaves a certain trace, characterised by effect. Here it is perfectly obvious that the constituted centre of excitation attracts excitation, in the form of a dominant, from other cortical areas.

Nevertheless, if, in the experiments, both associative reflexes are alternately evoked several times and are supported by electrical stimulation, we ultimately succeed in securing, under the influence of either stimulus, the appropriate, isolated reflex.

It is obvious that the same law of differentiation which operates in the inculcation of association reflexes in two different extremities operates also in the inculcation of an association-motor reflex in one extremity, for, in both cases, because of the diffusion of excitation in the central areas, we are concerned with the initial generalisation of the reflex in its afferent, as well as in its efferent, aspect ; but, when the initial excitation abates, and its field narrows and scope is given for the development of inhibition, which travels in a direction opposite to that of the development of excitation, the association-motor reflex increasingly differentiates both in its afferent and efferent aspects.

Let us now pass on to experiments investigating the interaction of various association reflexes in man.

According to Dr. Zhmichov's experiments in my laboratory, after the inculcation of an association-motor reflex to a sound in one (the right), and to light in the other (the left), extremity, both association reflexes are obtained to simultaneous stimulation by sound and light, *i.e.* the movement of the right, as well as the left, foot. In alternation of these stimulations, alternation of the corresponding association reflexes occurs.

But here, as also in experiments on animals, we discover a peculiarity consisting in the fact that when one series of identical stimuli is replaced by a different series also identical, then the first stimulus of the second series evokes either both association reflexes or the association reflex corresponding to the previous stimuli, and this is explained by the effect of the dominant.

But, if we several times alternate numerically equal series of both classes of stimuli, the association reflexes begin, in time, to be produced in the appropriate manner ; but if there is numerical change of those stimulations, which alternate with the others, for instance, if their number is increased, we again get the inappropriate association reflex. It is obvious that here there is adaptation of association reflexes to a definite number of stimulations. It is necessary to note also adaptation to the time interval to which the reflexes are realised, for the interval itself, even without a new stimulation, conditions the appearance of an association reflex already established. This is the so-called reflex to an interval.

It must be kept in mind, however, that when one set of stimuli replaces another and the time intervals are irregular, the association reflex to the interval is inhibited, and we then get complete correspondence of the association reflexes to their stimuli.

This inappropriateness of association reflexes, which prevails when one series of stimuli is regularly replaced by another, holds good not only for all personal, but also for all symbolic or verbal, reflexes. This has been proved by investigations made first by myself and then by those working in the laboratories under my supervision, and especially by Dr. Dobrotvorskaya in regard to personal reflexes, and by Fyodorov in regard to verbal reflexes.

According to Dr. Dobrotvorskaya's investigation, it transpired that, if it is agreed—in an experiment in which two consecutive stimuli are applied, for instance, light and sound—to execute a certain motor reaction (for example, a pressure of the index finger on a rubber ball) to one of these stimuli, this reaction, after a number of appropriate stimulations, is manifested for some time to the other stimuli also which succeed the first. On further repetitions of the second stimulation, this reaction is inhibited, but on fresh alternation of two different stimuli, it reappears at the time of the alternation.

The durability of this reaction stands in direct correlation with the number of the stimuli alternated and is, in general, increased in the course of experience, *i.e.* after a number of consecutive renewals of the given stimulations.

It must be noted that inappropriate association reflexes develop more quickly and are more durable when the stimulations succeed one another more rapidly. Previous and frequent inculcation of the association-motor reaction to one of the stimuli has an influence in the same direction.

In the same way, greater speed in the formation and greater durability of the inappropriate motor reaction is manifested in the above-mentioned experiments, when concentration is distracted by an incidental stimulus.

On the other hand, it was found, in investigations of verbal reflexes, that, if we present light and sound simultaneously after certain time intervals to the subject, with whom we have previously arranged that he should utter the word " sound," when he hears the sound, and should remain silent on the appearance of the light, we see that the subject pronounces the word " sound," even when, after a series of simultaneous stimulations, light alone is presented, and *vice versa*. In the contrary case the same thing occurs, only that sound is called light. If three simultaneous stimuli are presented instead of two (for instance, light, sound, and a tactual stimulation) slips of the tongue occur still oftener than in the previous case.

It was discovered that the appearance of inappropriate responses is favoured not only by the speed with which the stimulations succeed one another, but also by the number of the stimulations experienced before the replacement of one order of stimulation by another.

Needless to say, individual conditions, as well as conditions determined by personal experience, exert, in all the above-mentioned cases, considerable influence on the interaction of association-motor reflexes.

Thus, it is clear that interaction between different association reflexes is, in certain measure, conformable to law and that the greater or lesser correspondence of reflexes in alternating stimulations stands in relationship with previous experience, the speed of the replacement of stimulations, the greater or lesser regularity of the latter, and certain other concomitant, external stimulations ; and that the deviation from certain conditions leads to the development of inappropriate association-motor reflexes, the appearance of which conforms to the same law in regard both to frequency and number.

Lastly, the following interesting fact is worth noting : According to investigations made in my laboratory (Dr. Kunyayev), it was discovered that, if an association-motor reflex in one extremity, for instance a lower, is being inculcated by the usual method (*i.e.* with the application of an electric current) and simultaneously a movement of an upper extremity is performed, then, after a number of such movements, the movement of the hand occurs simultaneously with the excitation of the association reflex of the foot. Subsequent experiments, made in our laboratory by Dernova-Yermolenko, show that, in such experiments, the active movement of the hand has enormous significance, for, because of this movement, the association reflex is, in these cases, obtained with particular speed, while, when the movement is passive, the reflex is either not inculcated or is inculcated with great difficulty. Thus, it is obvious that active muscular contraction is, in this case, as a result of its connection established with the association-motor reflex, revived on the appearance of the association-motor reflex, and evokes a movement corresponding to it.

This may be understood thus : Active muscular contraction produced by the movement of the given limb inculcates in it, as it were, an association-motor reflex on the simultaneous electrical stimulation of the foot, and this reflex, on application of the appropriate stimulus, is revived at the same moment as the simultaneously inculcated association-motor reflex in the lower extremity. As every movement is accompanied by collateral muscular contractions, it is clear in what varied manner associations, in connection with the inculcation of association-motor reflexes constantly executed in the course of various life conditions, may be established. The association of a certain speech reflex with a certain movement is just as easily secured. If we arrange with the subject of experiment that he respond to a certain word by a certain movement, for instance of the hand or the foot, and if we accompany this word by some collateral stimulus, for instance a sound, we shall soon obtain the same responsive motor reflex to the sound alone.

There are analogous phenomena of interaction in other cases. It had been already discovered that the association reflex, after the initial unstable phase, is at first more or less general. But with exercise in one direction, for instance when an association reflex to a certain tone is supported (by the electrical stimulus) until differentiation is established, all other tones become inhibitory. However, this inhibition is not uniform, and the nearer a tone is to the tone supported, the weaker the inhibition. This may be observed in the effect of the respiratory curve. But, in this case, the harmony or discord of tones is, apparently, of great significance and this problem is at present being investigated in the laboratory supervised by me.

As every association reflex is an expression of the prevalence—at the period of its manifestation—of the exciting forces over the inhibiting, so also, in regard to the influence of qualitatively different stimuli in the case of an inculcated association reflex, the problem is reduced to the interaction of processes of inhibition and excitation. If an inculcated reflex has not been differentiated, it is easily released from inhibition by any incidental stimulation ; if differentiated, it is inhibited, to a greater extent, by incidental stimulation. But, generally speaking, any stimulus may be made an inhibitory force, even if, as an additional stimulus, it initially excited an association reflex. For this purpose, it is sufficient to repeat it often, without supporting it by the current ; after this, its exciting influence is gradually weakened and is finally replaced by an inhibitory influence.

It must be noted that, after such exercise, the inhibitory influence ensues more quickly in the case of other stimuli also. This consequence of the inhibitory process is usually observed during the inculcation of an association-motor reflex.

The above-mentioned phenomena must obviously be explained thus :
At first, during the inculcation of an association-motor reflex, the excitation diffuses over the whole cerebro-cortical area capable of excitation by the given order of stimulation, but then the wave of excitation is more and more limited and is replaced by an inhibitory wave travelling in the opposite direction. If this wave of inhibition, in the case of a differentiated reflex, does not diffuse over the area from which the reflex is invariably obtained, this is obviously due merely to the constant support of the excitation in this area by the current as a reflexogenous stimulus.

On the other hand, experiments in the inculcation of inhibition show that the wave of inhibition evoked by inhibitory stimuli initially diffuses over the whole area of the given function, then is gradually limited, and is replaced by a contrary wave of excitation. In all these phenomena, there is a striking manifestation of conformity to law—a conformity easily demonstrated in the inculcation of association-motor reflexes.

If the limitation of the wave of excitation corresponds to the process of inner inhibition, which begins to be manifested soonest where the wave of excitation, which diffuses over the region of the cortex, is weakest, there is regular replacement of excitation by inhibition. On the other hand, the wave of inhibition also, which initially diffuses from the point of inhibitory stimulation over the excited area of the cerebral cortex, later begins to be limited, the process beginning from those parts of this territory where it is weakest, and so we conclude that there is here regular replacement of inhibition by excitation. Sherrington has applied the term *induction* to an analogous process in the spinal cord. Thus the essence of this process consists in the regular replacement of exciting by inhibitory influences, and, *vice versa*, of inhibitory by exciting influences ; and irradiation and concentration are only a direct consequence of the replacement of excitation by inhibition, and *vice versa*.

Because of the above-mentioned circumstance in the investigation of cutaneo-tactual association reflexes, by taking advantage of the instability of a newly inculcated association reflex and inhibiting it by tactual stimulations in some other spot of the cutaneous surface, I have found it possible easily to transfer the reflex from one point to the other and thus to traverse the whole cutaneous surface. It must be noted, however, that investigations made in my laboratory show that this is not so simple in respect of stimulation of different sides of the body, for the inhibition of reflexes in symmetrical areas of the body is more difficult to procure than is the inhibition of reflexes in different points of the same side of the body, and the reason for this is, apparently, that, in life conditions, co-excitations reach the cerebral cortex oftener from symmetrical parts of the body than from other bodily areas.

But, generally speaking, if we take into account processes on the same side of the body, we see complete conformity to law in the development, course, and extension of the association reflex and in its replacement by the inhibitory wave, and, as the wave of excitation of the association reflex diffuses over that region of the cerebral cortex which receives the given stimulations, after which the wave is more and more confined, so also the wave of inhibition which rises to replace the first wave, beginning from the inhibition which initially appears at the periphery of the first wave, flows over the territory of the cerebral cortex in an analogous manner, but in a contrary direction.

On the other hand, all reflexes in the region of the inner organs, and among them the chemo-reflexes, of which we have spoken elsewhere, exhibit many-sided interactions between the appropriate organs, and this is another confirmation of the principle of interaction.

The organism, as a closed system of complex processes which interact, is so organised that a change in one organ evokes in the other organs changes of a kind which, in the course of time, lead back the organism to the established norm, and the latter is to be understood as the equilibration of its various functions.

I have duly approached this problem from the viewpoint of reflexology and come to the conclusion that the function, when operative, bears an element of self-regulation. Thus, the excitation of an organ leads to the development of inhibitory processes in it, and, on the contrary, the inhibition of an organ, an inhibition associated with its functional recuperation, produces subsequent reinforced activity on its part.

Ultimately, also, those changes (investigated by Dr. Belov, a collaborator in the laboratory supervised by me at the Institute for the Study of Brain) which occur at different periods of life, are a result of a number of interacting reflexes, some of which excite others, and these latter inhibit the former.

From my point of view, the whole of correlative activity is subject to that principle according to which the excitation of one functional activity leads to the co-excitation of the activity of another function and so produces inhibition of the first, and this ultimately conditions a functional levelling out and the appearance of appropriate functional equilibration.

The association reflex, as we have already said, must be understood thus : Side by side with processes of excitation in the appropriate neurons, processes of inhibition also develop, ultimately weaken the excitation, and lead the organism back to the norm.

Here, too, operates the same principle as we have mentioned above, which Dr. Belov calls the law of parallelo-intersectional dependence and formulates thus : " If, during changes in the state of one of two elements interacting in a closed space, a change in the other is observed, this latter change is such as leads to changes in the first element."[1]

If we take any kind of work, we invariably encounter the problem of interaction between the work itself, the instrument of work, and the object worked on, for the worker utilises certain qualities of the objects as forces,

[1] Dr. Belov : *Voprosi izutcheniya i vospitaniya litchnosti*, vol. IV, 1921.

so as to act with them on other objects, which, through resistance, act back on the instrument and, consequently, on the worker.

In the same way, in the performance of movements which overcome resistance, there is question not only of interaction between the contracting muscles and the objects towards which their activity is directed, these objects offering resistance, but also of the contrary action of the resistance on the contracting muscles.

CHAPTER XXXII

The principle of periodicity or rhythm. Discussion and examples.

IN one of the above-mentioned works, *The Fundamental Laws of the Universe*, I discussed the principle of rhythm as one of the universal laws the manifestation of which we see in all the movements of the inorganic, organic, and super-organic worlds. In my *Collective Reflexology*, I tried to explicate the manifestation of this principle in the social conditions of life. Therefore, we shall touch here only on the phenomena of rhythm in biological conditions and particularly in manifestations of correlative activity.

The whole of organic nature is characterised by periodicity. The periodicity of vegetable life, in dependence on the seasons and the alternation of day and night, is universally known. Animal life is characterised by a similar periodicity. The whole somatic sphere of animals, not excluding man, is periodic or rhythmic—from the heart-beat, the circulation of the blood, metabolism, and respiration, to temperature, the activity of the gastro-intestinal tract, and the sex sphere. For instance, periodicity in the activity of the female organism in connection with processes of ovulation is known to every one. Correlative activity also is rhythmic, first of all in the form of waking and sleeping, and, secondly, in its dependence on the different hours of the day and on the seasons. Even the nervous current, which lies at the basis of correlative activity, is, like muscular contraction, a wave-like movement with a certain rhythm.[1] In particular, higher or association-reflex activity also is rhythmic. For instance, we can prove that such phenomena as concentration manifest more or less regular periodic oscillations. Even creativeness is rhythmic. But rhythm is most clearly manifested in human movements. Alternations of movement and rest, of exhilaration and depression, and *vice versa* are manifestations of rhythm. Walking and running are, to a certain extent, rhythmic; all other movements executed during work are likewise rhythmic, some to a greater and some to a lesser extent. Such movements as walking, chopping wood, planing, sharpening implements, type-setting, needlework or machine sewing, printing, sheeting paper, and others are rhythmic, as may be readily observed.

A series of physiological investigations, for instance, those of Setchenov, Mosso, Atwater, Zuntz, Traves, Schowos, Omare, and others, study man as a working machine and determine the rhythm of his work.

---

[1] We have a number of investigations, concerning the rhythm of muscles and nervous currents, by Buchanan, Garten, Dittler, Tichomirov, Pieper, Weszi, Verworn, Hoffmann, Beritov, Pravdin-Neminsky, and others. It was discovered that every contraction of a human muscle consists of 50 oscillations a second. The smooth muscles, for instance, in the bowels, are characterised by a slower rhythm. A bibliography of this subject may be found in Pravdin-Neminsky's paper : *The Concept of Innervation Rhythm—Ekaterinoslav. Med. Zhurnal*, 15th October, nos. 13–14, 1923. According to Lazarev's theory, we are concerned here with periodic chemical reactions (pulsating catalysis).

Recently, it has been discovered that every human being has a peculiar movement tempo and, consequently, has a different rhythm (the school of Kraepelin, Dr. Shumkov from my laboratory, A. P. Netchayev, and others). According to Kollarits's investigations, all human beings manifest rhythmic oscillation of the extremities and there is peculiar disturbance of rhythm in psychopaths. In every activity, a tendency, as it were, to rhythm is manifested and each kind of work has its maximal rhythm. Marey, for instance, has calculated that 85 steps a minute is the limit after which further quickening of pace results neither in increase in the length of the step nor in advantage in propulsion. A number of investigations have been made in regard to military marching (Marey, for the French Army ; Mosso, for the Italian ; Billroth, for the Austrian ; the Secret Commission, for the German) and have determined the maximal rhythm in marching movements, the maximal march for a day, the maximal pack, etc., and these determinations are utilised in the training of soldiers and in military campaigns.

Besides, the frequency of rhythm varies in certain movements in accordance with the radius and weight of the particular organ. The speed of movement is in inverse ratio to the length of the radius and the weight of the organ. Therefore, the leg, for instance, moves at an average speed of one movement a second, while the finger-joints, being only two centimetres long, move at a speech of one movement in one-seventh second, and the eyelids can move even faster. But, apparently, a rhythm of one-seventh second is the maximal speed of movements which perform work. Our gestures and facial expressions are similarly rhythmic. Rhythm is manifested with particular clearness in our speech ; and rhythmic speech, in the form of verse, is, as a matter of fact, only a regulation of the rhythm of ordinary speech. The latter, in states of excitement, automatically passes over into regular rhythm. Written language also has its rhythm. Musical movements are based exclusively on rhythm. The subjection of movements to the rhythm of music—a subjection easily discovered in laboratory surroundings also, as has been proved in our laboratory by special investigations (Dr. Hirman, Reitz, and others)—is also explained by that rhythm which appertains to movement. However, not only movements, but also secretory functions are rhythmic, as has been proved by physiological data. Rhythm in general is a fundamental attribute of all the manifestations of nervous activity, as also of all work.

As all living and dead nature obeys the law of rhythm, it is quite natural that all the manifestations of correlative activity conform to the same principle, just as social life does. I have discussed this topic in my *Collective Reflexology* (Leningrad, 1921).

" Could solidarity and concerted action exist among such large human groups as military units—the brigade, the division, the army—if all individual and collective movements were not subordinated to the iron force of the rhythm of military life. At the emotive basis of any productive organisation lies combined rhythmical work. Social pedagogics has always derived support from certain measures which lend rhythm and regularity to social life." (I. Sokolov : *Industrio-rhythmic Gymnastics—Organizatziya truda*, vol. II.)

The manifestation of the association-reflex activity of individual persons also is not, as we have seen, devoid of rhythmic oscillations noted by various investigators. This statement may be verified in any man by such data as reveal the quantitative and the qualitative productivity of his activity. Besides, it has been observed that, in the creativeness of the talented, there occurs a periodicity or alternation of greater fitness for activity, when the talent is manifested with particular brilliancy, with periods of lesser quantitative and qualitative productivity in work.[1]

By the way, we often come across an abnormal state known as cyclothymia, characterised by constant alternation of enhancement and depression of energy, a state which is really, as it were, an exaggerated form of the normal change of the same kind in a healthy man.

Many other data, which lend support to the principle under consideration, might be adduced, but, in view of the incontrovertible character of the pertinent data, we shall confine ourselves here to what has been already said.

Let us only note that, as everything said above shows, we are concerned, also in the case of association reflexes under laboratory conditions of experiment, with a periodical alternation of excitation with inner inhibition, which, after rest, is replaced by release of inhibition, etc. By the way, it was found, in experiments in which composite colour-stimuli were used, that a certain periodicity, in the form of alternation of periods of excitation with depression, occurred in the fading of the reflexive response to the components.

---

[1] A work recently published by N. Pern : *Ritm, zhizn i tvortchestvo* (*Rhythm, Life, and Creativeness*, publ. by " Petrograd," 1925), contains data concerning a number of talented persons, and these prove that the rhythm of creativeness oscillates in time intervals of about seven years. These data have been derived from investigations of the biographies of Beethoven, Wagner, Mozart, Schubert, Schumann, Glinka, Goethe, Schiller, Pushkin, Byron, Heine, Gogol, Kant, Spinoza, Rembrandt, Helmholtz, Mayer, Girard, Davy, and Liebig.

CHAPTER XXXIII

The principle of historical sequence. Discussion and examples.

THE principle discussed here consists in the fact that no phenomenon in nature originates and is manifested until all the necessary preconditions have been realised. A field will not ear and ripen, if it has not been duly tilled and sown. So, also, the existence of water on the surface of the earth was precluded, before the temperature of the earth had fallen to a degree which made possible the condensation of water vapour into rain-drops, which fell on the earth in the form of rain precipitations. The same is true of correlative activity.

The most elementary association reflex could not have developed otherwise than on the basis of an ordinary reflex, and association reflexes of a generalising character cannot precede in their development the separate influences of the various stimuli, etc. No generalisation can develop until all the necessary facts are present and the necessary observations have been made. Thus, the invention of writing could not have developed before the development of oral language ; printing could not have been invented before the appearance of writing. Chemistry could not have developed before alchemy, and astronomy is the outcome of the attempts of the ancients to read their destiny in the starry sky. These attempts resulted in ancient astrology. Every process in the development of correlative activity obeys one universal principle, according to which no new and more complex form of existence can be realised before the appearance of the necessary simpler forms which determine it. The phylogenetic development of correlative activity also obeys this principle, as does the phylogenetic development of living beings in general.

The ontogenetic development of the person also obeys this principle, and even education and teaching must necessarily accord with it, for no enrichment of the mind is possible for the developing person until all the knowledge necessary for it has been previously acquired. This may be observed most clearly in the study of mathematics : Multiplication cannot be learned before addition ; division, before multiplication, etc.

The principle of historical sequence is manifested also in the fact that a discovery is often incomprehensible to contemporaries and, therefore, they do not recognise and accept it ; consequently, it is sometimes necessary for a generation or even a number of generations to pass before the importance of the discovery is appreciated. As examples of discoveries rejected in their time, we may mention the proof of the revolution of the earth round the sun, the principle of conservation of energy, Mendelism in hereditary transmission, the recognition of hypnosis as a real fact, etc.

Lastly, the principle of historical sequence may be traced in the ontogenetic development of association-reflex activity in individual men, from the very day of birth, as may be seen from a number of published investigations, and from the material adduced elsewhere (end of chapter XIX).

CHAPTER XXXIV

The principle of economy in expenditure of energy. Discussion and examples.

IT is necessary to discuss here another fundamental principle, in accordance with which every association reflex, since it is a result of individual experience, economises, as a consequence of exercise and habit, the energy which is being expended.

No higher or association reflex develops of itself, but is a result of individual experience and exercise. Man does not learn to walk, speak, perform various movements, even gesticulation, which is based on reproduction and imitation, without repeated experience ; in a word, without exercise and habit, there is no successive development of increasingly complex higher reflexes.

This has been confirmed by laboratory experiments also. The latter show that, for the realisation of an association reflex, numerous repetitions of a certain stimulus concomitant with that stimulus which produces an ordinary reflex are necessary.

Besides, every inculcated association reflex requires, for its fixation, personal or individual experience, consisting in repeated reproduction of the given association. And the more an association reflex is repeated with the support of the primary stimulus, which produces an ordinary reflex, the more it is fixed, and, finally, it becomes so stable that it can be reproduced without support during weeks and even many months, and that with extraordinary ease.

The capacity to reproduce association reflexes stands, *ceteris paribus*, in direct dependence on the frequency and number of the associations previously made. This is confirmed by everyday observation also, for all motor acts, which have been repeatedly renewed under appropriate conditions, are, broadly speaking, more easily reproducible as compared with movements which have, in the past, less frequently found the conditions necessary for their renewal.

For the explication of the principle discussed—a principle already pointed out by Avenarius—it is necessary to keep in mind that an association reflex is not a result of exciting forces alone. It is always a result of the interaction of exciting and inhibiting conditions. These latter appertain to that environment in which an association reflex develops, *i.e.* the nerve tissue, for every association reflex, stimulated after certain time intervals and not supported by the primary stimulus in association with which it has been inculcated, is inhibited, and this inhibition may depend merely on increase of resistance or inhibitory forces in the nerve tissue. Therefore, the early period of the inculcation of an association reflex, when it still remains latent or unexpressed, is to be regarded as a period of the prevalence of inner resistance or inhibitory forces antagonistic to the manifestation of the reflex. Nevertheless, here, too, exciting influences are not absent. But they are only gradually accumulated with every new associative stimulation, until they finally overcome the appropriate resistance.

With the first appearance of the association reflex, the exciting forces begin to preponderate over the inhibitory conditions, until, finally, they breach the latter, as it were, within the sphere of appropriate stimulations. In the course of time, when the association reflex, during its inculcation, reaches the highest point of development and, thus, the exciting influences preponderate to the maximum over the inhibiting conditions, the association reflex is undifferentiated and, consequently, there are no external forces to inhibit it, except, perhaps, stimuli, altogether different in character, which act on other centres.

However, the fact that this period also is characterised by inner inhibition, of which we have already spoken, proves that inhibitory forces are not absent here.

But, on repeated excitations of the association reflex, if it is supported from time to time by the primary stimulus, its differentiation develops ; in other words, the field of stimuli exciting it grows restricted and, at the same time, the influence of inhibiting conditions widens.

In this differentiation, the principle of economy of energy is manifested : the energy is not diffused, but is concentrated in the appropriate direction, so that the reflex becomes more fixed and is called out with extraordinary ease.

All dressage is based on the above-mentioned principle. In what, for instance, does the training of a dog consist ? According to the words of all trainers, it is first of all necessary to create in the dog the habit of obedience to the fullest possible extent. Then it is necessary to establish a mechanical chain of nerve stimulations, which must be so closely associated that one word, one appropriate gesture, is enough to produce a series of movements. It is clear that all training is based on the inculcation of association reflexes.

Habits acquired in this way are, to a certain extent, transmitted in the form of tendencies to posterity, since, for instance, young spaniels point before a sheep, a white stone, and a bird's nest. In other words, they have inherited the tendency to point, but this tendency does not receive its proper direction, until the latter is given it by education, i.e. by training. The same may be observed in regard to sheep-dogs, though any dog can be trained to become a sheep-dog. In such training, a piece of meat is tied to the sheep's ear, so as to train the dog to drag the stray sheep back by the ear. But well-trained dogs leave a progeny which acquire, even without special training, the necessary skill to deal with the flock ; by frolicking and playing, as it were, they acquire all the skill necessary for their work.

To illustrate this, we shall cite here a description of how sleuth-hounds are trained : " On the green within the enclosure, gymnastic apparatus are placed in position : a ladder, a high ' hill,' and, lastly, a special apparatus, like a wall, consisting of boards placed one on top of the other. This latter apparatus represents a fence. Here puppies about a year old are always being trained. They go through a ' course ' of training consisting of seventy separate exercises. When first seen, this process looks like a game. The trainer, to whom a particular dog is consigned from its early days, takes some object (a cap), and, trailing it over the grass, hides it somewhere under a bush. Then he guides the dog on a lead along the trail, and makes the animal smell to every inch of it, until, at last, he guides the puppy to the hidden object, while he continually repeats : ' At him, good dog ! ' Later, the dog itself finds the cap, seizes it, and fetches it for the master on the order, ' Fetch ! ' The explanation of the trick is simple. The dog, when it retrieves the cap, first gets a patting on the head, then a few words in a kind voice, and, in addition, a morsel of meat or sugar. After some time, the patting alone is sufficient.

When the first stage is finished, the second exercise begins : the dog is given to smell some object belonging to the master. This object is then taken some distance, up to about 200 yards. The dog, accompanied by the trainer, rushes along the fresh trail, until the object is found. Still later, when these exercises, too, have been finished—by the way, the animal in training returns daily to these ' bases,' as a pianist returns to his scales— exercises in which the trainer's assistant participates are begun.

This assistant is an important personage. He wears a special padded suit to protect him from the dog's teeth, and then the hunting-down of the ' criminal ' begins—jumping over ropes and fences (the height of the fence is gradually increased), swimming across a pond which represents a river, and many other exercises. The perception of the trail by scent is here, too, kept in the foreground, and the tasks presented to the animal are gradually increased in complexity.

One of the most difficult feats required in the course of training is the mounting guard over the discovered criminal, *i.e.* the assistant, who is hidden in a secluded spot.

The sleuth-hound must be well trained, so as not to betray the discovery he has made until the detectives approach—otherwise the criminal may easily escape. Having discovered the hiding-place, the dog remains rooted to the spot somewhere in the vicinity. It must suppress the reaction inculcated in it, and this inhibition is secured by special exercises resembling those used in training lap-dogs ' to die.' Then a special police-whistle is sounded, and the dog answers immediately by a characteristic bark. The criminal's hiding-place has been discovered. Now, if necessary, the dog is given, also by a special signal, the order to arrest the thief—and the animal hurls itself, with a splendid leap, on the criminal's back and throws him to the ground. It is unnecessary to attempt to demonstrate the enormity of the psychological effect of this ' gesture.' Some dogs are trained to seize the criminal by the legs, if he offers resistance—and then it is difficult to extract the victim from the animal's teeth." (Borovoi.)

This is how sleuth-hounds were trained at the time of negro-hunting— a practice instituted by Christopher Columbus, whose precedent was followed by the Spaniards and, later, by the French. From an early age, the dogs were fed chiefly on the blood of other animals. " When they

x

began to grow up, they were sometimes shown, over the cage, the figure of a negro made of plaited bamboo and filled with blood and the entrails of animals. The dogs were angered by the bars which imprisoned them, and the more their impatience grew, the nearer the effigy was pushed to the bars of the cage. Meanwhile, their rations were daily decreased. At last, the dummy negro was thrown to them and, at the moment when they ravenously devoured him and tried to tear out the entrails, their masters patted them encouragingly. Thus, their hatred of the negro developed proportionally to their attachment to the white. When this training was regarded as sufficient, they were sent hunting. The poor negro was in a hopeless plight. When he ran away, he was hunted down by the sleuth-hounds and torn to pieces. When he took refuge on a tree, the barking of the bloodthirsty animals betrayed him, and he fell into the hands of their still more cruel masters. But this was not all. Near Cap Français, these dogs, which were very carelessly supervised, often broke loose and attacked negro children, whom they met and devoured on the road. Often they also rushed to the neighbouring woods, caught a harmless family of negro peasants unawares, tore infants from the mothers' breasts, and even devoured man, woman, and child. Then, with the blood of poor negroes coagulated on their muzzles, these blood-hounds returned to their kennels." (C. Letourneaux : *L'évolution de la morale*.)

If, in the example cited, an example so terrible in its very nature that we cannot decide which is more amoral—beast or man—we are concerned with the production and strengthening of bloodthirstiness ; in other cases, the bloodthirsty tendencies of animals may be successfully subdued or mollified by special training. The subjugation and mollification of these tendencies may be effected by cultivating affection through kind treatment, proper care, and habituation ; by causing animals naturally inimical to live together from an early age ; and, above all, by education. According to Mantegazza, the best method of training sheep-dogs is to put the pups to the sheep's dugs and thus feed the future guardians of the flocks. A polecat brought up by a hen does not attack its foster-mother and is even slow to attack other hens. Many wild animals brought up under domestic conditions become quite tame. Examples of the transmission to posterity of this mollification of behaviour have also been observed and this transmission is, apparently, a result of upbringing. Obviously, in the case of man also, a similar tendency to transmit is manifested in regard to associative or so-called professional skill, but the question remains : To what extent may the part played by upbringing be excluded here ?

Finally, it must be noted that, within the bounds of the existing anatomical and physiological conditions of muscular activity and secretory functions, nature has set no limit to the development of association reflexes by exercise. Therefore, since, according to the amount of experience and exercise, there may be transmission of appropriate tendencies through heredity, man constantly develops his association reflexes in the most diverse directions, and some reflexes are developed with facility, others with difficulty, in accordance with the interrelation of external stimuli with constitutional conditions, as well as with other conditions including tendencies acquired from the parents.[1]

The principle of economy, as manifested in the form of routine and skill in the life of the individual, was first formulated by Zellner, in respect of the conditions which prevail in inorganic nature, as the principle of the least expenditure of means. Avenarius (*Philosphie als Denken der Welt gemäss dem Prinzip des kleinsten Kraftmasses*, Leipzig, 1876) has extended it to the "spiritual" sphere and maintained that, for the purpose of expediency, it secures its ends by the expenditure of the least quantity of force, as is manifested in all cases of routine and skill. Apart from this, it is incontrovertible that this principle is significant in respect of that function of the organism which we call correlative activity. Indeed, all our reflexes—the lower as well as the higher or association reflexes—are nothing but acts of adjustment and, consequently, acts directed towards possible economy in our correlations with the environment. Townsend (*Magic in the Study of Movements*) has already regarded economy and rhythm as general principles in the attainment of perfection of movement. We tend towards economy in all our movements, even though we may have to learn it. Our speech, like all symbolic reflexes, effects extraordinary economy not only of the internal activity of the central nervous apparatus, but also in the establishment of the external correlations of one individual with another. Modes of calculation and all mathematical procedures are, in turn, among the most important means of effecting economy of correlative activity, for, otherwise, we should be obliged to substitute the substraction or addition of concrete objects, which is possible, as we know, only in an extremely limited number of cases.

The formulation of general definitions, of every generalisation, and also of every dependence or law has the same aim : to effect economy in correlative activity.

Indeed, if, instead of naming the given generalisation or pointing out the given dependence or law, we had to reproduce every separate fact referring to a given generalisation or to a given law which has been

---

[1] It is interesting to note that exercise is significant in regard to the inorganic world also. In illustration, let us quote W. Ostwald's words : " I have two equal quantities of the same nitric acid, and these differ only in the fact that in one I have already dissolved a piece of copper. I put two equal, but thin, plates of copper into each of the acids, which are standing in water in the same vessel so that their temperature is equal. I see immediately that the acid which has already dissolved copper has " adapted " itself to the work of dissolving, and begins to continue it skilfully and quickly, while the other acid, inexperienced, as it were, does not know how to commence operations on the copper, and performs the work so inertly and bunglingly that we cannot wait for its consummation. If I add a certain quantity of natrium nitrite to the inert acid, the acid immediately acts on the copper, and the latter is dissolved. This fact shows that we are concerned here with catalysis produced by nitric acid." An analogy with habit in organised bodies naturally forces itself upon us here.

discovered, we should have to expend an incredible amount of energy unproductively.

It is clear that the development of all science and technique inevitably leads, in addition to the realisation of certain achievements, to the establishment of the principle of the least expenditure of force in the performance of certain tasks.

Lastly, in practical life also man acts in accordance with the same principle : in language (by appropriate condensed expressions, contracted forms of speech, abbreviations), in division of labour, in the uniting of individuals into groups, in the organisation of the latter, in the establishment of a general legislature, and in thousands of other forms of manifestation of the individual and collective activity of man.

CHAPTER XXXV

The principle of adaptation. Signalisation as a form of adaptation. Experimental data. Discussions and examples.

THE principle of adaptation must take its place beside the principle of economy. The former principle, since its significance is universal, has a direct bearing on correlative activity. As a matter of fact, the whole of correlative activity is only a kind of adaptation—the most complex and the highest kind—to the conditions of the physical and the social environment, if we take into consideration that the utilisation of the forces of nature is a kind of adaptation. Even the primitive reflexes of lower animals and plants—reflexes in the form of protoplasmic irritability—as well as acts of defence in the form of shrinking, contractions, etc., are defensive adaptations, just as the enveloping of external bodies, the ingestion, swallowing, and digestion of nutritive material are acts aggressive in character in the form of adaptations which secure existence. Further complications of these activities in the life of protozoa are adaptations more complex in character.

As we know, all the simple reflexes of higher animals are, to a certain extent, teleological ; they are acts of adaptation for defence or aggression.

In the higher manifestations of correlative activity, which consist in the development of association reflexes in the form of acts of defence, aggression, concentration, facial expressions, gestures, language, and those complex manifestations called action and conduct, we are concerned with nothing but various and complex adaptations to environmental conditions, and the highest form of these adaptations is doubtlessly the above-mentioned utilisation of external conditions in order the better to secure the existence of the individual.

Thus, what we refer to the so-called creative activity of a human individual must also be understood as higher acts of adaptation. There is no doubt that technical creativeness is adaptation, while artistic creativeness also must clearly be regarded as adaptation. If this creativeness " ennobles " or elevates man, if it teaches him something, enriches his mind, and " softens his heart," we cannot help seeing adaptation in it, but adaptation of the finest and highest kind imaginable.

This is why it must be postulated that, in the manifestations of a human individual, there is nothing which is not included in the scope of his adaptation to environmental conditions.

In laboratory investigations of association reflexes, the principle of adaptation is manifested in so-called set, a topic which we have already discussed.

But there are other facts concerned with the inculcation of association reflexes, and these facts do not leave any doubt that the principle of adaptation is fully operative here too, as in other cases.

The establishment of signals—a theme to which we have already referred—must be regarded as a special form of adaptation. This establishment means that if two stimuli follow each other, the first being more or less indifferent, but the second reflexogenous, then, after a number of consecutive repetitions of these stimuli, a reflex, which formerly appeared only to the second stimulus, occurs simultaneously with the indifferent stimulus which has been presented earlier. Thus, the first stimulus becomes, as it were, a signal for the second, and itself, as a signal-stimulus, becomes capable of evoking reflex phenomena which formerly were produced only by the later stimulus.

If, in these experiments, the reflexogenous stimulus is presented during the unbroken presentation of an indifferent associative stimulus (for instance, sound or light), the association reflex, when it appears to the indifferent stimulus, is invariably established at the moment when the indifferent associative stimulus is presented. In other words, the association reflex occurs before that moment at which the ordinary reflex originally appeared as a response to the reflexogenous stimulus, as if the latter were presented simultaneously with the beginning of the indifferent associative stimulus, although this beginning precedes it in time.

It transpires that if, in an experiment, the stimulus to be associated is not presented simultaneously with or before the fundamental stimulus, but somewhat after it, then, contrary to the tenets of I. Pavlov's school, the association reflex, as has been shown by experiments in my laboratory (Dr. A. L. Shnirman), can here also be evoked. This may be explained by the perseveration of the primary electro-cutaneous stimulus.

Thus, only a stimulus more or less simultaneous, or shortly preceding or closely following the reflexogenous stimulus, can call out an association reflex and thereby reproduce that reflex which was formerly evoked by the primary reflexogenous stimulus. In other words, the indifferent, associative stimulus reproduces such reflexive effects as more or less synchronise with it and are produced by another stimulus ; and it reproduces them in the form of reflexes which arise on the presentation of the associative stimulus.

May we speak here of a reversed order of excitation, according to Hachet-Souplet's theory ? It would be more correct to maintain that the reflex reproduced by association either precedes the ordinary reflex evoked by the primary stimulus or follows it, according to whether the associative stimulus is presented before or after the primary. That is why there is question here not of a law of recurrence, as Hachet-Souplet maintains, but only of an associative stimulus leading, by reproduction of the reflexogenous stimulation, to the adaptation of the reflex to the moment of the influence of the associative stimulus.

All training is really effected by means of associative stimuli, especially signals. A previous signal and a subsequent allurement cause the animals, in the course of time, to obey the signal only. In another case, the showing of a whip plays the rôle of a signal which incites the animal to run.

The same precisely is true of man. Let us assume that the repeated appearance of an enemy was preceded by a certain sound and produced readiness to fight. Later, this sound alone produces readiness to fight. Here the signal, in the form of a sound, which formerly produced no reflexes, gradually begins to produce readiness to fight, even when there is no aggression.

In another case, a man turned to flee when he had experienced a snake's bite preceded by rustling of the grass in which the snake moved. This is later sufficient to make him run when he merely hears a rustle. When a man sees a cloud in the sky, he provides himself with an umbrella, although he requires it only when rain is actually falling. When a pious person hears the tolling of the church bell, he crosses himself in readiness to go to church, although the service begins later. When a man is hungry and hears the rattle of plates, he begins to secrete saliva abundantly and experiences a gnawing in the stomach, etc.

The acquisition of skill, too, is based on signalisation and is accompanied by facilitated reproduction of successive reflexes. Everybody knows how quickly activities occurring consecutively are reproduced and how difficult their reproduction is in the reversed order, for instance the order of days, months, etc. This is explained thus : In the first case they are reproduced as a result of signals which habitually precede them, while, in the second case, this is not so.

The same is true of all the usual verbal combinations, for instance Jesus Christ, God help us ! etc.[1]

When we learn by heart the text of a book or a series of figures, they are relatively easily reproduced in their consecutive order, but with great difficulty in the reversed order. This again is similarly explained : In the first case, each preceding verbal stimulus is a signal for the subsequent one, while subsequent verbal stimuli do not serve as signals for the preceding stimuli.

The process of signals must be taken into account in all investigations of association reflexes ; otherwise the conclusions may be fallacious. Thus, in investigating the salivary reflex, Professor Orbeli (*Dissertation*, St. Petersburg) experimented on the reaction of dogs to colour and could not produce in them a differentiated reflex to a colour. This is equivalent to maintaining that the dog does not distinguish colour. But, in the arrangement of these experiments, a moving colour frame was used. Naturally, the very movement of the frame could have been a signal-stimulus in the experiment and this, apparently, sufficed to develop in the dog an association reflex to this movement, and this reflex was identical in respect of all the colours. This, however, does not mean that, under other experimental conditions, a differing reaction to colours could not have been obtained. Investigations made in my laboratory by Dr. Valker using the more precise method of association-motor reflexes showed that a dog can exhibit an association reflex to one colour, for instance blue, and not manifest it to another colour, for instance red. On the other hand, Pro-

[1] See also Professor Astvatzaturov's experimental investigations (my laboratory) of speech : *Dissertation*, St. Petersburg.

fessor Babkin's experiments have shown that the first tone is the decisive factor in the investigation of dogs in regard to tone combinations. If this first tone is the same in two different sound-combinations, the reaction to it by salivary secretion is in both cases positive, although, under other conditions, the dog reacts differently to different sound-combinations. But this holds good only at the beginning of the inculcation of an association reflex, for complex sound-stimulations, even if they begin with the same tone, can be differentiated according to the difference in the subsequent tones of the complex sound-stimulus.

It is clear from the aforesaid that, if the reflexogenous stimulus is preceded by some indifferent by-stimulus, the latter soon acquires the significance of an adequate stimulus, that is, one which is capable of evoking an association reflex identical in character with the primary reflex, and which is. in reality, a reproduction of the latter. This explains the influence of all methods of encouragements under the conditions of life, for these encouragements are secondary stimuli which, in life experience, are associated with primary stimuli. Thus, all marks, distinctions, orders, titles, ranks, etc., are in themselves indifferent stimuli, but, because of their immediately preceding favourable changes in the social position of the individual, changes effected by giving this individual certain privileges and more of the good things of life or what raises him in the esteem of others, they become adequate stimuli inciting many to strenuous work.

But, in addition to such purely external stimulation, we must also distinguish internal stimulation based on the store of energy possessed by every living being and on the needs resulting from life experience.

Every stimulation of reflexes is essentially based on the store of energy as the fundamental source of the individual's reacting, but, while external stimulation has an external stimulus to activate it, this stimulus acting, as a result of previously established connections, in the same direction as the primary reflexogenous stimulus, internal stimulation is based on the reproduction—or release from inhibition—of an internal stimulation resulting from a habit formed or an organic need. This internal stimulation is manifested, for instance, in the case of a man making a fire, for this act is correlated with the reproduction of a primary reflexogenous stimulus in the form of food prepared on the fire. The same internal stimulation incites a man to make efforts to receive education, for education stands in correlation with the reproduction of the social standing later acquired thereby, or of some of the good things of life, these amenities and this social status constituting primary, reflexogenous stimuli, etc. We often run across the same internal stimulation in the work of a scientist, who, because of his reproduction of the amenities which will accrue to mankind from his discovery, makes an effort to discover the truth, and these amenities, in addition to personal satisfaction, here constitute the primary, reflexogenous stimulus. We must similarly explain that inner battle which a man fights against the inherited, organic tendency to self-preservation, when he sacrifices his life for the good of his circle, his nation, or mankind in general.

These are essentially the chief modes of manifestation of the individuals' adaptation to environmental conditions.

CHAPTER XXXVI

The principle of reciprocal action. Discussion of this principle.

A S everybody knows, Newton's third law is as follows : "Action and reaction are always equal in magnitude and opposite in direction." We have seen that, if we take living substance, the action of an external stimulus which produces a reaction, produces a reaction in a living being—the intensity of the reaction being proportional to the intensity of the stimulus. If, at another time, the same reaction is obtained to a weaker stimulus, that is because the resistance of the substance has, to that extent, been diminished.

The above principle is everywhere applicable to correlative activity, but its application is naturally circumscribed by the limitations of the organism's powers. Within these limits, the principle admits of no exception. Thus, all influences harmful to the organism are opposed by an organic reaction equal to the action. Let us assume that an excessively stimulating influence is acting on some part of the body. It evokes the effect of a reaction proportional to its action, and the reaction takes the form of a defence reflex which mobilises the nearest muscular apparatus defending the organ in question from excessive stimulation. But, if this reflex is not sufficiently counteractive, more and more remote muscular mechanisms become operative for the same purpose. If, for instance, the influence of a pricking instrument on the cutaneous surface produces withdrawal of the stimulated organ by jerking it back, then, if this is not sufficient, the hands are brought into action and seize the pricking instrument in order to counteract further pricking stimulation, and the intensity of the reaction by the hands increases proportionally to the force of the action of the pricking instrument. If this reaction of the hands is not sufficient to remove the influence of the pricking instrument, other muscles of the body become operative for the purpose of increased counteraction, and if this also proves insufficient, almost the whole musculature, until exhausted, is invariably called into action for the purpose of defence.

The means at the disposal of the organism are everywhere mobilised to a degree equal to the external influence which is being experienced and which must be removed by force of a pre-established set to resistance, but, obviously, within the limits of the organism's powers and resources.

On the other hand, if there is question of action on the part of the organism when striving after an aim, here, too, reaction is equal to action. For instance, in the overcoming of an inert environment, the reaction is directly contrary and equal in force to the action. This may be easily proved of all mechanical work, for instance, agricultural labour, wood-chopping, etc., and the same holds good of the resistance offered by living beings when attacked : for instance, when they fight, pursue an enemy. Lastly, so-called mental work also obeys the same law, for, here too, mental tension increases more and more in order to overcome all obstacles, and, ultimately, reaction is equal and contrary to action or mental tension.

Thus, the above principle admits of no exceptions in its application to the manifestation of correlative activity and here receives the same kind of confirmation as in the manifestations of the inert inorganic environment.

CHAPTER XXXVII

A FURTHER important principle governing the phenomena of association-reflex activity is the principle of differentiation of association reflexes. We decisively reject the specificity of association reflexes, a doctrine at first propounded, as a result of the investigation of salivary conditioned reflexes, by the physiological school of I. P. Pavlov.

The principle of differentiation, which is general for the inorganic, the organic, and the super-organic world, prevails even in ordinary or innate reflexes.

When a living organism reacts in one way to rays of a certain wave-length and in another to rays of a different wave-length, there is, even here, differentiation of reflexes, just as there is differentiation when sound-energy produces a reflex in one receptive organ and light-energy in another.

The principle of differentiation of association reflexes consists in a narrowing—in respect both of the range and intensity of stimuli—of the circle of stimuli which produce the association reflex. This restriction proceeds hand in hand with exercise and, as a result, the production of the association reflex is restricted to an increasingly narrowing, and, consequently, special, range of external influences.

If we take a composite stimulus, all its components act at the beginning and each component can produce the same reflex as does the whole. But, in the course of time, only the composite stimulus can produce the reflex.

All the investigations of association-motor reflexes in my laboratory leave no doubt that, at the beginning, there are, indeed, no " specific " association or conditioned reflexes, as has been often maintained by those applying the salivary method in the physiological laboratory, but, on the contrary, every association reflex which is being inculcated is, to some extent, subject to differentiation, for differentiation is a fundamental attribute of every association reflex. The reflex is differentiated on every repetition, which is a necessary element of exercise, whether the latter is natural or artificial. It is obvious from this that differentiation, since it is a direct consequence of exercise, is a fundamental attribute of association reflexes in general.

In this respect, the difference between different association reflexes is only quantitative, in the sense of greater or lesser speed in the differentiation of individual association reflexes, and in the sense of the direction of their differentiation, and this speed and direction really depend on the character of that organ in which the association reflex is being inculcated. It is perfectly comprehensible that a reflex inculcated to stimulations of the cutaneous surface is differentiated from other similar reflexes in respect of intensity and topographical extension, while a reflex inculcated in the auditory organ is differentiated from other auditory association reflexes in respect of the timbre, as well as of the intensity and pitch of the sound, and also in respect of the position of its source in space.

It is, however, exceedingly important to explicate the laws to which the differentiation of association reflexes conforms.

The investigations of these organs—the auditory organ, the visual organ, and the cutaneous surface—are particularly instructive in this respect. In the first two, the differentiation of an association-motor reflex, in regard to the intensity and quality of the stimulation, in the third, the differentiation of an association reflex, in regard to the topography of the stimulation, may be satisfactorily studied.

Pertinent investigations made in my laboratory make possible a sufficiently complete elucidation of this problem. It was discovered by a number of investigations (Protopopov, Molotkov, Israelson, Shevalev, and others) that the differentiation of the association reflex is the essential aspect and the inalienable peculiarity of its development. Differentiation leads to greater and greater narrowing of the sphere of action of the reflex side by side with its repetition and, consequently, with its fixation, and, thus, a reflex develops from a more general and less stable, into a more particular and, at the same time, more stable, reflex. Later investigations, made in my laboratory, of cutaneo-tactual stimulations (Dr. Shevalev : *Dissertation*, St. Petersburg) have shown, however, that the law of differentiation operates only from the moment when the reflex has reached its initial generalisation or irradiation. It was discovered that there is at first a preparatory period in the development of a reflex and that this period, at the moment of the appearance of the association reflex, is expressed not in a process of differentiation, but, on the contrary, in a process of generalisation. This is that preparatory period—in the inculcation of an association reflex—which consists in the establishment of the reflex, when the latter is still characterised by great instability and a particular facility for release from inhibition, this release occurring under the influence of some incidental external stimulus.

Because of the latter circumstance, the reflexogenous area is not easy to determine at the beginning, but, anyhow, it is limited in extent and, only *pari passu* with the gradual establishment of the association reflex, is it quickly generalised, spreading over the whole cutaneous surface or the greater part of it.

However, here too, we are concerned not with equal reflexogenous excitability, but, on the contrary, with the fact that the area of origin, which is the locality of the usual stimulation, usually exhibits, when the stimulus is applied, a more stable reflex, often repeated many times on fresh stimulation without being supported by the current, while more distant areas produce less stable reflexes, which are, at the same time, more easily inhibited.

The period of generalisation, which concludes the first stage of the inculcation of an association-motor reflex, this first stage ending in greater or lesser fixation of the reflex, is that period from which the differentiation of the reflex begins in further inculcation. Besides, the generalisation of an association reflex is accompanied by the greatest reflexive excitability, for every new tactual stimulation of the cutaneous surface, wherever the stimulus is applied, has, at this period, no inhibitory influence in respect of the inculcation of association reflexes, but rather one which excites reflexes or releases inhibition and leads to enhancement of the strength of the association reflexes, while inhibitory influences are much weaker here.

As has been pointed out, after the period of generalisation or irradiation of the association reflex, the period of its differentiation really begins, and differentiation, which develops hand in hand with further repetition, is manifested particularly strongly when the given association reflex is supported by concurrence with its primary electric stimulus.

As a result of this, the reflexogenous excitability becomes more stable in the areas of influence of the stimulus and those neighbouring on the stimulus, which is supported by the electric current, and this excitability is gradually weakened or inhibited in proportion to distance from the point of stimulation.

However, differentiation or limitation of the reflexogenous area conforms to certain laws, as has been perfectly clearly demonstrated by the investigations made in my laboratory (Dr. Shevalev: *Dissertation*, St. Petersburg).

It has transpired that limitation begins in the areas more distant from the locality originally stimulated and that reflexes disappear more quickly on the opposite side of the body, but the symmetrical area of the opposite side retains reflexogenous excitability considerably longer than do the other parts of the opposite side, even when, on the original side of the body, there is such limitation of the reflexo-excitable area that the radius of the latter is much smaller than the distance between the area under investigation and the symmetrical part on the opposite side.

Further, it was discovered in the investigations that areas more stable in respect of reflexogenous excitability, both on the same and the opposite side, are, in external outline, by no means equal in shape in different parts of the body, but correspond to the segmentary distribution of cutaneous receptivity or the so-called dermatomes, but more often to some of their fragments. It is obvious from this that, in the differentiation of association reflexes, the reflexogenous areas, in their extent and outlines, correspond to anatomo-physiological conditions of cutaneous innervation.

It must be noted, however, that, at the beginning, these limited reflexogenous areas are not characterised by great stability, for, in attempts to support the inculcation of the association reflex in some more distant area, the reflex is easily generalised again.

However, in the course of time, when the above mentioned differentiation is continued, the reflexogenous area, in the form of a dermatome, becomes more stable, but, under the influence of certain stimulations, its boundaries oscillate, extending sometimes to one, sometimes to several, segments, until they become still more stable and definite, with some oscillations at their edges, but not to the same extent in all of them.

At this period, the differentiation of association reflexes is, generally speaking, characterised by greater stability, for the reflexogenous areas, in the form of dermatomes, remain, but with oscillations of their boundaries, for several months, when the investigations are interrupted for a longer or shorter time.

It is deserving of attention that, at this period, the influence of external incidental stimuli is manifested mainly as inhibition rather than excitation, but later the association reflex, limited to the area of dermatomes, becomes more and more independent of any kind of external incidental stimulations.

Further, experiment shows that differentiation of reflexogenous areas to the point when they coincide with dermatomes or their fragments is not final, for, in further differentiation through artificial support of the association reflex—in the area under investigation—by means of concomitant electro-cutaneous stimulation and through inhibition by means of repeatedly applied and unsupported stimulations of other areas, reflexogenous areas may be successfully reduced to still narrower limits which are not equal at different places and, according to investigations made in my laboratory by Dr. Israelson (*Dissertation*, St. Petersburg), tend to coincide with the boundaries of the so-called Weber circles. But these areas, too, are not stable and, during a longer or shorter interruption in the investigations, the reflexogenous areas may again expand to the size of dermatomes.

The circumstance that limitation of the reflexogenous area, as a result of inhibition of association reflexes from other areas, goes on side by side with exercise, shows that the absence of reflexes, under normal conditions, during cutaneous stimulations, is often a result of inhibition effected by life experience.

Observations on children, for whom every cutaneous stimulus is a source of various reflexes, may be taken as a proof of this. With advancing years, this excessive reflexive excitability is weakened and is manifested only to stronger external stimuli. On the other hand, in poisoning with certain poisons, for instance strychnine, the reflexive excitability of the cutaneous surface is released from inhibition, and this surface serves as a locality in which cutaneous reflexes develop even to weak external stimuli.

As regards investigations concerning other stimulations, for example sound (Dr. Protopopov) where we distinguish pitch, intensity, and timbre or quality of the sound, it is necessary to keep in view, as we have already mentioned, that, on the inculcation of an association reflex, the latter is, at first, generalised or irradiated, appearing to every sound regardless of its character and intensity, but, later, on the differentiation of the reflex in the usual manner, that is, by electrically supporting a sound-stimulation of a certain pitch, intensity, and timbre and leaving unsupported the association reflex to all other sound-stimulations, we obtain, at first, an association reflex only to a sound of a certain timbre, whatever the intensity and pitch of the sound, and, on further differentiation, only to a sound not only of a certain timbre, but also of a certain intensity ; and, lastly, in the final differentiation, we obtain an association reflex only to a sound of a certain timbre, a certain intensity, and a certain number of vibrations.

Thus, it is obvious that, at the time of the establishment of an association reflex during the period of its generalisation, it is associated, first of all, with the most general qualities of the given stimulus, but, during the period of the further development of the association reflex, its connection with the more particular qualities of the given stimulus, that is, the intensity of the sound and the number of vibrations, is consecutively established ; consequently, the association reflex inculcated is segregated from all other sound-stimulations.

It follows from the above that, as everyday observation and laboratory experiment show, every association reflex, being a reproduction of an ordinary reflex, is at first general, but, on further repetition, becomes gradually more and more particular—in other words, it is differentiated little by little, although, under certain conditions, it may be again generalised.

Let us assume that a man has been frightened by a gun-shot. He afterwards manifests fear at the sight of any gun and even at the sight of all firearms. But, in the course of time, having grown familiar with firearms, he becomes indifferent to them and fears only a loaded gun. A similar phenomenon may be observed in animals. Let us say, for instance, that a dog has been whipped. It is clear that after this it will turn to flee at the flourishing of anything which may happen to be held in the hand. However, in the course of time, having grown accustomed to threats, the dog will run only when threatened with the whip, and will not be frightened by, for instance, a paper fan.

Similarly, if investigations are made with colour stimuli, an association reflex inculcated to a certain colour stimulus appears, at first, to every colour stimulus and even to every stimulation by light, irrespective of its intensity. Only during repeated reproductions of the association reflex is it gradually differentiated, appearing only to the given colour stimulus, and, later, the differentiation reaches such a degree that the reflex is evoked only by coloured or white light of a certain intensity.[1]

Obviously, the same is true of association reflexes produced by other external stimuli.

If stimuli are applied under conditions of contiguity, for instance in

---

[1] Even in such animals as axolotls, which are the larval form of amblystoma, the differentiation of association-motor reflexes in regard to colours may be proved, as shown by investigations made in my laboratory by Dr. N. Studentzov ; and S. Michailov, a former collaborator in the Institute for the Study of Brain, has proved the differentiation of association reflexes to colour in a hermit-crab.

cases of cutaneous stimulations, the reflex inculcated is at first differentiated from all other stimulations, then from stimulations spatially more distant from, but qualitatively equal to, the initial stimulus, and, lastly, it is differentiated from qualitatively equal stimuli spatially more contiguous. The *modus operandi* of stimulations in the opposite side we shall not discuss here.

It is clear from the above that the differentiation of association reflexes always proceeds from the least similarity or the least contiguity to greater similarity and greater contiguity. Therefore, an association reflex is first of all differentiated from less similar stimulations and latest of all from more similar stimulations. Thus, for instance, an association reflex inculcated to a sound-stimulus is at first produced to every sound, only later to the sound of a certain instrument, and lastly to a particular sound of given intensity.[1]

The principle of differentiation is, as we have seen, easily demonstrated in experimental investigations of association-motor reflexes. On the basis of these investigations, this principle was orginally formulated by me as one of the fundamental laws of association-reflex activity.[2] Therefore, we deny the originally "specific" character of all conditioned reflexes, including the salivary. We have referred to this already.

But we must remember that the principle of differentiation is valid not only in respect of stimuli which excite reflexes, but also of the responsive aspect of the reflex, that is, of movements, for, at the beginning of the inculcation of a reflex, at least when the current is strong enough, the association reflex is, to a certain extent, more or less general in character when it appears, and only gradually, hand in hand with the fixation of the association reflex, does it become more and more local, until, finally, it is expressed in one defensive movement of the organ stimulated.

Further, it must be borne in mind that every differentiation of an association reflex is limited. As investigations of cutaneous and light-stimuli in my laboratory have shown, this limit corresponds approximately to the difference limen of sensation. Consequently, it must be unequal for qualitatively different stimuli, just as the difference limen of different sensations is not equal. We must also note that differentiation occurs more fully and easily when the experiments are always made with the same kind of stimulus of a given intensity and quality. On the contrary, if, in the course of the experiment, stimulation is effected by different stimuli, although they approximate in intensity or character, differentiation to a certain stimulus occurs with greater difficulty.

A further fact brought to light by the experiments made in our laboratory is that precision in differentiation is in direct dependence on the time which has passed between the primary stimulus and the associative

---

[1] Dr. E. A. Shevalev : *Dissertation* (my laboratory), St. Petersburg. See Dr. V. P. Protopopov : *Dissertation* (my laboratory), St. Petersburg.

[2] See V. Bechterev : *The Significance of the Investigation of the Motor Sphere,* etc.—*Russky Vratch,* nos. 33, 35, 36 ; 1909.

stimulus to be differentiated. Therefore, if a reflex is inculcated to a certain tone, for instance, the tone C, its differentiation from other tones will not be complete until the fundamental tone C, to which the association reflex was originally inculcated, begins to be repeated (Dr. Protopopov). This phenomenon, which has been observed in dogs, I have called " the behaviour process."[1]

The same may be proved in respect of cutaneous stimuli, the differentiation of which is more fully effected only by continuous repetition of the primary stimulus applied to a certain spot ; otherwise differentiation will not proceed to its full extent.

It is clear from the above that precision in the differentiation of external stimuli, to which an association reflex is being inculcated, from all other stimuli is, to a certain extent, a function of the time which passes between the stimuli to be differentiated.

We see from experiments with double stimuli—sound and light—as made in my laboratory (Dr. Platonov) that, after the inculcation of an association reflex to a composite stimulus, a more or less durable association reflex is produced by the action of one component of the stimulus—sound, while the action of the other component of the stimulus—light—is either ineffective or produces a less durable and a weaker association reflex. In precisely the same way, in experiments on new-born infants, the association of feeding with simultaneous sound (electric bell) and light (switching on an electric lamp) signalisation, gave analogous results. The groping movements of the lips, movements which appeared in the course of time to the composite associative stimulus (bell and light) could, after fixation of this association reflex, be evoked by each of the components of this composite stimulus, but the association reflex, in the form of groping movements of the lips, was much weaker and less durable when produced to light than when produced to sound. This fact indicates differentiation or analysis of composite stimuli and, as a result of this differentiation or analysis, it is possible to segregate one component of a composite stimulus from the other.[2]

Nevertheless, composite stimuli, after further numerous applications, are, also as a whole, differentiated from all other stimuli, including those particular stimuli of which they are composed. Consequently, the association reflex is ultimately produced only by the composite stimulus and not by any other stimuli—even by those which are components of the composite stimulus.

If we inculcate an association reflex to a composite stimulus, we succeed, as we have already said, in inculcating an association reflex fully differentiated from the association reflexes to its components, and these latter reflexes, which appeared during the period of differentiation, gradually

---

[1] *Translators' note :* The German translation (of 3rd ed.) has " the principle of induction." There may be a misprint.

[2] By the way, in the subjective world, processes of abstraction of a quality of a perception correspond to this process.

become extinct. In this case, before their extinction, the reflexes to the components are unequal in stability. The inhibition of the reflex to one of the components leads—in accordance with its greater or lesser stability —to the inhibition of the reflexes to the other components too, and also the reflex to the composite stimulus is weakened, and sometimes even disappears. On the other hand, the composite stimulus usually releases from inhibition the reflex to the components, just as a stronger reflex to a component weakens the weaker reflex to another component. Such are the results secured by a number of investigators (Eliason, Zeliony, Burmakin, Perelzweig, Kashenirnikova, Palladin—on animals, by the salivary method; Israelson, Platonov, Lukina, and others—on men, by the motor method; in the author's laboratory).[1]

Further, it must be noted that inhibitory influences also obey the same law of differentiation, in the sense that, if various stimuli have originally exerted an inhibitory influence on association reflexes produced by certain stimuli, a differentiated inhibitory force can, in the course of time, be inculcated from the same stimuli, this force acting only on the given association reflex produced by a certain stimulus.

Needless to say, influences which cause release from inhibition must also obey the general principle of differentiation, to which all stimuli which produce association reflexes are subjected.

Thus, the principle of differentiation means that, of the integration of external stimuli, one stimulus, as a result of an established connection, produces, or releases from inhibition, an association reflex, while all other stimuli suppress this reflex.

In other cases, a stimulus inhibits the given association reflex, while other stimuli release it from inhibition.

The fact that, at a certain period of the inculcation of an association

---

[1] We shall set down here the most important results of the investigations, the aim of which was the study of a composite colour stimulus in the form of sectors— white, red, and green for one group (seven persons), and red, green, and blue for another group (five persons). The topography of the colours was changed during the experiments. The results showed that, in the differentiation of the composite stimulus, the reflexes to the components were inhibited towards the end of the differentiation; but, when the differentiation was complete, the reflexes to the components were released from inhibition. This release from inhibition occurred in a definite order : the reflex to red was the first to appear, to white—the second, to green—the third, and to blue—the last, and these reflexes to the components were differentiated. On the other hand, reflexes to components disappeared earlier than reflexes to the composite stimulus, and their disappearance conforms to law in the following time order : red, white, blue, green. Further, the extinct reflex to the components was released from inhibition by the composite stimulus and by the other components. The power of the components to release the reflex from inhibition was also unequal. Green was the most powerful, then blue, white, and, least of all, red. On the extinction of all the reflexes to the components, the reflex to the composite colour stimulus was retained. But the extinct reflex to the composite stimulus could be released from inhibition by the components, while colours which were not included in the composite stimulus did not produce release from inhibition.

reflex, when the reflex is still undifferentiated in respect of the intensity of the stimulus, the intensity of the latter may be reduced to a certain minimum at which the reflex will, however, be still obtained, is related to the principle of differentiation, which our experiments have enabled us to formulate.

Thus, when an association reflex is inculcated, the stimulus evoking it may be gradually weakened until the stimulus reaches a certain minimum which may be called the lowest threshold of the association reflex.

This fact was observed by Hachet-Souplet later than by us in his dressage experiments and, in his opinion, corresponds to the fact that an habitual reaction is, generally speaking, manifested the more easily the oftener it is repeated.

By the way, Hachet-Souplet, in demonstrating this fact, used our method of applying an electric current to the dog's paw in training the animal to seize with its teeth and pull a leather strap at the moment when the current was applied. If the strap is attached to a dynamometer, it is possible to observe that, when the training is accomplished, the current may be weakened, while the animal's reaction will be of the same intensity.

In our arrangement of experiments in the production of association-motor reflexes, these facts may be still more simply proved and do not necessitate the training of the dog.[1]

In stimulations equal in intensity, but varying in their topography, as, for instance, the touching of different areas of the skin, the extent of the area stimulated may be reduced to a certain minimum, which may be called the association-reflex threshold of least extent.

In connection with the law of differentiation, we must not overlook the opposite effect, in the form of irradiation or generalisation of association reflexes, which is usually observed in their inhibition.

We have already stated that association reflexes proceed, in their development, from the general to the particular. On being established, they are general, and then gradually differentiate. On the contrary, in the case of inhibition, the differentiated association reflex gradually loses differentiation and is generalised, that is, arrives back at the initial state when it serves as a response not only to a definite stimulus, but to a number of dissimilar stimuli, although of the same kind, and, on greater generalisation, as a response even to a number of stimuli different in kind. This generalisation is a result not only of inner inhibition, but also of external inhibition, and is easily proved both by observation and experiment.

It is well known that an alarmed animal fears everything : both what is really dangerous and what is perfectly innocuous.

In experiments in association reflexes, the same fact is proved with especial clearness, for every differentiated reflex, whatever the cause of

[1] See V. Bechterev : *The Application of the Association-Motor Reflex in the Treatment of Psychic and Nervous Diseases—Obozrenie Psychiatrii*, no. 8, 1910. Also his *The Application of the Association-Motor Reflex in the Investigation of Simulation—Russky Vratch*, no. 14, 1912.

its inhibition, is inevitably accompanied, at the period of incomplete inhibition, by loss of differentiation, and, consequently, in the initial phase of inhibition, it is evoked by a stimulus of any intensity, and, on further inhibition, by any stimulus.

Laboratory experiment shows that the association reflex, during its inhibition, loses differentiation gradually, and recapitulates, as it were, all the stages of its development, but in reverse order. Thus, for instance, when a differentiated sound-association reflex is being inhibited, it is at first obtained to sounds which approximate in intensity and quality, then to sounds more remote in intensity. It still retains differentiation to sounds different in quality, but later loses differentiation to every sound. The same is true of cutaneous and other stimulations until the reflex becomes completely extinct. Thus, in the period of its inhibition, the association reflex passes from the particular to the general.

The same phenomena may be observed also in regard to the strength of the association reflex. At the period of inculcation, the association reflex is originally weak, and only in the course of time is it strengthened, to a certain extent, side by side with differentiation, while, at the period of inhibition, it gradually weakens more and more, and also its latent period is usually prolonged.

It is clear from the foregoing that the process of development or excitation and of fixation of the association reflex is accompanied by its differentiation, while the process of inhibition is connected with its generalisation or irradiation.

Moreover, the experiments of Krotkova, Tchegodayeva, and Dr. Schneerson, who have worked under my supervision, leave no doubt that the association reflex, if it is not evoked in the course of a certain time, is not only fixed, but also automatically differentiated without any exercise. I call this process " latent differentiation."[1] Thus, the state of the reflex is determined not only by exercise, but also by its age. This is in accord with the fact that, for intsance, after the fatiguing of our muscles, we are not able to continue exercises in the previous direction, but, after a day or two, when we again take up the unaccustomed work, we are often surprised at our success. I have frequently observed this phenomenon in myself.

We know that Ebbinghaus, who applied the method of learning meaningless syllables, came to the conclusion that the results are better on the following day than immediately after learning. Dr. Lazursky, who used the same method in the laboratory supervised by me, obtained similar results.

[1] Schneerson : *The Influence of Personal Efforts and Concentration on the Association Reflex—Vestnik Psychiatrii,* 1919.

CHAPTER XXXVIII

Selective generalisation. The principle of synthesis or combination of association reflexes.

IN addition to generalisation, which is invariably associated with inhibition of the association reflex, we must distinguish selective generalisation, which may occur at the period of development and fixation of the association reflex. The principle of selective generalisation may be formulated thus : every association reflex, at the period of its inculcation, can be associated not only with one definite stimulus, but with two or several stimuli by which it is constantly produced, while other stimuli, because of their inhibition, do not evoke the association reflex.

Everyday observation affords thousands of examples of this law. Let us, however, turn to the example we have already cited several times : the dog which has once been struck with a whip. Needless to say, the dog which has been struck with a whip and is more or less indifferent to any threat, immediately starts away at the mere sight of the whip. But if the same dog is struck with a cane, it will run away at the sight of the stick as well as of the whip. It is clear that here the association reflex, originally differentiated to one stimulus, is then generalised under the influence of a new stimulus of a different kind, but it is generalised in a selective manner, for now it is a responsive movement to two stimuli different in kind, while to other stimuli the reflex is not manifested. We stretch out our hand to take food, to examine a given object, and lastly to discover the source of a sound. We produce the same tone in G sharp and A flat. We turn to flee at the roar of a wild beast and at the sight of a snake crawling towards us. We listen to the howling of the wind, to a tuneful melody, and to the words of him with whom we are conversing, etc. In all these cases we are concerned with the principle of selective generalisation.

This principle of selective generalisation is also easily proved in laboratory experiments. Let us assume that you inculcate an association reflex to the tone C by its coincidence with the electro-cutaneous stimulation of the sole or of the fingers. After some time, you will see that the tone C evokes the association reflex, even without the electro-cutaneous stimulus, while no other tone evokes the reflex. But you can associate, simultaneously, not only the tone C with the electro-cutaneous stimulus, but, for instance, also the tone F. In this case, you will obtain an association reflex to the tones C and F, but you will not obtain it to the tone D or to the tone E or to any other tone. Thus we secure selective generalisation in laboratory experiment.

The original synthesis may be conditioned even by the character of the stimulation. If two stimuli are applied simultaneously and in the same posture, they naturally evoke a reflex common to both stimuli, and, consequently, on repetition of one of the stimuli, the same reflex is evoked, although quantitatively weaker. This has been proved in my laboratory by Dr. Platonov's experiments. On the other hand, the generalisation of different, but approximate, stimuli into one common stimulus appears to be possible. This process may be compared with the exceedingly interesting experiment in composite portraiture—an experiment which has succeeded as a result of the inventive faculty of the English scientist, Francis Galton, and the perseverance of Professor Bowditch, both of whom succeeded in obtaining on the photographic plate racial types and even types derived from the same face with different expressions. Under such conditions, traits common to the individuals photographed are more strongly imprinted, while rarer traits are shown less clearly, and individual features photographed once only do not appear at all. Thus, on the photograph there is a type which resembles each individual, but is nobody's portrait in particular.

To obtain such photographs, it is, of course, necessary that the lighting should be always the same, that the light should always affect the same area of the plate, that the exposure should be of the same duration in all cases, and should be a certain fraction of the time necessary to secure a clear photograph. As our retina with its rhodopsin is also a photographic plate or a similar apparatus, and in the occipital area of the cortex we have, as it were, the reproduction of the retina, and since, too, there is, in both cases, the same light-energy, it is quite natural, in this case, to hit on an analogy between the physico-chemical process which occurs on the photographic plate and the process on the retina, and, consequently, also on the cortical retina—the more so as, in both cases, there are physico-chemical processes.

Therefore, it is natural that an impression of types similarly occurs in the retina and the brain and that this impression makes possible the reproduction, with greater ease, of those parts of similar stimuli which are most often repeated, and not the reproduction, at least not with the same ease, of those parts of the stimuli which are repeated not oftener than once, twice, or thrice. One must not think, however, that the process in the cerebral cortex is the same as the photographic in the form of an impression or of a cliché, but it is indubitable that some elements of the retina are more often stimulated, others less often, and, consequently, that the fibres of the visual path leading to the striated area are also, some more and others less, stimulated. Therefore, it is quite natural that those neurons which have been more frequently excited are more capable than others of the reproduction of the stimulation under the appropriate impulses.

To this correspond, in language, the so-called common names—such as tree, horse, man, etc.—which we use at every step.

The principles of selective generalisation and synthesis are exceedingly important in life conditions, for these principles unite diverse stimuli in as much as the latter evoke the same responses, either positive or negative. Besides, our choice of acceptable and unacceptable objects as stimuli is based on the principle of generalisation.

It is necessary to keep in mind that differentiation and selective generalisation, as also analysis and synthesis, are those fundamental principles which condition the development of association-reflex activity in general, for, if the inculcation of every association reflex is inseparably connected with its differentiation and analysis, it is natural that differentiation and analysis may be manifested not only to one stimulus, but to several consecutively or simultaneously, and this is the characteristic of selective generalisation or synthesis.

And, indeed, I have shown in a special paper, that, in man's individual life, all special association reflexes, such as the inherited-organic or instincts, orientation, expressive movements, speech, and personal reflexes, obey, in their development, the principles of differentiation and selective generalisation from the earliest days of man's existence, and thus the way is paved, on the one hand, for variation in the manifestations of association-reflex activity and, on the other, for the establishment of the interrelation between various external influences and the individual, through the mediation of a common reaction associated with them.

The principle of selective generalisation is easily traced in the development of language also. According to Romanes, one of Darwin's grandsons called the duck " qua," and denoted water by the same word. Then the denomination was extended to all birds, all winged beings, and also to all fluids. Even the French sou, the American dollar, and other coins bearing an eagle were also called " qua." Thus such different objects as bird, angel, pond, river, medal, shilling, and others were denoted by one and the same word. Dr. Hun (*The Monthly Journal of Psychological Medicine*, 1868) tells of a girl who invented a language of her own and taught it to her little brother : " papa " and " mama " separately denoted father and mother, but combined into " papa-mama " denoted church, Prayer Book, prayer, and other religious acts, only because the child saw the parents always together going to church. " Dar odo " meant : send for the horse, or pen and ink-stand, for a written order was usually sent for the horse. " Bau " denoted bishop and soldier, because of the bright clothing of each. One of my children saw a crawfish in the water and called it " crawfish," according to my instruction, but when a piece of paper was thrown into the water and floated on it, he called it also " crawfish." I could cite a multitude of such examples from my observation. Here purely external indications serve as objects for selective generalisation by means of the same verbal denotations. However, we cannot deny that, in this denomination of different objects by a single vocal sign, the child's lack of adequate verbal expressions may play a rôle.

We know that metaphors in the language of adults are merely borrowings, because of the absence of special, appropriate denotations, from denotations applicable to motor and other reflexes. What are, for instance, such graphic expressions as : " to embrace all aspects of a subject," " to grasp an idea," " to keep to the point " but descriptive denotations borrowed, because there are no special denotations, from motor reflexes of a certain kind.

Needless to say, speech is not a result of individual creativeness, but of social life without which it would never have developed. Whitney is right when he says that speech is not a personal achievement, but a public institution, that nothing we say is language until acknowledged and made current by others, and that the development of speech is effected by the community acting together. Therefore, metaphors are not a result of individual creativeness, but of social life, which accepts the metaphor as one of the forms of language.

The principle of selective generalisation is often supplemented by the principle of generalisation, which we have mentioned above. Thus, for instance, in men's attitude towards a certain profession or group, the principle of generalisation is often manifested side by side with selective generalisation. Thus, some individuals have a positive or a negative attitude to a certain nation and are guided therein by personal contacts. It sometimes happens also that an event, which has produced a favourable or an unfavourable impression and has been experienced during social intercourse with a representative of a certain profession or of some social group, causes us to transfer the attitude corresponding to the reaction we have experienced on to other members of the given profession or even to those of a whole social group.

Such phenomena are manifested in the animal world also. According to Franklin, a little dog, which a policeman had saved from a newfoundland, afterwards idolised all policemen. It is also well known that some dogs, simply because they have witnessed animals being slaughtered, hate all butchers.

Processes of selective generalisation, like all other processes of association-reflex activity, are a result of life experience. Therefore, they are dissimilar in different individuals, not only in respect of the speed with which the processes develop, but also, to a certain extent, of their degree and character. A specialist will discover details where a layman will not notice any, just as the former makes a generalisation of some details, while the layman is not capable of doing so, etc. Let us also note that the process under discussion is directly connected with concentration, which is at first directed towards the stimulating object as a whole, but, on repetition of the stimulation, the object's separate parts also become stimuli and arouse concentration.

One and the same, or approximately equal, reaction is evoked by the simultaneous influence of two or several stimuli which have common details, while dissimilar details produce different reactions. This results in selective generalisation, which is based on experience.

Let us take two fluids. Let them be contained in vessels of the same size and shape, be equal in quantity, and, at the same time, have similar qualities, but let them differ from each other in colour. In this case, colour is a stimulus which will produce a special reaction, and this is the beginning of differentiation, but in every other respect the reaction will be the same. It is quite obvious that if, in the previous example, we had two fluids the same in all respects, including colour, differentiation would be impossible ; on the contrary, if both objectshad not one similar feature, selective generalisation would be impossible.

During the investigation of association reflexes, some other aspects of the principle in question were discovered, and among them what may be called synthesis or the process of addition or combination of stimuli.

In this case, we have the phenomenon in which two stimuli, different in kind and always simultaneously repeated, act as a whole and ultimately evoke a certain association-reaction, which neither of the separate, associative stimuli evokes or, rather, which either of them may evoke, but with lesser intensity.

The process of addition of stimuli is manifested everywhere in everyday life. Thus, a chord or even a certain temporal combination of sounds acts on us in a certain manner, while the individual sounds do not produce this reaction. In precisely the same way, the influence of white is different from that of any one of its component colours separately. The influence of grey is different from that of white and black taken separately. This principle is experimentally proved thus :

Let us assume that you inculcate an association reflex, as has been done in our laboratory, to two stimuli different in kind—sound and light. After some time, you obtain a reflex to sound and to light, and one is more stable than the other. Thus, if an association reflex is inculcated to some composite stimulus, the association reflex thus inculcated will be at first obtained also to its components. It is true that both the strength and the stability of these association reflexes are not equal. One of them becomes predominant, as it were, over the other in significance, in the sense that the association reflex to one of the stimuli can be evoked for a longer time than can the association reflex to the other stimulus. Nevertheless the intrinsic character of this phenomenon, according to which the association reflex is evoked by both components of the composite stimulus to which the association reflex has been originally inculcated, is not restricted by the unequal stability of these " partial " reflexes. But, during further inculcation of the association reflex in the above-mentioned example, the reflex is obtained only to the combination of sound and light, and no reflex whatever is obtained to sound or light acting separately (Dr. Platonov). Thus, addition of two stimuli of different kinds in regard to the given association reflex is obtained. Laboratory experiment shows that, at the period of inculcation of an association reflex to the simultaneous influence of two stimuli, when they begin to evoke an association reflex, the latter is always stronger than either of the reflexes obtained to the components.

CHAPTER XXXIX

The principle of substitution or compensation. Discussion and examples. Phenomena of symbolism. Gestures and other expressive movements as symbols. Speech symbolism.

OF the particularly important manifestations of association-reflex activity, we must call attention also to the principle of substitution or compensation, in other words, commutation, a principle which obtains in the most varied phenomena of this activity.[1] Thus, even in regard to the manifestation of muscular energy, we come across the principle of substitution.

The muscles of our body constitute a great working-power. If we measure separately the power of the flexors of each arm in the different joints, the power of the flexors of each leg also in the different joints, the power of the flexors of the neck and back separately, and then separately measure in the same way the power of the extensors of the arms and legs, the power of the efferent and afferent muscles and, lastly, the power of the rotators, the total power manifested by all these groups of muscles when contracting is enormous, and the work performed by all these muscular groups is colossal.

However, the organism cannot use all the muscles simultaneously : it uses them at different times. But even in those muscles which work in co-operation, the power of the muscles is not summated, but is appropriately distributed among the muscles participating in the work.

If we successively measure the grasping power of one hand and then the grasping power of the other, we shall see that the grasping power of both acting simultaneously by no means corresponds to the sum of the grasping powers of each hand separately, as one might think, but in reality is much smaller.

If, in addition to the grasping activity of both hands, we simultaneously bring the leg muscles also into action, we thereby further reduce the grasping power of the hands. The same may be observed in regard to all other work.

Obviously, there is here a distribution of nervous energy, which, by flowing towards one muscular apparatus, produces greater muscular force than when the same energy is distributed among several muscular apparatus, and this, in turn, is conditioned by the fact that the enhanced afflux of

---

[1] The principle of substitution is certainly manifested in inorganic nature also. Thus, to the principle of substitution are referable : the theory of equivalents, on the one hand, and, on the other, various chemical reactions based on substitution. According to Dumas, all bodies containing the same number of equivalents, combined in the same manner, and having the same chemical qualities, belong to one and the same chemical type. In complex chemical unions, as is known, various elements may be consecutively replaced by others and, in spite of these substitutions, the complex molecule remains intact. Even when a fortuitous group is substituted for a simple atom, the general structure of the system remains. (A. Grekov : *The Theory of Chemical Types—Dictionary*, ed. Brockhaus and Ephron, vol. XXXVIII, pp. 222–293, 1903.)

nervous energy to one muscular apparatus is compensated by the suppression of the energy in all other directions.

This principle of compensation is based on the equivalence of certain quanta of various kinds of energy, and, as a result, each quantum may be replaced by an equivalent quantum of other kinds of energy.

In association reflexes, the principle of substitution is manifested everywhere. First of all, the very inculcation of association reflexes is based on this principle, for the secondary stimulus here becomes reflexogenous, like the primary stimulus. The same principle also obtains whenever there is opposition to the manifestation of association reflexes.

Let us assume that an association reflex to cutaneous stimulations has been inculcated in a dog. This reflex is, through exercise, differentiated to a certain minimum of the cutaneous surface. If the appropriate cortical centre is then destroyed, we see that the association reflex is not produced in the earlier cutaneous area, but appears to stimulations of neighbouring and more distant cutaneous areas, and is less differentiated.

Through further exercise, it is possible again to secure a certain differentiation or limitation of the territory which produces the association reflex, but only within a certain limit. Thus, in regard to the reflex inculcated earlier, the original cutaneous area is compensated by the territory which surrounds it.

On the other hand, if, after the inculcation of a reflex in a dog, we remove the corresponding efferent or responsive area of the cerebral cortex, the association reflex, as has been shown by investigations made in my laboratory, does not occur in the extremity in which it has been inculcated, but becomes more general, and is manifested by movements of other parts of the body. In the course of time, however, on further revival of the reflex, it is again limited, and is manifested only in the paw on the opposite side.

Consequently, here again we have compensation or substitution, for one movement replaces another which has been lost.

Similarly, we know from observation how often an impeded movement is replaced by others.

This principle is manifested with particular clearness in speech movements, for every word, inhibited for some reason or other at the moment of speaking, is immediately replaced by another which is analogous, or by a number of words which explain the word temporarily inhibited.

On the other hand, when an orator speaks, he usually suppplements his speech by movements of the trunk, by facial expressions, and gesticulation. When a man cannot express everything in words, or when he cannot orally communicate certain necessary facts to someone, he has recourse to movements which take the form of writing. If a singer cannot reproduce the words of the song, he replaces them by meaningless sounds. If one in the mood for singing may not, because of the particular circumstances, sing aloud the words of the song, he replaces them by voiceless reproduction of the tones or by appropriate movements of the hands. If a man moving forward encounters an obstacle, he substitutes for this movement such movements as surmount the obstacle. If a man is forced to hold something and his hands are not sufficient for the task, he holds it, if possible, even with his teeth, etc.

In a word, in reflexes both of aggression and defence, when it is impossible to bring one of the organs into action, other organs unimpeded in their movements are inevitably brought into action.

This principle of compensation or substitution is familiar also in the pathology of cerebral functions and is manifested with special clearness in the common neuroses, for instance. It is, without doubt, a general principle in regard to nervous activity, but perhaps nowhere is this principle manifested so clearly as in regard to association reflexes, which, in the higher animals, are realised with the participation of the cerebral cortex.

CHAPTER XL

Phenomena of symbolism as expressions of the principle of substitution. Symbolism in the cultural life of nations.

WE find the principle of substitution everywhere in symbolic reflexes. Both gestures and verbal symbols serve as substitutes for other reflexes. Thus, we make a gesture instead of performing the complete action (a threat instead of an attack, blowing a kiss instead of giving a real kiss, etc.).

Similarly, verbal symbols, as signs, substitute descriptions of objects, actions, or states. Lastly, in speech also, we constantly come across the principle of substitution. Thus, to avoid detailed description, we refer to examples which are more or less familiar to everybody. When, for some reason, the utterance of a certain word or phrase is inhibited, we immediately have recourse to another mode of verbal expression, to an allegorical form, or to a descriptive mode of expression, etc.

The symbol is one of the important forms of the manifestations of association-reflex activity.

By symbols we understand those forms of association-reflex activity in which often even an accidental, or sometimes an extremely transformed, characteristic or part of an object, a phenomenon, or, in general, an action or movement, becomes a sign or symbol, which evokes a reaction equivalent to the reaction evoked by the whole object, phenomenon, action or movement. Thus, a child is frightened even by two fingers which project like horns on a hand approaching him, for this movement symbolises butting. It is sufficient to make a threatening grimace before an infant and utter sounds reminiscent, for instance, of a dog's barking, and he will cry. The same effect can be produced by a sound resembling the roar of a wild beast. Thus, the influence of symbolic stimuli is often identical with that of the real stimuli for which they are substitues.

Symbolic reflexes may be divided into verbal (speech, exclamations, writing), gesticulatory, and signal (signalling, for instance, on railways, on ships, etc. ; flags, pennants, etc.).

In the life of an adult, all gesticulation is based on symbolism, for every gesture is really a reproduction or sign of a certain movement. Thus the straightening of the index finger in a certain direction is part of a poking movement at an object ; a kiss is a sign of intimacy ; embraces are a sign of friendly relations ; shrugging the shoulders is a sign of helplessness, etc.[1]

Expressive movements also are signs or symbols of various inner processes and states, which, therefore, evoke a corresponding reaction in other people.

For instance, a cat comes to get food from its master. We know that it ingratiates itself by rubbing itself against something. But it ingratiates

---

[1] Those who wish to become more closely acquainted with the rôle of gestures as symbols I refer to my paper mentioned above : *The Biological Significance of Expressive Movements—Vestnik Znania*, 1912, and sep. ed.

itself not only by rubbing against its master's feet, but performs the same movements in regard to inanimate objects, for instance it rubs its body against a neighbouring post, or even against some projection, and performs the same bodily movements as when rubbing itself against its master's feet. Is not this symbolic of ingratiation?

When a turkey-cock puffs, spreads his wings, fans his tail, and so struts among a dozen turkey-hens absolutely submissive to him, is not that a kind of symbolism? When the woodcock, during the courtship period, performs strange bodily movements and utters peculiar sounds before copulation, is not that symbolism? When a man, who hates his enemy, bares his underdeveloped tusk even when he does not directly see him, and looks askance at him, is not that symbolism?

Thus, expressive movements, which, without doubt, have originally been purposeful, attain symbolic significance in many cases and thus denote just a certain state of the organism or its attitude to the environment, and this is doubtlessly useful in the social intercourse of animals, as human speech is useful in the social intercourse of men.

In human life, all the arts are based, to a considerable degree, on symbolism, manifested by some artists to a greater, by others to a lesser, extent.

Side by side with gesticulatory and facial-expressive symbolisation we may place tonal or musical symbolisation, colour and emblem symbolisation, and also pictorial symbolisation, to the extent to which such symbolisation may replace human speech.

Everybody knows that the boom of the cannon in Leningrad at 12 noon, the whistle of a steamer or a train, the ringing of a church bell, the factory hooter are all examples of sound-symbolisation with the same significance as human speech.

Poetry and singing supplement human speech by the picturesqueness of their presentation and by musicalness, and thus co-operate in the complication of verbal symbolism. Lastly, complex musical works, too, express in sound a correspondence to general mimico-somatic states, reproduce life and nature, and so are symbolisation, which, it is true, has a distant similarity to speech, but, in any case, music can, and really often does, denote symbolically what otherwise is expressed by speech.

Let us take any funeral march or, for instance, Tchaikovsky's *Autumn Song*. Does it not express in sound—and perhaps even better than words can—what may be expressed in words?

Further, painting and sculpture also are manifestations of symbolism in as far as they reproduce the general mimico-somatic state, the life, and the activity of human beings.

Lastly, architecture also serves, to a certain extent, as a symbolic sign of a certain aim and as a reflection of a general mimico-somatic state which the architect wished to express.

It is necessary to note that symbolism, nevertheless, reaches its highest point of development in human speech, which consists of signs or symbols not only of various objects and phenomena, of the interrelations of these objects and phenomena, and of our relations to them, but also of our actions and states. Setting aside special forms of symbolism in speech, for instance in poetry, it is necessary to keep the following in view : whether the word is an echoism—for instance : " skripet " (to creak), " pilit " (to saw), " svistat " (to whistle), etc.—or whether its origin is due to compensation or substitution, which gives it its figurative meaning—for instance " svistnut "[1] (to whistle) in the sense of " to strike " ; " vzdut " (to inflate) in the sense of " to flog," etc.—whether it is due to differentiation of the original echoistic roots—for instance " razuchabisty " (rutty), from the echoistic " uch," " uchab "—or to their welding in the sense of a combination of two or more roots in one whole—for instance " mirvolit " (to be indulgent ; *mir*—peace, *volya*—will), " zemnovodnie " (amphibians ; *zemlya*—earth, *voda*—water), " kosogor " (a slope ; *kosoi*—slanting, *gora*—mountain), etc.—or to symbolisation when the denotation of one characteristic part becomes a substitute for the denotation of the whole—for instance " zubtchatka " (a cog-wheel ; *zub*—tooth)—or, lastly, whether the word is a borrowing from a foreign language—for instance " inzhener " (engineer), " muzika " (music), etc. —in all these and other cases, words are sound-signs or written signs, which are substitutes for objects or phenomena, for the interrelations of these, for actions or states, for our relation to objects, etc.[2]

It is not difficult to see that, from the manner in which they are acquired by learning, speech reflexes are real association reflexes, but, as a normal child learns to speak at such an early age that he cannot give an account of it himself, we shall take as an example the famous blind-deaf-mute, Helen Keller, who began to learn to speak at a considerably later age, and could give an account of her learning. This is what she writes about herself.

" When I had played with it (the doll) a little while, Miss Sullivan slowly spelled into my hand the word ' d-o-l-l.' I was at once interested in this finger play and tried to imitate it. When I finally succeeded in making the letters correctly, I was flushed with childish pleasure and pride. Running downstairs to my mother, I held up my hand and made the letters for doll. I did not know that I was spelling a word or even that words existed ; I was simply making my fingers go in monkey-like imitation. In the days that followed I learned to spell in this uncomprehending way a great many words, among them pin, hat, cup, and a few verbs like sit, stand, and walk. . . .

---

[1] *Translators' note :* Russian infinitives have two forms. When one ends in -*at* and the other in -*nut*, the former denotes continuous state or action.

[2] The particularly subtle character of symbolic speech reflexes appears in the circumstance that a change of even one letter may sometimes radically alter the character of the entire content of a complex symbolic reaction and have a completely different influence on other individuals. Thus, for instance, in a telegram stating : " Our father passed away," the substitution of the word " your " for " our " may ruin the life of a family or, on the contrary, affect it only slightly.

" One day, while I was playing with my new doll, Miss Sullivan put my big rag doll into my lap also, spelled ' d-o-l-l ' and tried to make me understand that that ' d-o-l-l ' applied to both. Earlier in the day we had had a tussle over the words ' m-u-g ' and ' w-a-t-e-r.' Miss Sullivan had tried to impress it upon me that ' m-u-g ' is mug and that ' w-a-t-e-r ' is water, but I persisted in confounding the two. . . . She brought me my hat, and I knew I was going out into the warm sunshine. This thought, if a wordless sensation may be called a thought, made me hop and skip with pleasure.

" We walked down the path to the well-house, attracted by the fragrance of the honeysuckle with which it was covered. Someone was drawing water and my teacher placed my hand under the spout. As the cool stream gushed over one hand she spelled into the other the word water. . . . I stood still, my whole attention fixed upon the motions of her fingers. Suddenly . . . the mystery of language was revealed to me. I knew then that ' w-a-t-e-r ' meant the wonderful cool something that was flowing over my hand. . . .

" Everything had a name. . . . I saw everything with the strange, new sight that had come to me. . . .

" I learned a great many new words that day. I do not remember what they all were ; but I do know that mother, father, sister, teacher were among them—words that were to make the world blossom for me."[1]

This is a simple, but lucid, description of learning to speak. It is clear from this how the word as a sign or symbol is associated with its object, how the process of generalisation occurs when the same word " doll " is applied to two similar, though somewhat different, objects, and how differentiation of the verbal association reflex occurs in the example of " mug " and " water." When the first experience proved insufficient, special life experience at the well—the water flowing on the hand—was necessary finally to establish differentiation of objects and of their verbal symbols : " mug " and " water."

It is not difficult to see from this example that not only the development of human speech, but also all education is based on the development of association reflexes subjected to processes of generalisation and differentiation.

Needless to say, the reflexological principle of the association of the word as sign with objects and actions, a principle which Miss Sullivan applied so successfully, is applicable not only to physically defective children, such as the famous Helen Keller, but also to mentally defective children. On the other hand, normal children also, even before the school age, can be taught, in the course of their games, to associate words with objects and actions. To achieve this, it is sufficient to associate every toy and every play-activity with a written verbal denotation.

[1] *Translators' note :* Helen Keller : *The Story of My Life*, p. 22, Hodder and Stoughton, London, 1911.

z

All assimilation[1] in movements is based on the process of symbolism. When a word fails the speaker and is inhibited, it is replaced by gestures, which, when there is question of the substitution of the name of an object, are assimilations to the touching of the object, and which, when there is question of the inhibition of a word which should denote a certain action, are assimilations to the action. When an analogous reaction is represented by an organ not appropriate to the action, or by the appropriate organ, but by a different method, that is, the method of assimilation, compensation is, in these cases, supplemented by symbolism. Thus, in speech, in addition to the above-mentioned cases, metaphor, allegory, and, partly, hyperbole belong to this order of phenomena. Music also is based, to a considerable extent, on assimilation, still more so pantomime and, partly, dancing.

We also find, in the cultural life of nations, symbolism in the guise of flags, semaphores, and certain kinds of colour signalling, in regalia, decorations, all kinds of insignia, uniforms, the rituals of law and religion, graphic and plastic art, literature, especially poetry, and even traditions. In a word we find symbolism everywhere. It fills and permeates our life.

In some cases, even natural objects become symbols of certain phenomena or states. Everybody knows, for instance, the so-called " language of flowers " (a red rose symbolises passionate love ; a white lily, virginity ; etc.). Further, colours are also symbols. Thus, white denotes purity ; yellow, treachery ; etc. Even a simple line is not devoid of a certain symbolism : a wavy line is a symbol of gracefulness, a zig-zag line of abruptness and lack of balance, etc.

Perhaps we cannot better explain the significance of symbolism than by a concrete example. Let us take the national flag. What does it denote, or, more precisely, what does it personify ? In this context, the words of the well-known American social worker and minister, Mr. Lepp, in his article *The Creators of the Flag*, are admirably suited to our purpose. What is a flag, according to Lepp ? Let us express it in his own words. Let the flag itself speak, as it were :

" I am not a flag ; oh no ! I am only its shadow. I am everything you make me, and nothing more. I am your belief in yourselves and in what a nation can be. I live an ever-changing life—a life of passions and moods, of a fluttering heart, of straining muscles.

" Sometimes, in the pride of my spirit, I am strong when people pull together in collective work and clear a forward path. Sometimes I droop and hang inert, when I have no aim to pursue and cynically fête the coward. Sometimes I am boisterous, gay, and full of that self-confidence which censures others severely. But always, always I am what you hope to be and what you have the courage to strive for. I am the song and the fear, the struggle, the panic, and the ennobling hope. I am the working day of the weakest of men and the gorgeous dream of the boldest. I am the constitution and the tribunal, the law and the law-giver, the

[1] *Translators' note :* To be taken in the sense of making similar or being similar.

soldier and the ironclad, the layer of sewers, the crossing-sweeper, the cook, the lawyer, and the clerk. I am the battle of yesterday and the mistake of to-morrow. I am the crowd who work not knowing what impels them to create. I am the germ of hopes and ideas, and the premeditated revolutionary aim. I am what you make me, and nothing more. I wave before your eyes like a bright, coloured ray, as a symbol of your selves, as a pictorial idea of that great whole which constitutes a nation."[1]

It is clear from the above that symbolisation, which is sometimes wide generalisation, as in the foregoing case, and which plays a special part in the cultural life of nations, may be most diverse in its nature. Symbolism may be subdivided into expressive-motor, verbal (including letters and ciphers), general-motor, sound-, object-, colour-, light-symbolism, and others.

This important sphere of reflexology is accessible, of course, to experimental investigation also, especially in respect of verbal symbols and expressive movements. Concerning the investigations of these problems in my laboratory, I shall refer to the above-mentioned paper by my disciple, Professor Astvatzaturov, in regard to the speed of verbal symbols (*Dissertation*, St. Petersburg), to Dr. Vasilyeva's paper comparing the excitations of association reflexes by appropriate stimuli or their verbal symbols (in *Obozrenie Psychiatrii*), to Dr. Fedorin's paper on slips of the tongue, and to my own investigations of expressive movements and gestures in *The Biological Development of Expressive Movements* (*Vestnik Znania*, 1912), to investigations by V. Osipova, Dernova-Yermolenko, and others.

It is difficult to overestimate the significance of symbolism in life. Apart from its special significance in the development of association-reflex activity, it conforms to the principle of economy, a principle of great importance in the activity of the organism in general and in its expenditure of energy derived from the environment.

[1] *American Bulletin*, no. 25, February, 1918.

Translators' note : Translated from the Russian. Repeated efforts to obtain the periodical have, unfortunately, been in vain.

CHAPTER XLI

The principle of inertia or set in association reflexes. The verification of the principle of inertia in respect of association reflexes under various conditions. The verification of the same principle by the experimental method in respect of movements personal in character and of slips of the tongue.

EVERY association reflex, like every movement, conforms to the law of inertia, and, if the conditions were appropriate, this reflex, once developed, would be indefinitely sustained. If the association reflex is not indefinitely sustained, but gradually weakens and finally disappears, that is only because, on every repetition, inhibitory conditions develop in the nervous system. However, individual differences must be reckoned with here.

Thus, in some cases, as Dr. Vasilyeva has proved in my laboratory, the association reflex of the movement of the sole, a reflex established at one attempt in one of the subjects experimented on, was afterwards evoked a countless number of times, and could be inhibited only by artificially created conditions. The same happened in the case of one of the subjects experimented on by Dr. Platnov (*Dissertation*, St. Petersburg), who worked in my laboratory. In other cases, as, for instance, in the investigations of another collaborator of mine, Dr. Greker, an association reflex in one of the subjects could be inculcated only after an unusually large number of associations. Lastly, in some cases it may be completely and permanently inhibited.[1]

All this means that inhibitory conditions are different in different persons and, in some cases, are so strong as to be almost insuperable, while, in other cases, although not quite absent, they do not preponderate over the exciting conditions. The latter fact is usually observed during the inculcation of association reflexes. Therefore, a reflex, once evoked, may be reproduced *ad lib.* like an ordinary reflex.

Strong inhibition of association reflexes, as well as greater promptness in their appearance and greater stability, may be artificially produced by introducing into the organism toxic substances which exert a direct influence on the brain or even by employing certain physical measures, for instance, phototherapy,[2] bromides, etc. To produce greater stability, we artificially create in the organism those conditions under which the association reflex, when once inculcated, is evoked, under ordinary conditions, a greater number of times than usual.

But also, in the manifestations of all reflexes, the limitation of the extent of the movement is due exclusively to physical causes, on the one hand, and to physiological, on the other.

Among these physiological causes, as in all other physiological acts, we have not only activating, but also inhibitory, conditions. The moment

---

[1] In these cases, it is preferable, in the investigation of association reflexes, to use respiratory movements, which, in general, are exceedingly sensitive in respect of the manifestation of association reflexes.

[2] S. A. Brustein (my laboratory) : *Dissertation*, St. Petersburg.

at which the reflex reaches its maximal strength coincides with the greatest preponderance of the activating over the inhibitory forces. After this, the inhibitory conditions begin to prevail over the activating, and the reflex begins to disappear.[1]

But it is clear that, if it were possible for us to remove the inhibitory conditions, the reflex, in accordance with the law of inertia, would, like all other movements, continue indefinitely, at least until it encountered purely physical obstacles.

However, the principle of inertia is not merely a theoretical doctrine. It is frequently verified in practical life in the case of association reflexes. Thus, if one pushes a door forcibly and the door is suddenly opened, one inevitably falls forward, as a result of inertia. If one is running, one cannot stop abruptly. If one is running with very great speed, one falls forward, when one is compelled to stop suddenly. If one is running and trips over something, one inevitably falls. If one sets one's hand with force against something, the hand inevitably plunges forward when the obstacle is suddenly removed. If one rapidly knocks with one's finger on the table, one cannot desist immediately on hearing an agreed signal, but inevitably performs some superfluous movements. If one raises a weight with one's foot or hand and the weight suddenly falls, the foot or hand inevitably jerks upwards. If one is walking on even ground and does not notice a depression on the path, one inevitably lurches. If, on the contrary, under the same conditions, there is an elevation on the path, one stumbles. The same happens if, while climbing stairs, one encounters a step protruding beyond the others. Lastly, in making a speech, the speaker cannot suddenly stop in the middle of a word.

Even the incomplete enumeration of such cases shows how the law of inertia or motor set obtains in the various conditions of the manifestation of association reflexes. In addition to these conditions, we must also remember the rôle of habit, which we observe everywhere, and the significance of routine in man's behaviour. Habit and routine are essentially based on the part played by inertia in association reflexes.

The principle of inertia obtains also in the fact that all discoveries remain unaccepted and useless for a long time, when the human mind is unprepared for them, but when they are at last accepted, sometimes even one or two generations later, they are overvalued. Thus, the law of conservation of energy, rejected at first, was later overvalued to such an extent that it was used to make good, as it were, all the defects of natural science, and scientists were prepared to accept it as the only fundamental law of the universe. Important discoveries are, in the majority of cases, overvalued during the early period of their acceptance. As a weight placed on the pan of a scales produces more violent swinging at first as a result of inertia and gentle oscillations later, so, too, discoveries are exaggerated as a result of inertia, and this exaggeration consists in the

[1] See V. Bechterev : *Obozrenie Psychiatrii*, nos. 5–12, p. 46.

establishment of a certain attitude to them, this attitude being usually characterised by subsequent oscillations to one side or the other, and only gradually do these oscillations subside, until equilibrium is established.

But the principle of inertia may be verified by experiment also, first of all on movements personal in character. Thus, if we arrange with the subject of experiment that he associates a beat of one finger, for instance the index finger, with sounds methodically repeated at definite time intervals, for instance tickings of the metronome, sudden cessation of these tickings will not cause immediate cessation of the finger movements, but will be inevitably followed by one, two, or even three " superfluous " finger movements, when the tickings have ceased. We find that the tendency to make " superfluous " movements is still more marked, when, under the same conditions, the sound to which the subject reacts with a beat of his finger is associated with the switching on of a glow-lamp, the lamp continuing to be switched on at the usual tempo after the tickings have ceased.[1]

In these cases, the number of " superfluous " movements stands in direct correlation with the frequency of the sounds, with the number of associative movements previously made, with the intensity of the associative stimuli, and also with the regularity or irregularity of the sequence of these stimuli, with greater or lesser concentration on the stimuli, and, lastly, with individual conditions.

This problem was later investigated in greater detail in my laboratory by several persons, particularly by Doctor N. I. Dobrotvorskaya.[2]

We see from these experiments that, if it is arranged with the subject to press his finger on a rubber ball—his movements being recorded on a revolving drum—only in response to sound-stimuli methodically repeated at certain time intervals, then, when light-stimuli replace the sound-stimuli, the motor reaction of the finger will be continued for some time to the light-stimuli alone, although the sound-stimuli have ceased.

This reaction to light-stimuli, in experiments in which they are not occasionally supported by the fundamental sound-stimuli, tends gradually to disappear.

The revival of the extinct reaction, that is, the reaction to light-stimuli, generally requires the application of a fewer number of fundamental sound-stimuli than would be necessary to originate the reaction. But this associative reaction may also be revived independently of support by the fundamental sound-stimuli.

The relative durability of an association-motor reaction, that is, the greater or lesser number of " superfluous " movements, grows, in the course of experience, concomitantly with increase in the number of

[1] V. Bechterev : *Reproductive and Associative Activity—Obozrenie Psychiatrii*, 1908.
[2] Dr. N. I. Dobrotvorskaya : *Vestnik psychologii, criminologii, anthropologii i pedologii*, 1916.

combined stimulations, with increase in the intensity of the associative stimulus (for instance, light), with increase in the frequency of the combined stimulations, with previous learning of a responsive motor reaction, and with distraction of attention.

Increase in the intensity of the associative stimulus, greater frequency of the combined stimuli, distraction of concentration, and, lastly, previous learning of a responsive motor reaction to the fundamental stimulus are influential in speeding up the appearance of this reaction.

Besides, individuality exerts a certain influence on the durability of this reaction, as well as on the promptness with which it appears.

The principle of inertia obtains also in regard to slips of the tongue.[1] This fact has been experimentally verified in our laboratory. The experiments were arranged so that the subject of experiment had to designate the stimuli applied: sound of the bell; light; tactual stimulation—" sound," " light," " tap."

Here it transpired that, when the sound-frequency is half a second, a superfluous answer by the word " sound " always ensues, after the sound-stimuli have ceased. When sound-stimuli were replaced by light-stimuli, a slip of the tongue occurred, for the subject, in this case also, uttered the word " sound " instead of " light," and did so even when the frequency was lower.

When the cessation of sound-stimuli was to be signalled by the utterance of the word " no," in this case, too, the subject pronounced the word " sound," that is, a slip of the tongue occurred.

In other experiments, two series of stimuli were applied—light and sound, and the series were alternated without warning to the subject. It was observed that when two series of stimuli, with a frequency of $2\frac{1}{2}$ seconds, were alternated, the sound was called " light " and the light " sound." When three series of stimuli are alternated, slips of the tongue in the names occur even when the frequency of the stimuli is lower. Distraction of concentration had no influence on these slips of the tongue, but other slips occurred which corresponded to the name of some object to which concentration was directed.[2]

As a result of experiments, it may be stated that, setting aside those forms of slips just mentioned, the appearance of slips of the tongue is favoured by the frequency of the stimuli, the number of stimulations, the application of incidental stimuli after the cessation of stimulation, and also the alternation of various stimuli.

In addition to slips of the tongue, analogous slips in reading and writing may occur. They depend on diminished concentration and are expressions

[1] See V. Bechterev : *Golos i retch*, no. 9, 1913.
[2] This fact must be understood thus : concentration on an object is accompanied by its appropriate symbolic verbal reflex which, however, is inhibited in its external manifestation. Under the conditions of experiment, this verbal reflex, usually inhibited, is released from inhibition, and, consequently, in the above-mentioned experiments, the name of the object to which concentration is directed is uttered at the moment when the word " sound " should be uttered.

of habitual forms of writing and reading. As we know, slips of the pen are frequent, and, therefore, examples need not be adduced, but similar mistakes may occur in reading. Thus, as I receive many letters addressed : " Vladimir Michailovitch Bechterev," I took one of a number of letters, and, having glanced at the address, put the letter into my pocket to read it at leisure. After some time, I tore open the envelope and began to read the letter. When I saw that the contents did not refer to me, I again took the envelope and was surprised to see that it was addressed to my relative : " Vladimir Borisovitch Nikonov." Thus, the first word here—the name identical with my own—determined, according to the principle of inertia, the mistake in respect of the remainder.

After all that has been said, there can be no doubt that the manifestation of the principle of inertia may be proved in regard to other forms of association reflexes also. So, for instance, if we take the mimico-somatic reflexes, we know that they continue for some time after the stimulus evoking them has ceased, and, as a result, are transferred to other objects. In this way, a man angered by another is angry with innocent individuals, etc. The principle of inertia, in the form of a definite set, holds good of concentration also.

Consequently, a man who concentrates on an object and is set in a certain direction does not notice, or ignores, many of those facts which do not accord with his views. Finally, definite routine, which is an obstacle to new achievements, develops in scientific views. By the way, it is interesting to trace the part played by routine in regard to inventions. On this topic we borrow data from Reginald Fessenden, who has three hundred inventions to his credit. He says that no organisation, which embraces a particular field of activity, has ever made an important improvement in its own sphere of activity, has ever accepted an improvement when offered it, or has ever invented anything related to its own sphere of activity, until external competition has forced it to do so. Reginald Fessenden confirms this apparently paradoxical statement by weighty, incontrovertible facts from American practical life. The most characteristic of these are the following :

1. The telegraph company did not invent the submarine cable. Moreover, when the cable was invented, the telegraph company continued their attempts to form a connection with Europe through Alaska and Siberia,

2. Neither the telegraph nor the cable company invented the telephone and they even refused it when Bell offered his invention to them.

3. Neither the telegraph, nor the cable, nor the telephone company invented wireless telegraphy and they even refused to buy the invention.

4. None of the companies mentioned invented radio, which they refused when it was offered to them for a relatively trifling sum (250,000 dollars).

5. None of the motor-building companies invented the Diesel motor ; they even ridiculed the very practicability of such a motor.

6. None of the ship-building companies played a part in the invention of the gyroscope and the radio-compass.

7. When a German immigrant offered a soft collar to the manufacturers of stiff collars, he was shown the door.

In a word, we have here a phenomenon which is certainly general in character and is always manifested under the appropriate conditions.

Other experimental data confirmatory of the principle of inertia consist in the so-called set of motor impulses. Fechner,[1] in his papers, and later Müller and Schuhmann,[2] were the first to call attention to this motor set.

In his experiments on the determination of weights, Fechner noticed that if, after one had repeatedly lifted large weights, for instance of 2000 or 3000 grams, light weights were to be lifted, for instance of not more than several hundred grams, in lifting these lighter weights which, in this case, seemed particularly light, a quick and vigorous upward movement of the hand occurred, the hand, as it were, flying up with the weight. Müller and Schuhmann's experiments are based on the same principle. They used, to be lifted by the hand, two fundamental weights, the one of 2476 grams, the other of 676 grams, and observed that after the weight of 2476 grams had been lifted several times, its replacement, unknown to the subject of experiment, by a weight of 876 grams resulted in the subject's regarding this weight as lighter than the fundamental weight of 676 grams. This motor set depends on exercise.

When a certain movement is often repeated, an appropriate motor impulse is established, as it were. Therefore, after numerous liftings of the weight of 2476 grams, this impulse is adequate to lift this weight and too strong to lift a weight of 876 grams. That is why the latter is considered lighter than the weight of 676 grams.

Experiment shows that the more often a certain movement is repeated and the smaller the interval between two series of experiments, the longer the duration and the clearer the manifestation of the motor set. The strongest set is manifested immediately after the cessation of a certain movement ; then it is gradually weakened, but in experiments it may last for many hours, even longer than twenty-four hours.

Other observations in regard to motor set have been made by Lotze, and also by P. Ephrussi.[3]

The latter, by the way, has observed in her experiments that, when learning poems read at a certain speed, the subject of experiment has difficulty in adapting himself to a different way of reading and at first wanders back to the previous habitual tempo. We have seen above that

---

[1] Fechner : *Elemente der Psychophysik*, vol. I, p. 93.

[2] See *Archiv für die gesamte Physiol.*, 45, 1889.

[3] P. Ephrussi : *Perseveration as a Factor in Normal Psychic Life.* Address to the Russian Society of Normal and Pathological Psychology ; 12th May, 1909. (See *Vestnik Psychiatrii.*)

set is applicable also to concentration, this set resulting in a certain direction of intellectual activity.

Besides, from Steffens's[1] experiments we learn that set depends on temporal distribution of movements. Thus, the lifting of a weight sixty times at one bout results in a weaker set than the same sixty liftings at several bouts. Further, the same investigator's experiments show that the introduction of a counteractive set cancels the action of the first. Thus, if at first a light weight is lifted after a heavy one and in the subsequent series of experiments the same heavy weight is lifted after the light one the same number of times, no set is obtained.

Here we note that the phenomena of so-called perseveration, which consists in a tendency to reproduce the same processes, stand in definite correlation with the motor set discussed above and, consequently, with the law of inertia. In particular, perseveration of words and movements, as sometimes observed in normal people and also in certain types of patients, is, without doubt, a result of the same motor set. The so-called " circular reaction " in movements, a phenomenon observed especially in children, certainly belongs to the same category of phenomena.[2]

In conclusion, let us remark that the present physiological data force us to admit that the above-mentioned motor set is a result of the activity not only of the higher cortical centres, but also of lower centres, as may be seen from experiments on lower vertebrates. Thus, we know from Steiner's experiments that, if one side of the base of the mesencephalon is destroyed in a shark, the latter performs circular swimming movements in the direction of the intact side. But, after it has been decapitated, the same shark resumes its normal swimming movements. But if a shark, after unilateral impairment of the base of the mesencephalon, is allowed to perform circular swimming movements for a long time and is only then decapitated, the circular swimming movements will, in this case, continue as before decapitation, obviously because a set has been established in the lower motor centres. Mott's, Schäfer's, and Bethe's experiments accord with these data.

To an analogous order of phenomena belong the various kinds of faulty sets in the human motor sphere when some work is being done (for instance, faulty holding of the pen in writing). These sets become so stable that, as my observations show, they can be eliminated only by means of special exercise in relaxing the muscles and later in contracting them in the proper direction. Recently, one of my collaborators (Dr. Verbov) at the Institute for the Study of Brain supervised by me has successfully begun to apply a similar method to pathological conditions of contractures of central, and especially of cortical, origin.

[1] Laura Steffens : *Zeitschr. f. Psych. u. Phys. d. Sinnesorgane*, Bd. 23.
[2] V. Bechterev : *Objective Psychology*, 3rd pt.

CHAPTER XLII

The principle of selection. Examples and discussion.

FROM the time of C. Darwin, the principle of selection has been established in biology. This principle rests on the struggle for existence among living individuals competing with one another to secure the necessaries and amenities of life. No matter how this principle has been restricted by the conditions of community life and mutual aid, it is incontrovertible, on the one hand, that the communities themselves are partly a result of struggle and selection and, on the other, that, both between communities and between the various classes of human society, the struggle for existence continues, and there ensues a kind of natural selection, which brings some to deterioration and untimely extinction, others to victory and prosperity. I have shown elsewhere[1] that the principle of selection is valid for the inorganic world also and, consequently, has general, that is universal, significance. Therefore, it is important that we explicate here the applicability of this biological principle to association-reflex activity. In a word, the problem of how the principle of selection, resting on the struggle for existence, is manifested in processes of association-reflex activity deserves attention.

Even a cursory glance at the manifestations of association-reflex activity leaves no doubt of the fact that it is possible to trace the operation of this principle in various cases. First of all, let us dilate on the problem of how the external world affects our apparatus of correlation. What an enormous number of external influences we experience in the course of a day, even in the course of every hour, and what a negligible number of these influences, which have stimulated orientation reflexes, leave a more or less durable trace capable of reproduction or release from inhibition! On what does this rest, if not on the struggle between these influences, every one of which, as it were, disputes the right of the others to exist? Experiments in my laboratory show that the final determinant is not so much the external qualities of these influences as those relations in which the given person has, at the time, stood in respect of these influences. It is obvious that, if, in the biological world, the more adapted individuals survive as a result of natural selection and, in the community, the more socially adapted individuals survive as a result of social selection, a problem which I have discussed in detail in my papers on social selection (*l.c.*), of the external influences which give further impetus to association-reflex activity, chiefly those which have a more intimate or a closer connection with complexes of previous influences—these complexes having attained directive significance in the behaviour of a particular human being—and also those influences marked by novelty and great intensity enter into correlation with that particular human being, as has been proved in experiments in our laboratory.

---

[1] V. Bechterev : *The Fundamental Laws of the Universe*, etc.—*Voprosi izutcheniya i vospitaniya litchnosti*, vol. II and following.

The first and earliest influences which the infant experiences during the earliest period of its existence are influences disturbing the peace of the organism. These are influences of hunger and cold, and produce grimaces and a number of random reflex movements of the extremities, these movements being accompanied by vigorous shouting, pallor of the face, and, later, blueness. These reflexes cease immediately when the infant is warmed and is fed with mother's milk. Simultaneously with this tranquillisation, a peculiar expression of biological satisfaction appears on the infant's face and is characterised by the smoothing of all facial wrinkles, the stretching of the corners of the mouth, and the flushing of the cheeks. Thus, in the first case, we are concerned with a mimico-somatic reaction of biological dissatisfaction accompanied by a host of random reflex movements of the limbs; in the second, with a mimico-somatic reaction of satisfaction and with tranquillisation of motor activity.

These fundamental relations to external stimuli are, as it were, the prototype of many other relations of the developing individual, for various stimuli, with an unfavourable influence on the organism, produce facial pallor, grimaces, general restlessness, and shouting, but such as have a favourable influence produce general tranquillity, smoothing of the facial wrinkles, stretching of the corners of the mouth into a smile, and afflux of blood to the facial coatings. Thus, gradually, *pari passu* with the development of the individual, complexes of mimico-somatic reflexes, positive and negative in character, develop, and these complexes are particularly significant in the individual's later life.

Later, at the age of puberty, influences on the sex sphere begin to be manifested, here also in accordance with selection, and these influences result in mimico-somatic complexes of reflexes sexual in character and positive or negative. Besides, even from an early age—as a result of the child's correlation with his parents, family, and other persons—influences, familial, and later social, in character, follow, and these lead to a complex of mimico-somatic and social reflexes, the latter also being both positive and negative.

In connection with these complexes of reflexes, general-biological, marital, and social needs develop in man, and to these are added, in the course of individual development, complexes of reflexes evoked by the so-called esthetic and, later, " moral-religious " influences. Consequently, corresponding needs arise as a result of frequent repetition of stimulations which become habitual. Lack of satisfaction of these needs often, by causing reproduction of previous stimulations, directs concentration precisely to those external influences which stand in closest correlation with the stimulations reproduced. Thus, in the state of hunger, a man releases from inhibition his past habitual, nutritional reflexes and, concentrating on nutritive products, tries to find them in the environment.

A man afflicted by the needs of sexuality reproduces from his past the process by which he has satisfied those needs, concentrates on appropriate external stimuli, and searches for a suitable sex object for himself. Thus, the foundation of human behaviour is constituted by inner stimuli, which guide the direction of concentration, by the character of external influences, especially social, and by past experience.

Moreover, in satisfying the above-mentioned needs, the human individual may, in accordance with the conditions of upbringing and life experience, choose from among the influences called into being by social correlations. In this case, the results of past social influences are reproduced under the stress of environmental stimulation and, as a result of the consequent direction of concentration, the given complex is supplemented by reflexes responsive to those of the new external influences which stand in more or less close correlation with a previous complex of the same kind. Thus, naturally, the life experience of the individual is enhanced. In other cases, environmental conditions revive the complex of past esthetic influences, which direct concentration towards new influences of the same kind and, thus, the stock of appropriate reflexes is supplemented, etc.

It is clear from what has been said that the selection of new influences and the accumulation of reflexes in the human individual occur under the influence of the previously established biological needs of association-reflexive complexes, in connection with the reproduction of which concentration is directed to certain kinds of external influences.

However, it is necessary to observe that, in all the cases mentioned, there is question of concentration adapting itself somehow or other to external stimuli. But an external stimulus, even weak, when acting suddenly and thus remaining completely outside the sphere of concentration, leads to a very intense and general mimico-somatic reaction called fright. The stronger such an influence under conditions of suddenness and of lack of preparedness in respect of concentration, the more intense its action on the general mimico-somatic sphere and on the nervous system, so that the latter is more or less deranged and, thus, a so-called traumatic neurosis is produced.

Are all other stimuli, then, to which concentration is not directed devoid of influence, or, more precisely, are they irrevocably lost to the individual as factors of the external world ? It transpires that they are not lost. At least, experimental data prove that they, too, call out reflexes, but without the participation of active concentration and, therefore, they are later irreproducible through excitation and direction of active concentration on them. Thus, accumulated stores of past reflexes naturally fall into two categories : the first are revived by direction of concentration on them, for they stand in close associative connection with it ; the second cannot be thus revived. Therefore, a human being can give an account of the first at any moment and denote them by their corresponding verbal symbols, while the second, since they have no connection with active concentration, cannot be reproduced by means of excitation and direction of concentration and, therefore, no appropriate account can be given of them. But, from among these unaccountable influences also, those which are more closely related to past individual experience are selected. The others are not closely related to it and, therefore, do not leave behind them more or less durable traces.

Lastly, in the reflexes themselves, which are characterised by movement, appropriate selection is made for the purpose of economy. Therefore, in every complex movement, such muscular contractions as harmonise more or less with each other and as are necessary in the execution of a movement with a certain aim participate almost exclusively. All other muscular contractions are eliminated as movements impeding the execution of the complex act. In the same way, all superfluous movements are eliminated by natural selection, although, in natural conditions, perfection in this respect is nowise attained, just as perfection in the development of species which arise through natural selection is not attained. Therefore, scientific organisation of work, by the careful study of movements performed during work, introduces artificial selection by eliminating all superfluous movements as impeding the worker.

CHAPTER XLIII

The principle of relativity. The confirmation of this principle by experimental data. The universality of the principle of relativity. The relativity of processes of inhibition and excitation.

THE principle of relativity is a particularly important principle to which attention must be called. It consists in the fact that the influence of external stimuli is determined not so much by the qualities which appertain to them as by that correlation in which they stand with preceding stimuli, with established complexes of association reflexes, and with the state induced by the latter in the cortical centres. In accordance with this, the influence of the same external stimuli is exciting or depressing in dependence on, for instance, the exact period of differentiation which the given reflex has reached, or on the correlation in which the new stimulus stands with the stimulus to which the reflex has been inculcated. Thus, no stimulus whatever is, either in character or intensity, bound up with the process of inhibition alone or with the process of release from inhibition alone, but, on the contrary, all stimuli may lead either to the inhibition of an inherited association reflex or to its release from inhibition, in accordance with the degree of development of the given association reflex.

Thus, we have already seen that every association reflex is at first general and only after numerous reptitions does it become more and more differentiated. Therefore, at the beginning, as experiments show, an incidental external stimulus, especially if it is of the same order as that to which the association reflex is being inculcated, causes the latter to be released from inhibition, while, in the course of time, when the association reflex has been differentiated, all incidental stimuli, including those which have previously produced release from inhibition, act in an inhibitory manner on the association reflex. The same phenomenon is observed also in simple reflexes. Thus, a sharp sound disturbs a child sitting quietly, while the same sound tranquillises a moving child. Still more convincing examples of how inner conditions, in this case, influence external reactions are the difference in reaction of a sated and a hungry child to external stimuli, and the reaction with which a child, a eunuch, and a sexually mature person respond to the opposite sex. Here, more than anywhere else, the significance of the somatic sphere and of hormonism, in respect of the state of the nerve centres and the development and character of association reflexes, is apparent.

Thus, the correlation of association reflexes with incidental stimuli is not the same at different periods of inculcation and in different states of the individual.

In investigating association reflexes of the cutaneous surface, we have been able to see that, while, in the early period, before the development of generalisation or irradiation of the reflex, the effects of excitation, arising, as it were, from the summation of stimulations, predominate during incidental stimulations, the influence of incidental stimuli on the association reflex which is being inculcated is, from the beginning of the period of differentiation, predominantly inhibitory, and the inhibition of the reflex which is being inculcated is manifested by its becoming weakened to the minimum.

This may be very clearly demonstrated in respiration in the case of an association-motor reflex.

Let us assume that an association reflex has been inculcated to the tone C. At first, when the reflex is not yet differentiated, all other sounds are stimuli and release the association reflex from inhibition. In respiration, this is expressed by a rise in the curve. But, in the course of time, after further differentiation, other sounds act inhibitorily on the association reflex, and, consequently, the respiratory curve falls. Simultaneously, because of inhibition, the jerking back of the extremity is not exhibited.

On the other hand, we know that, at the period of development of a differentiated association reflex, an external stimulus which has not been previously associated with the given association reflex, acts inhibitorily on the latter, while the same stimulus may lead to its release from inhibition at the period of inhibition of the association reflex.

So it is clear that the same stimulus differs in its action on the same association reflex according to the developmental phase of the association reflex.

In one case, an incidental stimulus may act depressingly ; in another, the same stimulus may act excitingly or in a manner to release from inhibition.

In the cases we have discussed, we are concerned with what we call the principle of relativity, so called because the incidental stimulus has, broadly speaking, no absolute or unconditional, but only a relative, significance in regard to the association reflex, for everything depends on a certain correlation established, at a given moment, between the new stimulus and the state of the nervous apparatus which effects the association reflex.

In accordance with the same principle of relativity, the difference limen (to which we shall refer later) of the association reflex varies according to the intensity of the given stimuli.

But, in spite of variation in the difference limens of association reflexes when the intensity of the stimulation is different, the limits of differentiation must stand in approximately the same constant correlation with each other. This thesis is, in any case, a direct inference from the data at our disposal, but requires to be finally confirmed by experiment.

Lastly, the principle of relativity appears also in the fact that the action of a stimulus to which a given association reflex has been inculcated varies according to the preceding conditions, for instance excitation of the association reflex or rest. We know already that an association reflex is gradually weakened by the repeated impact of the same stimulus, but, after a sufficient pause, it is revived by the same stimulus. Consequently, it is clear that the action of all stimuli is nowise stable, nowise constant, but depends on the state induced in the centres by preceding stimulations or by a pause.

Everyday observation also confirms this principle of relativity. Thus, a distracting external stimulus disturbs reproduction of what has been learned, when reproduction follows its usual course, but when reproduction is disturbed and cannot follow its usual course, a distracting stimulus promotes correct reproduction.

The principle of relativity is one of the general laws of the functions of the nervous system and is applicable to association reflexes in particular. That some moderately strong stimuli in the natural environment are exciting and others—exceedingly intense—are depressing is because the former are usual stimuli to which the state of the given receptive organ has been co-ordinated, while the second, being unusual, depress the functions, at least until adaptation has been exstablished, that is, until the appropriate relation of the stimuli to the fuction of the given organ has developed. Weak stimuli which are unusual may be also inhibitory, but, as their intensity is low, this inhibitory influence exerts itself only when they are repeated and when they impinge over a long time.

Such relations between stimuli and the individual are established in a natural way in the course of life. Yet they are by no means absolute, but are relative, for, if a usual stimulus is applied for a long time, it ceases to be a stimulus. On the other hand, this same " extinct " stimulus resumes its rôle of stimulus after a time interval ; in other words, it enters into its former correlation with the receptive organ.

Even a usual stimulus impinging on the given receptive organ sometimes becomes an inhibitory force in respect of the association reflexes of that organ, if a reaction to another usual stimulus has been established.

Thus, indeed, every usual stimulus, irrespective of its character and intensity, may become an association-inhibitory force in respect of the organ functioning. But this inhibitory force is not constant ; it is relative, for, in the initial stage of the formation of the association reflex, it is not an inhibitory force, but becomes so simultaneously with differentiation of the association reflex and only during the occurrence of differentiation, but, when the latter becomes weaker, ceases to be an inhibitory force. Thus, everything in association reflexes is relative ; there is nothing absolute.

Further, if we evoke an association reflex by a certain stimulus, the latter, in the course of time, ceases to be a stimulus, but it is sufficient, in the initial stage of the association reflex, to add to this stimulus another, but indifferent, stimulus, and excitation reappears.

On the other hand, we know that an intense external stimulus, which at first acts inhibitorily on the receptive organ, later, on repetition, ceases to be an inhibitory force and, consequently, the extinct association reflex is re-established.

Further, a weak external stimulus, in certain cases, at once releases the extinct reflex from inhibition, though not always, but according to the state of the reflex, for, in the case mentioned, it revives the reflex, while,

2 A

in other cases, even a weak stimulus may become an effective inhibitory force.

Even the primary electro-cutaneous stimulus, under the conditions prevailing in the inculcation of association reflexes by our method, is not always a stimulus in respect of these ; it is so only in a certain temporal correlation with the preceding primary stimulus, as has been proved in my laboratory by Dr. Schwarzman's investigations.[1]

The interrelation between processes of inhibition and excitation also deserves attention.

In this case, when an association reflex is differentiated, all other incidental stimuli, even when of the same quality, are, as we know, forces inhibiting it, but not inhibiting any other reflex.

In the case of a generalised or irradiated cutaneous reflex, inhibition of the reflex in one point gradually diffuses, as we know, to more distant points, and then gradually disappears, beginning from the more distant areas. However, symmetrical areas, as we have seen, stand in a peculiar relation to each other, for a reflex of a symmetrical area is retained for a comparatively longer time.

Even those association reflexes which are produced by components of a composite stimulus to which the association reflex has been inculcated, stand, as we have seen, in mutual correlation with each other, in the sense that, if one of these reflexes responsive to one of the stimuli is inhibited, this inhibition, to some degree, influences inhibitorily the other " partial " association reflexes also. If the association reflex to a composite or compound stimulus is again revived or released from inhibition, the " partial " association reflexes dependent on it are also revived.

Needless to say, the principle of relativity stated above is one of the expressions of the universal law of relativity which obtains everywhere and which, as a result of Einstein's brilliant investigations, has been finally demonstrated in regard to the heavenly bodies.

It is ultimately impossible to picture anything absolute in the universe. Everything is relative. In precisely the same way, individuals are interrelated, not in absolute, but in relative forms, with the natural environment and with each other in the social environmental conditions.

[1] It follows from these investigations that electro-cutaneous stimuli, when they are repeated too often and exceed a certain limit in regard to frequency, hinder, because of their after-effect, the inculcation of an association reflex.

CHAPTER XLIV

The principle of dependent relations and the process of the connection or concatenation of association reflexes. Sthenic and asthenic influences of stimuli on the receptive organ, as well as on other organs. Experiments with the ergograph.

THE principle of dependent relations presupposes a process of connection or concatenation of association reflexes, a process in which one association reflex as stimulus is followed by other association reflexes connected by a sequence of stimuli. When we have inculcated an association-motor reflex to a double stimulus, for instance light and sound, we know from investigations made in my laboratory that the association reflex is obtained to each stimulus separately. When we then add to one of these stimuli a new collateral stimulus not depressing in character, we obtain the association reflex to this pair of stimuli also. And, again, when we add to one of this pair of stimuli a new stimulus not depressing in character, we obtain the association-motor reflex to this pair of stimuli also, etc.

Lastly, an association-motor reflex may be changed by substituting one reflex for another. Thus, if we inculcate a reflex by stimulating a certain area of the cutaneous surface, we can, by applying the stimulus to another cutaneous area, obtain the same association reflex by stimulating the other area, when strict differentiation of the original reflex is absent, and, at the same time, the reflex may become extinct in response to stimulation of the original area. The reflex may be again transferred from this new area to a different area, etc.

On the other hand, when an external stimulus produces a certain influence, this influence becomes associated with other more or less simultaneous external stimuli also.

The same is true of mimico-somatic reaction. The latter, being evoked by a certain stimulus, becomes associated with other simultaneously impinging stimuli also. Every association reflex enters into association with all influences acting more or less simultaneously on the organism, in as far as they do not inhibit the reflex, though these influences be external stimuli altogether impertinent and even by nature indifferent.

This is why a reaction once experienced may enter into association with other external influences and this is of special significance in regard to the so-called common neuroses in general and to psychasthenia in particular.

Thus, a mimico-somatic reaction once experienced enters into association with all simultaneous external stimuli and even with those past stimuli which stand in more or less stable connection with them. Let us assume that a man worried about his health and suffering from hypochondria, as I have observed in one of my cases, has experienced an intense mimico-somatic reaction at sight of a corpse passing by on a white hearse and covered with a white pall. He later reproduces this reaction not only at sight of all corpses and hearses, but also at sight of anything white, and also on reproduction of these.

As we know, the external manifestations of mimico-somatic reflexes may be more or less inhibited by certain external or internal stimuli and even by reproductive processes. In this case, the reflex is manifested in an intense inner reaction, notwithstanding inhibition of the external reaction. Here the principle of compensation appears, according to which, instead of external reaction, internal somatic reaction in the form of changes in heart beat, etc., is intensified.

However, an inhibited reflex, inhibited, for instance, by habituation to a certain stimulus, may be revived, and this not only independently after a certain time interval, but also in response to any other stimulus with which the reflex has been originally associated by contiguity.

This association of higher reflexes is found in life, just as in experiments, when a new stimulus, which later becomes capable of calling out the same association reflex, is added, during the period of incomplete differentiation, to the stimulus which calls out the inculcated association reflex.

In these cases, concatenation of association reflexes, which establishes their dependence one on the other, is transferred to incidental stimuli varied in character and associated with each other by contiguity. We have examples of such concatenation of association reflexes in other cases also, for instance in the execution of the same movement when we count one, two, three, etc.

In investigating speech, we often encounter phenomena referable to this concatenation of reflexes by contiguity.

In laboratory experiments, we can cause two different external stimuli to be associated, in the same individual, by means of the primary electro-cutaneous stimulation, into two different association reflexes. Thus, for instance, we can inculcate an association reflex in one foot to a given sound-stimulus and an association reflex in the other foot to a different sound-stimulus.

Experiments of this kind in our laboratory (Dr. Zhmichov) prove the possibility of connecting up different association reflexes evoked by different stimuli provided that there is a definite sequence of stimuli, and this, as we know, occurs at every step in life.

In complex speech movements and also in complex actions, the element which connects motor reflexes produced by different stimuli is the biological needs of the organism, which determine the direction and character of complex speech movements and complex actions, and lead to the production of a series of association-motor and other association reflexes.

We find such a phenomenon, for instance in all complex movements performed during the playing of instruments, during reading aloud, during dancing movements, in habitual speech movements such as the pronouncing of the words of a familiar song, in the execution of complex actions, etc.

In a word, life affords countless examples of how, under the influence of biological need, one movement, which we are justified in regarding not only as an association reflex, but also as a stimulus, is followed by another movement, then by the third, and so on.

Phenomena of concatenation prove that every external reaction is connected, that is, enters into dependent relations, not only with that reflex associated with the primary stimulus evoking it, but also with each preceding stimulus which becomes connected with the associative stimulus. This principle obtains in respect of all reactions, not only external but also internal.

The same is true of so-called personal actions, for instance acts of defence, of aggression, or of imitation.

Here we have the origin of obsessional actions, which are symbolic in character and arise on the slightest provocation, and also of obsessional imitation (echopraxia), both of which may be observed in neurotics.

Freud's doctrine of "strangulation of affects" (*Einklemmung der Affekte*) and their transference from one "psychic" content to another, a doctrine which Schultz[1] regards as "the cornerstone of the Freudian system," harmonises with these data.

Anyhow, the mimico-somatic reaction, like every reaction, is a result of the energic process which begins from some area of the receptive surface through external or internal stimulation exciting movement of the nervous current in the sympathic ganglia in the central apparatus, where the current revives previous processes through reproduction, consequently through a repeated excitation of the appropriate nerves, and is then transmitted to the periphery where it produces a certain effect expressed either in external muscular contractions or secretory phenomena ; or in inner muscular contractions or inner secretion.

This energic process is bound up with the expenditure of the stored energy of the central and peripheral neurons and this energy is replenished chiefly by the supply of nutritive material to the centres by means of the circulation of the blood and the lymph.

Muscular movements and secretion are, in turn, accompanied by stimulation of receptive nervous apparatus inlaid in the appropriate organs and excite a fresh nervous current directed towards the central organs, where, in the case of external movements, it promotes origination of the so-called circular reaction, but, in the case of inner reaction on the part of the heart, the vessels, respiration, inner movements, and inner secretion, it leads to the renewal and support of the same reaction for a considerable time.

The subjective process accompanying this inner somatic reaction is called feeling, but we prefer to use the term "temper," as equally applicable to the subjective and the objective process.

The mimico-somatic reaction referred to above may be sthenic or asthenic in character. In the first case, it is a positive mimico-somatic reaction ; in the second, a negative. But there may be reactions partly sthenic and

[1] *Zeitschr. f. ang. Psychologie*, II, p. 44.

partly asthenic, or mixed. There is reason to believe that there is, in general, a great variety of mimico-somatic reactions difficult to distinguish physiologically, but each of which is characterised by a special set and by peculiar changes bound up with the activity of the endocrine glands.[1]

The character of this set is conditioned not only by difference in the mimico-somatic reaction, but also by various associations of the given reaction with external stimuli. Thus, the state of alarm caused by fear of persecutors and that arising from the possibility of adultery on the part of the husband differ not so much in the character of the reaction, as in their connection with certain external conditions and the association-reflex processes corresponding to these conditions.

A mimico-somatic reflex, like all other reflexes, originates and runs its course. The difference between an ordinary motor reaction and a mimico-somatic reaction consists, however, in the fact that the latter is more lasting and spends itself only gradually. Although a mimico-somatic reaction is spent more slowly than any other reaction, still it is inevitably spent unless inhibited by some conditions, whether external or internal stimuli. But an inhibited mimico-somatic reaction may be revived under the influences of an external stimulus.

It must be noted here that all external stimuli, when exciting the receptive apparatus, necessarily lead not only to an external muscular or secretory reaction, but also to a mimico-somatic reaction of a certain degree.

Ultimately, every external and internal stimulus, in accordance with its character and intensity, produces, in addition to a special motor or secretory reaction, a general mimico-somatic tonus and a general sthenic and asthenic influence on the whole organism, as well as on the organ stimulated or operative.

Thus, stimuli, when acting on the appropriate organs and evoking a reflex in dependence on the character and intensity of the stimuli, exert, at the same time, a general exciting (sthenic) influence or a general depressing (asthenic) influence. Every organ apparently has certain limits—the optimum in regard to the intensity of the stimulus and the duration of its application. Within these limits, the given stimulus acts sthenically. Besides, the replacement of one stimulus by another is of great importance as regards sthenic influence.

Lastly, the general state of the organism as also of the organ stimulated— a state conditioned by preceding influences—is not without significance. It is clear to every one that a stimulus which usually acts sthenically may act asthenically on an organ previously fatigued, and *vice versa*.

Thus, every external stimulus produces, in addition to a local influence on the receptive apparatus, also a general influence sthenic or asthenic in character, and, here too, there is nothing absolute or unconditional in

[1] In investigations made on the respiratory reaction during various mimico-somatic states, we have, for instance, revealed a number of its peculiarities.

respect of these general influences, for one and the same external stimulus may, according to the state of the organism, exert at one time a sthenic, and at another an asthenic, influence.

It is perfectly comprehensible that these data are equally applicable to the receptive organs and those organs which execute work, for work itself, for instance muscular work, is invariably bound up with a certain stimulation arising from muscular contraction and from mechanical stimulation of the ligamental apparatus and of the joints.

In a word, every external and internal stimulus influences not only the appropriate organ, but diffuses to other organs, such as the muscular apparatus, the cardio-vascular and respiratory systems, the glands including the endocrine, and the nervous system. So local stimulations exert a general influence, which, as has been mentioned, may be sthenic or asthenic according to the character and intensity of the stimuli.

Experiments made by Féré[1] may be adduced to prove the sthenic and asthenic influence of external stimuli on other activities. We shall take only those which refer to sound-stimulations. His collaborator, Marie Jaëll, investigating the rôle of various stimuli including sounds, arranged her experiments thus :

Féré—a man " without an ear for music "—was required to lift a weight of three kilograms with his middle finger and to repeat this action at certain intervals to the point of exhaustion. The ergograph was employed in the experiment. It transpired that, under the influence of certain sound-stimuli, the weight seemed comparatively light to him and he could lift it a larger number of times in succession. Under the influence of other sound-stimuli, contrary results were obtained. Thus, the hand, as it were, distinguished the sounds in their influence on the muscular apparatus, while the brain was incapable of doing so.

Further investigations on the same person show that consonant intervals (octave, fifth, third) increase muscular energy, while dissonant intervals decrease it. The difference in the influence of perfect and imperfect fifths is particularly striking. So, under the influence of the perfect fifth (A–E), Féré could lift the weight 850 times in 16 experiments. This corresponds to lifting one kilogram to a height of 112 metres ; but, under the influence of the imperfect fifth (A–E flat), he could lift the weight not more than 50 times. This corresponds to lifting one kilogram to a height of 7 metres. Thus, a difference of a semitone in the one direction makes a strong man weak and, in the other direction, a weak man strong.

The exciting and depressing influences of music on the motor sphere have long been known. Every one is familiar with the fact that a funeral march produces a depressed state and slow gait, while a dashing march produces the opposite effect, and light pieces played in a major key incite us to dance. We know that, in regard to the influence of music on movement, the sequence of tones also is not indifferent. Thus, for instance, in

[1] See Féré : *Travail et plaisir*, Paris.

alternating a perfect second (A–B) and a diminished second (A–B flat), Féré performed the following work expressed in metre-kilograms :

Series 1 . . 19 kgs.   Series 2 . . 1·4 kgs.
   ,, 3 . . 26 ,,   ,, 4 . . 1·3 ,,
   ,, 5 . . 31 ,,   ,, 6 . . 0·6 ,,

Further, we have seen how depressingly the imperfect fifth (A–E flat) acted. But, after 32 experiments with a fourth (A–D), it became possible, with a fifth, to perform, in the course of 5 minutes, work of 44 metre-kilograms (260 liftings).

It is perfectly comprehensible that the general state of the organism expressed in fatigue or rest influences the result of the experiment. Thus, one and the same F minor chord from Beethoven's sonata proved in one case stimulating, in another, depressing.

Experiments in the sthenic and asthenic influence of music on muscular work have been made in my laboratory by Dr. Spirtov. But the above figures are striking in any case. Therefore, at my suggestion, the results were experimentally checked by L. L. Vasilyev in the reflexological laboratory supervised by me.

In general, we must say that the work of M. Jaëll and Féré must be corrected in certain details, although their fundamental contentions must be admitted. Their results, on being checked, prove to be less striking, and if M. Jaëll's results are striking, this may be accounted for by the influence of suggestion and auto-suggestion during the experiments, the aim of which was apparently known to the subject.

CHAPTER XLV

THE world is constructed in the form of closed systems which are individualities. Each individuality may differ in complexity, but always represents a certain harmony of parts, has its configuration, and is characterised by relative stability of system. Individuality ascends from the simplest to the complex : the electron, the atom, the molecule, the crystal, the organism, the community, the planetary world, the universe are each an individuality. Harmony of parts is the basis of individuality, and, therefore, the harmony of the universe is, in its way, a harmony of the parts of a large organism, a harmony based on correlation, interaction of parts. Every person is, in turn, individual and depends, on the one hand, on individual conditions of heredity and on inherited constitution and, on the other, on individual conditions of education and life experience in the social environment. As a result of these factors individual characters are created. Reactions to external stimuli here acquire a special individual character in the person.

It is necessary to take into account, in regard to sthenic or asthenic influences, the significance of individual conditions, as well as of conditions of education and habit. These conditions play a rôle here just as in other cases. In this respect, we must keep in mind the endless variety of conditions favourable and unfavourable to a certain activity. Sometimes, in this case, a peculiar set in work to a definite stimulus influence is observed. Thus, " one is incited to work when certain areas of the skin are rubbed ; another, by looking at a bright object, as was the case with Haydn, who looked at a diamond when he worked ; a third, by a certain colour, a musical fragment ; lastly, by smells, as with Schiller, who kept rotten apples in the drawer of his desk."[1]

Here we are really concerned with the rôle of external stimuli in regard to a general reaction evoked in the form of an association reflex in the given individual ; and, consequently, neither the duration nor the intensity of this general reaction depends directly on the duration and character of the stimulus.

Thus, the stimulation of the receptive organ may not exert a particularly significant influence on the receptive organ, but, by exciting a sthenic or an asthenic reflex, which has been inculcated by individual experience, it may evoke an intense reaction of some kind or other. In addition to the examples adduced above, we may indicate the sound of a tocsin, which causes general unrest, a funeral march which acts depressingly, and, lastly, a dinner-bell, which arouses a general sthenic reflex in all those even moderately hungry, notwithstanding the fact that these sounds of themselves, that is, originally, did not produce such a reaction.

[1] Many examples of this kind may be found in S. O. Grusenberg's book : *Geny i tvortchestvo* (*Genius and Creativeness*), Leningrad, 1924. Published P. P. Soikin.

Then, we must note that both the local and the general sthenic and asthenic reactions become connected, in the course of life, with a special attitude of motor-reflexes to external stimuli, for all sthenic stimuli excite the motor apparatus and so evoke a tendency to aggressive acts directed towards the possible retention and prolongation of the sthenic stimulus, and, on the contrary, all asthenic stimuli either depress the motor apparatus or evoke a tendency to defensive movements directed towards the possible elimination, weakening, or curtailing of the asthenic stimulus.[1] It is clear that, in this way, the attitude of the organism, too, to external stimuli of various kinds is determined. It must, however, be noted here that both sthenic and asthenic reactions depend, to a considerable extent, on the conditions of education.

Further, it must be observed that inner stimuli (from the surface of the gastro-intestinal canal, the cardio-vascular system, the lungs, the muscles, the uro-genital organs, etc.) excite general sthenic, as easily as local sthenic, reactions, both of which reactions may develop not only directly, but also in the form of an association reflex. It is clear from this that these reactions, which are excited by stimulations of internal organs, may also serve as stimuli to certain actions, which, in some cases, effect the removal or amelioration of the asthenic state and, in others, the prolongation and reinforcement of the sthenic state. The establishment of these attitudes determines the interrelation between organism and environment, this interrelation being always characterised by individual peculiarities.

Both observation and experiment lead to the conclusion that, in respect of association reflexes, we must take into consideration not only the environment, but also considerable individual differences in the inherited constitution and in other inherited conditions, which exert an influence on the speed with which association reflexes are inculcated, as well as on the stability of association reflexes established.

As we know, it is sufficient, in some cases, to present a stimulus suddenly to a man unprepared and unadjusted in regard to concentration, and a stable association reflex is established, as happens in the case of persons unusually impressionable because of unfavourable heredity and other conditions. This mode of development of durable association reflexes explains the origin of phobias in psychasthenics,[2] the development of nervous stammering, of hysterical attacks, and even of epilepsy. The so-called traumatic and other neuroses in impressionable children and in adults are conditioned precisely by the suddenness of some stimulus which causes a nervous shock, as we have discussed above. In these cases, the association reflex forces its way directly, that is, ignoring concentration, into the mimico-somatic sphere, the endocrine organs participating, and, consequently, is fixed with extraordinary ease.

[1] V. Bechterev : *Objective Psychology*, 2nd pt., St. Petersburg.
[2] V. Bechterev : *Obsessional Phobias and their Treatment—Russky Vratch*, no. 14, 1915. Also his *Development of Phobias*, etc.—*Obozrenie Psychiatrii*, 1917.

On the other hand, there are persons who are, in general, not easily influenced by certain external stimuli and, consequently, the inculcation of certain association reflexes is difficult in their case.

Thus, we have, as it were, two extreme poles of impressionability among human beings. Laboratory experiment shows the same. We have already said that there are cases in which it is sufficient to evoke an ordinary reflex under special experimental conditions and in one association with another external stimulus not exciting an ordinary reflex, and this stimulus immediately becomes a source of excitation of an association reflex, a source so real that no inhibition occurs on repeated application of the same stimulus, and so we are forced to have recourse to artificial methods of inhibition.

On the other hand, there are cases in which the inculcation of association reflexes encounters great difficulties and an unusually large number of associations of the two stimuli are required to establish and fix an association reflex. In some cases, we come across a remarkable set towards inhibition of association reflexes. There is reason to think that, here too, we have a special state of individuality, the reason for this state being hidden in unfavourable previous influences or in special hereditary or constitutional conditions.

In explicating the problem of the individual peculiarities of an organism, it must be noted that the very character of the stimulus often gives rise to unequal conditions in respect of the inculcation of higher or association reflexes. Thus, some influences are, generally speaking, unusually quick in evoking a durable association reflex, while other influences do not develop an association reflex so quickly, and the latter reflex, when inculcated, may be much less durable. Comparison of the influences of stimuli of light and sound shows that sound-stimuli, as a rule, produce an association reflex more quickly than do light-stimuli, and the reflex is in the first case more durable than in the second. But it is possible that, in this respect, the individual type of the given person (auditory, visual, etc.) is not without significance.

To conclude the discussion of conformity to law in the phenomena of association reflexes, it transpires that man, as an agent, is no exception to the correlation or dependence which prevails throughout both inanimate and animate nature, a conclusion which may be expected when the person is observed from the objective, bio-social standpoint. General cosmic laws are applicable equally to phenomena of the physico-chemical order and to those of the organic and super-organic worlds, including the correlative activity of man.[1]

[1] What has been said above does not exhaust all conformity to laws in the development and manifestations of association reflexes. Other correlations, for instance the subsequent influence of each stimulation on the development of association reflexes and the dependence of the duration of the latent period of the reflex on influences of inhibition and excitation, etc., are indicated here. But these more particular correlations are really developments of the same general principles, and this does not at all decrease their special significance for reflexology as a science.

CHAPTER XLVI

IT is necessary to touch here on the problem of the correlation between the objective data studied by reflexology and those subjective experiences dealt with in subjective psychology. But here we shall be as brief as possible, as it will be sufficient to confine ourselves to more or less general data.

Already when human reflexology was being established as a special science studying personality objectively, we relegated to the subjective method a sphere of investigations carried out on himself by the experimenter or the subject of experiment by means of the method of self-observation checked against objective data. We deny the right of subjectivist psychologists indiscriminately to extend, by using analogy with themselves, the conclusions of their self-observation to the subjective world of others and particularly to the subjective world of children, of psychopaths, and of animals. But as reflexology aims chiefly at the study of the objective manifestations of human personality, it is clear that, in this way, the parallel study on oneself of both aspects of human personality is possible,[1] the more so as reflexology investigates subjective experiences too from the standpoint of unexpressed reflexes. In this direction we may go further and speak of the possible, even the inevitable, future structure of reflexology, which will embrace the special investigation of subjective phenomena as unexpressed association reflexes verbally accountable, but it is perfectly comprehensible that, in this case, there must be appropriate procedure in investigations of this kind. But as the time is not yet ripe, we shall confine ourselves for the present to the more general pertinent data.

We must not overlook the fact that the earlier subjective psychology found no correspondence with the material aspect of the activity of the brain, which was regarded as consisting of cells and their projections, while the psychic process was regarded as a temporal sequence. However, as soon as we adopt the standpoint of movement of energy in the form of a nervous current externally manifested in the form of various reflexes, and internally, that is in oneself, characterised under certain conditions by so-called conscious phenomena, the correlation between subjective processes and objective manifestations in the form of association reflexes must appear in a different light.

Here it is necessary to note that even the initial and fundamental process of association-reflex activity, a process concerned with the

---

[1] Guided by this principle, I and Dr. Shumkov, working in collaboration, have recently investigated the reflex of alertness (Address to the Congress of Pedology, Experimental Pedagogics, and Psychoneurology, January, 1924) by the application of the autognostic method, by which the subject of experiment investigates on himself subjective phenomena in antithesis to objective.

acquisition of reflexes conditioned by certain external or internal influences —a topic to which we have already referred, does not dispense with association reflexes. Those subjective processes which are called perception cannot be at present explained without the participation of personal experience and without having recourse to the theory of reflexes. Indeed, all recent investigations in the sphere of the physiology of the receptive organs lead decisively to the predominance of the empirical theory initiated by Helmholtz's work and supplemented by W. Wundt's investigations and by those of other and more recent writers.

Wundt definitely opposed the view that the sensitivity of the retina is the basis of the visual process. He espoused the view that every stimulation of the retina evokes a nerve reflex which may associate with other reflexes traversing the same cerebral areas. According to Wundt, the chief rôle in visual perception is played by motor sensations which determine not only dimension, but also distance, and localisation in space.

According to Bourdon, the most elementary data of size and form are also determined by motor processes. In respect of the size of an object, the projection of an object means nothing unless the eyes explore the various parts of the object, unless the distance is determined, and unless we have an idea of the absolute size. The image on the retina is only the point from which motor processes originate. Indeed, this writer is less categorical in respect of form, for, while admitting the participation of muscular and tactual sensations, he finds them too imperfectly differentiated to give precision. Consequently, he consigns the chief rôle to the retina. But Mach's experiments do not harmonise with the latter view.

As a matter of fact, it is sufficient to turn letters or photographs upside down, and we have difficulty in recognising them. Obviously, it is not the retina which is involved, but those motor-reflexive processes which are associated with retinal stimulation.

Nuel's[1] views are still more decisive. He explains visual process without having recourse to self-observation or even to psychological terms, for which he substitutes the terms "light-reception," "light-reaction," etc. Finally, his view confirms the rôle of motor processes in the act of vision. For him the visual act is constituted of reactions, partly simple eye-reactions, partly somatic or cerebral reactions. The former modify the latter and, therefore, may be regarded as acting on the perception of distance, size, relief, etc., the conscious data being produced by the cerebral reaction alone, with participation of an associative process.

It is necessary to note that experiments made after operation on those blind from birth decidedly favour the empirical theory. Those operated on distinguish a circle from a square, but they cannot denote the difference either verbally or by gesticulation. Hirschberg showed a knife, a fork, and a spoon to a man blind from birth who had been operated on. He examined these objects attentively, indicated the colours correctly, but

[1] Dr. Nuel : *La vision*, 1904.

could not describe the objects, and could not indicate the significance of these objects which he had held in his hand so often.[1]

In Uthoff's experiments,[2] the man operated on, when shown two or more objects, was absolutely incapable of estimating, by vision alone, the difference in their size. Neither could he indicate with his hands the size of an object placed before him. Only on the eighth day after restoration of vision could he attempt to determine which of two apples given him was larger and which smaller. Determination of thickness came still later.

Fidèle, dilating on the phylogenetic development of vision, completely discards introspective data. He begins by describing heliotropism in the lower animals, discusses dermatotropism, and passes on to the special reactions of the eye and the gradual development of this organ. He then deals with the general somatic reactions consisting of simple reactions and of icono-reactions (*icono-réactions*), accompanied by nicer discrimination of the details of an object.

Then, touching on the direction of human vision, he holds that photo-reactions are most perfect only in the layer of cones in the yellow spot (macula lutea) and comes to the conclusion that progressive adaptation of the organ modifies the primitive mechanism in such a way that now a movement which turns the retina to the object occurs as the first effect of a reaction which is not macular. This supplementary mechanism consists of fixation movements of the body, the head, and the eyes, but the ocular effect, developing gradually, replaces all others. An analogous process occurs in the establishment of binocular vision.[3] It must be remarked that observations of new-born infants in our Pedological Institute leave no doubt that a light-stimulus from a lamp lit at the side of the eye, so that the light falls on the peripheral areas of the retina, produces in the new-born infant a slow and interrupted (ladder reaction) turning of the eyes towards the light and simultaneous turning of the head. Obviously, the stimulus which leads to the side-turning of the eyes issues from the peripheral retinal areas opposite the light.

As regards audition, the explication of its function from the view-point of the empirical theory has not advanced to the same extent, I regret to say, but at present the old theory of resonance is being subjected to severe criticism and it also is being replaced by the doctrine of reactive process.

Hermann's[4] pioneer attempt to replace mechanical resonators by organs capable of adaptation to vibrations of a certain rhythm has been already

[1] Bourdon : *La perception visuelle de l'espace*, 1902, p. 382.

[2] Bourdon : *loc. cit.*, p. 376.

[3] A more detailed account of the older literature concerning the empirical theory may be found in my papers, which have appeared also in separate editions : *The Theory of Our Conception of Space* (St. Petersburg, edited separately, and also in *Vestnik Psychiatrii*) and *The Significance of the Organs of Equilibrium in the Formation of Conceptions of Space* (edited separately and in *Nevrologitchesky Vestnik*).

[4] Hermann : *Zur Lehre von der Klangwahrnehmung—Pflügers Arch.*, Bd. 56.

abandoned, and now audition also has been reduced to a nervous process.

It is thought that the organ of Corti has no specific function, but that it distinguishes sounds in respect of the changes which they produce in the whole organ.

According to some writers (Ewald),[1] the distinction depends on the transverse propagation of waves in the organ of Corti ; according to others (Meyer),[2] it depends on the number of nerve endings stimulated.

According to Bonnier,[3] there are complex changes in all the media of the auditory apparatus from the tympanic membrane to the round window, which forms " *un appareil enregistreur.*" Later investigations disclose that the tympanic membrane is even accommodative in function. We shall not discuss other views and more recent investigations relevant in this respect.[4] Thus, we are concerned here with transformation of these stimulations into a certain form which some regard as concussion, others as pressure on the auditory nerve.

Although this empirical theory of audition is still insufficiently elucidated, it is certainly developing along the same lines as the theory of vision and reduces auditory functions to nervous reflexes, which, in the form of movements of the ear and head, are produced by sound-waves.

Needless to say, processes of touch, taste, and smell may easily be reduced to reflexes evoked by appropriate stimuli. In any case, the early development of touch, taste, and smell is most intimately associated with reflexive movements of the receptive organs.

It is clear from this that the functions of all the receptive organs, such as those of vision, audition, smell, taste, and touch, are based on reflexive processes, and, as we have already stated, processes of seeing, hearing, smelling, tasting, touching are merely a number of orientation association reflexes. In my book, *Objective Psychology*, I touch also on the determination of spatial and temporal relations[5] from the standpoint of motor reflexes which are intimately associated with the receptive organs, and, consequently, I refer the interested reader to the work mentioned.[6]

We conclude this chapter by an extract from a work of Meumann's, who

[1] Ewald : *Zur Physiologie d. Labyrinthes—Pflügers Arch.*, 1899.

[2] M. Meyer : *Über die Tonverschmelzung u. die Theorie d. Consonnanz.—Zeitsch f. Psych. u. Phys. d. Sinnesorgane*, Bd. XVIII.

[3] P. Bonnier : *L'audition*, 1901, p. 125.

[4] *Translators' note :* See Wheeler : *The Science of Psychology*, pp. 409–412, Jarrolds, London, 1931.

[5] The problems mentioned are more fully discussed in the German and French editions of *Objective Psychology*. These editions are more recent.

[6] Goldstein's latest and interesting investigations (*Zeitschr. f. d. ges. Neur. u. Psych.*, 1918) show that : (a) the localisation of tactual stimuli (extension, distance, and form), (b) the position of the limbs, (c) " local signs," and (d) even the capacity to execute movements independently and without looking depend on loss of the capacity to reproduce visual pictures (so-called images), while vision itself is retained. Concerning the determination of spatial relations, see also W. Woerkom's paper : *Journ. de Psych.*, nos. 8–9, 1921.

could not overlook this problem in discussing experimental pedagogics :
" As regards our receptive activity when we have sensations, general
psychology emphasises the fact that all our sensory organs are supplied
with motor apparatus and that each sensory organ is most efficient in
providing us with knowledge of the external world only when its perceptions
are associated with movements. A completely immobile eye would provide us with a much less perfect idea of the spatial world than a mobile
eyes does ; the immobile skin of our body provides us with fewer and
less precise percepts than does a mobile organ of touch ; the ear, as a
result of head movements not only in the direction of the source of a
sound, but also in the opposite direction, makes possible a nicer localisation
of sound.

Thus, in regard to the three main forms of sensation, we may speak of
three main sensory-motor ways of acquiring knowledge through our
receptive organs. These ways are : the tactual-motor, the auditory-motor,
and the visual-motor."[1]

[1] Meumann : *Vorlesungen über experimentelle Pädagogik*, Leipzig, 1911, Bd. I,
S. 201.

CHAPTER XLVII

The significance of the inhibition of associative processes for perception. The coincidence of thresholds of association reflexes with thresholds of sensation. The antithesis between conscious phenomena and the external manifestations of association-reflex activity. Experimental data in support of this thesis.

WHEN we speak of perception as a subjective process, we must keep in view not only the special tension of the activity of cerebral centres, as we observe, for instance, in concentration as a dominant process, but also, at the same time, processes of inhibition of other association reflexes. We know, on the other hand, that every impediment to, or inhibition of, association reflexes in respect of their external manifestations is accompanied by enhancement of the subjective state,[1] while the unimpeded discharge of association reflexes leads to weakening or even elimination of conscious or subjective phenomena.

And if this is so, we can make the following supposition : we have a number of stimuli acting on our cutaneous surface, on our eyes, ears, and other receptive organs, and exciting the appropriate subjective states, that is, sensations and ideas, while the motor and other association reflexes are, as a result of inhibition, not manifested to their full extent. Thus, we are perfectly justified in assuming, as we have said above, that we have here inhibited association reflexes which were originally manifested in their usual form of motor association reflexes, but were later inhibited in respect of their external manifestation. In the course of life, many association reflexes orginally evoked are later almost completely inhibited. Indeed, if we observe a new-born infant, we shall be struck by the multitude of movements he performs every minute, each external stimulus evoking in him a number of various movements.

Thus, stimulation even by moderate light causes, in the infant, a marked half-closing of the eyes, a number of grimaces, and also movements of the head and limbs. Obviously, these are reflexes which, as a result both of the development of the process of concentration and of the strengthening of inhibitory influences in respect of muscular contraction, are inhibited in the course of time.

The same holds good of other external stimulations which, in infancy, evoke a large number of various reflex movements, which are later suppressed. These reflexes are evoked, however, only when the infant is not engaged in sucking the breast, for sucking is a real dominant in the infant and counteracts the manifestation of other reflexes by suppressing them.

From the middle of the second to the middle of the third month approximately, visual and auditory concentration, which is a dominant repressing all other reflexes, becomes possible. This suppression of reflex movements promotes the greater intensity and distinctness of subjective states. Thus, it is clear that also in adults such stimulations of the receptive

---

[1] Intense subjective experiences under the influence of hypnotic suggestions (for instance, in the form of suggested hallucinations) and during ordinary sleep (in the form of dreams) are also bound up with inhibition of movement.

organs as produce appropriate sensations and ideas are conditioned by enhanced excitation of those cortical centres which are activated, and by concomitant inhibition of other reflexes, as we observe in concentration.

That this holds in actual life is proved by the fact that all pathological enhancement of reflexive excitability is immediately accompanied by the development of reflexes in response to such ordinary stimulations of the receptive organs as do not usually produce reflexes. This increase of reflexive excitability may also be produced artificially and with the same results, for example by strychnine poisoning. Here there is no question of increase in the intensity of sensations. At least, in these cases, the subjects do not complain of hyperesthesia and intense sensations.

Facts of another order show, on the other hand, that motor discharge weakens the intensity of sensation. Every one knows, for example, that when we have knocked our fingers against something, we repeatedly shake our fingers in the air and thus doubtlessly ease the pain.

Everything said above forces us to admit that our subjective states, in the forms of sensations and ideas, are conditioned by concentrated excitation of a certain centre—this excitation having been established in life experience—and by inhibition of other association reflexes.

So we see that even the explication of processes of subjective perception is impossible unless we admit concentrated excitation of appropriate cortical centres and inhibition of association-reflex processes in regard to all other stimulations. In other words, subjective processes of perception may be correctly explained only from the viewpoint of association reflexes evoked by external stimulation of the receptive organs.

We have said above that, from the standpoint of reflexology, the objective and the subjective aspects in association-reflex processes accompanied by reciprocation of energy stand in a certain interrelation with each other. To elucidate this interrelation, we shall dilate on the data bearing on the so-called thresholds of sensation. As we know, subjective psychology has established, on the basis of experiments in which external stimuli were applied, a minimal threshold as a measure of sensation. It has been proved by experiments in my laboratory that a minimal threshold can be determined for the association reflex also. It is sufficient, for this purpose, to inculcate an association reflex to some stimulation of an organ, and after this association reflex has been inculcated, the intensity of the associative stimulus may be decreased without eliminating or even weakening the reflex. However, this decrease may proceed only up to a certain minimum, after which further decrease will not be accompanied by production of the association reflex.

That minimal limit at which the association reflex can still be evoked we call the minimal or lowest threshold of the association reflex. By investigating this lowest threshold of the association reflex on oneself it may be seen that it approximately corresponds to the minimal threshold of sensation.

In cases of electro-cutaneous stimulation, however, we found that the objective differentiation of the association reflex proved nicer than the subjective and that the minimal stimulus evoking the association reflex proved to be unperceived (Krotkova and Tchegodayeva).

Further, it transpired from investigations made in my laboratory that differentiation of an association reflex in response to light-stimuli of different intensities may be carried to a limit corresponding to the difference limen of sensation (Dr. Molotkov). Lastly, topographical differentiation of an association reflex in response to cutaneous stimulations of touch may be carried to limits corresponding to Weber's tactual circles so-called (Dr. Israelson). This method, as well as other methods, of producing association reflexes may be used, by the way, not only for the detection of simulation of cutaneous anesthesia and disturbances in the activity of the receptive organs in general, but also for the detection of aggravation of such conditions. I have discussed this in detail in a special paper.[1] Lastly, what we have above called concentration and what in the physiological sense must be understood as a dominant is characterised in its subjective manifestation by the process of attention. The dominant is an expression of physiological tension of one centre with suppression of other centres—a tension which attracts co-excitations from neighbouring areas and, consequently, directs the course of the cerebral processes. This explains the determining tendencies discussed in subjective psychology, tendencies which the Würzburg school describes. It is clear from this that reflexology by no means identifies itself with association psychology, as some psychologists erroneously assume.

In the above cases there is, obviously, greater or lesser coincidence of objective phenomena, in the form of association reflexes, with subjective data discovered by self-observation.

However, is there, in every case, justification for speaking of interrelation between objective and subjective phenomena ? It transpires that this interrelation is somewhat different under certain conditions of association-reflex activity and requires explanation.

Just as our sensations may be regarded as phenomena resulting from concentrated excitation of a cortical area when reflexes are, at the same time, inhibited, so also we are justified in regarding all other subjective states as a result of concentrated excitation of the appropriate areas, when motor and other association reflexes are, at the same time, inhibited. Indeed, we have already seen that all association-reflex processes which discharge quickly in the form of movement are not accompanied by conscious, or at least intense, inner states. On the contrary, processes of excitation accompanied by inhibition of movement are inevitably accompanied by intense conscious or subjective states. This is precisely the case when intense mental activity or some difficult, though possible,

[1] V. Bechterev : *The Application of the Method of Association-motor Reflexes in the Investigation of Simulation—Russky Vratch*, no. 14, 1912. This method of investigating simulation was granted the highest award at the Dresden Physiological Exhibition.

mechanical work is being performed. Every one knows that if work is performed with attention, consequently consciously, it proceeds with great difficulty and comparatively slowly, while the same work performed without attention, consequently automatically, proceeds both more easily and more quickly.

Obviously, in these cases there is a disproportion between the conscious or subjective process and the objective process. The more conscious an activity is, the more the manifestation of the work is inhibited, and *vice versa*. But work is a reflex. Thus, it is clear that inhibition of reflexes with simultaneous excitation of a centre is accompanied by heightened consciousness, and *vice versa*.

Consequently, in association-reflex activity we are concerned with a process in which the external manifestations conditioned by the movement of the nervous current may come to preponderate over inner or conscious phenomena and, on the contrary, in other cases, inner or conscious phenomena may come to preponderate in intensity over various external manifestations.

It follows from this that we have here one and the same phenomenon in the form of movement of energy, in one case the external process being more marked at the expense of the intensity of the inner or subjective or " psychic " process ; in another case, the inner or " psychic " process being more marked at the expense of the manifestation and speed of the external motor process.

Thus, the inhibition of external motor manifestations, when it is simultaneous with the excitation of a centre, necessarily leads to intensification of consciousness, and *vice versa*.

This favours the view that subjective states—including mental processes—which are not accompanied by immediate external discharge in the form of movements are states which represent the excitation of cortical centres, when motor (speech and other) reflexes are externally unexpressed, a topic which we have already discussed.

As a matter of fact, we know that all ideas, thoughts, and, particularly, phantasy, which seem exclusively subjective phenomena, are, in fact, always accompanied by weak motor, vasomotor, and secretory effects easily detectible by means of suitable apparatus. Even a skilful thought-reader easily taps these movements and thereby determines the character of the thought, notwithstanding the fact that the movements are usually imperceptible to the thinker himself.[1] Obviously, these movements are, in a given case, external manifestations of association-reflex activity which are impeded and, consequently, reduced to a minimum.

Thus, we conclude that not only sensations, but also ideas and thoughts, are based on excitation of the central organs, this excitation being accompanied by inhibition of the motor aspect of association reflexes, which are given clear external expression only when the idea or thought passes into action.

[1] See Tarchanoff : *Tchtenie mislei*, etc. (*Thought Reading*, etc.), St. Petersburg.

A proof that subjective experiences are bound up with inhibition of motor and other nervous impulses, while discharge in movement leads to a lowering of consciousness, is afforded by the fact that, for instance in the course of mimico-somatic reflexes or emotional states, in which there is violent manifestation of motor effects, consciousness is lowered. On the contrary, consciousness is enhanced in the same person in a calmer state.

On the other hand, a number of incontrovertible facts show that external discharge of internal tension weakens the latter. Tears relieve sorrow. Confession eases an oppressive psychic state. Penance and remorse lighten the burden of guilt. Movements ease pain, etc.

All of this indicates that development of consciousness is bound up with development of processes of excitation, when, simultaneously, external movements are inhibited, while abundant and intense movement is obviously bound up with a lowering of consciousness, the latter gradually increasing *pari passu* with development and reinforcement of inhibitory processes.

In investigating association reflexes inculcated by the method in vogue in my laboratory (see above), we have repeatedly come across cases in which, in the first stage of the development of an association reflex, the subject answered the question why he jerked back his fingers or his foot, when in reality these were not stimulated by the current, by saying that he nevertheless experienced a shock ; in other words, under these conditions, a subjective process arose in the form of a hallucination, but disappeared in further experiments according as the motor association reflex became automatic.

This phenomenon of antithesis between the subjective aspect and the objective manifestation of association-reflex activity has recently come to light in K. N. Kornilov's investigations.[1] He succeeded in constructing a special apparatus—a dynamoscope, which is attached to the chain of Hipp's chronoscope ; and, consequently, in the investigation of so-called reactions, a triple record of the effect obtained—the temporal on the chronoscope, the dynamic and the motor on the dynamoscope—may be secured, the motor record indicating the form of the movement made by the hand in reacting.

Four series of experiments were made, with the following results : during a reaction performed naturally and without constraint, an exceedingly marked individual difference in respect of expenditure of energy is observed among different persons. Thus, one expends less than one dynamical unit ; another, under the same conditions, expends 22,500 dynamical units. This indicates the native passiveness or activeness.

In precisely the same way, different persons react unequally in respect both of speed and intensity ; in other words, a reaction may be weak and

[1] K. Kornilov : *The Method of the Application of Physical Energy to the Investigation of Psychical Processes.* The Moscow Society of Experimental Psychology. 19th March, 1914. *Vestnik Psychologii*, IV–V, 1914.

slow, weak and quick, strong and slow, or strong and quick. In so-called muscular reaction, in which "thought" activity is reduced to the minimum, it transpires that the external manifestation of energy reaches its maximum when the reaction is briefest, but, as soon as a complication is introduced into the experiment, for instance in the form of a "sensory" reaction or discriminating reaction, a certain quantum of the energy in the external manifestation of the reaction begins to be lost, and, at the same time, the reaction becomes slower.

It is clear from this that both tension of thought activity, such as is manifested in juridical proceedings, and external manifestation of energy are in inverse ratio. The external manifestation of association-reflex activity becomes less intense according as thought tension increases, and vice versa.

Even the quality of the thought process influences the amount of energy expended in movements. Let us assume that the external manifestation of energy during an elementary thought process is equal to 3600 dynamical units. As soon as we complicate the thought process, the energy falls to 2304 units, that is, there is a loss of 1296 dynamical units and, on further complication of the thought process, the energy falls to 650 units.

Here we note another interesting fact. When we calculate not the absolute, but the relative, decrease of energy during different thought processes, it transpires that, notwithstanding difference in the absolute store of energy, the same relative quantum of energy is always lost. Thus if, during a certain thought process, one expends 78,400 dynamical units, and another expends 4100, then, when the thought process is equally complicated for both, the relative decrease of energy is the same in both cases. However, it must be remarked that the latter fact has not yet been finally verified. The foregoing conclusions clearly accord with everyday observation. Thus, tense thinking stops all our movements. A man concentrating deeply on some problem is immobile. While walking, a man slackens his pace proportionally to the tension of his thought, etc. Thus, during a thought process, concentrated excitation of a cortical area, when this excitation is accompanied by muscular tension in the appropriate receptive organs, occurs with more or less complete inhibition of general movements. These phenomena, consequently, are explained by the process of dominant-formation.

CHAPTER XLVIII

Orientation and defence reflexes of the receptive organs. The close correlation in these reflexes between subjective and objective phenomena. The correlation between more complex association reflexes and associations in the sphere of subjective processes. The analysis of phenomena posited by the Würzburg school. The theory of association reflexes makes possible the positing of the correlation between complex psychical manifestations and objective processes of cerebral activity.

W E have already referred to the fact that every moderate influence, which affects one of the organs, necessarily excites a reflex in the receptive organ, this reflex placing the given organ in conditions more favourable to the reception of this influence.

Reflexes of this kind may, as we have already said, be called orientation reflexes of the receptive organs (Diagrams XII–XIX). However, the

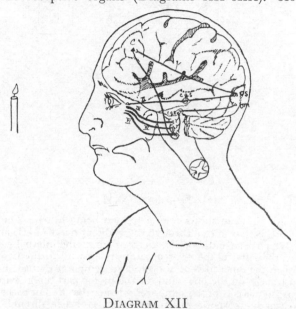

DIAGRAM XII

This schematic drawing shows how a human being sees. The retinal excitation evoked by light travels along the optic nerve (II) through the subcortical external geniculate body (*cgs*) to the retinal area of the cerebral cortex just on the fissura calcarina (*os*). Thence the excitation travels, on the one hand, along the associative conductors to the motor area (*om*) of the occipital lobe of the cerebral cortex, thence along the efferent conductors to the area of the anterior corpora quadrigemina (*cqs*), and through the posterior longitudinal bundle to the nuclei of the cranial nerves (VI, IV, III) and thus leads to the correct set of the eye. It travels, on the other hand, to the area of concentration in the frontal area of the cortex (*C*), whence it travels along the efferent conductors to the same nerves (VI, IV, III) which move the eyes, and produces active direction of the gaze, when there is concentration on the candle. In this, as in all the other schematic drawings, there is merely a representation of the fundamental direction of the nervous current, so as to make comprehensible, in the most general manner, the realisation of a reflex and to eliminate all other possible movements of the current along other channels. By the way, in this diagram, the process which we call a dominant is not represented.

excitation of positive orientation reflexes is observable only while the influence of the external stimulus is favourable to the organism. In the contrary case, a reflex of a different character is evoked in the same organ and leads, if possible, to removal or weakening of the external

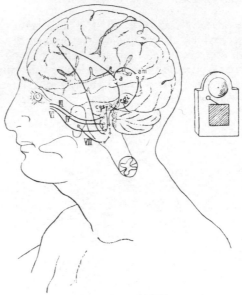

DIAGRAM XIII

This schematic drawing shows how a human being hears. The excitation of the organ of Corti is transmitted through the auditory nerve (VIII) and its cerebral continuation, which is an auditory conductive path, to the internal geniculate body (*cgi*), and from the latter to the cortical auditory area (*a*) in the two convolutions of Heschl and in the inner area of the superior temporal gyrus. From this area the excitation travels, on the one hand, to the motor part (*am*)—lying at the back (near the gyrus angularis)—of the same area whence the efferent paths are directed : (1) to the area of the corpora quadrigemina (*cqs*), thence through the posterior longitudinal bundle to the nuclei of the cranial nerves (VI, IV, III), and (2) to the colliculi inferiores and the lower-lying nuclei which give its set to the auditory organ (this latter direction of the current is not represented on this diagram). On the other hand, the excitation travels from the auditory area of active concentration, C (in the frontal area of the brain), the area whence the efferent conductors lead through the front part of the internal capsule and the cerebral peduncle to the nuclei of the same cranial nerves (VI, IV, III). The diagram shows the direction of the gaze towards the source of the sound, when there is active concentration on the sound-stimulus.

influence interfering with the activity of the organ and, if possible, to defence of the organ against the unfavourable influence. Such reflexes in the sphere of the organs of vision, audition, smell, taste, and touch, are so familiar to every one that we need not dilate on them.

These reflexes are doubtlessly acquired chiefly through individual

experience and may be called defence reflexes of the receptive
organs.

We have already mentioned that the majority of contemporary physiologists and psychologists explain the primary process of perception, which
is the basis of all other subjective processes in the human individual, by

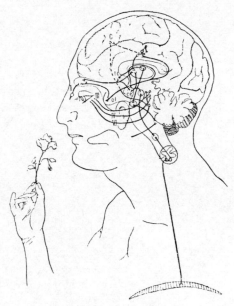

DIAGRAM XIV

This schematic drawing shows how a human being smells. (The inner surface
of the cerebral hemisphere is represented.) The excitation begins in the region
of the Schneider membrane, passes through the olfactory fibres (I) and the bulbus
olfactorius to the gyrus uncinatus (*ol*), to the tuber olfactorium (*tc*), and to the
corpus mammillare (*ce*). From the gyrus uncinatus (*ol*) the excitation travels
along the association fibres to the gyrus fornicatus (*gf*) whence it reaches the area
of active concentration (*C*) in the frontal part of the cortex and thence along the
efferent conductors to the nuclei of the cranial nerves (VI, IV, III) which set the
gaze on the object of smell. The other connections, namely of the tuber olfactorium (*tc*) and the corpus mammillare (*ce*) with other subcortical formations (the
thalamus opticus, the nucleus of Gudden, etc.) serve both the inhalation of air
into the nostrils and expressive movements of the face.

the participation of motor processes in the appropriate receptive organs ;
in other words, the process of perception is unrealisable in the absence
of those reflex movements which we have above described as orientation
reflexes.

Thus, on this first state of association-reflex activity, which establishes
the individual's correlation with the environment, subjective phenomena
are most intimately interwoven with those objective processes which,

under the influence of external stimuli, develop in the form of orientation association reflexes.

Consequently, there is a correlation the closest imaginable between subjective and objective phenomena. But what is the position in respect of complex processes of association-reflex activity ?

In this context, we must first of all ask to what extent all this activity,

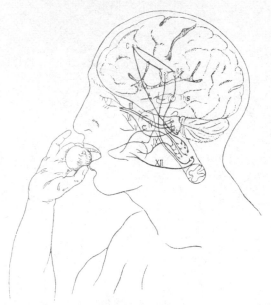

DIAGRAM XV

This schematic drawing shows how a human being tastes. The excitation, beginning in the tongue, is transmitted along nerves IX and V to the appropriate nuclei in the medulla oblongata and from the latter to the receptive subcortical nucleus in the thalamus opticus (*ths*), whence the excitation, by means of sub-cortical conductors, reaches the area in the neighbourhood of the posterior region of operculum (*gs*). Thence the excitation is transmitted partly to the motor cortical area serving the tongue and jaws, and then through efferent conductors to the nucleus of nerve XII so as to realise the act of eating, and partly to the frontal area of active concentration (*C*), whence the excitation travels along the efferent conductors to the nuclei of the cranial nerves (VI, IV, III), which effect appropriate direction of the gaze.

comprised of dominants and the development of association reflexes different in complexity and character, accords with the general character of the course of subjective processes, a course indicated by the data of subjective psychology.

We know that all authorities do not regard psychical processes as developing exclusively according to the laws of association. Some psychologists regard the logical process as one different in quality from the associative.

Yet the viewpoint which subsumes logical inference under the category of associative processes pursuing a definite course cannot be excluded.[1] Thus, Marbe's well-known investigations show that reasoning processes

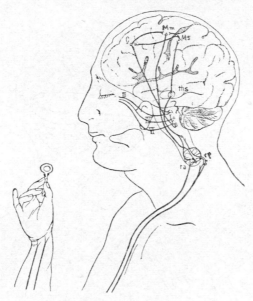

DIAGRAM XVI

This schematic drawing shows how a human being explores an object by touch. The excitation from the mechanical stimulation of the object touched travels along the centripetal nerves of the hand to the spinal ganglia and along the dorsal radices (*rp*) to the cells of the grey matter of the spinal cord and to the nuclei of the medulla oblongata (nuclei of Goll and Burdach). From here, along the spino-thalamic tract and the lemniscus, the excitation reaches the subcortical receptive nucleus in the thalamus opticus (*ths*), whence it ascends to the receptive manual centre (*Ms*) in the middle region of the postcentral and præcentral gyri, and thence, along the association conductors, it is transmitted to the appropriate manual motor centre (*Mm*) in the middle region of the præcentral gyrus. From the latter centre, the excitation then travels along the efferent pyramidal bundles to the ventral cornua of the cervical enlargement, and then, through the ventral radices (*ra*), to the muscles of the hand which operate in touch. Active touching presupposes, however, participation of the sphere of concentration (*C*) in the frontal region of the cerebral cortex, and this is realised by transmission of the impulse from the manual centre (*Ms*) in the cortex of the postcentral gyrus to the area of concentration (*C*), and from *C* the excitation travels along the efferent conductors to the nuclei of VI, IV, and III, which move the eyes, which, in this case, inevitably follow the movement of the hand.

do not essentially differ from associations either in respect of intrinsic character or sometimes even of the speed of their realisation. Anyhow, we are scarcely justified in denying that, at the basis of logical inference,

[1] See the discussion of these views in my *Objective Psychology*, 3rd pt.

lies the same associative process, which, however, is given a particular direction—in the form of the combination of a major and a minor premiss ; and, consequently, a definite direction of association is established. This

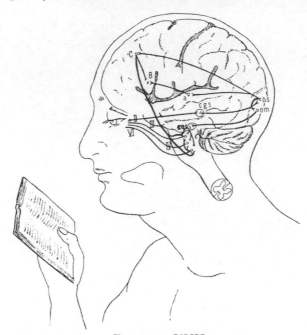

DIAGRAM XVII

This schematic drawing shows how a human being reads. The excitation, which, under the influence of printed signs, that is, symbolic stimuli, begins in the retina, travels along the optic nerve (II) to the subcortical external geniculate body (*cgs*), whence it ascends to the retinal area of the cerebral cortex in f. calcarina (*os*). From this area it travels, on the one hand, through the associative connections to the motor area (*om*) of the cortex of the lateral areas of the occipital lobe, thence along the efferent nerves to the anterior corpora quadrigemina (*cqs*), and thence, along the posterior longitudinal bundle, to the nuclei of the cranial nerves (VI, IV, III) which fix the gaze on the book. On the other hand, the excitation travels from the occipital area of the cerebral cortex partly to the speech centre of Wernicke (*a*), thence to Broca's centre (*B*), which is connected by efferent conductors (not represented in the drawing) with the nuclei of the medulla oblongata which control speech movements, and partly to the area of concentration (*C*) in the frontal region of the cerebral cortex, whence the excitation travels along the efferent conductors to the same cranial motor nuclei (VI, IV, III)—so that the eyes are actively adjusted and follow the letters—and simultaneously to Broca's centre (*B*) for active reproduction of the words.

may be explained only by admitting, in addition to the concatenation of association reflexes in this process, the participation of what we understand by the term dominant.

Nevertheless, some recent psychologists, especially those of the Würzburg school, posit the existence, as it were, of autonomous phenomena of " psychic " activity, phenomena which, as verbally unexpressed thoughts, as lightning-like inferences, so to speak, etc., suddenly burst into the course of the process. Still, it is impermissible to assume that they are

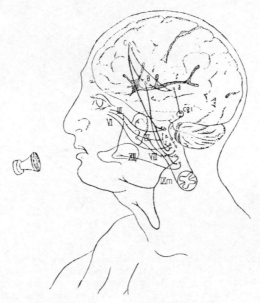

DIAGRAM XVIII

This schematic drawing shows how a human being speaks. The sound-waves received by the ear, when we converse with another person, reach the organ of Corti in the inner ear, whence the excitation is centripetally transmitted along nerve VIII and further along the auditory path to the subcortical internal geniculate nucleus (*cgi*), after which the excitation, travelling along the centripetal subcortical conductors, reaches the centre of Wernicke (*a*) in the middle region of the cortex of the left superior temporal gyrus, but from this centre the excitation is transmitted, on the one hand, to the area of concentration (*C*) in the frontal region of the cerebral cortex ; on the other, to the motor speech centre of Broca (*B*), from which the excitation is transmitted along the efferent conductors to the nuclei of nerves XII and IX *m*, which control the movements of the tongue and the larynx. Simultaneously, active concentration on the topic of conversation is conditioned by the travelling of the excitation from the area (*a*) of Wernicke to the centre of concentration (*C*) in the frontal region, and from this centre, on the one hand, to the area of Broca (*B*), and, on the other, along the efferent conductors to the nuclei of the cranial nerves (VI, IV, III), which turn the gaze in the appropriate direction.

something quite special, having not even a distant connection with perception produced by external stimulation. Is it inconceivable to assume that they are explicable by the attracting force of excitation, a force which characterises the process of the dominant and can extract appropriate products from unaccountable processes ?

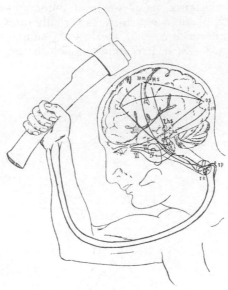

DIAGRAM XIX

This schematic drawing shows how a human being works. The peripheral excitation, arising under the influence of the cutaneo-muscular stimulations of gripping and holding the handle of the axe with the hand, travels along the centripetal peripheral nerves and the dorsal radices (*rp*), and reaches, on the one hand, the grey matter of the spinal cord (cutaneous stimulation), and, on the other, through the posterior fasciculi, reaches the appropriate nuclei of Goll and Burdach in the medulla oblongata (muscular stimulations) and thence, through the mediation of the stratum lemnisci, the receptive subcortical nucleus of the thalamus opticus (*ths*). Simultaneously, the excitation travels from the grey matter of the spinal cord, through the mediation of the spinothalamic tract, to the receptive subcortical nucleus in the thalamus opticus (*ths*). Thence the excitation, both from the skin and the muscles, reaches, through the subcortical centripetal conductors, the receptive cortical manual (*Ms*) area in the middle region of the postcentral gyrus. Then the excitation travels along the association paths to the appropriate manual motor area (*Mm*) in the præcentral gyrus and thence along the pyramidal bundle to the ventral cornua of the cervical enlargement of the spinal cord, whence the excitation travels through the ventral radices (*ra*) and motor nerves to the muscles of the arm and causes their contraction. Simultaneously, visual stimulation arises from the object of work, and this stimulation is transmitted through nerve II, travels to the subcortical external geniculate nucleus (*cgs*), and thence to the retinal area of the cerebral cortex in the fis. calcarina (*os*). From the latter, the excitation travels, on the one hand, to the lateral occipital motor region (*om*), thence to the area of the anterior corpora quadrigemina (*cqs*), and then to the nuclei of the cranial motor nerves (VI, IV, III) for the fixation of the gaze on the object of work, and, on the other hand, to the receptive manual area (*Ms*) for visual control of the movements of the hand. The impulses travel from the occipital area partly to the area of concentration in the frontal area (*C*), whence they go to the appropriate manual motor area (*Mm*) (for the active direction of manual movements issuing from inner stimulations) and partly along the efferent conductors to the nuclei of the cranial nerves (for direction of the gaze during concentration on the work).

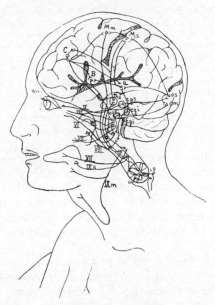

DIAGRAM XX

This schematic drawing illustrates cerebral reflexes in processes of sleep and wakefulness. The excitation, arising under the influence of cutaneous and muscular stimuli, ascends along the centripetal conductors of the peripheral nerves and the dorsal radices (*rp*), and then ascends in the spinal cord along the spinothalamic tract and the posterior fasciculi to the medulla oblongata and thence, by the same route, along the spinothalamic tract and the lemniscus to the receptive nucleus of the thalamus opticus (*ths*), to which the centripetal conductors from the organ of taste also lead running along nerve IX*s*. Thence the excitation, travelling from the nerves of the hand along the subcortical conductors, reaches the cerebral cortex of the postcentral (and the præcentral) gyrus (*Ms*), whence it travels along the association paths to the appropriate part (*Mm*) of the præcentral gyrus, and, from the latter, along the efferent bundles, the excitation reaches, on the one hand, the nuclei of the facial nerve and so causes contraction of the muscles of the face, and, on the other, descends along the ventral horns of the spinal cord and thence, through the ventral radices (*ra*), reaches the muscles of the extremities. Retinal stimulations travel centripetally along nerve II to *cgs*, and thence to the retinal cortex fis. calcarina (*os*), whence the excitation travels, on the one hand, to the adjoining area of the lateral region of the occipital lobe (*om*) ; thence it is transmitted along the efferent conductors to the anterior corpora quadrigemina (*cqs*) and then to the nuclei of nerves VI, IV, III, and through them to the corresponding cranial nerves. On the other hand, the excitation travels from the retinal cortex (*os*) to the centre of Wernicke (*a*) for the revival of the speech mechanism ; also to the receptive and motor centres (*Ms, Mm*) of both central gyri, and thus produces movements of the extremities. Further, under the influence of sound-stimuli, the excitation of the organ of Corti, travelling along nerve VIII and the central auditory conductors, reaches the subcortical posterior geniculate nucleus (*cgi*), whence it ascends along the centripetal subcortical conductors to the centre of Wernicke (*a*) ; from the latter, it travels along the association conductors partly to the receptive centre of the postcentral gyrus, and, being transmitted to the præcentral gyrus, produces gesticulatory movements and facial expressive movements, but it is mainly transmitted to Broca's gyrus (B), whence, travelling along the efferent conductors, it reaches nuclei XII and IXm, and through them the speech muscles which they innervate. But simultaneously with these excitations, impulses from the sympathetic sphere come into operation, and, being transmitted along the sympathetic afferent conductors of the spinal cord, the medulla oblongata, and the mesencephalon, reach the hypothalamic area of the diencephalon (which embraces *ths* in the diagram), and from this latter, travelling along the subcortical conductors, they reach the cortical area (C), whence they are transmitted along the association conductors to the motor areas of the cerebral cortex. During sleep, the area of active concentration (C) is depressed, and the cutaneo-muscular-motor sphere, which is free from internal stimulations from the area of C, is in a passive state.

We must admit that subjective analysis always recognises certain gaps in self-observation, for only part of the association-reflex process occurs in the conscious or accountable sphere, while the other part occurs in the subconscious or unaccountable. The determining tendencies of subjective processes, tendencies assumed by the Würzburg school, accord with the principle of the dominant, which doubtlessly participates in logical processes also.

Lastly, however subjective these processes may be in reality, the only question is whether they may be regarded as processes bearing no relation to the nervous current which travels along the nerve tissue, or whether they stand in correlation with cerebral processes, which, as physiology tells us, are accompanied by action-current. If their correlation with the nervous current cannot be excluded, and this correlation may, in the light of present-day science, be regarded as an incontrovertible truth (see diagrams XVI, XVII, and XVIII), we are justified, from the objective standpoint, in regarding them as higher or association reflexes, at the basis of which lies the movement of the nervous current along the cells and fibres of the cerebral hemispheres.

And if this is so, the theory of association reflexes makes possible, in this case also, the positing of an intimate correlation between the subjective processes mentioned and the objective processes of cerebral activity. However, the external manifestations of this latter activity are here reduced to a minimum, which, nevertheless, may be revealed in appropriate investigations, for, as we have said above, each more or less tense thought is divested neither of motor manifestations in the appropriate receptive organs nor of cardio-vascular and secretory effects.

CHAPTER XLIX

Psychical processes are a result of tension of nervous energy. Concentration, which is bound up with detention of the nervous current, is accompanied by conscious phenomena. Thought as an inhibited reflex. Setting aside the theory of parallelism, we must posit the existence of a unitary process, in which the external and internal phenomena are expressions of the same energy. Sense images develop in connection with a certain complex of motor impulses in the form of cerebral reflexes.

EVERYTHING said above leads to the conclusion that psychic or subjective processes are, as we have already mentioned, a result of tension of energy or of nervous current in certain areas of the cerebral cortex, while there is simultaneous inhibition of other areas. In cases in which the conditions of nervous conductivity are facilitated and the nervous current moves unimpeded, the subjective process or consciousness is weakened and even disappears. We have already said that, for instance, every action performed for the first time is mostly conscious, while every habitual action is unconscious. But even an habitual action may become conscious, if it is performed slowly and with concentration on each component movement.

Concentration, as a process of excitation of a definite centre, is invariably bound up with impediment or inhibition of other centres; hence it happens that everything that produces concentration is accompanied by conscious perception; everything that is not accompanied by concentration goes unperceived and, consequently, occurs without the participation of consciousness.

Active reproduction, too, stands in direct connection with concentration, which arises from inner impulses. Some of the phenomena of suggestion and hypnosis,[1] as well as many manifestations of such neuroses as hysteria and traumatic neurosis, may be explained by suppression of concentration.[2]

During concentration on an object, all other stimuli are non-existent, as it were, and we neither hear nor see what is going on around us, but, as soon as we are distracted from the object with which we have been preoccupied, we begin to hear and see everything happening around us.

[1] V. Bechterev : *Suggestion and its Rôle in Social Life*, 3rd ed., St. Petersburg. *Hypnosis, Suggestion, and Psychotherapy*, St. Petersburg. *La suggestion et son rôle dans la vie sociale*, Paris. In the French work, a chapter elucidating hypnosis and suggestion from the reflexological standpoint has been added.

[2] Clinical investigations recently carried out under my supervision lead to the conclusion that, in cases of hysteria and traumatic neurosis, speedy release from inhibition is produced by the artificial inculcation (by a method developed in my laboratory) of association reflexes in those organs whose function has been suppressed, this release from inhibition leading to a cure. Thus, neurotic anesthesias, deafness, etc., were removed. (V. Bechterev : *Obozrenie Psychiatrii*, nos. 1-12, 1917-18.) Besides, in those partially deaf, the method of calling out association-motor reflexes may be of practical significance in perfecting audition. I shall not here dilate on all these facts, for they belong to the sphere of pathological reflexology and reflexological therapy. I am preparing these facts for publication.

Translators' note : The German translation refers the reader to *Vestnik sovremennoi meditzini*, 1926, and *Therapia*, 1926.

Obviously, this process of distraction, by an influence to which concentration is not directed at the given moment, lies at the root of the phenomena of suggested anesthesia.[1] Fechner compared the distraction of concentration to a partial sleep of the centres and we may reasonably suppose that real sleep also, on whatever we may regard it as based bio-chemically, is ultimately related to processes of inhibition developed biologically for the purpose of defending the brain from further activity detrimental to it. Therefore, sleep may be reasonably regarded as a defence reflex biologically evolved (see above).

Our sensations, as Mach has already shown, are by no means passive processes. Even the lower organisms respond to external stimuli by reflexive movements. In the higher animals, too, stimuli evoke reflexes which, because of the inhibitory activity of the centres, are not always externally manifested. In the infant, reflexes are inevitable results of external stimulation, but in later life they are gradually inhibited, chiefly as a result of the development of concentration. Simultaneously, the subjective aspect of the ideational process develops, and becomes more and more marked as the child grows up.

Finally, what are what we call ideas and thoughts, by which we understand the subjective process which has attained a certain completeness and degree of development? Is this process distinct from other manifestations of association-reflex activity? As a matter of fact, every idea is accompanied either by weakly expressed external movements in the form of words or actions or by internal movements and secretions. When a person intensely thinks of something he must say to someone whom he will meet, he involuntarily says the words quietly, while he is thinking over what he is to say. Visualise a man yawning before sleep, and you will feel the approach of a fit of yawning. Imagine that you are listening to the strains of the *Marseillaise*, and you notice that you are quietly humming it. Imagine that you are playing a difficult piece on the piano, and your fingers begin lightly to play it on an imaginary key-board. Remember an insult which has been offered you, and you manifest movements expressive of anger and hate. When you hear a description of woeful events, tears fill your eyes. Imagine something that excites nausea, and you feel a salivary secretion such as one experiences before the onset of real nausea. Remember a sorrow suffered, and your throat constricts and your heart is wrung. Imagine the joy of an expected meeting, and your heart bounds and your respiration quickens.

According to Ribot, the " idea " of a movement is already the beginning of a movement or is a movement on the point of realisation. The bulbar centre becomes excited and the movement is performed whether this

---

[1] *Translators' note :* Here the German translation of the 3rd ed. has : " Obviously, this process of distraction, produced by a verbal influence to which concentration is at the moment not directed, lies at the root of the phenomena of suggestion."

idea is real (direct perception) or evoked by memory.[1] These are not only everyday observations, but facts accurately verified. I shall mention some of them.

A number of pertinent investigations have been made in the sphere of vascular and secretory activity, including cutaneo-secretory and cutaneo-galvanic currents.

Here belong the investigations of A. Mosso, Tarchanoff, Lehmann, Veraguth, Henkin (my laboratory), and many others on galvanic reactions, and also a number of investigations on so-called " psychic " salivary and gastric juice secretions.

These " psychic " secretions, by the way, attracted attention as early as the 18th century. Even then it was known that when oats is given to a horse, he secretes saliva before the oats enters his mouth. Mitscherlich's investigations, made in 1835 on a man suffering from fistula of a salivary duct, have been already mentioned. Much later, in 1905, Malloisel produced a dissertation on the " psychic " secretion of saliva.

In Russia, extensive investigations in this respect have been made on dogs by representatives of Pavlov's school. Some pertinent data have been studied in my laboratory also.

On the other hand, experiments made in my laboratory (Dr. Spirtov) show that if a finger is held in the Sommer apparatus designed to record finger movements and if, at the same time, the thoughts are concentrated on finger movements to the right or to the left, the indicatory levers immediately deviate in the appropriate direction. Interesting experiments in thought-reading and in the registration of the scarcely noticeable movements which then occur have been already mentioned.

What does all this signify ? It means that thought as a purely " spiritual " idea does not exist, that thought cannot be manifested in some cases without weak verbal expression ; in other cases without other scarcely noticeable movements ; in still other cases without some more or less weakly expressed respiratory, cardiac, and vascular changes, and movements of inner organs ; in other cases without the appearance of tears, secretion of saliva and of other juices of the alimentary tract, etc.

But all these manifestations are merely association reflexes more or less impeded in respect of their external manifestation. It is clear from this that thought also is a higher or association reflex, but a reflex inhibited in its external manifestation, as we have already said. Consequently, there is but one process, in which the inner phenomena, in the form of thought, are merely inhibited reflexes in which the subjective process is more marked in comparison with the external objective process.

For this reason, there is no justification for dilating further on the theory of parallelism. Our view of the problem of correlative activity is that there is a unitary process, viz. movement of energy in the form of nervous current. In this process, the external objective and the internal

[1] Ribot : *Psychologie des sentiments,* p. 29.

or psychic phenomena occur in perfect oneness, and the process of movement of energy along the nerve conductors is not even momentarily interrupted at any point.

We have seen that, in the sphere of so-called sense images, subjective analysis has come to the conclusion that they develop in connection with a definite complex of motor impulses. On the other hand, the physicist Mach,[1] like Wahle, has contended that psychic images are really a certain grouping of sensations. Their content is, however, fragmentary and inconstant. If we think, for instance, of a friend, he may be sad or gay, elegantly dressed or in *négligé*, etc., and we can mentally reproduce certain details, for instance, his eyes, his face, his gestures, etc. Thus, it is clear that mental images have no such fixity as a developed photographic plate has, but are really an imperfect trace left over from sensations,[2] or, more accurately, a moving trace, and the origin of sensations, as we have seen, cannot be explained without correlation with reflexive movements of the organs.

Thus, it is obvious that mental images must not be regarded as wholes, as indivisible units and that, in fact, they cannot be localised as such in the brain.

On further analysis, Mach concludes that mental images are composed of those motor sensations which accompany cerebral reflexes.

On the other hand, N. Kostyleff[3] concludes that mental images are merely cerebral reflexes and that they are not processes which perfectly reconstruct everything seen, heard, and touched, but only reproduce two or three of the more important features in the form of motor sensations, for instance in the form of sensations of measure, identification, etc.

We have already said that sensations are inhibited or unexpressed association reflexes of whatever kind. There are data in favour of the view that more complex subjective processes also, which are most intimately associated with these external sensations, are also unexpressed association reflexes, for these processes are reducible to internal revival of these same external sensations, but only in correlation with other external and internal conditions.

Ultimately, analysis shows that abstract ideas also are merely manifestations of the same reflexes reproduced according to a connection established. If we have, for instance, general concepts : man, horse, book, etc., we are really concerned here with what is common to visual-motor, auditory-motor, tactual-motor, and other reflexes, which have arisen from impressions made on us by different men, horses, books, etc.

Thus, it is obvious that complex subjective phenomena also, in their nature, may be understood only by adducing for their explanation a complex of reflexes. This gives a footing for the establishment of a close

---

[1] E. Mach : *Die ökonomische Natur der physikalischen Forschung*, 1882.
[2] E. Mach : *Analyse der Empfindungen*, Wien, 1885.
[3] N. Kostyleff : *Les substituts de l'âme dans la psychologie moderne*, Paris, 1906.

inner connection of these phenomena with cerebral reflexes, which are objective occurrences (diagrams XII–XIX).

However, the problem arises whether subjective phenomena, as, for instance, affective states, are primary or secondary in mimico-somatic reflexes. This question is tantamount to asking what is primary in man : metaphysically expressed—soul or body ? The James-Lange theory, as we know, regards somatic processes as primary in emotion. Others, taking the opposite view, stand for central localisation of these states in the cortex and in the thalamus opticus.[1] However, this question may be asked only by those holding the dualistic viewpoint. But for us, who hold the energic view, which we make the basis of reflexology, this question does not arise, for, as a result of the manifestation of the nervous current, we have simultaneously, in the given case, both external or objective phenomena manifested in the sympathico-somatic sphere and inner or subjective phenomena the origin of which may be, in one case, a result of a higher or association reflex, in another, a result of lower reflexes arising in the somatic sphere. Naturally, in both cases, the external and the internal phenomena go hand in hand, although it must be noted that the internal phenomena are not necessarily accountable and, in respect of intensity, do not completely accord with the external.

However this may be, both the internal and the external phenomena are alike specific. Let us take the sphere of feeling. Let us assume that we suffer from insufficiency of water in the body. Experience, elaborated by life and conditioned by the drinking of liquid to compensate for insufficiency of water in the body, leads to the production of an aggressive reflex in regard to liquid ; in other words, to a tendency to imbibe liquid, or to a need for drink. This reflex, which may be qualitatively defined as aggressive, is accompanied by inner signals, which we call a feeling of thirst. When we are thirsty, we say that the thirst makes us want to drink or causes a tendency to use water for the needs of the body, while, in reality, the aggressive reflex which has developed has here the same significance in respect of the realisation of drinking as has the inner process called the feeling of thirst. Both are specific and characterised by qualitative peculiarities.

In this case, the reflex has arisen from the somatic sphere, and having been realised also in the somatic sphere, produces an active condition— in the form of a somato-motor and visual-motor reflex—in the cortical areas also. But when we weep over the coffin of a dear person, the primary impulse arises under the influence of an external stimulus and, by establishing an association reflex, excites a reaction in the form of a general physical state which leads to tears. In this case, the beginning was a higher or association reflex, which evoked the same cardio-vascular reaction as appears in a physical state conditioned by strong external stimulations, for instance intense destructive processes. But it is clear that, in both examples, the subjective state stands in direct connection

[1] C. Dana : *Archives of Neurology and Psychology*, VI, p. 634, 1921.

with the changes in, and the state of, the somatic sphere. In the first case, we are thirsty because of lack of water in the body and because of changes, brought about by this lack, in the somatic sphere, for instance insufficiency of fluid in the vessels, etc. In the second case, we weep as a result of changes which have occurred in the form of a reflex in the cardio-vascular system, these changes reproducing changes which have already been produced by powerful destructive stimuli.

CHAPTER L

The complex phenomena of the inner world stand in definite correlation with external manifestations in the form of reflexes. An analysis—from this standpoint—of the main theses of the Würzburg school of experimental psychology.

IT must be remembered that the more complex internal phenomena also stand in correlation with external manifestations which take the form of reflexes. Details of this subject may be found in a work by Dr. Kostyleff,[1] the translator of my *Objective Psychology* into French. He analyses, from the standpoint mentioned, a number of the more important works of the Würzburg school, which clearly indicates the subjective trend of contemporary experimental psychology. Let us here discuss this analysis.

In Henry Watt's[2] investigations, the method was the same as that used by Scripture, Münsterberg, and others in their investigations, but with the one difference : that the reaction to the questions asked was not free, but was limited to logical responses and to an accurate description of everything the subject experienced in the course of the experiment. The data derived from these investigations permit us to distinguish, at the outset, in the psychic process : (1) attention ; (2) the perception of the stimulus-words ; (3) the search for an answer ; and (4) the appearance of the response-word. Each of these stages has its characteristics. The first stage is characterised by physical and moral tension ; the second, by the particular nature of the perception, which, in some cases, is simply visual, in others, is accompanied by sub-vocal utterance of the words ; the third, by the different degrees of the subject's activeness or passiveness ; the fourth, by the discovery of visual, auditory, or motor phenomena with a shade of emotionality.

The reactions fall into two main groups : direct answers and bifurcated answers. The reactions of the first group are divided into : responses by means of a visual image ; responses by means of a verbal symbol ; and purely mechanical responses without any intermediate phenomenon. The reactions of the second group are divided into : (a) answers with conscious direction, that is, when the subject searches for an answer in a certain direction, while it comes from another direction ; and (b) answers with unconscious direction, that is, when the subject searches for an answer, but without being able to determine what kind of answer, while the answer meantime comes quite independently. Let us take as an example the stimulus-word : " universe." Logical task : find a subordinate term.

[1] Kostyleff : *Le mécanisme cérébral de la pensée*, Paris. We note in passing that N. Kostyleff presents the subject in a wrong light, for he assumes that reflexology absolutely excludes subjective processes from its sphere, while it is clear from the foregoing that, in making objectivo-biosociological data the cornerstone, reflexology does not admit subjective phenomena as isolated data, but does not exclude them when they are derived by the method of direct self-observation and are investigated in direct relation to objective data, which should control them.
[2] Henry Watt : *Exper. Beiträge zu einer Theorie des Denkens*. *Arch. f. d. gesam. Psych.*, IV, 1904.

Answer : " Immediately after the perception of the stimulus-word, a number of vague terms flit through my head, and here I become aware of the futility of the search, and then, to my own surprise, answer : ' star.' "

The quickest responses are the mechanical ; then follow those with a visual or a verbal symbol ; while the slowest are those with unconscious tension. Besides, transition to a subordinate term requires more time than transition to a more general term.

Investigation shows that, apart from simple and direct reactions, the experiment excites processes which are characterised by the subjective quality of arbitrariness and represent impulses of the brain itself, as it were.

Ultimately, the results of the investigation justify the conclusion that the mental process is not a passive reaction ; on the contrary, the brain is endowed with its proper activeness setting in motion the individual's past experience, which is utilised as a result of the activeness of the process, an activeness which results from stimulations issuing from organic functions.

The same writer does not confine himself to phenomena of associations. Noticing that the majority of answers, excluding the mechanical, are, at the same time, reasoning, he begins by discussing Marbe's thesis that, from the viewpoint of inner observation, reasoning does not differ from association, and that in reasoning the answer follows as quickly as in association. But, from the objective standpoint, reasoning differs from association, viz., by the presence of a task as a precondition, for reasoning occurs only when association is directed. But this favours the view that reasoning is association also, but with this difference : that the direction of the association is conditioned by a given task which plays the part of a stimulus.

As a matter of fact, all the experimental data clearly approximate to the concept of reflex. The answers are verbal-motor reactions, and what is called facility or difficulty is merely a result of inner inhibitory conditions varying in degree. Impulses, since they are a result of excitation of past experience, are verbal-motor in character, for they consist in the utterance of one word in preference to another.

Here attention must be called to the automatism manifested both in the influence of the task and in the so-called " pure tendencies of the brain."

Watt points out that, under the same conditions, preference is always given from among many tendencies to that which, because it has been oftener reproduced, is the most speedily reproduced.

According to Kostyleff, if the rather vague term, " tendencies," is replaced by the scheme of verbal-motor or emotive reflexes, then Watt's formula perfectly fits the conditions of the functioning of the brain as a reflexive apparatus, for the oftener a reflex is produced, the more quickly and easily is it capable of being produced. Therefore, the given reflex has more chance of being reproduced than have other reflexes which have been less frequently produced. The tendency to the reproduction of previous processes or images corresponds to the functioning of the cerebral reflex.

Turning to A. Messer's[1] investigations, we must remember that the experimental procedure was almost the same, and even the subjects experimented on were the same, but the investigations were carried much further, for the investigator passed over from experiments with simple associations, to those with free and more varied reactions. In the first six groups of experiments, a single word was presented, as in Watt's experiments, but from the seventh to the eleventh group of experiments, two words were presented, and in the last three experiments the words were replaced by a sentence, an object, or a picture. This change necessitated change of the logical task, which, from the seventh group, no longer consisted in association, but required the formulation of relations between two reactions, and from the eleventh group onwards, there was a still more complex process of perception and reaction. Thus, for instance in the ninth group, the task required a comparison of two persons named by the investigator : such as " Plato-Aristotle." Answer : " The greater—the greater genius." In the eleventh group, the task consisted of a thesis or question and required the adoption of a personal standpoint. Example : " Nietzsche is systematic." Answer : " The opposite," etc. In the thirteenth group, the stimulus was an object or a picture, and the task required reacting with the first thought which presented itself. Example : " Archaic figures of Adam and Eve in the Hildesheim Cathedral." Answer : " Assyrian sculpture." This writer analyses his experimental results in greater detail than does Watt.

As regards reasoning, Messer discusses, in passing, the physiological basis of the process. The influence of the task, according to him, has special organic significance. It represents a certain enhancement of the activity through anticipation of a co-ordinated reaction and this enhancement or effort of attention distinguishes reasoning from simple association, for in the first case there is complete adaptation of reactions to the impulses received, and this is not true of the second.

It must be assumed that that impediment or inhibition which precedes the transition of a tendency into a strictly co-ordinated reaction corresponds to the enhancement mentioned and, in this respect, we again find that the data of subjective psychology accord with the data of reflexology.

Messer divides reasoning processes in the following way : according to their content—into positive and negative, analytic and synthetic, abstract and concrete ; according to their relation to the other phenomena of conscious life—into new and repeated, whole and fragmentary, intermediary and final ; according to the attitude of the subject—into theoretical and practical, proper and derived, categorical and problematic ; according to their relation to the external world—into perceptual and imaginative reasoning.

[1] A. Messer : *Experimentell-psychologische Untersuchungen über das Denken.* *Arch. f. d. gesam. Psych.*, 1906, Bd. VIII.

Needless to say, these subdivisions cannot be regarded as satisfactory from the objective standpoint, and, therefore, there is no necessity to dilate on them here. Messer's investigations concerning the " disposition of consciousness " (*Bewusstseinslage*), which Erdmann called " unformulated thoughts," deserve attention.

On the basis of his investigations, Messer concludes that the actual processes which form the basis of thought may be fragmentary both in psychological expression and in expenditure of psycho-physical energy. This formula again accords with the objective understanding of phenomena.

According to Dr. Kostyleff, the production of a reflex arc is, in this case, accompanied by fragmentary remnants of associative reactions. For instance, visual perception may incidentally release verbal-motor reactions. Therefore, the scheme of cerebral reflexes not only harmonises with phenomena of this kind, but makes them even inevitable. In an educated man, the cerebral mechanism in general is so mobile that it is almost impossible to evoke in him a homogeneous and strictly isolated reaction.

Further, let us dilate on Messer's attempts to determine the course of thought. This course is twofold : along the path of associations, and along the path of expansion (*Entfaltung*). Associations, which form the basis of reasoning, lead to a more complex logical process, but the process of expansion belongs to those phenomena which have been mentioned above and consist in unformulated thoughts.

Thus, here too, the scheme of cerebral or association reflexes, completely or partially developed, throws a perfectly satisfactory light on the problem.

Turning to Bühler's[1] investigations, it is necessary to keep in view that the interrogatory method is applied here to still more complex phenomena than in the investigations mentioned earlier, for the questions, which were presented to highly educated persons, required well-thought-out answers. Let us cite the following examples. Simpler questions : " Can you calculate the speed of a falling body ? " " Can Berlin be reached from here in seven hours ? " More complex questions : " Do you know what Eucken understands by the term ' world apperception ' ? " " Can we, by thinking, comprehend the essence of thought ? " " Do you believe that Fichte's philosophy was productive ? "

Besides, Bühler used paradoxes also in his investigations. Let us cite an example. Stimulus : " To give each what belongs to him means to desire justice and to create chaos." Response : " Yes." " At first, a moment of reflection with fixation on the surface in front of me. The echo of the words with special accentuation of the beginning and end of the sentence ; a tendency to make sense of everything said. Then suddenly the memory of a fragment of Spencer's criticism of altruism,

[1] Bühler : *Tatsachen und Probleme zu einer Psychologie der Denkvorgänge*— *Arch. f. d. gesam. Psych.*, 1907, IX ; 1908, XII.

in which he proves that altruism will never achieve its aim. After this I answered : ' Yes.' As idea, nothing but the word ' Spencer.' ''

On the basis of similar investigations, the same writer posits another process differing from association, a new process, which constitutes the " summit of thought." An example in the form of an aphorism : " The real rogues are to be found among criminals, but among those who have committed no crime." Answer : " Yes." At first the effort to explain : how can this be maintained ? Memories referring to Lombroso ; then suddenly the following thought completely imageless : " Don't those who are so cunning as to avoid conflict with the law commit a crime ? These are, therefore, the real rogues."

Bühler assumes that, in these cases, there are new processes, because there is something that " has no sensory quality and no sensory intensity, something that the subject designates as consciousness or what is more accurately and more commonly designated as thoughts." This pure act of thought or these data of pure ideation he classifies as follows : (1) *Regelbewusstsein* or the becoming conscious of a method of solving the problem ; (2) *Beziehungsbewusstsein* (consciousness of relationships) in which there is recognition of a class or of an indirect connection ; (3) *Intentionen* or consciousness of tension, that is, thoughts with no concrete index, but representing merely logical connections.

He thinks that this classification is not exhaustive, and finally concludes that thought develops according to laws quite different from those of associations.

Ultimately, he attempts to determine the psychic function which produces new elements.

It is unnecessary to follow Bühler into those psychological thickets to which the above-mentioned interpretation of phenomena leads. We shall merely remark here that both the results of these investigations concerned with new phenomena of consciousness and the results of the investigations of other subjective psychologists, on whose work we cannot dilate here, may be harmonised with the scheme of cerebral or association reflexes, while the pre-reflexological view, which was based on the activity of the brain cell, could find no way of harmonising the subjective and the objective world. Here, of course, it is necessary to take into consideration not only the passage of the nervous current along the nervous arc, but also the effect of the dominant, inhibition, stimulation, and substitution or the switching over of the current, which is then transmitted to other cerebral areas.

Each element of our knowledge must, according to Kostyleff, represent an association process from the part to the whole, from one part to another, etc. A well-developed child should be already supplied with many transmission systems. Let us suppose, for instance, that the child sees an apple. He may react by the judgment : " The apple is beautiful," or by transition to a general term : " fruit," or by transition from the part to the whole : " garden." This latter transition may be accompanied by the unformulated thought : " Our apples are worse than this," or by the wish : " I should like to have this apple."

All of these are, ultimately, products of external experience, remnants of past reactions, which, in the form of unexpressed reflexes, are later, in appropriate circumstances, reproduced to be given external manifestation in the form of action.

CHAPTER LI

Correlation of the investigations of the school of Jung-Freud with the doctrine of association reflexes : catharsis as the discharge of an inhibited reflex. The interpretation of psycho-analysis from the objective standpoint.

LET us now turn to a different order of investigations, also based on subjective analysis—to the school of Jung-Freud.

According to Jung,[1] every person forms one or several psychic complexes, which come to light in his associations. A complex, according to him, is merely a remnant of previous impressions more or less coloured by affective memories.

Needless to say, these complexes are ultimately traces of a number of co-ordinated and concatenated past association reflexes, ready to be discharged as a revival of past reflexes on the occurrence of an external impact. The stimulus-words in Jung's experiments are based on the excitation—produced by these words—of concentration processes and of mimico-somatic states, which lead to the inhibition of association reflexes. Thus, in Jung's doctrine of complexes we find complete agreement with the data of reflexology, which also recognises complexes of reflexes and complexes of traces of past reflexes, although in a different grouping.[2] Besides, Jung's method affords completely objective results in time-units.

Further, we shall dilate on the results of Freud's investigations in psycho-analysis.

We cannot help seeing the correlation of reflexology with Freud's doctrine, known as psycho-analysis, first of all in so-called catharsis (purification by confession) which is equivalent to discharge of a " strangulated " affect or of an inhibited mimico-somatic drive. Is not this the discharge of a reflex which, when inhibited, oppresses the personality, shackles and diseases it, while, when there is discharge of the reflex (catharsis), naturally the pathological condition disappears ? Is not the weeping out of a sorrow the discharge of an impeded reflex ?

Freud's method is based first on the disclosure of the condition by talking out, while concentration is directed to some pathological symptom or sometimes to a dream which reflects the pathological state ; in general, to anything referring to the illness, and then the disappearance of the pathological state is effected.

Hypnotism was at first used for this purpose, but later Freud abandoned it as a method of disclosing the pathological state and began to require the patients to concentrate on the pathological phenomena and simply talk out everything, no matter how trivial, that came into their head. These disclosures, as well as their detailed discussion, became the basis of psycho-analysis.

Freud sets out from the supposition that associations are grouped into complexes, and, consequently, neither the individual's words nor his

---

[1] Jung : *Psychoanalyse und Assoziationsexperiment*, etc. *Ass. Studien.*
Translators' note : See Jung : *Analytical Psychology* (tr. Long), ch. II, p. 94.
[2] V. Bechterev : *Objective Psychology*, 3rd pt., St. Petersburg.

gestures are casual when his thoughts are concentrated on anything, but refer to the complex to which concentration is directed.

Psychic trauma as a cause of neurosis is referred by Freud chiefly to the sexual sphere. This, however, cannot be accepted without very extensive reservations and has met with much opposition in scientific literature. Breuer and Freud began by discovering an " unconscious " state in respect of certain impressions in hysterics, and this state acts as a psychic trauma and leads to pathological symptoms. But that the impression remain concealed, it must be not only inhibited, that is, denied direct reaction, but must also be cut off from the associative activity of the ego.

This feature, by the way, approximates hysterical phenomena to hypnoidal, but the former are, for various reasons, not explicable as hypnoidal states, for, in many cases, the pathological phenomena develop from impressions consciously received by the patients. For this reason, Breuer developed the hypothesis of change in nervous tension, this change making " abnormal reflexes " possible, and, according to him, the abnormality is caused by over-tension of the neuro-psychical tonus, with weakening of resistance as a result either of organic disposition, or of temporary illness, or of exhaustion.[1]

These reflexes are abnormal partly because they are a pathological response to external impressions and partly because they are not a direct response to an impression received, but are a response only through the mediation of pathological memories. These latter, isolating themselves from the patient's own observation, or his ego, give hysterical symptoms their apparent arbitrariness and this, by the way, distinguishes hysteria from traumatic neuroses.

Dissociation of the ego is by no means unusual. On the contrary, even in the normal state, this splitting may be observed to a certain extent. We may look without seeing, hear without being accountable to ourselves in respect of what we hear. Needless to say, the splitting is much deeper and more considerable in pathological states. In hypnosis and suggestion, we have obviously a similar, only deepened, process of dissociation of the subject's ego or personality.

But, according to Breuer, the splitting of the ego in hysteria is conditioned not by the weakening of attention, but by a prepossession through which the field of consciousness is essentially narrowed and more scope is given to reflex activity. However Breuer's interpretation of the phenomena of hysteria may be regarded, it is obvious that it harmonises with the fundamental thesis of reflexology in regarding the higher manifestations of correlative activity from the standpoint of association reflexes, which, in the given case, take two directions, some entering into correlation with the personal complex of reflexes, others entering into no correlation with it. It is not necessary to dilate here on the basic causes of this diverse relation of association reflexes to the personality or to the complex of

[1] Breuer und Freud : *Studien über Hysterie ;* Deuticke, Wien, 1895.

personal reflexes, a theme to which we have already referred, but, anyhow, it is clear that there is here a dynamic, and not an anatomical, difference in the phenomena.

It must be noted here that Freud's method, since it is exclusively subjective, has led its initiator to the gravely erroneous conclusion that sexual trauma is the basic cause of the common neuroses. Such error frequently results when investigations are given a subjective basis. The Great War produced an enormous number of neurotics, and here the traumata were of a different kind, and rarely sexual.[1] Thereupon, Freud's disciple, Adler, advanced the doctrine, not of sexual trauma, propounded by his master as the cause of the common neuroses, but of social conflict, in which the neurotic manifests an active attitude towards the illness (" flight into illness "), which for him is something desired as an inevitable escape from the given situation. Adler's theory also, though considerably wider in fundamental principles than Freud's, is based, to a considerable extent, on subjective analysis, and therein lies its weakness. Let us point out, however, that Jung's investigations (mentioned above) in respect of the association method, which takes the form of stimulus-words, have afforded an important objective indication of what has been experienced and done, and this indication may be used in revealing both the causes of neuroses and of criminal acts, fields in which it is already beginning to be applied. For this purpose a special list may be compiled in which words relating to what has been experienced are inserted among indifferent words, and it transpires that, when a word is presented to the subject in order to stimulate free association with other words, a more or less marked delay results in respect of the reaction, when words bearing reference to grievous experiences are presented.

This objective method, which had been applied (Dr. Rosental) also by us in the Psychotherapeutical Hospital of the Institute for the Study of Brain supervised by me, gives much more valuable results than does subjective analysis alone. Here, too, it must be mentioned that, though facts are facts, precision in their interpretation, in the sense of the discrimination of subjective states, for instance, guilt, is exceedingly relative. On this point most writers agree. However this may be, the objective understanding of phenomena from the reflexological standpoint throws a light, hitherto unavailable, on Freud's theory, with its processes of repression (inhibition), conversion (substitution), etc., and, at the same time, through the scheme of abnormal reflexes, supplements those processes which were regarded as purely subjective states (Dr. Kostyleff).

Besides, as we have seen, the reflexological viewpoint affords the true explanation of psycho-analytic treatment. It is true that psycho-analysis as presented by Breuer, and more so as presented by Freud, who developed it into a system, is, as we have said, teeming with a subjectivism often too

---

[1] *Translators' note :* For the Freudian point of view, see *Psycho-analysis and the War Neuroses*—a series of papers by Ferenczi, Abraham, Simmel, and Jones. Introduction by Freud ; Internat. Psycho-analytical Press, 1921.

involved and difficult to be explained even from the viewpoint of contemporary subjective psychology. Nevertheless, it is clear from all that we have said above that the psycho-analytic method of treatment is easily understood by means of the reflexological doctrine of association-reflex activity.

It is unnecessary to enter here into the details of this problem. We merely state that, from the viewpoint of reflexology, a strangulated affect is just an inhibited, that is, externally unexpressed, mimico-somatic reflex, which is revived by the psycho-analytic method, that is verbal stimuli, is ultimately released from inhibition, and is liberated, so that there results a cure, which presupposes the liberation of other reflexes also, which have been suppressed on inhibition of the fundamental reflex.

CHAPTER LII

The Freudian theory of dreams. Criticism of Freud's views. Dreams a result of inhibition of external discharge of neuro-psychical processes. The mechanism of
phantasy. The mechanism of creativeness in poetry.

THERE is no doubt that dreams also, the detailed psychology of
which has been elucidated by psycho-analysis, may be harmonised
with the data of reflexology. Freud himself, when outlining the
scheme of dream development, remarks that the psychic apparatus is
constructed after the model of a reflex.[1] It is true that he intends this
comparison to be taken figuratively, but, clearly, in discussing complex
psychic phenomena, even he cannot dispense with the scheme of the
reflex.

According to Freud's view,[2] in dreams there is a process which consists
in a regression of the nervous current to the mechanism of perception.
The phenomenon of regression he regards as nothing new, for thought in
general often regresses along the path of memory, but usually does not
transgress the limits separating it from perception, for memory never
presents such vivid pictures as does perception. In dreams, on the contrary,
regression extends much farther, almost as far as in hallucinations.

But Freud thinks it impossible to answer definitely the question of how
dreams are to be explained or of how the regression reaches the vividness
of perception. He merely assumes that, in the waking state, the psychic
apparatus encounters obstacles preventing disturbance of the continuous
coursing stream of the nervous currents flowing from perception (P)
towards motility (M), while sleep, because of suppression of the psychic
activity, opens the way for regression.

Needless to say, this does not explain anything. But, from the reflexological viewpoint, the matter is altogether different, for there is no question of a regression of the movement or of a return to the original area, but
of a regression to the original form. Whatever the perception, the memory,
or the dream, the direction of the reflex remains the same and is not
reversed. A proof of this may be found in experiments in association
reflexes.

We know already that, after a certain number of associations of an
electrical stimulus applied to the fingers or to the sole with a sound-
stimulus, the sound-stimulus alone leads to a jerking back of the organ
stimulated. In some of these cases, when consecutive applications of the
sound-stimuli alone led to the jerking back of the fingers or the foot, the
subject answered the question why he could not help making this movement by maintaining quite decisively that he actually felt a pain in the
fingers or the sole, as if these were electrically stimulated. It is clear that
the initial stimulation, arising in the auditory apparatus and travelling
along the receptive part of the cutaneo-muscular area of the cortex (the

---

[1] *Translators' note :* See Freud : *The Interpretation of Dreams*, p. 426, tr.
Brill.

[2] *Translators' note :* Freud : *l.c.*, p. 430 ff.

postcentral gyrus) to its centrifugal conductors (the precentral gyrus), revives the trace of the past cutaneous stimulation to a degree almost equal to the initial intensity.

However, this phenomenon is observed only in some persons and only in the first stages of the association reflex, but, later, when the association reflex is fixed, this phenomenon usually ceases to be manifested. Therefore, we may maintain that the explanation of why the sound-stimulus revives the trace of the past cutaneous stimulation to a degree approaching the actual cutaneous stimulation consists in the fact that the inculcation of an association reflex at first encounters some resistance, which is expressed, when there is impediment of movement, in the development of heightened nervous tension, characterised by greater intensity of the subjective process.

Dreams are, like thoughts, reflexes inhibited in their external manifestation, but, in contradistinction to thoughts, dreams are distinguished by special vividness, because the suppressing influence of the active part of the personality—that part which controls internal stimulations—is removed.

But psychologists are mistaken in thinking that we have, in dreams, a process regressive in respect of the sequence of the process, for they maintain that here there is a regression to processes of perception.

We have referred above to the fact that processes freely discharged in motor reactions in the waking state occur without intense subjective images, while all inhibition of motor acts produces extreme tension and intensity of the subjective state. Therefore, there is no necessity to have recourse to the hypothesis of a regressive movement of the current in order to explain dreams, but we have only to recognise that, during sleep, there are conditions inhibiting external discharge in the form of movement, and this, under the influence of inflowing stimulations, enormously raises the intensity of subjective states.

And, indeed, in sleep we have obviously inhibition of all motor reactions, for, notwithstanding even vivid pictures of movement, conversation, etc., all the sleeper's motor organs remain motionless. We shall not here enter into an explanation of the causes of this phenomenon, which is obviously associated with suppression of the active part of the personality, this part being situated in the frontal areas. But a fact is a fact, and this fact explains the existence of dreams, for, according to the thesis propounded by us, inhibition of an external reaction, when this inhibition is accompanied by simultaneous excitation of a certain area, always raises somewhat the intensity of the inner or subjective experiences.

Therefore, everything experienced in the dream is as vivid as a hallucination, and the development of hallucinations in those psychically ill must obviously also be associated with the existence, in certain cases, of conditions of inhibition produced by pathological causes. Therefore in mania, since there is very much motility and facilitated movement of reflexes, hallucinations are usually not observed or are rare, while, in other disturbances accompanied by inhibition and suppression of movement, they are usually present, and, in stuprose conditions, sometimes apparently acquire extraordinary intensity, according to the accounts of the patients themselves.

Freud's assumption that dreams are always a fulfilment of the dreamer's wishes must be regarded as inadequate. True, childhood dreams may have this character, but, in respect of the dreams of adults, whose mental life is exceedingly complex, we cannot agree that the dream, as Freud assumes, is usually a fulfilment of wishes conserved in the unconscious or unaccountable sphere. At any rate, my observations indicate that the dreams of adults may be exceedingly varied in character and are connected with external stimulations and states which precede sleep, and, in other cases, with stimulations occurring during sleep and with concentration before sleep on some object whch may or may not be desirable to the dreamer, and, finally, with the general tone or mood in which the dreamer falls asleep, and with certain phenomena in the organic sphere.

Thus, we are here concerned with phenomena which develop from the same source as do inner experiences in the waking state and, consequently, there is no reason to have recourse to special hypotheses, as Freud has.

As regards the phenomenon which Freud calls "censorship," this process of non-acceptance of certain subjective experiences by the ego must be reduced to the inhibitory influence of that complex of association reflexes which is closely bound up with the personality of the given individual, this inhibitory influence being exerted in respect of such association reflexes as stand in opposition to the complex, are irreconcilable with it, and are, therefore, suppressed. In a word, there is here a special inhibitory act associated with the most stable group of personal reflexes, this group being always the most apt to revive and standing in the most intimate relation with the somatic sphere.

Ultimately, dreams, too, which Freud regards as a reanimation of latent wishes and, as it were, a sensory regression, are really only an internal manifestation of excitation during the inhibition of reflexes, this excitation resulting from certain influences and states accompanying or preceding sleep.

By the way, the mechanism of phantasy, according to Freud, resembles that of dreams, for there is a reanimation of traces of previous experiences, usually even childhood experiences, and these traces develop in accordance with the wishes of the person.

If we admit the conditional character of the last-mentioned statement, which is a tribute Freud pays to his one-sided domination by his theory, we are again confronted by the thcsis that in creativeness there is ultimately reproduction of results of past experience, and this reproduction takes the form of a revival of association reflexes, the revival being conditioned by the given problem as a stimulus establishing a dominant.

Obviously, the mechanism of poetic inspiration in literary creativeness may be interpreted from the viewpoint of reflexology. Without entering into the details of the problem of creativeness, a problem which we have already discussed, we shall dilate here on the conclusions reached by N. Kostyleff, who explicates the problem of the correlation of reflexological data with complex subjective processes.

Setting out from our fundamental thesis that all mental processes, including reasoning, are reflexes, this writer points out that confidence may no longer be placed in one who tries to show that there is no correspondence between the functioning of the cerebral mechanism and psychic phenomena discovered by self-observation. Kostyleff shows that inner or subjective processes of such a kind as, at first glance, appear heterogeneous, for instance mental images, including the most insensible, such as conscious states verbally unexpressed, still exhibit characteristics which approximate them to the mechanism of cerebral reflexes.

It must be recognised that images, as usually understood, do not exist, but that an image is a group which has originated from sensations. Adopting this position, we must naturally approximate the image to the scheme of cerebral reflexes.

Metaphysical concepts are now replaced by exact data : " spirit " by the mechanism of cerebral reflexes, the ego by a central complex of these reflexes. And even the unconscious is now truly and exactly explained, for it consists of reflexes whose paths have been beaten in the central nervous system, but which, in respect of reproduction at a given moment, do not depend on the active side of the personality, this active side being constituted of a complex of association reflexes which have originally issued from the somatic sphere. Therefore, certain reflexes remain unaccountable.[1]

We must add that even an habitual reflex accompanied by a conscious process may become an extroconscious or subconscious process, that is, an unaccountable process, in objective terminology. For this to happen, it is sufficient if the active side of the personality becomes incapable of evoking the reflex, as occurs when the active side is distracted to other processes. Consequently, the reflex will no longer be actively reproduced.

Bodily processes which constantly occur inside the organism produce impulses which flow unintermittently to the central organs and, on the one hand, determine the so-called inner needs of the organism and condition the active relation of the personality to the environment and, on the other, determine a certain direction of motor reactions, which take the form of concentration, orientation, defence, or aggression. Consequently, there are here processes which follow their usual course from the peripheral apparatus to the central organs and from the latter back to the periphery, but, as all inner processes which send impulses to the central organs are, as a result of inhibitory influences, characterised by a certain slowness in their development, they inevitably become conscious, their integration expressing itself in a subjective state known in psychology as the ego or self-consciousness.

[1] Apropos, see the development of these views in my book : *Suggestion and its Rôle in Social Life*, especially the latest, that is, the French, edition.

In this ego, also called " the conscious sphere," individual bodily processes are not reflected individually, but enter the general complex of the conscious ego, except when some inner function is emphasised because of its unusual excitation, depression, or pathological stimulation. When this occurs, this function stands out, as a special ingredient taking the form of inner perception, in the subject's conscious ego.

All so-called active movements and active concentration are also connected with the ego complex. Therefore, everything perceived under the influence of " voluntary " acts and active or " volitional " concentration becomes bound up with the subject's ego and becomes conscious. But all other perceptions in which active concentration does not participate remain outside the conscious complex.[1] However, this in nowise changes the essence of the energic process, that is, its fundamental scheme.

As every active process is accompanied by impediment and retardation of the whole process, it is possible that these, supplemented by the excitation, make it conscious, for being conscious is, as must be supposed, a result of inner tension of energy in the centres, and this tension is a direct result of impediment or inhibition.

Unconscious or unaccountable processes also enter into relation with the subject's ego or the active side of the personality from the moment when they become objects of active concentration, and so they become conscious or accountable. On the other hand, conscious processes cease to be conscious when attention is distracted or suppressed.

In view of everything that has been said, all association-reflex processes fall into two main groups : the conscious or accountable and the unconscious or unaccountable. Correlations between the former and the latter are established chiefly through active concentration. On the other hand, when concentration is suppressed in respect of conscious or accountable processes, they become unaccountable.

The unconscious or unaccountable group—" the subconscious " in subjective terminology—must not be confused with those purely nervous processes of the lower centres, processes which, in a developed organism, have nothing in common with consciousness. The unaccountable complex includes those processes which have been in the conscious or—in objective terminology—accountable complex and, later, on withdrawal of active concentration, have temporarily dropped out of that complex, but may re-enter it by means of active reproduction. On the other hand, this complex embraces those processes which, because of distraction of concentration at the moment of their development, have not entered the conscious or accountable group, but which will enter this group as soon as they arouse active concentration and enter into correlation with the latter.

The extroconscious group of reflexes, which we call unaccountable, may exert a certain influence on the accountable group, for the reflexes which

[1] See V. Bechterev : *Personal and General Consciousness—Vestnik Psychologii.*

remain in the unaccountable group are not completely devoid of connection with the accountable complex. This influence shows itself, for instance, in the individual's general mimico-somatic state.

It is clear from the above-said that both the accountable and the unaccountable activity conform to the same laws in respect of their manifestation.

Both the conscious or accountable and the extroconscious or unaccountable group are divisible, on the basis of the fundamental stimuli participating in the creation of personality, into association complexes.' Thus, we may distinguish somatic, sex, physico-cosmical, and social complexes, and these are divisible into still more particular complexes.

The reflexes which constitute each of these complexes are always inter-associated as a result of contiguity or of some other association in respect of the stimuli which have evoked them. Besides, the reflexes of one complex may, as a result of certain conditions, enter into correlation with those of different complexes.

The division of complexes according to affects (or mimico-somatic reflexes), as propounded by the Freudian school, cannot be accepted, because one and the same external influence may excite different affects according to the state of the organism. A sated man, for instance, experiences disgust and manifests a defence reflex at the sight of food, while a hungry man experiences an urge and manifests an aggressive reflex in regard to food. In the first case, the sight of food is accompanied by a positive general tonus, in the second, by a negative general tonus. Moreover, the dissociability of affects (that is, of mimico-somatic states), of which this school speaks, does not tally with such a division.

The receptive organs utilise by no means all the external energy, and, because of expenditure in overcoming obstacles in the receptive apparatus, only part of this energy is transformed into nervous current, the impeding of which in the central organs leads, when there is excitation, to enhanced tension of energy, and this, as we have said, makes the process accountable. In the normal state, the process encounters the greatest impediment in the cortex when there is active concentration on the external object which supports a continuous afflux of nervous excitation from the appropriate organ. Therefore, the process of active concentration is always strikingly accountable, but the reproductive process, since it is not accompanied by a supporting excitation on the part of the receptive organ, though it is accountable, is always less vivid than the process of concentration on an external object.

It must be assumed that transformation of external energies in the various organs leads to a development of current of different waves or rhythm, and this, together with the tension of energy, determines the qualities of fundamental sensations.

General tonus positive in character is, as experiment shows, associated with favourable, moderate influences and with the correlative activity of tension of such a degree that the cerebral apparatus operates with facility, the losses arising from its activity being, in the course of the work, fully restored as a result of arterial hyperemia.

Negative general tonus occurs when the conditions are the opposite, and here the apparatus does not succeed in restoring the losses which it suffers during work.

This may be stated of the activity of the brain, which is supplied with a vascular system regulating its work and sending to it impulses which depend on the state of the vascular system. But external influences become associated, through direct stimulation or association reflexes, with a certain vasomotor or other effect inside the body, and these effects, by influencing favourably or unfavourably the activity of the endocrine organs and of the brain, lead in turn to states of positive or negative general tonus.

Lastly, toxic influences also, entering from outside or developing inside the body, may act analogously on the cardio-vascular system and thus evoke states of positive or negative tonus. The above-mentioned are the chief sources of change in the general mimico-somatic tonus.

It must be noted, in respect of the character of external stimuli acting on the cardio-vascular system, that all unusually intense stimuli, especially those impinging without personal preparation (or unexpectedly), influence unfavourably the state of the cardio-vascular apparatus and produce a very marked sympathicotony associated with the subjective state of displeasure, while all moderate stimuli, acting favourably on the receptive organs, at the same time act favourably on the cardio-vascular system, produce moderate sympathico-vagotony, and are reflected in the subjective sphere by a state of pleasure. A similar influence may be reproductivo-associative in character and so support some state or other in the form of an association reflex.

Further, we note that if the associations so-called in subjective psychology correspond to association reflexes more elementary in character, the energic tension of the given association reflexes, ready to discharge in a certain direction, but temporarily impeded or inhibited, is manifested as tendency.

If this tendency is accompanied by a favourable reaction on the part of the cardio-vascular system, it is manifested as a wish in the subjective sphere.

We have already said that concentration is always associated with intensification of the subjective process, but weakening or even complete disappearance of subjective processes is conditioned by distraction of concentration. Every one knows that, by means of distraction of concentration, even a severe toothache may be mitigated, while direction of concentration to a painful area increases the pain. On the other hand, inhibition, as an objective fact and occurring in various cases, corresponds to forgetfulness in the subjective sphere and simultaneously leads to easing the suffering or weakening the pleasure, to lowering the speed of associations, to indecision, and to incapacity to act.

Substitution takes place in slips of the tongue, in the replacement of one movement or action by another, in the substitution of some meaningless or half-meaningless expression—for instance, " as it were," etc.—for a missing word, while in the subjective sphere we have the substitution of one memory for another, and substitution when, in searching for a word, we use an habitual and established association, etc.

Tarde (*Les lois de l'imitation*) refers the phenomena dealt with here to so-called interference. Referring to the fact that a casual thought, as if it were a solid statement, influences a parallel wish and increases its intensity, he cites the following example : " I should like very much to become an orator in parliament, and my friend's compliment convinces me that real oratorical talent will immediately develop in me. This conviction increases my vanity, which, by the way, has enhanced my aptitude to be convinced." In objective investigation, we are obviously concerned in this case with stimulation of association reflexes.

On the other hand, a contradictory or negative opinion does not promote one's tendency, but acts in the opposite direction. It is clear that the opinion, in this case, will prove an inhibtory force in respect of the manifestation of this tendency. How much real talent has thus been blighted through wrong education, when the harsh domination of an ungifted teacher has nipped in the bud talents which otherwise might have reached full flower !

CHAPTER LIII

The personal complex of association reflexes in its relationship with the subjective ego. Processes of inhibition and release from inhibition; and the subjective processes of distraction and attraction of attention. Differentiation, selective generalisation, and subjective analysis and synthesis. General conclusion.

EVERYTHING said above is, in many respects, a reproduction of what I have developed and proved in a number of papers. In order to explain the relation of the personal complex to the subjective ego, I shall here adduce what I have already said concerning this complex, which arises on the basis of somatic stimulations.

It is scarcely necessary to demonstrate that all those organic reflexes which secure the organism's existence develop in the earliest period of the individual's being, some of them even in the womb.[1] Therefore, the complex-organic association reflexes which develop on this basis also constitute a primary group of association reflexes as necessary for life as are all organic reflexes. Moreover, all interno-external association reflexes, since they stand in the most intimate correlation with them, naturally belong to them. These really form the somatic complex of association reflexes to which, in subjective psychology, corresponds the organic ego of each and every subject, with all its inner experiences and needs.

On the basis of this complex of association reflexes, other groups of association reflexes develop through further connections. The integration of somatic reflexes and of muscle-joint association reflexes developing in close connection with them may be called the personal complex, which consists of reflexes corresponding, in subjective psychology, to " volitional " movements, which are above all directed to the active expression of one's ego.

These " volitional " movements develop—in connection with the general mimico-somatic tonus—like all other association reflexes, on the basis of inter-association of organic muscle-joint stimulations. Let us take an example : As a result of reflex movements, a child pricks its hand with a pointed object ; consequently, an ordinary defence reflex naturally develops in respect of the prick. But the stimulation arising from the prick has become associated with the sight of the pointed object, with even momentary concentration on it, and with a negative mimico-somatic tonus. So, on another occasion, the mere sight of something pointed, although there is no prick, causes a precautionary movement of the hand, which reproduces the previous defence reflex, the reflex, in this case, being caused, in connection with a negative mimico-somatic tonus, not by a prick, but only by visual impulses. Afterwards, a similar reflex may be reproductively evoked through the mediumship of concentration on the pricking object or on its influence in the past, the concentration in question having participated in the reflex. In the same

[1] Minkowsky (Zürich) has recently, by means of experiments on embryos, made detailed investigations of these reflexes.

way, personal reflexes aggressive in character arise when reflexively produced muscle-joint stimulations become connected with a positive mimico-somatic tonus.

Further, we cannot refrain from noting here that the data at our disposal permit us to assume that processes of inhibition and release of association reflexes are correlated with the subjective processes of distraction and attraction of attention, as we have already mentioned. Indeed, proof may be adduced that processes of inner inhibition and of distraction of attention go hand in hand. Thus, we know that an irrelevant stimulus acts for the most part inhibitorily on an inculcated association reflex, and, at the same time, subjective analysis tells us that an irrelevant stimulus distracts attention. On the other hand, we know that attention is distracted particularly by new stimuli, while stimuli to which we are accustomed do not distract attention.

We know that personal reflexes, in turn, serve as a source from which other association reflexes spring. Let us assume that a man hears a familiar sound, goes towards it, discovers that its source is a sheep, and involuntarily exclaims : " Oh, this is a sheep ! " Here the bleating is, as a result of active movements, associated with the visual influence and a certain verbal symbol; consequently, the same sound on another occasion produces a symbolic association reflex, which is expressed in the verbal denotation " sheep ".

Thus, the personal complex of association reflexes, since it is the chief determinant of the organism's relations to the environment and is the immediate directer of its actions and conduct, gives rise to continuous enrichment in the form of new reflexes.

But this is not all. Preparation of the external organs for the reception of external stimuli and for the development of dominants in the appropriate centres—processes which we call personal or active concentration—develops in connection with the personal complex of association reflexes.

By means of this concentration, which is directed by the personal complex, a person may, to a certain extent and in connection with established needs, choose from among the external stimuli and make a personal choice in respect of his movements.

Here active concentration exerts a regulatory influence not only on the general motor sphere, where it leads to choice in respect of certain movements, but also on symbolic reflexes, and thus conditions a certain verbal connection called the logical connection or the logical combination of verbal symbols. Thus, the personal complex of association reflexes serves as a basis of those activities denoted by the word " cognitive " (the self as logical subject).

If we take into consideration that concentration may be directed to the manifestation of a person's own verbal or other association reflexes, we thus arrive at the self-determination of the personal complex or of what subjective psychologists call the empirical self.

We shall not dilate on other fundamental complexes of association reflexes. We shall merely note here that a general sthenic reaction (a heightened general tonus), manifesting itself in an enhancement of energy, is usually accompanied by a subjective state consisting in a facilitated flow of associations, while an asthenic reaction is accompanied by a lowering of energy and by sluggishness in the flow of associations.

Long ago, Spinoza defined pleasure as an enhancement of power or of capacity to act. Indeed, all pleasure is accompanied by enhancement of energy and increased circulation of the blood, particularly in the organ stimulated, and this increase raises the nervous tone of the organ. General pleasure is accompanied by general enhancement of energy and general quickening of the circulation of the blood, particularly in the brain. Displeasure, on the contrary, is accompanied by depression of nervous energy and of the circulation of the blood.

Bio-chemical reactions, hormonic and fermentative in character, are not without significance in regard to general sthenic or invigorating and asthenic or depressing reactions accompanied by subjective states, in the first case, of pleasure, in the second, of displeasure.

Further, the differentiation and the selective generalisation of association reflexes necessarily correlate with analysis and synthesis, which we find in subjective processes.

Indeed, it is not difficult to see that psychic processes or the subjective manifestations of association-reflex activity are conformable to the same fundamental laws of differentiation and selective generalisation as are all association reflexes. We know that analysis and synthesis are the bases of thinking and mental activity in general. It may be proved by experiment that even the development of sensation proceeds, on the one hand, through gradual analysis and, on the other, through synthesis, as Professor Lange's[1] experiments and Professor Nikitin's[2] (my laboratory) investigations show.

Lastly, we know from everyday observation that the sensations which we receive are split up by consciousness into their constituent parts and, on the other hand, a number of somewhat similar sensations are generalised by synthesis, so that we get so-called general notions.

If we compare with this the development of association-reflex activity in objective investigation, we shall here, too, find a correlation—perfectly conforming to law—of processes subjective and objective in character, in the form of analysis and synthesis, on the one hand, and differentiation and selective generalisation, on the other.

Lastly, the development of association reflexes in response to signal-stimuli finds corresponding expression in subjective states, for what are known as " pleasurable anticipation " and " preliminary pleasure " are the subjective expression of the phenomenon in question. This pleasurable anticipation or preliminary pleasure is, as every one knows, a result of experience and, what is more, of experience quite analogous in subjective

[1] N. Lange : *Voprosi philosophii i psychologii,* 1892, vols. XIII–XVI.
[2] Dr. Nikitin : *Vestnik psychologii,* 1905, vol. II.

perception to the experience which we reproduce objectively in our laboratories.

A man who has once experienced pleasure or displeasure anticipates this pleasure or displeasure in the future on the first hint of possible realisation of the given stimulus and the experience associated with it.

.   .   .   .

It is clear from the above-said that the objective bio-social study of personality and the study of psychic phenomena through direct self-observation should not clash with each other. Indeed, the study of subjective processes on oneself should supplement the study of the objective manifestations of personality, so that the interrelation between both may be elucidated.

Thus, it is clear that the reflexological method makes it possible not only to study the processes of man's association-reflex activity from the objective aspect, but, simultaneously, to elucidate the greater or lesser correspondence between these and the subjective processes and the greater or lesser completeness of the verbal account of the subjective processes.[1] Such a method of parallel investigation carried out on oneself, especially in respect of mimico-somatic reflexes, a method by which the objective, as well as the subjective, aspect of the process may be studied side by side, is very valuable. By the way, I and Dr. Shumkov, in a special paper addressed to the Congress of Pedology, Experimental Pedagogics, and Psychoneurology (January, 1924, Leningrad) described this method in its application to the investigation of the alertness reflex.[2]

But if, in complexes of association reflexes, we must recognise a certain correlation between the subjective data and the objective or external manifestations, it is obvious that reflexology or the objective bio-social study of personality, and the data of the subjective world studied through direct self-observation are complementary departments of knowledge, and the more closely we study the mutual relations between reflexes, the more completely we comprehend the correlations between the subjective phenomena corresponding to them.

For this reason, subjective phenomena should not be studied apart from their correlation with the data of reflexology as an objective science. Reflexology, which regards the change of dominants developing and replacing each other together with their association reflexes in their various manifestations and complexes as the fundamental manifestation of association-reflex activity, maintains that those inner phenomena which are accompanied by the development of subjective states studied by direct self-observation are merely association reflexes externally unexpressed, and, therefore, all these correlations, conformable to law and investigated

[1] V. Bechterev : *The Fundamental Manifestations of Neuro-psychical Activity Objectively Investigated—Russky Vratch*, No. 12, 1911.
[2] See *New Discoveries in the Reflexology and Physiology of the Nervous System*, State Publishers, Leningrad, 1925.

in association reflexes, bear directly on the corresponding inner or subjective processes. And it cannot be otherwise, for, in both cases, there is a unitary neuro-psychical process.

When we observe inhibition of a mimico-somatic anger reaction, this inhibition is conditioned either by distraction of concentration to other external stimuli or by reproduction of unexpressed, antagonistic complexes of association reflexes. These complexes, having arisen under the conditions of the social environment, take the form of duty, responsibility before the law and public opinion, fear of certain consequences of one's actions, etc. These inhibitory influences may issue also from outside, as when anger is mitigated by the threats or persuasion of a second person.

Here the nervous energy, in the form of a current realising association-reflex activity, encounters, in the cerebral cortex, obstacles to its conduction and, therefore, reaches its highest tension and leads to subjective phenomena, but, when the inhibition is removed and the energic tension falls, the accompanying subjective phenomena weaken and even disappear.

The source of this energy is to be found, as we know, in the external world, whence it enters the body, on the one hand, in the form of nutritive material, which travels along the alimentary paths and then enters the blood which nourishes the brain, while, on the other hand, light- and sound-stimuli, mechanical impacts, olfactory, gustatory and other stimuli act on the receptive organs—which are transformers of external energies—and are transmitted to the cerebral centres as nervous current, which, summating in the nerve cells during weak and infrequent stimulations, ultimately leads to appropriate discharges.

When inhibition is removed, the same nervous energy is transmitted along the efferent conductors to the skeletal and smooth muscles and the secretory cells of the glands and so is transformed into mechanical and molecular work.

In this way, in the personality of a human agent, an appropriate interrelation is established between, on the one hand, the various manifestations of the external, environmental energies, which act on him through the introduction of reserve energy in the form of food and through external stimulations of the receptive organs, and, on the other, various kinds of mechanical and molecular work performed by his bodily organs.

It is scarcely necessary to state that the prototype of such interrelation is already given in the cellular protoplasm of the amœba, the simplest living accumulator of energy, an accumulator in which no nervous system has hitherto been discovered and in which there are no other tissues, or, more exactly, in whose protoplasm we find the chemical elements of all the tissues of the higher animals, even the elements of nerve tissue, for only through evolution does gradual differentiation of the tissues of the organism occur in the phylogenetic animal scale.

Through evolution, a particular co-ordinating apparatus—the brain—as the chief accumulator of energy in the higher animals, also specially develops with its conductors in the form of epithelial neuro-muscular and epithelial neuro-glandular systems, while the connective tissue, which differentiates appropriately in the various organs, serves chiefly (though by no means exclusively) the static needs of the organism and secures for the organs a construction adapted to the more effective execution of their functions, including those functions bound up with the activity of the co-ordinating apparatus.

CHAPTER LIV

The lines along which the reflexological investigation of personality must be conducted.
General principle of the method of objective observation and investigation.

IN the investigation of personality, not only must attention be paid
to medical examination and to investigation of the general constitution, to the anthropological type, to various bio-chemical and, in
particular, hormonic and fermentative reactions, to ordinary or inherited
reflexes, but we must also take into consideration all the manifestations
of personality, under the various forms of association reflexes and
dominant processes or concentration, in their relationship with the external
and internal stimuli, both present and past. For this purpose, we have
elaborated a scheme to guide observation of the person's main reactions
—under the particular environmental conditions and in response to the
various environmental influences—in respect of his manifestations in the
sphere of complex-organic reflexes or instincts, in the mimico-somatic
sphere, in the sphere of established behaviour sets in general, in respect
of the character of his speech reactions and of his peculiar creative
activity. Uninterrupted observation of the person's manifestations and
their causes or stimuli, even over a period of ten days, is sufficient to
enable us to arrive at a more or less complete determination of his relation
to the environment and of his reactions dependent on various influences.
Missing links may be filled in by natural experiment, including the
artificial application of an appropriate stimulus, and we utilise this experiment in such cases. Here, of course, an analysis of the reactions is
necessary ; not, however, the subjective analysis in vogue among psychologists, but a correlation of the person's various manifestations one
with the other ; a correlation of aggressive, inhibitory, and defensive
reactions to certain stimuli, these reactions being results of past experience
and established set ; a correlation with the age, sex, constitution,
anthropological type, special talent, etc. Observation of the professional
work also and of the results achieved in it is of the utmost importance.
This necessitates special methods of observation and investigation.
Every such investigation demands, of course, some expenditure of time,
but always provides valuable material for the study of personality.

In empirico-psychological investigations, it is usual to apply special
tests so as to save time, and various psychologists have advanced methods
differing according to the individual psychologist's view of the psychic
sphere. Here belong the methods of Binet-Simon, Sante de Sanctis,
Rossolimo, Netchayev, Lazursky, Pierkovsky, and others. Let us note
that the very multiplicity of these methods shows that psychology affords
no firm footing for the investigation of personality, although the material
obtained is not devoid of a certain practical, scientific value, since it affords
an objective indication of the given personality in the given conditions
of the individual's activity.

It is self-evident that the reflexological investigation of personality
may also be applied in the form of tests, which make it possible to conduct

a personal investigation in the course of a relatively short time. For this purpose, it is, in my opinion, necessary above all to determine, by appropriate methods, the degree of refinement of audition, visual spatial discrimination, cutaneous sensibility, capacity to determine weight ; the physical strength of the wrist, the accuracy of its movements, its fatigability, as registered by the dynamometer ; and also the degree of professional skill in relationship with its acquisition in the past.

Next we should determine the person's capacity for work, that is, his exercisability, the development of excitation during the given work, subsequent fatigue, as well as the degree of inner effort and the stability of concentration on the work (by means of applying an irrelevant stimulus at a certain moment).[1] Lastly, speed in the formation and differentiation of association-motor reflexes must be investigated by laboratory methods. In addition, the individual peculiarities of creative activity in given conditions of work may be investigated by special methods.

All these indications may be utilised only in reference to the objective data, and we must not exclude creative activity, which is to be evaluated in respect of time, form, expression of personality, greater or lesser success in the solution of the task, the character of the work, the relation to the environment, etc.

It is always essential to consider not only the quantitative, but also the qualitative, aspect of the work, and to do so perfectly objectively, without excursions into the subjective sphere. Thus, in their connection with hereditary conditions, with peculiarities of the physical constitution and general reactivity connected with hormonic conditions discoverable by medical, anthropological, and bio-chemical investigations, the essential aspects of the personality of man as an agent in the social environment may be revealed, when his behaviour has been studied over a certain period of time.

In concluding the present work, let us briefly remark that reflexology, in its present state, is already, in the form of pathological reflexology, being widely applied to the pathology of personality, as I have described in a series of papers beginning from the middle of the 'nineties. Papers on the investigation of simulation and those on reflexo-therapy also belong here. Reflexology is particularly fruitful for the understanding of the common neuroses, and also of hypnosis and suggestion, both of which find a truer explanation precisely from the standpoint of reflexology, as I have shown many years ago in a special work (*La suggestion et son rôle dans la vie sociale*, Paris). Reflexology is no less fruitful in explaining the genesis of various pathological habits and phobias and also elucidates sexual

---

[1] This method was elaborated by me and my associate, V. I. Timofeyevsky, and consists in sounding a bell signal, which, in the course of mental work and before the onset of fatigue, produces temporarily heightened capacity for work in the case of those endowed with stronger powers of concentration, while it lowers capacity in the case of those endowed with weaker powers.

inversions and perversions. To this I have also devoted a number of separate papers.

Next we must recognise the particular significance of reflexology in applied science, for instance, in the study of work and of the person's professional peculiarities, a study to which, in the Institute for the Study of Brain supervised by me, a number of scientific collaborators and I devote ourselves.

Further, in the sphere of pedagogics, reflexology is being applied in the investigation of the conditions of development (genetic reflexology), and also of correct education and methods for the improvement of defects in the individual's behaviour (reflexological pedagogics and orthopedics). By the way, in the Educational Clinic (an Institute under my supervision) for nervous children—at the Psychoneurological Academy—a special training-college for the reflexological study and education of children was opened in the beginning of 1925.

In the sphere of biology, reflexology, side by side with behaviourism, is being extensively applied in the study of the functions of the receptive organs, and utilises here experiments in association reflexes and—in the case of the various species of the animal kingdom—dressage and various other manifestations.

Lastly, sociology also finds in the reflexology of the masses or " collective reflexology " one of the objective bases of the study of the development of communities, the characterology of social strata, classes, and professions, and their interrelations, and finds it in connection with the objective study of the economic factors in behaviour.

All that has been stated above is not exhaustive, but is sufficient to show to what extent reflexology, which always relies on the strictly objective method of investigation, is a fertilising factor in a number of theoretical and applied sciences.

In the course of time, it will doubtlessly provide a scientific basis for the other humanistic sciences, too. The time is not far distant when the most complex and subtle manifestations of human personality, such as the various branches of art, will be studied by a method as strictly objective as that applied in every department of natural science. Therefore, it is to be expected that the future will replace the modern psychology of art by the reflexology of art. The foundations of this branch of reflexology are already laid.

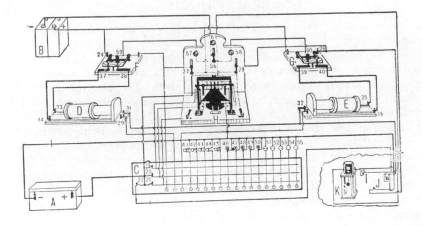

FIGURE 1 : Plan of Reflexological Apparatus (for experiments on human beings).

Laboratory for General Reflexology in the State Reflexological Institute for the Study of Brain, Leningrad.

PRINCIPAL PARTS OF THE APPARATUS :

A. Large accumulator (6 volts) : source of the continuous current for the whole apparatus.
B. Small accumulator (2 volts) for the signal lamps.
C. Main switch-board used by the investigator.
D. Induction-coil sending alternating current to the left switch (F).
E. Induction-coil sending alternating current to the right switch (G).
F. The left switch (Protopopov's) for the subject's right hand. ⎫ In the cabinet to be occupied by the subject.
G. The right switch (Protopopov's) for the subject's left hand. ⎰
H Automatic regulator of stimulus-sequence (" time relay ").
I. The chronoscopist's signal lamp.
J. Signal button from the chronoscopist to the investigator.
K Chronoscope.
L. Interrupter of the continuous current of the coils.

In the chronoscope room (denoted by a zigzag line).

434

FIGURE 2: General View of the Reflexological Apparatus of the State Reflexological Institute for the Study of Brain.

In the foreground, a table with a distributing-board and a "time relay." Behind (in the cabinet) may be seen the switches on which the subject's hands rest. On the right, a kymograph with an accessory for the recording of motor effect.

FIGURE 3 : Experimental Procedure in the Reflexological Laboratory of the State Reflexological Institute for the Study of Brain.

The shutter, behind which the subject is situated, is drawn down during the experiment. The movements are recorded according to the lightings of the signal lamps and are registered on the kymograph.

FIGURE 4 : Reflexological Apparatus in the Second Psychiatric Clinic (general view).

The investigator's table in front of the cabinet in which the subject is situated. On the table, a distributing-board (left) and a stand with apparatus for recording the movements of the hand, respiration, and pulse—by transmission through the air in the rubber tubes. On the right-hand upper corner, the drums and the kymograph.

FIGURE 5 : Reflexological Apparatus in the Second Psychiatric Clinic (details).

Below, a distributing-board ; left and somewhat higher, a general contact-breaker ; still higher, a distributer of faradic current. In the centre, an apparatus for changing the colour of the central lamp (the lever turns a circular plate of glass of various colours, the plate being hidden behind the board). Above the lever a box enclosing the central lamp. On each side of the box, a signal lamp from the switches.

FIGURE 6 : The " Time Relay " (front view) : an apparatus automatically regulating the duration of the stimuli and the intervals between them.

On the right and left sides of the floor of the apparatus, switches for the frame and the electromagnet. In the centre, the frame, the revolving drums (with a handle for winding them—on the right), collecters, and, under the drums, a vaseline container, in which the blades regulating the speed of movement revolve.

FIGURE 7 : The " Time Relay " (side view) :
Frame seen in profile.

The electromagnet which sets the mechanism
in motion. On the vertical board behind,
signal lamps : from the chronoscopist (top
centre), from the switches for the subject's
hand (at the sides). Below (centre), a switch
which cuts off the current to the signal lamps,
and (at the side) one which cuts off the
current to the chronoscope.

FIGURE 8 : A Switch for the Subject's Hand.

A special stand makes it possible to record the movements. (This switch is
made from a board, old nails, two copper plates, and several screws.)
All the movements of the hand are transmitted by mechanical conduction
(leads) to special springs which record these movements on the kymograph.
The subject's fingers rest on the head of two screws isolated from the switch.
These screws conduct the electric stimulus (faradic current). Behind the
fingers (to the right), a plate leads from the movable frame of the switch and
cuts off the current to the chronoscope (by means of the lower contact, when
the hand is pressed down) or to the signal lamp (by means of the upper contact, when the hand is withdrawn).

FIGURE 9 : Recording of Hand Movements on the Kymograph by means of
Springs to which are Attached Leads from the Subject's Hands.

Below, an electromagnetic indicator which records the stimulus time.

BIBLIOGRAPHY

List of the Author's Scientific Works on which the Present Work is Based.

THE AUTHOR'S WORKS ON GENERAL REFLEXOLOGY[1]

1. *An Apparatus for the Exact Investigation of Auditory Stimuli*—*Vestnik Psychologii*, 1905.

2. *Objective Psychology and its Subject Matter*—*Vestnik Psychologii*, 1904 ; *Revue scientifique*, 1906.

3. *Litchnost i usloviya eyo razvitiya i zdorovya.* (*Personality and the Conditions of Its Development and Health*), St. Petersburg, 1905.

4. *The Association-motor Reflex Method*—Address to the Scientific Meetings of the Hospital ; see *Minutes*, 1907.

5. *The Objective Investigation of Neuro-psychical Activity* (Address to the International Congress of Psychology, Amsterdam, 1907)—*Obozrenie Psychiatrii*, 1908, No. 1 ; and *Proceedings of the Congress*.

6. *The Reproductivo-associative Reaction in Movements*—*Obozrenie Psychiatrii*, 1908 ; *Über die reproduktive und assoziative Reaktion bei Bewegungen*—*Zeitschr. f. Therapie*, Bd. 1, H. 1, 1909.

7. *The Aim and Method of Objective Psychology*—*Novoye Slovo*, 1909 ; *Die objektive Psychologie und ihre Begründung*—*Journal f. Psychologie und Neurologie*, 1909, Bd. XIV.

8. *The Significance of the Investigation of the Motor Sphere in the Objective Study of the Neuro-psychical Activity of Man*—*Russky Vratch*, Nos. 33, 35, 36, 1909 ; *Folia neurobiologica*, Bd. IV, 1910.

9. *The Biological Development of Expressive Movements from the Objectivo-psychological Standpoint*—*Vestnik Znania*, 1910, and sep. ed. ; *Die biologische Entwicklung der Mimik vom objektivpsychologischen Standpunkt*—*Folia neurobiologica*, Bd. V, No. 8, 1911 ; *Le rôle biologique de la mimique*—*Journal de psychologie normale et pathologique*, Paris, septembre, 1910.

10. *The Fundamental Manifestations of the Neuro-psychical Activity in their Objective Study*—*Russky Vratch*, 1911 : *Über die Hauptäusserungen der neuro-psychichen Tätigkeit beim objektiven Studium derselben*, Leipzig—*Zeitschr. f. Psych. u. Physiologie der Sinnesorgane*, 1910.

11. *First Principles of the So-called Objective Psychology or Psychoreflexology*—*Obozrenie Psychiatrii*, 1912.

12. *Obyektivnaya psychologiya* (*Objective Psychology*), parts 1, 2, and 3 (1907–12) ; *Objektive Psychologie oder Psycho-Reflexologie*, Leipzig und Berlin, Verlag Teubner, 1913 ; *La psychologie objective*, Paris ; *Obyektivnoye izutcheniye litchnosti* (*The Objective Study of Personality*), part 1, pub. Grzhebin, 1923.

13. *The Causes of Slips of the Tongue*—*Golos i Retch*, No. 9, 1913.

14. *What is Objective Psychology?*—*Voprosi philosophii i psychologii*, 1913 ; *Was ist Psycho-Reflexologie?*—*Deutsch. med. Wochenschr.*, Leipzig, No. 32, 1912. *Qu'est-ce que la psycho-reflexologie?*—*Arch. internat. de neurologie*, août, 1913.

15. *The Interrelations of the Various Motor Association Reflexes*—*Obozrenie, Psychiatrii*, Nos. 10, 11, 12, 1914–15.

---

[1] It is regrettable that it has been found impossible to collect all the papers published in foreign periodicals.

444 BIBLIOGRAPHY

16. *The Correlation of the Objective Manifestations of Association Reflexes with the Subjective Account Rendered by the Subjects*—Obozrenie Psychiatrii, Nos. 10, 11, 12, 1914–15.

17. *The Alternation of the Phenomena of Excitation and Inhibition in the Inculcation of Association Reflexes*—Obozrenie Psychiatrii, Nos. 10, 11, 12, 1914–15.

18. *Conformity to Law in the Inculcation and Development of Motor Association Reflexes*—Obozrenie Psychiatrii, Nos. 5–12, 1916.

19. *General Principles of Reflexology as a Branch of Science*—Priroda, Moscow, 917, Nos. 11–12.

20. *The Strictly Objective Method in the Investigation of Neuro-psychical or Correlative Activity and its Rôle in the Founding of Human Reflexology*—Vestnik Znania, 1917 ; Address to the Petersburg Philosophical Society in 1917 ; see *Minutes* of the Society and *Obozrenie Psychiatrii*, 1917–18, p. 99.

21. *The Sex Urge as an Association Reflex*—Russky Vratch, 1918, Nos. 29–32, 33–36.

22. *Obshtchie osnovi reflexologii (General Principles of Reflexology)*, St. Petersburg, 1918, 1st ed. ; and 1923, 2nd ed.

23. *Reflexology as a Science Objectively Studying Human Personality*— Address to the joint meeting of the Conference on Defective Children and the Congress for the Protection of Children's Health, Moscow, 1920. See *Minutes* of the Congresses.

24. *Methods of Reflexological Investigation of Personality both Norma' and Abnormal*—Address to the Scientific Conference for the Study of Brain, 1921 ; *La methode objective appliquée a l'étude de personalité*—Scientia (Sep. ed.).

25. *Association Reflexes Obtained from Cutaneous Transformers* (based on the investigations of Krotkova, Tchegodayeva, and Dr. Shumkov)—Address to the Conference of the Institute for the Study of Brain, 26th February, 1923. See *Minutes* of the Conference.

26. *Objective or Subjective Investigation of Personality ?*—Address to the Medico-pedagogical Institute, Moscow, January, 1923.

27. *Creativeness from the Reflexological Standpoint.* See S. Grusenberg : *Geny i tvortchestvo (Genius and Creativeness)*, Leningrad, pub. Soikin, 1924.

28. *The Influence of Hypnosis and Suggestion on Association Reflexes* (in collaboration with N. M. Shtchelovanov)—Address to the Scientific Conference for the Study of Brain, 1920—*Novoye v reflexologii i physiologii nervnoi sistemi*, part I, p. 181, 1925.

29. *The Theory of the Spinal Vaso-adaptation Reflex for the Explanation of Trophism of the External Coatings*—Zhurnal po nevropatologii i psychiatrii, pt. I, Kiev, 1925.

30. (In collaboration with G. E. Shumkov) : *The Mimico-somatic Alertness Reflex*—Novoye v reflexologii i physiologii nervnoi sistemi, pt. I, p. 250, 1925.

31. *First Principles of the Functions of the Cerebral Cortex*—Sbornik, posvyashtchonny prof. V. Y. Danilevsky (*Symposium dedicated to Professor V. Y. Danilevsky*), Ukraina, 1925.

32. *Psychologia, reflexologia i marksizm.* (*Psychology, Reflexology, and Marxism*), Leningrad, 1925.

33. *The Development of the Sex Urge from the Standpoint of Reflexology*— Polovoi vopros, State Publishers, Moscow, 1925.

THE AUTHOR'S WORKS ON GENETIC REFLEXOLOGY

34. *The Objective Study of the Neuro-psychical Sphere in Infancy*—Address to the Committee of the Pedological Institute, 1908—*Vestnik Psychologii*, 1909, and sep. ed. ; *Objektive Untersuchung der neuropsychischen Sphäre im Kinde.-alter—Zeitschr. f. Psychotherapie u. med. Psych.*, Bd. II, H. 3, 1910.

35. *The Individual Development of the Neuro-psychical Sphere from the Standpoint of the Data of Objective Psychology—Vestnik Psychologii*, 1910, and sep. ed.

36. *Early Stages in the Evolution of Children's Drawings—Vestnik Psychologii*, 1910, and sep. ed.

37. *The Biological Development of Human Speech—Vestnik Psychologii*, 1910 ; *Über die biologische Entwicklung der menschlichen Sprache—Folia neurobiologica*, Bd. XIV, No. 7, 1913.

38. *The Development of Neuro-psychical Activity in the Course of the First Half-Year of the Child's Life—Vestnik Psychologii*, 1912.

39. *Vnushenie i vospitanie (Suggestion and Education)*—Address to the International Congress of Pedology, Brussels, 1911—*Vestnik Psychologii*, 1912 ; *L'éducation et la suggestion*, 1913—Premier Congrès international de pedologie, Bruxelles. ; sep. ed. pub. Vremya, Petrograd, 1923.

40. *The Evolution of the Neuro-psychical Sphere—Russky Vratch*, Nos. 14, 15 ; 1913.

41. In Collaboration with N. M. Shtchelovanov : *Principles of Genetic Reflexology—Novoye v reflexologii i physiologii nervnoi sistemi*, pt. I, p. 16, 1925.

THE AUTHOR'S WORKS ON PEDAGOGICAL REFLEXOLOGY

42. *Problems of Public Education—Pedagogitchesky Vestnik*, 1910 ; and sep. ed.

43. *O vospitanii v mladentcheskom vozraste (The Education of Infants)*, St. Petersburg, 1913.

44. *Problems of the Evolution of Neuro-psychical Activity and their Relation to Pedagogics :* Address to the Congress of Experimental Pedagogics, 1916—*Vestnik Psychologii*, 1916.

45. *Voprosi vospitaniya v vozraste pervovo detstva (Problems of Education in Early Childhood)*, St. Petersburg, 1916.

46. *O sotzialno-trudovom vospitanii (Education to Social Work) :* Address to the Congress of Experimental Pedagogics, 1917 ; and sep. ed., 1917, Petrograd.

47. *The Activity of the Psychoneurological Institute as a Higher Pedagogical Institution and its Rôle in Pedagogical Construction—Voprosi izutcheniya i vospitaniya litchnosti*, 1921.

48. *The Psychic Activity of Childhood and the Protection of Children's Health—Pervy zhensky kalendar*, 1st year.

THE AUTHOR'S WORKS ON THE REFLEXOLOGY OF PHYSICAL AND OF MENTAL WORK

49. *The Fundamental Aims of the Reflexology of Physical Work—Voprosi izutcheniya i vospitaniya litchnosti*, No. 1, 1919; *Die Grundaufgaben der Reflexologie der physischen Arbeit—Praktische Psychologie*, III Jahrgang, H. 10, 1922.

50. *Personality and Work—Nautchno-Technitchesky Vestnik*, No. 1, 1922.

51. *The Rational Utilisation of Human Energy in Work :* Address to the Initiatory Conference for the Scientific Organisation of Work, Moscow, 1921 ; see *Proceedings* of the Conference.

52. *What the Initiatory Conference for the Scientific Organisation of Work has Achieved—Voprosi izutcheniya truda*, Leningrad, State Publishers, 1922.

53. *The Medicinal Significance of Mental Work for Patients Suffering from Common Neuroses :* Address to the Balneological Congress, Moscow, 1921 ; pub. in *Voprosi psycho-physiologii, reflexologii i gigieni truda*, pt. I ; Kazan ; *Vom Heilwert der geistigen Arbeit bei den an allgemeinen Neurosen Leidenden*, Berlin— *Zeitschr. f. d. ges. Neurol. u. Psych.*, Bd. LXXXVIII, H. 1–3, 1924.

54. *Mental Work from the Reflexological Standpoint :* Address to the Commission for the Investigation of Artistic Work, 11th December, 1922 ; See *Minutes* of the Commission ; pub. in separate Symposium.

THE AUTHOR'S WORKS ON ZOOREFLEXOLOGY

55. *Zooreflexology as a Branch of Science ; and Parrot Speech from the Viewpoint of Objective Investigation—Voprosi izutcheniya i vospitaniya litchnosti*, vols. 4–5, 1922.

56. *Experiments in " Thought " Influence on Animal Behaviour—Voprosi izutcheniya i vospitaniya litchnosti*, 1920.

57. *The Direct or So-called " Thought " Influence on Animals—Voprosi izutcheniya*, etc., 1922.

58. *Von den Versuchen über die aus der Entfernung erfolgende " unmittelbare Einwirkung " einer Person auf das Verhalten der Tiere—Zeitschr. f. Psychotherapie u. med. Psychologie*, Stuttgart, 1924.

THE AUTHOR'S WORKS ON THE REFLEXOLOGY OF ART

59. *Reflexology in Art :* Speech at the *Actus* of the Psychoneurological Academy, 1922.

60. *General Scheme of the Reflexological Investigation of Workers in Art :* Address to the closed session of the Scientific Conference of the Institute for the Study of Brain, 22nd February, 1923 ; see *Minutes* of the Conference.

61. *The Personality of the Artist in the Light of Reflexology—Symposium :* *Arena*, 1923.

THE AUTHOR'S WORKS ON PATHOLOGICAL REFLEXOLOGY

62. *The Objective Indications of the Common Neuroses and of Hysteria—Obozrenie Psychiatrii*, 1897.

63. *The Objective Indications of Local Hyperesthesia and Anesthesia in Traumatic Neuroses and in Hysteria—Obozrenie Psychiatrii*, 1899 ; *Über objektive Symptome lokaler Hyperästhesie und Anästhesie bei den sog. traumatischen Neurosen und bei Hysterie—Neurolog. Zentr.*, No. 5, 1900 ; *Nevrop. i psychiatr. nab'yudeniya*, 1900.

64. *Something More about the Objective Indications of Hyperesthesia in Traumatic Neuroses—Obozrenie Psychiatrii*, No. 2, 1900.

65. *Objective Indications of Suggested Variations in Sensitivity under Hypnosis* (in collaboration with Dr. Narbut)—*Obozrenie Psychiatrii*, 1902.

66. *The Objective Indications of Suggestions during Hypnosis* (in collaboration with V. M. Narbut)—*Obozrenie Psychiatrii*, Nos. 1, 2 ; 1902 ; *Les signes objectifs de la suggestion pendant le sommeil hypnotique—Archives de psychologie*, 18 octobre, 1905.

67. *The Objective Indications of Suggestions Received during Hypnosis—Vestnik Psychologii*, 4, 1905.

68. *Partial Cortical and Subcortical Paralyses of Psycho-reflexive Functions—Obozrenie psychiatrii, nevrologii i experiment. psychologii*, October, 1906.

69. *The Objective Investigation of Psychopaths—Obozrenie Psychiatrii*, Nos. 10–12, 1907 ; *Die objektive Untersuchung der neuropsychischen Sphäre der Geisteskranken—Zeitschr. f. Psychotherapie u. med. Psychologie*, Bd. 1, H. 5, 1909.

70. *The Application of Association-motor Reflexes as an Objective Method of Investigation in the Treatment of Nervous and Psychic Diseases*, No. 8, 1910 ; *Über die Anwendung der assoziativ-motorischen Reflexe als objektive Untersuchungsverfahren in der klinischen Neuropathologie u. Psychiatrie—Zeitschr. f. d. ges. Neur. u. Psychiatrie*, Bd. 5, H. 3, Berlin, 1911.

71. *Contributions to the Method of the Objective Investigation of Psychopaths* (in collaboration with S. D. Vladyzko), St. Petersburg, 1910 ; *Beiträge zur Methodik der objektiven Untersuchung von Geisteskranken.*

72. *The Experimento-objective Investigation of Psychopaths* (in collaboration with S. D. Vladyzko)—*Obozrenie Psychiatrii*, 1911.

73. *Gipnoz, vnushenie i psychoterapia (Hypnosis, Suggestion, and Psychotherapy)—Vestnik Znania*, 1911 ; and sep. ed.

74. *The Fundamental Aims of Psychiatry as an Objective Science—Russky Vratch*, No. 6, 1912.

75. *The Treatment of Pathological Tendencies and Obsessional Conditions by Divertive Psychotherapeutical Methods—Obozrenie Psychiatrii*, Nos. 6–7, 1913.

76. *Reflexive Epilepsy under the Influence of Sound-stimuli—Obozrenie Psychiatrii*, Nos. 10–12 ; 1914–15.

77. *Sexual Perversions as Pathological Association Reflexes :* Address to the Psychoneurological Institute, 1913—*Obozrenie Psychiatrii*, Nos. 7–9 ; 1915.

78. *Obsessional Phobias and Their Treatment—Russky Vratch*, No. 14, 1915.

79. *The Development of Phobias, etc.—Obozrenie Psychiatrii*, 1916.

80. *The Therapeutic Significance of the Inculcation of Association Reflexes in Cases of Hysterical Anesthesias and Paralyses*—*Obozrenie Psychiatrii*, Nos. 1–12 ; 1917–18.

81. *Diseases of Personality from the Viewpoint of Reflexology* (*Contributions to Pathological Reflexology*) : Address to the Moscow Society of Neuropathologists and Psychiatrists, 1918—*Voprosi izutcheniya i vospitaniya litchnosti*, vol. II, 1921.

82. *The Objective Investigation of the Diseased Personality as the Basis of Pathological Reflexology*—*Nautchnaya Meditzina*, No. 9, 1912 ; *Die objektive Untersuchung kranker Persönlichkeit, als Grundlage der pathologischen Reflexologie*, Tartu (Dorpat), Estonia—*Folia neurologica Estoniana*, vols. III–IV, 1925 ; *Scientia*, 1925.

83. *Sexual Perversions and Inversions in the Light of Reflexology*—*Voprosi izutcheniya i vospitaniya litchnosti*, vols. IV–V, 1922 ; *Die Perversitäten und Inversitäten vom Standpunkt der Reflexologie*—*Archiv. f. Psychiatrie u. Nervenkrankheiten*, Bd. 68, H. 1–2, 1923.

84. *The Objective-biological Investigation of Those Suffering from Diseases of Personality* : Address to the Society of Normal and Pathological Reflexology and Neurology, 23rd December, 1922.

85. In collaboration with G. E. Shumkov : *Local Contusion Neurosis*—*Noviye dostizheniya v oblasti reflexologii*, etc., pt. I, p. 347, 1925 ; *Die Lokalkontusionsneurose*—*Arch. f. Psychiatrie*, 1925.

86. In collaboration with G. E. Shumkov : *The Symptom Complex of Nervous Functional Disturbances Caused by Influences Not Complicated by So-called " Psychic Trauma "*—*Novoye v reflexologii*, etc., pt. I, p. 351.

87. *Sexual Perversions as a Set Acquired by the Sex Reflex*—*Pedagogitchesky sbornik ;* pub. " Ephron," Leningrad, 1925.

88. *Principes de reflexologie pathologique*—*Scientia*, fasc. CLVIII, 6, 1925.

89. *Perversions and Inversions of the Sex Urge from the Viewpoint of Reflexology*—*Polovoi vopros*, State Publishers, Moscow, 1925.

90. In collaboration with Shumkov : *Change in the Functional Activity of the Nervous System in Dependence on the Influence of Cutaneous Stimuli*—*Novoye v reflexologii i physiologii nervnoi sistemi ; Sbornik*, 1925.

91. *Über die Behandlung der krankhaften Triebe und Zwangszustände durch Ablenkungspsychotherapie*—*Zeitschr. f. Neurol. u. Psych.*, 1922.

THE AUTHOR'S WORKS ON JURIDICAL PATHO-REFLEXOLOGY

92. *The Application of the Association-motor Reflex Method in the Investigation of Simulation*—*Russky Vratch*, 1912, and sep. ed. ; *Die Anwendung der Methode der motorischen Assoziations-reflexe zur Aufdeckung der Simulation*—*Zeitschr. f. d. ges. Neur. u. Psych.*, Bd. XIII, H. 2.

93. *The Murder of Yushtchinsky*[1] *and the Psychiatro-psychological Expert Evidence*—*Vratch. Gazeta*, 1913. (*The Application of the Objective Method in Elucidating Problems of Juridical Practice.*)

---

[1] The child Beilis was accused of having murdered. See Biography of Author, p. 7.—*Translators*.

THE AUTHOR'S WORKS ON COLLECTIVE AND SOCIAL REFLEXOLOGY

94. *The Subject and Aims of Social Psychology as an Objective Science—Vestnik Znania*, 1911 ; *La psychologie sociale considérée comme une science objective—Revue psychologique*, fasc. 3, 1911.

95. *Vnushenie i evo rol v obshtchestvennoi zhizni* (*Suggestion and its Rôle in Social Life*), St. Petersburg ; *Die Suggestion und ihre Rolle im sozialen Leben*, Wiesbaden ; *La suggestion et son rô'e dans la vie socia'e*, Paris.

96. *Social Selection and its Biological Significance—Vestnik Znania*, 1913 ; *Nord und Süd*, 1912.

97. *The Objectivo-psychological Method in its Application to the Study of Crime—Sbornik, posvyashtch. pamyati D. A. Drilya*, and sep. ed., St. Petersburg, 1912 ; *La psychologie objective appliquée a l'étude de la criminalité—Archives d'anthropologie*, 15 mars, 1910.

98. *Das Verbrechertum im Lichte der objektiven Psychologie*, Wiesbaden, 1914.

99. *The Significance of Hormonism and Social Selection in the Development of Organisms—Priroda*, 1916.

100. *The Immortality of Human Personality from the Scientific Viewpoint—Vestnik Znania*, 1918 ; and sep. ed.

101. *Kollektivnaya reflexologiya* (*Collective Reflexology*), pts. 1 and 2, 1921.

102. *The Significance of Experiment in Collective Reflexology—Nautchniye Izvestia*, pt. 1, Moscow State Publishers, 1922. (Address to the Conference of the Institute for the Study of Brain, 10th April, 1919.)

103. *The Fundamental Laws of the Universe in Connection with the Objective Investigation of Social Life from the Viewpoint of Reflexology—Voprosi izutcheniya i vospitaniya litchnosti*, vol. 3, 1922.

104. *Experimental Data in Collective Reflexology* : Address to the Congress of Psychoneurology in Moscow (in collaboration with M. V. Lange), 1913—*Novoye v reflexologii i physiologii nervnoi systemi*, pt. 1, p. 309 ; *Die Ergebnisse des Experiments auf dem Gebiete der kollektiven Reflexologie* (mit dem Assistenten des Instituts M. V. Lange)—*Arch. f. d. angewandte Psychologie*, Bd. XXIV, H. 5–6, 1924.

THE AUTHOR'S WORKS ON CEREBRAL STRUCTURE AND FUNCTIONS BEARING ON REFLEXOLOGY

105. *Die Functionen der Sehhügel* (*Thalamus opticus*) : *Experimentelle Untersuchung—Neur. Zentr.*, No. 4, 1883 ; *Vratch*, 1883.

106. *The Physiology of the Motor Area of the Cerebral Cortex—Arch. Psychiatrii*, 1886–87.

107. *Expressive Movements—Vratch*, 1883.

108. *The Functions of the Thalamus Opticus—Vestnik Psychiatrii*, 1885 ; *Die Bedeutung der Sehhügel auf Grund d. experimentellen und pathologischen Daten—Virchows Archiv. f. pathol., Anatomie u. Physiol., u. f. klinische Medizin*, Bd. 110, 1887.

109. *The Influence of the Cortex of the Cerebrum on the Act of Swallowing and on Respiration* (in collaboration with P. A. Ostankov)—*Nevrologitchesky Vestnik*, vol. II, pt. 2, 1894.

110. *The Problem of the Influence of the Cerebral Cortex and of the Thalamus Opticus on Swa'lowing—ibid.*

111. *The Voluntary Dilation of the Pupil—ibid.*, vol. III, pt. 1, 1895.

112. *Über die Gehörcentra der Gehirnrinde—Archiv f. Anat. u. Physiol.*, 1899.

113. *The Influence of the Human Cerebra Cortex on Heart Beat, Blood Pressure, and Respiration—Nevropatologitcheskiye i psychiatritcheskiye nablyudeniya*, 1900.

114. *Die Hirnzentren der Scheidenbewegungen bei Tieren* (in collaboration with N. A. Mislavsky), Leipzig, 1891 ; *The Brain Centres of Vaginal Movements in Animals* (Russian—in collaboration with the same).

115. *Provodyashtchiye puti spinnovo i golovnovo mozga* (*Conduction Paths in the Brain and Spinal Cord*), St. Petersburg, pts. 1–2, 1896 ; *Die Leitungsbahnen im Gehirn und Ruckenmark*, Berlin ; *Les voies de conduction*, Lyon, 1900.

116. *The Contact Theory ; and the Doctrine of Discharges of Nervous Energy as Conditions of the Conduction of Nervous Excitation—Obozrenie Psychiatrii*, No. 1, 1896.

117. *The Significance of the Epithelial Apparatus of the Sensory Nerves in respect of Qualitative Discrimination of Sensations which Are Being Received—Obozrenie Psychiatrii*, No. 1, 1896.

118. *Über die Lokalisation der Geschmackzentren in der Gehirnrinde—Archiv f. Anat. u. Physiol.*, 1900.

119. W. Bechterew und N. Mislawsky : *Über den Einfluss der Hirnrinde auf die Speichelsekretion—Neurolog. Zentralbl.*, No. 20, 1888.

120. Bechterew und Mislawsky : *Zur Frage der die Speichelsekretion anregenden Rindenfelder—ibid.*, No. 7, 1889.

121. Bechterew und Mislawsky : *Zur Frage der Innervation des Magens—ibid.*, No. 7, 1890.

122. Bechterev and Mislavsky : *The Innervation and the Cerebral Centres of Tear Secretion—Meditzinskoye Obozrenie*, No. 12, 1891 ; Bechterew und Mislawsky : *Über die Innervation und die Hirnzentren der Tränenabsonderung—Neurol. Zentralbl.*, No. 16, 1891.

123. *Über die kortikalen sekretorischen Zentren der wichtigsten Verdauungsdrüsen—Archiv f. Anatom. u. Physiol.*, 1902.

124. *Der Einfluss der Hirnrinde auf die Tränen-, Schweiss-, und Harnabsonderung—Arch. f. Anat. u. Physiol.*, 1905.

125. *Osnovi utcheniya o funktziyach mozga* (*Principles of the Study of the Nervous Centres*), pts. 1–7, St. Petersburg ; *Die Funktionen der Nervencentra*, H. 1–3, Jena.

126. *Psychika i zhizn* (*The Psychic and Life*), 2nd ed., St. Petersburg, 1904 ; *Psyche und Leben*, Wiesbaden ; *L'activité psychique et la vie*, Paris, 1907.

127. *The Significance of the Investigation of Local Reflexes in the Study of the Functions of the Cerebral Cortex—Nevrologitchesky Vestnik*, t. XV, 1908.

128. *The Investigation of the Cortical Functions by means of Natural Association Reflexes : The Significance of this Method in regard to the Investigation of*

the Cortical Centres of the Internal Organs and of Various Secretions—Obozrenie Psychiatrii, No. 8, 1908 ; *Untersuchung der Funktionen der Gehirnrinde auf Grund des Verhaltens der Assoziationsreflexe und die Bedeutung dieser Methode für die Erforschung der kortikalen Zentren der inneren Organe und Sekretionen— Folia neurobiologica*, Bd. II, 1908.

129. *Der Einfluss der Gehirnrinde auf die Geschlechtsorgane, die Prostata und die Milchdrüsen—Archiv f. Anat. u. Physiol.*, 1911.

130. *Principles of the Functional Activity of the Cerebral Cortex according to the Data of Psycho-reflexology—Russky Vratch*, No. 33, 1913.

131. *Bio-chemical Systems and their Rôle in the Development of Organisms— Russky Vratch*, 1913.

132. *The Study of Frontal and Other Areas of the Cerebral Cortex by means of Association-motor Reflexes—Obozrenie Psychiatrii*, Nos. 4, 5, 6, 7, 9, 1914 ; *Das Studium der Funktionen der frontalen und anderer Gebiete der Hirnrinde vermittelst der assoziativmotorischen Reflexe—Schweizer Archiv für Neurologie und Psychiatrie*, Bd. XIII, 1922.

133. *La localisation des psycho-réflexes dans l'écorce cérébrale—Scientia*, dec. 1916.

134. *Von den Versuchen über die aus der Entfernung erfolgende " unmittelbare Einwirkung " einer Persönlichkeit auf das Verhalten der Tiere*, Stuttgart, Bd. VIII, H. 5–6, 1924.

135. *General Plan of the Functioning of the Cerebral Cortex from the Reflexological Standpoint* : Address to the Scientific Conference of the Institute for the Study of Brain, 1921.

In addition to the above-mentioned works, the objective study of human and animal association-reflex activity has been prosecuted by a large number of collaborators, who, under my direction, worked at different times in my reflexological laboratory and in the scientific institutions supervised by me. The present circumstances make it impossible to enumerate all these works. They appeared as Dissertations and as papers published, during the past twenty years, in various periodicals, particularly in those publications edited by me— *Obozrenie Psychiatrii, Nevrologii i Experimentalnoi Psychologii ; Vestnik Psychologii, Nevrologii i Pedologii ; Nevrologitchesky Vestnik ; Trudi kliniki dushevnich i nervnich boleznei (Activities of the Hospital for Mental and Nervous Diseases) ; Minutes of the Scientific Meetings of the Hospital for Mental and Nervous Diseases ; Voprosi izutcheniya i vospitaniya litchnosti ; Voprosi psychologii i reflexologii truda* (Kazan) ; *Pedagogitchesky Vestnik* (Orel) ; *Novoye v reflexologii i physiologii nervnoi sistemi*—and in various symposiums and in other publications.

Of the works published from my laboratory I shall mention here the publications of Professors : Protopopov, Astvatzaturov, Osipov, Nikitin, Gerver, Zhukovsky, Rachmanov, Vladyzko, Lazursky, Povarnin, Brustein, Narbut, Ostankov, Shumkov, Vladimirsky, Agadzhanov, Belitzky, Anfimov, Shevalev, Platonov, Vasilyev, Belov, Lenz, and others ; of *privat-dozents* and lecturers : Molotkov, Golant, Sreznevsky, Kazatchenko-Trirodov, Ivanov-Smolensky, Shtchelovanov, Pavlovskaya, Schneerson, and many others ; of doctors, natural scientists, and pedagogues : Gutman, Erikson, Topalov, Voitzechovsky, Abramov, Zhmichov, Greker, Shirman, Ivanov, Gromik, Frenkel, Vasilyeva, Henkin,

Spirtov, Dobrotvorskaya, Osipova, Schwarzman, Kunyayev, Livshitz-Veselovskaya, Afanasyev, Tchaly, Ilyin, Israelson, Valker, Rosental, Pesker, Brazhas, Borishpolsky, Larionov, Trivus, Boldireva, Hirman, Myasishtchev, Kandaratzkaya, Studentzov, Solovtzova, Barankeyeva, Shnirman, Dernova-Yermolenko, Lukina, Smirnova, Kontarovitch, Lange, Fedorin, Krotkova, Tchegodayeva, V. Timofeyevsky, Gratzianov, Kushinnikov, Oparina, Polonsky, Dubrovsky, and many others.

I seize this opportunity to express my gratitude to all my collaborators and pupils for the interest they have shown in their work in that new scientific sphere the significance of which continues to grow *pari passu* with the extension of scientific investigation.

NAME INDEX

SUBJECT INDEX

CLASSICS IN PSYCHOLOGY

An Arno Press Collection

Morgan, C. Lloyd. **Habit and Instinct.** 1896

Münsterberg, Hugo. **Psychology and Industrial Efficiency.** 1913

Murchison, Carl, editor. **Psychologies of 1930.** 1930

Piéron, Henri. **Thought and the Brain.** 1927

Pillsbury, W[alter] B[owers]. **Attention.** 1908

[Poffenberger, A. T., editor]. **James McKeen Cattell:** Man of Science. 1947

Preyer, W[illiam] **The Mind of the Child:** Parts I and II. 1890/1889

The Psychology of Skill: Three Studies. 1973

Reymert, Martin L., editor. **Feelings and Emotions:** The Wittenberg Symposium. 1928

Ribot, Th[éodule Armand]. **Essay on the Creative Imagination.** 1906

Roback, A[braham] A[aron]. **The Psychology of Character.** 1927

I. M. Sechenov: Biographical Sketch and Essays. (Reprinted from *Selected Works* by I. Sechenov). 1935

Sherrington, Charles. **The Integrative Action of the Nervous System.** 2nd edition. 1947

Spearman, C[harles]. **The Nature of 'Intelligence' and the Principles of Cognition.** 1923

Thorndike, Edward L. **Education:** A First Book. 1912

Thorndike, Edward L., E. O. Bregman, M. V. Cobb, et al. **The Measurement of Intelligence.** [1927]

Titchener, Edward Bradford. **Lectures on the Elementary Psychology of Feeling and Attention.** 1908

Titchener, Edward Bradford. **Lectures on the Experimental Psychology of the Thought-Processes.** 1909

Washburn, Margaret Floy. **Movement and Mental Imagery.** 1916

Whipple, Guy Montrose. **Manual of Mental and Physical Tests:** Parts I and II. 2nd edition. 1914/1915

Woodworth, Robert Sessions. **Dynamic Psychology.** 1918

Wundt, Wilhelm. **An Introduction to Psychology.** 1912

Yerkes, Robert M. **The Dancing Mouse** and **The Mind of a Gorilla.** 1907/1926